Spiritual Practice, Occultism, and Extraterrestrial Intelligence

A Travel Guide for Beyond the Rainbow

by

Judy Kennedy

PaperWings Publishing

Published by:

Paper Wings Publishing, LLC
Post Office Box 1211
Maricopa, Arizona 85239-1211, USA
paperwingspublishing@excite.com
http://www.waywardmuse.com
(602) 361-6741

ISBN 0-9770132-0-0

Cover Design and Art by Judy Kennedy and John Halley, 2005.

Printed in the United States of America, North America, Earth on Recycled Paper

CONTENTS

The Land of Oz

The Cosmic Connection: UFOs, ETs, and our Origins

UFOs, ETs, and the Mystery Schools

Closing Encounters

Music is Key: The Magic of Sound, Color, and Imagery

Going Home

Dorothy Wakes Up: Meanwhile, Back at the Ranch...

Qabalistic Tree of Life

Cosmic Chronology

Tarot Key 0: The Fool

Acknowledgements

Every moment I've ever lived has gone into this book, so my acknowledgements must span a lifetime. Deep gratitude to my late parents, who shared a love and a flair for the written word, which I'm sure was passed down to me in some measure through their genes and guidance. Deep gratitude to my late grandmother ("Mamoo") and Ivy, who nurtured me when my parents could not. Deep gratitude to all the teachers, especially the muckraking authors and creative artists, who nurtured my muse and helped to shape my unique perspective on life. Deep gratitude to Builders of the Adytum, Dr. John D. Rankin, Lama Surya Das, Jiwanjonim, and other spiritual mentors. Deep gratitude to Marcia Schafer for her encouragement and helpful advice. Deep gratitude to Dr. Steven M. Greer for his monumental work and generous contribution to mine. Deep gratitude to Roger Waters and his publishers for allowing permission to reprint his inspirational lyrics. Deep gratitude to all the other publishers and authors who graciously granted permission to reprint their copyrighted material – you know who you are – (too many to list!) Deepest gratitude to all beings – great and small, human and nonhuman, seen and unseen -- who witnessed this event and added significantly to my inspiration when most needed, especially my animal children – Caesar, Panther, Jaz, Bluz, Shining Shooting Sugar Star Snowflake ("Star"), Raven Rapture of Rayi ("Raven"), Tara, Dalai Lama ("Dolly"), Ebony Dharma ("Ebony"), Mocha Kaya ("Mocha"), Gingerbread ("Ginger"), and Coconut ("Coco"). Let's not forget the incredibly diverse Sonoran wildlife frequenting my home. My deepest gratitude to John Halley for his undying love and friendship, and especially for his constructive criticism that provided just enough edge to push me past my comfort zone and closer to my personal best. Finally, deepest gratitude to the grace of my Holy Guardian Angel – the Higher Self – the Inner Teacher -- my very own wayward muse, without which this book could not have been written. And thank you to any and all who I might have missed. May all beings be blessed by this blessing – infinitely!

Judy Ann Kennedy
Vernal Equinox 2004
Somewhere in Arizona

Introduction

It's safe to say we're not in Kansas anymore. It is impossible to be just a "Texan" or an "American," or even just an "Earthling" now. In these crazy times, freedom calls out to each and every one of us, but it's as if we're still stuck in Oz. Now that we're over the rainbow, we must get beyond the rainbow. Only in renewing the cosmic connection do we find our way home.

A broad, diffuse, and overwhelming barrage of information, misinformation, and disinformation exists regarding Unidentified Flying Objects (UFOs), extraterrestrials (ETs), and their connection with occult conspiracy. Much of what is written on this subject stems from paranoia and a deep misunderstanding of these phenomena. Things are not what they appear to be, and few people seem willing to look beyond those appearances in order to see through and beneath the surface to the underlying spiritual principles that form the basis for these multidimensional realities.

On the other hand, many authors know precisely the value of such knowledge and the power that comes from such knowing. It's like the proverbial pot of gold at the end of the rainbow. Unfortunately, they don't want to share it. Therefore, they keep the truth about its whereabouts shrouded in secrecy while erecting intriguing signs that do nothing more than mislead. Some authors tell us that there is no pot of gold and that something else dreadfully evil and dangerous awaits us.

Why do they do this? Why don't they want us to know the truth? Because the truth is liberating. Genuine understanding of the underlying spiritual principles forming the basis for occultism leads to self-empowerment, autonomy and freethinking. The authors who don't want us to know the truth about it are the reactive authors with secret agendas. They point to various individuals and groups as either knowingly or unknowingly involved in their conspiracies, when the authors themselves are the true conspirators.

The word *occult* means "hidden" – "secret" –"mysterious." It is often associated with the so-called mystic arts like magic, astrology, alchemy, and any other endeavor that cannot be rationally explained in the context of current scientific understanding. Practical occultism is really a form of psychology – a spiritual science of mind. There was a time when reading, writing and arithmetic were considered occult arts. Today we use these tools on a daily basis. Does that make us evil Satanists, alien reptiles, or Illuminati conspirators? Of course not. The common sense approach is the only approach when attempting to understand what it's all about. And when the veil is parted we see a precious jewel reflecting the rainbow in the pure light of day -- no longer "occult" or hidden from view.

Supersensory awareness and the manifestation of seemingly supernormal abilities are just expressions of energies lying dormant within us all. These lesser-known aspects of spirituality are usually attributed to the world's great sages. Jesus and many spiritual leaders were trained in the esoteric mystery schools behind the veil of the world's spiritual traditions. These schools, for the most part, remain "occult" or hidden from ordinary view. The origin of these schools is extraterrestrial.

The purpose of the schools is the focus of all occult practice or engaged spirituality: the transformation of the individual into the new human -- a human who has awakened and unfolded inherent divinity for the greater benefit of one and all. This awakening involves the transmutation of the baser elements of personality into the spiritual gold of illumined awareness. The rainbow that leads us to it is a path that is already within us – awaiting actualization in the world around us. Nobody can keep us from it except ourselves. The muddlers will try to, but that's their job. The Rainbow Alliance is my term for all the rest who remain true to the truth, in service of the light. *Beyond the Rainbow* is a declaration of that truth.

This travel guide for *Beyond the Rainbow* comes directly from the way-showers and is the way of the hero's journey. My favorite hero whose journey is the model for this story is Dorothy from the movie, *The Wizard of Oz*.

The Wizard of Oz Mysteries refer to the sacred truths that are woven into the symbolism of this beautiful, much loved story. The only reason why anything remains a mystery is because the knowledge of our relationship to its creation is lost. That's why we must go the source – the origin of the teachings. When speaking about a tale expressed in a book or a movie, the meaning becomes a mystery when it gets lost behind all the metaphor and symbolism. As we unravel the metaphor, we solve the mystery.

The story of *The Wizard of Oz* as portrayed in the classic film was my earliest exposure to Ageless Wisdom. As a faithful disciple, each year as far back as I remember, I sat in front of the television set, absorbing the lessons in more ways than one, and loving every minute of it. It was a tradition. Though many authors have analyzed this tale from a spiritual perspective and done a marvelous job, none have yet to interpret certain symbols and scenes from it in quite the same way that I have. Therefore, I offer bits and pieces of what I've learned from these mysteries in the form of a unifying theme throughout the book.

Following this thread, we sort through the tangled web of information available regarding UFOs, ETs, and their connection with occult conspiracy. We dispel the disinformation, synthesize what remains, and arrive at a sound multidisciplinary overview of the truth with startling conclusions. The conclusions are timely and largely relevant to current sociopolitical problems that impact each and every one of us. The conclusions also point to specific solutions. It's up to each of us to implement these solutions uniquely, for we have our own gardens to grow – we must each follow the yellow brick road in our own ruby red slippers and at our own individual paces. The reason for this is because there is no greater teacher than the inner teacher who speaks through your heart alone, and there is no greater truth than the integrity of your own experience.

The journey has seven parts and is illustrated in ten chapters:

Part 1 is all about being over the rainbow. Leaving the purely personal perspective of our Kansas soap opera behind us, we venture over the rainbow to find ourselves thrust into the middle of a global perspective on the nature of reality. We are introduced to Ageless Wisdom through a discussion, overview and comparative analysis of the Western and Eastern esoteric mystery traditions. These traditions are the source of all so-called occult practices. Understanding these practices in this context is critical because it is the only way we can properly understand the role that these schools play in the cosmic connection with regard to UFO and ET phenomena.

Part two is all about following the yellow brick road. Once our feet are firmly set upon the Path, we find spiritual friends, tools and accessories to assist us on our magical journey. Therefore *Beyond the Rainbow* reveals that practical occultism is spiritual practice. It illustrates the basic principles in simple terms and offers practical instruction for personal confirmation. Though methodology may vary slightly from East to West, the basic truths – the spiritual principles founded on cosmic law, are the same.

Subsequently, a firm foundation is provided upon which to understand UFO/ET phenomena in itself because we are dealing primarily with psychology – the mechanics of consciousness and the more subtle processes of awareness – human and extraterrestrial. The underlying principles are explored to a sufficient degree for enabling an adequate comprehension of a new cosmology for integration into our current world view and any view to come.

In order to understand the roles of spirituality, religion, and occultism in our lives, we apply the principles of transpersonal psychology. Transpersonal psychology is a holistic approach to awareness and healing which integrates psychology, religion, and the study of consciousness. Derived from the Latin *trans* meaning beyond and through, and *persona* or mask, the transpersonal approach combines the metaphysical-mystical perspective of the world's perennial philosophy and the psychological research of modern times. It extends beyond focusing primarily on personal development by affirming the centrality of the spiritual quest.

Part Three is all about the Land of Oz. We get to know all the strange creatures that inhabit this land and how to communicate with them. All aspects of UFO and ET phenomena are fully addressed, especially in relation to the origin of the human species. The connection between these phenomena and the ancient mystery schools is revealed in a historical context and thoroughly explored.

Part Four is all about the flying monkeys and the haunted forest. This is the scary part. We meet the muddlers face to face – the true conspirators – the seemingly "evil ones" who work to keep us ignorant, enslaved, distracted, and paralyzed with fear. They place obstacles on the path. They erect misleading signs. They tamper with the truth by mixing it with untruth and scattering the pieces. We learn to separate the wheat from the tares, put the pieces of the map back together, and then proceed to the witch's castle where we confront our worst fears and free Dorothy from the nightmare.

In order to understand the politics of conspiracy, we unflinchingly explore the psychological dynamics operating behind those processes. This is social psychology – the study of the behavior of groups of people in contrast to the individual. Social psychology sheds much light on the politics of conspiracy, especially with regard to the UFO/ET phenomena in connection with occultism.

Part Five is all about reclaiming the broomstick. We cannot deny that our efforts to understand ourselves, as groups or individuals in relation to UFO/ET phenomena, is a spiritual quest in and of itself, for the concepts of cosmos and spirit are intimately related. The word *spirit* comes from the Latin *spirare*, meaning *to breathe*. Life requires breathing; the very life breath *is* Spirit – the animating principle behind all forms according to many spiritual traditions. No matter what planet we're from, we're all in this together because we all share space. We all have bodies or forms of some kind that intermingle with that space. The substance of cosmic energy, sometimes called *Ki,* fills that common field. Learning how this energy interacts with and permeates the world of form and physical manifestation is learning that mind or awareness is life itself. Awakening the dragon is understanding the physiology of awareness, which is essential if we are to heal and in turn heal the world. The ability to recognize and manifest this power in our lives for the benefit of one and all doesn't just belong to the few or the spiritually enlightened – it belongs to all of us. Reclaiming this truth about our spiritual heritage is reclaiming our bodies in more ways than one.

Part Six is all about closing encounters. We are rewarded for our efforts in Oz, and learn that our new powers must be wielded responsibly and with compassion. We learn to relate to ourselves and a world of diverse beings in ways we never dreamed. In order to communicate intergalacticly and co-exist peacefully, we master a universal language – the secret language of music – a language that has its origins in the esoteric mystery schools founded by our extraterrestrial ancestors. This language is based on sound, color, and imagery, which are the basic tools of every occultist and which comprise the very matrix of all mystical experience. This is the process – the most effective way – to make and renew the cosmic connection.

Part Seven is all about going home. Coming home to who and what we really are is waking up to an expanded, multidimensional reality. Kansas will never look the same again because we are transformed. A method often used in transpersonal psychology to understand the universe and ourselves involves the application of Jungian analysis to the interpretation of metaphor and symbolism in dreams, stories, myths and legends which often constitute the basis for world religion. Mythology, anthropology and cross-cultural studies are integral in this regard when exploring an interdisciplinary approach to truth. In the new millennium, however, we are finding that these stories, myths and legends have a dual meaning and existence when considering UFO/ET phenomena: they are both symbolic *and* literal. This concept is explained by the Hermetic Axiom – a universal law known to all occultists that basically goes, 'as above, so below – as within, so without.' Nearing our destination, we see the integration and actualization of our understanding of this concept from both Western and Eastern perspectives into our very lives throughout the entire journey, bringing us full circle and beyond the rainbow, ready to awaken from the dream. To truly understand what has happened on this magical journey, we look within once more – because that's where all projections of reality begin.

As is written on a plaque above the door to an ancient mystery school, we read the imperative that is timeless in essence: KNOW THYSELF. To that end, we begin our adventure.

PART 1

Over the Rainbow

It would seem that the most parsimonious position possible is simply to affirm that reality is experience, and nothing more. This means that any experience we have – sensory or otherwise – is real in that undeniably we have had it.

-- Dr. Steven M. Rosen

CHAPTER 1

SECRETS REVEALED

Colors of the Rainbow – Fulfilling the Promise

Spirituality and religion are not always the same. One can exist with or without the other. Yet social scientists and religious scholars from all faiths have long recognized commonalities among all religions and spiritual traditions. After all, it's just water – many waves and forms but one substance. The light reflecting on the surface of the water changes its color all the time. Color is the way we perceive light. Yet we don't see the colors of the rainbow in a fight for dominance. They co-exist peacefully to make up one of the most spectacular displays of hope, beauty, and harmony in the universe.

Politics and religion are usually forbidden topics of discussion in social circles, but the trend is changing. In a growing global economy and rapidly shrinking world, it must change. Interfaith work is essential for the sake of planetary survival -- we've got to get along.

It is possible to talk about important aspects of our lives without turning speech into a sales pitch. To better understand one another, we need to learn about all cultures and religions. The more we do this, the more we find we are not so different. The color of blood, sweat and tears is the same for everyone. Joy is still joy when loved and loving no matter who or where you are. Teaching tolerance, especially to young children, is essential if we're ever to experience world peace.

Of course there will always be political differences that tend to be divisive but they don't have to be. Not long ago I was pleasantly surprised to see pro-choice and anti-abortion advocates engaged in constructive dialogue. Without a doubt, both sides valued life and wanted to see a reduction in the number of abortions. They just couldn't agree on how to go about it. But at least they found common ground in one area, and that common ground is the foundation for a better world.

The best way to learn about an unfamiliar faith is to talk to its adherents. I moved to Mesa, Arizona in the late 1980s, a town founded and largely populated by Mormons. Mormons, like Jews, share a lively history of adventure and persecution that has given rise to many misperceptions about them. It wasn't until I went to work for a partnership between a Jew and a Mormon that many of my misperceptions about both religions were dispelled. In fact, I was surprised to learn that Mormonism shares some similarity to Gnosticism. Few people know that *The Seven Habits of Highly Effective People* by best-selling author Stephen J. Covey, is really a secularized version of a Mormon text made to appeal to all people of any or no faith. And yet it has changed the lives of countless individuals and organizations all over the world. How did he do this? Simple. He went to the source of the teachings – the underlying substance – the common threads that hold the entire tapestry together: principles.

Principles are divine laws that are substantiated by personal experience, above and beyond dogma. We discover these sacred principles underneath and behind the outer premise of all religions and spiritual traditions, yet it requires effort because we have to read between the lines and think abstractly. For one, we must start from a framework that rejects dogma at face value and that presupposes a common thread of truth. This does not mean that dogma has no purpose. Dogma sometimes provides structure and stability when a rest from ontological struggle is warranted. But eventually, the law of impermanence prevails, and those beliefs are seen to be inflexibly rigid and no longer effective when confronted with problems of a deeper and more complex nature. Then it's time to let go and allow the paradigm to shift into a more open-minded, less certain way of viewing things, yet a way that is more practically suited to our modern lifestyle. This does not necessarily invalidate the former version of truth – it just allows for a more expanded and universal interpretation of that truth – a wider, more inclusive perspective. This is the evolution of awareness. To quote a popular scripture from the Bible: *For now we see through a glass, darkly; but then face to face: now I know in part; but then shall I know even as also I am known.*

The spiritual Path has two major arteries of travel: the exoteric and the esoteric. Esoteric means, "meant for or understood by a few." Exoteric refers to everything else. In ancient Egypt, reading, writing and arithmetic were considered occult or esoteric arts exclusive to the few. Today these skills are common and accessible to everyone. Once esoteric, they are now exoteric. Another example: Centuries ago, witches used bandages of molded bread to heal wounds. Today we know that mold is a source of penicillin. Shamanistic peoples have always known about the medicinal value of herbs and plants. Modern science eventually catches up and validates that knowledge – turns the esoteric into the exoteric. These terms are relative however, and cannot always be clearly distinguished; just as a road may have highly variable patches of dirt and asphalt running together which at times overlap. But one thing is for sure: esotericism always recedes into exotericism; the dirt road usually ends up paved. The more people travel it, the more likely it is to get paved to make the way easier for others. We will always have preferences. Some people will always prefer the smooth surface and profuse camaraderie of the paved highways. Others like the relative seclusion and challenge of the dirt roads. To each his own. That's what makes the world so diverse and the rainbow so beautiful.

Fundamentalist Christians interpret the Bible literally. On the other hand, Christians attending Unity and the Unitarian Church interpret scripture figuratively, relying upon a less dogmatic analysis of the teachings of Jesus Christ. Some mystics and ascetics denounce the physical body and the material world. Satanists and nihilists say let's live it up while we can because the physical universe is all there is. Any approach can be carried to its extreme. This is why, as

Shakyamuni Buddha suggested having learned it by personal experience, it is sometimes best to follow the middle road.

Of course, hardy pioneers cut through the brush and bramble, making new paths – extending the road – way up ahead of most of us. Some of these pioneers become significant historical figures, like Jesus and Mohammed, yet some don't. That is not to say that those who are further down the road are somehow closer to the goal or God and therefore more holy, spiritually evolved or enlightened. That's spiritual elitism. A holier than thou attitude has no place on the Path except to serve as a rock on which to stub your toe.

For one, the issue of a goal is irrelevant, prescribes limitations, and can be misleading. The inner world like the outer world is more round and spatial than flat and linear. Furthermore, a seven-year-old child who is just learning rudimentary arithmetic would not be deemed innately dumb or somehow less capable because she has not yet mastered calculus. This is not a game, a race, or a contest. Great spiritual leaders all point to something inside each of us that is already completely pure, equally divine, and perfectly enlightened as it is. It's just a matter of becoming aware of it – of "unfolding" or "awakening" – so to speak. That's what traveling the road is all about, and that's what the esoteric orders or mystery schools behind all religions and spiritual traditions – East and West – have set out to help us do.

A Little Bit of History

On September 9, 1900, one of the greatest natural disasters in the recorded history of humankind occurred: the 1900 Galveston Storm. A hurricane of mass proportions swept across the most advanced city in Texas killing 6,000 people. Elsewhere around the world, a storm of similar strength was wreaking havoc, however people were not perishing, but ideas – outworn concepts and old thought forms. Remnants of separative consciousness were washed away clearing debris, making ground for the foundation of conceptual frameworks driven by an impetus toward unity, world peace and transformation. In particular, spiritual movements began to embody approaches that emphasize the integration of the so-called spiritual and material worlds in contradistinction to transcendence or a purely mystical psychosis that undervalues or ignores the realities of the physical plane of existence.

In the West, the Renaissance period and resulting age of reason culminating with the industrial revolution had given rise to schisms between science and religion, mind and spirit, for good reason. Sometimes a separation is necessary before a better grasp of truth can occur. With each tearing down comes a rebuilding of the structure that is more sound, reliable and useful than the last. In particular, these movements were cultivating a growing awareness of the importance of "spiritualizing" the mind. Recognizing the workings of the mind as the greatest enemy of a spiritually advancing humanity, they sought to make it their greatest ally. Their position all along was that spiritual sages such as Jesus and the Buddha had already done this, and they sought to explain *how* they did this, publicly for the first time. Of course, Buddhists had always been open in their teachings regarding the relationship between mind and spirit. But at the time, the East, particularly Tibet, was still a relatively insular society, closed off to the rest of the world and barely touched by the industrial revolution. Therefore it was not subject to the waves of persecution suffered by the spiritual iconoclasts of the West.

The Theosophical Society had been in full swing since the latter half of the 19th century as a major player in this trend. Madame Blavatsky, its most charismatic leader, wrote *Isis Unveiled* and *The Secret Doctrine* that were seminal in this regard. While Blavatsky's work is more Eastern in origin than Western, she was still one of the first westerners to publicly proclaim the existence of the esoteric orders and an inner plane adepti. In this way, she did more to promote an open-minded investigation into all the mysteries and the lesser-known aspects of spiritual reality than most. About this time, the term *occultism* began to be used to describe the study of these lesser-known aspects of spirituality and the so-called paranormal phenomena that resulted from their engagement.

The Theosophical Society had a mission statement with three primary aims:

1. To form a nucleus of the Universal Brotherhood of Humanity without distinction of race, creed, sex, caste, or color;
2. To encourage the study of Comparative Religion, Philosophy, and Science, and
3. To investigate the unexplained Laws of Nature and the Powers latent in man.

Previous to publishing this statement, part three originally read, "To make a systematic investigation into the mystic potencies of all life and matter, or what is usually termed occultism." There we have the true work of the Society.[1]

As previously stated, things that are labeled occult or esoteric usually don't stay that way. Annie Besant, a student of Blavatsky's who took over the leadership of the Society after Blavatsky's death in 1891, was gifted clairvoyantly. Fortunately, one of her clairvoyant visions was transcribed and diagramed for posterity. In later years with the advent of the electron microscope, this diagram was recognized as an accurate depiction of the structure of a subatomic particle, down to the level of quarks.[2]

Integrating Science and Spirituality

Multidimensional reality is best explained by Ed Witten's M Theory – a super theory to unify all string theories in modern physics. String theories say that subatomic particles are more like moving strings stretching to form membranes ("branes") that become worlds or universes of their own. The search is currently underway for a vanishing particle called the graviton, which when found, will shed much light on how travel between these dimensions occurs.[3] Ageless Wisdom or occultism has long known about these different dimensions and calls them "planes" rather than "branes." Recent research into what physicists call dark matter reveals more about what scientists don't know than what they do. It is estimated that current scientific knowledge only applies to about 7% of the universe. The remaining 93% is unknown. Additionally, science tells us that humans do not use their brains to their fullest potential. Yet the brain is not the be all or the end all, but merely an instrument. Occultists are trained to develop and finely tune that instrument, which more often than not obviates dependence on artificial ones. Therefore some of their accomplishments appear to be supernormal feats. In reality, these phenomena, if not already understood, are on the verge of explanation via continuing discoveries in physics and integrative medicine. Until then, they remain "occult" or hidden from view.

Albert Einstein said, "It is possible that there exist human emanations which are unknown to us. Do you remember how electrical current and "unseen waves" were laughed at? The knowledge about man is still in its infancy."[4] To learn about the magic of computers one studies computer science. To learn about the magical workings of the mind, such as telepathy, one studies occultism. These days, however, the lines between legitimized science and occultism are beginning to blur because both approaches to life and problem solving end and begin in the mind – the one field of mind – consciousness. Modern science for the first time is asking the same question occultism has explored for ages: *What is the nature of mind?*

For centuries, science subjugated pure reason and creative insight to the crippling superstition of absolute objectivity. Quantum physics demonstrated there was no such thing. We cannot observe reality without changing it. As popular author Gary Zukav states, "We cannot eliminate ourselves from the picture. We are a part of nature, and when we study nature, there is no way around the fact that nature is studying itself."[5]

One of the most respected and influential philosophers of the 20th century, Ken Wilber, is another pioneer in this area. His works have contributed much toward bridging the boundaries between science and religion. In a similar vein, he writes:

> We have seen that the philosophers of science are in widespread agreement that empirical science depends for its operation upon subjective and intersubjective structures that allow objective knowledge to emerge and stabilize in the first place. Put bluntly, knowledge of sensory exteriors depends upon nonsensory interiors, interiors that are just as real and just as important as the exteriors themselves. You don't get a message on the telephone, claim the message is real but the phone is illusory. To discredit one is to discredit the other.[6]

Being objective means being unbiased, having no prejudices – that there's an "out there" to be observed, totally separate from the observer, right? Well the problem that went unnoticed for three centuries, according to Zukav,

> …is that a person who carries such an attitude certainly is prejudiced. His prejudice is to be "objective," that is, to be without a preformed opinion. In fact, it is impossible to be without an opinion. An opinion is a point of view. *The point of view that we can be without a point of view is a point of view.* The decision itself to study one segment of reality instead of another is a subjective expression of the researcher who makes it. It affects his perceptions of reality, if nothing else. Since reality is what we're studying, the matter gets very sticky here. (Emphasis added.)[7]

As it certainly did when Madame Blavatsky tried to explain this to the public in the inadequate language of her day: "…matter is spirit at the lowest point of its cyclic activity" and "spirit is matter on the seventh plane."[8] Or as the ancient Hermetic Axiom puts it, "As above, so below." And as the great heart sutra goes, the Prajna Paramita of Tibetan

Buddhism: "Form is exactly emptiness; emptiness exactly form." All variations on modern field theory show that particles cannot be separated from the space surrounding them in accordance with this root principle. Fritjof Capra, author of *The Tao of Physics*, explains,

> The distinction between matter and empty space finally had to be abandoned when it became evident that virtual particles can come into being spontaneously out of the void, and vanish again into the void, without any nucleon or other strongly interacting particle being present... Here then, is the closest parallel to the Void of Eastern Mysticism in modern physics. Like the Eastern Void – the "physical vacuum" – as it is called in field theory – is not a state of mere nothingness, but contains the potentiality for all forms of the particle world. These forms, in turn, are not independent physical entities, but merely transient manifestations of the underlying Void.[9]

So does this mean that all opposites as we have come to know and love them are not real and serve no purpose in the scheme of things? Not exactly. It just points to the fact that there is something beyond all that – something that operates beyond the bounds of dualistic thinking – beyond the rainbow. Yet it is in the mind where we must realize this truth. As the Tibetan Djwal Khul reminds us in Alice Bailey's *Esoteric Psychology*, "It is in the realm of so-called mind that the great principle of separateness is found. It is also in the realm of mind that the great at-one-ment is made."[10]

This takes us back to Zukav who quotes Carl Jung: "The psychological rule says that when an inner situation is not made conscious, it happens outside, as fate. That is to say, when the individual remains undivided and does not become conscious of his inner contradictions, the world must perforce act out the conflict and be torn into opposite halves." Wolfgang Pauli, the Nobel prize-winning physicist who was also Jung's friend, similarly states, "From an inner center, the psyche seems to move outward, in the sense of an extraversion, into the physical world." Zukav concludes that if these men are correct, "... then physics is the study of consciousness."[11]

Now you know why occultism which has always had for its primary subject the study of consciousness has also been called metaphysics. This is where they finally meet. And these days, we have the ridiculous term, "New Age." This stuff is not "New Age." This stuff has been around for millenniums. This stuff is *Ageless Wisdom*. It was with the Druids; it was among early Egyptians. It was taught to Jesus by the Essenes and to the Jews in the form of the Mystical Qabalah. We find it in the shamanistic practices of indigenous peoples all over the world – from the Native American Indian and Australian Aborigine to the ancient Mayans and their unknown ancestors. The Buddha finally found peace in its limitless light, and in sharing its mysteries began the great Eastern lineages that continue to this day. We find its hidden treasure buried deep within the pages of folklore and myth – ancient and contemporary. The sacred story and its secrets are revealed to us in literature and modern movies for those who are receptive to its symbolism.

Still, I prefer the term 'occult' because even with the advent of scientific confirmation, it remains hidden from the masses in its purer forms. It also alludes that it is more of a science than a faith. This is the difference between the pure occultist and the pure mystic. "When the scientific temperament approaches the Unseen, it chooses the Occult Path of development, and when the artistic temperament approaches the Unseen, it chooses the Mystic Path; one progresses through right knowing, and the other through right feeling, and both meet in the end," says legendary occultist Dion Fortune in her classic treatise, *The Esoteric Orders and Their Work.*[12] However, this was more true yesterday than today. As stated previously, since the turn of the 20th century, the trend has been towards integration – balance – like the holistic merging, interdependence and cooperation that results when the hemispheres of the brain are acting in harmony. But what good is that harmony if we don't do something with it? Therefore in occultism, the emphasis is on practical application of this Ageless Wisdom to make the world a better place for self and others. As Lama Surya Das says, "Reality, after all, is spiritual enough. Spirit is meaningless without being grounded here and now in this plane of existence."[13]

Buddhism teaches that wisdom without compassion is just as incomplete as love without truth. This too is acknowledged by Fortune:

> We might speak of the mystic art and the occult science and in so speaking we are reminded that every art is based on a science, and every applied science partakes of the nature of art. The highest development is attained when the mystic has the knowledge and technique of an occultist, or when the occultist is at heart a mystic. The mystic can then express the teaching of the spirit in terms of the intellect and so render them available for those who have no higher consciousness than that of the mind; and the occultist who shares in the things of the spirit will have that element of devotion in his nature which is so often lacking in those in whom the intellect is dominant. Without this element the final synthesis is impossible; he will only be as the exoteric philosopher who follows an ever-receding horizon, because he only studies phenomena by means of the effect they produce on the senses. Noumenal consciousness, which is the ultimate aim of the esotericist, is only possible to those who can actually unite with that which they wish to know... To this all paths lead, and in this all aims find their realization.[14]

On a similar note, Carl Jung writes: "Science is the art of creating suitable illusions which the fool believes or argues against, but the wise man enjoys for their beauty or their ingenuity, without being blind to the fact that they are human veils and curtains concealing the abysmal darkness of the unknowable."[15] Then why the stigma attached to the occult, other than the fact that in general, most people fear the unknown? Well, as Dion Fortune explains,

> An immense mass of verbiage has gathered around the Sacred Science since Madame Blavatsky drew back the curtain of the sanctuary, and the Theosophical Society sought to popularize the ancient Mystery-teaching. Imagination, freed from the bonds of proof, has had free rein, and scoffers have found ample material that was legitimate game for their comments. The pseudo-occultism of the present day, with its dubious psychism, wild theorizing, and evidence that cannot stand up to the most cursory examination, is but the detritus which accumulates around the base of the Mount of Vision. All such worthless rubbish is not worth the power and shot of argument; in order to form a just estimate of the Sacred Science we must study originals, and try to penetrate the minds of the great mystics... whose works bear evidence of first-hand knowledge of the supersensible worlds.[16]

This is why, as all true Gnostics or *those who know* proclaim, the only real proof of anything comes from the integrity of one's own experience. We are given the tools and the means by which we realize this *Great Work* or *dharma* as it is called in the East – and demonstrate the underlying principles of this Ageless Wisdom in the ordinary trials and tribulations of our everyday lives. This is the only confirmation we need. It works – and that's all we need to know.

One Path: Three Great Traditions

Much is determined by personal experience because that is what influences us the most. Therefore, when Ageless Wisdom begins to filter down through human consciousness, it becomes colored by it as well – with all its idiosyncrasies. This phenomenon is what creates the seeming differences on the Path. But oddly enough, it's also what keeps it fresh and fun in any shape or form. It's what every artist knows by heart – that substance is nothing without style!

In order to most effectively examine the various styles through which Ageless Wisdom manifests, we need to touch on origins. Ageless Wisdom has no origin because it's ageless. The different ways by which it's revealed to humanity, however, do have origins, and this particular creation myth has many versions. Yet it's still the same story.

Dion Fortune reminds us, "Readers of esoteric literature will be aware that there are many different schools of occultism, and will find that the teachings and symbolism employed in all are fundamentally the same; so much so that by a mere translation of the terminology the initiate of one is enabled to understand the scriptures of another. Nevertheless, these schools are not identical, for although the form is the same owing to their common origin, the force that animates them is entirely different owing to the circumstance of their foundation."[17]

The common origin of these schools, according to Fortune, is the lost continent of Atlantis. According to her version of the story, there were three great cataclysms that shook Atlantis before it finally sank into the sea, coinciding with three major emigrations. The emigrations were led by what could be called the "high priests and priestesses" of this advanced civilization – highly awakened initiates who took with them their sacred records and teachings. These initiates gained their knowledge from something called *Manus*. Manus are not human, although Fortune says they are more closely related to us than other life forms. Isn't this starting to sound familiar? Whether it is angels, gods, deities, dakinis, or extraterrestrials – in all the different versions of this story across the world, a nonhuman element plays a vital role.

According to Fortune, these Manus operated under the different aspects or 'keynotes' of the rays of the sun which all came together in the Great Sun Temple in Atlantis. The three emigrations were colored by three major Manus and their energy specializations roughly corresponding to Love, Wisdom,

14

and Power. The first emigration traveled across the north of the land we know as Europe and Asia, and was responsible for such megalithic sites as Stonehenge. Research has established that Stonehenge predates the Druids.[18] Central to much Celtic mythology and Druidic lore is a reference to the Great Ones who came from across the sea. It is said that Merlin, for instance, was taught by one. At any rate, this first emigration settled in Southeast Asia where it came in contact with remnants of a more ancient magic associated with the lost continent of Lemuria. The Power aspect ruled this emigration, and according to Fortune, was the basis of what she calls "primitive cults" which work mainly with forces belonging to the astral plane or "etheric" levels of existence. Shamanistic practices utilizing blood and animal sacrifice are expressions of this force. Its influence can also be seen in the Bon religion that predated and had a significant impact upon the development of Tibetan Buddhism.

The second emigration went in the same direction, but more southerly due to the advancing polar ice. Ironically, it landed in the Himalayan region, and gave rise to all those schools that have that spiritual center as their source of inspiration. The Wisdom Manu was behind this movement and planted the seeds for its development in the Eastern Mystery Traditions. This Wisdom energy mingled with the Power energy that was already established; its elements most recognizable in the Eastern sects that are more shamanistic and tantric in nature. "Yet for the most part a remarkable degree of purity has been maintained in the inner Orders, and some of the profoundest knowledge in the world is guarded in its mountain strongholds," writes Fortune.[19]

Last but not least, we have the invasion of the Love brigade – the final emigration that had for its major task the socialization of humanity with the ideals of 'brotherhood' and compassion. Here we have the foundation for all the Western Mystery Schools and the major theme running through the story of Jesus. These folks headed south and landed in Egypt, settling mainly in the Middle East and Mediterranean Basin.

From this area arose the mysteries associated with ancient Egypt, Greece, and Israel. As Fortune describes,

> The Tyrian and Grecian Mysteries admit that their adepts were trained in the Egyptian temples; from the Tyrian we know that the Hebrew tradition derived its renaissance, and from the Grecian Mysteries grew that Gnosis which translated the spiritual concepts of Christianity into the language of the intellect; and from that Gnosis, crushed as it was by the Christian Church after the power had passed from the hands of those who knew nothing but the outer form of the truth they held, arose that long line of intellectual mystics who kept the fire alight in Europe and whom later generations have called the Alchemists.[20]

Fortune doesn't talk about a westward emigration. She doesn't explain how the mystery traditions of the indigenous peoples of the Americas emerged. If scholars are correct in saying that these people originated in Asia and came across the land bridge over the Bering Sea, that could explain the striking similarities between their shamanistic practices and those of the first emigration from Atlantis who filtered down the Asian plateau. Yet we have the ancient civilizations of the Maya and Inca in Central and South America, whose spiritual practices and architecture bear greater resemblance to those settlers from the Third Emigration in ancient Egypt. Many of these indigenous Americans also speak about their ancestors coming from across the sea. The *Book of the Hopi* refers to a third world that was destroyed by a flood. Spider woman guided them to safety where they could build the next world.[21]

All these early indigenous peoples, including European-based pagan tribes, worshipped nature and placed highest importance on protecting and respecting the Earth. One version of the legend says that although Atlantis may have been an advanced civilization, there were those who misused the power of the Sun Temple, and that abuse led to the destruction of their land, much like what could be done with nuclear energy today.

Could this be the reason why our native brothers and sisters so revere the Earth? Perhaps they share some dim racial memory of such an occurrence as reflected in their myths and legends.

At any rate, Fortune might have been giving us a clue when she wrote:

> American occultism will never come into its own until it ceases to import its systems from Europe and India, but goes back along the line of its own tradition, picking up the aboriginal contacts, and daring to bend them to its own evolutionary purposes. It must seek the contacts of the Sun Temple of Atlantis through the Maya tradition. Egypt has no message for the United States. Americans can learn esoteric philosophy and science from the Western tradition, just as Europeans can learn from the Eastern tradition, but the initiatory forces cannot be conveyed across the Atlantic or the Pacific. Some day there will come an American who will pick up the ancient Maya contacts, adapt them to modern needs, and express their forces in an initiatory ritual which shall be valid for the civilization to which he belongs.[22]

Pondering that statement at length, the first thing that came to my mind was the work of Carlos Castaneda. In recent decades, much research and analysis has gone into his work and that of other authors influenced by the Toltec tradition, such as Don Miguel Ruiz. Revealing insights are found in the work of Edward Plotkin, who has documented the similarities between the complex teachings of the Yaqui sorcerer, Don Juan, and the more esoteric tenets of Tibetan Buddhism, such as Vajrayana and Dzogchen.[23]

For the most part, however, I do not feel that Fortune is accurate in her assessment of esotericism in the United States. Though highly knowledgeable and insightful as her writings undoubtedly are, they partially reflect some of the social biases of her time. For instance, she talks about some races and cultures as better suited for certain mystical paths than others by virtue of the differences in their genetic makeup, metabolism, environment, and so on.

For one, this presumption fails to recognize that most Anglo-Saxon Americans have their roots in Europe. This heritage alone makes accessible to them the Western Mystery Traditions. Regarding the differences in temperament between the European races and Asian races, she states:

> The Eastern forces require very purified and rarefied vehicles for their operation, and therefore the primitive aspects of the nature have to be pruned away. The Western forces are much stronger and more drastic in their action, because they take hold of the primitive aspects and use them for their own ends, sublimating the base metal into gold, not precipitating the gold from the ether. You may enable yourself to receive wireless signals beyond normal range either by increasing the power of the transmitting apparatus or the sensitivity of the receiving apparatus. The Western method employs the former, the Eastern the latter... Meditation and asceticism will bring the Eastern chela to the foot of his Master, but the Western initiator, working in the much denser material conditions of that civilization, has to employ ritual to get his results – rituals that very few Eastern bodies could stand. The meditative methods of the East will not get results in the West unless the vitality is lowered, and it is a very risky thing to attempt to handle high potencies on a lowered vitality; nor will the aspirant fare well in the rush and drive of our civilization.[24]

While this might have been true at the beginning of the 20th century, it is hardly applicable in the new millennium. This is not theory -- we are beginning to see proof, particularly in the results that some Westerners are obtaining through the study of Eastern traditions such as Tibetan Buddhism.

Seventy-five to one hundred years ago, the Eastern spiritual methods were best adapted to the Eastern spiritual lifestyle, which was highly reclusive, hierarchical, completely in slow motion (if in motion at all) and without the distractions and stresses of a growing, industrialized civilization. As Fortune says, "If you wish to follow the yogi methods you must lead the yogi life; if you do not, you will break down."[25]

In the West, we can't go into a cave and meditate for three years. We have business to attend. In the 1960s and 70s many first generation Western dharma students who went to Asia to study were confronted with this dilemma even then. What these brave pioneers had to contend with and endure in order to learn the material well enough to translate it, adapt it to Western thinking, and then finally make it applicable to Western culture, is much underrated and unappreciated in my opinion. I'm talking about people like Lama Surya Das, Joan Halifax, Robert Thurman, Tsultrim Allione, and Catherine Ingram, just to name a few. Exposure to their work helped me to see the parallels between the Eastern esoteric schools and the Western schools that I've been trained in.

In fact, these Western dharma pioneers have been so successful at what they're doing that it is causing some individuals who know better to minimize if not outright dismiss the value and equal effectiveness of our Western Mystery Traditions. This trend is changing fortunately because of the synthesis and integration of the teachings happening on many levels in diverse fields all over the world. It is what going beyond the rainbow is all about.

This task of getting together and staying together has been one of the major difficulties confronting Western aspirants during the past two millenniums, and one of the major reasons why the West does not have a great body of esoteric literature like the East, comparatively speaking. The waves of persecution effectively dispersed and oppressed many seekers, causing many schools to go underground. Esoteric Christianity reveals that Jesus accepted and taught reincarnation. Early Church manuscripts asserted the same. Yet when Church and

State merged, the process was corrupted by the power elite. By the last council of Constantinople in 869, C.E., the Church had rewritten scripture and strictly banned the teachings of the esoteric truths that gave Christianity its original spark. This was one of the ugliest and most formidable experiments in social control, the effects of which still linger today. Those who shared the Ageless Wisdom had to go into hiding or else suffer merciless persecution and often death.

Therefore, the sacred flame was kept alive in secret societies formed by the Gnostics, Freemasons, Rosicrucians, Alchemists, Troubadours, Knights Templar, Celtic Church, and so on. Like their pagan brothers and sisters who were manifesting the mandates of the Love Ray Manu through nature contacts and polytheistic mysticism (for example, Briton and Nordic tribes), they had a rich oral tradition, because writing down these words was always risky. Any documents could be used as evidence of "witchcraft." Yet at the same time, much subtlety and many finer points were lost after generations of oral transmission, because this was not just an art – it was an experimental science.

Scientific methods and results must be preserved. Someone had to start writing it down. Therefore, what was written down was done so in a manner that did not make the truth completely obvious. So we find these silly stories and myths, medieval cartoons, fairy tales, and Tarot cards that make absolutely no sense to the casual observer – not to mention the openly esoteric manuscripts of the 18th and early 19th centuries fraught with deliberate blinds. But those who knew could decipher the secret symbolism, extrapolate its meanings and associations, and communicate in a language that evolved into a tradition so richly diverse, highly individualized and truly visionary – that it eventually gave birth to one of the most profound experiments of the Love Ray Manu in the history of humankind: democracy – the United States of America – the greatest legacy of the Western Mystery Tradition.[26]

The promise of the rainbow awaits us.

[1] Clayton Matthews, *Secret Psychic Organizations,* Sherbourne Press, 1969, p. 98.

[2] Robert Beutlich, "Quarks, Occult Chemistry and the String Model," a paper presented at the 1980 United States Psychotronics Association Conference.

[3] Brian Greene, *The Elegant Universe: Superstrings, Hidden Dimensions, and the Quest for the Ultimate Theory,* Vintage, 2000.

[4] Mikol Davis and Earle Lane, *Rainbows of Life,* Harper Colophon Books, 1978, p. 37.

[5] Gary Zukav, *The Dancing Wu Li Masters: An Overview of the New Physics,* Bantam Books, 1979, p. 31.

[6] Ken Wilber, *The Marriage of Sense and Soul: Integrating Science and Religion,* Random House, 1998, p. 150.

[7] Zukav, p. 30.

[8] Alice A. Bailey, *Esoteric Psychology, Vol. I,* Lucis Trust, 1936, p. 17. Reprinted with permission from Lucis Trust Publishing.

[9] Fritjof Capra, *The Tao of Physics,* Bantam Books, 1975, p. 209.

[10] Bailey, p. 16.

[11] Zukav, p. 31.

[12] Dion Fortune, *The Esoteric Orders and Their Work,* 1928, Llewellyn Publications, 1971, p. 138. Reprinted with permission from Red Wheel/Weiser.

[13] Lama Surya Das, *Awakening the Buddha Within,* Broadway Books, 1997, p. 233. Reprinted with permission.

[14] Fortune, p. 139.

[15] Davis, p. 45.

[16] Dion Fortune, *Sane Occultism,* Samuel Weiser, Inc., 1967, pp. 7-8. Reprinted with permission from Red Wheel/Weiser.

[17] Fortune, 1971, p. 45.

[18] Jean Markale, *The Druids: Celtic Priests of Nature,* Inner Traditions International, 1999.

[19] Fortune, 1971, p. 48.

[20] *Id.*

[21] Frank Waters, *Book of the Hopi,* Penguin Books, 1963.

[22] Fortune, 1967, p. 168.

[23] Edward Plotkin, *The Four Yogas of Enlightenment: Guide to Don Juan's Nagualism and Esoteric Buddhism,* http://www.FourYogas.com, 2000; see also Daniel Noel, ed., *Seeing Castaneda: Reactions to the "Don Juan" Writings of Carlos Castaneda,* Perigee Books, 1976; Tomas, *Creative Victory: Reflections on the Process of Power from the Collected Works of Carlos Castaneda,* Samuel Weiser, Inc., 1995; and http://www.nagual.org.

[24] Fortune, 1967, p. 168.

[25] *Id.*

[26] Dr. Paul Foster Case, *The Great Seal of the United States: Its History, Symbolism and Message for the New Age,* Builders of the Adytum, Ltd., 1976 (first published 1935).

CHAPTER 2

EAST MEETS WEST

Esoteric orders today: Who are they?

The Western Way

Around the same time Blavatsky was making headlines with her Eastern-flavored occultism, a truly Western order was established on this side of the fence – not the fence that divides East and West, but the veil between the seen and the unseen. Inner planes of being exist – no matter what we choose to call them – "the other side" – heaven – hell – purgatory --the astral plane – the bardos – the Elysian fields – other dimensions – other realities.

The Mystery Schools often call the ones who have gone before and who now reside on the inner planes, "Masters" – souls who have "graduated" from the physical plane of existence. Some people dislike the word master because of its association with slavery. In a way, the association is real because until we learn self-mastery, we are somewhat slaves to ignorance and suffering. I like to refer to these illustrious folks as *higher beans*. That's right -- beans, just beans – higher on the beanstalk than most of us, so they have a wider perspective -- a more majestic view, so to speak.

Now these are magical beans, not just ordinary beans – as Jack was soon to discover when he got home from the market. He'd traded their only cow -- for beans? His mother was furious. She threw the beans out the window and sent Jack to bed without supper. Some magic, Jack thought. Until the next day….   Jack looked out the window, and well, you know the rest of the story.

Jack was about to face the most significant challenge of his lifetime. He succeeded in overcoming this adversity and got the golden goose that benefited not only him and his family, but the entire village. It's your every day run of the mill hero myth, just like Dorothy's journey in *The Wizard of Oz*. The meritorious author, Joseph Campbell, has written about them extensively:

> …we have not even to risk the adventure alone, for the heroes of all time have gone before us. The labyrinth is thoroughly known. We have only to follow the thread of the hero path, and where we had thought to find an abomination, we shall find a god. And where we had thought to slay another, we shall slay ourselves. Where we had thought to travel outward, we will come to the center of our own existence. And where we had thought to be alone, we will be with all the world.[1]

The Dweller on the Threshold must be confronted before we can pass into the light. Those magical beans show the way. These beanstalks or magical schools spring up from time to time when most needed.

That's how *The Golden Dawn* got started – one of the most seminal Western esoteric orders of the 19th Century. For a while, it had its day in the sun. Some of its members were talented in other fields. We know them as W.B. Yeats, Florence Farr, A. E. Waite, Algernon Blackwood, Arthur Machen, Annie Horniman, S. L. MacGregor Mathers, Aleister Crowley, and of course, Dion Fortune.[2] But the Golden Dawn lost much of its appeal when it refused to change with the times. Many of its members became trapped in the web of spiritual elitism, placing undue emphasis on ritual and degree. *Neophytes*, meaning beginners, were treated arrogantly and selectively. As a result, the flame that served as the heart of the organization began to fizzle.

For example, a young fellow had sought them out and humbly submitted to their teaching. It wasn't long before he began to discover some secrets on his own and began to decipher things that, according to the Golden Dawn elders, were reserved for the highest grades of the Order. Appalled and outraged, these elders sent the young fellow packing. Well,

"Fine," he said. "I got my own magic beans. I'll plant my own garden."

So the old beanstalk got cut down, its rotting remains serving as fertile compost for the growth of another, more resilient and strongly resistant to pests than the previous one. It was planted here in the home of the free and the brave in the 1930s by that visionary young fellow, Paul Foster Case, and is called *Builders of the Adytum*, or B.O.T.A. ("BOTA" hereafter for short.)

After Paul Foster Case passed away in 1954, Dr. Ann Davies extended the BOTA work until she passed away in 1975. But the beanstalk continues to flourish and grows strong even today in the new millennium. The curriculum lessons currently disseminated are the original lessons that were written by Case and Davies.

BOTA is "...a non-profit, tax-exempt religious organization irrevocably dedicated to spiritual attunement through enlightened worship in the Tradition of the Western Mysteries."[3] Though not a formal religion, its members are part of a worldwide group of spiritual aspirants linked together by sharing common spiritual practices. Members pay nominal dues, and the teachings are distributed as a privilege of membership.

The name of the order is derived from antiquity:

> *Adytum* is Greek for "Inner Shrine" or "Holy of Holies" and *Builders* refers to the emulation of the Carpenter from Nazareth, Jesus, whom many people believe was versed in the Qabalistic Tradition. However, B.O.T.A. is not a strictly Christian organization, nor is it Jewish, as the Qabalah is thought to be. B.O.T.A. accepts the Qabalah as the mystical root of both ancient Judaism and the original Christianity, but people of all faiths should have no difficulty accepting B.O.T.A. teachings if they are mystically inclined.[4]

Most of the BOTA studies focus on the Qabalah and Tarot -- integrated, complex systems of symbolism that tell the story of Ageless Wisdom. These symbolism sets are highly effective because they communicate spiritual principles in the natural language of the subconciousness – image and symbol. Therefore, meditation on the symbolism of the Tarot keys is often enough to ascertain their meanings. The lessons and techniques provided by BOTA, however, accelerate this process for the attentive aspirant. Still, the student must do the work, as is true in most schools.

Many people believe that the Tarot began as a pack of playing cards used by the Gypsies in the 14th century. According to Case, the first pack appeared around 1200. A group of adepts (highly trained occultists about to become higher beans) representative of many spiritual traditions, met in Fez, Morocco after the great library at Alexandria was destroyed. The time was ripe, they thought, for preserving this Ageless Wisdom in a new form – a form that would be fluid and flexible enough to survive centuries of change and that could be interpreted and understood by anyone regardless of background or origin. Because they were all familiar with visualizing archetypal patterns and using sound, color, and imagery in the development of supernormal states of consciousness, these adepts decided to embed these ancient secrets and spiritual principles into an intricately designed series of images known collectively as the Tarot. BOTA prefers the term "keys" to cards when talking about individual Tarot images because they unlock the door to a greater understanding of these ancient principles.[5]

There are many versions of the Tarot. I cannot speak for their effectiveness because sometimes it's a matter of individual sensitivity. What I can say, however, is that BOTA's version, having stayed true to the original design, has proven to be the most effective version for me – as well as for a great majority of others, judging by the extensive membership of this order in countries all over the world.

26

What are some other branches of the Western Mystery Tradition in existence today? The Rosicrucians are still around. Wicca – a neopagan religion also thrives. There's an odd assortment of other lesser-known Hermetic and neopagan organizations doing their thing, some of them offshoots from larger organizations, not to mention American Indian shamans who have their equally valid esoteric systems. One only has to do a simple search on the Internet to find them. But as far as having genuine contact with higher beans on the other side goes, I cannot speak for them. I can't even speak for BOTA really. As Dr. Case discovered, we all have our own "magic beans" in the palm of our hands. If we want to share them with others, fine. But whatever we choose to do with them is up to us. As long as we are mindful and remember to watch our "P's and Q's" as the old trickster warned Jack, and to abide by the law of karma -- "what ye sow, ye shall also reap" – we'll be all right, at least for the moment.

We all have our own gardens to grow. Sometimes they may look like other gardens, sometimes they don't. Either way, the gardening is always up to each of us, individually.

Ego in the Land of Oz – A Reconciliation

If you were Dorothy in the adventure film "The Wizard of Oz," what scene in the movie would best fit your life as it is right now? Have you realized that there's no place like home? In a spiritual or mythological context, what does that phrase mean – *There's no place like home!* And what does it have to do with ego?

Jesse Stewart, author of *Secrets of the Yellow Brick Road,*[6] feels it is a difficult phrase to describe or understand with our limited vocabulary. It points to something that transcends ordinary experience so that it can only be alluded to with words, yet not fully recognized until experienced, unless you're already there. Well where is "there"? Wherever it is and how we get there depends on where we are. As the Good Witch says, "It's always best to start at the beginning." And better to begin than not at all.

Dorothy and her companions learn many lessons along the Yellow Brick Road. Their adventures shed light on the role of ego in spiritual development, reconciling Eastern and Western views. Assuming the Yellow Brick Road circles the entire globe, we realize that there really is no East or West and that most of what we experience is perspective. Views reconcile when the veil of duality is lifted and we see into this magic world called Oz. We are thus propelled into a state of being where paradigms shift and interdimensional experience is the norm. So we're off to see . . . the Ego in the Land of Oz.

Dorothy and house spinning inside the cyclone is one of the most critical scenes in the entire film. It shows how easily we become hypnotized by appearance. As Dorothy is sitting there with Toto on her bed, she is caught up in the inner turmoil, and passively watches as various items fly by outside the window. Suddenly she sees Ms. Gulch on a bicycle. We all know what happens to Ms. Gulch. The question is, how did she do it? Who or what turned Elmira Gulch into the Wicked Witch of the West? Was it you? Was it Dorothy? Actually, I believe it was the Wizard of Oz, or *ego*. And we all have one of those. So let's take a closer look at that man behind the curtain, and see what he's really all about.

Discussion of ego is important at this stage of our adventure, because how one handles the ego is key in all spiritual traditions and mystery schools. The ego is often seen as an obstacle on the Path. However, as we all know, you don't have to be on a spiritual path to encounter a serious challenge from the ego – one's own or another's.

Another reason this topic is timely is because it can appear that Eastern and Western views on the ego's rightful or wrongful place on the spiritual Path are at odds. These superficial differences are the source of all the confusion, misinterpretation, and downright disparaging of this enigmatic instrument. It is truly a stumbling block for many students, and that's just not necessary. We must reconcile with the ego as the

East must reconcile with the West, because that is where we meet and that is where we are, globally speaking. Therefore, let's agree on a clear definition of ego, for this discussion at least.

Ego is one of those catchall terms that can mean a lot of different things to a lot of different people, even in the secular world. A Webster's dictionary defines ego as "the 'I' or self as distinguished from others; the individual's mental states and sensual experiences, as known through direct introspection."[7] The etymology of the word suggests it comes from *eg* – one of the oldest personal pronouns of the first person singular, which grew into the Latin *ego*, meaning "I". "I" comes from the Old English, *ic*.[8] It is through the ego that we come to know ourselves as separate identities in the topside world of duality and relativity. Therefore, ego, in this sense, is neither good nor bad, but just something that is -- awareness of a "self" or individuality that appears separate from others.

Sigmund Freud, in his psychoanalytical theory, expanded on this definition. Freud viewed the ego as the mediating force between what he called the *id* and *superego* -- the age-old developmental conflict between the part of us which is purely instinctual and focused on pleasure versus the inhibiting part of us attributed to conscience. The whole stigma around repressed desires revolves around this conflict – the ego's inability to mediate and come to a healthy compromise. Instead of dealing with the problem head-on, the ego often runs away from it, according to Freud, eventually lapsing into denial which becomes a dysfunctional defense mechanism. So when things don't go exactly as the ego wants, it pulls a temper tantrum or hides behind smoke and mirrors shouting, "Pay no attention to that man behind the curtain!" In other words, pay no attention to that individual behind the mask.

Here the ego sometimes hardens into a mask -- another meaning for *persona* or personality. But reflect for a moment on the function of masks. Is a mask good or evil, or does it just serve a purpose? Is it a permanent fixture or can it be changed? Robbers wear masks. So do surgeons. Actors wear masks as do astronauts. Batman and Catwoman wear masks. Sunglasses are a form of mask. Make-up is a mask – one that can enhance or disguise. Any hat you wear is a subtle mask. But are you the mask? I don't think so. Carl Jung didn't either. He also didn't care for Freud's dim view of the ego.

Returning to its etymological roots, Jung viewed the ego as a person's basic self-awareness or sense of separate individuality – neither good nor bad but malleable all the same. An individual's ego consciousness is shaped by the integration of other aspects of the psyche often symbolized in story by forces beyond our control -- deities, giants, demons, dragons, animals, fairy-godmothers, and in Dorothy's case wicked witches and winged monkeys. It is through an individual's challenges by these elements that they learn their strengths and weaknesses. This is the mystery of the hero archetype.

However, things are not so black and white. There is no morality in ego play – there is just work to do. The hero who slays the dragon doesn't judge or condemn the dragon. In fact, without a dragon or a wicked witch, there could be no hero. Both roles are essential for the birth of higher consciousness as a result of this play. This is why coming to terms with the shadow archetype is so important. The editors of Carl Jung's *Man and His Symbols* reiterate:

> Dr. Jung has pointed out that the shadow cast by the conscious mind of the individual contains the hidden, repressed, and unfavorable (or nefarious) aspects of the personality. But this darkness is not just the simple converse of the conscious ego. Just as the ego contains the unfavorable and destructive attitudes, so the shadow has good qualities – normal instincts and creative impulses. Ego and shadow, indeed, although separate, are inextricably linked together in much the same way that thought and feeling are related to each other . . . The ego, nevertheless, is in conflict with the shadow, in what Dr. Jung called "the battle for deliverance." . . .For most people the dark or negative side of the personality remains unconscious. The

hero, on the contrary, must realize that the shadow exists and that he can draw strength from it. He must come to terms with its destructive powers if he is to become sufficiently terrible to overcome the dragon – *i.e.*, before the ego can triumph, it must master and *assimilate* the shadow. (Emphasis added.)[9]

Jung's analytical psychology places great importance on individuation as a means of realizing the Self. This is where the terminology begins to tangle. Yes, the ego is a self, but a "little" self, of which personality is a component. The big Self, sometimes called the *Higher Self,* is our essence or soul/spirit-identified Self and is often considered immortal. We view the Self as the center of our innermost being – a kind of divinity within. In *The Wizard of Oz*, Dorothy's Higher Self is symbolized by Glinda, the Good Witch of the North. A sense of separation is still implied by this identification. Even though we may know the separation to be illusory, it still manifests in this manner. A realm exists beyond all this that can't be adequately described with words.

That indescribable realm is represented by the sphere of Kether on the Tree of Life of the Mystical Qabalah. Kether is absolute, undifferentiated, and nondual. (See Appendix 1.) In the West it is known by many names including: *First Matter, Yekhidah, Spirit.* In the East it is like *Rigpa* – a Tibetan Buddhist term for nondual or ever-present naked awareness. Further down on the Tree of Life is the sphere of Tiphareth. Tiphareth is right below Kether on the middle pillar. This is the centered Self of wholeness that Jung talked about – the little ego awareness of a bigger Self or immortal soul that reflects back to us, like a mirror, the realm of Kether. This is the transcendental experience of Self-recognition – a conscious identification with the spiritual oneness we share with all beings.

It might appear that some Western esoteric literature adds to the confusion by calling this big Self or Higher Self, "the Ego" – ego with a capital "E" – in contrast to the little ego, otherwise known as the personality or lower-self. The Ego behind the egos is the Being behind the beings.

31

To illustrate, take Dr. Paul Foster Case's description of the 13th path on the Tree that links Kether to Tiphareth. The Tarot image attributed to this particular path is the *High Priestess* and the assigned Hebrew letter is *Gimel*, meaning "camel." Case translates as follows:

> Thus, it is a symbol of transportation, commerce, that which unites one point in space with other points and carries news from one place to another. In the Qabalistic system this letter is attributed to the Uniting Intelligence of the thirteenth path on the Tree of Life, joining Tiphareth, the seat of personal ego consciousness, to Kether, the seat of Yekhidah, the Universal Ego consciousness.[10]

As if we didn't already have enough egos to worry about, now we have another one, and it's a really big one! With all these egos running amuck, it's no wonder that some Eastern flavored mysticism advocates doing away with ego altogether. But frankly, that's throwing the baby out with the bath water. That's not really what the great Eastern sages intended. Again, it boils down to what we mean by ego – especially the little ego, since that's where all the fingers point.

A cursory review of the Eastern sacred literature reveals an even dimmer view of ego than Freud's, ranging from "let's get rid of this pesky ego" all the way to outright denial – "there is no ego." But remember, I said *cursory* review. Buddha didn't write those texts anymore than Jesus authored the New Testament. Human beings with good and bad intentions had a part in putting together all those various assemblages of the puzzle of truth. Therefore, as with everything else, one must look through, in between and underneath in order to find the appropriate clues and pieces that will help put it back together again.

For instance, Sogyal Rinpoche, one of the foremost experts in Tibetan Buddhism, defines ego as follows:

So ego, then, is the absence of the true knowledge of who we really are, together with its result: a doomed clutching on, at all costs, to a cobbled together and makeshift image of ourselves, an inevitably chameleon charlatan self that keeps alive the fiction of its existence. In Tibetan ego is called *dak dzin*, which means "grasping to a self." Ego is then defined as incessant movements of grasping at a delusory notion of "I" and "mine," self and other, and all the concepts, ideas, desire, and activity that will sustain that false construction. Such a grasping is futile from the start and condemned to frustration, for there is no basis or truth in it, and what we are grasping at is by its very nature ungraspable. The fact that we need to grasp at all and go on and on grasping shows that in the depths of our being we know that the self does not inherently exist. From this secretly, unnerving knowledge spring all our fundamental insecurities and fear.[11]

On the surface, it appears that Rinpoche is saying the little self does not exist, and this is misleading. I am told that what he really means is that the little self only exists in *relation* to other selves so that by itself the little self *is* illusory, and on one level this is true. Still, Westerners who don't think it out to that extent become easily confused. How can we have compassion for this little self if we don't believe it exists on some level? Therefore, I take issue with how some of these concepts are translated from the Eastern perspective.

At the time of death, the story of an illusory little self comes in real handy because it allows us to relinquish our grasp on what we think life is. But while we are living in flesh and blood, we better have a good sense of ego -- a well-defined, strong and healthy sense of separate identity, or *we will not survive – literally*. Thanks to all those saber-toothed tigers, we were able to do this. Therefore, taking *dak dzin* literally, "grasping to a self" can be useful and even essential from time to time.

The ego is the boundary maker. Without it, we *would* die, and because of it we still die. What do I mean by that? Well, think about guns. Sometimes a gun can save our lives, sometimes it can't. Does that make the gun good or bad? To parrot the cliché, guns don't kill people – people kill people. It's the same way with egos. Egos aren't barricades to spiritual enlightenment. Egos don't get in the way. It's what we do with the silly thing that makes all the difference in the world. The ego is a tool pure and simple – nothing more, nothing less. The ego is an instrument for functional thinking – a vital part of our being, but not the whole. It is when we mistake it for the whole that all hell breaks loose.

I think the best metaphor for the ego is one I heard many years ago attending a course in transmutation taught by the illustrious Dr. John D. Rankin at Unity Church of Christianity in Houston, Texas. Our textbook was *Self-Mastery* by the psychologist, David Seabury. Dr. Seabury likened the ego to a secretary. Anyone who's ever had the privilege of working with a secretary knows there are good ones and bad ones. Again, it's not really accurate to label the secretary good or bad, it's the *training*. And who is responsible for supervising the secretary? The boss. The secretary can only work within the limitations prescribed by the boss, and that requires acute observation and communication skills. So in a sense, the ego as secretary is the same as ego as computer – garbage in, garbage out. It's not the computer's fault. It's not the secretary's fault.

Secretaries who overstep their boundaries usually get fired. Our egos are the same. But unfortunately, you can't fire your ego. Instead, you must forge a workable truce – maybe do some reprogramming. The goal is to become a proficient *team* – a productive partnership, because it's true – the two must work together. Their roles are meaningless otherwise. Most power is defined by relationship, not inherent position. Training the ego to rightly relate is what practical magic or any form of engaged spirituality is all about. That means getting down to the business of integration.

Dorothy's three travel companions represent the three primary facets of her psyche: Scarecrow = brains (intellect); Tin Man = heart (emotions); and Lion = courage (will). All three must cooperate with her -- with self-consciousness, in order to effectively integrate their skills and get the job done. But if any of them take over the mission by their leadership alone, they fail.

I think that this is one area where Easterners and Westerners can learn much from each other. It would do well for many Americans to relinquish their overgrown sense of pride that results from a grossly misplaced cultural value on the little ego and its attachments. On the other hand, if the Tibetan people had initially developed a well-formed sense of ego and better "grasp" on its place in the scheme of things, they might not have succumbed to China's tyranny. But perhaps that was their saber-toothed tiger – their shadow – and as soon they fully assimilate it, they will be stronger for it. Who's to say? Still, like Dorothy, this is a lesson we must learn for ourselves, and often the hard way.

Dorothy's last mistake is thinking she has complete mastery over the situation when the Wizard decides to take her back to Kansas in his balloon. That was a lot of "hot air" indeed. It did nothing more than to launch the ego off into the stratosphere causing Dorothy to feel lost and alienated once more. When the Wizard admits he doesn't know how the balloon works and therefore cannot control it, the futility of grasping or relying on this little self for ultimate direction is made clear to Dorothy. Only then does the Higher Self reappear to show Dorothy the real solution to the problem. The good witch, Glinda, reassures Dorothy that she always had the power to go home by virtue of her ruby red slippers.

In the Western mystery schools, red is the color of desire. Only through desire or falling through to the "end" of desire (as it is sometimes similarly stated in the East), can we do this. To follow our heart's desire is to follow a natural path for each of us as unique individuals. In the chapter entitled "There's No

Place Like Home" in Joey Green's book, *The Zen of Oz*, the author explains:

> The Path to Enlightenment is a personal journey. No one can hand you the answer on a silver platter.[12]

So the ego must grow up, maybe even fly away to who knows where for a little while until it learns how to handle all that hot air. This is letting go and taking advantage of the present moment. This is exactly what Dorothy does – as soon as she realizes she can. As Lama Surya Das says, "If you cling to nothing, you can handle anything."[13]

Always, we must tend to our own gardens. No one can do it for us. The best way to deal with another person's out of control ego is to get control of one's own. Sometimes (but not always), getting control means just the opposite – letting go – seeing through – and smiling down on the little self that loves to make mountains out of molehills and who thinks it's the king of all of them, including the forest. In other words, sometimes we need to stop taking ourselves so seriously. Dorothy and her companions had to learn this lesson. So must we. Those three supporting forces must be integrated with the whole or the magic disappears like bubbles.

It's no coincidence that Glinda, the Good Witch of the North, travels in a bubble. The Higher Self is encapsulated in an utterly glistening transparent bubble. It is used for transportation and nothing more. It gets her from point A to point B in a rational, linear fashion, however it seems to appear out of nowhere. Something paradoxical, as essence and nonduality, begins to manifest when we call upon it to do so. In the words, of Lama Surya Das:

> The whole sea is in the bubble, the ego. The bubble is transparent. . . You don't have to get rid of your ego. Just see through it. You don't have to fight with it. The bubble is the sea. And it is dancing in and as the sea already. We don't have to figure it out: yes or no, right or wrong, smaller or bigger, or

many or one. These are all just intellectual concepts. It's a paradox, but only to the mind. Can we tolerate the paradox of yes and no, of will on one hand and allowing on the other? Of course, you can give your opinion and do your best, but you also have to be able to let go; you need to maintain the bigger perspective. It's a challenge. There's no easy answer. Better to keep the question alive than come up with some quick, superficial answer. Every moment try to investigate: Where is the Middle Way between the two sides of everything? . . . the model, the concepts, are very limiting. But those are like the bubbles, also. They can be there. You are not just that. This is the View. You are not just that. It's not really a limitation. It's just a momentary form of emptiness. You are not that. You are not stuck there. It's not you anyway. You momentarily experience feelings, thoughts, sensations, but they are not really yours, or anyone's.[14]

They're just there, those bubbles, and aren't they beautiful? Let us continue to enjoy this incredible diversity of display – to don these beautiful and horrifying masks, and parade about in our silly stories and myriad pageants of gore and glory. But when the show is over, let's not forget to place the costumes where they belong, and to remember, the actor could not act without the one who wrote the script. The soldier could not fight without the general giving orders. And the man behind the curtain is simply the man behind the curtain. The Land of Oz is what we make of it. The Wizard admits that he's actually a very good man committed to service; he's just a very poor wizard. The sooner we see through his shenanigans, the sooner we realize he isn't God – the sooner we can befriend him and allow him to bestow upon us the Self-recognition that we already have deep inside each of us whatever it takes, whatever we desire – to get us all back home.

The Eastern Way

The East is like an ocean whose underwater boundaries resemble an upside down bell curve. Visually, the slopes reveal a smooth descent to the bottom. Whereas the West is like a giant freshwater lake fed by secret underground springs with pockets of unfathomable depths encountered unexpectedly. The topography of the bottom is far less predictable. Reverse these images and the analogy still holds true. The Western mystery schools are like an irregular, jagged mountain range with peaks of all different shapes and sizes. The Eastern school is a solitary, majestic mountain. The Eastern higher beans have maintained their mountain strongholds for centuries, and clearly forged a way to the top for those who wish to climb. The paths leading to the ascent are many, and most of them are paved with intricate designs carved into the walls lining the path. An illiterate man may not know what those designs are all about, but he certainly knows that they're about something special. Therefore, he holds for them and for those who put them there a great reverence and respect – even though he cannot decipher the meanings. This is one of the major cultural differences between the East and the West.

Even in Eastern secular society, the emphasis on the family and community is greater than on the individual, and as a whole, they honor their elders and have a greater respect for authority than most Westerners. Of course, Americans know all about the down side to that or they wouldn't be Americans. But the up side is that it's probably that very element that has enabled the East to build up one of the most vast and richly documented storehouses of ancient wisdom teachings in the world.

Hinduism, Jainism and other Eastern religions all have their esoteric sides. My discoveries, however, have come from an exposure to Tibetan Buddhism, which is only one form of Buddhism. Therefore, an elementary introduction is in order.

Many Westerners are attracted to Buddhism for several reasons. One reason is that Buddhist values are similar to Christian values. Vietnamese Zen Buddhist Master, Thich Nhat Hanh, explores this idea at length in his bestseller, *Living Buddha; Living Christ.*[15] I think the best introductory book on Tibetan Buddhism is by Lama Surya Das, *Awakening the Buddha Within – Tibetan Wisdom for the Western World.*

Surya's birth name is Jeffrey Miller. He was born and raised in a middle-class Jewish family on Long Island in New York – a regular guy -- wanted to be a ball player. He even went to college. But then something happened: Kent State – friends murdered. The shock of that insanity propelled him eastward where he eventually landed in Nepal. After spending several decades overseas, he has become one of the most highly trained American-born lamas in the Tibetan tradition. But his Jewish mother still jokingly calls him, "the Deli Lama."

Surya simplifies complex Buddhist terms, like dharma. Dharma is a Sanskrit word meaning teaching or truth. Literally it means, "to support or uphold."[16] In the East the dharma generally refers to the teachings of the compassionate, enlightened Buddha who lived in northern India about 500 years before Jesus Christ. Let's not forget though that the West has its own 'dharma' not unlike that of the East. Yet enthusiastic new 'converts' often quote an ancient prophecy by Padma Sambhava, the founder of the first Tibetan monastery in the 1700s: "When the iron bird flies, and horses run on wheels, the Tibetan people will be scattered like ants across the World, and the Dharma will come to the land of red-faced people." Many historians speculate that the land of the red-faced people is code word for America.

While the part about the expulsion of the Tibetans came true, the other part is a little lame. The dharma has been here all along. We may call it by other names, but it's still the dharma. It didn't need to be imported. That's not to minimize the efforts of those pioneering Westerners who traveled overseas and brought back the teachings – quite the contrary. What those Westerners did was offer a different *version* of the dharma in order to enrich and reinvigorate our own. In the long run, I believe that the outcome will be the development of a unique expression of spirituality neither Eastern nor Western – but something entirely different, yet basic and integral. It is as yet without form.

A tendency towards overgeneralization and over-idealization is still prevalent in many dharma circles in the West. Buddhism in Tibet, much like Christianity in the United States or any religion anywhere, has an esoteric and exoteric side, and like all religion, it can be used as a tool for enlightenment or exploitation. Lama Surya Das, Robert Thurman, and other Western dharma teachers have extracted from the Buddhist teachings the *inner core* of the mysteries and compacted them into an essentialized but highly delectable dish that truly satiates the spiritually starved psyches of many Westerners. These teachers are charismatic and exceptionally eloquent in their delivery of this perfect dish, this completely *uncorrupted* jewel of wisdom. Unfortunately, some Westerners begin to think that everything about it and its country of origin must be completely pure and better than anything offered over here. Naively, they assume that all Tibetans are saints and that we're just a bunch of barbaric morons, even though a greedy, hierarchical faction of the ecclesiastical system in Tibet abusing privilege for personal power and gain has been exposed.[17] Yet anywhere we are, we must retain the maturity to remember that corrupted ministries do not invalidate the teachings or effectiveness of any religion – Christian, Buddhist, or otherwise.

Another false supposition is that Tibet spent centuries developing an inner technology of the mind focusing on enlightenment and liberation while the West refined an outer technology of machines for military purpose and material gain. Anyone who makes that argument is just not familiar with the Western Mystery Traditions. The same inner technology has been present all along over here, yet remained underground for long periods of time for reasons previously stated.

40

Finally, you may hear someone say, "Buddhism produces leaders like the Dalai Lama who would never advocate war; but Christianity produced George Bush!" This thinking is equally erroneous. For one, quality of political leadership is not contingent upon religion. Second, reducing a person to their religious affiliation is sadly shortsighted. A leader's actions are no more a reflection on their religion than the color of their eyes. While George Bush's Christian upbringing certainly influenced his ideas and values, it was not what motivated him to bomb Iraq. It is not even what put him in office. The religious group that was most instrumental in getting him elected was the cult of high finance – the people who worship the money god.

Having countered those arguments, it must be emphasized that we are extremely fortunate that these new leaders of Buddhism in the West are distilling these ancient mysteries into a new form as yet uncorrupted in its transmission, truly practical in its application, and genuinely spiritually transformative. It is a most welcome, refreshing and valuable contribution to Western spirituality.

Even though Buddhism is recognized as one of the world's major religions, it's more of a philosophy than a religion. Buddha's teaching does not acknowledge a supreme creator but neither is it completely atheistic. Buddha's main concern was suffering and figuring out how to end suffering; not theological issues like "Is there a God?" However, the development of compassion and wisdom are key to overcoming suffering, according to Buddhist doctrine, not unlike the teachings of other world religions.

Enlightenment or *nirvana* is a state of mind more than anything, yet still beyond mind as we know it, according to Buddhism. It's everywhere and nowhere – an all-inclusive awareness experienced when hearts, minds, and egos have been liberated from ignorance, the illusion of separateness, and over-attachment to people and things. According to some traditions, it IS the innate reality of everything and our own true nature, also known as Buddha nature. Lama Surya Das says we're all Buddhas. All we have to do is wake up.

You may be asking, what is the nature of this divine alarm clock that will awaken us? The nature of all clocks is to tell time. Time is conceptualized in three parts, as far as clocks are concerned: hours, minutes, and seconds. The Buddhist alarm clock also tells time in three parts: (1) wisdom training, (2) ethics training, and (3) meditation training.

What does the alarm on this clock sound like? Well, it's going off at this moment, and when we turn it off, we will be truly awake. The sound of the alarm clock is suffering. Thich Nat Hanh says that in order to end our suffering, we have to closely scrutinize the nature of our suffering. Buddhists have been doing this for a long time. In so doing, they found out that the sound of suffering also has three distinct qualities: (1) ignorance of the truth or denial; (2) unhealthy attachments – attachments which are formed as a result of putting one's ego before all else, and (3) aversion or dislike, which is negative thinking. For more detail on the inner workings of the clock, I recommend Surya's book.

What I think is most helpful to remember is that the clock has snooze control. It may be a while before you finally get up and stay awake, but that's part of the process too. Jesus and the Buddha both taught that the kingdom of heaven is within. We just get too caught up in living without.

Reincarnation and karma are integral parts of Buddhism, but those beliefs are not necessary to benefit from the teachings. In fact, it's not about believing at all. It's about experiencing. Yet once we fall deeply into the esoteric waters, we experience an inner confirmation of the law of cycles, and that usually translates into an awareness that we have lived before and that we will live again. That's why the law of karma is so important, irrespective of a belief in reincarnation. There's a price to pay for everything.

Buddhist leaders teach that tolerance is paramount. The Dalai Lama says to learn from everyone. He admonishes Buddhists to contribute – not convert. As Surya often says, quoting one of his teachers, "No one has a corner on the market of truth." A Christian need not convert to Buddhism to benefit from practicing Buddhist basics like mindfulness, meditation and chanting, and Buddhists need not become Christians to learn from the Sermon on the Mount. The truth belongs to everyone.

It is true that Buddhism, as the world has known it, is rapidly changing – especially in America. In fact, there's a huge conference held once a year dedicated to this very issue. There are specific trends, however, according to Surya. For one, American Buddhism is far more open, integral, and inclusive than the Asian branches. It is practice-oriented and trying to move past an authoritarian approach to one more egalitarian.[18]

That movement in particular is creating great controversy in Buddhist circles right now. Yet something beneficial and extraordinary is happening as a result. The movement is opening doors to some of the greatest treasures of the esoteric teachings secretly guarded by the high lamas for centuries. Teachers like Lama Surya Das are making these methods accessible to us right here and now with outstanding results and without requiring long years of study. These practices are loosely associated with the terms dzogchen and tantra. In the meantime (pun intended), pay attention to that stupid alarm clock. The awakening can be quite rude sometimes, as we shall see.

The Primordial Female

"Toto, I have a feeling we're not in Kansas anymore."

Ever feel that way? If so, good. It means you're half way home. How did Dorothy get to Oz? When did it all start? As with most things, it all started with a simple desire: the desire to be free -- to be free from suffering. "A place where there isn't any trouble... Do you suppose there is such a place, Toto? It's not a place you can get to by a boat or a train. It's far, far away. Behind the moon, beyond the rain..."

Dorothy gets her wish and travels via cyclone. Having barely arrived in this strange new land, she sees this great big bubble of light approaching, and out steps Glinda, the Witch of the North. Dorothy turns to Toto and says, "Now I know we're not in Kansas. We must be over the rainbow." Glinda says, "Are you a good witch or a bad witch?" And this is critical. For you see, we're all witches deep down, whether we want to be or not. Dorothy had to learn this the hard way. Being over the rainbow or in the Land of Oz, she just found more trouble. Yet through a series of tasks, she discovers that she always had the ability to stand forth on her own, and that it stemmed from the very thing that she thought was causing all the trouble to begin with – desire for freedom, symbolized by the ruby red slippers. Out of all the hero myths, none renders the telling of this truth clearer than the tale of Dorothy's quest.

Dorothy's home is transformed into the most important place in the world because now she looks at it with new eyes; eyes that see through, beyond, and in between -- eyes that see things the way they really are. This new vision transforms all pain and suffering because these are the eyes of a witch – a tantrika – and a master of dzogchen.

Home is a symbol for that source of wholeness, unity, absolute reality, nondual awareness where everything and everyone is rooted. We never leave home. We just think we do. We get so caught up in the world of duality, materialism, and personal soap opera that it appears we are anywhere but home. When we wake up in this dream that has turned into a nightmare, that's when we turn to Toto and say, "I have a feeling we're not in Kansas anymore." But as Dorothy found out, we don't get back home by running away from our problems, but by confronting them. She had to claim the witch's broomstick as her own. The broomstick is a symbol for what the Eastern schools refer to as the *kundalini* – the serpent energy coiled at the base of the spine that enervates the energy centers in the body known as *chakras*.

Many people flee their spiritual homes of origin in search of something better for the wrong reasons or under the wrong conditions. Many folks, disillusioned with Christianity, flock to alternative religions, New Age groups, or the exoticism of Eastern religions like Buddhism. While exploring other spiritual perspectives and traditions has its own merit, it usually doesn't solve the problem because the problem is in the person – not the religion or the spiritual tradition. Truth is truth. If human beings want to disregard the truth, distort the truth, and desecrate it with hypocrisy, even killing others in the name of it -- that doesn't do a damn thing to the truth. Doesn't change it one bit. The truth is still the truth. No religion or spiritual tradition is immune to human corruption and greed. That is why it is so important to find one's *own* way home. And that's what Dorothy does.

Dorothy recruits necessary friends along the way – Scarecrow (mind/intellect), Tin Man (emotion/feeling), and the Cowardly Lion (courage/will.) Though they each have a separate role, they all work together to accomplish a mutual goal. In the West, this working together, synthesis, and integration is accomplished through gnosis, ritual magic, alchemy, and transmutation. In the East, it's a result of practicing tantra, dzogchen, and esoteric yoga. Yet no matter how it's done, in a Western style or Eastern, the ultimate outcome is the realization of that nondual awareness we call home. It's easier than we think. The trick is learning how to sustain that realization through all our thoughts, feelings, and actions while living in the ephemeral state of duality. It's all about finding heaven in earth. Once this hidden treasure is found, it doesn't abnegate the need to work toward making the world a better place for others. On the contrary, one feels a greater need than ever to be of service because one sees more clearly how to be most effective in that regard.

In Christianity, the Garden of Eden symbolizes the state of nonduality where there is no good or evil. All creation myths are different versions of the same story. In *The Power of Myth*,[19] by Joseph Campbell with Bill Moyers, twelve pages contain examples that classically illustrate this truth. Bill Moyers reads a line out of the Book of Genesis, and Campbell responds with reciting text from another spiritual tradition or mythology with the same meaning. Unfortunately, the orthodox Christian interpretation is tainted with a great deception – not that of the devil, but of man: male supremacy and devaluation of the feminine aspect of the divine.

Patriarchy and/or dominator society has not always held the world in a stranglehold. Scholars, historians, and archeologists, such as Harriett Lerner and Riane Eisler, have unearthed more than enough evidence in support of this.[20] This is good news because what was created can be uncreated. Patriarchy is on its way out, thanks in part to these esoteric orders. But religion is a powerful tool that can be used to uplift or to crush, as we all know too well. Still, looking behind and underneath and through and beyond and in between, we find the ancient clues. The sacred feminine principle is still at the root of everything – no matter how some may want to redress her, disguise her, or eliminate her altogether.

The Wicked Witch of the West and Glinda the Good Witch of the North, in Eastern spiritual tradition, particularly Tibetan Buddhism, are obviously dakinis. One is a mean mother and the other is "the good guy." Both serve Dorothy in her journey. Therefore, one could not exist without the other. So what's a dakini? Generally, "the dakini represents the ever-changing flow of energy with which the yogic practitioner must work in order to become realized. She may appear as a human being, as a goddess – either peaceful or wrathful – or she may be perceived as the general play of energy in the phenomenal worlds."[21] Dakinis are important in Eastern esotericism because tradition says they brought the sacred mysteries to humanity.

In Tibetan Buddhism, the primordial female is the Great Mother of all things, but still something beyond even that. Buddhist author Tsultrim Allione quotes Trungpa Rinpoche:

> In phenomenal experience, whether pleasure or pain, birth or death, sanity or insanity, good or bad, it is necessary to have a basic ground. This basic ground is known in Buddhist literature as the mother principle. Prajnaparamita (the perfection of wisdom)

is called the mother-consort of all the Buddhas . . . As a principle of cosmic structure, the all-accommodating basic ground is neither male nor female. One might call it hermaphroditic, but due to its quality of fertility or potentiality, it is regarded as feminine.[22]

Allione points to a similar concept illustrated by Starhawk's description of the Great Mother Goddess from the Wiccan perspective: "In the beginning the Goddess is the All, virgin, meaning complete within herself. Although She is called *Goddess*, she could just as well be called *God* – sex has not yet come into being. . . . Yet the female nature of the ground of being is being stressed – because the process of creation that is about to occur is a *birth* process. . ."[23] And birth is seldom a pleasurable experience for the mother or the baby.

The Biblical fall can be interpreted in many ways on many levels. It even has a literal basis in truth in relation to our extraterrestrial origins. But here, figuratively speaking, we have the son, Adam, being expelled from the Garden of Eden – his mother's womb. In this way God (or the Goddess) is acting through Eve or is Eve. So women get a bad rap for this. When asked why, Campbell says because "They represent life. Man doesn't enter life except by woman, and so it is woman who brings us into this world of pairs of opposites and suffering."[24] In the Greek trilogy by Aeschylus, Orestes gets so upset about this that he kills his mother, and is later acquitted of the crime by the insane reasoning that he's not related to her. The jury was tied, however. The backstabbing goddess Athena – symbolizing female complicity in advocating male supremacy and establishing patriarchy – cast the tie-breaking vote. It was another instance of divide and conquer that worked for the time being.[25]

The serpent fares no better than the woman in the orthodox Biblical interpretation. However, the Old Religion reveres the Serpent. The great Serpent protectively hovered over the meditating Buddha. The mystical Qabalah teaches that Christ and the Serpent are two sides of the same force. Yet many

47

people revile the snake. Campbell reminds us that the Garden belonged to the Serpent long before the advent of the Judeo-Christian tradition. "We have Sumerian seals from as early as 3500 B.C. showing the serpent and the tree and the goddess, with the goddess giving the fruit of life to a visiting male. The old mythology of the goddess is right there."[26] Campbell also sees in the story of the fall a reflection of the historical conflict between the Hebrews and the people of Canaan. "The principle divinity of the people of Canaan was the Goddess, and associated with the Goddess is the serpent. This is the symbol of the mystery of life. The male-god-oriented group rejected it. In other words, there is a historical rejection of the Mother Goddess implied in the story of the Garden of Eden."[27]

With that said, what does the Serpent have to do with women? For one, snakes live a large part of their lives underground, and the Earth has always been associated with the Mother Goddess. In addition, the serpent is linked with recognizing and honoring the law of cycles that usually comes more naturally to women than men. This principle was the central organizing theme behind matriarchal society. The snake has the power to shed its own skin and still survive, just as women once a month shed their blood and continue to live. Yet the power of life within that blood and its shedding enables new life to come forth.

Sometimes the image of the serpent biting its own tail is used to represent eternity, immortality, and life in general. According to Campbell, it represents the primary function of life, which is eating. "Life consists in eating other creatures."[28] He continues, "The serpent is a traveling alimentary canal, that's about all it is. And it gives you that primary sense of shock, of life in its most primal quality. . . Life lives by killing and eating itself, casting off death and being reborn, like the moon. This is one of the mysteries that these symbolic, paradoxical forms try to represent."[29]

Even without the historical perspective, it all boils down to one thing: Taking one sacred fruit in its wholeness and dividing it into two pieces – duality – the world of opposites – the world

48

of phenomenal experience. There was a reason for that. Dorothy's journey is not in vain. Dakinis -- manifestations of this great feminine principle were to appear and teach her a valuable lesson. Not only that, they were going to show her how to use tools she didn't even know she had in ways she never imagined.

Esoteric Buddhism

The difference between the path of sutra and the path of tantra in Tibetan Buddhism is the difference between a theologian and an occultist on the Western path. In sutra and theology, one learns, studies, and contemplates truth. In tantra and occultism, one applies, experiences, and validates truth for oneself. Most of this experiencing requires working with the law of polarity – assimilating and integrating it into an awareness of the Greater Whole, right down to the fact that your actions and your words become an expression of this divine paradox.

Tantric practices have sometimes been associated with scandalous or questionable sexual activity. This is not a reflection on true tantra any more than the Baptist preacher having an affair with the choir director at my friend's church is a true reflection of Christianity. While there are teachings of "sacred sexuality" in both Eastern and Western traditions, it's only a small part of what tantra is all about.

In fact, true tantra cannot be taught, but only experienced. Lama Ngakpa Chogyam expresses it this way: "We are the dance of existence and non-existence. Unless we know this – Tantra is impossible. But, whether we understand it or not – Tantra is continually performing itself; it IS what is happening."[30] Lama Surya Das adds, "Tantra talks about integrating and assimilating all our life experiences into the path rather than excluding any aspect of life as monastics choose to do."[31]

Dzogchen, (pronounced "Zochin" – the "d" and "g" are silent), also known as Maha Ati, comes from an ancient school of meditation that teaches that we are already enlightened, and that there is a radical way to awaken to that. Some call it a short cut. Again, quoting from the dzogchen master, Lama Surya Das, "Dzogchen is a naked awareness practice; it doesn't depend on cultural forms or unfamiliar deities. In fact, nowness – awareness – is the true Buddha, as my own lamas said. Dzogchen's unique message is that, by nature, we are all Buddhas for whom enlightenment is possible within this lifetime. In the light of our speeded-up world, many believe that Dzogchen is the teaching for our time."[32]

The difference between dzogchen and tantra is subtle because both can overlap. There can be dzogchen tantras and tantric dzogchen.[33] Rather than unscramble that mouthful of seeming paradox, I'll let my Hermetic brethren explain it in their down home way from *The Kybalion*:

> The half-wise, recognizing the comparative unreality of the Universe, imagine that they may defy its Laws – such are vain and presumptuous fools, and they are broken against the rocks and torn asunder by the elements by reason of their folly. The truly wise, knowing the nature of the Universe, use Law against laws; transmute that which is undesirable into that which is worthy, and thus triumph. Mastery consists not in abnormal dreams, visions and fantastic imaginings or living, but in using the higher forces against the lower – escaping the pains of the lower planes by vibrating on the higher. Transmutation, not presumptuous denial, is the weapon of the Master.[34]

This is a warning against nihilism, a common trap that many students of Eastern mysticism fall into once they grasp intrinsic perfection. It takes more than intellectually grasping. It involves the opposite – letting go – and shedding all the skins of ego and separate identity. (Remember, I said identity – NOT individuality. There's a big difference.)

Transmutation, working that snake power, is in essence, western tantra. Dzogchen is a way of resting in the view of natural perfection, so that we may all the more realize it in our lives. That sounds like a contradiction because words are inadequate for describing this view. But remember, I'm not talking about the view. I'm telling a story. It's a story about a journey every bit as exciting, adventurous and transformative as Dorothy's.

To become more fully aware of this journey is to follow the yellow brick road.

The ruby red slippers await.

---

[1] Joseph Campbell, *The Power of Myth* with Bill Moyers, Anchor Books Doubleday, 1988, p. 151.

[2] Israel Regardie, *The Golden Dawn,* 6th ed., Llewellyn Books, 1993, p. ix. See also, Mary K. Greer, *Women of the Golden Dawn: Rebels and Priestesses,* Park Street Press, 1995.

[3] Builders of the Adytum, "The Open Door." Reprinted with permission. See Bibliography for contact information.

[4] *Id.*

[5] Paul Foster Case, *Highlights of Tarot*, Builders of the Adytum, Ltd., 1970, p. 9-10.

[6] Jesse Stewart, *Secrets of the Yellow Brick Road,* Sunshine Press, 1997, p. 147.

[7] Dana F. Kellerman, Ed., *New Webster's Dictionary,* Delair Publishing, 1981.

[8] Pickett, Joseph P. et al., Eds. *The American Heritage Dictionary of the English Language,* 4th Edition, Bartleby.com, 4th Edition, 2000.

[9] Conceived and edited by Carl G. Jung et al., *Man and His Symbols,* Aldus Books Ltd., 1964, pp. 119-121.

[10] Paul Foster Case, *The True and Invisible Rosicrucian Order*, Samuel Weiser, Inc., 1985, p. 246. Reprinted with permission from Red Wheel/Weiser.

[11] Sogyal Rinpoche, *The Tibetan Book of Living and Dying*, Rigpa Fellowship, 1992, pp. 116-117.

[12] Joey Green, *The Zen of Oz: Ten Spiritual Lessons from Over the Rainbow,* Los Angeles: Renaissance Books, 1998, p. 125.

[13] Lama Surya Das, *Awakening the Buddha Within,* Broadway Books, 1997, p. 103. Reprinted with permission.

[14] Lama Surya Das, *Dancing with Life: Dzogchen View, Meditation and Action,* Dzogchen Publications, 1996, p. 62. Reprinted with permission.

[15] Thich Nhat Hanh, *Living Buddha, Living Christ*, Riverhead Books, 1997.

[16] Lama Surya Das, 1997, p. 25.

[17] Alexandra David-Neel, *Initiations and Initiates in Tibet,* Dover Publications, 1993 (first published in 1931), and *Magic and Mystery in Tibet,* Dover Publications, 1971 (first published in 1931.)

[18] Lama Surya Das, 1997, pp. 384-385.

[19] Joseph Campbell, *The Power of Myth,* Anchor/Doubleday Books, 1998, pp. 50-61.

[20] Gerda Lerner, *The Creation of Patriarchy (Women & History, Vol. 1),* Oxford University Press, 1987; Riane Eisler, *The Chalice and the Blade,* Harper Collins, 1988.

[21] Tsultrim Allione, *Women of Wisdom,* Snow Lion Publications, 2000, p. 103. Reprinted with permission.

[22] *Id.*

[23] *Id.*, p. 109.

[24] Campbell, p. 55.

[25] Eisler, pp. 78-80; See also *Gyn/Ecology: The Metaethics of Radical Feminism* by Mary Daly (Beacon Press: 1978) for a brilliant and thoroughly detailed explanation about the function of Athena and her modern day emissaries.

[26] Campbell, pp. 54-55.

[27] *Id.* p. 55.

[28] *Id.*, p. 53.

[29] *Id.*

[30] Ngakpa Chogyam, *Wearing the Body of Visions,* Aro Books, 1995, p. 3. Reprinted with permission.

[31] Lama Surya Das, 1997, p. 211.

[32] *Id.*, p. 45.

[33] Chogyam, p. 19.

[34] Three Initiates, *The Kybalion: A Study of the Hermetic Philosophy of Ancient Egypt and Greece,* Yogi Publication Society, 1912, 1940 p. 77.

PART 2

Following the Yellow Brick Road

You must be the change you wish to see in the world.

-- Gandhi

CHAPTER 3

ESOTERIC PSYCHOLOGY
AND PRACTICAL OCCULTISM

Story, symbolism, and ritual enactment of myth play an important role in the deeper mysteries of East and West. It is easy to understand why watching young children play, or even baby animals. All creatures seem to learn best when having fun. Even most adults admit that material is easier to retain if taught in story form. Stories enrich, enliven, and fortify personal experience. They enable us to retain the experience longer in a way that left-brain linear learning by rote does not.

Why are stories so effective? Because most stories are told in the native language of subconsciousness – imagery and symbolism translated through simile and metaphor.

Enacting a story or myth through ritual binds us to its meaning on all levels – physical, emotional, mental, and spiritual. It is a way of purposely conditioning ourselves to be more effective in whatever we're trying to do. Ritual is universal as are archetypal symbols. Approaches may differ from East to West due to culture, but original intent is the same.

Cultural Conditioning

Are we culturally free or culturally bound, and to what extent? We are both to the extent that we think we are, for what we think – we are, or become, depending on how we look at it. It's a matter of consciousness.

Consciousness has three aspects or means of expression: subconsciousness, self-consciousness and superconsciouness. These three aspects are like streams in the water of mind. Subconsciousness is just below waking consciousness, however it is given full play during sleep in dreams. Self-consciousness is consciousness of awakefulness. Superconsciousness is awareness of the water itself – the top of the waterfall – the rim of the Angel's vase where the source is discerned – nondual awareness and perfect freedom.

These streams are not exactly separate from one another. They function individually and interdependently, much like ocean currents. An inspired artist or raptured mystic can get caught up in a surge of superconsciouness that is beyond words. A psychic, overwhelmed by a subconscious tidal wave, may become lost in a vision of mayhem. What keeps both streams in check is self-consciousness -- the mediator – the director. Self-consciousness interprets the experience according to purpose and desire. Self-consciousness defines the cultural symbols in the context of the ritual to be performed.

Human personality is largely conditioned how to think, feel, act, or even react. Most of us, at some point in our lives, learn it is impossible to change another person, and that we must resolve to changing our attitude towards that person if we want to experience any peace with it. Even if we believe we had a great deal of influence on another's action, it was still that other person's willingness that prompted such action. On the other hand, we can allow personality to be conditioned for so long that we seem to know no other way to be. But this too is illusory -- for what really is the personality?

The Mask of Personality

Personality is a mask. Masks being what they are can be changed, reshaped, and remodeled. Masks are made from whatever material is provided to us. Some masks are strong; some are weak. Some masks are pretty; some are ugly – all depending on how we individually perceive them. The fact remains that the mask can be changed or eventually will change – change being a natural law of the universe, the law of evolution. Sometimes we become dissatisfied with our masks and want new ones. In this case, the old ones are subjected to modifications for better adaptation to our current relationships and life circumstances.

Lee Whorf in his book, *Language, Thought, and Reality*, speaks of a similar principle – the Hopi Indians' concept of time as expressed through the verb 'tunatya' – "the action of hoping -- mental causal activity which is forever pressing upon and into the manifested realm." He elaborates, "It is the realm of expectancy, of desire and purpose, of vitalizing life of efficient causes, of thought thinking itself out from an inner realm (the Hopian heart) into manifestation. It's in a dynamic state, yet not a state of motion – it's not advancing toward us out of a future but already with (or within) us in vital and mental form and its dynamism is at work in the field of eventuating or manifesting, evolving without motion from the subjective by degrees to a result which is objective."[1] Here is another reference to the Hermetic Axiom – as above, so below; first within, then without. In the Eastern tradition, this principle is illustrated by Vimalakirti, and serves as the foundation for the quintessence of the Middle Way central to Mahayana Buddhist scripture: "Matter is not void because of voidness; voidness is not elsewhere from matter. Matter itself *is* voidness. Voidness itself *is* matter."[2]

But from where does this dynamism emerge? Where in us does this deep inner realm of purpose, the fount of desire force – the "vitalizing life of efficient causes" reside? Certainly not within the limited confines of personality – the mask that we created or let be created by conditioning. While the dynamism might express through the mask, the mask is not its source. The true source must be behind the mask. The personality must mask something which controls but does not – the fount of this desire force – the power of life itself. This source cannot be culturally bound for in essence it is the force that cannot be touched by anything but which touches all else in existence.

The Higher Self

Many eastern and western terms have been used to describe this force throughout the ages – God, spirit, cosmic energy, or what have you. In the West we refer to the Higher Self, sometimes called the Inner Teacher or Holy Guardian Angel, to explain how this force operates within human consciousness and to emphatically infer that it is *within* human consciousness. The Higher Self is what lies beneath and behind the mask of human personality. The mask may appear separate but is really more like an extension of the Higher Self – a vehicle through which it can express in the relational realm of culture and communication. The Higher Self is a divine representation or reflection of this source – this cosmic energy, God, or Force within us – the Christ or superhuman within us all as one; what Jung and others refer to as a superconscious Self.

The purpose of life on Earth is evolution of the soul -- spiritual development or unfoldment. Development is not creating anew. It's taking what is given and forming new artistic expressions out of that initial material – much like themes are developed in a musical sonata. The theme goes though many metamorphoses before it returns in its original seed form. We don't become 'more spiritual' – we just actualize that which is already inherent within us. The more attuned personality is to this Higher Self, the more it begins to resemble the instruments of those who have gone before. We follow in their footsteps while making our own. They will not be sterile copies. They will be as colorful as we desire, for we are all unique and individual as personalities, and that is how it should be. The story would be very boring otherwise.

Awareness of the Higher Self frees us from the spell of time and space. It enables us to break through the stranglehold of conditionings, thus widening the latitude of choice regarding personal reaction. Nevertheless, we must act *through* the personality -- the mask.

The personality is also an extension, reflection or projection of the Higher Self. Then why isn't it as perfect as the Higher Self? In essence it is. In other words, the materials we have been given with which to construct it are pure. It's the form we construct that falls short of our expectations. Like all artists, our craft must be learned well enough to make the art match the vision in our artist's eye. This takes time and practice. Sometimes we lose sight of that vision, and we make mistakes. That's okay. We ball up the clay and begin again. What compounds the problem is becoming so attached to the mask that we cannot bring ourselves to crush it and ball it up again. But we must -- because if we don't, life and death will do it for us, which brings us to the concept of duality.

When Adam and Eve halved the apple from the Tree of Knowledge, they suddenly knew good and evil. Figuratively speaking, this story is symbolic of Spirit or the Life Force as God deciding to manifest in form or relative existence – the world of duality (positive and negative, male and female, and so on), in order to become aware of heaven through hell and to show it can be done. Why? Well, that brings us back to the purpose of story. It's like two little girls who are bored and decide to play dress-up. That's what Spirit, Cosmic Energy, or God did. But no matter how much makeup and clothing those little girls put on, no matter how grown-up they pretend to be, they're still just little girls. In the world of make-believe, they truly think they are grown up, but as soon as they look in the mirror at the awkward sight, or better yet when Mommy discovers them, they awaken to the fact that they're really just little girls. But they don't cry about it. They giggle and say, "Oh well, that was fun!" That's what we're learning to do.

No matter how thick we cake our masks with cultural conditionings, we cannot change the fact that we're not what we're pretending to be. While we may have succeeded in fooling ourselves and perhaps others in our particular culture or symbol system, sooner or later we come to the realization that we are not what we do, act, think, or believe. That is the day that our true nature – our 'mother' – the Higher Self, gets our attention. Hopefully it will not be a painful experience. If it is painful, it is only because we have become too attached to the costume and so caught up in the game that we have forgotten it is a game. But do not condemn the masquerade. Nothing says we should not enjoy the parade. In seeing through it however, we know that like all forms – all things in the relative world of duality -- impermanence is a fact of life. That is why the Changeless One cannot be described in changing terms.

Again, the Wizard of Oz Mysteries set a good example for us. In that story, Dorothy always had the power to go home, to get back to the Godhead or become aware of her Higher Self. She just had to find out for herself. She took her little adventure so that she could find *meaning* in home and in going home. The real wizard was within. And what got her there? Her ruby red slippers. The color red symbolizes desire, the dynamic Life Force as in the blood. Desire equals action. The symbolic implication of the slippers is obvious then and tells us that the oneness of dualities is only realized through desire.

Desire determines just how culturally free or culturally bound we are. We collect cultural data -- these trimmings and ornaments with which to array our costumes, and sometimes become so enthralled with them we want to keep them forever. Captured by the outward appearance of things, we fail to realize that some of these ornaments or conditionings are no longer necessary and perhaps even detrimental. Therefore, we must choose whether we use cultural accouterments for clear, unobstructed communication or let them use us – hiding our true nature behind the overly done hardened masks of vain ego, prejudice, narrow-mindedness and superficiality.

Freedom is the choice of one's own disciplines. If we're talking about personality, that's the only freedom there is. We can't escape the responsibility of life on Earth just yet for the job's not finished. Until it is, we are culturally bound to that extent because we must use these cultural items and symbol systems as tools for expression and communication in the world of relativity. Sometimes these bindings wear out. In that case, we must let go of them.

The Creative Process

The theory of structuralism holds that truth arises from the external relationships of things. Carried to an extreme, this reasoning suggests that humans have no free will. Yet it doesn't have to be so black and white. In this light, we can compare the process of spiritual transformation to the process of creativity because it is a creative act – making something new out of something old. It is essentially reballing the clay of personality and making a new mask.

As an undergraduate, I was asked by one of my college professors to discuss creativity in the arts in the light of structuralism and oral formulaic theory in an answer to these questions: Is a poet, writer, graphic artist, or musician ever simply a craftsman, and what is the difference between a skill and an art, and how do we create – through inspiration or craft or both? I used the process of transmutation to explain my answer because transmutation is the drawing up out of the subconsciousness old conditioning and habit patterns of reaction and consciously converting them into new patterns for freer expression. This involves creative imagination to a large extent. In this sense we are all artists, painting the pictures of our lives and self-portraits with the paints and materials provided to us. We can just cop out and copy other people's patterns or we can create our own. Yet how can we do that when we have allowed our culture to influence us so? It is all a matter of interpretation, and the metaphysical interpretation of creativity brings both concepts of structuralism and free will into play for balance.

Jungian psychologists say that archetypal symbols are buried within the collective unconscious of humanity. Their energy serves to motivate and inspire us. Esoteric psychology explains that although these archetypal symbols reside in the subconsciousness, their source is in superconsciousness and the Higher Self. The symbols and images are embodiments of the force clothed in the substance of subconsciousness. This animating force is the same as the Life Force of libido that most often manifests in the desire to merge or create. The artist takes this energy, and instead of producing a biological baby with it, sublimates and redirects it into new forms or patterns of expression through thought and feeling. The end result is the art form.

Archetypal symbols and images don't make us do things. It is more a question of what we do with them. Psychological complexes are formed by how we react to persons, events, or experiences in our lives. It is energy that becomes frozen like a hardened mask. Though it may seem that these external forces mold us, it's how we think about them that makes the real difference. Conditioned thinking is a kind of reaction as well, however unconscious it may seem. Any reaction can be changed because it's one of the many functions of the mask, personality or game character we choose to play. This is the purpose of story. In order to break up the fixated energy, we just rewrite the script. The artist or storyteller expresses the Life Force through creative imagination in order to come up with new forms we call art. The scientist does the same thing with more detachment, yet it's still a story.

A Map for the Journey

The Western Mystery Tradition illustrates these archetypal energies in the 22 images or "keys" of the Tarot. The symbolism in the Tarot reveals the true nature of humanity and the universe and all their possible relationships. These keys represent 22 paths or modes of consciousness within each and every one of us – universal aspects of us all – like 22 major ways that the Life Force or God expresses through us and the cosmos as one.

Working with these keys accelerates conscious contact with the Higher Self, so that we become an actor instead of a reactor. The keys unlock the door purely through the power of suggestion with the aid of visual images and the vibratory rates of color. Subconsciousness responds more readily to images and symbols than words because imagery is its native language. This is the working principle behind the communicative power of Tarot. The symbols work on subconsciousness directly, and subconsciousness understands them whether the self-conscious mind does or not. There is a level of awareness where form as we understand it does not exist -- a superconsciousness which is the source of intuition. For most people, however, intuitional flashes of inspiration from superconsciousness must be mediated through subconsciousness.

Tarot tells the ultimate story through a series of relationships between the individual Tarot keys in addition to the interrelationships between the various symbols in each key and their equivalent astrological and numerical correspondences. Tarot is intimately linked with the Qabalah. An extensive system of numerical coding called gematria is embedded in the Qabalah. A Hebrew letter is assigned to each Tarot key, and each letter has a numerical value. Different combinations of Hebrew letters and the sum of their values can bring to light many hidden relationships between seemingly paradoxical concepts. For instance, the Hebrew word for the devil or serpent is called *naschash*, which has the numerical value of 358. The numerical value for *messiach* which means messiah is also 358. What does this mean? It means that the agency of temptation, testing, and bondage and the agency of liberation, release and redemption are one in the same. The devil is merely the testing side of the Christ. When we misunderstand this, the natural laws of the universe seem to be our adversaries, a self-created devil of ignorance. But when we finally realize that all manifestation comes from the one Life Force, we find that a reversal of this relationship is possible so that those things that seem to be against us are transformed into the means for our liberation and release from suffering.

In the traditional Tarot, Key 3 entitled *The Empress*, represents creative imagination. It is the natural outcome of the three preceding keys in the series. Key 0, *The Fool*, represents superconsciousness. Key 1, *The Magician*, represents self-consciousness. Key 2, *The High Priestess*, represents subconsciousness. What naturally follows and results from these keys is Key 3, *The Empress* -- creative imagination. Key 0 is seed potential – the cosmic egg from which all manifestation emerges. When self-consciousness, represented by Key 1, *The Magician*, is stimulated by superconsciousness, it receives the seed idea and plants it in the garden soil of subconsciousness, represented by Key 2, *The High Priestess*. The seed idea germinates there and soon sprouts, yielding a full harvest of wheat or tares, depending on how self-consciousness planted the seed – carefully or carelessly. This is why the empress appears pregnant.

Only careful cultivation of proper mental images yields a fruitful harvest. It is observing the way things really are. The Eastern traditions call this mindfulness practice. But subconsciousness does not know the difference – it has to be told. The power of suggestion is the power of self-consciousness. The subconsciousness, though reservoir of great knowledge that it is, is still amenable to the power of suggestion on the part of self-consciousness. The only real reasoning power subconsciousness has is deductive, meaning that it is only able to elaborate on what it is given. *The Magician* (self-consciousness) is the programmer. So if something goes wrong, it's not the fault of subconsciousness. It's the programmer who incorrectly observed and entered faulty data. How does *The Magician* separate true observation from false? By being mindful -- learning to see through appearances by being receptive to guidance from the superconsciousness or Higher Self. This is the story of the first four Tarot keys in the series, although their symbolism goes far deeper than what is offered here.

What we hold inside ourselves invariably manifests externally. We create our own circumstances according to the thought-patterns we choose to generate. The law of the harvest applies to all of us, not just artists. Inspiration is receptivity to the superconscious stream of Spirit – the sense of wonder in all things great and small – the beauty of the divine expression in everything. The Eastern mysteries call this sacred outlook.

Everything in the macrocosm is reflected in the microcosm. The universe perceived to be outside of us is actually a projection of the internal universe within. Therefore, patterns of structuralism do not need to replace a personalized deity; they simply explain and reveal the workings of the deity in the world of relativity. Even though the Life Force appears to clothe itself in form, the two are not really separate when viewed on the subatomic level. The Eastern Prajna Paramita also speaks to this: *form is exactly emptiness; emptiness exactly form.* The distinction between a spiritualist view and purely materialist view is irrelevant because it's just two ways of looking at the same thing. Matter is dense, crystallized spirit vibrating at slow rates, like ice is frozen water. Everything is composed of tiny vortices of energy vibrating at different wavelengths, and the higher the vibrational frequency, the less solid it appears.

It is impossible for anything to stay the same. This is why we are never completely bound to anything – culture or whatever -- because that would be unnatural. This is also why a creative artist is never simply a craftsman. Only in strict imitation does craft prevail over art, yet the act of interpretation is creative. Not being creative is being dead – not feeling it from within. Creation must utilize feeling for only feeling fertilizes mental images and brings them to life into forms for all to see, share, and experience. Skill alone is dull, automatic, technical, repetitious and requires astronomical amounts of discipline. Art is born of innovation, and innovation is simply deciding to apply skill in a different way than before. Truly creative artists use art and skill; same as the creative individual does in becoming free of inhibiting patterns of cultural conditioning.

The artist becomes inspired -- feels this superconscious driving force or urge to create – to express from within. Mental images and ideas are gathered, and through thinking and feeling about them they are manifested by means of the tools of craft and skill. The patterns are already there, and their combinations are infinitely inexhaustible – their relationships are endless. So we can always be creative. We can always come up with our own design, our own original patterns – and that is the elusive thing we call *style.*

We can't escape influence by patterns put together by our ancestors or contemporaries, however we don't have to let that influence dominate or obscure our own uniqueness. In listening to the music of Mahler, the influence of Wagner is clearly evident. Yet Mahler was able to produce new patterns definitive of his own style, discernable from all others, including Wagner. When creation is imbued with "personal touch" – it is embedded with soul quality. This personal sound or perspective is what makes the art original, for it has taken on a new and different purpose. So it is with life. This is one reason why all students of occultism are asked to make their own tools and ritual instruments by hand.

A craftsman simply looks and copies. A creative artist looks *through*, thinks, feels and then conveys a personal interpretation so that the artistic expression is enhanced by their uniqueness as an individual. Personality is the same. In order to become more expressive of the Higher Self, we must learn to create and express ourselves in terms of not what our peers, culture, parents or teachers tell us, but in terms of what we find to be wholly true within ourselves. This is what story, psychology and ritual help us do.

If you are acting out the hero's journey in your life, the details of that adventure will be different from all other versions of the hero myth. We must make the story our own and give it signature. Therefore in ritual, it is important to make your own implements or at least personalize them. The tools and props do not have power. The power is in the mind's ability to focus on what the tool, prop or symbol represents thereby magnifying the meaning. Ritual is a means of recreating ourselves in terms of what we aspire to be. It is how we reball the clay and make a new mask. It doesn't matter how you practice or with who you practice. Sometimes the most effective rituals are the ones you make up as you go because spontaneity is very magical if it is truly inspired.

Rituals do not have to be elaborate or grandstanding. Sometimes they can be as simple as creative visualization. What matters is the meaning – how they *move* us. Once when I was deeply depressed, the only spiritual practice I could bring myself to do was feed the birds. Yet this was a very significant ritual for me because it meant that there was still a part of me that was nurturing *the wild*. The wild symbolizes the spiritual

Life Force that best expresses through nature. Birds have long been a symbol of spirit because their wings carry them to greater heights in awareness. Therefore, that simple act of putting seed in the bird feeder each day was enough to help me continue to feel connected to my source of spiritual being when nothing else could, and that was all I needed.

You must feed your birds in whatever way seems most appropriate for you. If you prefer to join a formal thaumaturgical society which re-enacts elaborate rituals of the Golden Dawn with masks, robes, props and costumes, that's okay. Just make sure that the rituals remain fresh and meaningful; that they do not become stale and automatic, or else the power is lost. That applies to rituals of modern day life as well, such as work, marriage, and so on. Spiritual practice is inseparable from our personal lives. It must be integral and practical, especially in the West, or meaning is lost. If what we do in our spiritual practice does not improve character and have specific consequences outwardly, then what is it worth?

Sometimes asking for that elusive thing called spiritual enlightenment is like opening a can of worms. But that's good too. How can we feed those worms to the birds if we don't first open the can and deal with them?

The Truth About Transmutation

Transmutation is Practical Occultism 101. Transmutation is the process by which one form or substance is changed into another. Metaphysically speaking, it usually refers to the conversion of particular emotional states into their polar opposites. The Eastern equivalent of this practice is *tonglen*.[3]

When confronted with feeling an undesirable emotion, such as rage for instance, most people believe they have only three options. The first option is to deny it or ignore it, which modern psychology tells us is dangerous because the result is depression, repression, neurosis, or worse. The worse is usually the inevitable explosion that occurs when the steam kettle cannot contain the steam any longer. The lid blows off, and we hear about another "McDonalds® massacre."[4]

The second option is to go right ahead and express it – either upon the object of your rage or through some other activity, which only serves to let off the steam, such as an intense physical work out. This option is usually better than the first because it's a constructive use of the energy.

The third option is to pray or positively affirm the rage away. New Agers and fundamentalists love this one. They invoke Jesus Christ or some other higher power to take the rage away from them, and command that it leave in the name of whatever. The rage will leave *them* alone, but it won't go away. Like a flea scratched off a dog, it'll just sit there and wait for the next furry beast to come along.

All these options work to a limited extent, but they don't get rid of the energy. They just displace it. The energy will remain in the atmosphere in the form of negative psychic residue. The crappy vibes accumulate and take on a life of their own. So the next sensitive person who enters the room is likely to get slimed – especially if that person has a propensity towards that particular emotion. Maybe they're already mad about something. Then all it takes is stepping in someone else's "deposit" for something to snap and they reach for the gun. That's an extreme example but it gets the point across.

The only other alternative is transmutation. Transmutation actively engages the rage energy and *converts* it into a different form of energy that comes out clean and pure, leaving no negative psychic residue – similar to what modern day water treatment plants do, but far more effectively. Human-made machinery cannot hold a candle to the equipment we already have within us that enables us to accomplish this glorious task. We only need learn how to use it.

The technique of transmutation is one of the greatest gifts I ever received from a well-regarded spiritual mentor. Dr. John D. Rankin was the minister of the Golden Pyramid, Unity Church of Christianity in Houston, Texas, during the mid-1970s. He had a lively teaching style that incorporated much humor so his talks were as entertaining as they were instructive. Yet where he really excelled was in a superior command of the intricate nuances of language and the English vocabulary in particular. For off the cuff spontaneous verbal transmission – he could not be beat. He was truly phenomenal in that regard.

Dr. Rankin gave a five-week course on transmutation during the summer of 1976. He not only acknowledged the need for dispelling the myths and confusion about transmutation prevalent in metaphysical circles, but also stressed the urgent need for this instruction, given the present state of human affairs. He added that these teachings had never before been given out to the public at large. Therefore, the pyramid was packed during this course. On the evening he spoke on the topic of sex and the role of transmutation regarding those particular energies, there was standing room only.

To this day, I've never seen these teachings offered so comprehensively. The closest thing to it is the Eastern practice of tonglen. Many teachers talk about transmutation, but few actually give out specific techniques, let alone discuss the effects that result from the practice.

Transmutation is probably one of the most catalytic, practical and effective methods for spiritual transformation, along with dzogchen. It is no coincidence that transmutation and dzogchen, once considered to be the most secret and esoteric teachings of the Mystery Schools, are being revealed to the masses at the dawn of the new millennium.

The Law of Polarity

Painkillers like morphine work because we have certain cells in our nervous system specifically designed to "catch" them. The Hermetic law of gender is operative right down to cellular biology. Keys must be paired with specific locks. Plugs only fit into appropriate outlets and so on. For a key or a substance to work in our bodies, we've got to have the corresponding lock or receptacle for it. This reasoning led researchers to discover the body's own natural painkilling substance – endorphins.

Endorphins are neurological chemicals that can be stimulated naturally in various ways – by music, ritual, meditation, athletic activity, and traumatic experience to name a few. The blissful states associated with mysticism involve this biological component.

We all want out of pain. We all want to end suffering – at least for ourselves if not for others. This is what usually turns an ordinary person into a seeker on the Path. Promises of personal power and freedom from pain and circumstance often seduce the seeker into exploring particular techniques before they have developed sufficient wisdom, character, and experience to handle the extraordinary energies involved. Being "ready" for freedom, enlightenment and increased personal power is not the same thing as being "ready" to suffer the consequences from using those gifts irresponsibly. Therefore the question becomes. . . how badly do we want it?

Dr. Rankin told a story about a disciple who kept pestering his guru about wanting to know when he would become enlightened. One day they were sitting beside a lake when the disciple asked this question again. The master forcefully took the disciple's head, shoved it under the water, and just held it there. Finally, when the poor disciple had nearly drowned, the teacher let him up. The student was furious and shouted, "You almost killed me! What do you think you were doing?!?!" The master calmly replied, "When you want enlightenment as badly as you wanted air, then that's when you shall have it."

Learning how to transmute is dealing with occult forces directly. It is also taking on the true task at hand – the transmutation of the personality, which is the real objective of these studies. It's important to learn how to apply these principles in practical matters because for one, we learn these energies are real; and secondly, we receive an immediate gain. Finally, we realize that no matter how good we think we are at magic, ritual, chanting, prayer, visualization or any particular form of meditation, none of us will ever achieve full mastery over anything until we have it over ourselves. A person will never be able to transmute lead into gold, literally – until they are first able to transmute the corresponding energies in their personal psyche. Therefore, a basic review of the main principles is in order.

If we recall, everything that Dorothy, Scarecrow, Tin Man and the Cowardly Lion wanted – everything they thought they lacked – was within them from the very beginning. But nobody could tell them that. They had to learn it for themselves, and that is the purpose of the Path or yellow brick road. The true laboratory of the alchemist is the alchemist's own mind, soul, and body. The metals that the alchemist works with are the seven chakras or energy centers in the subtle energy body corresponding to specific endocrine glands in the physical body. The energy takes many forms -- specific emotional states and mental patterns are just a few. During transmutation, those patterns are broken up, freeing the energy to realign and resurface in its natural state – pure prana – pure spirit – pure cosmic energy.

Specific knowledge of the chakras or endocrinology is not necessary in order to transmute. It might be helpful to be familiar with the great wisdom teachings of the East concerning the workings of form and emptiness. The equivalent of these teachings from the Western perspective are found in a priceless little book called *The Kybalion – Hermetic Philosophy* by Three Initiates. But again, none of this is necessary. All that is needed is to feel and be open to the possibility.

Transmutation involves working with the Fourth Hermetic Principle – the Law of Polarity. All manifestation has two sides or poles – pairs of opposites with many degrees between the two extremes. In other words, when we're talking about our earthly existence, there is no such thing as absolute good or absolute evil. The truth usually lies somewhere in between. If good and evil are on the same continuum, they must be made of the same thing. What we call good and evil are merely degrees in the expression of a particular force, but it's the same energy. This truth is evident on the physical plane as well. "Cold" and

70

"heat" are identical in nature and only different by degree. The higher of the two degrees is always warmer and the lower is always colder – even if we're talking about sub-zero temperatures. As the Kybalion states, "There is no absolute standard – all is a matter of degree."[5]

Another way to explain this is in terms of the musical scale. Starting with the note "C" moving upward, another "C" is encountered, octave after octave. They differ in degree or frequency, but they're still "Cs". Someone circling the globe as far west as possible lands in the east. In addition, wherever we find hate, love's lurking around in there somewhere because it's the same energy. The trick of transmutation is to lift that energy up so that the so-called "hate" becomes "love." It's not easy. But if we're truly motivated, we can learn.

Transmutation only occurs in same substances or polar opposites. It is necessary to be in the same element or category stream. For instance, hate can't be changed into courage any more than fear can be changed into love. But fear can change into courage and hate into love. Cold can't change into sharpness any more than dullness can change into heat. It's the same principle.

In *The Mystic Keys of Hermes*, Dr. Rankin talks about reconciling the opposites through realizing that the universe is within you. I like to translate that as "The Force is with you," a phrase made popular by the Star Wars movies. If we *use* the *Force,* we're really opening up to the One Will or cosmic energy of the universe that's already on our side. The reason why total darkness or total evil ("the devil") is impossible is because it is natural for all energy to move toward the positive pole. The phrase "let go and let God" is all about this phenomenon.

A scene from the film *The Empire Strikes Back,* Episode V from the Star Wars series illustrates this principle. Master Yoda is training Luke, the protagonist, in the art of using the Force. Luke crashed his spacecraft into the swamp so he decides to apply his newly acquired skill of telekinesis to get it out. Luke begins to focus his mind, and the spacecraft begins to wobble.

But then Luke loses his concentration, and the movement stops. He throws up his hands in exasperation and goes off to pout. Little Yoda, not even half the size of Luke, proceeds to set an example, successfully transmuting the spaceship out of the swamp on to dry land. Luke exclaims, "I don't believe it!" Yoda replies, "And that is why you fail."

Luke didn't really believe the Force was on his side. It wasn't that he needed to believe something new as much as it was that his old belief about it not being possible was getting in the way. That is why it didn't work for him. Yet all along he was using the Force and didn't know it. The power of the Force was fueling his old belief because that's where he told it to go! It is WE who direct the Force – it always responds to our commands. That's why the antagonist in the Stars Wars movies, Darth Vader, could misuse it. But if we make it our ally and not our slave, it returns to its natural state conforming to the positive pole, and good overcomes evil.

This is what Jesus meant when he said, "Whoever will be chief among you, let him be your servant." As Rankin explains:

> Master and servant are really one being, for master and servant are but roles a person plays. The same individual must learn how to act successfully in both roles. In the master science of life, presented in the teachings of Jesus, the way to learn to act successfully as master is to learn to act successfully first as a servant. The more fully one serves the principle of love, the more fully one has mastered that principle. The more fully one masters the principle, the more opportunity and ability he has to serve through that principle.[6]

He continues,

> Apparent opposites, joining, lose the quality of opposition, and take on the appearance of unity. If I were able to take a pin, with its two obviously opposite poles, and were to apply certain pressures of

dynamics to it, one pole would become so electrified that it would draw the other over to it, to form a full circle in which the opposites meet. When the positive side of your being becomes so fully charged with understanding, dedication, and insight, it draws the other side of your being up into its aura and atmosphere.[7]

So a true master is a true servant. This is why intensive meditation retreats are so effective. As Lama Surya Das often explains, if you stew in those lofty juices long enough, you're surely to get pickled. But there's an easier, less expensive way. Transmutation, as a formal practice, has immediate results in terms of *feeling*. The good news is that it's free and takes less than five minutes a day.

The "Poof" is in the Pudding

How do we make all those little demons go "poof" and turn into delights? There are three basic techniques. You can use what works best for you or combine them. After you get proficient with one, you can even create your own. Anecdotal evidence suggests that it's best to work with the one you feel most comfortable with in the beginning.

Remember we are working with real energy. Call it what you may, but it's much like the Force in Star Wars mythology. It surrounds and penetrates everything. It *is* everything in one sense. Whether or not you can feel it is irrelevant. But for healthy skeptics, the proof is in the pudding. So here's a bit to sample, then we'll proceed with the actual technique.

Choose a willing and trustworthy partner who you feel comfortable around. Stand facing each other almost touching. Reach your arms out to your sides so that your left palms are open facing up and your right palms are open facing down. Now move into position to where you can easily place your right palm over the other person's left palm and vice versa. Hold the palms horizontally facing one another about four to five inches apart. Now one person takes a deep breath, holds it for a second or two, and then releases it. At the moment of release, the other person should feel the energy flowing into their left palm out of their partner's right palm. Take turns doing this. Then do it together. It may take a few times but you will actually begin to feel the energy tingling between the palms, flowing out the right palms and flowing into the left palms.

This little exercise helps you to get a sense of what it should feel like when doing the transmutation technique. People usually get excited because they realize they are dealing with an actual energy that they can feel. Eastern schools call this energy *prana* or *qi* (sometimes spelled *ki*.)

Feeding the Unfed Flame

In transmutation, we don't want to just suck energy in and blow it out. We want to *cleanse* the energy of its impurities, returning it to its essence before we release it again. Something inside of us already knows how to do that. It has many names. Rankin calls it by its Biblical term: "The Holy Shekinah" or *the unfed flame*. It's unfed because it's eternally burning – the divine spark of Spirit within us all. The mitochondria are the powerhouse of the physical cell. The Holy Shekinah is the equivalent in the spiritual realm. Rankin says to imagine it as a brilliantly burning etheric flame in four jewel-like colors – three flaming tongues flaring up from an amethyst base. The three tongues of flame are ruby red, yellow topaz in the middle, and blue sapphire. If you can visualize this triple flame right behind and slightly above your physical heart, excellent. If you can't, that's fine. Just know it's there.

Most of the so-called negative thought forms and destructive emotional patterns that we want to transmute reside in the *solar plexus* chakra, which is just above the navel and below the heart. It's where we feel butterflies and other sensations related to fear and anxiety. When someone reports a sickening feeling in the pit of their stomach, it's this energy-center that's stimulated. Memories are also stored there, according to occult theory. This might also explain why the solar plexus chakra is often called the *abdominal brain.* The star technique of transmutation involves lifting the unwanted thoughts, memories, and emotional patterns up from the abdominal brain and feeding them into the unfed flame where they are purified, transmuted and released forever. We enlist the services of the Force, the Holy Spirit, cosmic energy or whatever you want to call it, in order to help us do this, as follows.

Sit comfortably in a chair with armrests where you can sit up with your spine straight and rest your arms on the armrests without strain. If you don't have a chair with armrests, you can sit on the floor cross-legged (half-lotus posture) and rest your palms on your knees. Place your left palm up and your right palm down. Relax. Decide what you would like to transmute. It's easier at first if you name a specific emotion like lust, fear, anger or greed. In naming the emotion, you literally pin it down. The first step towards power over it is acceptance of it. Now feel it.

You're probably feeling it right in the pit of your stomach in your solar plexus chakra. It's in there all right, swirling around, all agitated like some kind of trapped reptile. Now let's set the little dragon free. Breathe deeply in and out and say this affirmation three times: *"I am one with Universal Life Energy. It is flowing through me now. I feel it."* As you inhale, visualize pulling or sucking that unwanted energy up from your abdominal brain into the triple flame of unfed fire, the Holy Shekinah, just slightly above and behind your heart. As you are doing this, the Force is directed through your left palm and it heads straight for the unfed flame in order to assist in the transmutation of that energy. As you exhale, the purified, cleansed energy is released downward through your right palm to be recycled into the atmosphere around you. That way, you leave no negative psychic residue for others to step into. Do this technique for at least three minutes or longer if you can.

If you don't feel anything at first, that's okay. Some people are more sensitive than others. But whatever you do, don't *imagine* you feel the energy flow when you don't because it will be all the more difficult to determine the real thing when you do begin to feel it. Usually those who don't feel anything at first will begin to feel the energy after about a week or so of practice. Don't try to force it. Just let the feeling happen all by itself in its own time. Just because you don't feel anything doesn't mean it's not working. But once you do begin to feel it and increase your sensitivity to the process, you can begin to measure the expanse of the aura or energy field around your head by just feeling it with the palms of your hands. It gets larger and larger as you tap into this infinite and limitless source of cosmic energy.

What I just described is the "modified star position" technique of transmutation. The original star position technique is the same, just standing up with legs and arms outstretched. That way the posture of the physical body more truly resembles a five-pointed star and therefore awakens the powerful suggestion behind that archetypal symbolism. The third technique is simply breathing in and out while visualizing pulling up the energy from the abdominal brain into the unfed flame. This is handy when you don't want to make a spectacle of yourself with the palm posture. You can even transmute with palms face up receiving the energy, and having the purified energy exit through the soles of the feet.

Play with these techniques for a while, and find which works best for you. A word of caution: Don't get overly ambitious. Start out slowly and work in moderation. Some folks get so excited with the immediate results and subsequent euphoria that they think that they can transmute the whole world in one week. Don't even think of it. You will find that the more stuff you dig out of your abdominal brain, the more stuff keeps coming out, like one of those unending party snakes that the clown keeps pulling out of a teensy weensy box. You've got enough stuff inside to keep you busy for quite some time. It doesn't all get transmuted at once. You're just beginning. But you've got to start somewhere, right?

Another thing to remember: If you begin to feel uncomfortable, stop the transmutation. As Rankin used to say, it's meant to be a pleasurable experience. It's not a dangerous process but you might experience some side effects like a temporary increase in body temperature, drowsiness, or light-headedness. If the technique is done to excess it can result in downright spaciness. Yes, you can get drunk on spirit. Western and Eastern literature is replete with stories about crazy yogis and wisdom masters. Just remember that the best rule of thumb is to trust your intuition and proceed with moderation. If you begin to experience any of those side effects and you don't like it, then stop. Most of the time they go away on their own.

Sometimes you might feel these effects several hours after the transmutation session. Your body is just readjusting and acclimating to the intensification of spirit. More often than not, it's trying to tell you it wants some more. It's a sweet champagne that's difficult to refuse. If it's not a good time, just say, "Later, sweetheart. I'm on duty." It's at your command, remember.

If you begin to feel pain or discomfort, stop and do something to ground yourself. Take a walk. Exercise. Sing. Do anything that will put you back in your body, so to speak. With me, I find that the more grounded I become, the more powerful and effective the transmutation session. The name of the game is balance, as always.

One more thing: You don't have to name a specific energy to transmute in order to benefit from transmutation. You can just say, "I'm going to let divine Spirit transmute whatever inside me needs to be transmuted." That will work, but again the outcome will be general and less specific, whereas if you put in a specific order, that's what you'll get.

I usually transmute first thing each morning just to feel the Presence. Each time I meditate or do dzogchen, I automatically assume the transmutation posture because it's healthy, vitalizing and enhances the experience. But if I've got a specific problem energy pattern or unpleasant memory that has outlived its purpose, I get specific and name it. When you name it, always remember that you're transmuting it into its polar opposite. If you are transmuting a fear for example, consciously affirm its transmutation into faith or courage as you are doing the transmutation technique.

Remember, you can get creative with this. You can even do it while you're singing or playing a musical instrument by simply letting your breathing in pull the energy up into the unfed flame behind your heart and exhaling the purified energy. You can do it while you're running or swimming. The important thing is to "just do it" as the commercial says. This is practical occultism at its best. Have fun!

---

[1]   Benjamin Lee Whorf, *Language, Thought, and Reality*, from Selected Writings of Benjamin Lee Whorf, published jointly by the Technology Press and John Wiley & Sons of New York, reprinted in Edward T. Hall, *The Silent Language,* Anchor Books, 1973.

[2]   Robert A.F. Thurman, *The Holy Teaching of Vimalakirti*, (a Mahayana scripture translated by Thurman), The Pennsylvania State University Press, 1988, p. 1.

[3]   For an excellent introduction to tonglen, go to http://www.americanbuddha.org. After entering the site, click on the area marked "meditation practice" and you'll be guided through the technique.

[4]   On July 18, 1984, James Hubert strolled into the local McDonalds® in San Ysidro, California and opened fire on the customers with automatic weapons. 21 people were killed, and 19 were wounded.. A similar incident occurred in a McDonalds® in Killeen, Texas during 1991.

[5]   Three Initiates, *The Kybalion – A Study of the Hermetic Philosophy of Ancient Egypt and Greece*, The Yogi Publication Society, 1912.

[6]   John D. Rankin, *The Mystic Keys of Hermes*, CSA Press, 1977, p. 49.

[7]   *Id.*

CHAPTER 4

CULTIVATING AWARENESS: SPIRITUAL GARDENING TOOLS IN THE EAST AND WEST

The basic principles governing the cultivation of spiritual awareness in the East and the West are the same, but the gardening tools are not. On closer examination, their function is the same. Substance is similar but style may be different. Ornamentation can vary widely. Basic truths are universal – practices differ. Therefore, comparative analysis between the sets of tools and practice methods is helpful. But first, what are the universal principles? When you take away the mythological and religious trappings from the East and West, what remains? When you strip the Tree of Life of all its decorations, what does it look like?

A New Cosmology

Over the rainbow, East meets West, and we've come full circle. To get *beyond* the rainbow to a place where Earth humans and other beings can find common ground, we need a new cosmology. This new cosmology provides the context for all that follows.

Dr. Steven Greer, author of *Extraterrestrial Contact: The Evidence and Implications*, proposes that the core principles of this new cosmology are:

- Linear, relative reality and non-local, non-linear reality both simultaneously exist as Reality; their perception and understanding is wholly dependent on the level of consciousness of the observer. Even physical matter has an aspect of its nature which is non-local, transcendent and conscious.

- Conscious, intelligent biological life forms, whether on Earth or from some other planet, have physical realities as well as spiritual realities; all have the potential to manifest physically and spiritually in a multitude of ways. Pure mind, or unbounded consciousness, is innate to all such life forms and is the ultimate highest common denominator which all life shares; it is essentially non-local, and is not bound by the constraints of time or space, but can manifest in time-space reality.
- Beings which do not have biological bodies (so-called astral or spirit beings) are also conscious, intelligent entities, and as such can interact with other conscious life forms, both biological and otherwise. On rare occasions they can even effect a physical manifestation. Once again, the highest common denominator linking these beings with other life forms and biological beings is that of unbounded consciousness, or non-local mind.
- The universe consists of both linear and non-linear, or transcendent aspects, which while seeming paradoxical, simultaneously exist at every point in time/space and non-time/space. From this point of view, every point in time and space exists in every other point in time and space, through the quality of non-locality.
- The concept of God, or of a Universal, All-Knowing Being, is enhanced and not diminished by the recognition of the vast multiplicity of life in the universe. The glory of God is magnified by the recognition of the infinite diversity and limitless scope of life in the cosmos.[1]

Non-locality is another way to describe the realm of nonduality. I prefer the term nonduality because it is both local and non-local. It is a way of saying that the Absolute or the great silent mirror of Cosmic Mind is everywhere. It's the First Matter of the alchemists and the Rigpa of the yogis:

80

And the earth was without form, and void; and darkness was upon the face of the deep. And the Spirit of God moved upon the face of the waters...

On this great silent still mirror of a sea, the first motion – the breath of Spirit -- sets up a vibration – the first wave -- the Cosmic Word – the original sound, and that's when things begin to manifest. Spirit saw its reflection on the face of the waters -- darkness begat the light -- and things have never been the same since. God's projection became our reality. The universe is born as a consequence of the Life Force's reflecting on its own nature, essentially. We create our own little realities in the same way. At this point, we enter the world of duality and relativity – the world of manifestation in all its multidimensional aspects. In this world, seven Hermetic principles[2] or cosmic laws are always in operation:

1. The Principle of Mentalism: The truth that every observable phenomenon is a mental creation of the All or Infinite;

2. The Principle of Correspondence: The truth that correspondences always exist between the laws, beings, and phenomena in all dimensions of reality; in other words, "As above, so below; as below, so above" – the Hermetic Axiom;

3. The Principle of Vibration: The truth that everything is in motion – everything vibrates – and nothing is at complete rest;

4. The Principle of Polarity: The truth that everything is dual or has two poles or opposites;

5. The Principle of Rhythm: The truth that all energy flows between all polarities in a pendulum-like movement or cyclical nature – a measurable motion;

6. The Principle of Cause and Effect: The truth that for every cause there is an effect and an effect from every cause, and that there is choice; and

7. The Principle of Gender: The truth that all manifestation is created and is expressed as a result

of the relationship and interplay between masculine and feminine forces.

None of the above is theory or simple philosophy. Science continues to verify these ancient principles regularly. This fact alone complies with the principle of correspondence mentioned above.

Therefore, in the new cosmology, it is too simplistic to use the terms 'spiritual' and 'material' as the extreme ends of a polarity because we don't live at those extremes – we are usually somewhere in between or all over the place. Reality is a spectrum, and few things are entirely black or white. According to the law of correspondence, as Blavatsky points out, spirit *is* matter on the highest plane, and matter on the lowest plane is simply condensed spirit. It's all a matter of degree. So it does not matter whether you call this new cosmology spirituality or science. Dr. Greer reminds us, "Truth is beyond labels anyway."[3]

Dr. Greer's model of the cosmos and how extraterrestrials (ETs) and other life forms interact in that cosmos explains how witches, yogis, alchemists, magicians, tantrikas, and other occultists do their thing as well. The technology of the mind that Tibetan yogis and other occultists have developed and refined over the centuries has already been mastered by most extraterrestrial civilizations. It also explains why so much of what we observe as UFO and ET phenomena appears to be magical. It is only because we do not completely understand it yet that it appears so.

A UFO that materializes and dematerializes before our very eyes is using the same technology that a witch or a yogi uses to do the same. They are shifting in and out of that aspect of material reality mystics and occultists call the astral plane using the technology of Cosmic or "non-local" Mind. They are using this technology on a portion of the reality spectrum that science has not yet fully discovered or explained. For instance, hundreds of years ago humanity did not have the technology by which to measure x-rays, gammas rays or microwaves. That's not to say those rays and waves did not exist because they did. Similarly, ETs use aspects of the universe that we cannot detect with our current scientific instruments. We can either develop those instruments or use the one we already have – the mind – or both. ETs use both. It's called CAT and TAC – consciousness assisted technology and technology assisted consciousness. Dr. Greer writes about these methodologies extensively in his book, *Extraterrestrial Contact.*

If an ET wanted to travel to Earth from a star system 1000 light years away, even moving at the speed of light (186,000 miles per second) it would take 1000 years to get here, then another 1000 to get back home. Now that's downright silly. There's got to be a better way. That way just happens to be beyond the electromagnetic portion of the spectrum of reality and our current understanding of physics. They must be using technologies that bypass linear time and space as we know them. They must be using the full spectrum of reality – slipping in and out of multidimensional planes through various densities of materialization. How can this be? They do this by venturing beyond "the crossing point of light" and by becoming masters of the Hermetic principles described above, especially the law of vibration.

The main thing to remember is that this magic is no illusion – it is real. The only illusion that exists is the illusion of separateness. To believe in the lie that we are separate beings from each other -- all objects -- and especially separate from "God" or our Creator prevents us from thinking and acting in accordance with the truth, and so in thinking we become. The Cosmic Mind never lets us down – it always conforms to our expectations. It always responds to the power of suggestion. This remember, is illustrated by the first four keys of the Tarot. Dr. Greer emphasizes,

> The human being (and this would include other non-homo-sapiens higher intelligent life forms, i.e. ETs) has every aspect (or dimension) folded within him. Human consciousness, or spirit, is always connected,

however unknowingly by the individual, to the Absolute conscious being. In fact, as mentioned earlier, consciousness or pure mind in its essential aspect is simply that whereby we are awake – or that whereby we are. It is a unitive state and is not divisible. It is always essentially one with the Absolute, but we are trained to see only multiplicity and separation. Thus individuation overwhelms the unitive state – and we think we are separate. *It is a perceptual defect which the practices of all religions, in the form of rituals, prayer, and meditation, attempt to correct.* (Emphasis added.)[4]

This is the meaning behind the statement made by Aleister Crowley, a notorious magician of The Golden Dawn: "Do What Thou Wilt Shall Be the Whole of the Law."[5] There is but One Will. All our little wills are but expressions of that One Will. It takes continued effort to train ourselves to think and feel this way until all our actions and expectations begin to conform to that truth. It's not easy. As Lama Surya Das likes to say, it's easy to reach enlightenment but far more difficult to stay there.

That's why schools of occultism – both Eastern and Western -- emphasize repetitive ritual, mantra, prayer, and meditation. If you're not a natural crazy mystic, that's the only way to wake up.

Alchemy and Yoga

Chemistry is the science dealing with the composition and properties of substances, and with the reactions by which substances are produced from or converted into other substances. If there is one major area of agreement among Western and Eastern adepts, it's that changes in awareness are always accompanied by changes in the physical body. This conforms to the Hermetic Axiom – 'As above, so below. As below, so above.' But the changes in the physical body always follow a change in the mind, and then the change in the physical body will trigger another change in the mind, and so forth. It's hard to tell which comes first because the changes are so inextricably linked. However, it's just good enough to know that this is no longer metaphor – it's actual chemistry taking place.

To become an expert in 'spiritual chemistry' in the West, one studies alchemy. In the East, one studies yoga. Remember that yoga, in this instance, is not just hatha yoga that focuses on mastering body postures, but yoga in the true sense of the word – union – becoming aware of an intrinsic oneness with all that is. So although there are different names, different tools, it's the same process with the same results.

If you were to take a master of alchemy and a master yogi and cut their brains open, you would find in the place where the pineal gland once resided, a small crystallized structure of brain sand resembling a jewel. This is the fabled magical stone of the alchemists – the Philosopher's Stone that is hidden from ordinary view. This little organ is what enables them to accomplish what appear to be superhuman feats.

A Buddhist chant which is almost always on the lips of the most devotional adherents of that faith is *om mani pedme hung*. It is the ultimate blessing of all blessings and literally means 'the jewel is in the lotus.' The jewel is the crystallized third eye and the lotus is the fully blossomed, actualized spiritual being residing within us all. To chant this phrase is to wish that most blessed of all realizations on every living being.

The points of agreement between alchemy and yoga are as follows:

- A prerequisite for performing the work is the development of purity in health (physical, emotional and mental) and strong ethics.

- All things are expressions of one force or fundamental energy.

- The seven main areas where the work is done are called metals by alchemists and chakras by yogis.

85

- All things are combinations of three specific qualities:

Alchemical Term	Yogic Term
Wisdom (Mercury)	Sattva
Desire (Sulphur)	Rajas
Inertia (Salt)	Tamas

- The three specific agencies at work are:

Alchemical Term	Yogic Term
Sun (Ruach)	Surya or Prana (masculine/conscious)
Moon	Rayi (feminine/subconscious)
Mercury (Wisdom)	Sattva (superconsiousness)

- Five types of expression or elemental manifestations of the one energy are:

Alchemical Term	Yogic Term
Spirit or Quintessence	Akasha
Fire	Tejas or Agni
Water	Apas
Air	Vayu
Earth	Prithivi

- The transmutation or sublimation of the chakras or metals results from the rising of a secret force that is fiery in nature. In the East, this force is known as the kundalini, or "serpent power."

- Success in all operations is characterized by the performance of extraordinary feats in awareness, including the ability to direct the forces of nature and heal all disease.

Books on the yogic system do not hide the fact that the main laboratory for this work is the human being itself. However, books on alchemy, especially the ancient ones, read like the work is to be performed on actual material objects

86

external to oneself. Remember, there was a good reason for this. To tell the truth about the process in those days would have resulted in persecution if not outright death. Therefore, alchemists had to write in metaphor. As Eliphas Levi would later disclose, "The Magus is truly that which the Hebrew Kabalists term Microprosopus – otherwise, the creator of the little world. The first of all magical sciences being the knowledge of one's self, so is one's own creation first of all works of science; it comprehends the others and is the beginning of the Great Work."[6]

Transmuting lead into gold is symbolic of completing the Great Work. It you want to study this from the Western perspective, I suggest enrolling in BOTA mentioned previously, whose address is provided in the Bibliography. If you want to study this from the Eastern perspective, I still recommend BOTA because they incorporate much of the Eastern terminology and understanding into their work. The great Eastern sages Nagarjuna and Patanjali are quoted extensively, and their esoteric texts are demystified and essentialized for practical application. That's what occultism is all about – practical application. If you can't use it, then what good is it? If knowledge is not used, the brain gets constipated. People are more familiar with the Eastern terminology these days anyway. You hardly hear anyone refer to your metals – it's always your chakras.

The Western mysteries have also thoroughly incorporated into their practice methodologies the use of *tattvas*. Tattva (pronounced TUT-wuh) is a Sanskrit word meaning "thatness" - - referring to the reality behind an appearance. Tattvas are the modes of motion – the organizing impulse behind rates of vibration. There are five basic archetypal tattvas of which numerous combinations can be made. These five basic forms correlate to the five basic elements and principles of sensation as follows:

Form	Tattva	Element	Sense
Blue-Violet Ellipse	Akasha	Ether	Hearing
Blue Circle	Vayu	Air	Touch
Red Triangle	Tejas	Fire	Sight
White Crescent	Apas	Water	Taste
Yellow Square	Prithivi	Earth	Smell

These tattvas are the causative and sustaining forces of the universe, and each one proceeds from the other. Since sound or vibration is the foundation for everything, it makes sense that Akasha corresponding to the subtle principle of hearing is first. Akasha is all-pervading like pure space and is the cosmic egg out of which all else emerges, like a big mixing bowl. Alchemists sometimes refer to it as the Quintessence.

Out of Akasha comes Vayu – the principle of whirling motion whose expression throughout the universe is observed from electrons to solar systems, generating all perceptible forms and forces. From Vayu emerges Tejas – the fiery principle of sight. From Tejas comes the contractive quality of Apas or water. Finally, we have Prithivi or the cohesive quality of Earth. Then all return to Akasha in a cycle that repeats endlessly in countless ways.

All perceptible forms are made up of combinations of these tattvas, which also correlate to astrological signs. Each of the interior metals, stars or chakras has its own combination. For instance, the Jupiter center or solar plexus is Vayu-Apas which is a blue circle enclosing a white crescent moon. The zodiacal signs attributed to fire are permutations of the Tejas tattva: Aries is Tejas-Tejas, Leo is Prithivi-Tejas, and Sagittarius is Vayu-Tejas. And so on.

Using these tattvas in meditation breeds insight into these formative energies. Visualizing them in conjunction with their proper tones and colors cultivates sensitivity and power in their manipulation. It's learning to direct the subtle vibratory forces that enter into the composition of everything. Therefore, these practices can unleash psychic energy for which an aspirant may not be properly prepared. That's why it's important to make sure motives are pure. Power always returns to its source. Therefore, benevolence, humility, courage, and compassion can protect us from potential harm. This is not child's play. Occult practices speed up the individual wheel of evolution. One of my teachers likened it to opening a can of worms. I think it's more like opting for the roller coaster ride over the merry-go-round at the amusement park. Not only is there the potential for dizziness – but also the rough and the dizzy. It's not for everyone. But it's certainly more exciting!

Astrology is a symbol system that all students should learn. Fortunately, many Western orders like BOTA include instruction in astrology in their curriculum because it is intimately interconnected with the alchemical symbolism of Qabalah and Tarot. Also, do not underestimate the importance of exercise and nutrition. Those aspects of personal development are essential for providing a healthy foundation for these magical endeavors.

Meditation and Visualization

While there are many different types and styles of meditation, there is no one "right way" to do it. It is not as difficult as it might seem. Most people probably do it without even knowing it at times. Just contemplating or concentrating on anything can be a form of meditation. Though most people associate meditation with cultivating a quiet, calm state of mind, it is not limited to that, nor should it be. The Western tradition likens meditation to a fishing process. It's a way to catch the truth on your own – by yourself – finding out things without anyone's help. It's learning to listen to your inner teacher, which is the most important one. The deepest teachings come through this way, and they're radiant and joyful. As Lama Surya Das says, "If all you want is a quiet mind, there is a huge pharmaceutical industry that would be happy to serve that need."[7] Surya's books contain excellent ideas and instructions for different types of meditation.

The important thing about meditation is that the more you do it, the better you get at it. Refining receptivity is crucial to occult training. Much more happens during meditation than one may be aware. I always get the sense that I'm "downloading" important information, even if I can't see it right at that moment. It's usually routed into a "folder" for later access, but it's in there, and will come out sooner or later.

There are many different types of visualization exercises. Guided visualizations by teachers in person or on tape are very helpful, especially for beginners. Later you can embellish, improvise and create your own. In the mystery traditions, specific forms are visualized in conjunction with corresponding chants and colors. The more detailed the visualization, the more effective the result, usually. But the key here is in the power that results from the combination of feeling and active imagination. Bringing all five senses into the visualization as vividly as possible makes it most real to the subconsciousness where it is processed. It's better to cultivate a strong feeling for the energy behind the visualization than to be super precise in seeing all the details. Without feeling, the visualization remains an empty form, like a colorless painting with no life, no matter how well it's sketched. This is especially true when visualizing saints or deities in prayer or invocation. Whether or not these saints or deities exist is irrelevant. What's important is to feel their presence. They represent actual archetypal energies which embody specific powers and qualities that we're trying to cultivate within ourselves. In becoming "them" – they bestow the blessings of those qualities and powers upon us. When people ask Surya if these deities exist outside and independent of our minds, he replies, "…they are as real, or unreal, as we are."[8]

Prayer and Mantra

Prayer is very powerful if done with faith, as faith is evidence of things unseen. Mantra or chanting words is powerful because it focuses the mind and also works up physical energy that can be directed into the intent or purpose of the mantra. Prayers and mantras don't always have to be said out loud. Saying them in your head sets up a vibration all its own that is equally reinforcing. Also, "sacred" or magical words with specific vibratory rates have specific effects. Even in ordinary religious settings, the repetitive use of certain words and phrases builds up a special power, especially when fueled with passion. Praying "in Jesus' name" is not for nothing. Calling upon anyone or anything in prayer is a way to contact that energy. Sometimes it's the only way.

The most important prayer is the prayer of gratitude. Counting our blessings and expressing thanks is a way of acknowledging and perpetuating those blessings. It is also a reminder not to take them for granted. One of the most powerful and personally gratifying practices for me is from the Buddhist tradition. It's dedicating the merits of each and every blessing to the benefit of all beings. When I began to do this, my life changed radically, and I began to feel so much better. Research in integral medicine shows that the healing benefits of prayer are not to be underestimated.[9]

Dream Yoga / Lucid Dreaming

Many occultists and spiritual practitioners use dreams as a primary form of communication with deeper aspects of themselves and with beings in other dimensions. Many people involved with extraterrestrial communication have made initial contact in their dreams.

Lucid dreaming is "waking up" during the dream in order to control the events of the dream. Most people who dream will usually have a dream of this kind at least once or twice in their lives. We all have this ability, and there are those to whom it comes more easily. The good news is that this skill can be developed, but like all skills, it takes practice. Various techniques are employed, and several universities and institutions teach them for a fee. One of the foremost experts in this field is Stephen LaBerge of the Lucidity Institute in California.

Dream yoga is the Tibetan Buddhist version of lucid dreaming. However, dream yoga is primarily a deliberate form of spiritual practice with its own tradition. Spiritual teachers will often appear in dreams and leave specific messages. Sometimes these dreams are lucid, sometimes they're embedded in metaphor, and sometimes it's a combination of both. All the same, these dreams usually carry great import for the dreamer. Lama Surya Das' audiocassette tapes on this subject are excellent instruction tools and easy to follow.[10]

Psychological literature is replete with instances whereby artists and scientists have made important discoveries while dreaming. Dreams provide a rich field for mining and unraveling one's deeper self and spiritual potentialities.

Who They Are

What do we call these practical occultists and spiritual practitioners? Well, there are many names. All persons who are seekers on the Path are spiritual aspirants – aspiring to a greater goal. All seekers are students, but not all students or seekers are adepts. By adept, we mean someone who has had very advanced training in these matters to the extent that they are "adept" in the usage of spiritual powers thus far unfolded within them. It is difficult to say that such and so is an adept and such and so is not. The only way I can tell is by an inner sensing – a strong, intuitive knowing and feeling that cannot be expressed with words. I don't think I've met many adepts in my life, but I automatically recognized the few that I have. Of course, these individuals would probably deny that they are adepts at all, and in some cases this is all the more proof that they are, for the true spiritual adept appears to be somewhat egoless. They may be intensely charismatic yet retain an invisible presence about them. It's paradoxical and difficult to describe. Meeting a *Master* in the strict sense of the word as used by Blavatsky and other authors is rare. And although I believe I have met a master of compassion in the flesh, I *feel* these presences inwardly more often than outwardly, as few of them operate on the physical plane.

According to Paul Foster Case, co-founder of BOTA, each master is a magus or magician, but not each magician is a master:

> The Magic of Light is the practical application of the science of Reality. A Magus is not a mountebank, nor a producer of illusions, nor a caster of glamour. He has mastered the sphinxes of sensation by the invisible reins of his mind. He has perfected himself in the art of occult speech, so that he transmits, from higher planes to lower, the creative Word of the One Identity. His path of life is one with the highway of the stars. His thought and word embody the truth of Reality as opposed to the lie of appearances.[11]

Any student of Ageless Wisdom, any spiritual aspirant, if they attempt to apply these principles – is by definition a witch, yogi, magician, or tantrika – because they practice the tantric, magical, or shamanistic arts. Therefore, when you see a lama or a student of Tibetan Buddhism doing the Green Tara chant with vajra and bell in hand, that's the equivalent of seeing a witch casting her magic circle and drawing down the moon during Beltane. No difference. The ritual instruments and the words might be different – but the energy and the intent behind the practice is the same. I'm saying this to illustrate an important point. Some spiritual practitioners of the tantric path of Vajrayana Buddhism may tend to distance themselves from practicing neopagans and witches, as if what they're doing as Buddhists is somehow above and beyond such superstitious hogwash because it comes under the umbrella of a bonafide world religion (as if paganism doesn't). This is sad and highly elitist. Tantric practitioners are the eastern counterparts to witches and magicians in the West and always have been. Both spiritual orientations have their roots in indigenous, shamanistic practices with the same end in mind. When I first met Lama

Surya Das, I knew he was a witch. Maybe it takes one to know one. But don't be deceived. Jesus was a witch too. We are all the same when it comes down to this. Take away the years of training, the ceremonial robes, the ritual implements, the fancy mantras and the visualizations, and what remains is a human being directing their will with the express purpose of transforming consciousness. And that's magic -- nothing more, nothing less.

Some Wiccan groups do rituals in the nude precisely for this reason – to remind us that we all came into the world the same way and that's the way we're all going out. No distinction can be made regarding social class due to fashion: It puts everyone on equal footing with no distractions. It's also natural and nearer to Mother Earth. If you want to strip everything away, then Aleister Crowley's bare bones definition of magic works even better: "Magick is the Science and Art of causing Change to occur in conformity with Will."[12] Therefore, intending to walk across the room in order to turn on the stereo and then doing so is a magical act. Crowley and other authors spell magic with a 'k' on the end to distinguish it from stage magic – the art of producing illusions as a form of entertainment. But I'm not that particular about it.

Witchcraft, Magic and Vajrayana Buddhism

The distinction between theory and practicum is important when trying to put hats on people. A great scholar on alchemy and occultism is not necessarily a *practicing* occultist or a magician. This same distinction can be applied to Buddhists, Hindus and students of other Eastern schools. Some Buddhists concentrate on the study of sutras – knowledge and wisdom texts. They might engage in prayer and mantra but not tantric ritual and visualization. *Sutra* in Sanskrit means *thread*. Tantra, on the other hand, means *woven*. It is the art of doing something with those threads -- just like witchcraft, magic, and alchemy are applications of Ageless Wisdom. Some Buddhist scholars, such as Vessantara, plainly recognize this similarity:

The Tantras are all attributed to Shakyamuni –
usually under his Tantric name of Buddha Vajradhara
– and it is claimed that their teachings were given by
him secretly. When you attempt to relate to the
everyday through the archetypal, or to manipulate
spiritual forces through natural ones, what you are
involved in is magic. The contents of the Tantras are
a witch's brew of magical spells and rituals, yogic
instructions and profound teachings, often in jumbled
fragments which make them unintelligible to the
uninitiated. They are like grimoires of an
Enlightened wizard – who practices a transcendental
magic which cannot be said to be either black or
white.[13]

Yet the practice of magic is not for everyone. Even His
Holiness the Dalai Lama admits,

The Secret Mantra Vehicle is hidden because it is not
appropriate for the minds of many persons. Practices
for achieving activities of pacification, increase,
control and fierceness, which are not even presented
in the perfection Vehicle, are taught in the Mantra
Vehicle but in hiding because those with impure
motivation would harm both themselves and others
by engaging in them. If one's mental continuum has
not been ripened by the practices common to both
Sutra and Tantra Mahayana – realisation of suffering,
impermanence, refuge, love, compassion, altruistic
mind generation, and emptiness of inherent existence
– practice of the Mantra Vehicle can be ruinous
through one's assuming an advanced practice
inappropriate to one's capacity. Therefore, its open
dissemination is prohibited; practitioners must
maintain secrecy from those who are not vessels of
this path.[14]

Old schools of occultism in the West used this same
rationalization for grading the levels of advancement for

initiates. While adhering to a strict grading scale and sworn secrecy are no longer valid issues for true esoteric orders in the current millennium, it was useful as a screening device when knowledge was not so readily available. Unfortunately, some branches of the Western mysteries, particularly the Freemasons, became corrupted in their use of these devices as a means of withholding privilege and political power. This has often led to their wholesale indictment by conspiracy theorists. While a suspicion of overemphasis on secrecy and selectiveness is warranted today, it does a disservice to all branches of the esoteric orders to insist that they are all guilty of this when they are not. Each organization, each school, should be judged on its own merits and not subject to paranoid, conspiratorial overgeneralization.

The basic ritual implements used by all Western magicians and witches correspond to the four elements: The wand corresponds to fire (spirit, belief, will, intent.) The sword corresponds to air (the incisive and defining power of mind, reason, intellect). The cup corresponds to water (feeling, the emotional flow or energy.) And finally, the pentacle corresponds to earth (substance, form, solidity.) Supplemental items and props also have their own significance. While no magical power is attributed to the props or instruments in and of themselves, they can be magnetized with signature energy. The power mostly comes from the mental association with the symbolic significance of the object. These tools aid the practitioner in narrowing focus and concentration.

The same principle of association and symbolism is at work in Vajrayana or tantric ritual. In fact, a Buddhist altar can be just as busy as a witch's with a wide assortment of ritual implements. Two primary instruments used in Vajrayana ritual conform to the Hermetic laws of polarity and gender: the vajra and the hand bell. The vajra or thunderbolt sceptre, of which there are many types, is masculine and basically represents the perfection of method or skillful means. The lightening bolt has the same symbolic significance as the sword. The bell is feminine and represents the perfection of wisdom, impermanence and emptiness (empty of intrinsic separateness). It loosely corresponds to the cup or grail of the Western tradition. Both traditions make use of a ritual dagger or athamé as it's called by witches. There is even a tantric staff to match the magician's wand.

In the West, we have Tarot keys. In the East, they have thangkas and mandalas. Thangkas are huge tapestries of various Buddhas, deities and dharma protectors. The Buddha manifests in many forms, and each form has its own meaning. Each item in the thangka has symbolic significance, as does every item in a Tarot key. A utilitarian difference between thangkas and the Tarot is that each thangka is self-contained and does not directly relate to other thangkas, at least to my knowledge. The Tarot is a *sequence* of images or keys that when considered collectively illustrates a pattern and tells a story, and the relationships between the symbols in each image or key extend to all the other keys in the sequence as well. Innumerable combinations of these keys contain their own stories in addition to the meanings they hold on their own as individual keys. For instance, different stages of spiritual development are represented by different combination sequences of the keys. These combinations are woven together in such a way as to elicit elaborate and detailed interpretations of these symbols and their interrelationships in the context of those particular combinations. I have never heard of thangkas or mandalas being used this way. In other words, Tarot is a *system* of symbolism. You can work a Tarot key by itself or in combination with other Tarot keys. Each thangka is pretty much on its own.

A common tantric synchronicity often experienced by beginning students while working with the Tarot, is that nine times out of ten, the particular key that is the object of study will be all about a specific principle that has great bearing on a current problem in the student's life. It's as if the Tarot key has come to life and is teaching the lesson of its inner meaning through the circumstances of the student's life in real time. This is subtle, intricate stuff. This is also why BOTA students are asked to keep an occult diary. The more this stuff gets written down, the easier it becomes to see how these principles manifest in ordinary day to day events. Pattern recognition becomes very important to the practicing occultist. The students practice as they learn, like real apprentices. There's no waiting to graduate. Hands on experience is the only way to grow. This is what distinguishes a spiritual *practitioner* from a spiritual scholar.

In the West, we learn to visualize and *become* Tarot keys, gods, goddesses, or whatever we want. A Native American shaman might choose to become a bear or a mountain lion, for instance. This process helps to activate the corresponding dormant abilities and powers of that deity or animal within us in a way that nothing else can, especially when enhanced by intoning sacred words of power. Tantric practitioners do precisely the same in their rituals with their chants and visualizations. A popular tantric ritual is a purification practice called Vajrasattva. Of course, as with all occult practices, rituals are only as detailed and complicated as we make them. That's why beginners usually start out with simple visualizations which help to cultivate intent and feeling first. When visualizing deities, this process can be especially powerful because it unlocks the powers of that deity within us ideally. In Wicca, the high priestess in drawing down the moon actually becomes an embodiment of the Goddess. Similarly, in tantra one becomes the deity that is being visualized, tapping into nonlocal mind where those powers exist. Ability to handle them and then bring them forth to effect a change or materialization on the physical plane externally is another story. That takes skill, time, focus, practice and precision. But in any event, doing this to even a small degree can profoundly affect the individual psyche. Author Bokar Rinpoche reminds us:

> In meditation, one replaces this ordinary pride by the
> "pride of the deity"; one engenders the conviction "I
> am Chenrezig."

Ordinary pride is the base on which conflicting emotions, illusory thoughts, and the ensuing sufferings develop. The pride of the deity helps us to stop these productions. When "I am Chenrezig," I am no longer the one with ordinary desires, aversions, and projects. The impure appearances with which we usually identify ourselves are replaced by pure appearances that are Chenrezig's body, his pure land of manifestation, his *mantra*, and so on.

One may think that replacing an identification – the one of our ordinary individuality – by another – the one of the deity – is not a significant change. The difference is, however, very great. In the first case, there are conflicting emotions and suffering and in the second case, there are none.[15]

Though the concept of Chenrezig in Tibetan Buddhism goes deeper than deity – it is also the *essence* of bodhicitta -- that's the general idea of what goes on.

Assuming god forms and similar practices in ritual and meditation are good ways to train, condition, and wean the psyche from too much reliance on ritual props and symbols. In other words, some day we won't need to use radios in order to hear radio waves. Instruments are no longer needed when the physical body becomes the fully realized expression of the energy itself. Dion Fortune reminds us,

It must be emphasized that the study of occultism is only a means to an end, and that end is the Way of Divine Union. Some there are who can take that journey direct, but others have to proceed by stages through the planes of form, of which the mental plane is not the least, and for them the mind has to be trained and raised and taught to function under new forms that shall more nearly approximate to the spiritual actuality. But let it never be forgotten that all forms but obscure the light, and we only know them by the shadows they throw upon a lower plane.

> The aspirant should use the symbols of occultism to train consciousness, not to furnish it, and it should be his aim to cast them aside at the earliest possible moment that pure consciousness can dawn upon him.[16]

This is one reason why I don't have a permanent altar. I like to improvise and make wherever I am my altar or meditation space. Witches actually had to do this in times of persecution. This is the real origin of how broomsticks got to be associated with them. In the dark days of the inquisition, spiritual practitioners had to disguise their ritual implements in order to avoid possible detection and certain death. Therefore, loosely attached broomsticks became wands, ordinary cups became chalices, kitchen knives became athamés, and coins or discs made of wax became pentacles or symbols for earth. Molded wax was especially useful in this regard because magical signs and symbols could be drawn on it with a sharp object. In the event of a bust, the witch could simply melt or crumble the waxen object.

This is also why I like the practice of dzogchen. It can be done anywhere with eyes fully open and requires nothing. So often you can be doing it and nobody can tell you're doing it, because ironically, it is more like "not-doing." It is a way to bring about that "pure consciousness" or "naked awareness" that Dion Fortune mentions above.

Do all adepts, gurus, lamas, Masters and spiritual teachers have *siddhis* – the Eastern term for supersensory powers? Have they all unfolded and developed their innate telepathic abilities, for example? Some of them have; some of them haven't. It all depends on focus, orientation, and specialization. There's a scene from the movie *Interview with the Vampire* that alludes to this. The vampire Lestat is telling the vampire Louie all about the devious deeds of the countess sitting a short distance from them at a ball. Louie says, "How do you know that?" Lestat answers, "Read her mind." Louie replies, "I can't." To which

Lestat sighs, "Oh well. The dark gift is different for each of us." And so it is.

An overemphasis on any form of psychism, however, may serve as a dangerous distraction for the serious student. Though these powers may be helpful in some instances, demonstration of these abilities is not required for progress on the Path. This is what the tales about going down to Egypt are all about. Egypt, an early Atlantean stronghold, was a major center of learning for the esoteric mysteries for so long, that naturally it became associated with the attainment of supersensory powers that have their basis in the lower levels of consciousness. Animals are closer to operating in these realms than we; therefore many creatures appear to be psychic. The Biblical tales about Jesus, Moses, and the Israelites, along with the modern tale of the Rosicrucian adept C.R.C., going down into Egypt, symbolize entering these realms in order to learn about these powers head on. Yet if the sojourn into those lands is prolonged, the danger of slavery becomes imminent. Paul Foster Case states,

> Psychism of this kind is so great an obstacle to liberation that Buddha not only agreed with Patanjali as to its dangers but actually made the exercise of such powers in any form of miracle working cause for expulsion from the Buddhist brotherhood. Yet C.R.C. goes to Egypt for a short time. Psychic powers must be investigated, and the laws of subhuman forces that are part of our makeup must be understood. There is a danger here, but it must be met, not avoided.

> Cowardly refusal to make oneself acquainted with subhuman powers is not the way to mastery. The business of the occult teacher is to warn his pupils against the dangers of "Egypt," and even Buddha's strict rule is only against the public performance of marvels of thaumaturgy and against public claims to the possession of the *Siddhis*. But that teacher is remiss in his duty who utters words of

discouragement. It is both false and cowardly to make people *afraid* of the "powers of Egypt." It is even worse to malign those powers as being in themselves evil. We repeat, the evil is in returning to the level represented by those powers, not in the powers themselves.[17]

It is also important to remember that just because a person may manifest supersensory powers – that doesn't necessarily make them a Master, bodhisattva, spiritual adept, or illumined being. As John Rankin once told me, "We don't grow evenly. We grow lopsidedly." It is possible to meet charismatic individuals who may have cultivated great psychic or natural healing abilities but who may leave a lot to be desired in ethics and character. This is why the development of your own inner sense of discernment is paramount when dealing with people of this kind. It is so easy to become misled and possibly hurt by them. This is why folks like Lama Surya Das and other teachers worth their salt will tell you that great discretion should be exercised in choosing a spiritual teacher. Ann Davies, one of the co-founders of BOTA, offered this invaluable insight: *An adept is only an adept when acting as one.* That brings us to a general discussion of the differences between teaching styles in the East and West.

How They Teach

> When the student is ready, the teacher disappears, and reality remains.
>
> *-- unknown*

And so it is. As with any relationship, it is not relationship that is the problem, but inauthentic relationship. We know each other by degree, and by degree we incur joy or suffering because of it. The teacher-student or guru-disciple relationship can be as complicated as any other relationship, depending on the level of intimacy between the two individuals. A teacher can be anything and anyone in our lives. Yet because humans for the most part are social animals, we like to learn from other humans. Therefore, we tend to formalize these relationships, especially when it comes to spiritual study and practice.

With regard to the esoteric traditions and mystery schools, the teaching patterns in the East and West *appeared* radically different up until the last one hundred years or so. I say appeared because again, these teaching styles are more similar than they are different. Any differences are usually the result of cultural conflict and confusion, and must be examined in the limited context of psychology, not universal principle. But because in the West, the Eastern based guru-disciple relationship has bred so much confusion and controversy, we'll begin there in offering some simple explanations.

In Asia, the traditional way to enlightenment has always involved becoming a student and then a disciple of a guru, yogi, or lama of some kind. Generally, the word "guru" has a negative connotation in America because of all the scandals surrounding cult leaders which surface in the media from time to time. Guru is a Sanskrit word meaning "heavy-weight." *Gu* comes from *guna* meaning good qualities, and *ru* comes from *ruchi* meaning collection. Therefore, a guru is a heavy collection of good qualities, hopefully. *Ru* and *gu* are also seed syllables for the opposing forces of light and darkness, male and female. Therefore, an adept is one who has achieved the union of these polarities within themselves. The Tibetan translation of guru is *lama*. *La* means sublime, unsurpassed – compassion and love; and *ma* means mother. Lamas are said to be like divine mothers because they give birth to the sublime attributes of love and compassion. *La* also refers to *bodhicitta* – "a heart fully focused on enlightenment and totally dedicated to achieving it to benefit others."[18] *La* is also attributed to "cosmic force." So the meaning of the word lama as teacher is pretty packed.

A student, of course, can have more than one guru or lama, but usually, there are few because of all the obligations entailed with *samaya* – a word loosely translated as bondage. In this

103

context, a high level of commitment or devotion characterizes the relationship. In my eyes, samaya should always be interpreted as bondage to the work – not the teacher. However, the guru-disciple relationship becomes intense and intimate, and some traditionalists require an unwavering obedience to the guru. Of course, in the West, the most popular example of a guru-disciple relationship was Jesus and his twelve disciples. To the masses, Jesus spoke in parables. To his disciples, however, he revealed the inner truths and deeper secrets of the mysteries. In exchange, his disciples followed him and usually did as he asked – even if it meant risking death. The plan, after all, was for his disciples to continue the work after he was gone. In the East, the relationship is identical. The disciple becomes what's known as a "lineage holder" and is eventually empowered by the guru to continue the teachings in the same manner as the guru and his gurus before him.

These kinds of relationships have been rare in the West, but they have existed and continue to exist. They're just not talked about much. In fact, the role of disciple is often misunderstood; it does not always include an intimate relationship with a guru. Disciple is defined simply as, "an individual pledged to serve Humanity, to cooperate with the Plan and the Masters of Planetary Hierarchy, and to develop the powers of the soul."[19] And humanity and the Masters can certainly be served without knowing them individually. That's why such a student in the West is more likely to be called an *aspirant* -- one who not only studies for the sake of gaining knowledge alone, but who aspires to wield that knowledge in service to a greater cause. An aspirant is also known as an *initiate*. An initiate is one who has taken an initiation, and initiation is simply a critical awakening in consciousness that leads to a commitment of action. That's all it is. No one has to do it or give it to you. Initiations are never "conferred" -- they are taken. Authentic initiation is made by the Self and the Self alone. If you want to ritually formalize it in a group setting, that's okay but it's not necessary. The same can be said of so-called "empowerments" from lamas and Rinpoches to perform certain spiritual practices.

They are helpful but not at all necessary. No one needs permission to actualize their spirituality in any way. Fortune reminds us,

> The teacher who asks you to follow blindly is no more training you than a mathematician who uses the same method. If a suggestion does not appeal to your reason and conscience, reject it. Those who climb high are subject to great temptations, and we never know when the vertigo of the heights may seize even the greatest; there are matters in which onlookers often see most of the game, and the wayfaring man, though a fool, may sometimes form a clearer judgment than those whose eyes are blinded by too much light.
>
> Questions of principle have nothing to do with the intellect, they concern character; and however little you know of occultism, you are competent to decide a question of principle by the guidance of your conscience, which, for you, is the voice of the Master.[20]

So for the most part, the trend in the West has involved a more indirect transmission of the mysteries not requiring the kind of commitment or intimate relationship with a teacher typical of Eastern traditions. One of the benefits to this is that it places the burden of responsibility more on the student than the teacher, leading to far fewer abuses on the part of the teacher and less co-dependency on the part of the student. The Western schools also stress reliance upon one's own inner teacher for ultimate guidance. This is surely more compatible with Western culture's glorification of individuality.

But again, this appearance is deceptive because if the words of the Buddha and the lineage Masters of the East are deeply studied, it's obvious that their motives are the same. Ideally, the lama or guru is supposed to serve as a mirror for the student's or disciple's own inner teacher. Devotion is therefore translated into a feeling of love like a child has for a parent --

not blind obedience. Of course, teachers being human are not infallible. As Lama Surya Das often says, there is no such thing as enlightened people – only enlightened activity.[21]

The Buddha said, "Don't rely on the teacher-person, but rely on the teachings. Don't rely on the words of the teachings, but on the spirit of the words, their meaning."[22] Take that down one more notch in the context of the teacher-student relationship, and the meaning gets insidious: Don't rely on the *words* of the teacher either. On the Vajrayanic path, this is especially important if the student has cultivated a tantric or *magical* relationship with the teacher. The nuances to the inner dynamics of this kind of relationship are too subtle to describe. To put it bluntly, the teacher can do some really weird shit to your head that you may or may not be able to associate with some specific teaching, but rest assured that it is, in some way or another. Because after all, the Vajra Master is:

> ... the ecstatic, wild, and gentle figure who short-circuits your systems of self-referencing... the only person in your life who cannot be manipulated... the invasion of unpredictability you allow into your life, to enable you to cut through the convolutions of interminable psychological and emotional processes... the terrifying compassionate gamester who reshuffles the deck of your carefully arranged rationale.[23]

Whatever buttons the teacher pushes are ultimately spurs to spiritual growth. This is no license for abuse, however. Again, one has to listen to the inner teacher for the ultimate guidance and final verdict on any outer teacher's behavior.

Added problems and perplexity arise when a group or sangha must share a guru. Personally, I find this to be one of the best advantages to working in the West where the aspirant has more choice regarding participation in group work and need not rely on a teacher so much. For the most part, I've practiced solo and consider the world to be my sangha. Of course, that works best for me but may not be for everyone. Some people need the kind of support, camaraderie and sense of belonging that only a group or sangha of like-minded people can provide.

BOTA and many Western extensions of the Third Order Mystery School offer the opportunity for self-initiation and a comprehensive curriculum through a correspondence course provided as a privilege of membership. A live link to the inner school is established and cultivated through individual study, practice and meditation, and at a later stage, participation in group ritual if desired. Temple advisors are available for counseling and healing requests, and group events are held all over the world. So the aspirant is not completely isolated, but still bears full responsibility for completing the course work on their own. In the early years at the end of each course, a written test is given to the student as a measure of determining comprehension of the material. No one is barred, however, from continued progress in the school. If an aspirant is just not getting it or not putting in the required time and effort to achieve the desired results, they usually drop out on their own accord. A temporary breaking way is another luxury in this system. Lessons can be put on hold or one can walk away from the curriculum altogether for a while. The student is never pressured to return or continue, yet the option is always available. The door is always open.

Years ago, when I initially began a comparative analysis of the Western and Eastern teaching styles, I corresponded with one of the temple advisors of BOTA by e-mail about this very issue. I include the dialogue (though edited for clarity) because it illustrates these points in a colorful and critical manner. To provide some contextual background, keep in mind that Ann Davies and Paul Foster Case were the primary founders of BOTA. Their relationship exemplifies the paradox mentioned above, and that these relationships can vary widely with regard to purpose and intensity in the East and West.

JK: I am researching the relationship between gurus/disciples, teachers/students...

TA: I personally view these situations as vastly different, gurus are not teachers, and disciples are nothing like students...

JK: ...and the psychological dynamics that ensue...

TA: Essentially neurosis, schizophrenia, delusions of grandeur, paranoia, and psychosis are just par for the course when people form attachments and dependencies to individuals they feel turn the wheel of life for them

JK: ...particularly in groups.

TA: This issue is most important in your research question. Remember, where there are people there are personalities, where there are personalities there are problems, and problems are just unrecognized potential for growth. This dynamic is unavoidable in group work. Just as group work is a splendid way to amplify our own bad patterns so they are more readily recognized and broken up, it also increases the intensity of the adjustments, which I must admit is at times almost all I can take, but bring it on! The personality defects that bother us the most in others are the ones we recognize and dislike in ourselves. So group work is likely to put us in close contact with persons who have the same problems that bug us so much, therefore just accelerating the growth process.

JK: A friend of mine is very involved with a lama. Love-hate relationships seem to ensue between everyone in the sangha, and sometimes between the lama and the student. Even the sangha groups fight over the lama's time. Also, interesting things begin to happen with couples and their relationships who become students of this lama...

TA: Yeah, like they split up. This often happens in a guru disciple set.

JK: I recently had a meeting with this lama where we discussed this phenomenon. He said it is very typical for these dynamics to occur.

TA: Not only typical but necessary.

JK: I told him about BOTA, and while there are disadvantages to not having this kind of personal guidance and contact in BOTA, there seem to be advantages as well.

TA: This is the difference between the Western and Eastern paths, and what type of system suits the personality of the aspirant is the true measure of the merits of the system. This comes back to the difference between the teacher and the guru.

JK: Seems like the problems are mostly political in nature.

TA: Any work without politics and schism is dead. It is extremely difficult to get a group of people to agree on the best way to administer any agenda, even with a massive point of unity. Personalities have rough edges that eventually get worn down in the tumbler of group work. So we persist with love in our hearts because life is a self-regulating process. We don't tell anyone how to live or express themselves until they enter group work, at which time we impose a code of social behavior through the facilitator that allows for harmonious disagreement and discussion while keeping a safe respectful space for aspirants to experience, express and question -- a safe forum for new people with an ethical conduct code. However, at BOTA we avoid dogmatic indoctrination of an individual into a particular lifestyle or situation.

JK: I remember reading about the intensity of the relationship between Case and Davies in the beginning of their partnership.

TA: When Ann met Paul she was sick, crippled, low
       energy, but very spiritually motivated, after her
       near death experience in the hospital, which she
       said was her turning point. Paul suggested that she
       eat a nice steak because she looked weak and
       sickly. She was indignant at his suggestion, as she
       was attached to her conception of a vegetarian diet
       as more spiritual. Paul told her of his experiences
       as a Veggie, and blankly stated that she needed
       more Mars force, and a steak would be a good
       source of that energy. Basically, the early part of
       their relationship involved Case whittling away at
       her intellectual misapprehensions. Ann was a
       natural mystic and psychic. She didn't need to
       study to experience supersensory states. Paul
       insisted that she diligently apply herself to the
       curriculum to develop discrimination and self-
       control over her faculties. Paul even moved her
       into his own home to monitor her studies more
       closely. He saw a diamond in the rough and
       nurtured her carefully. Ann was strong-minded,
       and I am sure she and Paul did not immediately see
       eye to eye on everything. This is highly
       exceptional, almost Eastern style training. Not
       everyone gets singled out by an adept for personal
       lessons, but the same thing roughly happened to
       Case with Master R. There is some kind of pattern
       there, but we are not talking about entry-level
       aspirants here. The key theme in the West is self-
       initiation, contacting the inner teacher (intuition),
       perfecting the personality, forming linkage to the
       inner school through the individual, not the group
       consciousness. Still when the student is ready the
       teacher appears. Actually, my opinion is that
       everyone in our lives is our teacher of some sort or
       another. That's how intuition works if we are
       receptive to embracing reality. A guru is an
       individual established in a structured setting to
       which the aspirant is attached like an apprentice.

110

The guru takes responsibility for the disciple, like a parent. The children ultimately grow up to reflect the personality of the parent, both good and bad. Now any good guru knows that he is merely a helpful illusion or prop to externalize the disciple's contact with intuition, but disciples become attached to the guru and resist individuation, just as a baby cries when the breast is taken away at the time of weaning. The precious security blanket is to be given up or will ultimately be taken away by the life process, which will grow you up if you just hang out long enough. Many people feel more comfortable knowing that someone they love is making their decisions for them so they are not responsible for their mistakes. It is a very subtle form of victimization. On the Qabalistic Tree of Life, this is the desire to stay in Netzach, in service to the central ego in Tiphareth, living in the past, refusing to change, individuate, and ultimately reparent themselves. LOOK AT WHAT YOU HAVE TO FACE TO GET OUT OF THAT PIT – KEYS 13, 14, AND 15! A lot of people have a hard time volunteering to do the work of those Keys. It's scary, painful, probationary, aggressive, and messy! So often the guru has to utilize and accentuate the negative aspects of personality and relationship to stimulate the disciple to abandon their attachments and embrace this part of the individuation process, even if it means ending their personal relationship with what appears to be an ungraceful severance or failure on the part of the guru. I think people progress much faster at first with a guru or participating in group work. However, the down side to that is the tendency to form attachments which only lead to suffering and that are counter-productive when it comes to the critical moment when the aspirant must embrace reality and volunteer willingly and happily to shoulder the responsibility for their entire

111

existence. Bottom line is no one knows more about you than you! Anyone who says otherwise is not to be trusted! We are all whole and complete even in our ignorance. The soul is already perfect and requires no development. The work is to remove the errors of the body, heart, mind, and personality, which prevent the free flow of light down to this plane from the soul. You get out of it what you put into it. The master doesn't withhold the workman's wages, and he who serves is served. It's a process of unfoldment, not attainment.[24]

Trust is important in these relationships as well – trusting the teacher, trusting others in the group, but especially trusting oneself. This particularly applies to individuals who do not accept the title of guru yet act like one anyway. I am a member of such a group that uses an online discussion group as its major forum. The leader of the group is a high profile individual, yet occasionally offers private training retreats for members in order to facilitate the group's work. Not long ago, one of the members sharing the role and responsibility of public liaison was complaining about the leader's unavailability and lack of sustained guidance to the extent that it was leading to dangerous divisiveness. Wisely, the member asked for feedback from other members about this particular situation. Without revealing the names of the individuals or of the group, this is what I wrote:

Dear [Member],

I've been watching this dialogue with great interest. You asked for others' thoughts on this, so I am giving you my take on it for whatever it's worth. I had a similar experience I'd like to share, which may be helpful. Great leaders are teachers/gurus, whether or not they accept that title, because they serve as role models when they take on such great responsibilities. I've studied these dynamics for quite some time and been personally impacted by them as well. I've learned that these kinds of relationships, like most all others, must be founded on trust. [Leader] is an adept and a spiritual warrior in the true sense of the word. In his particular area of expertise, he's much farther down the road than we are. Like you, I view him as a personal hero and a spiritual mentor. However, no matter how much we may look up to him for guidance and leadership, he still has clay feet like the rest of us. And like all of us, he is far from perfect. Therefore, tolerance is also key.

I felt very privileged to attend the last [Group] retreat so that I could meet him personally and see him in action close up. Though he decries the role of guru, he takes it on nonetheless when he sticks his neck out to train students in the powerful techniques that he does. And if he is a guru, we must be his disciples. Now what does that mean? Does that mean we are devoted to him? WRONG. A disciple is devoted and committed to the *ideal* or the *principle* for which the teacher stands. A disciple is an individual who has pledged to serve humanity, especially through the unfolding of his or her own spiritual potential. That is precisely what [Leader] teaches us to do. I don't know how many times he said that over and over – that we already have within us the power to do the things that he does. He sets the example – we tend to our own gardens. The teacher's responsibility then is to provide guidance when and if it's needed in a context that is appropriate for the kinds of relationships he's cultivating. And each individual relationship is judged on the merits of how it serves the ideal or principle – not for how it serves the student or the teacher. That's what the dharma or Great Work is all about.

Therefore, I feel that one of our main responsibilities is to trust [Leader] to do what's right and to assume he knows best with regard to what, when and how to communicate with us or anybody. If you feel you need a more intimate response from him regarding your concerns and it's not forthcoming on the physical plane, I suggest you do what I do – rise upon the planes to the place where your mind and [Leader's] mind are one in order to get your own answers. And then this is where we take it to a deeper level and turn the question back around onto ourselves – can we trust ourselves to establish that kind of connection with the truth and act on it? Can you trust the integrity of your own experience and act on your intuition? I could be wrong about all of this, but I must go with my intuition because I've learned the hard way by ignoring it that it's usually right. [Leader] talked about this at length in the training – about how we must exercise faith and act on courage to go out on that limb – because that's the only way we learn to develop and hone our own abilities.

My experience is that my relationships and sense of satisfaction with them deepens when I allow my spiritual mentors the space, time and freedom to do their work. They are very busy and so efficiency is paramount. But there is more than one way to communicate with someone. Outer communication with words and writing is only necessary when and if outer action is required concerning more than one person who may not be on the same wavelength, so to speak. Now you might feel that as a [Group] representative, that's precisely what you're talking about. But is it really? Are you really needing guidance on an *action* that requires the decision-making authority of more than one person, or are you really fishing for information that's not critical -- details you don't really need to know right now, confirmation, assurance, or maybe a pat on the head? Sorry to be so blunt, but this is where true adepts really test our patience. Their seeming unavailability on the outer planes can drive you crazy if you let it. But not if you recognize it for the spur that it is –

prodding you to seek your own confirmation from within yourself – your inner teacher – to rely on your own inner resources, rather than depending on those of another. I believe this is what [other member] meant by the word maturity. We're all kids, spiritually speaking. Still it's our own responsibility to grow up – no one else can do it for us!

So go within – ask your questions – relay your concerns. You will get a response, sooner or later. It may not come in the manner that you desire, for instance, directly from [Leader], but you will get it. Any good guru knows he's just a reflection of the student's own inner teacher anyway. He's a great big mirror. If you don't like what you see, then look within and you will begin to see more clearly.

So that's my two cents for whatever it's worth. I've been in your shoes – I know how frustrating it is, especially when it involves the politics of group work. But that's what really grows us. Without it, we stagnate and get stale. If you're not getting what you want, best to let go and see what happens. I trust [Leader]. I trust the [Group] people. Moreover, I've learned to trust myself – and that's the hardest (but most rewarding) thing of all.

Many blessings to you --
Judy

So obviously, many things must be considered when seeking a spiritual guide, teacher or guru. Many books talk about this process if you need guidance. If you're not quite ready to put both feet on the Path, then maybe what's called a spiritual friend, mentor or study group will do. But if you're ready for the big league, you need to ask yourself if a teacher in a formal, structured setting is actually what you need. It is possible to be what's called in the Eastern tradition a *snow lion*. A snow lion is a person who treads the Path on their own for the most part, without structured guidance from others. It's a rough road because they're not given maps. But remember, a lion is a wild, instinctual animal. It's especially adapted to survive harsh conditions, and can sniff out what it needs on its own. Therefore, it can usually navigate the territory with little impairment. Personally, I feel we're all snow lions deep down and that's the mark of a true connection with your inner teacher. Still, as stated, it helps to be given a map by someone else most of the time. That way, if you need it, you have it.

If you want a teacher or guru to provide such a map, then ask yourself, why? Motivations are the most important issues in any relationship and particularly in this one. Any motives less than pure become ineffectual, especially in a tantric relationship. Not only are the consequences of your actions inescapable, but your thoughts and your feelings must be accounted for as well.

Remember too that the most important school is the inner school without walls or physical dimensions. A teacher must have true linkage with an inner school. Do not take anyone's word for it. Find out for yourself. How do you do that? Simply pray and meditate on it. Expect the answer or confirmation to come to you and it will. You will know when you know, and that's all there is to it.

If you find a teacher or a guru on this outer, material plane that has connections to the inner school, be it through a traceable lineage, spiritual order or what have you, then always remember that once you make a commitment or vow to follow that teacher or order, your ties to the school on the inner planes are permanent, no matter what happens on the outer. For instance, a student may become the victim of a political power struggle in an organization, and therefore exiled from the group. That is not the same thing as being excommunicated from the spiritual order. In fact, excommunication can never occur if true initiation on the inner planes took place. And again, by initiation, I mean a personal awakening in that individual that they are beyond a doubt committed to the Great Work or the dharma in the deepest levels of their being. So even if that student has no further outer contact with the group or teacher, he will always have an abiding telepathic relationship with the teacher and others in the school in spite of what transpires on the material plane. He may never even talk to that teacher again in the flesh – still the relationship can continue to grow and operate on inner levels. Much work on the inner planes is done at night anyway while sleeping. Whether or not the student becomes aware of this in a dream or remembers it upon awakening is not critical.

Sometimes these severances on the outer plane must occur to get the student to begin relying more on their own inner faculties. This boils down to learning to trust your inner teacher and the integrity of your own experience. As Glinda says at the end of the movie, Dorothy had to discover the powers of her ruby red slippers on her own and that she always had them. In other words, she no longer needed Glinda's magic wand because she had her own.

This complicated dynamic operates similar to the addiction process. Relying on a drug to achieve calmness, for instance, will actually diminish a person's intrinsic ability to become calm without the drug. The more a person relies on outer, verbal confirmation from a teacher, the less they are able to maintain an intuitive awareness of that link on their own. It's a tricky business but an essential part of the path if the student truly wants to progress toward full adeptship.

This takes us to protocol – what's proper and what's not in discussing these strange things and goings on between strange people. Well, this again is determined by culture more than curriculum. The Eastern traditionalists are more conservative in this regard, and usually discourage students from discussing these things simply because they view these things as mere 'phenomena' that rise and fall. Westerners, on the other hand, sometimes find it helpful to share their experiences. This can be carried to an embarrassing extreme, however. As with most behavior, it is wisest to take the middle road. It's true that sometimes sharing these experiences often diminishes their magic, meaning, and mystery. However, there are times when such experiences need to be demystified so that they're not shrouded in doubt, delusion, or self-serving secrecy. Some people feel better when they know they're not the only ones having such strange experiences, for one. Secondly, sometimes sharing these experiences with others helps to elucidate the processes by which these events occur. For instance, if someone had a contact experience in a meditation with another being but they're not sure whether the contact was with a disembodied soul, an extraterrestrial, or perhaps a projection from their own subconsciousness, it helps to talk about it with someone who can provide guidance in discerning such things. It all depends on the merits of the situation. Therefore, it's up to the student to decide whether or not such sharing is appropriate, the proper timing of the sharing, and their individual comfort level with it.

Again, the main thing to remember is best summed up in the words of Dion Fortune:

> ... no one has the power to give you initiation or deny it to you; as soon as you are entitled to it you claim it by right, not by grace. If one channel closes, another will open up. Claim your initiation from the Masters, not from any Lodge, Fraternity, or Order upon the physical plane; and although the vote of such an assembly has the power to close any particular Lodge to you, it has not the power to close the Order if that Order be a true occult fraternity, for in such case the decision does not rest with those upon this plane, but with those upon the Inner Planes where the Order derives its power. If those who are guardians of the gates on the physical side persistently deny access to those to whom it is due, the stream of force issuing through those gates will be deflected to another channel, a bare and boulder-strewn bed will lie where there once had been a navigable course, and the Waters of Life will flow elsewhere; but the Waters of Life will not cease to flow because human judgment declares them private. No seeker after truth need fear human judgment; the

issue lies between him and his Master and none other.

Never hesitate to take your stand boldly upon a principle in occult matters, for you are dealing in principles, and if you take not your stand upon these, where shall you set your foot and find it firm?[25]

We've discussed how to choose a teacher. Now how do we choose a school? Because I'm writing about renewing the cosmic connection that closes the circle and takes us beyond East and West, I've taken the liberty to mix and match symbol and metaphor throughout the writing in this book. But is it wise to study in both traditions as you are progressing on the Path? The answer to that question depends on where you are on the Path. As reiterated from the beginning Chapter, the differences between the traditions are not as marked as they used to be – in practice or principle. However, like learning language, it is common sense to master one language or symbol system before proceeding to another. I had been studying Qabalah for over 25 years before I began serious study of Tibetan Buddhism. What's more, I had the advantage of building up a knowledge base of Eastern terminology that had already been adapted by my particular order. The Western occultist and author, W.E. Butler, has similar advice:

> A common symbol code which both the mediator and the communicator know and can use is the basis for all successful unions between the higher and lower levels. In the West we use as a foundation the Tree of Life with all its associated symbols and ... associated ideas. If there is that within you that wishes to act as a channel for the Teachers of the Light then such a foundation is mandatory. Perfect yourself in the ways of the QBL [Qabalah]. It is because of the necessity of having such a mutually agreed symbol language be it between the medium and the higher self, or the medium and a greater Entity that we caution students against working with

a combination of the Eastern and Western systems. Once you have learned, assimilated and properly grounded yourself in the Western Way, then you may if you wish go on to learn another system, possibly that of Eastern origin which you can learn to use in the same way and maybe draw to you a Teacher from that system. If you try to become an esoteric Jack of all Trades without firmly stablising yourself in your own system first, you will come to grief.

Do not misunderstand what I say, the Masters are ALL brothers and engaged in the great work. But the work is along what we might call departmental lines in order to achieve the greatest results from the minimum expenditure of energy. If you are wise you will follow their example. Dion Fortune said in her training papers, "A fraternity is simply an association of people on the physical plane who are being trained themselves and helping to train others in a symbol system used as a method of notation in the Mystery Tradition. When a student reaches a certain degree of development he can operate any symbol system with ease, and beyond that may dispense with symbols altogether. But in the early stages of training a symbol system is essential for balanced development."

The secret key consists in knowing how to use the system and is taught like violin playing, NOT revealed like a password. It cannot therefore be betrayed, but one can either use the mystery technique or one cannot. The work should be taught grade by grade in order that it is fully understood. But although the outer grades may be given formally with instruction and ceremony, it is the inner awakening and development alone that leads to adepthood.[26]

Remember, the Masters or "those who have gone before" can communicate with us and we with them in many ways. The

120

way I feel is most effective yet most often overlooked is when the vibrations are "stepped down" through the levels of the Higher Self as opposed to coming through a medium or other channel. For the individual, this indirect way insures direct access. It also obviates the need for determining or confirming the source. Those unfamiliar with this process will attribute credit and causation to the individual. That is fine and sometimes as it should be, because truth can only be shared -- it can never be owned.

A final note on how to be a great student: Listen always to the still small voice of the Higher Self and trust it. The more advanced the spiritual aspirant, the subtler the lessons. There comes a point when we can no longer give ourselves the kind of slack that we once did at the beginning of occult training. When it comes to what my Buddhist friend calls 'ego blunders' this is particularly true. Remember, the ego only blunders when it mistakes itself for king of the hill. The illusion of separateness is fine and dandy. Without it we could not navigate on this plane or relate to others. It's being *deluded* by the illusion that is problematic.

Personality tendencies rooted in the lie of separation are often veiled in a sense of self-righteousness. Spiritual pride is one of the biggest ego blunders of all and can take many forms. For example, rationalization of overly criticizing others as being honest and helpful is one such form. Another is when we feel as if we are more unselfish and benevolent than others, and therefore deserving of better karma or privilege. Refusing help from others when such help is warranted is another behavior based on delusion. To minimize one's minor transgressions as insignificant or rooted in the righteousness of principle is another.

Giving love and serving others with invisible strings attached is one of the most difficult transgressions to recognize. Love is truly a part of our souls that we cannot understand until we give and expect nothing in return. To do otherwise is continuing to be caught up in the trap of wanting to be important, respected, and recognized. This is not the same as allowing others to take advantage of us, however. That's the opposite extreme, sometimes called 'idiot compassion' and can be just as damaging. We must strike a balance between mercy and severity. Difficult? Yes – that's what I mean by subtle. It's not always straightforward at all. This is when we need to let go and give it up to the Higher Self in asking for guidance while trying to refrain from being unduly harsh or judgmental towards ourselves. There's no room for guilt in this process. The kind of firmness that's needed is like a mother's stern but forceful action in pulling her child out of the street. She doesn't punish the child for this transgression, but she let's the child know, in no uncertain terms, that such behavior will not be tolerated in the future.

Then let's not forget the most useful antidote for any and all ego blunders – humor and mirth. The personality is like the Higher Self's pet. It needs moderate discipline, yet we can still laugh at its silly antics. If we can't have fun while we're doing this, what's the point? That's the true secret to survival!

Reclaiming the Garden

Dr. Greer, Jelaila Starr, and many others feel the time for the priest and the rabbi and the mullah and the guru is over; that institutionalized religion is completely off the timeline. We are at least one hundred years into the time where each individual should be their own priest, rabbi, mullah, guru or whatever.[27] This is surely and ideally the goal. Sadly, I don't feel that everyone is there quite yet. But each day someone picks up a book like this one they are getting closer and might be closer than they think. In the meantime, present day guides and spiritual teachers can be just that – guides or counselors who advise and help us out along the way. There's always a place for that – no matter who you are or how far down the road you think you've come. The problem comes about from elevating these teachers and preachers to God-like status or creating a personality cult around them. The problem arises when they are set apart from us as somehow above, hopelessly beyond and better than us. The problem comes from giving away our personal power to them -- sacrificing our autonomy, spiritual integrity and creative self-worth. The problem comes from allowing them to make our decisions for us – telling us what to read, what to do, how to act, what to say, how to think, how to feel, how to live and how to be – without critically thinking about it first. The problem arises when we allow them to grow their enormous centralized power structures that corrupt the true teachings of the spiritual masters. The problem arises when religion takes precedence over spirituality, and when preserving the church, the sangha, the circle or the synagogue is more important than the sanctity of the individual. The problem comes when we accept their authority without question thinking they know what's best for us and consider ourselves spiritually incompetent. The problem arises when we believe the lie that the divine only speaks through certain prophets or emissaries separate from us. Make no mistake – you are the Buddha. You are Jesus. You are the Goddess. You are God. You are all these things and everything deep down and more than you can possibly imagine at this time. We only need awaken to it. If others can help us wake up, that's fine. But the waking up is all your own. No one can do it for you.

And that's what occultism is all about. That's what the esoteric mystery traditions are trying to teach us – that we already have what we need to wake up. We only have to recognize it and take advantage of the clues and the keys they've left behind. This is the major reason why the conspiracy theorists try to lump all these occult "secret societies" together into one great big boogey man. They know, on some level, that these teachings are self-empowering and lead to freedom. And they don't want that. They want you to continue to believe in the lie, which is the real devil. Well, as my BOTA mentors are fond of saying, "Laugh at the devil and he shall flee." For the devil is only the testing side to the light. See through the darkness – see through the shadows – the light is still there. It is yours to gather in Truth.

Dorothy ends her journey as empty-handed as she began it. Toto is still with her though. I like to think that Toto represents her intuition – the still small voice inside – the divinity within that's sometimes difficult to recognize at first. That's the ultimate gardening tool really, if you think about it. Dogs are the best diggers around. And if you recall, the problem arose when Toto ran through Ms. Gulch's garden to begin with. Dorothy allowed that part of herself to run out of control and mess up other people's gardens instead of being mindful and tending to her own. As a result, Ms. Gulch comes to take Toto away. Ms. Gulch, the Wicked Witch, is our shadow side – the internal psychic predator we always have to be watching out for. It's as if that unlikely ally is saying, if you don't learn to value your gifts, they will be taken away until you learn not to take them for granted.

Dorothy fully acknowledges her mistake and admits she let Toto run through the garden and that she should be punished instead. But it's too late. A lesson must be learned. The authorities – her inauthentic custodians – succumb to the predator and they take Toto away anyway, or try to. But it can't be done. Intuition cannot be denied – it cannot be confined -- and always returns to us. With this newfound value, we vow to never let go of it again. But that is not enough. We enter the hero's journey where we find out who we really are and learn the real meaning and purpose behind our deepest loves and spiritual values.

Perhaps if you take up some of the gardening tools mentioned in this chapter, you'll never have to lose Toto and suffer to the extent that Dorothy did. But if it's too late -- if you're already up in the cyclone or being carted away to the witch's castle, congratulate yourself. The ruby red slippers are already on your feet and you're halfway home!

---

[1]   Steven M. Greer, M.D., *Extraterrestrial Contact: The Evidence and Implications*, Crossing Point, Inc., 1999, pp. 67-68.   Reprinted with permission.

[2]   Three Initiates, *The Kybalion*, Yogi Publication Society, 1940, pp. 25-26.

[3] Greer, p. 83.

[4] *Id.*, pp. 89-90.

[5] Aleister Crowley, *Magick in Theory and Practice*, Castle Books.

[6] Eliphas Levi, *Transcendental Magic*, Samuel Weiser, Inc., 1972, p. 30.

[7] Lama Surya Das, *Awakening the Buddha Within: Tibetan Wisdom for the Western World*, Broadway Books, 1997, p. 21. Reprinted with permission.

[8] *Id.*, p. 367.

[9] Larry Dossey, M.D., *Prayer is Good Medicine: How to Reap the Healing Benefits of Prayer,* Harper San Francisco, 1996; *Healing Words: The Power of Prayer and the Practice of Medicine,* Harper San Francisco, 1993.

[10] Lama Surya Das, *Tibetan Dream Yoga: A Complete System for Becoming Conscious in Your Dreams*, Sounds True, 2002.

[11] Paul Foster Case, *The True and Invisible Rosicrucian Order*, Samuel Weiser, Inc., 1985, p. 292. Reprinted with permission from Red Wheel/Weiser.

[12] Crowley, p. XII.

[13] Vessantara, *Meeting the Buddhas: A Guide to Buddhas, Bodhisattvas, and Tantric Deities,* Windhorse Publications, 1993, p. 207.

[14] H.H. the Dalai Lama, Tsong-ka-pa and Jeffrey Hopkins, *Tantra in Tibet*, Snow Lion Publications, 1977, p. 47. Reprinted with permission.

[15] Bokar Rinpoche, *Chenrezig Lord of Love: Principles and Methods of Deity Meditation*, ClearPoint Press, 2001, pp. 64-65.

[16] Dion Fortune, *The Esoteric Orders and Their* Work, 1928, Llewellyn Publications, 1971.p. 98. Reprinted with permission from Red Wheel/Weiser.

[17] Case, p. 82.

[18] Alexander Berzin, *Relating to a Spiritual Teacher,* Snow Lion Publications, 2000, p. 35.

[19] M. Temple Richmond, *Sirius*, Source Publications, 1997, p. 373.

[20] Fortune, p. 108.

[21] Lama Surya Das, "Taking Refuge and Awakening Compassion," *Dancing with Life: New Dharma Talks by Lama Surya Das,* Dzogchen Publications, 1996, p. 11.

[22] Lama Surya Das, 'The Teacher: Learning from Both the Foolish and the Wise," *Dancing with Life: New Dharma Talks by Lama Surya Das,* Dzogchen Publications, 1996, p. 89. Reprinted with permission.

[23] Ngakpa Chogyam, *Wearing the Body of Visions*, Aro Books, 1995, p. 141. Reprinted with permission.

[24] From e-mail correspondence with a temple advisor of BOTA, July 24, 1995.

[25] Fortune, p. 132.

[26] W.E. Butler, from "Concerning Contacts, Control, and Communication," published at http://www.houseofthehorizion.org/public/documents.php?id=172.

[27] From comments made by Dr. Greer in February of 2003, and from a personal dialogue with Jelaila Starr in January of 2003.

PART 3

The Land of Oz

We tend to view nature through a tiny slot from a narrow angle; others see it from another angle and describe it in a different language. It sounds different, but it is not. The universe is so rich in diversity that almost anything one says about it is correct, provided one takes a broad enough view.

-- Itzhak Bentov

CHAPTER 5

THE COSMIC CONNECTION:
UFOS, ETS, AND OUR ORIGINS

The Land of Oz is a strange place, no doubt, especially for first time visitors. One meets all kinds of bizarre creatures that act and communicate much like we do. And so it is with outer space -- and inner for that matter.

This book is written on the assumption that UFO and extraterrestrial (ET) phenomena are real; that they represent beings that exist and events that take place both inside and outside our personal sphere of awareness; that there are many different ways to categorize and analyze these phenomena, and that all ways are valid attempts at understanding it. Some of these phenomena are produced by humans and appear to be strictly psychological in origin, but most are not. So first let's briefly examine the types of literature currently available on this subject, and then focus on which approaches are providing the basis for my particular view.

Finding the Truth

Most bookstores do not have a particular section devoted to "Ufology." They usually lump such books under sections entitled "New Age" or "Speculative." On those shelves are a wide variety of books by an equally diverse range of authors. Writers like John Mack and Budd Hopkins focus strictly on documenting and explaining abduction phenomena. Authors like Whitley Strieber focus on their personal experience with ETs, their general ideas regarding contact and the reasons why they believe ETs are here. Some authors take an archeological and linguistic approach to analyzing the data, like Zecharia Sitchin. Books by conspiracy theorists, like David Icke, tell a story about a world covertly controlled by a reptilian race of aliens in collusion with a secret world government based on particular family bloodlines. Other conspiracy theorists generally tow the same line but may not be so colorful in their descriptions of the aliens. Much conspiracy literature links secret societies – particularly those that practice occultism – with the manipulative agenda of the aliens and/or secret government. Then there are many books devoted to simply unearthing physical evidence of visitations by extraterrestrials – from Roswell to Von Daniken's description of archeological sites related to his theory of ancient astronauts. On the other extreme, some authors take a purely scientific or psychological approach to the subject, coming to the conclusion that all these phenomena are exclusively the result of psychotic delusion or anomalous neurophysiological events in the brain. Finally, numerous "New Age" books give voice to channelings purporting to be messages from various ETs who may or may not be "Ascended Masters." Barbara Hand Clow is a popular author in this genre.

The Internet is another story. Not only are websites categorized in similar veins, but many pages resemble disjointed mish-mash hodge-podges that are difficult if not impossible to pin down to any approach at all. Some sites attempt to classify hundreds of alien races according to physical typology; others simply talk about the physics and mathematical theories involved in understanding intergalactic travel and exploration of other dimensions. Many sites are dedicated to monitoring government activity and suppression of UFO information. However, one can never be too careful in evaluating online material. Double-check the source before you rely on it for anything, and you can save yourself some time and embarrassment. According to Dr. Steven Greer, the majority of the literature on this subject, including Internet web sites, is 95% disinformation. Therefore it's good advice to be wary of everything you read initially.

With all that's available, it is difficult to sort out what's true and what's not; what's useful and what's merely entertaining. It is my hope that someday someone will come along and put together a comprehensive compendium covering all aspects of these phenomena. It certainly merits a discipline of its own.

The ideas I present and use as a foundation for my view are based on my personal experience, research and insight, and the work of authors I get the most "truth-sense" from. I don't completely reject any author for it seems they all have something worthwhile to contribute, no matter how small. Similarly, there are few authors whose work I would wholeheartedly endorse because of what I perceive to be misinformation, disinformation or impure motives laced into their presentation of the material. There may be one exception, however. Dr. Steven M. Greer is the author offering the most reasonable and comprehensive view of this vast subject, in my opinion.

Dr. Greer is one of the most courageous, tenacious, and visionary pioneers of our time. He is a spiritual warrior who's already done much of the dirty work in getting to the bottom of all this. Outside of a historical context, his books, *Extraterrestrial Contact: The Evidence and Implications* and *Disclosure* tell you essentially most of what you need to know to truly understand these phenomena.

Dr. Greer is a specialist in emergency medicine and former chairman of the department of emergency medicine at Caldwell Memorial Hospital in North Carolina. He is a lifetime member of Alpha Omega Alpha, the nation's most prestigious medical honor society. Dr. Greer left a successful career in medicine to fully devote himself to the study of extraterrestrial intelligence (ETI), by founding the Center for the Study of Extraterrestrial Intelligence (CSETI) in 1990, and then later the Disclosure Project in June of 2000.

For over a decade, CSETI has trained and deployed teams of investigators out in the field to observe, record, and often times interact with ETI. Having experienced a great deal of success in these endeavors, CSETI has grown into a worldwide organization that continues to investigate, analyze, educate and promote understanding of ETI with compelling results.

The principles of CSETI are as follows:[1]

- There is strong evidence for the existence of ETI, civilizations and spacecraft.
- ETI/ETS have been and are currently visiting the Earth.
- Careful bilateral communications between ETI and humans is of continuing importance and will increase in the future.
- CSETI approaches the study of ETI with cooperative, peaceful, non-harmful intentions and procedures.
- The establishment of a lasting world peace is essential to the full development of the ETI-Human relationship.
- Both humans and ETI, as conscious, intelligent beings, are essentially more alike than dissimilar; CSETI is dedicated to the study of both our shared and unique characteristics.
- CSETI operates on the premise that ETI net motives and ultimate intentions are peaceful and non-hostile.
- It appears probable that more than one extraterrestrial civilization is responsible for the ETI/ETs contact so far observed. It is likely that this represents a cooperative effort.
- CSETI will attempt to cultivate bilateral ETI-human contact and relations which will serve peaceful, cooperative goals. It is NOT a goal of CSETI to acquire ET advanced technologies which may have a potential harmful or military application if disclosed prematurely.

In order to help you sort through the rest of what's available online and in print, I suggest trying my general rule of thumb: Any site, author, or teacher that focuses on separateness, xenophobia (specieism/racism), conspiracy without solution, or that feeds off fear, prejudice and paranoia, is a good sign you're in a shit hole swimming in newage. Not

131

that these authors don't have something to offer because many of them do. For one, how are you going to know what disinformation/misinformation is unless you're exposed to it, right? It's a wonderful way to study how the "secret government" has successfully infiltrated the UFO community and is actually posing as part of the anti-secret government movement. The ominous thing about these sites is that a sprinkling of truth-bytes mingled with a knowledgeable amount of the jargon makes them seem authentic. Their tactics and true motivations, however, are insidious.

The only way to determine truth-sense is to listen with your heart and ask these questions: Who is the messenger? What is the motivation behind the message? Who benefits from the message? Is the message proactive or is it reactionary? Does it promote free will or is it fatalistic? Also, anyone who tells you that all religion, spirituality of any kind, and secret societies related to ancient mystery schools are simply methods of human enslavement and thought-control, consider their fruits. One bad apple doesn't make the whole barrel bad, as previously discussed. A distortion or misuse of religion, occultism or spiritual teaching does not invalidate the teachings in themselves. Again, consider the source and most importantly – who is funding it. Follow the money. It works every time. Nothing is good or bad in itself – but can be used either way -- even the truth. And sometimes, that's the most difficult pill to swallow.

Until the advent of archeology in the 1800s, the Roman Catholic Church controlled the documentation of history in the West. The Church decided that life on Earth, according to Genesis, began around 4004 B.C.E. We only learned that this was not true in the last century. Before then, anyone who claimed otherwise was deemed a heretic and often times destroyed. Well if that small piece of information was not true, might there be other bits and pieces that are also misleading in the entire historical overview? Turns out such is the case. Archeology initially appeared as a real threat to religion. Even now, while it may seem that academia (science) and religion are at odds, that's only on the surface. Many scholars have revealed covert collusion between the two with regard to how particular archeological findings are presented.[2] There seems to be a highly selective process at work – one which is deeply disturbing and unfair to the citizens of this planet.

The following historical overview follows a timeline that I feel is more accurate according to my research. By the end of this life, I hope to see many more corrections trickling out into the historical mainstream. Until then, we must continue to push for complete disclosure.

Basic Origins: The Anunnaki

Zecharia Sitchin is a pioneering scholar whose genius will surely someday be recognized without question. Russian born, Sitchin grew up in the area we know as Israel. He attained a degree in Economic History from the University of London, and had a successful career as a leading journalist and editor in Israel for many years. Eventually he moved to New York where he continues to write today.

While living in the Middle East, Sitchin extensively studied the Old Testament and the history and archeology of the area. He also became fluent in many ancient and modern Semitic and European languages so that he could understand first hand the ancient texts to which he was exposed. Only about 200 people in the world can read and interpret clay tablets in these ancient languages, and he is one of them. His comparison of the original Hebrew Biblical text with the parallel Sumerian and Akkadian texts yielded startling and extraordinary revelations about what really happened way back then and exactly how we came into the picture. These revolutionary conclusions about our cosmic history are presented in his series of books entitled, *The Earth Chronicles*.

Therefore, most of the following summary derives from scientific, scholarly examination and translation of hundreds of clay tablets and cuneiform texts originally unearthed from the ancient sites in the Middle East. Sitchin never claimed to have records at his disposal that anyone else did not have. All his data is based upon archeological findings that were shared and made public. None of his assertions come from "channeling" or pure speculation. He bases everything he proposes on his thorough examination and incisive interpretation of these historical records.

Over 500,000 years ago, planet Earth was seeded by extraterrestrials in many ways and in many forms. Some Earth primates had evolved to the level of homo erectus, yet humanity as we know it today did not exist. Our souls may have lived in other life forms, some which might have been humanoid in appearance, but the physical species of homo sapiens had not yet arrived on this planet. In the next 50,000 years, a particular migration of ETs would come to Earth, known by Sumerians as the Anunnaki and the Nefilim by the Hebrews. Anunnaki in Sumerian means, "those who came down from the heavens." Therefore, the term Anunnaki refers to a group of extraterrestrials of several races, not just one race.

The Anunnaki came from the 10th planet in our solar system, called Nibiru by the Sumerians. The 10th planet is sometimes called "Planet X" in the popular media. Proof of its existence is conclusive, yet Nibiru has not yet been "officially" recognized by any government or academic institution. Many folks agree, however, that this information will be properly authenticated by the powers that be within the next ten years.[3]

The Anunnaki came in search of gold for the maintenance of the atmospheric conditions of their planet, and formed several colonies on Earth for the purpose of gold mining. Anu, one of the main rulers of Nibiru, placed two of his children in charge of Earth operations – the half-brothers Enlil and Enki. The brothers' sister Ninhursag, the chief medical officer of the mission, assisted them and played a major role in the events that spawned humanity. Enlil's initial job was to oversee the major colonial settlements, and Enki was given the gold mines to supervise. The area known as Mesopotamia became a lush, prosperous settlement and was literally the original Garden of Eden. Everyone lived in harmony until approximately 250,000

B.C.E., when the Anunnaki miners revolted. The solution, they decided, was to genetically engineer a "worker race" to take their place. Initially, experiments were conducted merging the genes of various animals with homo erectus. When that didn't work, they decided to splice their own genes into the primate. Ninhursag is the Anunnaki female primarily responsible for our creation. She was the living archetype for the Mother Goddess. Homo sapiens was born by her hands and turned out to be quite an intelligent creature.

Various prehistoric hominids roamed the Earth prior to the arrival of homo erectus. Homo neanderthalensis (Neanderthals) and homo sapiens (CroMagnon) emerged after homo erectus. Some scientists say, based on DNA studies, that the Neanderthal were an entirely separate species from the CroMagnon or modern human, and probably became extinct at the hands of the more populous CroMagnon. Yet some scientists believe the two species were not that different, and that they interbred until all the unique Neanderthal genetic characteristics were swamped out. What is certain is that Neanderthal did not survive.[4] There is a theory that the Neanderthals were the result of an earlier, yet failed genetic experiment on the part of an extraterrestrial civilization, and were discarded or left on their own to fend for themselves as a species. We may never know.

What we do know is that both Darwin and the creationists are correct. It had taken millions of years for an existing primate to evolve into homo erectus. Then homo sapiens suddenly appeared on the scene 300,000 years ago virtually overnight – a million years too soon given the pace at which homo erectus was evolving. Therefore, man was literally made in the image of the gods. I said "gods" for a reason. The archeological evidence reveals that the Old Testament of the Bible was taken directly from older Sumerian records. Modern linguists have discovered several mistranslations – many which may have been deliberate – which resulted in the compilation of the books of the Bible as we know them today. The original records clearly state the way it really happened for anyone who wants to know. And the correct translation is "gods" – not God.[5]

Homo sapiens could not initially breed, being a hybrid. The demand for more workers created a need to make some modifications to the species so it could reproduce. We get our first "DNA upgrade" and the rest is history. We became homo sapiens sapiens according to the literature. We proliferated to the point of being expelled from the Garden and left to our own devices for survival. About this time some of the male Anunnaki began to mate with human women producing strange offspring as indicated in the Bible and original texts. In fact, things got so strange, ugly and out of hand that Enlil deemed the entire human project a failure. His solution? Wipe if off the face of the Earth.

So about 12,000 years ago Earth suffered a great catastrophe that was partly engineered by the Nibiruans. The planet Nibiru comes close enough to the Earth's orbit approximately every 3,600 years and produces a profound effect on its gravitational field. With a little bit of nuclear tampering, it was easy to create conditions that would set off the great flood of all world legends.[6] Therefore the timing was perfect. But Enki had compassion for his human children and deemed them worthy of saving. Therefore, a few humans were secretly salvaged along with vital genetic material for reseeding the planet, spawning the tale of "Noah's ark."

Enlil was pissed. Things never were quite the same between the half-brothers from that point onward. The dissension between them was reflected in the conflicts between their followers. For instance, Enki had created what was known as the "Brotherhood of the Serpent." This brotherhood was the beginning of all our modern day mystery schools, including the ones that tutored such spiritual sages as Jesus and others of similar stature. Within these schools, select humans were taught reading, writing, healing, sacred geometry, and other spiritual practices. This was the legacy of *Adonai* – Hebrew for "God in man." Enlil and his followers did not want to see humans so empowered. Therefore this tradition would eventually go underground because of persecution. It is also why over the course of time the Book of Genesis was revised to depict the Serpent as an evil creature who later became known as Satan.

Around 4000 B.C.E., the Anunnaki began to phase off the planet. They had given the gift of civilization to humans, which culminated in the great cultures of Mesopotamia, Egypt, India, and the Americas. Earthly kings were appointed as intermediaries between the Anunnaki and humans. Mathematics, technology and astronomy were taught to the ruling clans, which is evident in the ancient civilizations they left behind. Most of the Anunnaki had left the planet by 1250 B.C.E. By then the earthly factions were well on their own way to dissipating, degenerating, and destroying each other. The old palaces of the Anunnaki became the temples of the new custodial religions named after whatever "god" was being followed and venerated. Enki and Enlil were not the only ones – there were others. However, the influence of the two half-brothers had the greatest impact on the evolution of human civilization as reflected in the Judeo-Christian tradition.

On close examination of the Old Testament, some scholars have noted that whenever something bad was happening to the Hebrews, it was all "Jehovah's" fault. Jehovah was a Hebrew name for Enlil who became known as the mean, wrathful god instilling fear in his subjects. Whenever something beneficial happened to them, however, it was a blessing from the good Lord, Adonai – a Hebrew reference to Enki.

Much of what follows corresponds to Sitchin's findings, yet the source information may have been channeled and will be distinguished as such accordingly.

Horses of Different Colors

Channeling is difficult to define. I think the best explanation of channeling comes from Marcia Schafer, an intuitive who sometimes engages in this practice. This is what she says about her channeling:

137

When the information comes through, it can be compared to entering a connective formation. I ascend into an altered state, and my consciousness rises up as I become increasingly relaxed and enter into a deep meditative state. At a unique point, there is a connection, a silent "click," described only as a sound without sound. At this juncture we become a hybrid of a collective essence. There is no "me" or "them." Just "we," just "us," just all that is.

It is misleading when others refer to being "only a channel" and take no responsibility for the information that comes through. It's a little like the ventriloquist blaming the dummy. . . the person is a filter through which all information borrows his or her color of bias and knowledge. This needs to be acknowledged.

I will not identify a name or source for these messages that come through, because labels tend to cloud one's mind and develop predetermined associations. It is the message, not the messenger that carries import here. Profound speech can come from a young child, an old fool, or an ordinary citizen with no outstanding public acclaim. It doesn't matter.

As a society, we tend to deify our messengers, and I refuse to let that happen. It is of no consequence whether the source is George of New Jersey, Avedon of Aventura, Ascended Masters, or Intergalactic Warriors. I ask only that you listen to the harmonies; if the song is sweet to your ears, hold it within your heart. If it carries no import, discard it.[7]

Unfortunately, everyone does not share her understanding of this phenomenon. Much channeled information that I've read may ring right with me in general, but there will be something a little bit off about it. It usually involves a label like she says. A name, a date, or a place where they're trying to be specific just doesn't match up with previous data, or some other inconsistency jars to reason. Just as one of her channelings indicated: "A channeled entity is not the ultimate resource for knowledge. There is absolute truth, universal truth, and personal truth. The channeling source can only share what is known from its sources and experiences gained from its travels. While it may provide good information in some areas, please regard it as only an adjunct resource, and not an end-all, be-all omnipotent fount of knowledge."[8] And that is what I try to remember as I'm sifting through all this.

Some say the Anunnaki never really left, but just went undercover. There are those who speculate that they continue to control us through the manipulations of particular groups of people and government. Regardless of whether that's true or not, it is evident that the Anunnaki are not the only visitors to Earth from outer space.

Information on these others can be found in numerous books and Internet sites. A few are particularly worth mentioning. First, we must clarify how important context is when discussing planets, star systems, alien races, and intergalactic travel. Much of the channeled information does not elucidate context, which can be confusing. For instance, when authors speak of particular races colonizing certain areas of intergalactic space, naturally we cannot even begin to imagine how that happened in our current technological paradigm. Therefore it's important to recognize that many of these assertions may well be describing events that transpired in other dimensions – not necessarily manifesting in the physical universe as we know it three dimensionally. Much space travel is interdimensional in nature and not specifically limited to physical vehicles described as UFOs. This does not preclude space travel with physical 3-D UFOs in our known universe. It just establishes a wider range of experience and possibility within which to view these phenomena. It is also possible that entities from other planets and stellar systems can weave in and out of dimensions with relative ease so that it may appear as physical phenomena on some occasions and upper dimensional on others. They may or may not need any particular kind of vehicle to do this. So it's important to keep these many variables in mind when discussing these phenomena.

Jelaila Starr wrote *We Are the Nibiruans*,[9] a semi-channeled work that has some very interesting information in it. As with much work of this type, I question some of the minor details, such as dates and the attribution of certain characters to specific mythological entities, yet overall I get a lot of truth-sense from it. Jelaila is what's called in UFO/ET circles, a "walk-in." A walk-in is an ET who has literally walked into the physical body of a human being lending their vehicle for a contractual period of time. The soul of the human being is not unconscious or unwilling as in possession; the relationship is considered a consensual partnership. The walk-in usually occurs when the person experiences some great trauma or near-death experience. Such incidents make it easier for the two to make the trade, according to Jelaila.

Jelaila's human name is Jocelyn. Jelaila is the messenger for the "Nibiruan Council." Therefore it may not be fair to call her a channeler since she regards herself as a Nibiruan ET. Regardless of who she is, Jelaila's work is practical and inspirational. Her multidimensionality is evident in her humility, honesty, generosity, compassion, and her courage to express and share all aspects of her "humanity" – the light and the dark. Such traits are rare in teachers on the 3-D plane. She fully acknowledges the polarity game for the game that it is, and openly encourages integration in a friendly, nonjudgmental forum through her workshops and online activities.

In Jelaila's book, Anu provides not only the history of the Nibiruan influence on Earth, which is largely consistent with Sitchin's interpretation of the Sumerian records, but also a prehistory regarding a "universal hierarchy." According to Anu via Jelaila, in simplistic terms, our universe had a "divine creator" who fragmented, and those fragments became the souls of every living thing in the universe. The way these souls come to recognize their essential divinity is through playing the game of polarity integration. In other words, souls must adopt both roles of light and dark in order to learn to integrate them. Some of those souls became major "founders" and "game engineers" who are like administrators of cosmic divine plans. These founders and engineers are of two main races from another universe that already finished the game: Felines and Carians. The Felines were responsible for the genetic engineering of all life forms, while the Carians magnetically engineered all the grids, portals, stargates, and dimensions. Evidently there are several dimensions, and in one of these dimensions reside the "Council of Nine" who are directors of the game for us. The Council of Nine has been mentioned in other channeled works as well, such as *The Only Planet of Choice*[10] by Phyllis V. Schlemmer and Palden Jenkins.

Anu through Jelaila says that our galaxy has a divine plan all its own with four major players or races involved in the polarity integration game: Humans, Reptiles, Felines and Carians. Felines and Carians created the Humans and Reptiles with all the other incarnate beings in our universe. Basically, the Humans were assigned to represent the forces of Light and the Reptiles the forces of Darkness. Yet Anu emphasizes that all souls must experience both at some time in their evolution. In order to do this, their genetic codes were embedded with the Formula of Compassion so they could eventually learn to love and appreciate each other's differences. Obviously, the game isn't over yet.

When Jelaila talks about Humans as being one of the major four races, she describes them as having originated on the Lyran constellation. We know that homo sapiens sapiens arrived rather recently on this planet. Therefore she probably means entities in humanoid form. Reptiles would obviously refer to embodiment in some kind of reptilian form. And that fits precisely the descriptions of some beings made by a number of contactees.

Jelaila says the Felines come from Sirius A. Three major bodies comprise the Sirius system: Sirius A, Sirius B, and Sirius C. Sirius B was the main body that imploded to create

Sirius A and Sirius C. Felines are natural healers who are involved with repairing the great psychic wounds created by war. They do not take sides because they have already completed the lessons of polarity integration and unconditional love. Although they are higher dimensional beings, they reside in the 6th dimension of creation because that's where energy becomes physical, according to Jelaila.[11]

Many early civilizations were acutely aware of the sacred Feline presence on our planet, as exemplified by the Egyptian cat goddesses, Bast and Sekhmet. Jelaila says, "The Felines left the lions, and all cats, to be transmitters of information back to Sirius A. The lions, in particular, were made king of the jungle so that they would not be killed off and could, therefore, continue being transmitters of information throughout the many thousands of years that Earth and mankind would need to complete their Divine Plan. Cats are the information link between the 3rd and 6th dimension."[12] This may sound absolutely silly to some people, but to me it is profound based on my personal experience with my own cats. They are far more than mere pets or even children. I have been attuned to this since I was a child. It also may be one of the main reasons why cats far outnumber dogs today as the number one pet in America. They may be preparing us for something.

While the spark of divinity is within all life forms, not all cats are essentially "gods from outer space." It reminds me of the lovely series of books in children's literature called *The Chronicles of Narnia* by C.S. Lewis. C.S. Lewis was a Christian writer whose stories are more like parables steeped in lessons involving ethics and spiritual principle. In the fantasy land of Narnia, the deity-like ruler is a great lion called Aslan, which is obviously a Christ figure. The children who travel to Narnia go on adventures where they are morally and spiritually challenged. Aslan is a presence who always overshadows them in a protective, loving way, but who can be quite stern when the situation merits, just like any reasonable parent. The interesting thing about Narnia is that all its creatures, including animals, are able to talk. Therefore they are not eaten or subjected to servitude like animals outside of Narnia. C.S. Lewis was probably subconsciously tapping into a deeper truth here. It is possible that many life forms are capable of hosting a presence whose awareness may be substantially greater than what we normally associate with that particular life form. Many Eastern religions also teach this. Therefore, this should give us pause when reconsidering our relationships to all species on this planet – particularly animals, and may help us to overcome specieism in general.

According to Jelaila, the civil engineers of the universe are a bird-like race called Carians. They also do a lot of protecting – not with weapons, but with manipulation of energy. Their influence is punctuated by the sacred bird symbols of many peoples on this planet.[13]

The Reptiles were created long before the Humans, and that's one reason why their technology is superior, according to Jelaila. They come from the constellations of Orion and Sigma Draconi. Jelaila says they were given a creation myth that teaches that they're superior to all other races, which naturally causes discord. They tend to want to take over and run any planet they colonize.[14] This doesn't make them bad, however, because they're simply playing a role. According to much of the recent literature, Reptilians are breaking through their creation myth as we are ours, and learning to rise above certain separatist tendencies rooted in past conflicts.

Humans were seeded and developed on a planet called Avyon, according to Jelaila. They began as aquatic primates (similar to whales and dolphins) that were taken on to the land where they were genetically modified to become bipedal. The remaining aquatic primates were left in the ocean for maintaining the planetary biosphere.[15] Interestingly, some literature suggests that whales and dolphins on Earth are acting in similar capacity. One school of thought says that many of these great ocean mammals are actually guardian beings from Sirius who are still intimately involved with our spiritual evolution.

Jelaila says that eventually the Humans were moved to Sirius B and became known as Sirian Humans. At this time Humans had a choice between becoming physical or remaining on the etheric level of the astral plane. These etheric Sirians became devoted to pursuing healing methodologies and other spiritual practices. The physical Sirians moved to a planet in the Orion constellation and became known as the Orion Humans. This planet was too close to a planet controlled by Reptilians. Therefore, the Reptilians invaded, conquered and enslaved these Humans. Sirians and Orions ended up on Tiamat, a planet that was eventually blown apart in intergalactic warfare. A huge portion of that planet is what became modern day Earth, with the remaining remnant an asteroid belt. An immigration to the Pleiades took place. Then a Galactic Federation was formed, and Nibiru was established as a kind of major command center for the Federation.

This is an extremely abbreviated version of Jelaila's story. The history is much more complex, and the events take place over millions of years. For more details, read Jelaila's book or please refer to the Cosmic Chronology in Appendix 2.

One of Jelaila's main assertions is that several different races inhabit Nibiru. Therefore the Anunnaki may not have been as pure a genetic pool as represented. Enki and Enlil had different mothers. Enki's mother was a Reptilian – a "Dragon Queen." Jelaila says that Earth humans are made up from genetic material of all four major races. Recent information channeled by Marcia Schafer indicates there may have been as many as twelve different races involved in the original experiments.[16] Other indicators point to multiple genetic upgrades received by humanity – not just the one referred to in the records exposed by Sitchin.

According to Dr. Greer, humans have so far identified at least 57 different species or phenotypes (different body types) of extraterrestrials.[17] Some of these visiting races are known as the Andromedans, Pleiadians, Arcturians, various other humanoids, and everyone's "favorite" – the Zeta Reticuli, otherwise know as the "Grays." I say "favorite" facetiously because those are the ETs who get the worst press. Unfortunately, they are frequently associated with many unpleasant abduction type experiences. Many contactees feel that these Grays are working under the supervision of another race. Sometimes androids are seen with them – machines that look humanoid like robots. According to Dr. Greer, there is evidence that a significant number of sighted Grays are not extraterrestrial at all but actually biological beings genetically engineered by humans as a result of secret government unacknowledged special access projects (USAPS) conducted in underground military bases, particularly in a location near Dulce, New Mexico.[18]

It is apparent that there is even greater diversity among ET races than there is among human races on Earth. For instance, many subgroups of the Reptilian race are reported. This makes perfect sense considering the infinite expanse of all possible universes. Many authors overgeneralize concerning racial characteristics, just as we humans unfortunately tend to do with each other. This is unfair and misleading. Each human and ET should be regarded on the merits of their individuality regardless of what race or planet they represent. It is sad to see the vehement demonization of the Reptilians by followers of David Icke and others of a paranoid mindset. Once you demonize a group of beings and make them "less than human" – that leaves the door open for all kinds of trouble, including genocide. Okay, so they may not be "human" as we understand the term -- that doesn't make them less worthy of existence than we are. All life is equally sacred – no matter what form it takes. Yet it seems we're still working on that one.

Of course there is a theory that many UFOs and aliens may not be extraterrestrial in origin at all, but instead come from inside a hollow Earth. The experiences of some abductees and contactees seem to support this to some extent. According to Jelaila, at one point in Earth's history, the Reptilians moved underground in order to avoid detection by their enemies. In the 1950s, U.S. military personnel were contacted by a purported alien from Venus who goes by the name of Valiant

Thor. Thor explained that his people lived underneath the surface of Venus and indicated that there were other races living beneath the surface of Earth, Mars and the Moon.

Many conspiracy models include a theory about a network of underground bases where all sorts of ominous events take place. The more negative faction of these conspiracists contend that many missing children have been abducted by agents of the secret government in collusion with evil aliens who take these children to their underground bases for slave labor and for harvesting their glands and tissues. When the children are no longer useful, they are simply "fed" to the Reptilians according to rumor. They say that these particular Reptilians do not consider themselves aliens at all because they colonized the planet long before humans arrived. These alarmists add that during a great intergalactic war, the Reptilians headed underground to conduct their operations covertly. They feel this war is still waged right beneath our feet as we speak. So yes, there is supposed to be a "good" faction of these intraterrestrial beings fighting on behalf of the light and humanity -- even some "friendly lizards" that don't eat people.

The existence of underground bases has been confirmed. But according to Dr. Greer, this rumor about "man-eating lizzies" is just that – a malicious lie contrived by the shadow government to make us fear all extraterrestrials. He also contends that 95% of all abductions are carried out by the military for the purpose of USAPS. The aliens witnessed by abductees in underground bases are for the most part human beings in costumes acting out a staged scenario for mind-control purposes. This premise is corroborated by much evidence and witness testimony.[19]

Speaking of the intermingling of humans and ETs, we come to the matter of hybrids and starseeds. This is an ambiguous topic that is problematic and seems to raise more questions than answers. Jelaila's definition of a starseed is someone from another planet or civilization walking around in a human body or some other life form. She says that many people may be drawn to certain animal forms that really resemble their true form. A person belonging to the race of aquatic beings from Sirius, for example, would have a strong affinity for whales and dolphins. At any rate, Jelaila lists many factors that hint at starseed identity, such as intense feelings of loneliness; being drawn to metaphysics; not "belonging" in one's biological family, and so on. Actually, these states describe most of us at one stage or another in our lives. My feeling is that on some level, we're all starseeds due to our extremely diverse genetic backgrounds. Because I believe in spiritual evolution as well as physical, I do not think it is reasonable to accept the premise that we may be culturally or even spiritually bound to a specific planetary identity or anything for that matter. For instance, a soul might spend the majority of their evolutionary development on planet Earth as an Earth human but may have recently had an incarnation on some other planetary system. Would this make them a starseed or could it be past life memory? On the other hand, the opposite scenario may present itself; the majority of their development occurring on a specific system such as, say, Planet Claire. They decide to come to Earth for a lifetime. Are they a starseed from Planet Claire or just a member of the B-52s?[20]

I asked Dr. Greer what his feelings were on the subject of walk-ins and starseeds, and he said he was not impressed. Personally he sees no need to distinguish ourselves in that way. It's a mythology or understanding that's just not necessary.[21] After all, the CSETI motto is "one people – one universe." These kinds of labels can work against synergy and social integration if we're not careful. So why use them if we don't have to? We're all made up of the same cosmic energy, light substance or Spirit, so what does it matter?

The issue of biological human/ET hybrids is equally complex. We know that homo sapiens began as a hybrid. Historically, tales regarding the "fairy folk" and incidents where they coupled with humans resulting in a strange child or a changeling might refer to this phenomenon. When the "sons of the gods" mated with the "daughters of man" this too occurred. But what about today? Many abductees report being taken

147

aboard ships where they are shown laboratories filled with rows of containers housing live fetuses. Many of them are told that these fetuses are hybrids between humans and ETs. A common abductee experience involves ETs extracting what appears to be ovum or sperm from the reproductive organs of the abductee. Some women have reported a sense of being artificially inseminated and do indeed become pregnant without recalling having intercourse with a human partner. A common story is that these fetuses are miscarried or extracted by the ETs in a later abduction. Again, however, remember that the shadow government is staging many of these scenarios for nefarious purposes, and that observed fetuses may simply be the products of covert cloning experiments conducted by the military. To what degree these reports are truthful representations of what is really going on remains largely unknown.

Much has been written about implants. Some people claim that there are many different kinds of implants, and that aliens and/or our government implant abductees for different reasons – anything from simply tagging a specimen like livestock to the implant being a type of mind control device.[22] Some individuals claim to have found these implants and extracted them. One might think that if any of these implants were made of a material substance not of this planet, then that would be the smoking gun. However, Marcia Schafer says that most of them are made of biological substance, which enables them to remain undetected for long periods of time.[23]

Meanwhile, it is unhealthy to dwell on such negative events, especially when they are so speculative. Discretion is advised when exploring this darker side of these phenomena. No doubt, horrible things happen in the world, and surely there are enough human serial killers to put any blood-drinking alien reptile to shame. Yet as with any form of negativity, dwelling on it without working to eliminate it is counter-productive and helps no one. Individuals who have endured such terrifying experiences are entitled to get all the help, support, and relief from their suffering that they can, and we should encourage them to do so. But fostering fear and paranoia only feeds whatever negative forces are playing upon our universe. Balancing compassion with severity is the solution, as always.

The Sirius Mystery

Sirius is a triple-star system in the constellation of Canis Major near Orion. Sirius A is the brightest star visible second to our Sun, about eight light-years away, and can be seen in the northern hemisphere from November through April.

Much esoteric literature discusses Sirius, sometimes called Sothis or the "Dog Star." It's probably no coincidence that a major breakthrough has occurred regarding evidence into extraterrestrial visitation from Sirius. This information can be found in *The Sirius Mystery* by Robert Temple.[24]

Robert Temple is a respected Fellow of the Royal Astronomical Society and a recognized scholar and author of classical antiquities. As a result of his interdisciplinary approach, he was able to decipher particular clues and codes embedded in ancient mythology that contain precise astronomical data revealing that an extraterrestrial race from Sirius once visited the Earth.

Temple references the African Dogon tribe who already possessed precise astronomical data about Sirius long before we were privy to such knowledge via scientific instrumentation. The Dogon say that their ancestors received this information from the Nommo, an amphibious type people from the Sirius star system. The Dogon's creation myth describes the genetic engineering of humanity. They believe that the elliptical orbit created by two stars in the Sirius system is a replication of the pattern of our DNA.

Amphibious gods are found in cultures all around the world – they are not specific to the Dogon. The Hindu Vishnu was part man/part fish, along with the Chinese Fuxi, the Sumerian Oannes, the Philistine Dagon, the Greek Nereus and Triton – son of Poseidon and Amphitrite. Folklore talks about mermen and mermaids. In Hindu and Buddhist literature, reference to the Nagas abound – a serpentine race inhabiting waterways.

149

The Babylonians wrote that each night their "gods" retired to the water. Certainly these descriptions may act as metaphors in some cases, and in the least allude to the possibility of some kind of extraterrestrial watercraft. Let's not forget that Jonah in the Bible was in the belly of a "great fish" for three days before he was "spit out." Still, there seems to be a lot of evidence, according to Temple, that some of these beings literally had physical features that required them to spend a great deal of their time in water for survival.

We don't know but that there may be a planetary body in the vicinity of the Sirius star system that is partially water. If not, then these beings may have chosen this particular form to materialize in for some other reason. Several historical events appear to be staged for our benefit in order to create a story or legend in which spiritual truths or principles are transmitted through symbol and metaphor. Perhaps the Sirians were up to that. Or maybe an aquatic form was simply the best fit for negotiating our particular ecosphere. Who knows? At any rate, this issue is probably not as important as others in relation to the deeper connection between the Earth and Sirius.

Where did these Sirian visitors go and when are they coming back, if at all? A possible answer to this question came through the channeler, Lyssa Royal, from a source purporting to be Sirian. It is a beautiful message that merits repeating here:

> We have been silent for a long time so you could begin learning the idea of self-empowerment, and learn that all you need is within you. You needn't look to any of us to do it for you. We can encourage you, but we won't do it for you. 3D, the old sleep cycle, was a cycle of deification. It was a cycle where God, seemingly, was outside of you. That was the illusion. That was the old pattern. That, in and of itself, can no longer be maintained as you now poke the holes through that thick fabric and begin creating the new paradigm. Now you begin touching the idea of All – the interconnectedness of All.

The beautiful beings that you speak to [in channelings all over the world] exist inside of you. They are not outside of you, they are a part of you. You have their wisdom within you and they are simply reflecting that which you already know. It is now why, at this time, we can return at some point soon (within your lifetime) and assist you. The choice now in the mass consciousness is such that you will no longer travel the road of deification. Finally, we will meet as equals. Until that day happens, landings in the mass way that you have envisioned will not occur. We will no longer perpetuate the idea that you are separate from us and that we are more knowledgeable than you.[25]

Intergalactic Communication

As we have seen, channeling is one way ETs communicate with us. Other interactions occur through materialization, lucid dreams, telepathy, implants, altered states, holographic communication, shared consciousness, and even ordinary technology from time to time. They can also communicate through music and sound – just as we can. However, as with communicating with anyone in any kind of relationship, the potential for abuse, projection, illusion and manipulation always exists. Here again, using one's own judgment in determining the effect of the specific communication is recommended. For instance, historically speaking, it appears that the use of illusion in terms of holographic projection by extraterrestrials may have played a major role in some religious visions experienced by certain saints and prophets. Overall, it would do us well to take the advice of Marcia Schafer in these matters:

It's imperative to note that if we hear a voice from another realm, it is still our responsibility to carefully exercise two of the most valuable gifts of the human condition: discernment and discretion. We must use our judgment to determine what is best for our reality and the beliefs we establish for our lives.[26]

151

Remember that ETs will more often than not tend to appear to us in a manner which seems magical or supernatural. We talked about this phenomenon in the previous chapter as it relates to natural law that we just don't have a complete handle on yet. Radio and television waves are passing through us continuously. We're not aware of them until we turn on a TV or a radio. Waves and frequencies from higher dimensions are continuously passing through us as well. The mind is the natural instrument for picking up these transmissions. The esoteric mystery schools have been teaching how to use it for that purpose for centuries in an effort to speed up the evolutionary process. Yet even without that instruction, the development of these states of consciousness would occur naturally at some point in an individual's life -- maybe not in this incarnation, but possibly the next. Therefore, telepathy, precognition, lucid and precognitive dreams, remote viewing, telekinesis, teleportation, transmutation, natural healing abilities, celestial perception, levitation, out of body experiences, materialization/dematerialization, bi-location, and other so-called supernormal abilities and states of awareness would be completely natural to peoples more advanced than we are in terms of technology. It helps to keep this in mind when encountering and interacting with extraterrestrials so that they are neither deified nor demonized.

CSETI Contact Protocols

For over a decade under the direction of Dr. Steven M. Greer, CSETI has developed and refined a systematic, innovative program for establishing contact in fieldwork with UFOs and ETs. CSETI members use both traditional and nontraditional technology in their contact efforts with specific but flexible guidelines. Traditional technology involves the use of sound, light, lasers, and equipment suitable for broadcasting tones believed to be extraterrestrial in origin. But because ETs use technologies beyond our current understanding of the laws of physics, we cannot depend on traditional technologies alone. It is, in fact, nontraditional technologies which have proven to be most successful in contact efforts; specifically, *thought*.

ETs use technologies that directly interface with mind and thought. For instance, someone might be outside and see a UFO up in the sky. Then they think to themselves, "I sure wish that thing would come closer," and it does. These kinds of scenarios have happened more than once in a manner that excludes the possibility of chance.[27] Therefore, CSETI has developed a technique known as CTS or "coherent thought sequencing" as a proven, effective method for establishing contact.

CTS is a structured group meditation with the sole intent of telepathically broadcasting to any ETs or UFOs which might be "listening" -- an invitation to visit complete with directions. The meditation begins with guided relaxation and then progresses to a state whereby unbounded, nonlocal or universal mind is accessed. Next, the exact location of the group's whereabouts is visualized in a sequential process, like a giant cinematic cosmic zooming lens. The Milky Way Galaxy is visualized. Next, the solar system's exact location on the appropriate spiral arm of the galaxy is seen, then exactly where Earth is located within the solar system, the specific continent upon Earth, the country, the region, down to the actual locale with as much detail and geographical precision as possible. This process is repeated as often as necessary to obtain results.

When I first began practicing dzogchen, I immediately recognized that it produces this required state of awareness – a state in which one is aware of awareness in a nondual sense. I instinctively knew that this "state" was fundamental for establishing contact with any extraterrestrial, assuming that they already operate from such a state -- a natural assumption given their advanced technologies. This was long before I'd ever heard of Dr. Greer's CTS technique. Sure enough, when I first listened to the guided meditation by Dr. Greer used as a prelude to CTS, it was practically identical to how Lama Surya Das introduces students to dzogchen. Surya and Dr. Greer even use the same words: "aware of awareness." Therefore, this may be one of the secret purposes or reasons behind the timely introduction of dzogchen to the masses by Surya and others.

After a period of CTS, UFOs are more likely to appear, however, they may not always arrive as expected. Sometimes they never quite materialize on the physical plane, but their presence can be felt and seen by those who have developed sufficient sensitivity. Naturally, the degree or intensity of the contact experience varies greatly from individual to individual. Of course, it is wonderful when an ET craft completely manifests and can be vectored in on a level that everyone can experience and appreciate, but this is not always the case.

When an ET craft fully materializes on the physical plane, researchers recognize five different kinds of possible *close encounters*, a phrase coined by Dr. J. Allen Hynek in the early days of UFOlogy:

> A Close Encounter of the First Kind, or CE-1, is described as the observation of a UFO within 500 feet. A Close Encounter of the Second Kind, or CE-2, is one where some form of trace evidence is obtained, such as in a landing case or radar case. A Close Encounter of the Third Kind, or CE-3, denotes the observation of a humanoid, generally but not necessarily in the vicinity of or within a UFO. In more recent years, the category of a Close Encounter of the Fourth Kind, or CE-4, has generally been accepted as an interaction where a human is taken on board a UFO, presumably in the presence of humanoids... A Close Encounter of the Fifth Kind, or CE-5, is characterized by human-initiated and/or voluntary human interactive encounters. That is, encounters with UFOs or their occupants are initiated or furthered by voluntary, direct and willful means by human observers.[28]

It was from examining the data resulting from CE-5s that Dr. Greer concluded that there are three main components to these interactive episodes: light, sound, and thought. Therefore

CSETI implemented a project called the CE-5 Initiative synthesizing scientific research, diplomatic, and inter-species relations goals. The main intent was to establish interactive communication and peaceful relationships with our extraterrestrial neighbors. Since its inception, CSETI has employed select working groups in field research around the world with remarkable results. Training seminars for these working groups have been highly successful in creating a new breed of "ambassadors to the universe."

The Case for Non-Hostility

It must be stressed that in spite of the negative reports concerning abductions and animal mutilations, there is no real evidence that ET motivations are hostile. The shadow government has staged many events and seeded popular culture with many scary movies and television shows in order to paint such a picture in an effort to cover up what's really going on. Dr. Greer and CSETI have experienced nothing but peaceful intentions, kindness, healing, and benevolence from these beings. Still, Dr. Greer rationally concludes,

> The polarizing tendency to declare ETI as either sinister intruders or perfect god-like saviors is unwise at best, and probably dangerous to the long-term health of the ETI-human relationship. This does NOT mean, however, that we must view this phenomenon in a "motive vacuum," and I feel that a strong case for assumed non-hostility can, and indeed must, be made. The assumption of non-hostility means that in our research, analysis and ETI interactions, we assume non-hostility until clearly proven otherwise. It does not mean that we regard ETI as necessarily godlike saviors, but it clearly avoids the premature characterization of ETI actions and motives as hostile or sinister. Such a moderate positivity and optimism is essential for the emerging

ETI/human relationship to develop with the least chance of conflict.[29]

Several other arguments support the case for non-hostility. If we are in fact, in some ways, their "children," this may account for the reason why they're here in the first place. It's as if we, as a race, are at a critical point in our social development. Perhaps we've reached a stage comparable to cosmic adolescence, and they're just watching us, realizing that we have free will and must learn from our own mistakes. This is also a main reason cited for their non-interference in global affairs. Indeed, it is juvenile to believe that they should come down and rescue us from ourselves. No, we made this mess and we're the ones responsible for cleaning it up. However, interesting behaviors on their part have been observed indicating a reluctance to just sit back and watch us destroy the planet.

Dr. Greer has obtained testimony from hundreds of credible witnesses, many of them ex-military, to events such as these. One such witness is Captain Robert Salas of the United States Air Force. Salas was an air traffic controller and missile launch officer and engineer. On March 16, 1967, he observed 16 nuclear missiles simultaneously becoming non-operational right after UFOs were sighted at these facilities.[30]

Lieutenant Colonel Dwynne Arneson of the US Air Force witnessed a similar event at Malmstrom Air Force Base in Montana during 1967. He saw a document reporting that all the missiles went off-line destroying launch capability after a UFO had been seen hovering near the missile silos. Bob Kaminsky, the Boeing engineer assigned to check out the missiles, confirmed that the missiles were in top working order and could not have possibly malfunctioned on their own.[31]

Obviously no "war of the worlds" resulted from these interactions. Greer is quick to point out that with their superior technology, if ETs had any intentions of taking over the Earth and enslaving the human race, they could've done so long ago. Therefore, it is his feeling and also the feeling of these witnesses that they were simply trying to tell us something – that maybe having those kinds of weapons around is not such a good idea. It could also have been in part a measure of self-defense, as there have been several instances where human military forces have deliberately shot down ET craft.[32] Through such actions ETs could simply be showing us the futility of even considering that we could successfully use weapons against them in any event. What has been observed is probably only a minute fraction of their complete defensive capabilities.

Then there's the completely convincing argument of karma, when considering spiritual law. Dr. Greer has proposed that there might be an evolutionary selection of non-aggression in intelligent beings, and that this alone precludes the possibility of ETs exercising such aggression against us in any form:

> Briefly put, this theory holds that an intelligent species cannot evolve past a certain technological level without concomitant and essential development of non-aggression. That is, malevolent aggression is an attribute which ensures the self-destruction of a species if retained past a certain point in technological and cultural evolution. It stands to reason that any intelligent species such as humans, who operate from a paradigm of malevolent aggression will first turn that aggression on themselves, thus resulting in their "mutually assured destruction" if retained much past the point of developing nuclear technology. Such aggression would perforce severely incapacitate or destroy intelligent species, thus limiting their ability to persist long enough to develop technologies capable of interplanetary or interstellar flight. It is, therefore, unlikely that a species would evolve to possess space travel capabilities while maintaining unchecked aggressive and malevolent tendencies. It is most likely that at some point in the evolution of a technological society (perhaps at the advent of nuclear technology), a species is required to transcend their own aggressiveness in order to

157

survive. There is, then a self-limiting dynamic which protects other planetary systems from aggressive species since the establishment of non-aggression is a requirement for significant and long-term technological development. The evolution of the consciousness of non-aggression is an absolute prerequisite for the long-term survival of a technologically advanced civilization.[33]

This thinking partially conflicts with the chronological paradigm presented by Jelaila Starr, but maybe not. After all, that was billions, millions, and thousands of years ago. There is much evidence that the wars between Anu's descendants in the Middle East and Southeast Asia were nuclear in nature.[34] The Biblical story of Lot and Sodom and Gomorrah infers one such war. Sitchin and others have verified that a form of space technology existed in that region during those years.[35] Yet the descriptions of that technology in the ancient records sound remarkably similar to what we possess today. This makes sense when considering that the extraterrestrial engineers of that weaponry were likely to be at a level of psychosocial development comparable to where we are now at this stage of the game in the early 21st century.

It is possible that the development of technology is not the most important evolutionary variable when considering motive and intent. Maybe there's something else. Still, Dr. Greer's theory is rational and very attractive. Even if it were not true, the law of cause and effect eventually balances everything out. What we sow, we certainly reap, and that's reason enough to end all war, violence and malevolent aggression right now.

The Problem of Identity

So what does it mean to be a human being now – an Earth human, no less? Neil Freer, author of *Breaking the Godspell* and *God Games: What Do You Do Forever?* – says that, "…unless and until we restore our true history, attain a generic, consensual definition of what a human being is and step out of species adolescence thereby, we shall not resolve the current UFO/alien questions fully because we will not have the species maturity and planetary unity to be able to interact gracefully with a strange species, knowing easily what is acceptable and unacceptable for both of us."[36]

But do we really need to define "human being" in order to do that? I don't think so.

To replace one definition with another is futile, for that definition will forever be changing. Can you really honestly answer the questions – who am I? – what am I? – with absolute certitude? Any worldly definition, in my opinion, is unduly restrictive and irrelevant, given our modern day perspectives on the nature of reality. It is going backwards – not forward. This is best explained by the Buddhist perspective – a perspective in which the concept of God plays no great role anyway.

The Buddha said that there are five components to individuality called the Five Skandhas: form; feelings or sensations; perceptions; intentionality or will; and consciousness. As individuals, none of us are just one of those things, but instead aggregates of all of them. Qabalistic teachings support this idea as well, as described previously. The divine purpose of these skandhas is to illustrate the tenuous, unreliable nature of the shifting conditional reality we call life. We are not our impermanent, ever-changing bodies. Neither are we our ephemeral thoughts, feelings, or perceptions. Conventional existence is not permanent – it is conditional. However, there is something else that we are that brings us closer to understanding ourselves and also species from other planets – because they are that too. This truth unites us on common ground that cannot be shaken. To quote Lama Surya Das:

> On the other hand, your innate, ineffable Buddha-nature is not impermanent; it is not subject to change. This inner light is unbound, untrammeled, and immaculate. It can be relied on; it can be depended upon. It is perfect, inherently wise and warm, free and complete from the beginningless beginning.

159

Actualizing that luminous, formless, and intangible core is what awakening is all about.[37]

That ineffable Buddha-nature, Qabalistically speaking, is not the individual "I" separate from all the others, but awareness of that "I" as the "I" of all humanity. We are as rays in the central Sun of Spirit, which is cosmic energy – awareness. What we have in common with all creatures is awareness. Becoming aware of that awareness is the hallmark of humanity. As Dr. Greer reminds us,

> Our deepest point of unity transcends race, culture, gender, profession, life roles, even level of intelligence or emotional make-up, since all these attributes vary widely among people. Rather the foundation of human oneness is consciousness itself, the ability to be conscious, self-aware, intelligent sentient beings. All other human qualities arise from this mother of all attributes. Conscious intelligence is the root essence from which all other human qualities emanate. It is the universal and fundamentally pure canvas on which the dazzling array of human life manifests. The firmest, most enduring and transcendent foundation on which human unity is based then is consciousness itself; for we are all sentient beings, conscious, self-aware and intelligent. No matter how diverse two people or two cultures may be, this foundation of consciousness will enable unity to prevail, as it is the simplest yet most profound common ground which all humans share.[38]

It doesn't matter where we came from. What matters is that we awaken to that divine spark within us all, call it what we may. It is that spark which animates all things – organic and inorganic. Organic beings are sentient beings – beings capable of *feeling* aware. Inorganic matter is still living – it's just not sentient in the vegetable or animal sense. But it's all life as Ageless Wisdom proclaims.

Looking back on our extraterrestrial origins is harmless if we don't get bogged down in the details. Overindulging in tedious typology tends to perpetuate a separatist view. Souls or divine "sparks" must eventually travel through all planes or dimensions – especially the physical – in order to achieve mastery over conditioned existence. "Fully enlightened" means a shedding of density no longer needed and returning to a *lighter* state literally. It's a raising of overall frequency. Consciousness is frequency -- vibration.

It doesn't matter what planet or star system the soul or divine spark decides to take its physical lessons on, just as long as it completes the lessons. A soul can have a string of incarnations on another star system, and then return to Earth. In so doing, the individuality might very well appear to identify primarily with that other star system, but that's still a false identity. Why not just go to the source in the first place? The value or merit in determining origin of major cycles of evolution lies in helping us to understand why we have particular affinities, aversions, and karmic reactions to things. But it is not the most important facet of our beingness. What's at the core of beingness is pure being.

Therefore, many Masters and spiritual adepts could truly be souls who have ascended from the animal Earth Sirian/human bodies that once inhabited Atlantis. There are others who might have evolved directly on Sirius or other systems. For instance, Jelaila Starr asserts that the Nibiruan Amelius incarnated as Adam on Earth.[39] So we probably switch around all the time and just don't remember, thanks to the blessings of Earth amnesia. It's confusing enough trying to figure out who we think we are in this one lifetime without having to take into account countless prior existences on other planets!

We must be wary of using our ET ancestry as a cloak or instrument of projection so that it doesn't become just another ego shell of separateness that must inevitably crumble. We have enough of those in the form of ordinary cultural conditionings to deal with as it is. How many times have we heard, "Well I was raised a Republican (or fill in the blank) so that's who I am." We don't have to stick with our ET conditionings any more than our earthly ones, fortunately.

No matter what we call ourselves, most of us are still in human bodies at this time, so that makes us all human in one sense. Therefore we all share that same group karma. We are all a part of one humanity. Based on the evidence and the channelings, it appears that Earth is just one great big cosmic melting pot anyway. We're all spiritual mutts when you get down to it. And we all pretty much have to play with what cards got dealt to us – these miraculous combinations of human DNA. We definitely owe allegiance to the Earth in that regard. Earth is common ground for all humans. It's Gaia who holds us in her arms and nurtures us now. She is our biological mother in this lifetime whether we like it or not. She gave us our physical bodies. Our father is the Sun – literally a star – giving us the energy that fuels those physical bodies. We are all "extraterrestrial" in that regard. We are all stars deep down. Like the CSETI logo says, "One Universe, One People."

To look no further than conditioned existence for a handle on what we really are, is continuing to live in the nightmare of the illusion of separateness. It's time to wake up – period. Once that occurs, nobody and nothing can ever enslave us again. It is possible for all beings of all possible universes to realize oneness. And finally, the cosmic connection will be renewed, and Oz will not look so strange after all.

---

[1]   From a brochure published by CSETI, reprinted with permission.

[2]   Among the many, see the following: Laurence Gardner, *Genesis of the Grail Kings*, Fair Winds Press, 2001; Zecharia Sitchin, *The 12th Planet*, Avon Books, 1976; Robert Temple, *The Sirius Mystery*, Destiny Books, 1998; Erich Von Daniken, *The Return of the Gods*, Vega, 1995; William Bramley, *The Gods of Eden*, Avon Books, 1990.

[3]   See "The Case of the Lurking Planet" and "The Case of the Layered Asteroid" by Sitchin at http://www.sitchin.com.

[4]   Various articles on "Origins" and "Emergence" from a special edition of *Scientific American*: *New Look at Human Evolution*, August 25, 2003.

[5]   Zecharia Sitchin, *The 12th Planet: Book I of the Earth Chronicles*, Avon Books, 1976. See also "The Case of Adam's Alien Genes" and "The Case of the 'Intelligent Designer'" by Sitchin at www.sitchin.com.

[6]   Sitchin, 1976. See Also "The Case of the Evil Wind" by Sitchin at www.sitchin.com.

[7]   Marcia Schafer, *Confessions of an Intergalactic Anthropologist*, Cosmic Destiny Press, 1999, p. 115. Reprinted with permission.

[8]   *Id.*, p. 116.

[9]   Jelaila Starr, *We Are the Nibiruans*, Granite Publishing, 1999.

[10]   Phyllis V. Schlemmer, *The Only Planet of Choice*, Gateway Books, 1994.

[11]   Starr, p. 63.

[12]   *Id.*, p. 64. Reprinted with permission.

[13]   *Id.*, p. 64.

[14]   *Id.*, p. 65.

[15]   *Id.*, p. 67.

[16]   Schafer, p. 74, 81.

[17]   From personal conversation with Dr. Steven Greer in February of 2003.

[18]   See Steven M. Greer, M.D., *Extraterrestrial Contact: The Evidence and Implications*, Granite Publishing, 1999, and Dr. Helmut Lammer and Marion Lammer, *MILABS: Military Mind Control and Alien Abduction*, IllumiNet Press, 1999, and Chapter 9 of this book.

[19]   Greer, 1999 and 2001.

[20]   This is a tongue-in-cheek reference to a song entitled "Planet Claire" by the popular alternative music group, *The B52s*.

[21]   From personal conversation with Dr. Steven Greer in February of 2003.

[22]   Lammer and Lammer, 1999.

[23]   Schafer, p. 50.

[24]   Robert Temple, *The Sirius Mystery,* Destiny Books, 1998.

[25]   Transmission dated August 29, 1995 through Lyssa Royal published on the Internet at http://www.lyssaroyal.com by Royal Priest Research. Reprinted with permission.

[26]   Schafer, p. 110.

[27]   Greer, 1999.

[28]   Greer, 1999, pp. 167-168. Reprinted with permission.

[29]   *Id.,* pp. 51-52.

[30]   Greer, 2001, p. 167.

[31]   *Id.*, p. 176.

[32]   Greer, 1999 and 2001.

[33]   Greer, 1999, p. 53.

[34]   See "The Case of the Evil Wind" by Sitchin at www.sitchin.com.

[35]   See Zecharia Sitchin, *The Wars of Gods and Men,* Bear & Co., Inc., 1985; and David Hatcher Childress, *Vimana Aircraft of Ancient India & Atlantis*, Adventures Unlimited Press, 2001.

[36] Neil Freer, *The Alien Question: An Expanded Perspective*, a white paper that can be obtained online at http://www.neilfreer.com/index20.htm.

[37] Lama Surya Das, *Awakening the Buddha Within*, Broadway Books, 1997, p. 82. Reprinted with permission.

[38] Greer, 1999, p. 18.

[39] Starr, p. 75.

CHAPTER 6

UFOS, ETS, AND THE MYSTERY SCHOOLS

The beloved character, E.T., from the Steven Spielberg movie of the same name, became a delightful cultural icon during the 1980s. For those not familiar with the story line, E.T. was an extraterrestrial child who became stranded on Earth when his ship had to take off suddenly to avoid detection. Some kids secretly shelter him, and the movie is all about their adventures. An especially poignant scene shows E.T. putting together a makeshift communication device out of toys and scraps in order to "phone home" to his mother planet. Well as we know, E.T.'s family really did land on Earth – deliberately – thousands of years ago. And they did more than just leave the telephone – they left the instructions on how to use it.

> I am a Qabalistic temple. I am dedicated to the perpetuation and dispensation of the Holy Qabalah and secret wisdom of the Tarot. I have an amazing history whose beginning is lost in the mists of time. It is said the angels brought my message to man. . .[1]

Angels can be many different things to many different people. They can be real and figurative. However, one thing is certain: Some angels are extraterrestrial.

Much of our ancient history and prehistory has been passed down to us in stories and myths. Many gods and demi-gods were actually ETs who once walked on the Earth same as we do now. Accounts of angels and other supernatural beings, such as Tibetan dakinis, have also been manifestations of ET and UFO phenomena. This is not to say, however, that all gods, demi-gods, angels and dakinis are ETs. The peculiar thing about consciousness is that it too conforms to the Hermetic axiom so that much of what goes on outside of us is truly a projection of events happening within. Many myths and ancient tales have deep metaphoric meaning when analyzed intellectually. That alone does not preclude them from having a material reality as well. In other words, it doesn't have to be "either–or." It can be both; not in all instances, but many, maybe the majority. Jesus Christ was a historical figure. At the same time, he symbolizes a crucial component of our innermost being that we all recognize, sooner or later. His life events mirror trials similar to our own, yet we can still believe those events had a literal reality if we so choose. What's important is what we get out of it.

The evidence demonstrates that humanity is the result of genetic crossbreeding between extraterrestrials and a prehistoric hominid. Civilization on Earth was seeded by extraterrestrials. Like human beings, these extraterrestrials didn't always get along with each other or agree on everything. Therefore we have the wars between the gods, the subsequent deluge, and all manner of Earth-shaking events that seemed to change the course of history. The story is told in many versions all over the world.

Much of the information has been suppressed or simply discounted because of what author Palden Jenkins calls a taboo:

> ...the taboo against knowing who we are and the taboo against acknowledging extraterrestrial life are themselves rooted in ancient man-made myths designed to disempower humanity, cut it off from its roots and reinforce the dominant position of controlling elites.[2]

Not only that, but the work of Dr. Greer among others emphatically reveals that a shadow government is involved. As a result of contact with extraterrestrials, the United States government has in its possession technology to eliminate all world poverty, hunger, and dependence on fossil fuels, thereby saving the planet. But the world is deprived of it because of one trait: greed.[3]

Jenkins continues:

If we are descended from ET genes, then it implies that the observable qualities ETs possess, as demonstrated in repeated close encounters, belong to us too. Close encounter testimonials and follow-up research catalogue capacities such as levitation, direct manifestation, holographic projection, telekinesis, teleportation, override of human motor functions or consciousness and adepthood in manipulating light, energy and gravity, direct mind-to-mind communication and profound healing and transformative abilities. Logically these abilities are available to humans too, even though we are repeatedly taught such things are impossible. Yet records of yogic feats, saintly miracles and parapsychological research illustrate that many such abilities are within our grasp. Many traditions of ancient ET encounters underline a large-scale educational effort on the part of ETs to initiate us into such abilities, as well as into language and literacy, advanced agriculture and species propagation, technologies, laws and social forms, medicine, social and spiritual matters.[4]

This is precisely what any kind of spiritual and especially occult training is supposed to do. Therefore, it only makes sense that our celestial ancestors would leave behind the materials and methods with which to do it.

Few spiritual leaders will publicly admit this, yet history and the esoteric literature abound with clues. I suspect that many of them secretly believe that extraterrestrials are the origin of the teachings but they keep quiet about it because of what it might do to their credibility. But I'm not a great spiritual sage so I have nothing to lose. I'm just a storyteller, and after I'm finished with the story, it's up to you to decide what you believe.

The Rainbow Alliance

In the first few chapters of this book I briefly mention the "Masters" and talk about an inner plane adepti. Much of the esoteric literature refers to this group of elusive souls as "the Great White Brotherhood," also known as the Collegium Spiritum Sanctum. It is politically incorrect to call them a 'great white brotherhood.' The group is neither white nor an exclusive brotherhood. Nor is the term 'white' meant to suggest race, as the members of this group cut across all races and creeds. The term was meant to designate them as the "good guys" or the ones who wear the white hats. Brotherhood excludes women, though this group does not. Therefore from here on out, I'm going to call them the *Rainbow Alliance*, not to be confused with the political groups bearing the same name promoting gay rights, deaf rights, or any other worthy cause.

This broader Rainbow Alliance is comprised of human souls who have advanced in awareness to the degree that further incarnation on the physical plane is not necessary for whatever reason. Still, they choose to stay close by in service to those who follow. Nonhumans are members of this Alliance as well, though not all ETs are a part of this alliance. Life is incredibly diverse and the scale of awareness has countless degrees for all beings – whether from this planet or elsewhere.

Dion Fortune refers to the Manus as being the source of this Alliance as it relates to Earth. She calls them "the Great Ones" who appeared upon the Earth when Atlantis was in full swing. She states,

> These are the "High Priests after the Order of Melchisedec," being without father or mother and building their physical vehicles without human assistance. It was their office to communicate with the concrete mind of humanity, and forge a connecting chain of associated ideas from consciousness to sub-consciousness, thereby enabling

man to pick up the subtler vibrations which are the voices of the higher spheres.

> In order to do this they had to appear to concrete consciousness in concrete form; hence with infinite difficulty they had to build a vehicle that concrete consciousness could cognise. These anthropoid forms were so unsuited to the highly evolved forces they had to carry that they were only held together with the greatest difficulty and for short periods of time. Hence the accounts of the sudden appearances and disappearances of the gods which form part of all primitive traditions. For these Great Ones were the actual gods of myth and fable, the Divine Founders of racial cultures to which all primitive traditions look back.[5]

Fortune says that these Manus selected promising students from the infant race to whom were taught all the secrets of cosmic evolution. After a while, the Manus withdrew from this world, having instructed their students on how to "rise upon the planes" for further instruction. And that's how the mystery schools got started. Not once does she ever use the terms UFO or extraterrestrial, but her words could be read in that light.

Karl von Eckhartshausen writes thus about the Rainbow Alliance:

> This community of light has existed since the first days of the world's creation, and its duration will be to the end of time. It is the society of those elect who know the Light in the Darkness and separate what is pure therein... This community possesses a School, in which all who thirst for knowledge are instructed by the Spirit of Wisdom itself; and all the mysteries of God and of nature are preserved therein for the children of light. . . . It was formed immediately after the fall of man, and received from God at first-hand the revelation of those means by which fallen humanity could be again raised to its rights and delivered from the misery. . . . This society of sages

169

communicated, according to time and circumstances, unto the exterior societies their symbolic hieroglyphs, in order to attract external man to the great truths of the interior.[6]

This is the inner sanctuary behind all outer sanctuaries. It was established to anchor and preserve the teachings for those weathering the turbulent transitional times during and after "the fall."

The fall is an interesting concept. The traditional Biblical interpretation of the fall is that this is the time when humanity fell from innocence into sin. What really occurred is that Adam awakened to a brutal realization of his place in the scheme of things, practically reduced to the status of slave animal in the eyes of most of the Anunnaki. He instinctively knew he was more than that, and began to wear clothing in order to demonstrate his likeness to his creators. Significantly, this occurred *after* he was given the ability to procreate and to become a co-creator in the world around him. The fire of libido – the quickening of the life force within his brain profoundly transformed human awareness in a way not foreseen by the Anunnaki. Enki saw the true potential of this diamond in the rough, and in accordance with karmic law, took it upon himself to nurture, protect and mentor this new being. These were their children, after all. The Sumerian texts indicate that humans never called the Anunnaki 'God.' They called them the equivalent of master or teacher, which was later translated to 'gods' collectively. Centuries later, 'gods' became 'God,' and then finally 'Lord' by the pen of King James.

In true form to the Hermetic axiom, the fall is also a literal description of events in addition to a figurative one -- a prolonged geophysical process not typically recognized in history. When Earth was an infant after the explosion of Tiamat, its crust and atmosphere were highly unstable until a gradual cooling off occurred. During this time the original land masses known as Atlantis, Lemuria, and Mu congealed, and life began to evolve. But the Earth was not fully materialized as we

170

know it today -- it was actually vibrating at higher frequencies. As a result, the separation between land, water, and air was not clearly distinct. The ground was not yet solid enough to support physical bodies in the dense forms we know today. The planet was a gaseous, misty, surreal place. The veil between the etheric and physical dimension was extraordinarily thin. It was as if the world was a giant container that had been shaken up, and it took a while before all the sediment fully settled at the bottom of the glass. A canopy of cloud and mist surrounded the planet for millions of years. The sun did not become fully visible until after the great cataclysm and resulting flood which spawned the climatic changes that shaped the Earth we know today.[7]

During solidification, the planet became increasingly dense, meaning lower and slower frequencies. So early on, there was a time when beings of light moved more freely among beings of flesh. This was when the great Manus of Atlantis and Lemuria appeared. Some authors feel that Atlantis vibrated in a frequency band that was about three times higher than ours today. If an Atlantean in that original frequency presented himself to us today, he would be invisible. Therefore the fall also refers to the solidification of the planet -- literally the *fall in frequency*. This phenomenon may also be the basis for the legend of Avalon of Arthurian lore becoming lost in the mists of time. Of course the "dust" didn't settle at the same rate over the entire planet. There were some places where it took much longer to settle, and these are the sacred places long associated with magic, vortexes and interdimensional portholes. For example, when a UFO is described as "bleeding through" into full materialization, it is going through a kind of fall of its own, creating its own porthole, so to speak.

The above quote from Karl von Eckhartshausen emphasizes that the establishment of the Mystery Schools happened immediately *after* the fall. This is probably accurate in a formal sense. Although the Manus were dispensing their teachings early on during the fall, the formal school that gave rise to the Western and Eastern lineages still active today, was not established until after Adam's symbolic expulsion from the Garden of Eden, meaning after humanity was pushed out of the cosmic nest to begin the long process of species maturation through procreation. This was after the great flood, approximately 10,000 B.C.E. The first students eventually became adepts and then what are commonly referred to as the "Masters" in the esoteric literature, whether "ascended" or not. Again, ascension in this sense only refers to a rising in frequency – the rebuilding of a body of light that no longer requires karmic attachment to the physical plane. Though they can choose to remain embodied in physical form for the completion of certain work, they are no longer bound by that form. Therefore, it is possible and moreover probable that many Masters are extraterrestrial as well.

The Alice Bailey books talk a great deal about the Masters. Alice Bailey transcribed the books from the words of an identity that chose to be known only as the Tibetan. In an extract from a statement by the Tibetan published in August of 1934, he claims to be merely a disciple and not a Master. He admits that this tells us little because "all are disciples from the humblest aspirant up to, and beyond, the Christ Himself."[8] He says he's just a brother of ours who has traveled a little longer on the Path than the average Joe, and therefore has earned greater responsibilities. His work is to spread the Ageless Wisdom to all who might by receptive, and claims to work closely with the Master M. and the Master K.H. He qualifies that by immediately following up with, "In all the above, I have told you much; yet at the same time I have told you nothing which would lead you to offer me that blind obedience and the foolish devotion which the emotional aspirant offers to the Guru and Master Whom he is as yet unable to contact. Nor will he make that desired contact until he has transmuted emotional devotion into unselfish service to humanity, -- not to the Master."[9] The Tibetan says that neither him nor Alice Bailey desire to have their books acclaimed as inspired writings or as being the work of the Masters. He concludes, "If they present truth in such a way that it follows sequentially upon that already offered in the world teachings, if the information given raises the aspiration and the will-to-serve from the plane of emotions to that of the mind (the plane whereon the Masters *can* be found) then they will have served their purpose."[10]

According to the Tibetan, the three requirements of a disciple who wishes to further the work of the Rainbow Alliance are as follows: "They are taught to attach no importance to recognition. They are trained not to judge from the appearance but from the inner vision. Capacity to recognize the Master's purpose and the ability to love are counted of paramount importance."[11] Therefore it might be difficult to truly pinpoint those working with the Alliance. It may not always be in an area as obvious as teaching. Service can take many different forms. There are those who even work with the Alliance unknowingly.

The Significance of Sirius

There are no references to UFOs or ETs in the Bailey books either. But there are many references to the importance of certain stellar bodies, such as Sirius, with regard to human evolution. Dion Fortune mentions Sirius in her book, *The Cosmic Doctrine:*

> The star Sirius has always been held in esoteric teaching to have much influence on Solar evolution. Astronomically speaking, of course, the position in space of Sirius is far outside the solar system but from a Cosmic standpoint Sirius and many other stars "condition" the Solar Logos and, since the Solar Logos is Itself Conditioner of and conditioned by Its universe, the influences of Sirius and other stars are transmuted correspondingly before being communicated to the universe. Therefore, in the purely esoteric sense, stars in general and Sirius in particular (because of its special influence) can be considered in relation to Solar evolution – more especially those which, like Sirius, have had a

marked effect on it. The individual, however, must have completed the cycle of Solar development before he can experience the *pure* influence of Sirius or other stars.[12]

Occultist and author, Gareth Knight, a former student of Fortune's, reminds us that the solar disk worn on the hat of Isis or Hathor, refers to Sothis, also known as Sirius or the Dog Star, a star that was especially sacred to Isis for reasons that Robert Temple explores at length in *The Sirius Mystery*. Knight further asserts, "Esoteric students of some experience will see the implications of this, for Sothis, along with the Great Bear and Pleiades, is a source of power behind the twelve zodiacal constellations, which in turn radiate influences to our Solar System via the mediation of the Solar Logos – our God."[13] In fact, he claims that Sirius is the heavenly body most closely connected with our solar system.

In his discussion of the zodiac sign Taurus in relation to the 16th Path of the Tree of Life of the Holy Qabalah, Knight again points out the significance of the Pleiades, the Great Bear, and Sirius:

> Just as Sirius bears similar relationship to our Solar Logos as the Individuality does to the personality. . . and the Great Bear holds the patterns for the seven Planetary Logoi of our Solar Logoidal jurisdiction; so do the Seven Sisters of the Pleiades have an important esoteric link with our Planetary Logoi. Not much can be given about the exact nature of the link because the factors involved are too vast for a detailed human understanding. . . Alcyone, the brightest star of the Pleiades, is a particularly important star as far as our Solar system is concerned, and was believed, in ancient times, to be the **hub** of the universe." (Emphasis added.)[14]

Hub? Excuse me, but that sounds like some kind of central airport or docking station. For one, how can a star be any kind of docking station being just a giant ball of gas and fire? Obviously, we're talking about other dimensions here. Only recently have physicists begun to study possibilities regarding travel to other dimensions in the parameters of string theory.

The Bailey books get a bit more specific regarding Sirius:

> Sirius is the home of that greater Lodge to which our fifth initiation admits a man and to which it brings him, as a humble disciple.[15] Sirius, the Pleiades and our Sun form a cosmic triangle. . . Vibrations reach us from Sirius, via the cosmic mental plane. . . The Lords of Karma on our system are under the rule of a greater Lord of Karma on Sirius. . . Cosmic Avatars . . .represent embodied forces from the following cosmic centres: Sirius, and that one of the seven stars of the Great Bear which is ensouled by the Prototype of the Lord of the third Ray, and our own cosmic centre.. . Only one Being (from Sirius) has visited our solar system and that was at the time of individualisation.[16]

Indeed, according to many UFOlogists, we've been visited more than once by beings from Sirius. However no further detail is offered by Fortune, Knight, or the Tibetan. As those books were written in the first half of the 20th century, maybe they thought we just weren't ready for the details.

M. Temple Richmond, a writer, researcher, and student of the Bailey books, authored a book of her own simply entitled, *Sirius*, in 1997. In this book she summarizes and synthesizes all the Bailey book teachings concerning Sirius, confirming what has long been suspected about the celestial system. Briefly, she concludes that

- Sirius is the origin of all the esoteric mystery traditions, the inner school and serves as home base for the planetary 'hierarchy' in charge of Earth.
- The Sirian Lodge is the prototype for the Masonic traditions in particular.

- Sirius is the 'higher-self' of our Sun or Solar Logos, and a major power center or "chakra" in the body of a transcendent cosmic being, along with the Great Bear, Draco, and the Pleiades.
- Sirian energy is the universal energy of love-wisdom.
- Sirian energy is distributed through the agency of the triangle, symbolizing the reconciliation of opposites. These triangles are formed with multiple star systems, each having their own significance and effect on the evolution of humanity.
- Sirian energy is primarily focused on the principle of freedom from form through initiation and karmic processes.
- Sirian beings were intimately involved in the seeding and cultivation of humanity on Earth.
- Sirian culture is void of all sense of separation, duality, and evil.
- Sirius is the origin of karmic law and the principle of periodicity, around which the mysteries of death revolve.
- Sirius is the place of origin for many great avatars.
- Sirian evolution is proceeding in ways in which humans cannot yet grasp.[17]

Pertaining to the individual, Sirian energy is first felt when awareness of the soul is awakened in self-consciousness. Contact on a subliminal level is established, and the aspirant is subsequently guided by that energy in all future initiations. Sirian influence enables us to grasp transcendent truth, leading the way to emerging nondual awareness. Blavatsky calls Sirius the star of Mercury or Buddha, the first great instructor of humanity before all other Buddhas. Richmond elaborates,

> But the fact that Blavatsky calls Sirius "the great instructor of mankind" indicates something additionally significant. This moniker for Sirius hails back not only to the knowledge and wisdom gods of antiquity associated with this star (Anubis, Thoth, Hermes, and Mercury), but also to the initiatory traditions established under Sirian tutelage, traditions that did much to accelerate the progress of disciples

throughout the ages toward affiliation with the Hierarchy. Thus, Sirius is the great instructor of mankind not only because its god figures are the givers of astronomy, mathematics, geometry, languages, music, art, medicine, and architecture through Anubis, Thoth, Hermes, and Mercury, but also because it spawned the wisdom tradition which spread from various points in the ancient world through history to the present time.[18]

So there we have it. The source for it all is supposed to be Sirius. Not that this means all is harmony and light, for the reception of a force so strong necessitates the breakdown of outworn forms and the elimination of obstacles. Therefore, the path for the individual initiate as well as for humanity as a race is not supposed to be easy. The acceleration of evolution on a personal and a cosmic scale has advantages and disadvantages. The Tibetan says that the tumultuous 20th century was a direct result of a "welling up of magnetic force on Sirius." According to Richmond,

> The fact that the Tibetan associates the impact of Sirius with massive turbulence tells us that when the higher quality energies of Sirius interact with the unregenerate material of Humanity, disruption of previous patterns based upon a materialistic focus is inevitable. The same thing happens when the individual person is impacted by the vibration of the Soul or the Monad: the previous fixations of the lower self are necessarily disrupted. But as we know, this is all to the good, for eventually the necessary transformations are accomplished, and then the way is made clear for a greater expression of the Good, the True, and the Beautiful.[19]

In one version of Key 13 of the Tarot named *Death*, a curiously twisted skeleton is reaping the black soil upon which dismembered body parts are spread among tender shoots of early spring grass. A river flows into a sunrise, and the entire sky is red. Up in the left hand corner, there is a tiny little ovoid, seed-shaped object that looks very much like a UFO. BOTA lessons explain the esoteric significance of this seed-like object, but I have yet to come across a deliberate attribution to UFOs. The Dogon tribe (discussed in the previous chapter) named a seed they revere after their professed planet of origin, Sirius. The Bailey books, as mentioned above, speak of a specific correlation between the esoteric cycles related to death and rebirth and Sirius. Key 13 in Tarot is all about that – regeneration and more. Could that seed in the corner also be an indirect reference to Sirius? Highly probable I think.

Another clue from the Tarot: In Key 14, the archangel Michael wears a seven-pointed gold star on his chest. Some researchers have associated the seven-pointed star with Sirius and the Pleiades.

Beware of what you read on the Internet regarding Sirius. There is a very slick web site purporting to be divine messages direct to you from the Sirian hierarchy through channeling. While many excerpts ring with truth, a close examination of the material reveals that it is not new information. Most of what is transmitted is a rehashing of ideas and discoveries from other researchers in the field presented in such a way that they appear original, but they aren't. And even though this source fully acknowledges the harmful effects of the government's lies and secrecy about UFO phenomena (thereby seducing one into thinking that they're an ally in the struggle for complete disclosure) a dead giveaway that this site may really be a DDT operation (decoy, distract and trash by government disinformants) in disguise, is the listing of another website in its "recommended links" section that feeds on fear and paranoia. Conveniently, all reviews and comments published on this site are positive. There are no critical remarks.

If you want to establish contact with beings from Sirius or "the hierarchy" – go within and do your own soul/sky mingling. As was stated in the previous chapter, you need not rely on the purported authority of anyone else. The voice of the Absolute is your own to claim – for you are an instrument in your own right and are equally sustained by those energies.

Serpents of Wisdom

Mark Amaru Pinkham is one of the few authors who fully acknowledges the extraterrestrial origin of the Mystery Schools. In his book, *The Return of the Serpents of Wisdom*, he reveals that the symbol of the serpent is the universal trademark for all the adepts and sages of the world's spiritual traditions, and recounts their long history on Earth, beginning with their extraterrestrial origin up to the present day.[20] He traces their influence through the appearance of the dragon cultures of China, the Nagas of Southeast Asia, the Amarus of Peru, the Quetzalcoatls and Kukulcans of Mesoamerica, the Serpent Clans and Tribes of North America, the Anunnaki of the Middle East, the Djedhi of Egypt, the Serpent Goddess cults of Europe, the Gnostics and Essenes, the Druids of Great Britain, and the Sufis, up through the modern mystery traditions in the West having their basis in Freemasonry and the Rosicrucian system.

The relationship of the serpent symbolism to Enki and the esoteric mysteries was previously discussed. The androgynous nature of the serpent also represents the conciliation and transcendence of opposites into the realm of nondual awareness. The serpent is also correlated to the kundalini or serpent fire energy uncoiling at the base of the spine and traveling upwards toward the brain through all the chakras, resulting in illumined states. Pinkham explains,

> As the first tangible form assumed by Spirit, the Primal Serpent was the vehicle of all God's powers, including the triune powers of creation, preservation and destruction. Through it, God created the entire universe... The Primal Serpent was also the possessor of God's Divine Mind, the wellspring of all knowledge and wisdom. For this reason, the Serpents of Wisdom worldwide have traditionally

venerated the Primal Serpent as the premier and archetypal teacher...[21]

Therefore, it was convenient that Enki assumed the form of a Serpent, already half-Reptilian. The original extraterrestrial Serpents of Wisdom -- the Atlantean and Lemurian Manus – existed in high frequency forms known as "dragon bodies." We all have a dragon body which can be strengthened through various esoteric practices. This dragon body will carry us through the bardos at the time of death. Tibetan monks refer to it as the *rainbow body of light*. This is the body that feeds upon the grids of the energy force field surrounding the Earth, needing no other nourishment.

Pinkham admits that many early spiritual teachers came from Sirius and the Pleiades.[22] In Atlantis and Lemuria their mission was to help infant humanity develop individuated mind and survival skills. As certain members of humanity advanced in awareness, ancient forms of spiritual practice were introduced to them, which evolved into systems giving rise to the great mystery traditions of the East and the West. Religion was born when the original Masters departed from the planet or headed underground, and the direct link to the teachings was lost or deliberately obscured or distorted by corrupted priest-kings that were appointed to serve as new custodians for the human race. But no matter how hard these greedy rulers tried to stamp out the "evil serpents" -- it was too late. The Serpents of Wisdom had already left their undeniable mark on the world's perennial philosophy in countless clues, songs, stories and symbols that would inevitably lead any persistent seeker to the inner school.

The Hermetic Legacy

A particularly strong lineage of Atlantean Serpents of Wisdom emerged from the region associated with Northern Africa and the Mediterranean inspired by the historic figure known in Egypt as Thoth; in Rome as Mercury; and in Greece

180

as Hermes Trismegistus. This great sage has also been equated with Enoch in the Middle East, Quetzalkoatl in Meso-America, and even Merlin in Great Britain, but these links are not succinct in my mind. Sitchin and others have confirmed a migration of the Anunnaki from the Middle East to Meso-America led by the exiled Marduk, as evidenced by the establishment of the pyramids, various Olmec artifacts, and other archeological clues.[23]   Sitchin equates Ningishzidda, another son of Enki, with the Egyptian god Thoth, and speculates he may have been the original Quetzalkoatl -- the "plumed-serpent" god of the Aztecs. I don't know if we'll ever know precisely who was who and where and how, but for certain we have a branch of Ageless Wisdom inspired by such a figure that has lasted to this day, and that's what's important.

Traditionally, Hermes is thought of as the Greek god of magic, language, and medicine. To the Gnostics he was known as the wise serpent of the world, wrapped around the terrestrial egg. In the Gnostic Gospels, Jesus instructs Mary in the symbolism of the serpent surrounding the world with its tail in its mouth, and holding within its body the twelve houses of the zodiac.[24]   This archetypal symbolism pervades all the mystery schools. The Druid's ouroboros, for example, is one such manifestation.

Enki's symbol was a snake coiled around a staff, which later evolved into the caduceus, symbol for the American and British Medical Associations. The image of two coiled snakes around the winged staff also alludes to the miracle of DNA and the Anunnaki's genetic engineering of humanity. The symbol for the planet, Nibiru, is a winged disk. A plumed serpent or a serpent with wings is a dragon – a creature symbolizing the unification of heaven and earth.

Hermes is said to have been the founder of alchemy, which is also intimately connected with healing. Alchemy is all about learning how to work with the kundalini or fiery serpent power and skillfully managing its flow through all the chakras (metals) and meridians of the human energy system.   Therefore

Hermeticism became the study of the so-called psychic sciences such as magic, astrology, and alchemy.

Mercury, being the Roman equivalent of Hermes, is also an important astrological sign in the Great Work. Among its many levels of meaning, Mercury is most significantly attributed to the mind or self-consciousness. All magic begins and ends in the mind. Self-consciousness directs the secret life force into the appropriate channels for the transmutation of personality. An alchemical treatise from the Middle Ages indicates that a Hermetic vessel is "a uterus for the spiritual renewal or rebirth of the individual…"[25] The symbolism of Mercury being the messenger of the gods also alludes to the primary importance of the role of self-consciousness in spiritual matters. It is all about being aware, attentive and focused on the here and now. It is mindfulness practice 101. The equivalent of Mercury in the Tarot is Key 1, *The Magician*. The Magician holds his wand up high in his right hand bringing down the powers from superconsciousness and channeling them through his outstretched left hand into the garden of subconsciousness below. That is how the garden is grown. The Hebrew root for serpent, *naschash,* meaning to decipher, find out or divine, plays into this well. Going one step further, we remember that the word *naschach* is the numerical equivalent in Qabalistic gematria to *messiach*, meaning savior or Christ. It is, indeed, the "Christed" mind that saves us from our "sins" or errors. The Christed mind is a pure, unobstructed, clear vessel for the fiery, transformative light of Spirit.

When the Serpent Enki coaxed Eve into sharing the apple with Adam, they suddenly knew what Enlil knew – that they had the same powers – the innate capacity to become gods themselves. And so the jealous god evicted them from Eden. Under the protective wings of Enki, they managed to survive and thrive, thank the "Lord" (pun intended), and so here we are today.

The interplay of polarities is also expressed in the tale of Adam and Eve, figuratively as well as literally. One of the attributes of Hermes was androgyny – the reconciliation of opposites, giving rise to equilibrium between the male and female principles. Mercury, the mind, works with both male and female energies in the human body or alchemical vessel. It is through their harmonious blending and ultimate synthesis that regeneration occurs. There is, however, a greater feminine principle that initiates this process involving a refinement of receptivity. Therefore, the serpent has always been closely aligned with the Mother Goddess in mythology. We see how this directly manifests in the conflict between the half-brothers Enlil and Enki, as portrayed in the Gnostic Gospels.

Elaine Pagels, in her extensive study of the Nag Hammadi Library, found that Eve represents the spiritual principle in humanity that raises Adam from the limitations of material conditions. Enlil, later translated as "God" – warned Eve that she and Adam would die if they ate the forbidden fruit of the tree of knowledge. Quoting from the *Hypostasis of the Archons*, Pagels writes:

> And the spirit-endowed Woman came to [Adam] and spoke with him, saying, "Arise, Adam." And when he saw her, he said, "It is you who have given me life; you shall be called "Mother of the living" – for it is she who is my mother. It is she who is the Physician, and the Woman, and She Who Has Given Birth." ... Then the Female Spiritual Principle came in the Snake, the Instructor, and it taught them, saying, "... you shall not die; for it was out of jealousy that he said this to you. Rather, your eyes shall open, and you shall become like gods, recognizing evil and good." ... And the arrogant Ruler cursed the Woman... [and]... the Snake.[26]

Enlil, or "God," was asserting himself as sole authority or ruler of the realm over Enki and the other Anunnaki. Therefore, we see all these displays of him wanting to be known as the only God as an expression of his jealousy and insecurity. He was threatened and challenged by Enki and Ninhursag's superior skills and wisdom in their genetic modifications to the human creature – an *intelligent* creature that was now able to procreate and aspire toward spiritual enlightenment. A story from the Gnostic Gospels illustrates the arrogance of Enlil and perhaps his chastisement by Ninhursag. In the following excerpt, read "God" and "Samael" as Enlil, "the angels" and "immortal ones" as the extraterrestrial Anunnaki, and "Faith" as Ninhursag:

> ... he boasted continually, saying to (the angels) ... "I am God, and no other one exists except me." But when he said these things, he sinned against all of the immortal ones... when Faith saw the impiety of the chief ruler, she was angry.... She said, "You err, Samael (i.e., "blind god"). An enlightened, immortal humanity [*anthropos*] exists before you!"[27]

Ninhursag, as the chief medical officer of the Anunnaki, is one of our archetypal models for the Mother Goddess. The serpent - symbol of divine wisdom - encouraged the humans to resist Enlil's tyranny. This directly points to humanity's first step toward independence as an authentic, autonomous species, ever bit as divine and potentially intelligent as the Anunnaki. Sure enough, they ate of the divine fruit and they were awakened, as promised by Enki. The Gnostic Gospels report that the serpent actually said, "On the day when you eat from the tree which is in the midst of paradise, the *eyes of your mind* will be opened." (Emphasis added.) And then God said, ... "Behold, Adam has become like one of us..."[28]

Clues suggest that the Biblical Eve in this story might have two identities. One reason for an additional genetic upgrade to *homo sapiens sapiens* was so that the Anunnaki could splice more of their genes into the human creature, making it more capable of achieving self-rule and mastery. Therefore, this experiment was supposed to provide the basis for a bloodline of royal "priest-kings" who would rule on their behalf. Individuals within the bloodline would also possess a heightened psychic sensitivity for this purpose.

Ninhursag agreed to carry the newly cultured embryo in her womb so that it would get an extra dose of Anunnaki blood. Therefore, she became the surrogate mother to the new human creature whose real mother was mortal, but whose father was immortal or divine, as it was Enki's sperm that was used to fertilize the embryo. The *Adama* (Sumerian for "Earthling") was born and named Adapa. The Biblical word for "clay" was a mistranslation of a more ancient Sumerian word meaning "life." It is also closely related to the Hebrew name for Eve that when translated from Sumerian, approximates another title for Ninhursag.[29] Therefore, some speculate that the original Eve was Ninhursag – mother of the new human race. Ninhursag also gave birth to a surrogate daughter to be a mate for Adapa. This was Eve number two or "Eve, Jr." Little Eve was also called "Nin-ti" -- a shortened name for Ninhursag. The last syllable – "ti" – had two meanings in Sumerian – "to live" and "rib." In subsequent translations from the Sumerian, scribes used their word for "rib" rather than "to live."[30] That's where the ludicrous idea about Eve being created from Adam's rib came from. It actually had nothing to do with a rib.

In Hebrew, the name for Eve was *Hawah*, taken from the root *hayah*, meaning, "to live." This is similar to the Arabic word *hayya* meaning "female serpent" and *hayat*, meaning "life."[31] Therefore, linguistically, the esoteric teachings about the special connection between the Life Force and the serpent, especially a female one, are fully supported. Ninhursag was strong in the dragon or Reptilian blood. Therefore, it makes sense that our original Mother Goddess was undeniably a true Serpent of Wisdom.

The Tree of Knowledge is not just a simple allegory about succumbing to the world of duality either. It is also a direct reference to the Holy Qabalah and its Tree of Life. By studying the Qabalah, we learn how to become even more like them – the gods – or more accurately put, unfolding the divinity within -- because its Ageless Wisdom is the essence of alchemy, taught by the original Serpents of Wisdom such as Enki and Hermes, and passed down through the ages by their followers. The fruit of knowledge has another subtler meaning in connection with the sublimated use of the energies normally associated with reproduction. The word 'knowing' in its sexual context hints at these deeper mysteries and their application to the role of sexual polarity in practical occultism.

The systems of the Western lineage of the Serpents of Wisdom were practically codified by this Hermes-Thoth character. Joseph Campbell, using Jung's comparative exploration of psychology and alchemy as a general platform, comments as follows:

> During Hellenistic times an amalgamation of Hermes and Thoth was effected in the figure of Hermes Trismegistus, "Hermes Thrice Greatest," who was regarded as the patron and teacher of all the arts, and especially of alchemy. The "hermetically" sealed retort, in which were placed the mystical metals, was regarded as a realm apart – a special region of heightened forces comparable to the mythological realm; and therein the metals underwent strange metamorphoses and transmutations, symbolical of the transfigurations of the soul under the tutelage of the supernatural. Hermes was the master of the ancient mysteries and initiation, and represented that coming-down of divine wisdom into the world which is represented also in the incarnations of divine saviors...[32]

Perhaps the greatest blessing bestowed upon humanity by this enigmatic personage is *The Emerald Tablet of Hermes.* The origin of this ancient alchemical text is disputed. Some writers claim it was smuggled directly out of Atlantis by the original author. The antiquities scholar, Sir Laurence Gardner, contends that it might have been the original Tables of Testimony that were written directly by "God" at the same time Moses transcribed the Ten Commandments. These tables were closely related to *The Table of Destiny*, one of the Anunnaki's most highly prized texts. Gardner's interpretation of the

Egyptian alchemical records leads him to believe that the original author of this Tablet was the biblical Ham, one of the descendants of the royal bloodline that began with Adapa.[33] In addition, he comments,

> The revered Emerald Tablet contains the most ancient of all alchemical formulae, which were of great significance to the early mystery schools. But the secrets have long been withheld from the brethren of modern Freemasonry whose leaders, for the past two centuries or more, have elected to pursue a spurious and strategically contrived allegorical ritual which teaches nothing of the true art of the original Master Craftsmen.[34]

The true art of the original Master Craftsmen is both literal and allegorical. The Rosicrucian branch of the Third Order of the Western Mystery Tradition became the custodian of an unflawed version of the Emerald Tablet, which is published by Builders of the Adytum. BOTA also provides extended interpretation and in-depth instruction in the ancient principles revealed by the treatise in their course work. An essentialized, abbreviated version of the text is as follows:

The Emerald Tablet of Hermes

> True, without falsehood, certain and most true, that which is above is that which is below, and that which is below is that which is above, for the performance of the miracles of the One Thing. And as all things are from One, by the mediation of One, so all things have their birth from this One Thing by adaptation. The Sun is its father, the Moon its mother, the Wind carries it in its belly, its nurse is the Earth. This is the father of all perfection, or consummation of the whole world. Its power is integrating, if it be turned into Earth.

Thou shalt separate the earth from the fire, the subtle from the gross, suavely, and with great ingenuity. It ascends from earth to heaven and descends again to earth, and receives the power of the superiors and of the inferiors. So thou hast the glory of the whole world, therefore let all obscurity flee before thee. This is the strong force of all forces, overcoming every subtle and penetrating every solid thing. So the world was created. Hence were all wonderful adaptations of which this is the manner. Therefore am I called Hermes Trismegistus, having the three parts of the philosophy of the whole world. What I have to tell is completed, concerning the Operation of the Sun.[35]

Another interesting manifestation of the Hermetic androgyny came through the female serpents of wisdom traditionally known as the Amazons. The legend of the Amazon warrior women was resurrected in our modern minds through the popular 1990s television series, *Xena – Warrior Princess*. Although there were plenty of corny episodes, there were just as many that took on some serious, difficult esoteric issues far surpassing what any other television series has ever attempted. It was an extraordinary creative blending of serious thematic material with special effects and action-packed adventure.

Xena and her sidekick Gabriel received training from the Greek Amazon tribes. In fact, Gabriel was an Amazon Queen for a time. Though most of what we know about the Amazons is relegated to legend now, many authors contend they were a very real and special female faction of the ancient serpents of wisdom.[36] Originally they migrated from Atlantis to settle in the Mediterranean area, establishing territory and trade routes. Adorned in snake skins and highly skilled in the martial arts, they chose to emphasize the androgynous nature of the Hermetic sage by expressing an ordinarily male, aggressive spirit through their female bodies. Ferocious and courageous warriors, they were renown for their fairness, loyalty to their leaders, and an ability to defeat even the bravest men in battle. As an exclusive sisterhood, they rarely associated with men except in battle and when mating. Male offspring were usually shipped off to integrated tribes. Female offspring were kept to be trained as Amazons. Asia Minor was one of their most heavily settled areas, and in that region sprang up strongholds of the goddesses Hecate and Medusa, personifications of the dark, destructive and transformative aspects of the feminine power.

Some authors, such as Pinkham, contemplate that in the early days of Earth's ancient history, the lost continents were polarized in their development. For instance, Atlantis was supposed to be psychically oriented toward the masculine pole, and Lemuria toward the feminine, in terms of spiritual expression. The reason for this was so that their inhabitants could specialize in these forces for later integration on a global scale. The only evidence suggestive of this that I see is in the outward appearance of the trappings that dress up the Eastern and Western mystery schools today. The Eastern way, having been predominantly influenced by migrating Lemurians, incorporates styles that suggest a greater amount of feeling and passivity than the West. The Western styles, under Atlantean influence, seem more action and ritual oriented, adopting a linear approach to learning. Also, the symbols and magical icons of the West are more angular in shape; whereas in the East there is a flourishing of circles, spheres, and curly-cue designs. The only place where this is not so distinct is in the Druid or Celtic branch of the Western mysteries. Yet a strong link between that school and the Eastern esoteric schools has been documented. At any rate, maybe the Amazons were partly acting in reaction to what they experienced on Atlantis with regard to their gender. Patriarchal systems probably originated on Atlantis, and maybe these female serpents of wisdom rebelled against it. Intuitively, that's what I suspect. Sadly, dominator society only continued to spread until even the Amazons were claimed, co-opted and then extinguished to become just more memory food for legend.

Druids and the Mists of Avalon

Many serpents of wisdom from Atlantis migrated to Great Britain. In legend they are called the Tuatha de Danaan, and their descendants were the Druids. The history of the mysteries on the British Isles is rich and complex. The islands seemed to be an attractive target for many seafaring peoples who settled there and merged with the native populations. For instance, the Celts were "Indo-European" in origin, and did not arrive until the end of the Bronze Age, somewhere between 900-500 B.C.E. Yet megalithic monuments such as Stonehenge had stood as long ago as 4000 B.C.E. The Atlantean serpents of wisdom erected those monuments, having the extraterrestrial technology at hand to do so. The time period between 4000 B.C.E. and 2000 B.C.E. is thought to be the era of Tolkien's Middle Earth. Again, we have a legend that might have some basis in reality. The elves leaving Middle Earth in *The Lord of the Rings* is reminiscent of the Anunnaki beginning to phase off the planet. It is the dawning of the "Age of Man" as Elrond proclaims, and coincides with the same time period.

Tuatha de Danaan means "folk of the Goddess Dana." The oldest written testimony about the source of Druidism is from Caesar who says that its doctrine was established in Britain and then exported to Gaul and the surrounding areas. Though Druidism has much in common with the science of Pythagorus and Hinduism, no direct link between those regions has been established. Therefore scholars conclude that Druidism was a doctrine handed down by the Tuatha de Danaan – whoever they were.[37] An ancient Irish text states that the Tuatha de Danaan "…were in the Isles of the North of the World, learning science, magic, druidism, sorcery, and wisdom, and they surpassed all the sages in the pagan arts."[38] This posed a problem to historians because there were no islands to the north during the current era. But Ageless Wisdom tells us that the antediluvian world did not look like the world of our modern day maps. In fact, Atlantis may not have been just one big insular continent stuck in the middle of the Atlantic ocean as most imagine, but instead a string of large island masses stretching from the Caribbean Sea to as far east as the Indian Ocean. To the north it could have extended above what is known today as Great Britain.

The Tuatha brought with them four fundamental talismans representing the four elements -- tools that every practiced sage in the West was to inherit in their tradition: the Stone of Fal or Coronation Stone corresponding to the pentacle representing earth; the fiery Spear of Lugh corresponding to the wand, representing fire; the Sword of Nuada, which can only be yielded by its rightful owner like Arthur's Excalibur, representing air; and the Dagda's inexhaustible cauldron, prototype of the grail, representing water. The Tuatha were credited with bringing social structure to the primitive inhabitants of the islands. One of the primary motivating factors of the Druid religion was to make the kingdom on Earth reflective of the kingdom on high, indicating a thorough understanding of the Hermetic axiom. Merlin was one magician in a long line of wizards, the word merlin meaning wise one or sage.

According to Gareth Knight, Merlin represents:

> … a humanized Western form of the ancient gods of learning and civilization, such as the Greek Hermes or the Egyptian Thoth. He is, furthermore, one of those, akin to Melchizedek in the Old Testament, 'without father or mother, without descent'.

> These are the great superhuman figures who work behind the scenes of planetary evolution, sometimes appearing physically to selected disciples at particular times of opportunity or crisis, but for the most part unseen, working through chosen human intermediaries. They are known in Eastern esoteric literature as *Manus*.

In this role Merlin brought the secret teaching of doomed Atlantis, at the end of its phase, to the new world of Europe, and founded first the Hibernian Mysteries, the vestiges of which come down to us in the mythology of Ireland. Following this, and from other Western seaboard outposts, the same teaching spread to the rest of the islands of Britain and Continental Europe.[39]

Merlin was a great spiritual leader whose main assignment was to lead humanity out of the hive mentality subordinate to hierarchy that characterized the Atlantean epoch to a higher level of group responsibility through individualization. This new paradigm was symbolized by the Round Table of Arthurian legend, and its earliest realizations were seen in the formation of circles made of stone, wood, or lines in the earth. Taliesin is a name often interchangeable with Merlin, and usually represents a bard or one who has been thoroughly trained in the art of music, writing, and storytelling.

Lugh, like Hermes-Thoth, was the Tuatha with the greatest stature, expertly skilled in the art of war, magic, medicine, carpentry, and metallurgy. The Triple Goddess reigned supreme, so the religion was predominantly nature-based. Druids saw the sexes as equal, and took it upon themselves to be proper custodians of their natural resources. Nature was sacred, respected, and played an important role in all facets of life. All trees represented the Tree of Life that unites heaven and earth, and the oak especially came to be associated with divine power and cosmic energy. Mistletoe was thought to be the 'water of the oak' and had a special place in Druid spiritual practice, representing the essence of the deity. The plant was harvested with the utmost mindfulness during select times to ensure its potency. Drinking the 'magic potion' made from the mistletoe was an act of assimilating and integrating into their bodies the power of the deity.[40] The symbolism of this magical act manifests in the mysteries of other Western practices, such as Christian communion, where the blood of Jesus is taken into the body from the Holy Grail.

There is a darker side to this aspect of shamanism that is reflected in legends of the vampire. Interestingly, mistletoe is a parasite, the vampire plant that feeds off the life force of other plants; in particular, the oak tree representing the deity. Of course, another perspective is that it "frees" the energy of the oak or deity so that it can be continually recycled into higher forms. It may also be symbolic of the recognition that all life is interdependent and unified by a common energy force field.

The ritual of sacrifice was another common spiritual practice of Druidism and early Judaism. To sacrifice means, "to make sacred." It is an act of exchanging energy with the divine. Whether human sacrifice actually occurred among the Druids is still debated among scholars. There are those who feel that human sacrifice also occurred in the Middle East, and that the burnt offerings of animal flesh practiced by the Hebrews are reminiscent of this tradition. Some believe that a faction of the Anunnaki regarded humans as inferior animals and so fed on their flesh.[41] The Biblical story regarding God relieving Abraham of the duty to sacrifice his son may mark the time when such a practice was discontinued, for whatever reason.

A central Druid doctrine was that a universal harmony exists behind all the seeming opposites of the world – a kind of great natural perfection. Tuning into to that Life Force or "dragon energy" enabled them to accomplish what appeared to be supernatural feats. The sanctity of the individual was cherished, and good and evil were relative concepts. Scholar Jean Markale writes,

> The druidic religion showed people the path to take in order to attain the degree of understanding at which false oppositions would be revealed for what they were, a dialectical quarrel. From such an understanding comes the necessity of affirming the all-powerful nature of the mind and spirit, the necessity for the ritual that in symbolic terms induces the human being to always go beyond the horizon. In a world the real is an illusory barrier that through laziness or ignorance the human being imagines is in

front of him. But there is no barrier. The horizon does not exist.[42]

Hence, integrative continuous patterns of round shapes and curves abound in Celtic art and design, much like Tibetan Buddhist iconography. There are also other ways in which Druidism resembles the Eastern mystery schools more than those that took root in the Mediterranean area. The Greeks and Romans had difficulty understanding druid logic because it was paradoxical, retaining much of the original esoteric teaching rejecting dualism. Balance, like Buddha's middle way, was key – balance between the prey and predator, the individual and the collective, the unity and the multiplicities. God was a Creator Goddess and was whole, complete, and not separate from anything. This idea is further developed in the Arthurian mysteries: If the king and the land are not one, the land dies and so does the king.

Therefore, the Druids for a long time were able to perpetuate a vast metaphysical and theological system of thought that surpassed a primary naturalism. Their influence can still be felt in today's neopagan religions, particularly those originating on the British Isles. Druidism did not immediately conflict with Christianity. Elements from both traditions were assimilated into an esoteric Celtic Christianity which is undergoing a modern revival. The legend regarding the Holy Grail finding sanctuary in Glastonbury was at one time merged with the legend of a pre-Christian Avalon, representing an entire consummation of the Western mystery traditions. That area in England is still a powerful center for those energies. Unfortunately, a power hungry elite seeking to dismiss the importance of the mysteries and the power of the sacred feminine corrupted many legends and stories, including the modern Bible. So we have Morgan Le Fay often portrayed as an evil sorceress. For a correction of these errors, Marion Zimmer Bradley's fictional account entitled, *The Mists of Avalon,* is highly recommended. It comes closer to the truth than most nonfiction texts.[43]

Tara was the name of the Tuatha's capital city in ancient Ireland. It was established around 3000 B.C.E., and was the crown jewel of European civilized culture. The city had an extensive library and was a center of exchange between writers, bards, musicians, alchemists, and other important functionaries of the time. Those familiar with Buddhism will recognize that Tara is the name of the preeminent female Buddha. Her name means "Star" and she has her own chant. Tara practice is quite popular these days, as she tends to attract those who wish to promote recognition of the divine feminine in Buddhism. Could this just be coincidence? Mark Roberts doesn't think so.

In ancient India, a matriarchal pre-Vedic people called the Dravidians once thrived. Aspects of their culture bear striking resemblance to the Celtic tradition of the Druids. Roberts, a versatile, thorough and tenacious researcher in this area, comments as follows regarding this lost connection:

> However appealing the title Gentle Wizard may seem, there is an important clue within their name ~ the Tuatha de' Danaan ~ the people of the Goddess Dana or Danu, a Goddess name that is directly linked to the Dravidians and archaic Tantra. Then, we have the shamrock, the most well known symbol of Ireland, symbolically inscribed all over the Emerald Isle as the triple spiral, representing Ireland's primal, three-fold Goddess. That same shamrock was equally honored by the Dravidians, and as the symbol of the "three yonis" it can be found inscribed upon many of the artifacts of the Indus Valley culture. For those deeply involved in Irish history, the word Tara stands apart in importance. It is the ancient capital of Ireland, named for the Goddess Tara. An identical Dravidian Goddess was named Tara. BOTH were known by their title, "Star Goddess."[44]

How did this happen? Well, the Anunnaki were not confined to Africa and the Middle East. The second and third generations, kids and grand kids of Enlil and Enki, spread out colonizing specific areas of the globe. The goddess associated with the name Inanna was one of these descendents. She was a true feminist and did not always get along with her male siblings who enjoyed creating havoc and playing war games. So she headed east, establishing the matrifocal culture associated with the Dravidians in the Indus Valley.[45] Most likely she was the original "star goddess" referred to above. We do not know for certain that the Tuatha were specifically Anunnaki, but it is likely, as they migrated from Atlantis as well. Other extraterrestrial civilizations were involved with colonization of the globe, and therefore the Anunnaki faction was not alone.

At this point, it would be well to remember that the dispersion of settlements from Atlantis and Lemuria were probably not as straightforward as some writers suggest. Most authors overgeneralize, correlating the Far East with Lemurian influence and the West and Middle East with Atlantean. But authors such as Pinkham have pointed out that again, these continents were probably disjointed strings of landmasses circling the globe. Lemuria could have stretched across the entire Pacific. Therefore, common sense dictates that western migrations from Lemuria landed in what became the Far East and eastern migrations landed on what became the North and South American continents. For example, Pinkham feels the area around Sedona, Arizona was an ancient Lemurian outpost. Similarly, Atlanteans could have dispersed as widely as the Lemurians. The connection is evident in comparative study of several Native American and Eastern cultures, and the Middle Eastern and Mesoamerican cultures.

In searching out commonalities between all these civilizations, however, it might make more sense to trace them to their extraterrestrial origins than their earthly domains. In doing so, there is one constellation that seems to stick out above all others in terms of universal prevalence and spiritual significance. That constellation is known as the Pleiades.

The Pleiades Connection

The following list is just a sample of the influence of the Pleiades all over the globe:

- Chinese records dating to 2537 B.C.E. regard the Pleiades as a sacred focal point, especially for young women, calling them the Seven Sisters.
- Huang-ti, regarded by historians as one of the greatest rulers of China, readily gave credit for his accomplishments to beings from the Pleiades. Under his rule (sometime between 3000 and 2500 B.C.E.) China developed the manufacturing of wood, clay, boats, carts, metal, a medium of currency, cartography, acupuncture and other methods of holistic healing.
- Practically all Polynesian peoples on islands spread over the entire Pacific, including Hawaii, have songs and religious rituals celebrating the Pleiades.
- The Australian Aborigines called the Pleiades "the Seven Maidens" who gave them the magic of the art of music. This sacred event was recorded in a series of rock-art paintings that present the Sisters as having heads with abnormally huge eyes, not dissimilar to some modern day depictions of aliens.
- Several South American tribes recognize the Pleiades, using their progression through the sky to mark important seasonal changes. One tribe calls them "the Seven Rain Maidens." The Brazilian Amazonian tribe of the Apibones claims the Pleiades as the home of their ancestors. Pre-Incan civilization claimed that their gods came from the Pleiades to teach them agriculture, mathematics and astronomy. The Incas, at Machu Picchu, constructed an astronomical observatory with a special window aligned to the rising point for the Pleiades. The

primary Nazca Lines also pointed to the rising point of the Pleiades during 500-700 C.E.

- The native Cunas of the Caribbean islands said that their deity lived at the exact center of the universe believed by them to be the Pleiades.
- Both the Aztec and Mayan cultures of ancient Mexico venerated the Pleiades, which play a predominant role in their calendar systems. Two great pyramids and a river at Teotihuacan were aligned to the setting of the Pleiades, and depictions of the stars are carved into the Temple walls and floors. In Palenque, the Mayans painted a beautiful mural of the Pleiades on a ceiling with script indicating that their deity, taking pity on them, sent a divine son to Earth called Quetzalcoatl to instruct them and care for them.
- Many Greek temples are aligned to the rising and setting of the Pleiades, including the Parthenon.
- Early Arab civilization regarded the Pleiades as the center of the universe and the seat of immortality. Mohammad even wrote about them.
- Many North African tribes, including the Berbers, also viewed the Pleiades as the center of the universe where immortality could be found.
- Many Native American tribes recognize the sacredness of the Pleiades. The Lakota believe it's where they go when they die. The Cheyenne and Kiowa say that seven maidens ascended to the sky to become the Pleiades for the purpose of protecting them from a great bear. Both tribes also view Devil's Tower in Wyoming as a sacred place for the Pleiades. (Is it a coincidence that this icon was used in the movie "Close Encounters of the Third Kind"?) The Cherokee shaman Rolling Thunder states that their traditional headdress was not made of feathers, but was a hat with an emblem of a seven-pointed star representing the Pleiades, their place of origin. An ancient drawing of the Pleiadian star

cluster is on a cave wall in Texas. The Hopi calendar also marks points in the cycle of our solar system around the Pleiades. As late as 1970, Hopi chief, Dan Katchongva, was quoted in the Arizona *Prescott Courier* as saying that a sighting of UFOs over their sacred mesas pointed to the fulfillment of an ancient prophecy. Evidently, there is a petroglyph on second mesa showing flying saucers traveling through space. Chief Katchongva said that the Hopi believe they are direct descendants of the people from the Pleiades, and that a "purification day" will arrive when they will all return to their place of origin.

- The Egyptian pyramids are constructed according to several complex mathematical formulations in connection with the Pleiades. In the Temple of Hathor, there is a star clock with the Pleiades representing the center, and the perimeter representing one cycle of 25,827.5 years, the length of time it takes our solar system to completely revolve around the Pleiades.
- The Judeo-Christian Bible contains passages referencing the Pleiades (Job 9:9 and Job 38:32.) The Jewish Menorah's seven candles are thought by some to originally represent the Seven Sisters of the Pleiades, evolving through the seven "men-horac" meaning "moon priestesses" linked to the Egyptian goddess Hathor.
- The Babylonian calendar was oriented to the Pleiades.
- The Dravidians of ancient India called the Pleiades "the Seven Mothers of the World" who took on the role of seven priestesses passing judgment on men. The month of November in their calendar was named for the Pleiades. In modern India, the Pleiades are still known as the "six nurses."
- Many ancient cultures revered the bull. Curiously, the small cluster of stars known as the Pleiades are positioned right on the shoulder of

the bull in the night sky otherwise known as the constellation of Taurus.

Therefore, it is not surprising that many New Age cults and UFOlogists focus on the Pleiades as playing a major role in the phenomena. The general consensus is that the Pleiades are the good guys. But if there are good guys, there must be bad guys, and unfortunately, most fingers point to Orion. While it is true that many world legends portray the Orion constellation in a negative light, basing all judgments in such simplistic terms is naive. Perhaps in the early days of colonizing the planet, conflicts arose between the inhabitants of these two systems. But that is no indication that such hostilities exist today.

As far as the mystery schools are concerned, the connection to the Pleiades and Sirius is direct. The Anunnaki came from Nibiru, an artificial planet comprised of peoples from several different star systems, especially the Pleiades. According to Jelaila Starr's chronology, Enki was the offspring of a union between the Pleiadian Anu and the Reptilian Dragon Queen Dramin. The marriage was the result of a treaty between the two civilizations. Therefore, the Pleiadian link to the origin of the mystery schools through Enki is secured.

On the surface, one might see a discrepancy between the legends of the seven maidens, priestesses or sisters, with the fact that depictions of the constellation usually show only six stars in the cluster. The naked eye can only see six or seven stars clearly, however, a telescope reveals hundreds of stars in the constellation. The number seven probably refers to the fact that the original female emissaries from the Pleiades were seven in number. These beings might have chosen to appear as a group of seven for several reasons. The number seven has many significant correspondences in esoteric lore. For example, it's the number of the major chakras in the human energy body and the major planets in our solar system. Extraterrestrial visitors deliberately staged many important events in such a way that the inner significance of such events would be forever retained in their symbolic configuration. That way, in case an accurate recording of the historical event became lost, as it frequently did as a result of the passage of time or deliberate distortion or obscuration on the part of humanity's power elite, a myth, story, or legend would remain in its place with the appropriate clues.

In a way, this is a brilliant demonstration of the Creator's artistic genius vividly illustrating the Hermetic Axiom through the laws of consciousness. All the gods and goddesses are expressions of the One, and everything that has been said about them is true on some level. None of the above conflicts with Joseph Campbell's attributing them to Jungian archetypes. They were that too and more. An academic scholar of mythology professing that they were "unreal" is not totally false. In many ways, they appeared very unreal to the primitive human minds that could not yet grasp their technology. Julian Jaynes relegating them to schizophrenic hallucinations is not far from the mark either, as some researchers have suggested that schizophrenia may result from unresolved subconscious memories of our alien genetic past.[46]

Much literature suggests that what we call schizophrenia is more often than not profound mystical experience gone awry. The stages of schizophrenic process often parallel those experienced by mystics such as St. Teresa.[47] The main difference between the two is that most of the time the mystic knows that what they are experiencing is a mystic revelation, and so they retain some level of functional ability in consensual reality. This is not always the case with schizophrenia, yet neither is it strictly uniform. Sometime the communication modalities change in schizophrenia so that the person is not able to convey the experience except through gestures, imagery and metaphor. Most individuals diagnosed with schizophrenia are very intelligent and have no problems learning to function in life, provided they are not subjected to stressors that push them over the edge, precipitating the "split mind" episodes.

When I was studying psychology in graduate school, R.D. Laing quickly became my hero. I thought, finally – here is someone who speaks my language. As a radical existential psychiatrist, this is what a diagnosis of schizophrenia means to him:

> To regard the gambits of ..[the patient diagnosed as schizophrenic] as due *primarily* to some psychological deficit is rather like supposing that a man doing a hand-stand on a bicycle on a tightrope 100 feet up with no safety net is suffering from an inability to stand on his own two feet.[48]

These people are coping with the fact that something in them is remembering that they are not and can never be confined to mainstream society's definition of human. When they begin to fully conform to their experience instead of the dictates of those around them and adjust their behavior to their own inner reality, it becomes strange and incomprehensible to most people, sometimes even themselves. When they seek help, they are told they have an illness. The illness really lies in a society that cannot cope with what it is. This goes back to acknowledging true gnosis, which psychiatrists seldom do in their patients. As Dr. Laing laments, "I think, however, that schizophrenics have more to teach psychiatrists about the inner world than psychiatrists their patients."[49]

For a more recent example of Pleiadian influence on the collective fabric of our experience, consider the emblem on the back of Subaru vehicles. It is a depiction of the Pleiadian constellation, as Subaru is the Japanese term for the Pleiades. One wonders what the chief executives of the Subaru automobile company were thinking when they decided on that name for their line of vehicles. On some level, a subliminal programming effect cannot be dismissed when we're often forced to view it on the back of vehicles that pass us on the road. Maybe this is just another way we're being prepared for the return of the Pleiadians to this planet. We know that this has been the plan of the shadow government for some time. Knowing they could not keep the alien presence a secret forever, ideas are introduced through media, film, and popular culture in order to prepare the mass mind of humanity for the direct revelation.[50]

When looking at the constellation of the Pleiades on its side, it resembles the Christian cross. The Teutons make an interesting connection between Jesus Christ and the Pleiades. One of their myths talks about a time when Jesus, while walking past a bakery, was attracted by the delicious aroma of fresh bread. He asked the baker for a loaf but the baker refused. The baker's wife and daughters secretly snuck a loaf to Jesus. As a reward for their generosity, the mother and her six daughters were placed in the heavens as the seven stars of the Pleiades, but the baker was changed into a cuckoo. As long as the cuckoo continues to sing from St. Tibutius' Day (April 14th) to St. John's Day (June 24th,) his wife and daughters, in the form of the constellation of the Pleiades, remain visible to him.

The Pleiades are often correlated with bird symbolism. The Iroquois Indians assigned a bird to each star. Far away on Easter Island, the natives have a special bird ritual marking the growing season which is oriented to the Pleiades. They also make use of an interesting alphabet keyed to large flying birds with huge eyes. Finally, let's not forget that Greek legend tells us that Zeus turned the seven sisters into a flock of birds that transformed into the Pleiades.

Cosmic Code and Sacred Language

It makes sense that a non-earthly higher culture in custody of a burgeoning new race like humanity would employ a method of communication that could be easily taught and yet malleable enough to embed within it codes containing secret knowledge for the advanced members of the species. Therefore one of the first written languages, Sumerian, was pictorial and visually descriptive, like later hieroglyphics. These early languages were also structured in accordance with the laws of number.

David Allen Hulse has compiled an exhaustive overview of all the sacred languages of the planet into a massive compendium entitled, *The Key of It All: An Encyclopedic Guide to the Sacred Languages and Magickal Systems of the World*. Volume I is devoted to the Eastern Mysteries, and Volume II to the Western Mysteries. These languages from the beginning of time have been described in terms such as 'the Angelic Language' or 'the language of the Gods.' This 'magickal language' as he chooses to call it, is a hybrid of many ancient languages. Hulse sums up its logical basis as follows:

1. It is the assumption that language evolved in a multidimensional manner on both a numerical basis and a phonetic basis.
2. That every number possesses a nature and character which is distinct and unique from every other number and is infinite unto itself in nuance and meaning.
3. Yet in their numerical interrelationships, each individual number develops a further set of characteristics and correspondences, which is brought out and reinforced by every individual number's position in the infinite range of numbers.
4. That the very letters of the alphabet of every esoteric language are numbers in themselves imbuing a sense of beauty and poetry into motion, number, and measure.
5. That every letter, word, phrase, verse, sentence, paragraph, chapter, even every book, contains a precise number described by the numerical values of the original language in which the words appear.
6. That every language, in its original format in accordance with the correct esoteric numeration of its alphabet, generates a set of poetic metaphors for the range of the number series zero to infinity, which is consistent, correct, and ever expanding in content and meaning.
7. That the essence of the numerical metaphors for all languages must be combined to completely flesh out and clearly define the number series.
8. In this sense no language leads or is the primary metaphor for the language of numbers, but each in its own unique alphabet, grammar, and numeration

bestows a special set of definitions for certain numbers in the infinite number series which are sympathetic to that specific language.

9. So that all languages of the world from all previous times unite at the ever-present moment as one gargantuan poetic series of word images, for every number conceivable to the mind of Man.[51]

Volume 1, *The Eastern Mysteries*, covers the occult keys to Cuneiform, Hebrew, Arabic, Sanskrit, Tibetan and Chinese. Volume 2, *The Western Mysteries*, does the same with Greek, Coptic, Runes, Latin, Enochian, Tarot, English, Aztec and Mayan. Though far from complete in terms of Hulse's exclusion of the languages of most indigenous peoples, each volume is a great reference book in addition to supplying over 500 pages of esoteric material for prolonged in-depth study.

One script appears to have a strong connection with UFO/ET phenomena all over the globe and is included by Hulse as a subtopic under Runes -- the mysterious script of *Ogam*. All scholars agree that Ogam, sometimes spelled 'ogham,' is the oldest form of writing found on the British Isles. It may also be one of the oldest runic representations of a universal Neolithic method of communication pervading the planet, but few scholars today are ready to accept that premise.

The Celtic myth is that Ogma, short for Oghaim Ghuaim, was the father of the alphabet, and the mother was the hand and the knife. Ogma's name means "sun-faced wisdom."[52] The alphabet could be signed with hand signals or alternatively carved into material objects such as bones, stones, and wood. The characters are composites of short simple line strokes crossed over a stem line drawn vertically, and in rare cases, horizontally. The characters also have numerical correspondences, making it the original Universal Product Code (popularly known as the bar code.)

In the Celtic form of Ogam, a number, color, bird, saint and time of the year is assigned to each character in the alphabet. Therefore, an inscription may have many different layers of interpretation. Ogam eventually evolved into the Beth-Luis-

Nion alphabet used by the Druids. This alphabet is patterned on a series of sacred numbers with emphasis on the number 32, which is also the number of paths on the Qabalistic Tree of Life.

First of all, Ogam, like many scripts, has evolved through many forms. In one version, it consisted of thirteen consonants and five vowels. The consonants corresponded to lunar months, and the vowels were attributed to the four solar seasons, with the fifth vowel representing the day after the Winter Solstice. This phenomenon explains the many references to "a year and a day" in the ancient Celtic literature. Therefore, Ogam was used as an astronomical calendar as well as for writing. Ogam is found on many megalithic monuments in the British Isles. It is also found in other places such as Africa and the North American continent.

The inscriptions found in the United States have caused much controversy. Evidence that the Celts visited the North American continent is seen in findings of Ogam inscriptions and other artifacts dating from the Bronze Age in the New England area. These findings have been easier for academics to accept by virtue of the fact that they are on the east coast, making it more likely that ancient seafaring peoples visited there. The Ogam petroglyphs found in ancient cave dwellings in Oklahoma, Colorado and Arkansas are not as well received.

Archeoastronomy is the study of ancient astronomy. Epigraphy is the art of deciphering ancient languages. A group of archeoastronomers and epigraphers found an Ogam inscription in a cave in Colorado that translates to "The sun strikes here on the day of Bel... At sunset this shadow will reach nearly to the jaw of the image of the jackal divinity..."[53] The image of the jackal divinity accompanying this inscription bears semblance to ancient Egyptian depictions of Anubis, the Jackal-headed god known as one of the sons of the Egyptian sun god, Ra. Bel is a Celtic sun god. The sun does exactly what the inscription says it will do at a time roughly corresponding to the day of the spring equinox. Another inscription says, "The Sun belongs to Bel. The cavern on the days of the equinox is for chanting prayers to Bel."[54] These inscriptions are dated before

Common Era, and it is thought that the caves may have had ritual purpose.

Most archeological sites having astronomical significance in the American Southwest are believed to be Anasazi in origin – Anasazi being the ancient Indian pueblo dwellers. Then why are Celtic and Egyptian-like pictographs in some of these places? The epigraphers believe that the Celts and other sea-faring peoples like the Phoenicians who would bear the Egyptian influence sailed up the Arkansas River and left their influence on Native American settlements. This assertion outrages many modern archeologists because they believe the charge is racist and has the effect of diminishing the rich, important cultural contributions of the Native Americans. In fact, they point to a proliferation of tiny figures such as the one in the Anubis cave wearing the headdress of Ra all over the American Southwest. To interpret these figures as having a European or Egyptian base is narrow and jumping the gun, scholars say. Nevertheless, the Ogam inscription's translation fits.

Although there may be some individuals who, for whatever reason, would like to believe that our earliest American ancestors were European in origin predating the Native American cultures, these epigraphers deny that motivation. It appears that both the epigraphers and archeologists are missing the point and framing the debate in the wrong context. The issue is not whether the Celts, Phoenicians or other Old World peoples were here first, but whether these inscriptions and pictographs reveal a universal connection in the Ogam script and its symbolism, globally speaking. If so, then the findings make sense when considering that these peoples all represent migrations from extraterrestrially seeded cultures. It may be that academia sees this relationship and is using the race card as part of a DDT operation – decoy, distract, and trash. No one wants to be considered racist in these days of political correctness, and so will avoid any consideration of an idea that has been even remotely linked to such charges by the powers that be. It's a good way to get people to look the other way, and unfortunately, it works more often than not. Yet the evidence plainly speaks for itself.

Take African Ogam for instance. There is a bone, called the Ishango bone because it was found in that region of Africa, which is at least 10,000 years old. On this bone are groups of carved notchings representing the oldest table of prime numbers found in the world thus far. (Believe it or not, this is still not the earliest mathematical artifact found. That title belongs to a section of baboon fibula with 29 notches dated 35,000 B.C.E.) The notchings on the Ishango bone closely resemble Ogam. For a more recent version, however, that is undisputedly Ogam, one only needs to visit a tribe of the Amazigh people in Saharan Morocco in Northern Africa, otherwise known as *the Berbers*.

The Berbers have a long rich history carrying heavy Mediterranean influence. Most of them have converted to Islam, yet a few isolated villages still practice ancient tribal customs which are surprisingly matriarchal. For instance, only women lead and own property. They do all the marriage proposing and divorcing, and they exclude all males from learning how to read and write their ancient script. That script happens to be Ogam.

Mark Roberts, a connoisseur of 'stargates,' discovered this by accident while on a research expedition in Cairo.[55] While visiting an outlying desert marketplace, he sighted an unusual looking native woman without a veil who sported a tattoo on her chin. The tattoo was written in Ogam. Excitedly, he ran toward her, shouting out the word on her chin. Immediately, several other women with chin tattoos in Ogam surrounded him, obviously upset and shouting angrily. Fortunately, his friends came to the rescue, dragging him away and admonishing him to never do that again. Fascinated by his new find, he vowed to return at a later date to follow the trail. It was an ordeal locating and traveling to the tribal settlement in the remote Atlas Mountains, yet Roberts says it was all worth it. He found many similarities between the Berbers and the Hopi Indians of the American Southwest, even down to their aversion to being photographed.

According to pioneering linguistic archeologist, Edo Nyland, Ogam probably originated in Northern Africa and was later exported to the British Isles by early Gnostic missionaries. According to his research the name Ogam likely comes from the Basque *oga-ama, ogasun* (property, wealth) and *ama* (Priestess, mother) meaning that the alphabet was the property of the priestess, indicating pre-Christian origin. This dovetails nicely with the vestiges of such a culture as seen in the isolated Berber tribe.

What does the Basque language have to do with Ogam? Well, according to Nyland, Ogam is not an original neolithic language or even a root script. Neither is Sanskrit as many believe. The universal language whence most all modern languages originate is an ancient Saharan language that became Basque. In other words, Basque has retained a linguistic purity all its own and contains the seed elements of most other languages. Most words can be deconstructed to their Basque roots (and therefore their original meanings) by using a decoding formula based on a vowel-consonant-vowel interlocking system called the "VCV formula" because these languages were artificially constructed with Basque root syllables.

The Tower of Babel and the Benedictine Curse

What? How did this happen? What on earth am I talking about?!? Well, consider the Biblical tale of the Tower of Babel out of the Book of Genesis:

> And the whole earth was of one language, and of one speech. . . And the Lord said, Behold, the people is one, and they have all one language; and this they begin to do: and now nothing will be restrained from them, which they have imagined to do. Go to, let us go down, and there confound their language, that they may not understand one another's speech.

In this context, the Lord was the extraterrestrial Enlil and the forces of patriarchal domination. Yet later generations of European priests took the command to heart and continued the ugly tradition. The priestly organization most responsible for this task was the Order of the Benedictines – language inventors supreme.

First, let's return to about 2000 B.C.E. and consider what it was that the people were doing that so angered their lordly rulers to the extent that those rulers would go to such great lengths to change the way the people communicated. The traditional interpretation of the story is that the people were building a tower to heaven so that they could make a name for themselves -- so they could be "as great as God." True, they were trying to get to "heaven" but not merely for recognition.

According to Sitchin, the tower of Babel was actually a great ziggurat or *shem* where rockets could be launched. Early scholars mistranslated this word to 'name.' The Anunnaki or Nefilim were known as "the people of the shem." Shem translates to "sky-borne vehicle."[56] Now the people's intent becomes clear. This was during a tumultuous time when the adversarial factions of Enlil and Enki were well underway. The people were caught in the crossfire and genuinely afraid that they would be dispersed and separated from each other as pawns in the game. Therefore, they decided to develop their own flying capabilities so they could get away and find a place of their own, under the supervision of sympathetic ETs, of course. But in the end, the 'gods' would not allow it. The supportive Anunnaki crumbled under the mounting force of the opposition, and the humans and facilities were abandoned to the conquering invaders. The invaders adopted the anti-human political position of 'divide and conquer' in order to maintain control of the population. A united humanity was too much of a threat to the patriarchal powers that be back then, even as it is today.

The first generation languages were constructed from the original language with the main goal of making it more difficult for people to communicate with each other. In the process of constructing these first generation languages, however, sympathetic forces embedded within them the secret science of numbers and symbolism. In other words, clues to deciphering the inner meanings were left in the languages, and these languages and symbol systems were subsequently taught in secret to initiates of the early mystery schools. These early languages were the sacred languages that Hulse lists in his two-volume compendium. When the dominators consolidated power in the Roman Catholic Church a millennium later, a second wave of language distortion and reconstruction was needed in order to preserve their power, which resulted in what was to become most of our European-based modern languages spoken today.

This is Edo Nyland's theory:

> All highly developed languages on earth (except possibly Chinese) can be shown to have been developed from the original Saharan language, which in itself was scholarly enhanced from the Neolithic substratum. There exists no "family" of Indo-European or Semitic languages. There are no Indo-Europeans or a proto-I-E. language; all these unstable languages are invented by scholars. Only Saharan has remained relatively unchanged and is now spoken as Basque.[57]

The hypotheses or suppositions that form the foundation for his theory are as follows:

1. The Saharan language was the language of the peoples living in the Sahara during the last Ice Age, who had created the first true civilization on earth, possibly centered around Lake Chad. As a result of deglaciation, starting about 18,000 before present (B.P.), resulting in ever expanding desertification, these tribes were forced to flee for their lives, creating an exodus culminating between 9,000 and 5,500 B.P. These refugees created four main

secondary civilizations in Mesopotamia, Egypt, the Indus Valley and Anatolia.

2. The Saharan language is still spoken as Dravidian in India (170 million speakers), as Ainu on the island of Hokkaido (18,000 speakers) and as Basque in Euskadi, Spain (800,000 speakers). Basque is likely the closest resembling the original language of the exodus.

3. The people of the exodus from the Sahara brought with them a matrilineally organized society, the nature based Goddess religion and the first highly developed language, maintained by very strong oral traditions.

4. As a result of several major advances in a number of fields such as agriculture, metallurgy, domestication of the horse and camel, astronomy, etc., the female-based religion was weakened and male domination arrived ca 5,000 B.P. in Egypt, Mesopotamia and Anatolia, and about 3,500 B.P. in India. The newcomers brought along learned priesthoods who proceeded to invert all aspects of the old religion, society, language, legends, etc. A new language was invented for each large area and placed under the control of a king, e.g. Sumerian and Akadian in Mesopotamia, Old Egyptian in Egypt, Samskrta and Hindi in India, Hebrew in Palestine, Hittite and Luvian in Anatolia, etc. All these were the product of formulaic distortion and scholarly manipulation of the original Saharan language. The Bible repeats the command to distort the original language in Gen. 11:7.

5. These newly created languages were then introduced to the local populations by taking young boys into residential schools and forcing the new order onto them, where they were often brutally treated. The purpose was to destroy the old religion and language and the traditional oral teaching of wisdom, religion and legends, replacing it with a patriarchal vision of the world and civilization. They almost succeeded. The hidden sentences in the invented words can be

decoded with the use of the Basque dictionary and a simple formula.[58]

In the early years of the first millennium CE, Gnostic Christianity flourished in Europe, merging well with the ancient Goddess religion because they were recognized as one and the same. The Old Religion threatened the growing power of the Roman Catholic Church. Therefore the Church took deliberate measures to squash it. Changing the language of the people proved to be an insidious yet very effective way to do this. The Pope chose Benedict of Nursia to head up a new monastic Order with this specific purpose in mind.

In order to distinguish themselves from the white-robed Gnostics, these Benedictine monks wore black. The white-robed priests had been named 'druids' – a derogatory title that stuck, which really means "get out, you deceitful idolater" when deconstructed with Nyland's formula. The name 'Benedict of Nursia' when decoded is a combination of "come to me under the cross and find learning to take with you" and "he inspires and touches beginners to respond."

Therefore, the Benedictine Order was really given the task of altering history by altering the language of the pre-Christian literature. The ancient writings were often retranslated with deliberate distortions, and then the original texts were burned or destroyed. This is especially seen with classical Roman and Greek literature. Any references to the Old Religion were twisted and tainted with negative terms like "pagan – savage – heathen – cultish – barbaric -- idolatrous."

Charlemagne officially formalized this policy of censorship in his Edict Number 78 dated March 23, 789:

> "…let no false writings and doubtful narratives, records which entirely contradict the Catholic Faith… let not such documents be believed or read, but be destroyed by fire, lest they lead people into error. Only the canonical books and Catholic treatises and the sayings of sacred writers are to be read and delivered…"[59]

The famous library at Alexandria originally founded around 300 B.C.E. was burned in 300 C.E. Ninety-one years later, its satellite library in the Temple of Saragis was attacked and burned. This is the root of the seeming inconsistency throughout the modern renditions of classic literature. Fortunately, the ancient oral tradition continued, and accurate renderings of the stories and legends were preserved and passed down in the mystery schools, and embedded in simple folktales and mythology.

For those who doubt this really happened or who think it's just another crazy conspiracy theory, looking directly at the Benedictine's operation manual may provide convincing proof. This book was once an extremely confidential resource called the *Auraicept Na n'Ecez*. Over time, parts of it have leaked out, with the original manuscript preserved in climatically controlled containers at the British Museum in London and Trinity College in Dublin. George Calder published a printed version of the manual in 1917. The original manual is written in the coded Basque language as suspected. In it the Benedictine grammarians boastfully and thoroughly describe how they invented the new languages in compliance with the Biblical mandate.

The Benedictine curse on language is not an isolated historical event. A power elite privy to the code still employs the practice. Famous political figures and members of royalty have had their names changed in order to reflect a desired identity in accordance with the code. The Windsor family of Great Britain is a prime example.

Queen Victoria's German-born husband's name, Saxen-Coburg and Gotha, was changed to Windsor on July 17, 1917 by their grandson, King George V. Historians say that the family did this in reaction to the anti-German sentiment of World War I. In choosing their new name, however, they obviously consulted a linguist who knew the code, because the new name when translated means "bequeath a thoroughly united nobility."

214

Here's a more fun one. Around 1913, A Russian by the name of Joseph Dzhugashvili wanted to be known as the "man of steel" so he changed his last name to Stalin. The linguist told him that Stalin came from the Russian word "stal" meaning steel. What the linguist did not tell him was that when decoded with the Basque formula, it really means "in a brutish way he kills people any way possible"![60]

Edo Nyland calls Indo-European linguistics a "conspicuously contrived, counterfeit science." He reminds us that for one, anthropologists now agree that there never really were any "Indo-European" people, and second, the family of languages labeled "Indo-European" is a long perpetuated academic fraud by a select group of religious scholars to whom modern academia still hold allegiance. That most scholars today do not yet uniformly accept Nyland's theory is no surprise. First, Nyland admits that his analysis so far is only preliminary. More research is needed. He provides solid evidence that most modern languages have the Saharan/Basque language as their core. However, Sino-Tibetan, Amerind, Australian and Khoisian language groups appear to remain untouched by the distortion effort. Second, Nyland is an academic outsider. That alone, however, should not bar eventual recognition of his great contribution to this field of study. As Thomas Kuhn wrote in his ground-breaking treatise, *The Structure of Scientific Revolutions:*

> Almost always the men who achieve these fundamental inventions of a new paradigm have either been very young or very new to the field whose paradigm they change.[61]

Edo Nyland never mentions the Anunnaki or even acknowledges the existence of UFOs. Still, he has accurately picked up on a pattern left behind by our extraterrestrial ancestors in following the evolution of language. The Saharan/Basque original core language had its origins on the African continent as did humanity. The ancestors of the

215

Berbers were among the tribes of ancient sea peoples who explored the Atlantic Ocean, eventually settling in the area populated by the Basques before migrating northward. The Saharan tribal peoples, along with the coastal populations of Scotland, Ireland, and Norway, have a higher than average incidence of Rh-negative blood. Some researchers in the field of UFOlogy feel that this may be a throw back to a time when the Anunnaki Reptilian traits were still strong in our genetic makeup. At any rate, these coastal areas were closely linked to settlements by the first migrations from Atlantis. These populations also hosted the old Goddess religion far longer than other cultures.

The first Serpents of Wisdom taught that the Earth was a living being, our natural mother, and an embodiment of the Goddess. This is no creation myth: It is scientific fact. The Earth could not support any life were it not receptive to the seeding of the Life Force from the Sun. The Sun literally impregnates the Earth from which issues all life on the planet. Yet physical manifestation is nurtured and sustained primarily by the Earth and her energy known as *Qi* (sometimes spelled *Ki.*) The Sun alone is not enough. Therefore, the feminine principle reigned supreme in lives, as did the earthly and heavenly representatives of that principle in the female Anunnaki, such as the one who eventually became known as Inanna. By changing the dominant focus to the Sun and the male principle to the exclusion of the feminine, balance and an important link to our humanity were lost. The Earth has been scorched by ignorance of our origins ever since.

Neurosurgeon Leonard Shlain, in his book, *The Alphabet Versus the Goddess*, says that a cultural predominance of writing over image served to advance and perpetuate patriarchy and dominator society.[62] Essentially, Shlain argues that literacy reinforces left-brain thinking (linear, digitalized) more closely related to masculine values, at the expense of right-brain activity related to the feminine values of holism and iconography. In other words (no pun intended), focusing on words more than imagery rewired the human brain for patriarchal culture. He points out that spiritual sages, such as Socrates, Buddha and Jesus, *orally* taught kindess, equality, and compassion, emphasizing a balance between masculine and feminine values. It wasn't until their words were committed to writing that their teachings were distorted and twisted into a patriarchal belief system.

After the invention of writing in Mesopotamian Sumer, worship of the Goddess declines, and eventually she is harshly rejected by the Israelites. In one of the first alphabetic books, the Hebrew Bible, God's image is obscured by words. The worshiper is further distanced from the divinity by an exclusive priesthood who preach that knowledge of the Lord is confined to what is written about him. In Asia, when the more masculine doctrine of Confucianism with its emphasis on "father-culture" replaced the more holistic, integrative, natural practice of Taoism, the torturing of women through foot binding became a common practice. In contrast, during the Dark Ages in Europe when illiteracy flourished, there was a rise in the worship of images of the Virgin Mary as a substitute version of the Goddess, and the protection and veneration of women was encouraged through the practice of chivalry and courtly love. During the Renaissance, the tide turned again. With the invention of the printing press, literacy was on the rise along with a focus on science, commerce, and Protestant scripture. Wise women and mystics were tortured and burned at the stake. The invention of photography in the 19th century sparking a renewed interest in the all-powerful image, promoted a resurgence in egalitarian values, and women's rights movements begin in earnest. In the 20th century, the television as a powerful medium becomes responsible for iconic information superseding text information. It is no wonder that the seminal milestones attained by feminists in the 1960s occurred during the first television generation.[63]

It is unlikely that writing and the use of alphabets rewired the brain *causing* patriarchy and dominator society. In observing the animal kingdom, male primates can occasionally become very aggressive and dominating absent any alphabet or written language. Therefore, it is probably more accurate to say that an emphasis on left-brain functions tends to reinforce patriarchal or dominator values already in place. Though Shlain's correlations are convincing, they merely point to the cyclical nature of evolutionary trends. The Tao is always seeking balance, and sometimes extremes come about as a means of correcting imbalance. This happens as a result of the Hermetic laws of rhythm and polarity. The pendulum is always swinging.

For instance, even during the intensely patriarchal reigns of the Egyptian pharaohs, a surprising feminine backlash emerged in the figure of Nefertiti. Egyptian patriarchy and military might reached its zenith during the reigns of Thutmose IV and his son, Amenhotep III. But then along came Amenhotep IV around 1353 B.C.E. with his beautiful wife, Nefertiti. With evangelistic zeal, the bold couple fostered a renewal of the ancient monotheistic Goddess religion, banning the worship of the Egyptian pantheons of dominant male gods and subservient goddesses. Amenhotep changed his name to Akhenaten, which when broken down by the Basque code, means "the Great Goddess, my refuge always." Nefertiti's name decoded is "reform the cursed patriarchy and discover faithfulness." But the new age was only temporary. Akhenaten died rather young, and Nefertiti alone could not restrain the new pharaoh from reinstating the previous patriarchal pantheon and resuming dominance.[64]

Sporadic events like these can be found throughout all history if the records are examined closely. Yet no matter how they tried to stamp it out, the ancient language of the Goddess remains with us today, and can be unveiled to all with open eyes, thanks to Edo Nyland.

Dr. John Dee and the Enochian Enigma

Dr. John Dee, born in 1527, became a prominent Protestant mathematician, magician and astrologer, and a beloved confident to Queen Elizabeth. He was also a member of the

Rosicrucian Order and owned the most extensive library in all of Europe. Some evidence suggests that he might have been one of the first secret agents of the British government, given his natural affinity for codes and secret language.

Dee is also an important figure in occult history because he openly relied upon his esoteric skill and knowledge to gain influence in political affairs. He was an imperialist, and genuinely concerned about Spain's intentions toward his country. Therefore, it only made sense that the magical language he received and transcribed would also reflect geographical concerns.

Dee also believed that humans were "star-daemons" – spirits connected to the stars. While he never wrote of seeing flying craft or anything else that could be construed as UFO phenomena, he had a remarkable experience with a being who had all the identifying marks of an extraterrestrial intelligence.

One day, Dee heard a knock at his window. Upon opening it, he saw what he described as a brilliant angelic being floating about twelve feet up in the air. The angel handed him a large smoky quartz egg, which by the way, is still on display today at the British Museum.

Dee and an acquaintance, Edward Kelly, used the crystal as a scrying tool for talking with angelic beings purporting to convey an ancient, secret magical language they called "Enochian." The angels said that Enoch had once been given this magical language, but it was withdrawn when humanity began to grow farther away from God. Now was the time, they indicated, to restore the ancient secrets to humanity for the benefit of one and all. We know that Enoch, according to Sitchin's research, was one of the first humans to gain significant favor from the Anunnaki.

The language system subsequently dictated to Dee by the angels and transcribed by Kelly is a complex, elaborate system of letters, numbers, sigils, and combinations that only a lover of puzzles could appreciate. The purpose of the language is ritual invocation of hidden dimensions of the Self and/or supernatural beings in order to produce material change and certain states of consciousness. A special sigil is assigned to each major geographical location in the world. The angels said that these signs were for invoking the guardian spirits of those particular areas of the planet in order to control them. The problem was that the spirit could be angelic or demonic, depending on the chosen magical formula or combination. Even if the magician believes that the angels and demons merely represent hidden dimensions of the Self, he or she must still accept responsibility for invoking them. We are all interconnected, and in unlocking a hidden dimension of ourselves, we are surely exposed to hidden dimensions of others whether they reside within us, outside of us, in a separate dimension or in outer space.

Much controversy exists over this magical language. There are those who feel it is a very real and powerful tool that was given to Dee by supernatural beings for whatever reason. Some believe it might be the original language of Atlantis. Other folks believe that the angels were really malicious, deceptive spirits who gave this formula to Dee in order to manipulate us. Then there are those who have decided that it is simply a completely artificial language constructed by Dee and Kelly from esoteric texts and resources already available to them.

Those contending that Enochian is an artificial language agree it has no recognizable grammar or syntax, but cannot agree on whether it is based on Latin or Hebrew. Correlations have been made between its alphabetical characters to the I Ching, the codons of DNA, and the Tzolkin calendar of the ancient Mayans. Some of the texts and tables also resemble elaborate Tibetan mandalas, complete with a phonetic patterning, rhyme, repetition and alliteration not found in normal speech. What is certain is that those who work with the alphabet, especially its sonic aspects, have strange and profound changes in consciousness. When Kelly was initially receiving the letters from the angels, he remarked to Dee, "My head is on fire." Researchers familiar with the effects of prematurely awakened Kundalini energy will recognize this symptom.

Some authors speculate that the Enochian signs and letters are deliberately designed to force consciousness into resonance with a language pattern coded into our very DNA, producing a rapid expansion of consciousness and an increase in symbol coherent cognition.[65] This is interesting because some folks theorize that the Anunnaki made additional genetic modifications to homo sapiens sapiens resulting in the deactivation of certain codes that originally enabled us to actualize supersensory powers. If this is true, then it makes sense that an extraterrestrial intelligence would grant us a way to *re-activate* the codes. I contend that they did this long ago through the ancient teachings of the mystery schools, and that what Kelly was experiencing was just a short-circuiting to that state directly triggered by the intensity of the CE-5 experience.

Funny thing though is that Dee or Kelly never used the language for any purpose after it was transcribed. The reason often cited for this is that one of the angels told Dee that he should not use it without their specific authorization. Evidently, he never received that permission. That did not stop others from coming along and attempting to make use of it. One of those individuals was the illustrious occultist Aleister Crowley of 19th century Golden Dawn notoriety.

Enochian is probably some kind of comprehensive communication system for use in magic and for making specific contact with extraterrestrial intelligence. Whether it is a true and ancient language or artificially constructed is not important. As every medial artist knows, original ideas and masterpieces often appearing to be divinely inspired can reflect not so original influences. The fact that Beethoven's music was to some extent influenced by Mozart and other composers preceding him does not diminish the originality and genius of his own special musical contribution. The muse works with whatever materials are provided to it. This is the principle on which any form of channeling is based. A spirit talking through a human medium is often limited by the medium's own vocabulary or scope of knowledge. This is not always the case but often is. Likewise, anything received will be colored by the medium's own consciousness and preconceptions to some extent. Therefore, it is understandable that Dee's magical

221

language would resemble languages he already knew. The fact that some of the words reflect Sanskrit or Egyptian roots, languages Dee did not know, is likewise inconsequential. The collective unconscious or astral vault of the "Akashic Records" is vast, and you can find anything there if you look long and hard enough.

Has the language ever been used to establish contact with ETs? That of course depends on what you mean by ET. Many magicians do not distinguish between discarnate entities, angels, demons, and elementals. To them it's all "extraterrestrial intelligence" in some context. Aleister Crowley, as previously mentioned, revived, modified and used the Enochian system of magic in his rituals. In doing so he established contact with Aiwass, a being with definite extraterrestrial connections, if not extraterrestrial himself.

Dee's angels continuously spoke of an apocalypse held in check by "gates" or "watchtowers." They professed to give the "keys" to these gates to Dee so that he could preserve them until the appropriate time for their use arrived. The angels repeatedly emphasized that they could not intervene in this process because it was the ultimate responsibility of humans to determine humanity's fate. One angel stated, "I dwell not in the soul of man."[66] This brings to mind many messages received from extraterrestrials explaining the reasons why they cannot just come forth and save us from our sins. We are in a process of species maturation where we must learn to take responsibility for all our actions. For them to directly intervene would deny us the opportunity for spiritual growth. According to Dee's angels, the purpose of the keys was for establishing communication with the spirits or guardian angels of all the nations of Earth. Then by passing through these "gates of understanding" the ability to move through all the other gates into all the other "Cities" would be granted. At that point, the keys would reveal all the secrets to their Cities and enable Dee to completely comprehend the mysteries contained in their tables.[67]

The pattern here is clear. Joseph Smith, the American prophet and founder of Mormonism, was also told a similar story by an angel. The golden plates containing his revelations had been hidden until the appointed time. Dee, unlike Smith however, was unable to do anything with his prophetic keys, much less base a new religion on them. William Bramley, in his fascinating little book, *The Gods of Eden,* theorizes that all religious or mystical experiences with apocalyptic flavor are probably holographic projections from extraterrestrials trying to maintain covert control over the minds of men. The allusion to gates and watchtowers in the Enochian system might well mean stargates and wormholes into other dimensions for all we know. If this sounds like some kind of sinister plot on the part of malevolent beings like the extraterrestrials portrayed in the movie *Stargate*, consider this: Author Donald Tyson believes that there are dark forces who want to see humanity destroyed or at least seriously crippled in some sort of apocalypse. He believes that the angels who spoke to Dee might represent those forces. So when Aleister Crowley (who conveniently believed himself to be the reincarnation of Edward Kelly) came along and began actually *practicing* the ancient Enochian magical system in 1909, he was partly successful. Soon afterwards the Earth saw two world wars, and the looming spectacle of a nuclear holocaust is never far away.[68]

To me, Tyson's fears and assumptions are largely naïve, unwarranted and unduly pessimistic. Though I agree that the apocalypse might also symbolize a much needed transformation in the collective unconscious of humanity, I do not believe it need manifest in large scale chaos and destruction. We have enough of that to work with as it is. To dwell on more only brings it to us. Again, the repeated message conveyed from other contactees is to think positive because all actions proceed from our thoughts. We cannot effectively change things if we do not believe it is possible to do so. By now, that should be common sense.

Whatever the reason and purpose behind the Enochian language, it remains an enigma for all those who wish to take its challenge. I would like to see CSETI or some other organization put it to use in their contact efforts. Yet because of its complexity and the negativity surrounding its history, it might be better to begin with a less controversial code or a sacred language that is more user-friendly!

The Secret Cipher of the UFOnauts

When I first began searching for a direct connection between occultism and UFOlogy, for the longest time I found absolutely nothing. There were vague allusions in the Bailey books and in some Qabalistic literature, but nothing that actually came out and used the words "UFO" or "extraterrestrial." Suddenly I came across an intriguing article posted on the Internet entitled, "The Men in Black and their Magical Origins." Turns out it was an excerpt from an obscure out of print book, *Secret Cipher of the UFOnauts,* by Allen H. Greenfield. Allen Greenfield is a Bishop of a Gnostic tradition with roots in the Golden Dawn, a practitioner of ceremonial magic, and co-founder of the National UFO Conference. His little book is seen by some as a cult classic.

He opens it with something that Aleister Crowley said in 1944 towards the end of his life:

> My observation of the Universe convinces me that there are beings of intelligence and power of a far higher quality than anything we can conceive of as human – the one and only chance for mankind to advance as a whole is for individuals to make contact with such beings.[69]

Greenfield believes that Crowley was contacted by some of these beings and given a secret cipher that would eventually be decoded and used to solve the UFO mystery. Several factors are supportive of this premise. For one, the physical description of the supernatural entity, Aiwass, who mysteriously appeared and dictated the code to Crowley, matches that of the modern-day "men in black." Second, Crowley had another interesting meeting with two "little men" in the Swiss Alps, which is listed in Jacque Vallee's catalogue of close encounter cases. Third, a sketch Crowley made of one of the "secret chiefs" or masters connected with his work called LAM, has common alien-type features. Finally, Crowley had a favorite magic mountain in Scotland, Mt. Mealfuorvonie near Loch Ness, an area currently associated with an underground UFO base.

While Crowley was on his honeymoon in Cairo, Aiwass, as a messenger from the "secret chiefs" appeared to him and asked him to transcribe what became known as *Liber Al vel Legis* or *The Book of the Law*. Crowley was told that this text was a comprehensive "holy book" for a new aeon. Part of this book contained a mysterious cipher. Aiwass told Crowley he would never be able to decode it, but that someone else would come along and do so at an appointed time. Already, we see a pattern paralleling the experiences of John Dee and Joseph Smith.

Initially, the code looked very much like an old mystical cipher having its origins in Freemasonry. According to Greenfield, such ciphers are often used to decode the original meanings behind words, names and places received in trance channeling. Traditionally, many western esoteric texts are written in code and symbolism anyway because of the long years of religious persecution by the Roman Catholic Church. *The Alchymical Wedding of Christian Rosenkrutz* out of the 1600s, often considered to be one of the most important seminal works related to the Rosicrucian movement, is a good example.

Crowley's code was broken long after his passing, however a computer program, Lexicon, was ultimately required to decipher it. When certain mystical names of beings and places related to UFOs and ETs were subjected to translation through the code, Greenfield found many interesting revelations regarding the nature of such phenomena. It's intriguing that the terms "UFO" and "ET" were not even coined until the official period of contact lore that began after 1947, the year of Crowley's death.

Greenfield discovered that the cipher uses the classical decoding techniques of the Qabalah but that it is based on the

English language rather than Hebrew or Aramaic. He provides a copy of the code with instructions on how to use it in his book. However, he reminds us that tradition shows that as soon as one code is broken, it is discontinued and eventually replaced by another. The ultimate purpose of such codes, he says, is the same as the purpose of all secret ciphers – to enable select groups of individuals to communicate with each other secretly. He contends that Crowley's code was specially used for contact and communication between extraterrestrial intelligences, which he calls "UFOnauts" -- the secret chiefs, including adepts and initiates of the inner school.

I've often thought that the Qabalah is like a direct line to higher intelligence(s) both inwardly and outwardly. It appears that Greenfield feels this way too:

> The story of our interaction with the UFOnauts begins with the Qabalistic Tree of Life, and the Chakra system of the body.
>
> According to the primal occult and frequently secret and subversive view, the manifest universe emerges from an Ultimate NOT-Thing, a Consciousness or Beingness beyond words or expressions sometimes referred to as the Unmanifest or The Limitless Light. This Unmanifest cannot be understood in the external sense, but can be Known in the Gnostic sense by the initiate or perfected sentient being . . . It can be plugged into.
>
> For reasons equally inexpressible, this uniqueness unfolds itself in manifestation. Thus, the limitless light becomes a series of emanations or expressions of Intelligences that devolve increasingly toward our material form of existence and thus towards accessibility in the conventional sense. But the manifestations also increasingly become subject to subdivision into arbitrary concepts such as "good" and "evil" as these are commonly understood. And they also become closer and closer in form and

content to our own mundane reality, though, in the relativity of things, these Higher Intelligences may seem unspeakably powerful, mythic and divine.[70]

Traditionally, prophets, seers, and oracles have been the ones to exercise the ability to "plug into" these intelligences, ultimately receiving messages and divine revelations as a result. In the past, it has been the responsibility of the mystery schools to train people to do this. But now we have secularists like Dr. Greer and psychologists teaching people to remote view. Esoteric skill and knowledge are neutral and can be used for either good or bad. Used with love and compassion, wisdom springs forth. But if it is gained with all head and no heart, we observe what has been called "the black lodge" or dark brotherhood, resulting in a misuse or abuse of such powers. Distinguishing between the two is easy. The work of the "good guys" benefits one and all. The work of the "bad guys" only serves the small self – the ego -- and/or a small enclave of associates related to that small self.

The good guys are traditionally called the Great White Brotherhood, but if you recall, I choose to call them the Rainbow Alliance. The so-called "black lodge" with impure motives I call the *muddlers*. The light of the rainbow cannot be muddled – only its reflection in pigment can. And as any artist knows, when you mix up colors, you get a big brownish gray muddle – like mud. When you want to make the water unclear, you muddy it. Polluting, diluting, distorting, soiling, DDT – all muddling techniques. Hence, the muddlers. That's basically what they do – muddle things up, and it's usually a very subtle process. As Crowley stated in his book, *Magick Without Tears*,

> What I am out to complain of is what I seriously believe to be an organized conspiracy of the Black Lodges to prevent people from thinking...[71]

On the occult path or any path really, when an aspirant is about to make an important breakthrough or truly awesome discovery of some paradigm shifting pearl of wisdom to share

227

with others, nine times out of ten an adversary or "man in black" will show up in order to thwart the process. Greenfield relates, "That they need to do this, and that they often fail in their efforts, is an indication that (A) the Black Lodge is opposed by Something Else, equally as strong, and (B) they are afraid of something we might find out – about them, about their opposition, about ourselves or all three."[72]

And lo and behold – I find an occultist besides me who finally admits the connection:

> Concurrently, and not coincidently, the two great initiatory bodies, or orders have generated and regenerated throughout history. The so-called Great White Brotherhood, when undistorted, appears (according to legend) guided by Intelligences associated with the dual star system Sirius or Sothis in some manner. This brotherhood also seems to have the purpose of uplifting the human character and initiating biological and social evolution designed to move toward identification with Ultimate Being. What is sometimes called "the Black Lodge" ... is generated to keep humanity in a state of materialist trance and evolutionary stagnation.[73]

Again, the muddlers don't do this just because they're "evil" or just because they like to see us suffer. Perhaps some do, but that's not their main motive. The underlying motive is a trait shared by *all* humanity – simple greed. They would not want to slow us down or keep us in a state of materialist trance if they were not gaining something from it.

The point that Greenfield makes is that the Rainbow Alliance and the muddlers have their corresponding allies or sponsors in outer space. It is clear that orders on both sides may greatly resemble one another. To put it simplistically, yes there are "good witches" and "bad witches" and "good Masons" and "bad Masons" – just as there are "good lawyers" and "bad lawyers" and "good priests" and "bad priests." An individual can cycle between "good" and "bad" in one lifetime because it's all energy – neither good nor bad. All depends on how it's used.

Unfortunately, Greenfield reveals a xenophobic tendency because he appears to blame all the bad on the so-called race of extraterrestrials known as "the Grays." For one, the existence of such a race is largely in question due to the probability that the U.S. military manufactures the majority of these biological entities. Therefore, like androids or robots, they probably have no soul, free will, or intelligence of their own. So how can you demonize a race that does not really exist? Perhaps there are those who might point to this as the ominous beginnings of artificial intelligence – that these Grays are in all likelihood the equivalent of the diabolical machines portrayed in the motion picture *The Matrix* that will someday enslave us all. Of course, David Icke would agree with that and would add that it's already happened – that we are already enslaved and that the Grays are merely tools for a higher order of malicious intelligent beings. If so, again, I say those malicious beings are none other than our brothers and sisters – other Earth Humans who are in it and in on it – whatever "it" is – for themselves. There is nothing conspiratorial about that.

It is unfortunate that almost all unpleasant, sinister abduction-type experiences in modern times seem to involve these Grays. And it is honorable to want to fight against that force, but demonizing them only plays into the hands of the muddlers. Such polarized overgeneralization generates fear, paranoia, and incredulousness. It will be even more so when the cat gets out of the bag and the whole abduction scenario is shown for the stage-magic that it is. Besides, even if there is a race (i.e., Zeta Reticuli) that is the prototype for the Grays – not all those who have had contact with them have had negative experiences. Author Marcia Schafer, for instance, says they're always friendly with her and treat her very well.[74]

Greenfield in his analysis at least retains a pure and exact definition of what black magic is:

The magick of the Black Lodge can be defined and thus identified in only one way and by one set standard: the subversion of the True Will. *This is the essence of Black Magick,* and is its only true definition. Aleister Crowley explained it this way:

"The Magical Will is in its essence twofold, for it presupposes a beginning and an end; to will to be a thing is to admit you are not that thing. Hence to will anything but the supreme thing is to wander still further from it – *any will but that to give up the self to the beloved is black magick* – yet the surrender is so simple an act that to our complex minds it is the most difficult of all acts, and hence training is necessary…"[75]

The True Will is the One Will of which all our little wills are but reflections. Being deluded by the illusion of separateness is what keeps us from the beloved, *i.e.,* the Higher Self. It is just an illusion from which we must awaken. And there are many different degrees of awakening.

Greenfield agrees that our best psychic self-defense against all unwanted invaders of space (both inner and outer) is actualizing our inherent divinity:

In elevated mystical states, the very secretions, psychic and otherwise, which humans emit and which desperate vampire-aliens consume like the soul-famished pathetic creatures they are, become poison to them in the Transformed Human. Cosmic Consciousness is literally poison to them.[76]

Likewise, he is not a total pessimist, as he fully acknowledges the superiority of inherent divinity above all other intelligence:

The transformed Adept, greater than the most advanced aliens, is the ultimate victor in the Battle of

Conquest. Not merely Earth, but the Omniverse is his domain.[77]

Greenfield's polarizing tendency is of marginal concern, however, when considering the sum total of his efforts. The extraordinary originality and resourcefulness of his research make his book a valuable gem of a contribution that should not go unrecognized.

The Gnostic Vision of Joseph Smith

On April 7, 1844, Joseph Smith wrote,

> You don't know me – you never will. You never knew my heart. No man knows my history. I cannot tell it; I shall never undertake it. I don't blame anyone for not believing my history. If I had not experienced what I have, I could not have believed it myself.[78]

That phrase right there was perhaps the truest prophecy Joseph Smith ever made. For over a century, his own religion never even recognized him for the true Gnostic that he was.

Whatever you may think of Mormonism, the Church of Jesus Christ of Latter Day Saints as it is officially called, it is the fastest growing religion in the world. Its church is one of the most influential and wealthiest institutions in the United States. Its flock is comprised of individuals whose mainly conservative values stem from a belief in inherent divinity and the expression of that divinity through principle-centered living. What most churches preach, Mormons practice. Like Buddhists living the dharma, Mormon lifestyle is centered on religious belief. Church is not something that just happens on Sundays. It permeates every aspect of their lives – particularly the family. Church happens at home, and home happens at church. While each individual church or ward as they call it, has its own Bishop, the Bishop does not give sermons. The members of the church, even the children, share their testimonials each Sunday in place of a sermon. So everyone is encouraged to participate in church activities from a very early age.

Mormonism is still relatively young – not even 200 years old yet. Already, it carries many unresolved contradictions in its law and scripture. Like all new religions, it's had to struggle and evolve to where it is today, and it's still changing. Due to the controversial nature of early Mormon teachings, the church has also suffered from internal division, and today there exist many churches which are offshoots from the main body. One of the most noted is a fundamentalist branch that still practices polygamy in remote areas of Utah and northern Arizona, even though that practice is illegal and no longer condoned by the main LDS Church.

Though outsiders and ex-Mormons alike have criticized the church for legitimate reasons, it must be offering an attractive package because membership is growing at an astonishing rate. Most Mormons I've met have been exceptionally friendly, hard working and principle-centered. For community outreach and helping their own, they can't be beat.

Some Christian fundamentalists do not recognize Mormonism as an authentic denomination of Christianity. They claim it is just a large cult founded on occult practices. On the outside, the LDS Church is anything but a cult with its emphasis on family values, tradition, and patriotism. Yet allegations about occult influence are correct, though most Mormons might disagree with that assertion.

Joseph Smith was born in 1805. Early on, it was evident that he was psychically sensitive and prone to emotional intensity. While an adolescent living in Palmyra, New York, he became disillusioned by the hypocrisy and petty disputes prevalent among the various church denominations in his community. A born nature mystic, he went to the woods seeking guidance. This is more significant than perhaps realized because it reinforces Smith's sacred outlook on nature and the Cosmos that would be pivotal in formulating the foundation of Mormon doctrine. It is also not the first time a spiritual sage in the making would seek refuge in a forest, a

232

sacred grove or under a special tree for divine revelation. In his words (and original spelling):

> For I looked upon the sun the glorious luminary of the earth and also the moon rolling in their magesty through the heavens and also the stars shining in their courses and the earth also upon which I stood and the beast of the field and the fowls of heaven and the fish of the waters and also man walking forth upon the face of the earth in magesty and in the strength and beauty whose power and intiligence in governing the things which are so exeding great and marvilous even in the likeness of him who created them and when I considered upon these things my heart exclaimed well hath the wise man said it is a fool that saith in his heart there is no God my heart exclaimed all these bear testimony and bespeak an omnipotent and omnipresent power a being that makith Laws and decreeeth and bindeth all things in their bounds who filleth Eternity who was and is and will be from All Eternity to Eternity.[79]

While he was praying in the midst of these trees, a brilliant pillar of light descended through the forest canopy and enveloped him. Luminous beings appeared in answer to his prayer. They instructed him to stay away from all churches, deeming them not genuine. Several years later, while praying in his room, Joseph had another mystical experience involving a descending beam of brilliant light. This time the luminous being was Moroni – an angel whose presence and appearance was like lightening Smith said. Moroni appeared to him three times during the same night, repeating verbatim the same message as the first.

Essentially, Moroni directed Smith to some gold plates hidden in a nearby hill that contained the history of the ancient people of North America. Smith eventually translated these ancient texts into what we now know as the Book of Mormon. Mormons believe that this book is an addendum to the Old and New Testament of the Bible, that Jesus appeared in the

Americas shortly after his resurrection to teach, and that their church is the restoration of the true church intended by Christ. And that's how the religion got started.

From the very beginning, the religion and its practices were controversial. Smith's bold and unorthodox behavior only added fuel to the fire. Subsequently, he and his brother were assassinated on June 27, 1844 by an angry mob.

Regardless of what you may believe about the religion and the accuracy of the events that led up to it, it is undisputed that Smith had an authentic mystical experience that had a profoundly transformative effect on himself and those around him. Joseph Smith was a modern Gnostic prophet. What is a Gnostic? Gnostic comes from the Greek word *gnosis* meaning knowing based on experience. Therefore, Gnostics don't *believe* anything that they haven't experienced for themselves. As Jung or some other Gnostic used to say, "I don't believe. I *know.*" Hence, consider Joseph Smith's statement.

A sect of early Christians felt this very same way, and produced the *Gnostic Gospels* discovered at Nag Hammadi, Egypt in 1945. The texts are closer to the true teachings of Jesus Christ and his disciples than anything found thus far. These early Christians recognized the divine feminine, and there is much evidence to support that their culture did not devalue women nor bar them from taking on leadership roles in the spiritual community. In fact, Mary Magdalene was the author of one of these texts.

Joseph Smith's involvement with occultism is historically documented. He often practiced divination by gazing into a "seer stone." He soon fell into a group that practiced ceremonial magic and went treasure digging. He began associating with Masons and other influential people with an occult background. In fact, his wife's cousin, a physician named Dr. Luman Walter, toured Europe as a popular mesmerist well versed in alchemy, Hermetic lore, and naturopathy. After Smith died, his family, as was tradition, preserved all his sacred relics. Among these was a ceremonial dagger bearing the occult sigil for Mars, and a silver medallion that probably served as a special talisman inscribed with the magic square and symbol for Jupiter, an astrological force associated with the time of his birth.

Significantly, Moroni appeared to Smith during the evening of the fall equinox between the hours of midnight and dawn -- traditionally the best hours for magical invocation. Smith's participation in a Masonic lodge lends further evidence to the importance of ritual and symbolism in his spiritual practice. Many Mormon rites reflect this occult influence. Freemasonry had already left a bad taste in the mouths of many Americans. But Smith recognized it for the corrupted remnant of the ancient mysteries that it was, and explained to his followers that his efforts were towards restoring the sacred mysteries to their fullness.[80] Smith also associated with a Qabalist that probably exposed him to the classic text, *The Zohar*, from which Smith quotes in his April 7, 1844 public declaration of the plurality of the Gods. It was from the Qabalah that Smith got his teaching about the spiritual evolution of humanity -- that we are destined to become as gods ourselves by virtue of the divine spark within us all. It is also where he gathered the concepts of pre-existent spirits, the unity of matter and spirit, and the covenant of celestial marriage as the ultimate vehicle for manifesting these truths. For instance, the divine paradox – a kind of Zen koan -- is revealed by these words out of the Book of Mormon: "His paths are straight, and his course is one eternal round." (Alma 37:12). The Mormon version of the Hermetic Axiom is out of Moses 6:63:

> And behold, all things have their likeness, and all things are created and made to bear record of me, both things which are temporal, and things which are spiritual; things which are in the heavens above, and things which are on the earth, and things are in the earth; both things which are under the earth, both above and beneath: all things bear record of me.

The tendency for humans to grow lopsidedly, however, becomes apparent when Smith took license to misinterpret some of the esoteric teachings. For instance, the secret alchemical practices concerning sexual polarity and sacred union became debased in the practice of polygamy. Smith was rightly picking up on the fact that yes, we can all have more than one mate, spiritually speaking, as sex doesn't only happen between bodies. Intimate relations can occur, and more often than not do, on the planes of emotion, mind, and pure spirit. Yet indiscriminate sexual intercourse on the physical plane does not automatically ensure that the mating is secured on the higher planes. And this is when the trouble ensued.

After Smith's death, his disciple Brigham Young emerged as the next natural leader of the church. Young, like Smith, was a full-fledged master Mason. In order to escape continued persecution, he led his people on their own spiritual Exodus to the valley of the great Salt Lake in Utah, which is a Mormon stronghold to this day. Though Young was a staunch defender of the practice of polygamy, pressure from the United States government forced the church to publicly abandon the practice in 1890. The church has never been the same since.

How it evolved into the conservative, dogmatic institution that it is today is another story, and a complex one at that. The life of Joseph Smith very much followed the pattern of earlier saints and mystics, to the point where the events in his life came to symbolize and represent the integration of spiritual archetype into principles of practice, much like the life of Jesus Christ or the Rosicrucian equivalent, Christian Rosenkreutz. Whether Smith was fully aware that the events in his personal life were staged for creating a new mythology of lasting religious significance is arguable. Nonetheless, that's exactly what occurred. Being the fully trained occultist that he was, he was undeniably familiar with the use of metaphor and symbolism in revealing spiritual principle. Therefore, it is equally certain that he intended his followers to focus more on the inner meaning of the symbols and the allegory than a strict literal interpretation. But this is not what happened. His indolent flock began to relinquish the personal knowing of gnosis and divine self-revelation to blind faith, belief and obedience to religious authority. Richard Smoley and Jay Kinney, authors of *Hidden Wisdom: A Guide to the Western Inner Traditions*, explain that gnosis, being based on experiential reality, is a vital and dynamic process. When that energy is subject to systematization, metaphors are mistaken for facts and spiritual reality becomes static.[81]

Therefore, the imaginative vitality of the prophet's original revelations was effectively drained by Mormons looking to the church before the teaching and by valuing the preservation of the collective over the sanctity of the individual. However, the religion is still evolving, and there are signs that a revitalization of some of these sacred principles may be underway. For instance, when potential new members are investigating the church, they are encouraged by the elders to invoke the "Holy Ghost" directly for guidance on whether the teachings as presented by the church are true. I find this fascinating because it appears to be a throwback to their Gnostic roots. Yet once baptized into the church, you are beholden to the church – never mind what the "Holy Ghost" tells you. Excommunication is church policy for those who go astray. The administration of other church protocol is similarly rife with inconsistencies. But this does not seem to bother most members, who for the most part, remain blissfully unaware of the religion's deep roots in the occult tradition of the Western mysteries.

Still, the Book of Mormon continues to lend itself to both a literal and symbolic view of reality, which makes it a useful instrument indeed. As stated in 1 Nephi 22:2-3, "For by the Spirit are all things made known unto the prophets, which shall come upon the children of men according to the flesh. Wherefore, the things of which I have read are things pertaining to things both temporal and spiritual."

Kevin Christensen has written a wonderful essay on the numinous and mystical qualities of Mormon spiritual experience. He explains it like this:

> The Book of Mormon sets the pattern for
> Mormonism by combining the physical and the

spiritual, the literal and the symbolic, the unique historic event and the mythic recurrence. Nephi tells us that he is writing a history, but that history is organized around the vision of the tree of life. We can neither separate the history from the symbols of the vision, nor the symbolic vision from the narrative history. The vision is a historic event, and the symbols of the vision come from the physical landscape. Yet the vision enacts current tensions and future events in the history of Lehi's family, just as it depicts eternal realities. Even when Nephi refers to history, he does so, not to merely recite facts, but to "liken" the history to his people, that is, to relive the patterns of creation and Exodus, and make them actual in the lives of his people and his readers… The literal and the symbolic illuminate and give meaning to each other; attempts to separate them make no sense at all.[82]

Yet unfortunately, both members and non-members of the church appear to do just that more often than not. Nevertheless, Mormons derive great strength from the fact that they have a rich, special history that alone belongs to them. Sharing the spiritual significance of that recent historical journey sustains and reinforces their immovable faith more than scripture alone. Many modern Mormon families take great pride and joy in re-enacting the Exodus from Nauvoo, Illinois to their Salt Lake mecca on a yearly basis. It is truly a rewarding religious pilgrimage.

The circumstances surrounding the creation of this religion has sparked the interest of UFOlogists. It brings to mind the occult tradition of invoking extraterrestrial intelligence by means of ceremonial magic, such as was described with John Dee and Aleister Crowley. I believe this is precisely what transpired with Joseph Smith, especially given his background in Hermetic science. Moroni was more than likely an extraterrestrial intelligence that was trying to convey an important message through Smith.

There is a negative faction that believes that Moroni was a Satanic "false angel" who deliberately set out to deceive Smith, regardless of whether he was invoked or not. One of the luminous beings and important figures in the Mormon texts is Nephi, whose name has been said to be shorthand for Nefilim, sometimes spelled Nephilim, otherwise known as our dear Anunnaki. The manner in which the vision occurred persuades some researchers to believe that it was a holographic projection played to Smith by the manipulative aliens.[83] They surely had this technology, though it would be a hundred years or more before we developed it for use in the entertainment industry and psychotronic weaponry. As author William Bramley states,

> Joseph's angel, Moroni, was different than the angels described by Ezekiel and John in the Bible. Smith's angel did not wear items that could be interpreted as a helmet and boots. Moroni was a figure in a true robe. However, Joseph appears to have been looking at a recorded image projected through the window into his room. The clue to this lies in Joseph's words that Moroni had repeated the second message "without the least variation." This suggests a recorded message. The manner in which Moroni disappeared indicates a projected light image from a source in the sky outside the house. When Moroni returned for a third time that same night, Smith "heard him rehearse or repeat over again… the same things – as before…" … If Smith's account is accurate and UFO-related, there would be tremendous humor in it. Today we can go to Disneyland and marvel at remarkable, life-like, projected images of talking heads in the Haunted House ride. A similar projection viewed by a young country bumpkin in the 19th century would no doubt be considered nothing less than a true vision from God… Joseph's testimony that he felt seized and unable to move is identical to several modern UFO encounters in which eyewitnesses report being immobilized, especially before an abduction.[84]

In addition, Mormon doctrines speak openly of inhabited planets in the universe, which was quite visionary for the 19th century. Certain scripture specifically describes a celestial body called "Kolob" having special significance in the cosmic order:

> And I saw the stars, that they were very great, and that one of them was nearest unto the throne of God; and there were many great ones which were near unto it; And the Lord said unto me: These are the governing ones; and the name of the great one is Kolob, because it is near unto me, for I am the Lord thy God: I have set this one to govern all those which belong to the same order as that upon which thou standest.[85]

Mormon academia employ archeologists and astronomers to search for clues that might lead to the verification of their scriptural claims. Speculation that Kolob is really Sirius has been made. I would like one of our sacred language or secret cipher experts to decode the name and see what comes up! At any rate, most Mormons I've questioned believe that extraterrestrials inhabit other worlds, that they look just like us, and that they are every bit as much God's children as we are.

Suppose Joseph Smith was really visited by an extraterrestrial. The Book of Mormon is a record of prolonged fratricidal oppositions, apocalyptic vision, and a witness to salvation through Christ. If Moroni was an Anunnaki, perhaps the stories about fratricidal opposition stem from the "wars of the gods" instigated by the conflicts between Enlil and Enki factions. There are countless other similarities, too numerous to explore here, between the story as told to Smith by Moroni and what's being uncovered by Sitchin and other researchers in Mesoamerica where Mormons hope to find hard evidence of their ancient Americans. For instance, 3 Nephi 8:5-23 in the Book of Mormon contains a description of an event that can be no less than a nuclear holocaust and a subsequent nuclear winter. A widespread deluge with sinking cities is also related resembling the story of Atlantis. But was this visitation a malicious manipulation by sinister aliens with an evil agenda? I doubt it.

The Internet is full of such conspiracies and speculations. There is also mixed information and disinformation published about obscure Mormon sects openly practicing a Gnostic, occult Essene tradition. These sects are said to be cult-like and abusive toward their members. Of course sensational stories of unusual ritualized sexual practices are a major theme. Again, if these stories are true, rest assured that these followers are continuing to misinterpret the esoteric teachings concerning alchemy and sacred sexuality. No esoteric spiritual tradition with a genuine connection to the Inner School would engage in harmful practices. Also, not all child abusers and sexual predators are Mormon. Each religion has its share of bad apples. "Ye shall know them by their fruits."

I suspect a Machiavellian disinformation campaign on the part of the muddlers to distract people from the truth. Both the professed cult and the anti-culters are really the same people pretending to play opposite sides to throw people off. Why? Because the more the truth gets out about the Gnostic origins of the church and the esoteric teachings lying beneath and behind the outer temple, the more likely it is that members will begin to seek out the truth for themselves. Potentially, this could inspire a beautiful mass awakening of sorts resulting in a decisive shift from slavery and dogma to genuine gnosis resulting in self-empowerment and enlightenment. The powers that be who want to preserve the status quo for self-serving reasons – whether sanctioned by a corrupted Mormon Church or not – are threatened by such movements and will do whatever they can to squash them. And by planting the seeds of dissension, disinformation, and deliberate misrepresentation, they can succeed.

Go with your heart and apply common sense when investigating any religion. Don't be misled by disinformation or scandalous misrepresentation. Hopefully, someday the whole truth about all this will be known so that all the disputes and controversy will finally be put to rest. In the meantime, I choose to take what is good, useful, and beneficial and leave behind the rest. Bramley recommends the same:

> No individual or organization is purely good or purely bad. In our crazy universe, "absolute" good and "absolute" evil just do not appear to exist. In the worst of people one will always find a tiny ember of good (*e.g.*, the psychopath Adolf Hitler was kind to children), and in the best of individuals there is always at least one thing that should change. The majority of people who join a group or follow a leader do so for the right reasons: they have heard an element of truth or they seek the solution to a genuine problem. The real trick in judging a person or group is to determine whether more good is being done than bad, and how the bad may be corrected without destroying whatever good there might be. The task is not usually an easy one.[86]

As has been said countless times before, there is no such thing as a perfect person or a perfect religion. Just a perfect perfection – which ultimately all true spiritual tradition seeks to awaken within us.

Freemasonry and "Secret Society"

Let's set the record straight. In this day of pervasive mass media and invasive communication technology, there is no longer any such thing as a "secret society." It's virtually impossible. I repeat: THERE ARE NO SECRET SOCIETIES. There are, however, groups of individuals who like to pretend that they belong to one and groups of individuals who like to play along and perpetuate the lie. But all in all, there are no secret societies.

That is not the same thing as saying that there are no select groups of individuals monopolizing control of the world's political and economic affairs, because there are. Neither do they operate in total secrecy or else we would not know about them. And finally, they're not exclusively Masons any more than they're all Mexican food lovers, cross-eyed, or American Idol fans!

Now that we have that out of the way, let's talk about what freemasonry really is. Freemasonry has ancient origins, and like most other esoteric groups and orders, its history is complex and convoluted. In spirit, it's just another branch of the Western mystery school with the same purpose as all the others. In practice, it has become the subject of much debate, controversy, and misinformation.

From a modern web site (www.freemasonry.org), a California Grand Lodge defines it like this:

> Freemasonry is the world's oldest and largest Fraternity. Its history and tradition date to antiquity. Its singular purpose is to make good men better. Its bonds of friendship, compassion, and brotherly love have survived even the most divisive political, military and religious conflicts through the centuries. Freemasonry is neither a forum nor a place for worship. Instead, it is a friend of all religions which are based on the belief in one God.

Like most mystery schools in the West, in order to survive during the days of persecution, this tradition like a cetaceas creature hid submerged in the depths of the ocean, only occasionally surfacing for air. Over the centuries this creature evolved in such a way that by the 18th century it had grown legs and become a land creature. It was such a beautiful creature that men everywhere began to follow it in order to emulate its grace and freedom. A source of great inspiration, it gave meaning to the lives of many. Of course there were some men who wanted to capture the creature so that they could have it all to themselves, and use it for economic gain rather than the uplifting of souls.

What has happened is this. Any organization – whether religious, political, charitable, or merely social – is going to reflect the personality of its leaders. Therefore, if such an organization is co-opted by a leader with impure motives, these motives will influence the members of that organization accordingly; the result being an imperfect reflection or distortion of original purpose, particularly in the public's eye. This can happen anywhere – a church, a university, a corporation – you name it. Within the past two hundred years, as a result of internal corruption and smear tactics by outsiders, many Masonic lodges are today but empty shells of what they used to be. Once important centers for dissemination of the sacred mysteries, so many are now merely social clubs for influential businessmen with personal agendas. It is a waste of words to write about them. Instead, I choose to focus on the origins of this great tradition, and how it has influenced almost all other Western occult traditions to this day.

The terms *masonry* and *freemasonry* are basically interchangeable. Essentially, the term "freemason" was coined in the Middle Ages to indicate that these mystical masons were free from political and religious dogma. But the real source of it all was, again, extraterrestrial.

According to the Tibetan of the Bailey books, "Masonry, as originally instituted far back in the very night of time and long ante-dating the Jewish dispensation, was organized under direct Sirian influence and modeled as far as possible on certain Sirian institutions."[87] Masonry was one of the systematic teaching methods adopted by our extraterrestrial ancestors for conveying the ancient mysteries to humanity. Its probable origin on this planet was the Atlantean continent, for several sources indicate that the Biblical figure known as Lamech, an antediluvian patriarch, was the first Mason.[88] He was an expert in the sacred science of geometry, which was said to represent the universal order of the cosmos.

The rituals of Freemasonry are symbolic expressions of spiritual principle, designed for transmuting the personality and transforming consciousness, as all ritual is supposed to be. The symbolism is intimately tied into the mysteries surrounding the central character of Hiram Abiff, supposedly the master builder of King Solomon's temple. Abiff is a Christ figure, much like Christian Rosenkreutz and the Egyptian god Osiris, who all underwent a gruesome death, resurrection, and transfiguration. Therefore, this mystery school's practices, like all others, are directed toward the central goal of the Great Work – spiritual transformation. The temple that is built represents the fully spiritually awakened human being – it is the "house not made with hands." According to one Mason, freemasonry is a "system of morality, veiled in allegory, illustrated by symbols."[89] Like all true mystery schools, freemasonry has always sought to inspire seekers to engage spiritual reality in a way that benefits one and all.

Whether or not freemasonry emerged in the dark ages of Europe as builders' guilds is debated and disputed. We know that several secret societies were formed around its principles throughout the centuries and often dedicated to seeing those principles actualized in revolutionary activities. Freemasonry is intimately associated with the activities of the occult organizations known as the Knights Templar and the Rosicrucians, both groups known to have participated in subversive politics in order to overthrow autocracy. In fact, if it were not for these groups and their revolutionary efforts, we would not have the democracy we so cherish today. Their egalitarian ideals were inspired by ancient memories of a pre-Egyptian time when all men and women were treated equally because they were created equally. For an enlightening and thorough accounting of the role that these occult traditions played in world political history, I recommend Michael Howard's book, *The Occult Conspiracy*. Even though, as said before, there is and never has been a conspiracy. The plan to make the world a better place to live by becoming better people is something that's openly revealed in all spiritual traditions – occult or otherwise. It's never been a secret in spite of what anyone might tell you. Precise methodology and strategy has been shrouded in secrecy from time to time, for good reason, as mentioned before. But the goal and purpose – never.

Today, there are probably some Masonic lodges that have preserved the ancient teachings and practice them in principle. It is not my intention to discredit them entirely. They have suffered from smear tactics and persecutions for centuries, because like all genuine mystery schools, they held the keys to spiritual and social liberation. They still do, whether the members are aware of it or not. I hope that some day their members will take it upon themselves to find out the truth about the esoteric origins and deeper meaning behind their rituals, rather than continue to be subsumed by the not so altruistic motives of their leaders. In the meantime, it is wisest to ignore most everything published about them on the Internet because most of it is negative. Again I suspect a Machiavellian campaign. In short, if anyone getting into Freemasonry were to really do their homework, they would find those keys that the muddlers don't want them to have. They don't want you to go there. So how do they keep you away? DDT – decoy, distract and trash. Therefore, the "powers that be" (the muddlers) are pretending to be "anti-powers that be" -- placing all the blame on the Freemasons and a now defunct group of men previously known as the Illuminati.

Therefore, for anyone wanting to get involved in a genuine esoteric order, I would not recommend Freemasonry because it is simply easier to find one that has not been tainted with so much negativity and that remains focused on the inner side of the Great Work. Spiritual groups openly engaged in political activism are rare because it is so easy for them to become corrupted. It is wisest, in this day and age, to keep these important activities separated in terms of operating as a collective in order to give the individual more freedom of choice while maintaining a high level of tolerance, plurality and diversity.

The Other Tibetans

Michael Howard, in his riveting little book, *The Occult Conspiracy,* never discusses ETs or UFOs anywhere in the entire text except for two curious entries in his chronology. The first one says, "10,000 B.C.E.. Evidence suggestive of early contact between extraterrestrials and Stone Age tribes in Tibet." The other entry says, "5,000 B.C.E.. First primitive cities established in the Middle East. Agriculture begins with domestication of animals such as sheep and goats. Possible contact between extraterrestrials and early Sumerian culture."[90] The contact between ETs and Sumerian culture is the topic of Zecharia Sitchin's book, *The 12th Planet.* Not much can be found on the Tibetan connection, so I did a little research.

There is a Buddhist "Genesis."[91] What is interesting about this text is that it shows people to exist for some time before they attain the ability to procreate. When they finally begin to multiply, they suffer shame, exile, and persecution from the elders in the village. Remember, a large faction of the Anunnaki were against the idea of giving humans this ability because they knew it would lead to trouble. Subsequently these same Anunnaki shunned the new humans and treated them with contempt. But then there were those who didn't, of course, and I think that important part of the story is reflected in another Tibetan version of Genesis in the form of a folktale. It is a story about the descent of the Tibetan people from a monkey and a rock-ogress, and comes from The Seventh Chapter of Shankara Pati's Ancient Scripts.[92] Elements in both these creation accounts parallel those of the ancient Sumerians and Amerindians.

The Tibetan and Indian cosmologies contain several pantheons of greater and lesser gods, goddesses and demons all ranked and pegged according to purpose. There is no reason why we cannot assume these entities represent extraterrestrials, just as in the Sumerian cosmology. The Anunnaki were rigidly hierarchical in their "government" if you can call it that, and everyone had their place. Marital and succession laws were strict, and those who violated them were harshly punished. It was very difficult to move up in the echelons, and the rare times it happened were attributed to royal favor more than merit.[93] The ways of the gods were to become the ways of men, of course, for better or worse. So it wouldn't surprise me if the caste system were some dim reflection of this kind of mind set.

During the early 20th century, the Russian mystic-artist-explorer, Nicholas Roerich, was traveling through Nepal and Tibet searching for the legendary city of Shambala. Roerich studied with various lamas in the Tibetan monasteries and suspected that the heads of the "Great White Brotherhood" lived in Shambala. Coincidentally, Roerich reported seeing a "flying saucer" flying over northern Tibet during 1926:

> On August 5th – something remarkable! We were in our camp in the Kukunor district not far from the Humboldt Chain. In the morning about half-past nine some of our caravaneers noticed a remarkably big black eagle flying above us. Seven of us began to watch this unusual bird. At the same moment another of our caravaneers remarked, "There is something far above the bird." And he shouted in his astonishment. We all saw, in a direction from north to south, something big and shiny reflecting the sun, like a huge oval moving at great speed. Crossing our camp this thing changed in its direction from south to southwest. And we saw how it disappeared in the intense blue sky. We even had time to take our field glasses and saw quite distinctly an oval form with shiny surface, one side of which was brilliant from the sun.[94]

Another famous Russian, the occultist George Gurdjieff, also made the rounds in Tibet where he tutored the 13th Dalai Lama among others for nearly a decade.[95] Gurdjieff was fascinated by the legend of an underground kingdom called Agarthi. One legend states that survivors of the sunken continent of Atlantis built Agarthi over 60,000 years ago, and hidden there were rare manuscripts of esoteric lore. This secret, magical hidden land also goes by other names and spellings, such as Shambhala, Agartha, Valley of the Immortals and the land of Hsi Wang Mu – an important Chinese goddess who was probably extraterrestrial by all accounts. Many visitors have established that there are many mysterious caves and underground tunnels in Tibet and Mongolia. One of these tunnels is said to lead right up to an opening inside the Potala Palace in Lhasa, the Dalai Lama's former residence. There has been much speculation that the Rainbow Alliance and the muddlers have access to these caves and tunnels, so that one never knows what might pop out of them. As is the case with many underground tunnels in the United States, there have been ominous stories of people going in and never coming out.

On the brighter side, ever wonder why nearly every single Tibetan sage you read about gets enlightened in a cave? Yeshe Tsogyel was awoken by a sonorous voice that led her to a secret cave. Once in the cave, she had several mystical visions that soon melted away to leave her in a complete state of enlightenment. Pema O-Zer and her consort Rangrig Togden found a cave called 'Tiger Space of Rainbow Light' where they experienced a transcendental state and remained there as life-long practitioners of dzogchen. Even more recent lamas and masters have spent a considerable amount of time meditating in or near a cave. Students often seek out the caves where great adepts previously stayed. On Lama Surya Das' website, there is a picture of him standing outside of one. If there is an underground network of passages and caves leading to areas where our extraterrestrial friends might still reside as the legends hint, well we know what this means.

Atlantis and the Rama Empire of ancient India had a very advanced technology that included various sorts of flying machines.[96] Current UFOlogy research supports the viability of underground bases of ETs, perhaps in conjunction with the shadow government. There is some speculation that Agarthi is one of those ancient underground bases that may still be active.

Riding the Kalachakra

The constellation Ursa Major (the Great Bear) figures prominently in Tibetan mythology as having a special

connection with Shambala through a Universal Tree.[97]
Shambala is an allegorical kingdom and a literal one. One of its
kings is said to have traveled to India to meet the Buddha who
gave him the Kalachakra teachings to take back to Shambala for
safekeeping. Later, several noted adepts and disciples returned
to Shambala to retrieve the teachings for integration into the
Buddhist literature.

Kalachakra is a Sanskrit word meaning "time-wheel." It is
an esoteric teaching and practice based on ancient texts that
deeply reflect upon the cyclical nature of the universe – inner
and outer. Considered to be one of the highest yogic tantras in
Mahayana Buddhism, the Kalachakra's origins reflect the
influence of other Asian spiritual traditions as well. The outer
and inner Kalachakras refer to the macrocosm and microcosm,
and are the Eastern equivalent of the Hermetic Axiom. A third
Kalachakra refers to the practice steps or spiritual method
leading up to a Kalachakra awakening. One of these methods
involves a Tibetan form of astrology.

The Tibetan word for Shambala is *bde 'byung* which means
"the source of happiness." Just like there are two main
Kalachakras, there are two main Shambalas – the external city
of Shambala associated with legend, and the inner Shambala
that is within the vessel of the human mind and body. Some
descriptions of journeys to Shambala symbolically represent the
transformation of the mind and body, much like the allegorical
tales of Western alchemy:

> The outer journey to Shambhala bears close relation
> to the completion stage practice of Kalachakra, the
> physical obstacles on the way represent inner barriers
> that must be faced at the psychic centers. These
> barriers form the knots that block the proper energy
> flow through the psychic nervous system, as such,
> they correspond to mental *defilements*, such as
> ignorance and lust, that limit our awareness… In
> taking the inner journey to Shambhala, we strive to
> regain this direct awareness of a child with all its
> sense of wonder and awe. But we cannot do so by

retreating in the past and attempting to become children again. We have lost the innocence that enabled us to experience the world directly. We cannot simply ignore or wish away the screen of preconceptions that now obscures our vision. We have to face ourselves and see what we have done to our minds. Only by becoming aware of our illusions and how we cling to them can we free ourselves from their power and awaken a fresh and direct awareness of the world around us. Rather than to go back, we have to go forward to a new and wiser innocence – one that combines the wonder of a child with the wisdom of a sage. By treating the ordinary events of daily life as we did the magical features of the journey to Shambhala, we may be able to uncover the hidden aspects of ourselves that we need to know in order to awaken the deeper mind.[98]

I suspect it is those hidden aspects that also enable one to find the external Shambala. This ancient spiritual center may be like the Atlantean Avalon – lost in the mists of time, and only accessible through an interdimensional porthole. Even His Holiness the Dalai Lama hints at this. During his 1985 Kalachakra empowerment in Bodhgaya, he told the audience that Shambala is not an ordinary place:

Although those with special affiliation may actually be able to go there through their karmic connection, nevertheless it is not a physical place that we can actually find. We can only say that it is a pure land, a pure land in the human realm. And unless one has the merit and the actual karmic association, one cannot actually arrive there.[99]

Yet he admits to having come close, because on several occasions during repeated trips to Mongolia, his caravan always stopped at a particular location where the horses became very uneasy. The Dalai Lama attributed their skittish behavior to the fact that they were "passing through the forbidden territory of

Shambhala."[100]   The Hungarian philologist, Csoma de Koros, who lived in a Tibetan Buddhist monastery from 1827 to 1830, also confirmed the location of Shambhala in southern Mongolia. It was said that the Panchen Lama, head of the Tashi Lhunpo monastery near Shigatse, actually issued passports to Shambhala, but never disclosed its true location.[101]   The Shigatse monastery is supposed to be near one of the main entrances to the underground kingdom of Agarthi.

The Kalachakra also has a dark side reflected in some of its stranger teachings.   The fact that Shambala probably was an ancient extraterrestrial outpost at one time is revealed by these teachings because they deal extensively with machines, aircraft, and other devices.

UFOlogist, Sally Sheridan, asserts that the Kalachakra predicts an invasion during our time and provides advice on how to handle it.   The Kalachakra evidently gives detailed instructions on how to build various machines to use in defense against the invaders.

> The Kalachakra predicts that one of our worse problems will be that the powers of negativity will be "tampering with the tables."   They are referring to astrological tables and Dr. Berzin specifically says on the tape that in our times that would mean messing with the programming of our computers! . . .   This dark age will last until the year 2424 A.D. when a "great war" will begin in India.   The human race will be rescued from total destruction by the armies of Shambhala riding "flying horses" and "boats that fly in the air."   A Golden Age will begin in A.D. 2424.[102]

Sheridan compiled this information from three sources: a tape of a lecture given in English by Dr. Alexander Berzin at Thubten Dhargye Ling, a Tibetan Buddhist Center in Los Angeles on May 3, 1988; tapes of a series of lectures given at the same center by the Venerable Geshe Gyeltsen on March 2, 1989; and a book she received from the center.   The words in quotation marks are the words of Dr. Berzin and Ven. Geshe Gyeltsen.

One can only wonder if the flying boats and horses refer to extraterrestrial craft piloted by members of the Rainbow Alliance. That means the invasion has already begun and that it's most likely a metaphor representing the pernicious activities of the muddlers.

Researcher Bernard Roy left an interesting message on an Internet message board on the Asian link. He said, "The late Karmapa lama . . . once told me outright that Tibetans have been in touch with extraterrestrial civilizations for centuries, and that the vehicles in which the E.T.'s travel can move as easily to and from other dimensions as they can maneuver in this one."[103] One might question such an assertion if another student of the late Karmapa had not asserted something similar.

Palden Jenkins, in an incisive essay on the topic, reveals that he was a student of the late Karmapa. The late lama may have revealed similar secrets to him. Jenkins speaks of the Council of Nine, a collective of higher beings who communicated through Phyllis Schlemmer some details about our cosmic existence and our future. He claims that the Council of Nine are not necessarily ETs, but moreover "cosmic beings of a high order who seem to act in the universe as a sort of executive committee (for want of a better analogy) dealing with the balance-of-energy aspect of universal creation and maintenance."[104] This sounds largely like our Rainbow Alliance. Jenkins adds that this Council of Nine works through all sorts of beings – including but not limited to ETs and humans, especially creative teachers and artistic geniuses. Again, these agents may or may not be aware of the Council of Nine, for much is being accomplished on subliminal levels.

One more interesting note about the Karmapa: Buddhist tradition says that seeing the Karmapa in his black hat is especially auspicious. There is a photograph of the Karmapa where he is pointing to this black hat on top of his head. Right above his head on the wall hanging behind him is an emblem that looks very much like the Anunnaki winged symbol for the planet Nibiru.

Rama and the Blue-Skinned People

Oral history, legend and lore all reflect that there was once a great pre-Vedic empire in the Indus Valley called Rama. It was an advanced, matriarchal civilization with all the markings of a planned community that seemingly suddenly appeared out of nowhere. Archeologists are still unearthing evidence of it, especially in the ancient cities of Harrapa and Mohenjo-Daro. This empire was ruled by the figure we associate with Inanna of Anunnaki royalty, previously mentioned, probably known as Tara in the Indus Valley region. In the Indus Valley as in the Sinai Peninsula there is evidence of a catastrophic nuclear war. When Mohenjo-Daro was first excavated, archeologists were surprised to find numerous skeletons scattered about the city, just lying in the streets, holding hands. "It was as if some horrible doom had taken place, annihilating the inhabitants in one fell swoop."[105] Scholars reported these skeletons to be among the most radioactive ever found, some having levels in excess of fifty times that which is normal, putting them on par with those found at Nagasaki and Hiroshima.[106] Besides other archeological evidence of a nuclear blast, such as fused walls and green glass, records of Mesopotamian, Egyptian and Indian origin talk about these wars.

Any differentiation that exists between these ancient cultures is slight. For instance, building materials vary due to differences in region and climate. But the unmistakable imprint left by the Anunnaki is clearly seen in the symbols, artifacts and life style patterns. For that it was a very advanced civilization is evidenced by the fact that every house had a bathroom as part of a well designed sewer system.

Curiously, a text written in a mysterious undeciphered pictographic script has been found in the ancient city of Harrapa, possibly indicating a foreign presence antedating the Anunnaki.[107] The same script has also been found on Easter

254

Island. Easter Island, famous for its monolithic heads, is thousands of miles away in a remote part of the south Pacific, and has long been thought to be a remnant of the lost continent of Lemuria or Mu.

Unlike the Mesopotamian and Egyptian civilizations that lasted for several thousand years, Inanna's kingdom was short-lived. Sitchin gives a fascinating account of the various Anunnaki escapades of that time in his book, *The Wars of Gods and Men*. It appears that the warmongering brothers were not solely responsible for the decline and destruction of the new Indus Valley settlement. Inanna, after having been promoted to the council of the twelve ruling Anunnaki, felt that she was short-changed and wanted to put her new domain on equal footing with that of Mesopotamia. So she flew back there in one of her "flying boats" and allegedly stole some pretty significant "MEs" from Enki. According to Sitchin,

> Though they are constantly referred to, the nature of the ME is not clear, and scholars translate the term as "divine commandments," "divine powers," or even "mythic virtues." The ME, however, are described as physical objects that one could pick up and carry, or even put on, and which contained secret knowledge or data. Perhaps they were something like our present-day computer chips, on which data, programs, and operational orders have been minutely recorded. On them the essentials of civilization were encoded.[108]

This incident only escalated hostilities between the siblings leading to all out war.

Speaking of "flying boats," an ancient Sanskrit text called the *Vimaanika Shastra* or "Science of Aeronautics" was translated into English during the mid-seventies by G. R. Joyser, founder and former director of the International Academy of Sanskrit Research. It is basically a comprehensive manual and instructional guide for building, maintaining, and piloting anti-gravitic aircraft used during the Raman empire. It is so detailed that it even includes instructions on how to manufacture food in a concentrated, condensed pill-like form for the pilots or astronauts. It also includes extensive sections on different kinds of metals and how to work with them, and how to manufacture specific high tech weaponry for employing aboard the *vimanas* or ancient aircraft. The descriptions and instructions are so elaborate, that the anxiously awaited newly translated transcript was circulated among interested parties all over the world, many noted for their affiliation with research in related fields of science. The complete text accompanied with detailed diagrams is included in *Vimana Aircraft of Ancient India and Atlantis* by David Hatcher Childress.

Childress feels that the Caduceus, also known as the "magic wand of Mercury" (one of the symbols for Enki) also representing electromagnetic flight and cosmic energy, is a simplified diagram of a Mercury Vortex Engine. The Mercury Vortex Engine is just one of many anti-gravitic propulsion devices that were used in the vimanas.[109] He also points to modern technological research derived from the interaction of high frequency sound waves with liquid mercury. This is significant because Atlantis was known for its sonic technology, remnants of which remain in the various esoteric traditions.

For the short time that Inanna ruled in the Indus Valley, a cultured people emerged known as the Dravidians that were peaceful, matrifocal, and devoutly faithful to their goddess. Inanna was responsible for instituting *the Great Rite* or "sacred marriage" which became a central practice for all goddess-centered traditions around the world. She was also responsible for establishing the matrifocal faith of Dakini Tantra that continues to influence all Eastern esoteric traditions to this day. Tantra is a mystical and magical practice of the perception that everything everywhere is interconnected and woven together, reinforcing the Hermetic Axiom: "What is Here is Elsewhere. What is not Here, is Nowhere."

Sadly, much of the pre-Vedic feminine focus of tantric practice today has been minimized, if not outright dismissed. Large-scale destruction of sacred statues depicting unconsorted goddesses and female oral sexuality has been ongoing for some time. The majority of latter day patriarchal Buddhist tangkhas show the female partner as smaller, squashed, and subsumed – as if she is totally overshadowed, engulfed and consumed by the dominant male. Her neck is uncomfortably and abnormally stretched back as if she is being forced to submit. And she's never smiling. I always cringe when I see those contorted forms. Of course, to be fair, I suppose there is a counter-balance with statues and images of wrathful yoginis triumphantly stepping on top of men drinking blood from skullcaps!

An interesting pervasive imagery throughout the Eastern literature is that of blue-skinned people or blue Buddha forms and dakinis. The one with which many people are familiar is the figure of Krishna in the *Bhagavad Gita*. This could be based on an ancient memory of extraterrestrials who appeared to have a blue cast about them. Modern contact experiences have also involved similar looking extraterrestrials. Short humanoids no more than three feet tall with a bluish cast to their skin have been sighted frequently in northern Mexico. At any rate, the Vedas and other ancient texts contain many references to these blue-skinned beings. Some folks claim that their descendants still live in the Himalayas. It is also speculated that the expression "true blue blood" may have originated from references to the "royal" bloodline established by the Anunnaki consisting of their blood combined with human blood.

In her travels throughout Tibet, Lama Alexandra David-Neel once encountered a woman considered to be a "lhano" – a goddess "who has assumed human form."[110] She was told that the distinguishing mark of such a character from the "fairy race" is a face with a bluish tint. The woman indeed had skin that appeared more mauve or bluish than normal, and had an unusual presence about her.

Dragons, Nagas, and Snakes, Oh My!

When the Kurgans invaded lower Asia around 2000 B.C.E., they found a peaceful, matriarchal civilization inhabited by strange beings including Nagas and their dragon culture. These days, Easterners think of nagas as symbolically representing serpent spirits that inhabit waterways and the underworld. Some believe they are real creatures. In *The Sirius Mystery*, Robert Temple discusses at length Sirian extraterrestrials that were aquatic in nature. Many other writers on UFO/ET phenomena have indicated that whales and dolphins might be descendants of these beings, if not actual manifestations of them from time to time.

Some historical texts speculate that the nagas were an ancient Indian race about which little is known, though their influence is evident in all the serpent-centered iconography, snake temples, and snake charmers of the region. According to *The Encyclopedia of Tibetan Symbols and Motifs*, "The cosmology, domains, activities, qualities, and castes of the nagas define them as inhabiting a realm of existence and social structure approaching the complexity of the human realm."[111] All accounts are probably correct to some degree, because nagas, like many mystical beings, are truly shape-shifters at heart. According to Pinkham,

> The Serpents of Wisdom of India's Dragon Culture were called Nagas, meaning Serpents. Their definitive symbol was the Royal Cobra, a version of the "evolved serpent," which represented Spirit united with and accelerating the vibratory frequency of matter. While serving as priest kings and hierophants in Bharata Varsha (India's ancient name), these Nagas preserved sacred traditions which stretched back to the very dawn of time. Some of their predecessors had arrived as missionaries from the Motherlands, while others had received inspiration directly from Spirit while meditating in the solitary retreats within their native India. With

258

their timeless wisdom, the Nagas formulated many of
the spiritual philosophies and practices of the current
cycle, such as Yoga and Buddhism, which have led
much of the world's population down a path of
enlightenment.[112]

Of course, the esoteric teaching is that the early nagas were
genuine serpents of wisdom of extraterrestrial origin.
Nagarjuna, the great Indian Buddhist sage who lived around
100 B.C.E., was responsible for giving us the quintessential
Prajna Paramita, the sutra on the perfection of wisdom. The
eminent Buddhist scholar Robert Thurman informs us,

> The legend goes that Nagarjuna was approached by
> *nagas* (dragons) in human form after one of his
> lectures at the monastery of Nalanda. They invited
> him to their undersea kingdom to see some texts they
> thought would be of great interest to him. He went
> with them magically under the sea and discovered a
> vast treasure trove of the Mahayana Sutras – not only
> the many versions of the *Prajnaparamita* but also the
> *Inconceivable Liberation*, the *Jewel Heap*, the *Lotus*,
> and the *Pure Land* Sutras. Nagarjuna spent fifty
> earth years studying these texts, and then he brought
> them back into human society and promulgated them
> throughout India.
>
> He later wrote under his own authorship the
> masterwork *Wisdom: The Root Verses of the Central
> Way*, in which he elaborated a systematic program of
> critical meditations that lead the practitioner into the
> understanding of samadhi of emptiness and relativity.
> He wrote other philosophical, meditational and
> ethical works over the next centuries, until going
> away with the *nagas* a second time, this time to the
> "Northern Continent," Uttarakuru (maybe what we
> now call *America*). There he discovered other
> treasured teachings and taught the local populations
> many spiritual and practical things. When he
> returned to India for the last time, he taught the

Unexcelled Yoga Tantras, especially the *Esoteric Communion*, founding the seminal "Noble" tradition of the practice of perfection stage yoga. His Tantric great adept persona is also included in the semi-esoteric "direct mind transmission" tradition known as Ch'an and Zen in East Asia. Overall, Nagarjuna is associated with the angelic bodhisattva Manjushri, the archetype of transcendent wisdom, and is considered the pioneer of the wisdom teachings in the human realm.[113]

Thurman uses code phrases like "earth years" -- "human realm" -- "undersea kingdom" and speaks of a mysterious continent called "Uttarakuru" which he suggests might be America, but could just as well be Atlantis, as they could have been one and the same before the flood. Many Buddhist sages were visited frequently by extraterrestrials that maintained a UFO base under the sea, as they still do today. I suspect that Nagarjuna was a hybrid or a full-blooded naga himself, as it is said he lived over 600 years.[114] The Anunnaki and their Biblical offspring were known for their long life spans. At any rate, the work of Nagarjuna and another great naga sage, Patanjali, did much to establish one of the most influential schools of Eastern wisdom known today. The tenets of Patanjali's *Yoga-Sutras* are the Eastern equivalent of the principles of Western alchemy.

The *Mahanagas*, meaning great nagas, were exceptional *siddhas* – spiritual sages and adepts with fully developed "siddhis" or extrasensory powers, and were regarded as perfected human beings. Lord Shiva was a powerful naga of possible Atlantean origin, as some scholars speculate he was associated with the Egyptian figure of Osiris. The sacred mysteries of sexual polarity, represented by the snake, became the foundation for all forms of yoga, which means union. Many ancient god forms are androgynous, meaning that they have united all polarities within themselves. Hatha yoga, the yoga that focuses on physical body postures, is a spiritual practice that seeks to realize the essence of the spiritual or energy body through the material, uniting the personal with the universal.

Awakening the kundalini is a process closely associated with these ancient spiritual practices. The kundalini has long been referred to as the "serpent power" that travels up the spine stimulating all the chakras until they are fully opened, precipitating cosmic awareness. The human spine closely resembles an undulating serpent. The earliest traces of yoga, not surprisingly, have been found in the ancient Raman cities of Harrapa and Mohenjo-Daro, the cities over which Inanna presided. Shiva, associated with Osiris, was more than likely one of Inanna's main consorts, as she is sometimes associated with the Egyptian Isis.

Buddhism was born in India before it spread to Tibet and other Asian countries. Therefore, its roots have intimate connections with the remains of the Raman empire. The Raman empire was so named after Rama, the hero in the ancient Hindu epic called the *Ramayana*.

Rama was a holy prince. His bride, Sita, was kidnapped by Ravan, the serpent king of Ceylon. Rama chases Ravan's army across India with his own army of monkeys under the command of the monkey-general Hanuman. Hanuman and his monkey soldiers enabled Rama to rescue his bride by building a bridge of boulders across the water to the mainland of the island kingdom of Ceylon. Now get this: Hanuman was conceived as a result of Shiva feeding a sacred cake to Anjan, the ape. The author R.A. Boulay believes this is a direct reference to the Anunnaki's genetic experiments in the creation of humankind.[115]

Boulay has a Master's degree in history and is a former cryptologist for the National Security Agency (NSA). He published a unique little book called *Flying Serpents and Dragons*, all about humanity's reptilian past. Many of his conclusions parallel those made by Sitchin and others. But because of his association with the NSA, much information in his book is open to question. The NSA is one of the major muddlers in the UFO/ET cover-up. Yet overall, his insights into the truth behind the myths and folktales of the time, for example, are probably harmless.

Boulay writes that early Chinese traders regarded Ceylon as the home of the nagas -- a land where strange serpent-like beings dwelled.[116] Ravan is described as an evil naga who fed on humans and drank the blood of his enemies. In battle he would sometimes use a special "naga weapon" that allowed him to paralyze his foes and then drain their life force. This sounds like an early form of vampirism. Boulay asserts that a faction of the Anunnaki became cannibalistic. Evidence that cannibalism was practiced in early Neolithic cultures where the Anunnaki settled has been found in archeological sites in the Anatolia region. Other authors speculate that the origin of the vampire legend is based on such creatures living in this neighboring region to the area later known as Transylvania.

D.J. Conway, in her book, *Dancing with Dragons,* writes:

> The Nagas were known for their great magickal powers and the *pearls of great price that they carried in their foreheads.* The Nagas, also patrons of lakes, rivers, rain, and clouds, lived in wonderful palaces, often visited by the gods. But as with all dragons in whatever form, the Nagas were capable of killing people and causing problems when annoyed. There are stories of their creating drought, pestilence, and great suffering when humans broke their rules. (Emphasis added.)[117]

Although many of these early nagas and Serpents of Wisdom were often highly regarded as spiritual sages, there were some bad apples too. Even modern day Buddhists consider the invocation of nagas in their rituals to be a risky endeavor not to be taken lightly because of their problematic nature. Boulay reports that early contacts with these nagas as reported in the literature reflect they had friendly and hostile natures. The Indian epic, the *Mahabharata*, tells a story about a great snake sacrifice. Boulay feels that it was deliberately construed to symbolically destroy the nagas and erase them from history.[118]

Nagas featured prominently among the Dravidians, who were said to be the result of matings between the serpent-gods and humanity, paralleling the Sumerian and Biblical accounts. Boulay relates,

> The ancient *Book of Dzyan*, probably the oldest of Sanskrit sources, speaks of a serpent race which descended from the skies and taught mankind. The recovery of this ancient source from obscurity was accomplished by the theosophist, Madam H.P. Blavatsky who spent three years in Tibet, Bhutan, and Sikkim accumulating the thousands of Sanskrit sources which were compiled into the *Book of Dzyan*. According to this book, the Sarpa or Great Dragons were the Fifth Race to inhabit the world. The Fourth Race was a race of giants who had lived before the Deluge but were wiped out by that catastrophe. The book relates how the serpent gods or dragons redescended after the Deluge and instructed man in the arts of civilization. These serpent-gods had a human face and the tail of a dragon; they founded the divine dynasties on Earth and are believed to be the ancestors of our current civilization, the Fifth Race of the *Book of Dzyan*. The leader of these gods was called "The Great Dragon."[119]

The serpent god with a human face and a reptilian tale closely resembles the description given to the fishtailed Babylonian Oannes. An artifact excavated from the Graeco-Roman era shows the gods Isis and Osiris with serpent tales intertwined. Serapis was a later name for Osiris, similar to the term Sarpa referenced above. Cecrops, the mythical founder and first king of Athens is shown with a fish or serpent-like tail. Figures like these can be found all over the world.

Pinkham writes about an early extremist sect of nagas called the Kapalikas, who in their efforts to actualize a more direct way of accessing nondual awareness, were responsible for developing the symbolic use of skullcaps or *kapalas* as begging bowls, pots and ceremonial implements.[120] This tradition continues to this day and is important to the spiritual iconography of Tibetan Buddhism. Generally, the skullcap represents wisdom. Yet in tantric ritual, the meaning can be more complex and multilayered, as with any other symbol.

Then came Shakyamuni Buddha, otherwise known as Siddhartha and later Gautama Buddha. He gets his name from the fact that his family was part of the royal lineage of Shakya kings in fifth century B.C.E. The Shakyas were naga kings. Their symbol, the golden cobra, was found in the casket of one of Siddhartha's royal family members.[121] Several nagas were instrumental in providing guidance to the young Buddha throughout his life. The great naga Shiva eventually became a symbol for the cosmic void or transcendental state associated with nirvana. When Siddhartha awakened to his true nature and realized oneness with this cosmic void, a great cobra with seven heads protectively hovered over him. This cobra is said to represent the "Primal Serpent Goddess" who "always attends to the needs of those united with her lord, Shiva."[122]

China had its share of great serpents of wisdom whose forms became immortalized in the beautiful diversity of the Chinese dragon. A clay human head with a snake slithering up to its crown dated around 4500 B.C.E. suggests knowledge of the kundalini force in the Neolithic era in that region. The early Chinese serpents of wisdom were called the Lung Dragons, also known as the Wu or Immortals.[123] Their sacred teachings about oneness and polarity are best represented by the ancient symbol of yin yang. Around 500 B.C.E., a special spiritual philosophy known as Taoism or "the way" emerged from the notable dragon sage, Lao Tzu. This beautiful spiritual perspective eventually influenced almost every other spiritual tradition in Asia, especially the ones dealing with the development of martial arts and esoteric energy anatomy.

The great dragon sage, Hsu, is known for reviving the ancient practice of internal alchemy. In the east as in the west, alchemy suffered a degree of debasement by shortsighted materialists trying to effectuate immortality by external means only. To one of these deluded alchemists, Hsu remarked, "The only effective furnace is the one you carry behind your navel and the only safe receptacle for the completed pill lies within your skull a few hairs breaths' from the crown."[124] This statement contains direct references to important parts of the body intimately associated with the physiology of enlightenment.

In Vajrayana Buddhism, tantric rituals are introduced to students in the form of "empowerments." One of these rituals is called "The Rite of the Naga." This practice is a direct invocation of the nagas. Buddhists view nagas as potentially problematic, therefore they have developed a specific protocol for contacting them. Accordingly, there are specific days and times that are best for doing this. The contemporary Buddhist adept, Chogyal Namkhai Norbu, explains, "It's never a good idea to go to a person to say or do something when that person is very busy or nervous. It's better to go when he or she is happy, relaxed and feels good. We call this *lutheb*, and the practice should be done only on days which are favorable or neutral for the Nagas."[125]

The fact that they view these nagas as very real beings is evidenced by a little manual by Norbu entitled *The Practice for the Naga*. The manual describes the ritual of transmission used to evoke the Nagas. Norbu describes eight different classes of Nagas in detail, and indicates that offerings to them should be made through *samaya*. He further indicates that communication with these beings is potentially very disruptive, and that "great realized beings" have manifested in the form of powerful entities, such as Avalokitesvara in the Mahakala form and Vajrapani in the Rahula form, in order to maintain control over these Nagas. Again, he stresses the importance of making sure that the *samaya* is in place in terms of the Naga's promise of obedience to these greater illumined beings, and that this is the only suitable way to contact them.[126]

First of all, *samaya* is the Sanskrit word for commitment, bond or vow, generally referring to the Bodhisattva vow, or in

Western terms, a commitment to the Great Work. Taking that vow enables us to contact intelligence from higher realms, including other beings. Norbu then openly speaks of calling upon the aid of enlightened beings in order to "control" the nagas. This is probably just a methodology to ensure that the "right" nagas are contacted. As with other sentient beings, there are helpful ones and not so helpful ones. Some can be downright mischievous. Therefore, in invoking the energy of the Higher Self in the form of a Buddha, protective measures are taken. This is done in Western ritual as well: The Holy Guardian Angel is always called upon as a preliminary measure in order to protect and seal the magic circle. Also, this guarantees that any communication received will be filtered through consciousness with a minimum amount of distortion and impurity.

In practice, this is precisely what all sages and magicians around the globe have done and continue to do in order to establish other worldly contact. Norbu continues the tradition in the manner of John Dee, Aleister Crowley, and Joseph Smith. What Norbu has described is no different. While he contends that only "lower-level" nagas can be contacted through this ritual, that does not preclude the possibility of contacting nagas of higher intelligence in ways that he does not immediately reveal. Some Buddhist schools are overly traditional and authoritative in their approach, insisting on spoon-feeding their students, underestimating the ability of those students to awaken on their own without the direct supervision of the teacher. Fortunately, this trend is changing with the advent of more open-minded and progressive teachers, such as Lama Surya Das.

At any rate, let's not forget that ritual has a symbolic component as well as a literal one. The best way to contact any "other-worldly" beings such as nagas or extraterrestrials is by contacting the nature they represent already deep within ourselves. Thus do we realize our oneness with the universe and all beings in the cosmos.

Machig Lapdron and Mystical Sky-Dancers

This brings us to the topic of angels, dakinis, and other supposedly "supernatural" beings and what their true identities might be. Dakinis are especially interesting when considering UFO/ET phenomena because the word dakini literally means "sky goer." Tsultrim Allione, an expert on the divine feminine in Buddhism, says that the dakini "represents the everchanging flow of energy with which the yogic practitioner must work in order to become realized. She may appear as a human being, as a goddess – either peaceful or wrathful – or she may be perceived as the general play of energy in the phenomenal world."[127] Allione goes on to say that under certain conditions, even an "unenlightened" woman or situation could suddenly appear as a dakini, so that the dakini experience is not just limited to paranormal expressions of energy or very realized women. Yet they can and do exist as very real separate entities on their own, she admits, in her tapes on the Chod practice. Call them and they'll come, she says. And you better be ready when they do because by their very nature they will precipitate some very strange experiences. "The world is not as solid as we think it is, and the more we open to the gaps, the more wisdom can shine through and the more the play of the dakini energy can be experienced. The primary way to relax the ego's grasp is to practice meditation."[128] And as we've learned, meditation is the primary spiritual practice in all mystery schools. Allione continues,

> Being a dynamic principle, the dakini is energy itself; a positive contact with her brings about a sense of freshness and magic. She becomes a guide and a consort who activates intuitive understanding and profound awareness, but this energy can turn suddenly and pull the rug out from under you if you become too attached and fixated. This can be painful. When the energy becomes blocked and we feel the pain caused by our fixation, this is the

267

> wrathful dakini. Her anger pushes us to let go of this
> clinging and enter her mysterious home.[129]

Allione asserts that the dakini often makes her first appearance in someone's life when that person is progressing to an experiential understanding of reality from a previously intellectual approach. How often do we hear of ordinary, practical persons immersed in the world of duality having a UFO/ET experience, and suddenly their lives are changed forever. They cannot adequately understand what happened with their minds, but they know the experience to be deeply real and perhaps even paradigm shifting.

Tibetan lamas speak of "the twilight language" of the dakinis as being a series of symbols that cannot be translated by the rational mind, and therefore comprehended by the few, historically speaking. The Buddhist sage Milarepa said, "The teaching of the whispered lineage is the Dakini's breath." Although there appears to be a specific methodology for interpreting the language according to Buddhist scholars, it would make sense that any language used by ETs in an attempt to communicate with Earthlings would consist of symbols, sounds, colors, and pictures – the native language of the subconscious requiring an intuitive awareness for assimilation.

Machig Lapdron was a historical figure of profound significance in Tibetan Buddhism. Much beloved by Tibetans, she was considered a saint and a mystic, and has become known to many as the divine mother of all Buddhas. For details about her life, I recommend reading the biography written by Tsultrim Allione in *Women of Wisdom*, of which the following is a summary.

The events in Machig's life resemble those of a "star seed" or "walk-in" in UFOlogy terms. Machig Lapdron epitomizes the life of a dakini as well, because her major contribution to Tibetan Buddhism was developing the Chod practice. Chod means "to cut" – the sole purpose of the practice is to help the practitioner relinquish attachment to the sense of separateness and to cultivate a sense of egolessness and compassion for all sentient beings. The visualization used in this practice is pretty intense because it involves wrathful dakinis cutting up your body and offering it to hungry demons. Once you give the demons your most precious possession – your body, they are satiated and do not bother you anymore. Of course these demons are figurative and represent specific ways the ego attaches to unskillful ways of being in the world. The demons are thus overcome, making way for clear, unattached awareness to manifest. The Chod practice also involves the use of sound (a drum and a bell) in breaking up the blockages for the establishment of a higher vibratory rate. It's a practical ritual for overcoming fears of all kinds.

The conception of Machig Lapdron reads like a classic tale of abduction. That fateful night, Machig's mother, Bum Cham, dreamt of four white dakinis pouring purifying water over her head. Several dakinis then surrounded her up in the sky. The leader, a wrathful dark-blue dakini, cut Bum Cham's heart out, and all the dakinis ate it. Then they handled a conch shell that spiraled to the right. It made a strange sound that went all over the world projecting a luminous white "A[h]" – the universal sacred sound of oneness. The dakinis implanted this conch shell in Bum Cham's chest where her heart was. As they were doing this, Bum Cham had the sensation of colored lights coming from the dakinis and dissolving into her body. The dakinis then left with their light-filled leader, dissolving into the sky. The abduction was witnessed by Bum Cham's 16-year-old daughter, Bumme, who said, "Last night I also saw a white light in the sky and it entered into my mother illuminating the whole house." Though Bum Cham was 48 years old, she appeared to grow younger after the abduction.

The birth of Machig was an extraordinary experience with rainbow light and beautiful sounds, and the baby herself was an extraordinary newborn. She immediately inquired as to her mother's well-being, followed by another "A[h]." Machig sported a blazing red HRI (a sacred Tibetan syllable) on her tongue, and threads of rainbow-colored light emanated from her forehead. In fact, the little creature had three eyes, which delighted big sister Bumme. Bumme worried about what Dad would say about all this. Much to her relief, Dad, after examining the baby, acknowledged that Machig had all the signs of a dakini, even down to webbed hands and red luminous finger nails on which sacred letters magically appeared. The family decided to keep her at home in relative seclusion.

Machig grew into a child prodigy chanting complex mantras by heart by the age of three. When she learned to read and write, she became a very fast reader and advanced rapidly in her studies. Her teacher was so amazed that he proclaimed she was an extraordinary dakini. The family finally let her out in the world. Everyone who met her loved her, and the King even asked to meet her.

Machig began to evidence supernormal abilities and profound realizations. Once after a deep meditation, a group of special dakinis appeared before her in the sky and transmitted four special empowerments to her. The dakini leader predicted that Machig would have a profound, positive influence over humans and non-humans alike.

Machig eventually went to study with a lama who taught her dzogchen and the secrets of sound. It wasn't long before she mastered both. The teacher told her that she was the phantom body of the Great Mother Dakini. She received a specific teaching on "how to open the door to the sky for transference." When Machig was a teenager, her mother and sister Bumme "passed into the dimension of the sky" to join the dakinis.

Machig dreamed a dakini told her she would marry an Indian master. She wasn't convinced of this until two more dakinis appeared and repeated the same. After the marriage, she conceived a son -- another seemingly paranormal event characterized by luminous color and celestial vibrations. Machig had a daughter who, of course, was also a dakini.

Machig had several experiences with Nagas. On one occasion, the King of Nagas visited Machig. Her webbed hands present at birth suggest a possible genetic link to the Nagas.

Machig was eventually challenged by some skeptical teachers, yet she succeeded in proving herself credible and worthy of their respect. She did much to promote the practice of dzogchen, which is a meditation (or really non-meditation) technique that helps to open awareness to the realm of nonduality which is essential for understanding and developing multidimensional awareness, a prerequisite for meaningful extraterrestrial contact.

Machig passed on her teachings through her children and disciples. She ascended to the land of the dakinis at the age of 99. Before she left, her son who was also her main disciple, asked how he could contact her after she was gone. She responded with a beautiful song that is chanted to this day by Buddhist practitioners wishing to invoke her presence and the Divine Feminine she represents, which is sorely needed in this day and age.

The fact that no specific images of aircraft are described in the biography of Machig does not discount the idea that she could have been a hybrid or that her experiences with dakinis were extraterrestrial in nature. Many abductees do not always remember aircraft involved as much as they might remember beams of light coming through walls and similar phenomena. As the late Karmapa admitted, extraterrestrial travel doesn't always have to involve aircraft as we know it. Interdimensional travel can and often is characterized by transformations of light, sound, and material, and these experiences can be as varied as the individuals who experience them.

Amerindian Stardust

An extensive network of varieties of Serpents of Wisdom run up and down the North and South American continents. In South America, predominantly in the region of Peru, the ancient dragon culture of the Amarus emerged. Amaru is a Quechuan term meaning snake or serpent.[130] These Serpents of Wisdom directly influenced other South American cultures, such as the Incan empire. The scenic temple of Machu Picchu in the old language means "City of the Bird of Lightning." Machu Picchu was an ancient observatory. Local shamans refer to it as the "Crystal City" because of a high concentration of resonating quartz crystal in its granite. According to Pinkham, the quartz combined with the temple's unique geographical location on top of a secluded mountain make it ideal as a receiving/transmitting station for planetary and extraterrestrial communication.[131]

Eventually, the vast civilizations of the Olmec, Mayan, Aztec and Toltec spawned esoteric mysteries of their own. The writings of Carlos Castaneda and Miguel Ruiz run deep in these traditions. In fact, Castaneda's way of the Nagual is very similar to tantric Vajrayana Buddhism. Edward Plotkin has done a meticulous comparative study of these traditions in his delightful little book, *The Four Yogas of Enlightenment: Guide to Don Juan's Nagualism and Esoteric Buddhism.*[132]

The Olmec and Mayan civilizations yield the best evidence of extraterrestrial origination. The Olmec artifacts provide a direct link to visitors from the African continent. When the Anunnaki spread out all over the world looking for other places to settle and mine for gold, they visited the American continents and left their imprint. Sitchin provides convincing evidence for this in his Book IV of the Earth Chronicles, *The Lost Realms.*[133]

One of the major Central American gods was Quetzalkoatl, "the plumed serpent." Legend said that he would return some day. Therefore, when the Spaniards landed on the coast looking for gold, the Aztecs mistook them for representatives of Quetzalkoatl for two reasons: One, they knew Quetzalkoatl was considerably paler than them, as were the Spaniards, and two, the Spaniards made it clear they wanted gold. To the Aztecs and many Amerindians, gold was considered the property or gift of the gods, not a currency for exchange. We must ask ourselves how they came to believe this. Indeed, Sitchin provides the answer. Therefore, they were more than willing to give back to the gods what they believed originally belonged to the gods. Everyone knows the sad ending to that tale.

Sitchin theorizes that Quetzalkoatl was Anunnaki for several reasons; the most salient being that the Aztecs had a

272

creation myth that was identical to the Sumerian version about how we were genetically engineered:

> In the Sumerian text... the god Ea, collaborating with the goddess Ninti, "prepared a purifying bath." "Let one god be bled into it," he ordered; "from his flesh and blood, let Ninti mix the clay." From this mixture, men and women were created.[134]

The Aztec myth explains how Quetzalkoatl created humans by bringing precious bones to Cihuacoatl ("Serpent Woman"), a special goddess, who then mixed them with the god's blood into a special claylike substance:

> He gathered the precious bones; The bones of man were put together on one side, the bones of woman were put together on the other side. Quetzalkoatl took them and made a bundle... She ground up the bones and put them in a fine earthen tub. Quetzalkoatl bled his male organ on them.[135]

There could have been more than one Quetzalkoatl, as there was more than one Merlin and one Buddha. Sitchin equates the Mesoamerican god to the Egyptian god Thoth. The Egyptian and Mayan calendars and their pyramids among other textual and archeological artifacts provide an important link between the two cultures.

On the North American continent, Native American tribes were also steeped in "Serpent Wisdom." In tribes too numerous to mention evidence of a serpent clan abounds. As migrants from Atlantis and Lemuria, many native tribes retained much of the lore and wisdom from the lost civilizations, including knowledge of the great flood.

Mormons consider that the pale Mesoamerican god known as Quetzalkoatl could have been Jesus during his visit to the Americas after his resurrection. Mormon scholars have discovered striking similarities between Biblical tales and Amerindian legend. Could Jesus have, in fact, been one in a long line of "gods" to have visited the Americas? In order to ascertain that, we need to take a closer look at who Jesus really was.

Jesus the Globetrotter and "Buddhist Christianity"

The Essenes were a Hebrew religious sect formed to revive the esoteric wisdom school of the original serpent of wisdom, Enki. Therefore they were well versed in the Holy Qabalah and Hermetic Science. The Jewish priesthood was rife with hypocrisy and power struggle, prompting the Essenes to break away from the mainstream. They chose their spiritual leaders from the direct descendants of King David. Historian and author, Sir Laurence Gardner, has traced the hidden lineage of Jesus from that line all the way back to the original Anunnaki-bred Priest-Kings. Their human progeny were the heirs to that special "royal bloodline" supposedly enriched with a surplus of Anunnaki genetic material.[136]

The birth of Jesus was not the result of an accident or a true "immaculate conception." The Essenes followed many ancient customs, including the rite of the sacred marriage. They were also advocates of the philosophy of the Greek sage, Pythagorus, whom many believe was an earlier incarnation of Jesus. Pythagorus taught the esoteric side to astronomy and mathematics. Therefore, the conception and birth of their special King was predetermined and auspiciously timed. The event, as we know, wasn't confined to the headlines in Israel, but spread all over the world. Adepts everywhere knew that something big was about to happen, and sent their representatives to witness it. This wasn't about the birth of another exceptional sage -- the presence of a divine avatar was presaged. Pinkham relates,

> When the birth of Jesus finally occurred, news of a Messiah and future Grandmaster of both the Hebrew and worldwide Order of Serpents rapidly spread throughout Asia, Europe and Africa. Some branches

of the Serpents sent representatives laden with gifts for the divine infant. According to the Hindu Siddha, Swami Yogananda Paramahansa, three Indian Mahanagas or "wise men" were led to Bethlehem via signals broadcast from the heavens (perhaps by the Extraterrestrial Serpents).[137]

UFOlogists have long speculated that the star of Bethlehem may have been some type of extraterrestrial craft. There is also a painting from the Middle Ages showing the Madonna and child with UFOs flying in the background.

Most Christians know that Jesus obtained much of his training as a youngster in Egypt. What is not as well known is that he also traveled to east Asia to study with great sages there. Evidence of this fact was unearthed in 1887 by the Russian, Nicholas Notavich, during his visit to a Tibetan monastery. Jesus was known there as "Issa." According to Pinkham,

> The first leg of Jesus's journey, a two years passage through the arid deserts of Asia, ended safely in India. In the land of Bharat Jesus proceeded to become a faithful student of the ancient Vedanta philosophy and learned the path of yoga from numerous Mahanagas and Siddhas. Jesus also went on pilgrimages and visited many of India's holy cities and shrines, including the holy city of Serpents, Kashi, and the famous Jaganath temple in Orissa. At some point he is reputed to have traveled to a Buddhist monastery in the Himalayas and studied the doctrines and philosophy of the Shakyamuni.

> Leaving India at the age of 26, Jesus traveled first to Persepolis, the capital of Persia, where he studied the teachings of Zoroaster under the tutelage of the Magi priests. Continuing west, he journeyed to Athens in order to study with the renowned Greek philosophers and from there passed into Egypt via the port of Alexandria. Once upon the soil of ancient Khem, Jesus was escorted by high ranking Djedhi initiates to

Heliopolis where he learned the wisdom of the Thoth-Hermes Masters while preparing for his final initiation within the Great Pyramid.[138]

So here we see that East met West long ago, and that a most beautiful synthesis and consummation of the essence of both traditions is best exemplified in the life and teachings of Jesus Christ. A great place to gather insight into this approach to the mysteries is the web site of the Order of Nazorean Essenes – "a Buddhist branch of original Christianity seeking to explore and restore the ancient vegan, gnostic and tantric teachings of Yeshu, Miryai, and Mani."[139] Yeshu is the Nazorean name for Jesus, Miryai for Mary Magdalene, and Mani for the prophet of the Manicheans. One of the biggest cover-ups in religious history is the suppression of the truth about Mary Magdalene. Clues have surfaced from time to time in popular culture about the possibility of a sexual relationship between Jesus and Mary. That she might also have been one of his disciples is clear from the fact that he chose to appear first to her after his resurrection, much to the chagrin of his male disciples. The Order of Nazorean Essenes does even more to restore Mary to her rightful place. She is not only student and wife of Jesus, yet more accurately his equal – a spiritual consort in the tantric tradition of Padmasambhava and Yeshe Tsogyel.

The Order of Nazorean Essenes was founded by an intriguing fellow who goes by several names such as Abba Yesai, Yesai Nasrai, Davied Asia Israel, yet he prefers to be called Yesai Nasrai. Yesai was born in 1955 near San Antonio, Texas. It appears that his first exposure to gnostic teachings may have come through the Mormon Church as he was growing up. At any rate, he has a diverse background and is no dilettante. His website alone is an enormous library of original sacred texts and authoritative essays, articles, and documents from respected sources on this vast subject. The tenets of his religious order are well researched and comprehensive. The focus of their purpose and spiritual practice integrates the esoteric with the practical. For instance, on a page describing the difference between a true Essene order and a counterfeit, he says:

> A true Order does not focus on the crucifixion of Christ on the Cross of Golgotha. A true Holy Order focuses on the crucifixion of the Heavenly Christ (Hibil-Ziwa & Zabriel) on the cross of light, and His/Her redemption from material imprisonment through the liberation of light particles entrapped in our world. It is not through the shed blood of a dying Savior 2000 years ago that we are "saved", but by liberation of the shed soul essence of Christ hidden within us that is saved from ignorance and darkness through the inner illumination of Nazirutha Enlightenment. The Blood of Christ that is shared in the sacramental chalice is the Light of Christ, the life-force of Jesus Palibitis, that is gathered from the world and sent upward to heaven once more. Certainly the death of Yeshua the Nazorean on the Cross represents his more universal crucifixion of Christ on the cross of the material universe, and certainly the person called Yeshua the Nazorean (Jesus of Nazareth) was an earthly incarnation of the heavenly Christ (also called Primal Man and Hibil Ziwa), but the death of his flesh on Golgotha was not the significant redeeming factor in our salvation. Our salvation is a result of the combined effects of our own spiritual endeavors to become enlightened and pure, balanced with the grace and assistance afforded us by the redeeming program of the Heavenly Christ and His and Her Primeval sacrifice on the Cross of Light.[140]

The Cross of Light, according to the Manicheans, is the Buddha nature of the ecosystem:

> Manichaeans taught that the "Suffering Christ" latent within matter was a result of an original fall of the Primordial Pair (Yeshu and Miryai). This Primordial Pair is an archetype of each of our own souls and the

> Cross of Light represents the scattered remains of our decomposed spiritual bodies lost when we descended down into these darkened universes.[141]

As mentioned previously, it is highly probable that humanity was genetically demoted by the Anunnaki. An impairment to the genes was made, much like a mechanic might disable a vital part of an automobile engine, but it was not *removed* – just disabled. In other words, certain switches inside the brain were turned off. However, in learning how to correctly adjust and realign specific physiological processes, the switches can be turned back on – the so-called spiritual organs can be reactivated. That is the purpose of all true mystery schools. Clark's order has picked up on this, and like other occult schools, devised an elaborate training program complete with ritual endowments in conjunction with eating consecrated vegan foods for this purpose. In consecrating the vegan foods on an altar, they gather latent light sparks for later weaving into what they call a spiritual *Rainbow Robe*. The Rainbow Robe is equivalent to the rainbow body of light from the Buddhist literature and the dragon body of the Serpents of Wisdom. It also represents the resurrected body of Christ:

> It is a subtle spiritual body woven from the subtle living portion of the Light Cross. It is not visible to the physical eye. Like later Qabbalists, Manichaeans sought to redeem the fallen world by returning these sparks of the fragmented spiritual body of the first Primal Pair back to Heaven. By this process they hoped to amass sufficient merit, as well as the raw material itself, toward a reconstitution of their original spiritual body.[142]

Yesai's Order also advocates the practice of dzogchen. Most of what's printed about dzogchen states that its origins are in the shamanistic Bon roots of Tibetan Buddhism. According to Yesai, the prophet Mani was responsible for bringing the original teachings to Zhang-zhung (now northwestern Tibet) from Tazik in Central Asia, formerly Persia or present day Iran. Later, Indian sages like Padmasambhava were instrumental in restoring the teachings as a systematic practice into the transmission of the Nyingmapa lineage of Tibetan Buddhism.

Mar Mani Hayya was an enlightened adept born on April 14, 216 C.E. in a little village in southern Iraq. His name means "Living Spirit" or "Vessel of Life." According to Yesai, Mani claimed to synthesize and restore the true teachings of Gnostic Nazorean Christianity, Zurvan Zoroasterism, and Mahayana Buddhism. The vegan Manichaean faith profoundly influenced the Tibetan Buddhist, Taoist and Sufi traditions. His Christian disciples knew him as Paraclete, his Persian disciples believed he was the Zoroastrian savior Saoshyant, and his Buddhist followers saw him as the Avatar Maitreya.

Yesai says that the middle eastern influence on the development of dzogchen and Tibetan Buddhism, specifically that of the Hermetic Qabalists, is evident in the 32 paths of the Bon tradition corresponding to the 32 paths of the Qabalistic Tree of Life. It makes sense that the major impulse for the transmission of these esoteric teachings would come from the "cradle of life" – the area where civilization was cultivated under the influence of the Anunnaki.

Yesai's Order of the Nazorean Essenes is not without controversy. It appears that he is testing the same waters that engulfed Joseph Smith. Because his religion promotes the study and practice of tantric spirituality, great importance is placed upon the dynamics of sexual polarity and gender balance, especially in ritual. Recognizing the ancient teachings regarding sacred sexuality, they too believe that souls can engage in simultaneous multiple unions. In fact, Yesai states that both women and men practiced multiple marriages in ancient Tibet. Not only that, but other independent sources have witnessed polygamy and polyandry practices in Tibet as recently as the 1930s.[143]

The main headquarters for Yesai's Nazoreans is located in northern Arizona near Colorado City, a haven for Mormon fundamentalists practicing polygamy. A traditional Latter Day

Saints watchdog group alleges that Yesai's Order is a Satanic cult engaging in kidnapping, slavery, polygamy, and perverse sexual rituals. I doubt this is factual, as I cannot find any other reports to substantiate that claim.

It is true that Yesai's Order of Nazorean Essenes lives communally and endorses a liberal view of sexuality. They admit as much on their web site. They encourage strong matrimonial bonds and sanction heterosexual partnership. Though they tolerate lesbian affiliations, male homosexuality is discouraged because they claim it has adverse effects on the subtle energy body thus hampering the development of the Rainbow Robe. Yet essentially they respect personal freedom of choice and condemn no one for any belief or sexual practice.

The Nazorean Essenes follow the path of the *Lotus Born* which has a close affinity to the *White Sangha* of the early Nyingmapa school of Tibetan Buddhism that was heavily influenced by the Manichaean priests. Female adepts are prized and revered for their unique contributions and treated with the same respect as male initiates.

> Padmasambhava is understood, in the Ngakphang Sangha of the Nyimgma School, to represent Form or active-compassion (Ziwa radiance), and Yeshe Tsogyel is Emptiness or wisdom (Noorah Luminosity). All reality is seen as the dance of Padmasambhava and Yeshe Tsogyel. The male and female heads of the Lotus Born can be seen as earthly manifestations of these two Buddhas in cosmic dance. They represent the embodiment of Wisdom and Compassion. In the Lotus Born expression of the Mother Essence Lineage one needs a teacher of the opposite gender. It is said that: "Female teachers are role models for women and teachers for men – whereas male teachers are teachers for women and role models for men." Without due honor being given to Yeshe Tsogyel and her earthly representatives, males within the Lotus Born would be bereft of instructors.[144]

Therefore, the Nazorean Essenes see the Divine Feminine as an integral part of spiritual reality. Yesai speculates that the Mother Essence lineage was lost in 11th century Tibet when large monastic institutions began to encode the teachings and bias them toward the ever-encroaching forces of patriarchal control. The lineage that began with Yeshe Tsogyel ended with the death of Aro Lingma who had no daughters, yet had a son, Aro Yeshe. Therefore he inherited the position of lineage holder. It was at this time that the direct daughter line or matrifocal succession passed indirectly to the male-dominated institutions. For a time, however, a woman teacher's transmissions were still considered more powerful than a man's. Therefore Aro Yeshe entrusted most of the responsibility of teaching to his female disciples and rarely gave out instructions himself. This, however, was not enough to stem the tide that would eventually consolidate the power of dharma transmission and lineage holding in the hands of men. Ngak'chang Rinpoche states that the direct daughter line will re-emerge with greater power if a sufficient number of women become accomplished in these visionary methods. Therefore, the Nazorean Essenes are dedicated to restoring this ancient lineage of Mother Essence.

As is evident by the experiences of the early Mormons and other spiritual zealots with good intentions, sometimes teachings based on genuine truth can be distorted or misapplied in practice. Hopefully, this is not what is happening with the Nazorean Essenes. Ultimately, whatever this Buddhist branch of original Christianity is doing or not doing does not diminish the immense contribution already made by the Order toward restoring the deeper esoteric teachings of Gnostic Christianity and Mahayana Buddhism in a public forum that truly brings together the mystical origin of all the Eastern and Western mystery schools. As Jesus expressed: I am the way (Buddha), the truth (dharma), and the Life (sangha.)

The Extraterrestrial Telephone

Occult practices, such as yoga, Hermetic science, alchemy, astrology, especially the Qabalah, Tarot, and dzogchen, are ways in which we can attune ourselves to the higher vibrational frequencies by which we complete the Great Work and further the evolution of humanity as a whole. The study and practice of these disciplines also prepares us for conscious contact with ETs. Surely individuals who have caught a glimpse into other planes or dimensions of reality and who have had some experience with nonduality will be in much better shape to handle contact than those who haven't. They will also be better equipped to communicate with these beings, having been fully versed in the original language of sound, color, symbol, and vibration.

The Qabalah may be more than just a system to help humanity evolve to the level of our extraterrestrial ancestors -- it may actually represent their own cosmology. Author Neil Freer writes:

> Although for many centuries, due to the loss of its true meaning by the Rabbis, it has been interpreted as myth, metaphor, poetry, magic, mystery, allegory, the Cabalistic tradition has been rediscovered... to be a coherent body of high science. That high science, it appears, was based on a unified field concept of the universe that was taught to us by the Nefilim. The universe, understood as a cosmic field working according to an all-pervading law couched in the metaphor of self-reference, seems to have been viewed as a transcendental Unity. Previous to the departure of the Nefilim it was understood correctly by those humans who were taught it as a science and as a view of the universe. It may also have been correctly viewed as the closest thing to "religion," in our terms, that the Nefilim possessed. That is to say that the Nefilim had a respectful philosophical-scientific view of reality but they do not appear to

282

have practiced anything that we would call worshipful religion of a transcendental Being.[145]

An extensive study of the Qabalah requires exposure to Gematria, which is the art or science of determining relationships between the meanings of words based on their numerical values. The Hebrew and Greek alphabets attribute specific numerical values to each letter of the alphabet, which when added give a word a numerical value as well. Much insight can be gained from studying words with the same numerical values. Recently, the human genome was discovered by using mathematics and combinations of letters. Some UFOlogists feel that these codes were given to us long ago by our extraterrestrial ancestors and guarded by those who were initiated into the mystery schools. The Greek Hermes is the equivalent of the Egyptian Thoth – the god who presided over astronomy, mathematics, and the building of the pyramids. All of that depends on code and measurement, the supreme knowledge gifted to Earthlings by our extraterrestrial ancestors. Sitchin reminds us,

> "Everything that we know was taught to us by the gods," the Sumerians stated in their writings; and therein lies the foundation, throughout the millennia and unto our own times, of Science and Religion, of the discovered and the occult.[146]

Sitchin explores this presupposition at length in *The Cosmic Code*. Robert Temple in *The Sirius Mystery* has also touched upon the true identity of Hermes Trismegistus. Speaking from one of the ancient treatises, he writes, "Hermes came to earth to teach men civilization and then again 'mounted to the stars', going back to his home and leaving behind the mystery religion of Egypt with its celestial secrets which were some day to be decoded."[147] A correlation between the Egyptian god Anubis and Hermes is also made. Anubis had the body of a man and the head of a dog or jackal. Temple makes a good argument that the Sphinx is not a man with a lion's body at all but with a dog's body, hence a giant statue of Anubis. This would go along well with the fact that Sirius is often called the Dog Star. Anubis is also a figure that can be seen on Key 10 of the Tarot, *The Wheel of Fortune*. If the wheel is perceived to be the sphere of Earth, Anubis is positioned so that he is just ascending to the horizon. Temple points out an observation made by Plutarch:

> When Nephthys gave birth to Anubis, Isis treated the child as if it were her own; for Nephthys is that which is beneath the Earth and invisible, Isis that which is above the earth and visible; and the circle which touches these, called the horizon, being common to both, has received the name Anubis, and is represented in form like a dog; for the dog can see with his eyes both by night and by day alike. And among the Egyptians Anubis is thought to possess this faculty, which is similar to that which Hecate is thought to possess among the Greeks, for Anubis is a deity of the lower world as well as a god of Olympus.[148]

Temple explains:

> Isis represents the visible component of Sirius (Sirius A) while Nephthys, Isis's sister, the 'dark goddess', represents the invisible component, Sirius B. As we have seen previously, 'the circle' is the orbit of Sirius B, called Anubis. Anubis was also called 'the horizon'. 'Horizon' in Egyptian is *aakh-t*, and what has come to interest me more recently is that *aakh-t* is also the name of the Great Pyramid. It would seem therefore that another name for Anubis was *Aakhuti*, since it was used to mean 'the god who dwelleth in the horizon', and as we have seen from Plutarch, this is Anubis.[149]

Therefore we again see that truth is like an onion with many layers. The descent of spirit into the planes of form or involution is met with the ascent of flesh and the evolution or unfolding of awareness. Extraterrestrials may be able to pass so easily between dimensions simply because in their past evolution, they completed the descent and mastered the physical plane elsewhere. It might be that most of them are not on a separate journey than we are, but merely beyond us on the ascending angle of the arc. This is what the New Age term "ascension" really means.

Initiates of the Eastern and Western mystery schools become thoroughly familiar with the basic tools of sound, color and visualization. Students are taught these techniques perhaps never realizing another purpose behind what they're originally told. Of course the main work is to make our minds and bodies better instruments for service in furthering the evolution of all creatures. It only makes sense that one of the byproducts of that would be an increasing sensitivity to those creatures and an ability to communicate with them – those of this Earth and those who are beyond.

Return of the Holy Grail

In our exploration of extraterrestrial influence on the origin and development of the Mystery Schools, we've covered many angles and perspectives on process and theory. We've established that there were connections that cannot be ignored. We've seen how the connections were made and how the circle completes itself. East and West have been sharing and exchanging esoteric treasures for some time. It began long ago with the progeny of the Anunnaki and the forging of the new frontiers of an infant race. We saw how the race began to grow and bloom until the cosmic promise of divinity that was bestowed initially materialized through our great sages and spiritual leaders. Those seekers and sages began to spread out all over the globe. We've celebrated the incredible journeys of Jesus, Nagarjuna, Mani, Gurdjieff, Blavatsky and others too numerous to mention. And we've seen how many of these adepts inevitably impacted and manipulated the world's political affairs.

One such intriguing character was the colorful Italian, Comte Cagliostro, who was instrumental in bringing about the French revolution.[150] In the mid-1700s, he became a disciple of the Armenian mystic and alchemist, Althotas. He also became a Mason, a member of the Illuminati, and studied hypnosis under a fellow Mason, Dr. Mesmer. Cagliostro is credited for reviving Egyptian symbolism in Freemasonry, which he believed was the true source of the teachings. Under his influence, Freemasonry witnessed a resurgence in popularity and the establishment of lodges throughout Europe where the Qabalistic mysteries could be realized through ceremonial magic. After becoming embroiled in one too many political scandals, Cagliostro was exiled and eventually settled in England. One of his most important mentors was the illustrious legendary Comte de Saint-Germain. Regarding Saint-Germain, Howard writes,

> This mysterious occultist claimed Russian, Polish and Italian blood, and was an alchemist, spy, industrialist, diplomat and Rosicrucian. Saint-Germain was active in Europe from 1710 to 1789, during which time he always had the appearance of a man in his early forties. It is said that while studying occultism in the East Comte was introduced to the secret rites of Tantric sex magic which provided him with a technique to prolong his youth. In 1743 he lived for several years in London writing music, and he became a close friend of the Prince of Wales. He was forced to flee from London after becoming entangled in a Jacobite plot to restore the Stuarts, and was exposed as an agent of the French Secret Service. In 1755 he traveled to the Far East to become a pupil of occult adepts in Tibet but he also found time to engage in spying operations against the British India Company.[151]

It is significant that Saint-Germain was involved with trying to restore the Stuarts to the throne. According to historian Sir Laurence Gardner, the Royal Scottish family members are direct descendants in the long bloodline of the Holy Grail, meaning that they are part of the hidden lineage that began with the offspring of Jesus Christ and Mary Magdalene. Gardner states:

> Although the Stuarts have been ignored by the British authorities since the death of Cardinal Henry, the descendants of Prince Edward James, Count Stuarton, Second Count of Albany, have been actively engaged in social, political, military and sovereign affairs for the past two centuries. They have often advised governments on constitutional and diplomatic matters in an effort to promote the ideals of *public service* and *religious toleration* upheld by their own reigning house, and they have been particularly concerned with matters of trade, welfare and education.[152]

The basic ideals that inspired all revolutions toward democracy, equality and public service are rooted in the esoteric traditions of the world's great mystery schools. That is the legacy of the Holy Grail. It was the original vision of a small faction of our Anunnaki ancestry that had our best interests in mind. It was the principle reason they established the age-old tradition of priest-kings and a royal bloodline.

Since those early days which surely seem lost in the mists of time, humanity has not honored the sacred vow. The bloodline was diluted, divine right was usurped by ignorance and greed, truth was mixed with untruth, and apathy reigns supreme. Elitism obstructs the way and is reinforced by self-perpetuating lies about who we really are. We bow to tyranny because we have not yet subdued the tyrant within. As Gardner reminds us,

No minister can honestly expound an ideal of equality in society when that minister is deemed to possess some form of prior lordship over society. Class structure is always decided from above, never from below. It is therefore for those on self-made pedestals to be seen to kick them aside in the interests of harmony and unity. Jesus was not in the least humbled when he washed his Apostles' feet; he was raised to the realm of a true Grail King – the realm of *equality* and *princely service*. This is the eternal 'Precept of the Sangreal', and it is expressed in Grail lore with the utmost clarity: only by asking 'Whom does the Grail serve?' will the wound of the Fisher King be healed, and the Wasteland returned to fertility.[153]

Our extraterrestrial ancestors will return. Some of them have already arrived and are making their presence known in ever so subtle and not so subtle ways. It is still too dangerous for a mass appearance. But rest assured, there will be one. Much depends on the maturity of the human race. This time, they wish to greet us as equal companions on the cosmic journey – not as our lords, masters, or gods, for they too have grown. In order to be ready for them, we must reassess everything and be willing to admit that we are more than we've allowed ourselves to be. This is our divine right -- our legacy -- and the divine message from the schools of Ageless Wisdom.

To that end, we summon our courage, turn our attention toward the witch's castle, enter the haunted forest, and come face to face with the flying monkeys who take us one step closer to realizing the truth.

---

[1]   From a recording of Ann Davies made by Builders of the Adytum entitled "A Qabalistic Service."

[2]   Internet article by Palden Jenkins entitled "The Great Taboo – It's the Neighbours! ETs and Humanity," http://www.palden.co.uk. Reprinted with permission.

[3] Steven M. Greer, M.D., *Disclosure: Military and Government Witnesses Reveal the Greatest Secrets in Modern History*, Crossing Point, Inc., 2001. See also, http://www.disclosureproject.org.

[4] Jenkins.

[5] Dion Fortune, *The Esoteric Orders and Their Work*, Llewellyn Publications, 3rd printing, 1971, p. 43. Reprinted with permission from Red Wheel/Weiser.

[6] Paul Foster Case, *The True and Invisible Rosicrucian Order*, Samuel Weiser, Inc., 1985, quoting from Eckhartshausen's *The Cloud Upon the Sanctuary* (London: George Redway, 1896), pp. 313-314. Reprinted with permission from Red Wheel/Weiser.

[7] Zecharia Sitchin, *The 12th Planet,* Avon Books, 1976.

[8] Alice A. Bailey, *A Treatise on White Magic*, Lucis Publishing Company, 1951, p. vii. Reprinted with permission.

[9] *Id.*, p. viii.

[10] *Id.*

[11] *Id.*, p. 350.

[12] Dion Fortune, *The Cosmic Doctrine*, Helios Book Service, Ltd., 1966, p.144.

[13] Gareth Knight, *A Practical Guide to Qabalistic Symbolism, Vol. I,* Helios Book Service, 1965, p. 64.

[14] Gareth Knight, *A Practical Guide to Qabalistic Symbolism, Vol. II*, Helios Book Service, 1965, p. 181-182.

[15] Alice A. Bailey, *Esoteric Astrology*, Lucis Publishing Company, 1951, p. 299. Reprinted with permission.

[16] *Id.*, pp. 658-660.

[17] M. Temple Richmond, *Sirius,* Source Publications, 1997.

[18] *Id.*, pp. 347-348.

[19] *Id.*, p. 349.

[20] Mark Amaru Pinkham, *The Return of the Serpents of Wisdom,* Adventures Unlimited Press, 1997.

[21] *Id.*, p. 3. Reprinted with permission.

[22] *Id.*, p. 24.

[23] Zecharia Sitchin, *The Lost Realms: Book IV of the Earth Chronicles*, Avon Books, 1990; see also "The Olmec Enigma" at www.sitchin.com.

[24] Barbara G. Walker, *The Woman's Encyclopedia of Myths and Secrets*, Harper San Francisco, 1983, p. 396.

[25] *Id.*, p. 397.

[26] Elaine Pagels, *The Gnostic Gospels,* Vintage Books, 1981, p. 36.

[27] *Id.*, p. 34.

[28] *Id.*, p. 35.

[29] Laurence Gardner, *Genesis of the Grail Kings*, Fair Winds Press, 2002, p. 104.

[30] *Id.*, pp. 104-105.

[31] *Id.*

[32] Joseph Campbell, *The Hero With A Thousand Faces*, MJF Books, 1949, p. 73.

[33] Gardner, p. 272.

[34] *Id.* Reprinted with permission.

[35] Builders of the Adytum, 5101 N. Figueroa St., Los Angeles, CA. 90042-0278. Reprinted with permission.

[36] Pinkham, pp. 41-42.

[37] Jean Markale, *The Druids: Celtic Priests of Nature*, Inner Traditions, 1999, p. 51.

[38] *Id.*

[39] Gareth Knight, *The Secret Tradition in Arthurian Legend*, Samuel Weiser, Inc., 1996, p. 121. Reprinted with permission from Red Wheel/Weiser.

[40] Markale.

[41] R.A. Boulay, *Flying Serpents and Dragons,* The Book Tree, 1999.

[42] Markale, p. 226.

[43] Marion Zimmer Bradley, *The Mists of Avalon*, Ballantine Books, 1982.

[44] Mark Roberts, from his website at http://home.earthlink.net/~pleiadesx. Reprinted with permission.

[45] Sitchin, 1976.

[46] Max H. Flindt and Otto O. Binder, *Mankind: Child of the Stars*, Ozark Mountain Publishing, 1999, pp. 189-192.

[47] Kenneth Wapnick, "Mysticism and Schizophrenia," *The Journal of Transpersonal Psychology*, Fall 1969, Vol. 1, No. 2, pp. 49-66.

[48] R.D. Laing, *The Politics of Experience*, Ballantine Books, 1967, p. 102.

[49] *Id.*, p. 109.

[50] Steven M. Greer, M.D., *Extraterrestrial Contact: The Evidence and Implications*, Crossing Point, Inc., 1999.

[51] David Allen Hulse © 1993 & 2000, *The Eastern Mysteries,* Llewellyn Worldwide, Ltd., PO Box 64383, St. Paul, MN 55164, all rights reserved, pp. xxx-xxxi.

[52] David Allen Hulse © 1993 & 2000, *The Western Mysteries*, Llewellyn Worldwide, Ltd., PO Box 64383, St. Paul, MN 55164, all rights reserved, p. 107.

[53] See http://archaeoastronomy.com/doctrans.html which contains a transcription of the Rocky Mountain PBS documentary called "History on

the Rocks" with a debate between the archeoastronomers/epigraphers and archeologists over the continuing controversy.

[54] *Id.*

[55] See http://home.earthlink.net/~pleiadesx/index.htm for more information.

[56] Sitchin, 1976, p. 149.

[57] Edo Nyland, *Linguistic Archeology,* Trafford Publishing, 2001; *Odysseus and the Sea Peoples,* Trafford Publishing, 2001; see also http://www.islandnet.com/~edonon/linguist.htm. Reprinted with permission.

[58] *Id.*

[59] *Id.*, quoting from Eleanor Shipley-Ducket's *Alcuin, Friend of Charlemagne*, The Macmillan Co., 1951.

[60] *Id.*

[61] *Id.* Quoting Kuhn, p. 90.

[62] Leonard Schlain, *The Alphabet Versus the Goddess: The Conflict Between Word and Image*, Viking, 1998.

[63] *Id.*

[64] Nyland.

[65] Vincent Bridges, *The UFO Enigma (Part 3),* at www.magicjourney.com/artandarchives/SS3.html.

[66] Donald Tyson, "The Enochian Apocalypse," from *Gnosis Magazine,* Summer 1996, at www.noveltynet.org/content/paranormal/www.brotherblue.org/libers/enoch-ap.htm, quoting from Meric Casaubon, ed., *A True and Faithful Relation of What Passed for Many Years Between Dr. John Dee and Some Spirits,* Glasgow: Antione Publishing, 1974, p. 188.

[67] *Id.*

[68] *Id.*

[69] Allen H. Greenfield, *Secret Cipher of the Ufonauts*, IllumiNet Press, 1994, p. 16. Reprinted with permission.

[70] *Id.*, p. 81.

[71] *Id.*, p. 80.

[72] *Id.*, pp. 80-81.

[73] *Id.*, p. 82.

[74] Marcia Schafer, *Confessions of an Intergalactic Anthropologist*, Cosmic Destiny Press, 2001, p. 49.

[75] Greenfield, p. 87.

[76] *Id.*, p. 96.

[77] *Id.*, p. 97.

[78] Lance Owens, "Joseph Smith: America's Hermetic Prophet" originally published in *Gnosis: A Journal of Western Inner Traditions*, Spring, 1995. Reprinted with permission from the Lumen Foundation.

[79]   Kevin Christensen, "A Model of Mormon Spiritual Experience." (February, 2002) published at http://www2.ida.net/graphics/shirtail/spiritua.htm.

[80]   *Id.*

[81]   Richard Smoley and Jay Kinney, *Hidden Wisdom: A Guide to the Western Inner Traditions*, Arkana, 1999, p. 41.

[82]   Christensen at http://www2.ida.net/graphics/shirtail/spiritua.htm.

[83]   William Bramley, *The Gods of Eden,* Avon Books, 1990, p. 309.

[84]   *Id.*

[85]   Joseph Smith, Chapter 3, verses 2-3 from the Book of Abraham in *The Pearl of Great Price.*

[86]   Bramley, p. 322.

[87]   Richmond, p. 197.

[88]   Michael Howard, *The Occult Conspiracy*, Destiny Books, 1989, p. 4.

[89]   Smoley and Kinney, p. 265.

[90]   Howard, 1989.

[91]   Albert J. Edmunds, "A Buddhist Genesis, " translated from Digha Nikaya 27, published at http://essenes.crosswinds.net/budgenesis.html.

[92]   "A Tibetan Genesis" can be found at http://essenes.crosswinds.net/tibgenesis.html.

[93]   Sitchin, 1985.

[94]   D.H. Childress and Ivan T. Sanderson, *Vimana Aircraft of Ancient India and Atlantis*, Adventures Unlimited Press, 2001, quoting Nicholas Roerich, *Altai-Himalaya: A Travel Diary,* pp. 361-362. Reprinted with permission.

[95]   *Id.*, p. 129.

[96]   *Id.*

[97]   Kathy Jones, "Spinning the Wheel of Ana," 1990, 2000 at http://www.isleofavalon.uk/local/h-pages/kathyj/ap-ana.html.

[98]   International Kalachakra Network, http://www.kalachakranet.org/resources/shambhala.html.   Reprinted with permission.

[99]   *Id.*

[100] Childress, p. 302.

[101] *Id.*

[102] Sally Sheridan, "Tibet, Shambhala and UFO's," http://www.sacred-texts.com/ufo/tibetufo.htm.

[103] http://www.korrnet.org/pipermail/levnet/2000-July/014959.html.

[104] Jenkins, see above.

[105] Childress, p. 81.

[106] *Id.*

[107] Zecharia Sitchin, *The Wars of Gods and Men*, Bear & Company, 1985, p. 233. See also Childress, 2001, p. 31, for an actual picture of the script.

[108] Sitchin, 1985, p. 239.

[109] Childress, p. 249.

[110] Alexandra David-Neel, *Initiations and Initiates in Tibet*, 1931, 1993, p. 164.

[111] Robert Beer, *The Encyclopedia of Tibetan Symbols and Motifs*, Serindia Publications, 1999. p. 72.

[112] Pinkham, p. 110.

[113] Lex Hixon, *Mother of the Buddhas: Meditation on the Prajnaparamita Sutra*, Foreword by Robert A.F. Thurman, Ph.D., Quest Books, 1993, p. xii. Reprinted by permission of Quest Books/The Theosophical Publishing House, Wheaton, Ill., www.questbooks.net.

[114] Pinkham, p. 136.

[115] Boulay, p. 42.

[116] *Id.*

[117] D. J. Conway, *Dancing with Dragons*, Llewellyn Publications, 1997, p. 22.

[118] Boulay, p. 43.

[119] *Id., p. 41.*

[120] Pinkham, p. 118.

[121] *Id.*, p. 132.

[122] *Id.*, p. 133.

[123] *Id.*, p. 138.

[124] *Id.*, p. 148.

[125] Chogyal Namkhai Norbu, *The Practice for the Naga*, Shang-Shung Edizioni (Italy), 1995, p. 5.

[126] *Id.*, pp. 5-6.

[127] Tsultrim Allione, *Women of Wisdom*, Snow Lion Publications, 2000, p. 99. Reprinted with permission.

[128] *Id.*

[129] *Id.*

[130] Pinkham, p. 154.

[131] *Id.*, p. 161.

[132] Edward Plotkin, *The Four Yogas of Enlightenment: Guide to Don Juan's Nagualism and Esoteric Buddhism*, 2000, available exclusively at http://www.FourYogas.com.

[133] Zecharia Sitchin, *The Lost Realms*, Avon Books, 1990.

[134] *Id.*, p. 35.

[135] *Id.*, p. 36.

[136] Gardner, 2002.

[137] Pinkham, p. 230.

[138] *Id.*, p. 231.

[139] Yesai Nasrai, The Order of the Nazorean Essenes can be found at http://www.essenes.net. Reprinted with permission.

[140] *Id.*

[141] *Id.*

[142] *Id.*

[143] Alexandra David-Neel, *Magic and Mystery in Tibet*, Dover Publications, 1971, (originally published in 1932.)

[144] Nasrai.

[145] Neil Freer, *God Games: What Do You Do Forever?*, The Book Tree, 1999, p. 113. Reprinted with permission.

[146] Zecharia Sitchin, *The Cosmic Code*, Avon Books, 1998, p. 125.

[147] Temple *The Sirius Mystery,* Destiny Books, 1998,, p. 112.

[148] Plutarch, 'Isis and Osiris', translated by Babbitt, in Vol V of *Plutarch's Moralia*, Harvard University Press, 1962, reprinted in Temple, p. 282.

[149] Temple, p. 283.

[150] Howard, pp. 64-65.

[151] *Id.*, p. 66.

[152] Laurence Gardner, *Bloodline of the Holy Grail: The Hidden Lineage of Jesus Revealed*, Barnes & Noble Books, 1997, p. 343. Reprinted with permission.

[153] *Id.*, p. 350.

PART 4

Flying Monkeys and the Haunted Forest

No building is too tall for even the smallest dog to lift its leg on.

    --   Jim Hightower

CHAPTER 7

GOVERNMENTS, GOBLINS, AND GODFATHERS

Good and Evil

A scene from the movie, *The Empire Strikes Back*, Episode V of the Star Wars story, places this problem of evil in proper perspective: Luke's experience in the cave while being trained by the Master Jedi Yoda. Luke is drawn to the cave and senses something unusual. He asks Yoda what's in there. Yoda replies, "Only that which you take with you." Luke fastens his weapons to his belt as he prepares to enter the cave. Yoda says, "Your weapons – you will not need them." Luke chooses to take them anyway despite Yoda's assurance. Luke encounters what appears to be Darth Vader inside the cave. They immediately draw light sabers and begin to battle. Luke is the victor, beheading Vader. He approaches the head on the ground that is still concealed by the dark mask. The front of the mask explodes, and Luke is startled to see the image of his own face beneath it – not Vader's.

This incident has many meanings, as do most. On one hand, it represents a failure and on the other hand, a success. Perhaps most importantly, it demonstrates that all evil begins inside of us – not on the outside. We must confront the shadow aspects of ourselves before we can fully embrace the light, and realize that it is absolutely essential to the process. In fact, the shadow – the darkness – must be embraced and integrated into the light before we can be blessed with true freedom from suffering. In order to realize this, we must first get a handle on what evil really is.

Evil cannot be confined to a religious concept such as original sin. Evil presents itself in phenomena that most people experience as unpleasant and obstructive. I don't believe in absolute evil, but evil is somehow more than just less than

296

good. Evil is often interpreted as error – not hitting the mark. Yet heinous crimes and common cruelty seem not only deliberate, but pointless – as if there is no mark to hit. Evil is often a point of view. We may not be able to define it precisely, but most of us know it when we see it. Sometimes I don't think it really matters what it is as much as how we react to it. As wonderful as a world without evil might be, how would be ever know good? The cliché is true: We can't appreciate sunshine without rain. Therefore evil has a divine purpose. It is here to teach – to instruct – to inform – and to grow us. Moreover, evil is just one end of another polarity.

The law of polarity was briefly discussed in Chapter 3. Darkness is the shadow of the light. Esoterically, Satan is the testing side of Christ. In Qabalistic gematria, the names for the Messiah and the Serpent are numerically equivalent. In fact, if a separate being like the devil truly existed, one would be fully justified in feeling sorry for him, for he has the most difficult job of all. No matter what he does – no matter how his horrible acts help us grow stronger and more spiritually aware – he gets no credit for it. No one likes him. They just want him to go away. But he never listens. You know why? Remember the mask. We all have our own caves to explore.

Most people who believe in evil also believe that good will overcome evil, and there is reason to believe that. Opposites are given to us for one purpose – to reconcile. It is through their integration that we finally experience unconditional pure Being. It's the way we get things done on the material plane. Without playing this game, we could not progress. In the words of John Rankin:

> Every stick has two ends. There is no way that you can have a pencil without its having two ends, no matter how close together you place those ends. You may think that if we get the ends of the pencil closer and closer together, that we can overcome the problem of having opposites. So we chop it and chop it, and if you chop far enough, there is nothing left materially! For there to be anything materially, there

must be pairs of opposites. As soon as we eliminate opposition, materiality and visibility disappear.[1]

Changing the negative polarity of evil into the positive polarity of good is simply a change in degree of the same thing – the same energy or substance. This is why wherever there is great hatred there is also potential for great love. It is not possible to feel hatred for anything we do not care about. So how does this work? Rankin explains it like this:

> If I were able to take a pin, with its two obviously opposite poles, and were to apply certain pressures of dynamics to it, one pole would become so electrified that it would draw the other over to it, to form a full circle in which the opposites meet. When the positive side of your being becomes so fully charged with understanding, dedication, and insight, it draws the other side of your being up into its aura and atmosphere.[2]

"Evil" becomes "good" through transmutation, not force. The change must come about in the very substance of evil – the *heart* of evil. Evil must turn of its own accord. And when you're dealing with other people, this change must come from within them.

In the classic motion picture, *Mr. Smith Goes to Washington* starring Jimmy Stewart, this lesson is profoundly illustrated. Mr. Smith uncovers political corruption in his fellow senators and threatens to expose it. But his enemies are on to him and strike the first blow. They engage in smear tactics, forgery, and outright lying to discredit Mr. Smith making it appear that he is the real bad guy, not them. No matter what Mr. Smith does to expose their scheme, they always manage to undermine and derail him somehow. Finally, nothing remains but to plead his case in the all too familiar tactic of filibustering. After countless hours, Mr. Smith delivers one final exceptionally eloquent plea to the integrity of every man for truth, justice, and honesty. He is exhausted and near the point of giving up. Suddenly, the corrupt Senator -- the bad guy – cannot stand it anymore and crumbles with a change of heart. He admits the error of his ways and completely exonerates Mr. Smith. What this says is that evil itself must change the error of its ways – we cannot force it. The political change and revolution that emerges from a change in heart and not by force of arms has the innate strength to last.

Therefore, when we see evil in the outside world that inspires us to battle, the fighting, if possible, should focus on winning over the heart of evil – not destroying it. Surely certain times and situations call for more immediate measures where force is warranted in order to prevent harm to self and others – but in the long run, the ultimate goal should be non-violent transformation.

How do we help to change the heart of others? By first changing our own of course – setting an example, as Jesus Christ taught so masterfully. After all, most evil is an outward projection of our own inadequacies and neglected social ills manifesting in a way that forces us to recognize them. So what is the inner evil that keeps corrupted governments, goblins and godfathers in place – that enables our so-called oppressors to continue to oppress and exploit us and the Earth's natural resources?

Greed – giving in to the illusion of separateness. But the antidote to that is not in just opening our hearts and our wallets and giving everything away. It's far more complex. We have to look at what causes greed – where its roots are buried and the social dynamics that ensue.

Authoritarianism, Obedience, and Repression

> The serious threat to our democracy is not the existence of foreign totalitarian states. It is the existence within our own personal attitudes and within our own institutions of conditions, which have

given a victory to external authority, discipline, uniformity and dependence upon The Leader . . .

-- John Dewey

Fascism is a form of government that manifests as extreme authoritarianism. Governments traditionally drift toward the right when increasing complexity of lifestyle coincides with economic unrest and changes in public awareness that threaten cherished institutions. This is because the powers that be always strive to maintain the status quo. Those in power always hate to relinquish it – even if it means a more just society for everyone. Unfortunately, they usually encounter little resistance to their efforts – not because the people don't know how to organize and impact but because they seldom see the need to. They seldom see the need because the powers that be automatically feed them lies and false promises that simply stifle and appease. We want to believe that those in power have our best interests at heart, and that makes it easier to believe their lies. So the vicious circle remains unbroken; not so much due to naiveté as much as to ingrained social attitudes and conditionings having their root in the basic structural unit of our society – the patriarchal family and by extension its surrogate clones in the form of private corporations and government institutions.

Authoritarianism begins with the individual. It is a basic personality style or syndrome of organized beliefs and symptoms characterized by several components. These components were defined by a group of social psychologists working out of Berkeley University in the early 1940s as a result of a landmark study. The components are: conventionalism, authoritarian aggression, authoritarian submission, power and toughness, anti-intraception, superstition and stereotypy, destructiveness and cynicism, projectivity, and overconcern with sex. The following table elaborates:[3]

300

1. *Conventionalism.* Extreme and strict adherence to middle-class values, and overresponsiveness to outside contemporary social pressures.
2. *Authoritarian submission.* Overwhelming emotional need to submit to others, and uncritical acceptance of strong, decisive leader figures and their orders.
3. *Authoritarian aggression.* Tendency to deal with people whose behavior deviates from conventional values by condemnation, total rejection, stern discipline, or severe punishment.
4. *Anti-intraception.* Emotionally inflexible and overly-suspicious of intellectual, theoretical, and impractical ideas while maintaining a narrow range of consciousness; disapproving of subjective reactions and fantasy, therefore feeling threatened by their own emotions and freedom of expression.
5. *Superstition and stereotypy.* A tendency to shift responsibility from within to outside one's sphere of influence; tendency to oversimplify and think in unambiguous terms of black and white, especially with regard to psychological and social matters.
6. *Power and toughness.* Identifies with power figures out of a need to have power and a need to submit to it, often denying personal weakness.
7. *Destruction and cynicism.* Rationalizes and justifies aggression enabling them to be aggressive because "everybody is doing it" or often modeling an admired dominant role figure.
8. *Projectivity.* Tendency to believe that the world is not safe; undesirable impulses that cannot be admitted by them consciously are often projected on to minority groups and vulnerable victims.
9. *Sex.* Seemingly obsessed with sexual activities often feeling punitive toward violators of sex mores.

Researchers later applied a measurement scale for determining the traits and tendencies of authoritarian personalities. Individuals who scored high on the scale tended to be prejudiced or ethnocentric; perceived others as possessing the same beliefs and attitudes that they have; had a low tolerance for ambiguity (e.g., were reluctant to believe that "good people" could possess both good and bad traits); and had a more traditional family ideology which included strong parental control over family decisions, highly rigid and separate roles for mother and father, and restrictions on the rights of children to disagree. They also tended to be less educated and appeared to gravitate toward religious and political groups that espoused strict dogma. Perhaps the most disturbing behavior they found most pronounced in authoritarian personalities was the ease at which such individuals engaged in the phenomenon of *destructive obedience.*

Destructive obedience occurs when obeying the demands of others requires the violation of one's moral responsibilities. Naturally this brings to mind particular war scenarios that transpired in Nazi Germany and Viet Nam. However, the behavior can range from the extreme to more subtle instances – such as a worker being forced to choose between manufacturing a dangerously defective product and risking the loss of a job. A controversial study was conducted in the 1960s by social psychologist, Stanley Milgram, to determine how many people would continue to obey the commands of an authority figure, even when they believed that they were endangering the life of another person. This experimental study entailed asking the participating subjects to give increasingly powerful electric shocks to other participating students whenever those students made a mistake on a learning task. 65% of the subjects obeyed the authority figure's instructions, knowing that they were hurting a powerless person. The subjects obeyed more often when the authority figure was present. Though Milgram's study was criticized on ethical grounds, the results merited further research into the principle of destructive obedience.

Sometimes mob mentality comes into play when tendencies toward destructive obedience are triggered. Recall the outrageous incidents that occurred soon after 9-11 including all out assaults on individuals who merely looked like they could be of Arab descent. Threats circulated on the Internet by "groups" of people who as individuals would never have the courage to follow through on them. It was a sad and dangerous time. But in the end, the American spirit of good will prevailed, and the forces of evil were again turned back by a rising tide of compassion and tolerance in the hearts of most Americans.

But back to these outer "forces of evil." Who or what are they and what is their goal? When, how, where, and what will they do next?

Dominator Society and the Godfathers of Patriarchy

Our understanding of prehistory is in the midst of profound transition. Traditional archeologists and modern linguists are redefining it in terms of new discoveries. One of these recent finds revealed a time when certain Neolithic tribes experienced harmony and equality between the sexes. No clearer illustration of this seeming anomaly exists than in the ancient culture of Minoan Crete, a highly developed agrarian civilization that sprung up around 6000 B.C.E. These gentle people worshiped the Goddess as Mother Nature – source of all beauty, harmony and creation. Over the next 4000 years, they developed architecture, and peacefully traded in pottery, metallurgy, weaving, arts and crafts. Ruins suggest a similar standard of living for everyone, which included a public works system and an equitable sharing of wealth. Male and female participated equally in political and religious ceremony. As author Riane Eisler notes,

> The equal partnership between women and men that seems to have characterized Minoan society is perhaps nowhere so vividly illustrated as in these sacred bull-games, where young women and men performed together and entrusted their lives to each other. These rituals, which combined excitement, skill, and religious fervor, also appear to have been characteristic of the Minoan spirit in another important aspect; they were designed not only for individual pleasure or salvation but to invoke the

divine power to bring well-being to the entire society.[4]

This was one of the last holdouts of a successful egalitarian society. It was neither patriarchal nor based on domination. For all across the continent, well into the Bronze Age, violent waves of territorial invasions were transforming the face of human culture and society, creating discrepancy and disharmony between the tribes and the sexes. Patriarchy was being born, or as Eisler prefers to call it, dominator society.

Between 4300 and 2800 B.C.E., the Kurgans assumed dominance by violent force. Scholars refer to them as the Indo-European or Aryan language speaking peoples, but they were not the original Indians or Europeans. The Dravidian people lived in India long before the Aryan invasion. Although these Aryan Kurgans descended from the European northeast and Asia, academia still insists on calling them "Indo-European." At any rate, these Aryan Kurgans, along with the ancient Hebrews, had one thing in common: a social system where male dominance, violence, and authoritarianism prevailed.

The old European culture was matrifocal and matrilineal, and its economy was based on farming. They worshiped the feminine principle or Mother Goddess as expressed through the agricultural cycle of birth, death and regeneration. The chosen symbol was the feminine chalice – the nurturing giver of life. In contrast, the Kurgan culture was patrilineal, hierarchical, and their economy was based on stockbreeding. Their religion "exalted virile, heroic warrior gods of the shining and thunderous sky." The chosen symbol was therefore the masculine weapon – a dagger or battle axe, glorifying the life-taking power of the blade. It was inevitable that the two social systems would clash.

How the Kurgans got the upper hand is simple: violent use of force. Unfortunately, the older culture was neither prepared nor equipped to resist. These invasions also marked the beginning of slavery, the first slaves being women. After the Kurgans killed off the men and children, women became chattel, though often valuable and treated as such. Friedrich Engels attributes the rise of patriarchy to a dominator society characterized by social hierarchies based on the distribution of private property. However, most scholars today feel that the rise is more closely correlated to the development of metallurgy and the redirection of that specific technology from hunting to war. From a larger perspective, this fails to explain how the egalitarian peaceful lifestyle was forsaken for an oppressive social system based on domination. That objective could only be accomplished through a gradual ideological obliteration of religious symbols and cultural traditions taking decades and even centuries. The myths and stories are deliberately distorted, and after several generations their deeper meanings get lost. Truth is forgotten and history ("his story") begins. Suffice it to say, as scholar Gerda Lerner points out in her groundbreaking treatise, *The Creation of Patriarchy* -- since patriarchy was *created*, it can be *uncreated.*[5] And there we have it. As we see – the weaving is unraveling, and the Goddess is revealing her presence to us all.

Patriarchy/dominator society is the basis for all other oppressions, tyrannies, and exploitations on the planet. It predates racism, specieism, and homophobia. All suffering springs from that – the original delusion of the illusion of separateness. Men as a group are not solely responsible for any of this because evil cannot exist without all of us holding it inside to some degree. Women are partially responsible for allowing this to happen – for tolerating inequality – for forgetting our ancient past – and for our silent complicity and refusal to take corrective action. But blaming is unproductive and serves no useful purpose. Besides, today we have many women who wholeheartedly subscribe to a dominator ideology, personally and politically. Mary Daly writes about these tokens and backstabbing "Athenas" in her brilliant book, *Gyn/Ecology: The Metaethics of Radical Feminism.*[6] Still, I don't want to point fingers at them either. For as always, the finger points both ways. It doesn't have to be an "either/or" dilemma. It can be a "both-both" solution. Yes, we are partly responsible and they are partly responsible. And yes, we can work to change the system while working to change ourselves. This work *must* be done simultaneously in the personal *and* political sphere, or else we get burned out and discouraged.

Changes in the heart change relationships, and families begin to embody purpose and values more closely aligned with principle. Up to now, the family has traditionally served as a factory for authoritarian ideologies and conservative structures, according to Wilhelm Reich.[7] Why? Because the family was an outgrowth and extension of earlier social structures developed and reinforced under dominator society. Classically authoritarian, the oppressed identify with their oppressors and internalize their oppression to the degree that they forget they are oppressed. Children are brought up to know no better and resign to thinking that life is supposed to be that way because it is. They become robots, programmed not to rebel against the existing social order. If they do show signs of autonomy and freethinking at an early age, they are often ostracized.

The question becomes then, is this human nature? Is this how humans naturally are – warlike, exploitive and dominating? Well evidently not, as suggested by earlier Neolithic cultures. Then where did the Kurgans – the original Aryan invaders -- get this insane idea? What made them so different from the older European culture?

The Original Gods: Godfathers and Goblins from Outer Space

Yes – you guessed it. Our friends from Nibiru and various assorted planets. This does not mean that the majority of our ET ancestors are bad guys – quite the contrary. But in the context of personal psychology we can all make mistakes. It always helps me to think about what one of my teachers once said: We don't grow evenly – we grow lopsidedly. Sometimes we meet someone who may be an expert in their chosen field, yet their character leaves much to be desired. No doubt some folks are way ahead of us in terms of technology and understanding how the universe works, yet they may be lacking in wisdom, compassion, and even what we Earthlings call common sense.

It all goes back to the ego. As long as we relate to one another in the context of separate identities, we will always have those ego shells of separateness to deal with. There's nothing to indicate that ETs don't have the same problems as we do in that regard. By looking at ancient history, it is evident that they did have conflicts and that something like egos were definitely involved. So it is easy to see how our initial role as homo sapiens sapiens colored the entire future of politics from the beginning.

We were bred to be slaves – to be subservient. It is our primal conditioning. The diligent scholarship of Zecharia Sitchin and others shows us that organized religion was a natural outgrowth and consequence of the Anunnaki-human relationship dynamic which was based on a master/slave – king/subject – parent/child – teacher/student paradigm. When the Anunnaki phased off the planet, their chosen representatives bearing the title of kings and priests took it upon themselves to formulate a methodology by which the teaching tradition continued and could perhaps be used to persuade our star parents to return. If we think we have problems with our egos these days, imagine what it must have been like for early generation humanity. Inevitably, we built a real and figurative tower of Babel that was doomed from the beginning. Infantile humanity continued to refuse to share, resulting in the splintering of the human race into hostile religious factions. Some folks still hope that "God" or the "gods" will return someday to pick us up in their arms, wipe our tears, and make everything all right. And this is what they pray for. *But it ain't gonna happen.* Like all young men and women emerging from adolescence – this species is on its own now. It's time to grow up.

Centuries passed and Mommy and Daddy never came home. But that was all right because the kids were busy enough trying to solve problems on their own. And what once was used to uplift and inspire became a tool of oppression – a weapon by which they could conquer and keep each other captive and under control.

Followers of Enlil's way mythologized him into a wrathful god known as Jehovah in the Old Testament. Followers of Enki's way established the cult of the Serpent and referred to him as Adonai. In Qabalistic gematria, Adonai means "God in Man." Well think about that for a moment. That's telling us that God is not a separate being outside of us but something within us. If God is within us, that must mean that all powers associated with God must be inside us too. In the least it suggests that we have the innate ability to become like God someday. And we did – we had their genes!

You don't have to be a rocket scientist to understand how such an idea could threaten the ruling powers that eventually became the Roman Catholic Church. Naturally, such knowledge leads to freethinking, autonomy and self-empowerment. Why would a person need to rely on a priest or other kind of surrogate parent or third person intermediary for spiritual salvation when they could do it on their own? To do so would threaten the existing social order and it did, as it still does today to some extent.

For a detailed understanding of how the Gospels were created, compiled, and forever revised sometimes leaving out vital information, the series of books by Zecharia Sitchin entitled *The Earth Chronicles* and *Genesis of the Grail Kings* by Laurence Gardner are recommended. Briefly, I will summarize some of their major points in order to describe how the early godfathers and goblins came to be, and how a selected few continue to attempt to control human activities to this day.

The 1850s through the 1920s marked an exciting time of discovery when all the ancient documents, stone tablets and cylinders from Bible land were placed in the public domain. As previously mentioned, it became evident that the stories preserved in these artifacts were models for the ones that appeared in the Old Testament. There was, however, huge discrepancy between the ways certain facts were presented.

Suddenly, as Gardner asserts, "...it was clear that the long-supposed authentic history of the Bible was not authentic at all: it had been contrived by adjusting original records to suit an emergent religious movement from 2500 years ago."[8]   This movement originally began as a small Hebrew cult but later expanded into mainstream Judaism and eventually Christianity.

One of the most frequent mistranslations occurring in the Biblical texts was the name for God himself.   Jehovah was supplanted where Elohim often appeared.   Elohim is a plural word meaning 'lofty ones' or 'gods'.

> *I have said, Ye are gods; and all of you are*
> *children of the most High.*
> -- Psalm 82

This mistranslation was not a singular event – it continued to occur during the early centuries after the death of Jesus.

A Royal Bloodline

Adam comes from *Adama* meaning earthling. If you recall, he was the result of the second genetic breeding experiment where Anunnaki blood was injected into the new human previously created.   Next, "Eve" was created on this same model. "Adam" and "Eve" were educated by Enki and had an awakening of sorts.   The slaves and servants of the Anunnaki did not wear clothes. Suddenly, Adam and Eve realized their subordinate status. They covered themselves not because they were ashamed of their sexuality but because they were striving to become like the 'gods' themselves, as they were destined to be.   Abel was the result of a mating between the two homo sapiens sapiens, but Cain had a different father. According to Gardner, Cain represented an advancement on the earlier cloning experiments because he was made with Enki's blood. This was the beginning of the royal priestly bloodline. Cain was not the bad guy he was made out to be, and he did not slay

Abel. He was elevated to kingly status over Abel because of his bloodline. Again, Gardner explains,

> ...but the word indirectly translated to 'slew' was *yaqam*, and the text should read that Cain (Q'ayin) was 'elevated' (raised or exalted) above Abel. The terminology that Cain 'rose up' against Abel is used in the English translation, but in quite the wrong context. Abel was a man conditioned according to his station, time and location. His blood was, therefore, figuratively swallowed into the ground (Genesis 4:10) – which is to say that he became so mundane as to be indistinguishable from his toil. The historical insignificance of Abel (or more correctly, Hevel) is qualified by the name by which he was identified, for a *hevel* was a puff of vapour.[9]

Gardner's thesis is that from Cain onward, there existed a royal bloodline that eventually spawned Jesus himself. His exhaustive research has shown, indeed, that such a bloodline existed, and that it continued long after the death of Jesus and Mary Magdalene through their descendants. And this is where the legend of the Holy Grail begins. The rulers of this bloodline were meant to be custodians of the people in service to a higher purpose for the benefit of all.

While the intentions of these early royal progenitors might have been sincere and fraught with good motives, it is in that very reasoning that lies the seed of separateness that we still suffer from today. Ability to govern is not contingent on physiology. This truth became clearly evident long before the medieval period when the rebelling peasants chanted, "When Adam delved and Eve span, who was then the gentleman?"

While the Anunnaki possessed esoteric knowledge regarding immortality and supersensory powers, it seems that something about Earth's atmosphere triggered a tendency to take short cuts. Instead of opting for the natural route, they began to depend on outside substances similar to drugs in order to achieve superior states of consciousness. By doing so, their natural ability to regenerate was diminished. Their obsession with creating this sacred bloodline was just another outgrowth of this misplaced thinking.

Today this bloodline is so diluted that it has lost its significance. Yet with or without the bloodline, we each have within us the original genetic material that enables us to accomplish what they did. The question is -- are we going to continue to believe the lie? Do we want to be just "puffs of air" as Abel is described? Or will we hear the lion within us roar and reclaim our rightful heritage?

The conflicts between the followers of Enlil and Enki continued to grow. Enki recognized the logic behind instituting Nibiruan matrilineal rules of descent. Along with his sisters, he also recognized the advantage of continuing to encourage reverence of the feminine principle in nature as the source of the divine creative power in the form of a Mother Goddess. Yet Enlil and Marduk (Enki's son) were beginning to follow the dominator impulses of other ancestry. We cannot definitively say this was due to the Reptilian factor as asserted by some authors because Enki was half Reptilian. Whatever it was, it was clear that the blade was garnering favor over the chalice resulting in the decline of Mesopotamian culture and the birth of patriarchal Judaism.

Some evidence suggests Kurgans predated Mesopotamian civilization. So where did they come from? My guess is that they were descendants of ETs of a more hostile nature from a prior colonization. Whether those were Reptilian colonies or mixed colonies, we may never know. Some Sumerian statues of the Anunnaki reveal physical features that are decidedly Reptilian in nature. Similar statues were found as far north as the Carpathian Mountains where Scythian warlords ruled. A Scythian settlement existed near Mesopotamia prior to Sumer whose dominator ideology may have influenced the early Hebrew tribes. It is interesting to note that the ancient Scottish Gaels migrated to Ireland from Scythia. And *sumaire* is an old Irish word that means dragon or serpent.[10]

From this dominator society sprung all custodial religions whose main focus became controlling the people for the benefit of the dominators. Some channeled messages indicate that upon the expulsion of Adam and Eve from the Garden of Eden, they were again genetically altered to make it more difficult for them to access their innate spiritual abilities. This was, of course, because the Enlil faction wanted to keep them as slaves. However, forcing the children out on their own without constant custodial care would be enough to accomplish that objective. Primary preoccupation with material survival does not leave much time for studying and spiritual practice even today.

William Bramley wrote an intriguing little book called, *The Gods of Eden*.[11] His historical analysis focuses on a malevolent faction of ET ancestry that he says continues to control the world. He tends to overgeneralize and portrays the evolution of the mystery schools in a negative light. However, he concedes that not all religion is a result of custodial interference, and that spirituality in itself does more good than harm. Again, it is as with anything else – nothing is good or bad – it depends on how it's used. Unfortunately, religion in many respects continues to be misused for social control.

The Muddlers

Bramley acknowledges that the Brotherhood of the Snake founded by Enki was dedicated to the dissemination of spiritual knowledge and the attainment of freedom for all. This organization promoted art, science and healing. The Brotherhood also opposed slavery. In fact, the early Egyptian writings indicate that it specifically sought to free humans from custodial bondage.[12] As was mentioned before, this might be the root of the deeper animosity between Enki and Enlil, giving rise to civil war. Bramley feels that this Brotherhood was eventually corrupted and taken over by the malevolent custodial faction of Enlil. Actually, it just split into different branches – one devoted to good and the other to evil.

312

The side devoted to the original principles, the Rainbow Alliance, exists to this day. The side with impure motives is also alive and well, and I call them the *muddlers*. "Muddlers" makes more sense than calling it the dark side, the black brotherhood, or the left-hand path. Besides not wanting to discriminate against lefties, darkness and blackness are not bad. The light could not exist without them. The light of the rainbow cannot be muddled – only its reflection in pigment can. And as any painter knows, when you mix up all the colors indiscriminately, you get a big puddle of mud. When you want to make the water unclear, you muddy it. Polluting, diluting, distorting, and soiling – all muddling techniques. Hence – the muddlers.

Anybody can be a muddler. It doesn't require membership in a religion, secret society, or political party. Anytime we lie outright or by omission, we're muddling. It's that simple. Therefore, not all muddling is evil because in rare instances it might save yours or a loved one's life. But in general, muddling is bad. It is a very effective strategy for winning wars and political campaigns, and it is the best strategy by far for distracting people from the real issues at hand. Our world wouldn't be what it is today without it, that's for sure.

The weapon of choice for the most sophisticated of muddlers, historically speaking, has been Machiavellianism. Niccolo Machiavelli, a 16th century philosopher, wrote a policy manual for a prince who wanted advice on how to control his subjects. Machiavelli suggested the prince should keep them fighting against each other so they would never mount a rebellion against the prince. He then advised against using this technique because it could easily backfire. "The success of the technique depends upon at least one of the manipulated parties not being aware of the true source of the problem."[13] If both parties find out they're being manipulated, they are likely to unite against the perpetrator and cause him real harm. Bramley says that most of our wars have been started just this way, and there's evidence to support his claim.

In order for this method of social control to be effective, the Machiavellian perpetrator must do the following:

1. Erect conflicts and "issues" which will cause people to fight among themselves rather than against the perpetrator.
2. Remain hidden from view as the true instigator of the conflicts.
3. Lend support to all warring parties.
4. Be viewed as the benevolent source that can solve the conflicts.[14]

Naturally, not all conflicts are Machiavellian in nature. The ones that are, however, tend to revolve around issues that are never completely resolved so that the perpetrator is continuously benefiting from the conflict. Our own government, through its intelligence agencies, has mastered this technique. The military industrial complex in conjunction with the corporate monarchy has profited immensely from both sides of several wars. General Electric helped to arm Hitler, and then armed the allies in opposition to him. The United States was responsible for building up the military of Saddam Hussein, and then both Bushes bring a war against him.

War in itself is a Machiavellian methodology because war seldom solves the problems that originally provoked the war. It just gives one dominator temporary power over the other one. The rules of force operate on entirely different principles than the rules of ethics. War may sometimes bind a bleeding wound, but the wound cannot heal as long as it continues to be afflicted. This is why, at least in the 20th century, there was never any lasting peace between the Israelis and the Palestinians or between the Serbs and the Croatians. Truces? Perhaps. But no substantial peace. Why? Because the hearts did not change. Tolerance is better than nothing but tolerance alone is no substitute for cooperation, understanding, and compassion. As Bramley reiterates, "War is the institutionalization of criminality. War can never bring about spiritual improvement because criminality is one of the main causes of mental and spiritual deterioration."[15]

So who is the main perpetrator benefiting from the continuation of wars on this planet? Bramley thinks it is our ET ancestors and the custodial pawns (ruling elite) acting on their behalf. If this were true, however, then what is their gain after all is said and done? I don't see that we're a major food or fuel source for them anymore. So what could it be?

No, I think at this point in our history, ET involvement becomes irrelevant. Our star parents simply left a bad seed in our genes, and that seed continues to play out in our global conflicts and sociopolitical strife. We are weird beings – almost like viruses – threatening to destroy the planet along with ourselves. But we have choice. We don't have to go down that road. It's not too late to turn around.

Conspiracy Theories

The conspiracy comes in when we allege that more than one person, usually a specific group of people, is behind this attempt to control the world. Some people claim to have named this group, but I think their accusations are too narrow and simplistic. Bramley and other authors draw a thread linking together many different secret societies into a complicated network of custodial control. Among the named "secret societies" having links to the original "Brotherhood" are the Illuminati, the Templar Knights, the Rosicrucians, and the Freemasons. It is true that several members of these formerly secret societies have attempted on occasion to wield political influence in international affairs for better or worse. The best source for learning more about this is the excellent book by Michael Howard entitled, *The Occult Conspiracy: Secret Societies – Their Influence and Power in World History.*[16] But remember there are two sides to every coin. Seeking political influence on governments in itself is not a bad thing. Surely, we, as citizens should do more of that on a regular basis. In order to accomplish common goals, people organize into groups because it is far more effective. It is when these groups become corrupted by ill-meaning factions or power hungry egomaniacs that the influence has a menacing tone to it.

The purity of the spiritual ideals behind the esoteric traditions of the mystery schools cannot be impugned. The Rainbow Alliance stands together just as strongly today than it ever has, if not stronger. The unfortunate efforts of a few should not minimize, diminish or detract from the fortunate efforts of that Alliance. As Howard reminds us,

> Many renegade elements have attempted to use the secret societies as a cover for their own power games and some of these have worn the masks of initiates. Prejudiced observers who had their own reasons for wanting these efforts to end in failure have often grossly misrepresented the legitimate efforts by the secret societies and the occult fraternities to advance social progress and eradicate ignorance. In our study of the hidden events which have shaped history, we have not ignored these negative aspects. They provide an invaluable, if depressing, insight into these human minds who work for the downfall of civilization. However, the reader can be assured that even in the crisis torn 1980s initiates of the Great White Brotherhood [sic] are still working behind the scenes, even if their existence is not recognized or is even denied by those who have no knowledge of their activities and little awareness of the spiritual reality beyond the physical world.[17]

Because far more is written about the unfortunate influence of the negative few in the UFO/ET literature, I set out to write this book partly in an effort to show how the muddlers have orchestrated this biased perspective and more importantly, why.

It is very simple and not inconsistent with what was said before. Cultivating spiritual awareness breeds self-knowledge, knowledge of others, and the ability to see through outer appearances to underlying principles of truth and wisdom. The initiate becomes more powerful through self-mastery – not mastery over others -- and thus becomes empowered to free themselves and others from the slavery that results from acquiescing to the muddling powers that be. Though it may seem that they can influence and even direct events and objects seemingly beyond their personal control -- that too is an illusion. Experiencing the interconnectedness of all makes all things possible. This is why the initiate muddler can go only so far in their efforts to control others. Inevitably they run headlong into the brick wall of their own ignorance and inability to relinquish their separatist view of the universe. Their karma rebounds on them threefold. And like an impatient, self-centered child who tries to cut in line before others, they are sent to the back of the queue to wait their proper turn. They are not sent there by some disapproving spiritual elder but by their own Holy Guardian Angel -- the Higher Self who inescapably abides by the natural laws of the universe, such as the law of karma. And *no one* is above that law.

The Misappropriation of Symbol

Infiltration is a favorite muddling technique and is self-explanatory. It is related to a more powerful technique that can really damage the collective psyche – the misappropriation and co-optation of symbol. Co-optation is when a muddler takes a sacred symbol, for instance, and misapplies it with impure motives. Similarly, misappropriation is when a muddler takes a symbol and corrupts its true meaning. Early Christian churches were often built on top of hills or sacred places where the Old Religion was practiced. In order to attract and co-opt pagans, they erected steeples on top of the churches to serve as substitute phallic symbols. In Mexico, Central and South America, Roman Catholicism absorbed many native Indian rituals, which diluted the power of the older religion. Worship of Mary was strategically emphasized where worship of the Mother Goddess had been strong. Though not a pure misappropriation on its own as Mary was a real person, it had a similar effect. At least it kept the sacred feminine alive, however minimized or tokenized it became in practice.

A more recent example of misappropriation is the Nazi swastika. The swastika is an ancient esoteric power symbol that is prevalent in cultures all over the world. It symbolizes the first swirlings of the universe, the four directions, and the four elements among other things. Adolph Hitler merely reversed the swirlings. The original sign shows the arms going in the other direction.

Why did he do this? Hitler was deeply interested in occultism, and felt that he had the right to exploit cosmic forces for his own ends. He became intimate with Karl Haushofer, a German militarist who had traveled extensively in the Far East in search of secret knowledge. It was during these travels that Haushofer met the famous Russian sage, Gurdjieff, who tutored the 13th Dalai Lama and was instrumental in conspiring a conversion of Czar Nicholas II to Buddhism.[18] Gurdjieff taught Haushofer all about the ancient subterranean kingdom of Agarthi supposedly constructed over 60,000 years ago by superhuman adepts from Atlantis. Haushofer excitedly shared this legend of a "master race" and Buddhist esoteric teachings on "awakening" with Hitler. About the same time, Hitler had discovered the anti-Jewish text, *The Protocols of the Elders of Zion*, which was later proven to be a forgery. At any rate, we can see how this all came together in Hitler's misapplication of these ideas with the Nazi slogan, "Germany Awake."

An example of outright misappropriation by the Roman Catholic Church is what they did to the Goat of Mendes – a sacred symbol to the early Knights Templar and other occultists. Sometimes called Baphomet, this figure is an incongruous goat-headed being with deep symbolic meaning. Originally, Baphomet is androgynous, seated on a cube, with a torch blazing between the horns. The torch represents cosmic intelligence and spiritual illumination. If you look closely at the head, however, it has the characteristics of a dog and a bull in addition to the goat. These three animals represent the origin of the mystery traditions. The horns make reference to the lunar headdress of a high priestess symbolizing receptivity to that which is above. A pentagram is on the forehead of Baphomet, representing the site where the perfected human remembers the cosmic origin of its divinity – the pineal gland or the third eye. The pentagram also has a connection to Venus, the morning star, associated with Lucifer and the goddess figures of Ishtar and Astarte. The androgyny of Baphomet is represented by female breasts and an erect penis hidden by a cloth, shrouding the mysteries of generation. Also, one arm appears female and the other male. One points down and the other up, a direct reference to the Hermetic Axiom, "As above – so below." The caduceus rises up from the cloth with phallic connotations and reinforcing the association with Hermes. Baphomet's belly is covered with scales, representing the reptilian origin of the human race. A black crescent moon and a white crescent moon are sometimes seen in the picture, paying further homage to the law of polarity and the cyclical nature of the universe. Later the figure of Baphomet was transformed into the goat-foot god of the witches.

The actual figure of Baphomet probably originated with the Essenes. Dr. Hugh Schonfield, an expert on the Dead Sea Scrolls, has linked the Gnostic sages to the Templars.[19] The Templars revered the sacred feminine, and when the word Baphomet is translated by a secret Essenic code, it reads "Sophia." Sophia means wisdom in Greek and was the name of a Gnostic goddess. The Templars also revered the symbol of the black cat, which probably represented the Egyptian cat goddess, Bast, also related to the lion-headed goddess, Sekhmet, and our extraterrestrial Feline ancestry.

The Roman Catholic Church took the symbol of Baphomet and turned it into a devil with horns. And we all know what happened to the black cat -- it became a symbol of bad luck and the Satanic familiar of the witch caricatured at Halloween.

Satan did not have horns until after the persecution of the Templars. How convenient for the church to claim Baphomet, twisting it and perverting it until it became the foundation for the familiar image of the modern day devil, a caricature of

319

Lucifer.   That Baphomet was connected to Lucifer was already a given – but it was the Lucifer understood by the Gnostics as the *light-bringer* -- not the Lord of Evil that today's fundamentalists call Satan.

The esoteric teachings about the true identity of Lucifer as a fallen angel run deep.   Decoding certain relevant Hebrew terms Qabalistically suggests that Jesus Christ may have been a later incarnation of this spiritual being or force.   The legend from the Gnostic Gospels provides fertile food for meditation that bears significantly on our discussion of good and evil.   In fact, I feel it is so powerful in its import, that I must include it here.

The origin of this particular quote is not fully known.   It is published in *Transcendental Magic,* an occult classic by the great 19th century sage, Eliphas Levi.   Arthur E. Waite translated the original text from French, and admits that the beginning and end of this quotation is unclear.   So we don't know how much of it is out of the Gnostic Gospels and how much of it may be Levi's own ramblings.   At any rate, I feel it is worth reproducing here for its eloquent expression of profound truth:

> "Self-conscious truth is living thought.   Truth is thought as it is in itself, and formulated thought is speech.   When Eternal Thought desired a form, it said: 'Let there be light.'   Now, this Thought which speaks is the Word, and the Word said: 'Let there be light,' because the Word itself is the light of minds. The uncreated light, which is the Divine Word, shines because it desires to be seen.   When it says: 'Let there be light!' it ordains that eyes shall open; it creates intelligences.   When God said: 'Let there be light!' Intelligence was made, and the light appeared. Now, the Intelligence which God diffused by the breath of His mouth, like a star given off from the sun, took the form of a splendid angel, who was saluted by heaven under the name of Lucifer. Intelligence awakened, and comprehended its nature

completely by the understanding of that utterance of the Divine Word: 'Let there be light!' It felt itself to be free because God had called it into being, and, raising up its head, with both wings extended, it replied: 'I will not be slavery.' 'Then shalt thou be suffering,' said the Uncreated Voice. 'I will be liberty,' replied the light. 'Pride will seduce thee,' said the Supreme Voice, 'and thou wilt bring forth death.' 'I needs must strive with death to conquer life,' again responded the created light. Thereupon God loosed from His bosom the shining cord which restrained the superb angel, and beholding him plunge through the night, which he furrowed with glory, He loved the offspring of His thought, and said with an ineffable smile: 'How beautiful was the light!'

God has not created suffering; intelligence has accepted it to be free. And suffering has been the condition imposed upon freedom of being by Him who alone cannot err, because He is infinite. For the essence of intelligence is judgement, and the essence of judgement is liberty. The eye does not really possess light except by the faculty of closing or opening. Were it forced to be always open, it would be the slave and victim of the light, and would cease to see in order to escape the torment. Thus, created Intelligence is not happy in affirming God, except by its liberty to deny Him. Now, the Intelligence which denies, invariably affirms something, since it is asserting its liberty. It is for this reason that blasphemy glorifies God and that hell was indispensable to the happiness of heaven. Were the light unrepelled by shadow, there would be no visible forms. If the first angels had not encountered the depths of darkness, the child-birth of God would have been incomplete, and there could have been no separation between the created and essential light. Never would Intelligence have known the goodness of God if it had never lost Him. Never would God's infinite love have shone forth in the joys of His mercy had the prodigal Son of Heaven remained in the House of His Father. When all was light, there was light nowhere; it filled the breast of God, who was labouring to bring it forth. And when He said: 'Let there be light!' He permitted the darkness to repel the light, and the universe issued from chaos. The negation of the angel who at birth refused slavery constituted the equilibrium of the world, and the motion of the spheres commenced. The infinite distances admired this love of liberty, which was vast enough to fill the void of eternal night and strong enough to bear the hatred of God. But God could hate not the noblest of His children, and He proved him by His wrath only to confirm him in His power. So also the Word of God Himself, as if jealous of Lucifer, willed to come down from heaven and pass triumphantly through the shadows of hell. He willed to be proscribed and condemned; He premeditated that terrible hour when He should cry, in the throes of His agony: 'My God, My God, why hast Thou forsaken Me?' As the star of the morning goes before the sun, the rebellion of Lucifer announced to new-born Nature the coming incarnation of God. Possibly Lucifer, in his fall through night, carried with him a rain of suns and stars by the attraction of his glory. Possibly our sun is a demon among the stars, as Lucifer is a star among the angels. Doubtless it is for this reason that it lights so calmly the horrible anguish of humanity and the long agony of earth – because it is free in its solitude and possesses its light."[20]

In the Waite and BOTA versions of the Tarot, the symbol of Baphomet is adopted for the depiction of the Devil in Key 15. This is a further co-optation of the symbol, but not without revealing additional esoteric significance. The pentagram on the forehead is inverted representing man's misunderstanding of his own divine nature resulting from slavery to appearance and the illusion of separateness. It is said that the devil is only God misunderstood. The Great Work involves readjusting the pentagram so that it is right side up like the original Baphomet. Once the male and female figures unchain themselves to this incongruous illusion of reality, they are free to do just that. The Devil is so absurd in appearance that it must be recognized as a creature that is not real. Therefore, laughter is what dispels the delusion which is only dependence on the illusion, and the truth behind the façade sets us free. The Hebrew letter assigned to the Devil is *Ayin*, meaning eye, the single eye that sees through all appearance, leading us appropriately to....

The Eye in the Triangle

Liberty – freedom – and justice for all. Just as Lucifer promised. Yes, that was the legacy of the United States of America. And to prove it, we have a reminder of our origins on our common currency – the dollar bill.

Everything that America stands for is deeply rooted in the Western Mystery Tradition. Esoteric occult symbolism permeates every aspect of our national culture. Americans see these symbols every day though few are overtly familiar with their meanings.

From the ancient Atlantean magic of our Native Americans to our founding fathers being Freemason initiates, it's all there. There's even a connection with Christopher Columbus. Columbus belonged to an esoteric Order called the Knights of Christ which was just a remnant and reorganization of the Knights Templar. [21]

Many early American pilgrims and settlers were Rosicrucians and Freemasons. Paul Revere was a Mason and began his famous ride at a Masonic lodge at the conclusion of an emotionally charged meeting. All the members of the Boston Tea Party were Freemasons belonging to the Boston St. Andrew's lodge. The American Revolution was directly inspired by the ideals of liberty and equality precious to every student of spiritual truth, particularly Freemasons. Benjamin Franklin was a Quaker who became a Freemason in 1731 in

Philadelphia. American Freemasons kept in touch with their brethren in Europe, and Freemasons on both sides of the Atlantic were instrumental in bringing about the French and American revolutions. Fifty out of the fifty-six American rebels who signed the Declaration of Independence were Freemasons, including John Adams and George Washington.

The occult symbolism of the first American flag was designed under auspicious circumstances. Michael Howard, as a result of his meticulous research, relates the following story. Benjamin Franklin and George Washington were members of a committee responsible for designing the American flag. The committee met at the house of one of the rebel leaders in Cambridge, Massachusetts during December of 1775. Evidently, a stranger staying with the rebel leader's family had a great deal of influence over the design. The stranger, whose identity is unknown, was an elderly professor very knowledgeable about the historical events of the previous century. He was also vegetarian and carried a large oak chest full of rare books and ancient manuscripts. When the meeting was over, all the committee members left except for Franklin and Washington who remained in conversation with the strange professor for several hours. The professor confided that America was destined to become a future leader of civilization.[22]

In addition, the Great Seal of America, our symbolic coat-of-arms, was deliberately designed in like manner. Many members of the committee were familiar with the occult teachings concerning sacred number/letter codes such as Qabalistic gematria. Therefore it is no surprise that the significance of number would play prominently in the design of the symbolism and the history of the nation, the most important one being in this case the number 13.[23] Just a short list here:

1. The digits of the year of the Declaration – "the spirit of '76" – equal 13.
2. The phrase "July the Fourth" -- the nation's birthday -- is comprised of 13 letters.

3. The phrase "The American Eagle" has 13 letters.
4. The revolutionary flag of Massachusetts had two mottos on it, both consisting of 13 letters: "An Appeal to God" and "Don't Tread on Me."
5. The Masonic phrase, "In God We Trust" can be numerologically reduced to 58, and $5 + 8 = 13$.
6. Washington, a Freemason in conjunction with 12 of his generals who were also Freemasons, made up an intimidating force of 13.
7. The first American Navy had 13 ships.
8. Even though only 11 states made up the Confederacy in the Civil War, its flag had 13 stars.
9. During WW1, the first expedition to France sailed on June 13, 1917 in 13 ships, taking 13 days to cross the Atlantic. The president during that time, Woodrow Wilson, signed his name just so in 13 letters.
10. When the Declaration of Independence was signed on July 4, 1775, the sun was in 13 degrees of the sign Cancer, and the ascendant 13 degrees in the sign of Scorpio. Key 13 in both the Rosicrucian, Masonic, Waite, and BOTA versions of the Tarot is correlated with Scorpio.
11. A deliberate repetition of 13 is seen in the Great Seal of the United States: 13 pieces for the escutcheon, 13 arrows bundled together in the eagle's talons, and the motto "E Pluribus Unum" is 13 letters. There are 13 stars and 39 (3 X 13) letters, and the berries and leaves on the olive branch total 13.
12. Early sketches of the pyramid show 13 courses.
13. The original colonies were 13 in number.

The eagle is one of the symbols for the astrological sign of Scorpio, associated with the number 13 and the concepts of death, rebirth, sexuality and regeneration. It also represents forces in the human body that once redirected and sublimated can give birth to higher vision. This process is known as spiritual alchemy, the subject of the Great Work. These early Freemasons knew that this process would be essential for the actualization and perpetuation of their spiritual vision. The olive branch symbolizing peace and the arrows symbolizing war represent the balance between mercy and severity. The phrase *E PLURIBUS UNUM* is Latin for "one out of many" representing the creation of one nation from the many colonies. It's also a reference to all gods being reflections of the One.

The other side of the Seal contains the image of a truncated pyramid with the eye in the triangle. According to Howard, the truncated pyramid represents "the loss of the Ancient Wisdom which occurred when the Christian Church achieved political power and began to repress the old pagan religions which were driven underground into secret societies."[24] Pyramids in ancient Egypt were originally initiation chambers and aerospace facilities, not tombs. At the top of each pyramid was a special capstone made of crystal and precious metals that served to concentrate and direct cosmic forces into the inner chambers for magical ceremonies. The pyramid on the Great Seal separated from its capstone infers that the adytum or temple is still incomplete. The eye in the triangle is the all-seeing eye of God. This symbol was also chosen by the Illuminist movement as their logo and was published on the cover of all radical political texts during the French revolution.

The motto "Annuit Coeptis" above the eye translates to "He favours our undertaking." The revolutionaries felt that their cause was divinely inspired and that the revolution was a fulfillment of divine prophecy. According to Howard, Washington had a corresponding mystical experience. At Valley Forge, an angel approached him and showed him a vision of an American Utopia governing the world in centuries to come. Further evidence of this vision rests in the words "Novus Ordo Seclorum" beneath the pyramid, meaning "New Order of the Ages." Could the angel have been an extraterrestrial?

The revolutionary occultists believed that America would guide the world through the transition from the Age of Pisces to the Age of Aquarius. This transition period roughly corresponds to 250 years, beginning with the American Revolution in 1776 to the year 2025 C.E. Interestingly, 2025 is the approximate date for the return of the planet Nibiru, home of our extraterrestrial ancestors.

Many things have been said about that eye in the triangle. Muddling conspiracy theorists will tell you that it is the symbol of the ruling Illuminati whose secret agents are building a New World Order for the enslavement of humanity. They will tell you that the Illuminati comprise an organization of evil men who are simply the pawns of evil aliens. Yet according to Howard,

> More sensational nonsense has been written about the Illuminati than any other secret society, yet the real facts about this mysterious organization and its role in the revolutionary movements of eighteenth-century Europe are extraordinary.[25]

At one time there was a group called the Illuminati. Adam Weishaupt, a young professor at the Bavarian University in Germany, founded it in 1776. Weishaupt was highly educated with a diverse background. Although born Jewish, as a child he was educated by Catholic Jesuits. Later he turned Protestant and became a student of the ancient mysteries and pagan religions. He soon discovered Freemasonry. Howard explains,

> Weishaupt first made contact with a Masonic lodge in either Hanover or Munich in 1774 but was sadly disappointed by what he discovered. In his opinion the other members of the lodge were ignorant of the occult significance of Masonry and knew nothing about its pagan symbolism. His contact with the Masonic tradition had, however, given Weishaupt an insight into the structure and organization of a secret society and he used his experience in Masonry to found his own clandestine fraternity.[26]

The Illuminati began as a small group of influential Bavarians united around egalitarian and socialist political ideas. In order to recruit more members, Weishaupt encouraged infiltration of Masonic lodges until he had a huge power base all over Europe. The Illuminati shared a Utopian vision of a society without nationality, private property, or social authority. Therefore, autocrats and despots of the monarchy and clergy were their first political targets.

Weishaupt did not hesitate to initiate women into the group because he taught they were equal to men. He also advocated religious freedom, invoking the wrath of the Church. He believed that the secret teachings of Jesus were preserved in the Rosicrucian and Masonic traditions. What made him different, however, was his belief that the political system should be overthrown, even if it meant resorting to violence. Therefore the Illuminati were very much a part of revolutionary movements.

But then an interesting thing happened. The group became so radical that the pendulum had to swing the other way. Post-revolutionary France saw substantial reforms domestically, yet the threat of foreign invasion and counter-revolution still loomed over everything. A new centralized dictatorship arose to take the place of the old one, and terror became the rule of the day, betraying the original goals of the Revolution. Howard reiterates,

> As with all radical political movements, those who advocated the replacement of the *status quo* were soon seduced by the power they had gained and became oppressors worse than the tyrants they replaced.[27]

In pre-revolutionary Europe, Masonry once had a strong traditional following among the aristocracy. After infiltration by radicals, however, the lodges began to splinter into reactionary traditionalists and radical revolutionaries both claiming to be upholders of "the way." It wasn't long then before Freemasonry became the scapegoat for anyone dissatisfied with the current political situation. To this day the scapegoating continues.

328

The Illuminati no longer exist as an organized force. However, their ideas have been picked up and misapplied on occasion by groups such as the German Thule Society. Modern conspiracy theorists feel the Illuminati still exist as a sinister force in political affairs. They say that the Council on Foreign Relations, the Trilateral Commission, and all the other muddling agencies are fronts for this force. But no one can offer definitive proof.

Some conspiracy theorists take a cynical yet more realistic view of this controlling elite, by whatever name, stating that they are completely devoid of commitment, working both sides for personal advantage irrespective of any belief at all. This is probably closer to the truth. The only society of the ruling elite is the society of high finance, and that is no secret. The lust for money and power is not exclusive to any one group – whether religious, political, neither or both. Those who share such lust often switch sides, depending on which way the wind blows. A prestigious law firm known for its aggressive insurance defense will just as quickly turn into the plaintiff's hero if a poor man was seriously injured by a negligent deep pocket. Wealthy corporations funnel money into both political parties to ensure that their interests are protected in spite of who is elected. It's not about belief and principle anymore. It's about the almighty dollar, which brings us back to that eye in the triangle.

The eye can look both ways but it is neither one way nor the other. Our founding fathers were not completely true to their Masonic ideals of justice, liberty, and brotherhood or else our Constitution would not have initially excluded women and people of color. Still, we must start somewhere. And like children learning to walk, we will fall many times before we learn to do it well. We are still learning as I speak.

Naming the Powers that Be

As we will see, the ruling elite pulling the strings behind the scenes is not so obscure. Their mechanisms for muddling are the mainstream politics of government bureaucracies and corporate boards of directors. Yet there seems to be a gathering of faces and events that can be connected to these mechanisms, and once we put a name to the faces, it's much easier to keep track of them. They loosely fall into three main groupings known as (1) The Trilateral Commission; (2) The Council on Foreign Relations; and (3) The Bilderberg Group. Though these three groups have been the focus of many conspiracy theories, their existence and their activities are really no conspiracy at all. They're certainly not secret societies, although the Bilderberg meetings are closed to the public.

Zbignew Brzezinski (former chairman of Manhattan Bank and national security adviser to President Carter), David Rockefeller, and other eminent, wealthy men founded the Trilateral Commission in 1973. Originally there were about 300 members, all coming from the upper echelons of international banking and industry, government, academia, and conservative factions of the media and labor organizations. Their common goal was to advance the doctrine of world order known as "trilaterialism." The term "trilateral" refers to the partnership among the ruling elite of the three main economic powers of the world: North America, Western Europe and Japan. Their program is to protect the interests of capitalism at all costs. Their strategy relies on some basic points of agreement:

1. The people, governments, and economies of all the nations must serve the needs of multinational banks and corporations;
2. Control over economic resources spells power in modern politics; and
3. The leaders of capitalist democracies -- systems where economic control and profit, and thus political power, rest with the few – must resist movements toward a truly popular democracy.[28]

Trilaterialism has its origins in the two older institutions of managing worldview: The Council on Foreign Relations and the Bilderberg Group. The Council on Foreign Relations is not a government agency – it is a private organization founded in 1918 in the United States for shaping public policy along similar ideological lines. Its European counterpart, the elite organization known as the Bilderberg Group, was founded in 1954. This group refers to select heads-of-state and influential individuals in business and academia who meet once a year to determine specific ideological goals consistent with Trilaterialism. The name comes from the physical location where this group first met: The Bilderberg Hotel in Holland.

None of these three groups alone controls the world. Yet all three of them and their diverse membership present a picture of a tightly organized multinational coordination of world management efforts rooted in capitalist imperialism. Of course they don't call it "imperialism" because that was a dirty word in a time of resurgent nationalism. But that did not keep them from openly addressing this delicate dilemma in one of their meetings. Isaiah Bowman, at a CFR meeting in May 1942, said that the United States had to exercise the strength needed to assure "security," and at the same time "avoid conventional forms of imperialism." The way to do this, he argued, was to make the exercise of that power international in character through a united national body.[29] And so the United Nations was born.

The Council on Foreign Relations strategically substituted the words "national interests" for "capitalist imperialism" and "neocolonialism." So foreign policy cannot be divorced from economic reality. U.S. Secretary of State Charles Evans Hughes admitted this as early as the 1920s:

> ...foreign policies are not built upon abstractions. They are the result of practical conceptions of national interest. The national interest is rarely an objective fact, however, as is indicated by the truism that in every country it is always redefined after a revolution... Since those in power define the national interest as the preservation of the existing set of economic, social, and political relationships and of their own rule, the national interest in a capitalist

331

society is little more than the interest of the upper class...[30]

No secrecy or conspiracy needs dismantling to discover this trend because historically managing matters of economic and political policy has always been reserved for a wealthy, elite force of individuals in society. It's just that as the ages progress, modern technology has contributed significantly to the compaction of such efforts. That same technology, however, guarantees a more widespread dissemination of information to the masses, so that at least the means to make these connections is more readily available to us than before.

By examining this information, we find that these institutions "propagate the resulting policy positions through their network of authoritative channels (university publications, public officials, forums, etc.) setting the limits of respectable foreign policy debate."[31] It is no secret that several members of the Bilderberg group are high administrative heads of our leading academic institutions such as MIT, Harvard, and Columbia. Innovation in these institutions is only encouraged if it furthers the status quo. Therefore, mainstream education goes a long way in preserving these power structures. The theory even trickles down into elementary grades where children learn that even in the midst of great economic disparity between social classes, we can still have what appears to be a "thriving democracy." Keeping up that appearance is a major way that the muddlers secure the status quo.

Because the nations joined together by the Trilateral Commission are the most prosperous and productive, a major concern of the Trilateral Commission was that these nations remain the "vital center" of managerial control over the world's affairs and resources. Therefore Brzezinski proclaimed the need for a world economy for which the Trilateral Commission would be the custodian. This economy would "embrace" and "co-opt" the Third World and gradually reintegrate the Soviet Union, Eastern Europe, and China, which were originally known as Trilateral "dropouts."[32] This, as we see, has already

332

happened to a large extent as predicted by Brzezinski. Communist forces have all but crumbled in those countries to be replaced by an unprecedented influx of corporate influence: Those 'golden arches' are everywhere!

> Trilaterialism is the creed of an international ruling class whose locus of power is the global corporation. The owners and managers of global corporations view the entire world as their factory, farm, supermarket, and playground. The Trilateral Commission is seeking to strengthen and rationalize the world economy in their interest.[33]

The Trilateral Commission divides the world into third world and fourth world regions. Third World countries are those nations that are basically client states to the United States tied to the U.S. by economic indebtedness, yet not so poor as to be totally uninfluential. These are countries such as Mexico, Brazil, and Saudi Arabia that possess some political clout, substantial foreign exchange reserves and needed exports. Fourth World countries are the poorest and weakest, easily manipulated or pacified with international welfare programs focusing on meeting basic human needs because they have no political clout. Any trend that these countries might show towards self-reliance or greater independence is perceived as a threat to the new global economy, and promptly thwarted by the Trilateral Commission forces in acts designed to induce greater "cooperation" on the part of these countries. And how is this "cooperation" coerced? According to political scholar and analyst Holly Sklar,

> In the wake of World War II, old-style colonialism gave way to neocolonialism. The neocolonial state has formal political independence but in reality its economic system and thus its political policy is directed from the outside. Instead of a single colonial master, the neocolonial state may have many new masters: Western governments (especially the U.S.),

333

the International Monetary Fund, banking consortiums, global corporations. Western powers have intervened repeatedly to sabotage and smash governments which challenged the tightly woven fabric of dependency: Iran, 1953; Guatemala, 1954; the Congo (now Zaire), 1960; Brazil, 1964; Dominican Republic and Indonesia, 1965; Bolivia, 1970-71; Chile, 1973... Debt dependency is one of the neocolonial leashes around a Third World Country's neck. The leash is let out to allow Western-directed development projects to gallop ahead – returning enormous profits to foreign corporations and banks. Or, the debt leash can be pulled in tight – as part of an economic and political destabilization campaign – to strangle a rebellious nation into submission.[34]

As nations are enslaved by indebtedness to the World Bank, so we are enslaved by our indebtedness to banks through credit and other funny money machinations. The Trilateral Commission controls the International Monetary Fund, and as long as people and nations are enslaved by debt, the ruling elite can afford to profess encouragement of human rights and democratic ideals because they know that we're too busy working to pay off those debts to fight for anything more. Therefore any trilateral strategy of "democratization" is one of co-optation. Limited democracy is governable democracy. Reform is tolerated, but never revolution.

So if we want to look for people who may be attempting to manipulate world affairs behind the scenes to their own benefit, we need look no further than our own government and its legally sanctioned corporations. These people need not resort to conspiracy to do this. The ruling elite more often muddle in plain view of everyone or anyone who has eyes to see. Laws, loopholes, and high court decisions are written in their favor in full public view as a result of their influence. Yet where is the public? That is the question.

A Call for an Informed Electorate

John Q – where are you? Shopping at the mall? Watching football? Drinking beer? At the kids' soccer game? Watching *Fearfactor*? Gossiping on the telephone? Working late at the office to pay off the astronomical credit card bills? Resenting the boss? Catching up on e-mail? Mindlessly surfing the Internet? Washing the SUV? Mowing the grass – again? Plotting the overthrow of an unwary coworker? Arguing with the spouse over something stupid and trivial? Planning an expensive wedding? Yelling at the dog? Getting high? Getting baptized? Getting nowhere? The list is endless.

Of course the above activities mostly apply to the citizens of the most economically advantaged country in the world – the United States of America. Assuming that most of my readers reside in that great nation, I will continue along those lines.

Several years ago, a black professor at Berkeley published an article saying that all that minorities needed to do to take back the reigns of power from an indifferent elite was to simply organize around a common cause. I responded saying that she entirely missed the point. The real minority is people who give a damn. People must have a change of heart before they can change anything. And that is the most serious problem facing the US of A today. Not crime – not the economy – not even the muddlers. It's apathy. Of course the muddlers encourage apathy, and we'll soon see how. First let's get rid of a popular misconception.

Americans live in the freest country in the world. Yet I wonder how many of us truly appreciate those freedoms when most of us have never had to fight for them. Maybe that's why we are losing them left and right. Voting does little to correct the problem because voting usually only ratifies a policy or decision made by an elite that is dedicated to preserving its power and privilege. Most of us have no part in making that policy or decision. And until we do, true democracy will remain a dream – not a reality.

How did this happen? How did we become mere consumers of a political system and not true participants? Leaders in democratic states cannot use violence to control people like totalitarian states (Waco excluded as an isolated event). Our rulers have had to use more sophisticated forms of indoctrination – propaganda; the manufacturing of consent through the popular media.[35]

Other than outright lies, misplaced emphasis, manipulated data and selective programming, the propaganda is usually subtler. An example of this is how the media portrayed American intervention in Nicaragua. That we should be there was a shared assumption. The only issue was *how* should we be there: violently or diplomatically? The issue of whether we should be there at all was never challenged. However, the ongoing debate made it appear that we had an independent press expressing opposing viewpoints, but only within the limited framework of that shared assumption. The truth is we have a press that is only as free as its corporate sponsors allow it to be. And the last thing they'll ever tell you is who your real enemy is. It's not aliens, gangs, unions, the Feds, greedy managers, North Korea, Saddam Hussein, Osama Bin Laden, creeping socialism, terrorism or any other "ism". The enemy is within – it's apathy.

So there is no conspiracy here. The government and corporations are only doing a job we abandoned. How do we get it back? Well, it won't be easy.

The first thing we have to do is care, and we have to care enough to act beyond our words, and most important -- beyond the little soap opera of "me, my games, my job, my family, and my possessions." Now those are valid self-interests. However, I believe that acting to preserve those self-interests means seeing that we are all connected and interdependent. The survival of the entire planet depends on developing and expressing human values other than those based on personal greed and personal gain.

Term limits or voting out incumbents will not solve the problem because in order to get elected, a candidate needs money. Corporations buy them out before they get there, and the majority of Americans have little influence over corporate agenda. Therefore we are further marginalized from the process of making decisions that affect us, our pocketbooks, and our future.

So beyond caring and a commitment to action, what's next? As isolated individuals with limited resources, the need for organization is given. But this organization cannot be imposed upon us from above. We have to discover it by trial and error, and base it on a commitment to principle-centered values. These voluntary organizations should also be dedicated to eliminating structures of hierarchy and domination and their basis in ownership and control. This is grass-roots democracy that insists on win/win or no deal. It doesn't require special training or unusual intelligence. It just takes honesty and hard work.

We deserve not to be lied to anymore the moment we no longer fear to look at the truth. We deserve the promise of true democracy the moment we are willing to fight to preserve what little we have. Fulfilling the dream for everyone happens when true spiritual values of principle-centered living direct everything we do. The darkness currently enveloping the corridors of power cannot extinguish the still small flame inside of you. Let that flame grow and dare to let it reach out and touch the flame within someone else. Then the fire will continue to spread until those corridors of power are lit with the light of a truth-loving citizenry who are not afraid to take responsibility – who are no longer afraid to be free.

The Illusion of Freedom and the Funny Money System

What is freedom? Freedom is the choice of one's own disciplines. So we must choose wisely. The freedom that most people live is counterfeit compared with what we are promised. And again, I'm talking about Americans here. We live in a partial democracy -- it is not complete. In order for it to be a complete democracy, it must also be an economic democracy.

It is a sad commentary on our educational system when adults do not know the difference between the terms 'democracy' and 'capitalism.' Or maybe they know but they don't act like it for fear of being called unpatriotic. Democracy is a form of government -- "Literally, government by the people as a whole rather than by any section, class or interest within it."[36] Capitalism is an "...economic arrangement, defined by the predominant existence of capital and wage labour, the former consisting of accumulations in the hands of private (i.e. non-government) owners, including corporations and joint stock companies, the latter consisting in the activities of labourers, who exchange their labour hours... (...labour power) for wages, paid from the stock of capital."[37] So capitalism is not a form of government but a form of economy. But "'Capitalist democracy,' which exists only in the political sphere, is a device which *prevents* the emergence of democracy at the economic and social level; 'true democracy' can come about only when the conditions for it are prepared at those more basic levels – hence the need for a (provisional) directed democracy in the political sphere." (Emphasis added.)[38] Therefore, democracy and capitalism are not really compatible. That is why we're struggling with it so today. The points of view are at odds with each other. A form of government that promises equality and control by the people cannot co-exist with an economy that is based on such inequality as exists between owner and worker, where the owner controls (governs) everything, including the worker.

How did this happen? Where did these strange bedfellows come from? What does it mean in relation to our particular topic? Well, a review of a little history is in order. The roots of capitalism reach farther back than the roots of democracy, so we'll start there.

Money was created to facilitate the bartering process. In olden days, folks traded goods and services directly. This exchange could involve many things and take many forms -- for example, two horses for three goats; a loaf of bread for cleaning out the barn, and so on. Coins and paper bills were invented so

338

that goods wouldn't have to be carried around everywhere or services immediately delivered. It was simply a matter of convenience. Paper bills in particular had the same effect as a promissory note – a written promise to pay a debt. A problem arose, however, when the goat farmer wrote more notes than he had goats to pay them off with. So many things could be at stake here, the least of which are the farmer's reputation and ability to perform well in the market in the future.

Coins operated a little differently. The value of these units of exchange was directly linked to the value of their metal. Our modern monetary system was founded in the 1600s when the goldsmiths established places to hold the strongest lockboxes for safekeeping the community's metal. These establishments were the first banks. The goldsmiths gave receipts to the depositors, and every receipt was really a promissory note which could be circulated as money until the note holder returned to the goldsmith to redeem the note for the metal. We know what happened next. Ordinarily, only about 15% of the notes were ever redeemed at a given time. The rest were still circulating about the community. So the goldsmiths discovered they could loan unredeemed metals and charge interest, making money on the loans. It was a risky business because timing was everything. If too many notes came back all at once or the borrowers were too slow to repay, the goldsmith could be ruined. But if he ran his business carefully, he could accrue considerable wealth without ever having to produce anything of value. As Bramley indicates,

> The injustice of this system is obvious. If for every sack of gold the smith had on deposit people now owed him the equivalent of four sacks, someone had to lose. As public debt to the goldsmith increased, more and more true wealth and resources were owed to him. Since the goldsmith was not producing any true wealth or resources, but was demanding an ever-increasing share of them because of his paper notes, he easily became a parasite upon the economy. The inevitable result was the enrichment of the careful

goldsmith-turned-banker at the cost of the impoverishment of other people in the community. The impoverishment was manifested either in the people's need to give up things of value or in their need to toil longer to create the wealth needed to repay the banker. If the goldsmith was not careful and his monetary bubble burst, the people around him suffered anyway due to the disruption caused by the collapse of his bank and the loss of the value of his notes still in circulation.[39]

So now you know why the whole world of credit, finance, and banking stinks and feels essentially dishonest. It is! When our fortune rises and falls with the economy, instability and helplessness prevail. It's not fun for anyone – rich or poor. The rich worry about holding on to it while the poor worry about getting enough of it. There seems to be no middle road.

Soon certain families became known for their expertise and control in the banking world. The Medici banking house in Italy established the "gold standard" by which all goods and services were valued. People thought their notes were "as good as gold" when they were not. The more gold notes that were issued, the less valuable they became, resulting in inflation. These "created out of nothing" gold notes engendered incredible indebtedness that would in turn slow down the economy. So this

> ...method of creating money clearly destroyed the true purpose of money: to represent the existence of actual tradable commodities. Inflatable paper money allows a handful of people to absorb and manipulate a great deal of true wealth, which are the valuable goods and services people produce, simply through the act of printing paper and then slowly destroying the value of that paper with inflation. It causes money to become its own commodity that can be manipulated on its own terms, usually to the detriment of the production-and-barter system.

Money was meant to assist that system, not to dominate and control it.[40]

But hey – what could you expect in a dominator society? I mean, duh! Bramley points to evil "Brotherhood" members as originating this system -- in other words, muddlers. The real reason behind instigating such a system, however, is far more sinister, in terms of global impact, according to Bramley. Evidently an experimental version of this system was developed in Holland in 1609, the year that Holland signed a peace treaty with Spain, marking the emergence of the new independent Dutch Republic. A wealthy group of gentlemen who wanted to renew the wars with Spain founded the Bank of Amsterdam. The bank then issued notes four times in excess of the Bank's asset base. This enabled the Dutch to draw on three quarters of this "created-out-of-nothing" money to finance their wars. Per Bramley,

> This reveals the primary reason why the inflatable paper money system was created: it enables nations to fight and prolong their wars. It also makes the human struggle for physical existence in a modern economy more difficult due to the massive debt and parasitic absorption of wealth that the system causes. Furthermore, steady inflation reduces the value of people's money so that their accumulated wealth is gradually eroded. The Custodial aims expressed in the Garden of Eden and Tower of Babel stories were greatly furthered by the new paper money system.[41]

Frightening, isn't it? This funny money syndrome was to spawn the oppressive economic arrangement known as capitalism in order to further enslave the people.

Targeting Marx

Author Rius says,

341

> Actually, Marxism today divides the world into two
> camps: Those who hate him and those who place all
> their hopes in him. . . and I'd mention a third group:
> those who don't know him. . . Because Charlie Marx
> is just like the Bible or the Koran: Many quote him,
> but very few know him, and even fewer understand
> him. . . [42]

Marx is not wholly responsible for communism. But he is largely responsible for social security, pensions, paid holidays, the protection of unions, and various other social victories directly improving the lives of those who must work for a living. Marx was born in Germany in 1818 of Jewish descent but raised Lutheran. Marx made friends with the prominent philosopher Friedrich Engels. Together they joined a secret society in London and co-authored *The Communist Manifesto*. Communism is a "...social and economic arrangement defined by the fact that no participant owns significantly more than any other. . . because ownership is confined to the means of consumption and is excluded from the means of production and exchange."[43] In the *Manifesto*, Marx described his materialist version of history and the future, and the role that the Communist Party as an international organization would play in bringing about that future. Interestingly, Marx eventually left the secret society because its very existence was contrary to his communist ideals. He disliked the romantic elitism and conspiratorial overtones he found there.

Marx made a clear distinction between socialism and communism. Socialism is supposed to be a transitional stage to communism, a state in which social classes cease to exist. Therefore communism has never truly existed anywhere on the Earth. Countries called communist such as China, Cuba, and the former Soviet Union are not really communist at all because class struggle still prevails and ownership is not excluded from the means of production and exchange. The State owns the means of production in those governments, making them more a form of state capitalism than true communism or even socialism. Socialism, on the other hand, is a social, economic, and political doctrine that promotes a more equitable distribution of wealth achieved by social ownership of the means of production, exchange and diffusion. A good example of this would be a factory owned and controlled by the workers.

This is the area where Marx is most misunderstood. Marx made it clear as did Rosa Luxemburg and other advocates of socialism after him, that this more equitable system called socialism could only be brought about by the workers as a result of their own activities; that nobody could ever bring socialism to them on their behalf. To retain the false hope that someone else could liberate them was to fall back into the age-old conditioning of master/slave subservience giving rise to such dictators as Stalin and Lenin. People get lazy, looking for a savior, and instead, just end up with another muddler. Those men, like most muddlers, were wolves in sheep's clothing making promises they never intended to keep – all under the cover of the communist ideal. But it wasn't communism. It never even got close. It was just another form of totalitarianism. If Marx could see what all the so-called revolutionaries have done in his name, he would be appalled.

But the masses are hypnotized by the words repeatedly recited by their rulers, and their minds close down as if thinking is no longer required. Why? Because somebody already did their thinking for them. American children were never given the opportunity to discover the true ideas of Marx and other great iconoclasts because from day one they are brainwashed to believe that such original thinkers are evil, crazy, anti-American, or not worth their time. And if our government says so as expressed through our state-controlled educational institutions, it must be so, right? Not!

Marx's finest contribution was the writing and publication of *Das Kapital*. In this book he takes the funny money system apart and shreds it to pieces, concluding that capitalism is based on the exploitation of labor following the sale of labor-power. There are two kinds of capitalism: Private capitalism -- competition between profit-seeking companies controlled by members of the "bourgeoisie" or owners of capital, and state capitalism, which is production-for-profit by state (government) enterprises controlled by members of the state bureaucracy, like the former Soviet Union.

Before capitalism, all items possessed use-value, not exchange-value. Dresses were made to be worn, not sold. Bread was baked to be eaten, not bought. And so on. As a matter of fact, seeking to profit from the production of these items was regarded as immoral and gluttonous. It was only after the funny money system was securely established that items began to have an exchange-value in addition to use-value. Use-value and exchange-value don't mix well. "The capitalist quest for profit – for ever greater sums of value – radically clashes with human desires for food, shelter, and other use-values."[44] This misuse results in a product's alienation as a use-value. Items then become commodities – products which must be sold to be used. If they cannot be sold, they cannot be used. So an unsold loaf of bread on the grocer's shelf just rots and goes to waste while millions starve. Another way that capitalists distort use-value in order to increase profits is by sabotaging the product – skimping on quality and safety – which may eventually render the product useless and defective.

If value exists only in exchange, we must understand the true nature of exchange. Goats are not really the same as horses, so how can they be equal? As Aristotle discovered long ago, exchanging items only gives the *appearance* of equality between them because that equality is false. So where do we come up with the notion of just the right price for just the right item? Where is the hidden value in items that are inherently unequal? According to Marx, the answer is labor. And when labor gets embodied into material objects, it becomes objectified. Once labor is objectified, it can be alienated from the worker, and this is where the problem begins.

Have you ever watched *Antiques Roadshow* on television? Do you really think those antiques are as valuable as they are estimated to be? The original movie poster for some old movie may have been worth thirty cents when first manufactured. But now, it could be worth hundreds of dollars. Why? The material properties of the object never changed. Certainly the time taken to produce it never changed. So how did it suddenly become worth hundreds of dollars? Scarcity and age? Well then why isn't it worth thousands of dollars instead of hundreds? Why not millions instead of thousands? Any value placed upon that poster is an artificial value that is socially contrived, not inherent in the object itself. If it can be socially fabricated, then it can be socially unfabricated because it was never real to begin with.

This is what happened to labor. Useful labor is any labor that enhances the useful properties of use-values, like the particular labor and skill required to make a pair of shoes. Making shoes though requires a different kind of labor than that required for making dresses. Yet someone might wish to exchange a pair of shoes for a dress for whatever reason – maybe the time to produce each was the same. We know that the labor was materially different because both objects are materially different and required different skills. Yet the persons who want to make the exchange treat the labor as equal to facilitate the exchange. Is this still useful labor? NO. Once the element of exchange is introduced, useful labor becomes abstract labor because the work activities are treated as if they had no distinguishing qualities.[45] The labor is reduced to time and becomes a commodity in itself. But wait a minute. It gets even more complicated. What if the shoemaker wants to do this again and decides to go more slowly, taking five days to make one pair of shoes instead of five hours, thinking he could get more dresses for his one pair of shoes. Do you think the dressmaker is going to go for this? Hell no. That's because most people will only pay for the *average* amount of labor that it really took to produce the commodity. The actual time spent making the object is not the point. The abstract labor is further deformed into socially *standard* labor.

This is what happens when technology replaces human hands. When the cotton gin was introduced, the value of handpicked cotton was cut in half. The actual labor did not change – just the level of socially standard labor. Therefore there is no such animal as real, material, 'equal' labor. It's all contrived – it's *socially abstract* labor. But if you look at a microwave oven, can you actually see this abstract labor? No, and you never will.

No useful object materially embodies abstract labor. It is only a commodity – an object produced for exchange. Useful labor is alienated from the worker because commodities become the measuring units of abstract labor. Labor determines nothing – only exchange value matters. And since this value is not material, it cannot be materially perceived. It is reduced to a phantom social reality created in our heads – literally a *figment* of our imagination. So not only did Buddha point to the empty nature of the material world – so did Marx.

Similarly, a celebrity is a celebrity as a result of social practice only. Nothing in their physiology inherently makes them a celebrity. We make them. And if we can make them, we can break them as we often do. It is the same way with the stock market. It is a ludicrous absurdity subject to the ever-changing whims of the select few, mainly investors, who allow themselves to be influenced by other phenomena which may or may not have a material base in reality. This is Marx's concept of fetishism. Fetishism is the belief that particular objects can have mystical powers – like gold, celebrities, and religious idols. Those objects then become fetishes. All commodities are fetishes. Money is the universal commodity. And the money that is invested to generate more money is capital. Therefore, capitalism really resembles a primitive religion.

Joseph Campbell said that the tallest buildings reflect a society's highest values. In medieval times, the tallest building was the cathedral paying homage to God. Now the tallest buildings are skyscrapers – paying homage to the money god -- the god of the ruling elite. The twin towers in New York did not represent America – they were the temple of the money god and the religion of capitalism. If America were truly a full democracy, both politically and economically, the attack on the World Trade Center would not have so deeply wounded its psyche. Unfortunately, human lives are lost each day in equally

346

senseless fashion. Death at the hands of drunk drivers, negligent surgeons, gang members, cancer caused by corporate environmental pollution, heart attacks brought on by work induced stress – these deaths are just as senseless and as outrageous as the deaths caused by terrorists. And these deaths happen everyday. Why aren't we as deeply affected by them? Because they did not occur as a result of an attack on the cherished religious institution of our country which is capitalism. And if the media had not biased the event out of proportion in service to a government who wishes its citizens to equate capitalism with what it means to be an American, we could have been spared a lot of unnecessary psychic trauma.

Capitalism is about accumulating more capital, and that is done by making profits. Where do profits come from? From creating something called surplus value. An even more valuable commodity than money is labor power. Surplus value comes from the alienation of labor – the subordination of the worker to an alien power, usually the boss. This happened through what Marx calls expropriation.

The great expropriation occurred during the dawn of the funny money system when the producer was divorced from the means of production. But throughout history, whenever a harmonious community is replaced with slavery and domination, we find expropriation. Expropriation is exploitation: the control of surplus labor by an armed oppressor class. This is the hallmark of every class society, including ours. Any labor beyond that necessary for survival resulting in a surplus product is surplus labor.

Workers (those who do not own their business) usually have no say about what to produce, how to produce it and why. Their only freedom lies in their ability to sell their labor power, which is not really a freedom at all because they are surrendering their control of it. That is the alienation of labor. Everyone knows there are only two kinds of workers: employed and unemployed. The value of labor power is not found in the hours a worker can labor, but in the time required to 'produce' the worker – to keep the worker alive and

347

productive – whatever it costs to replenish the worker's energy so that the worker can put out about the same amount of labor power each day. So the value of labor power can be less than the value of the labor product. This is the secret of surplus value – the exploitation of labor power. The commodities that result from this process are more valuable than the labor power that was sold to make them. This is where profits come from. Therefore, there is no such thing as a fair wage. Living wage perhaps, but never fair.

We are duped into thinking we are paid for our labor instead of our labor power. This makes the concept of a fair wage seem possible. But it's not. The nature of the employer-employee relationship obscures this reality, which of course was the intention of the original muddlers. Authors Smith and Evans summarize:

> In reality, workers are *not* paid for their 'labour' – nor is there such a thing as a 'fair wage.' Capitalist production is based on *exploitation*. Once labour-power is sold, the capitalist uses it as he likes. Workers are paid not for their *own* labour, either useful or 'socially average,' but for the average labour-time required to *reproduce labour-power*. This payment is equivalent in value only to part of the average labour performed by the worker – beyond this, there is *unpaid surplus labour.* Workers seldom realise this. Instead, it is common to believe that working people are paid for *all* their labour – so that profits *do not* result from the exploitation of labour. The wage-form thus extinguishes every trace of the divisions of the working day into necessary labour and surplus labour, into paid and unpaid labour. All labour appears as paid labour.[46]

It's really a reverse form of slavery. At least under the feudal system, we knew when we were working for ourselves and when we were working for the king. Under slavery, we know we're always working for someone else. But under the wage system, we're still working for someone else -- it just appears we're working for ourselves. Now you know why it's so difficult to get ahead. Even if you want to go into business for yourself and become your own 'capitalist,' it is almost impossible to do that without borrowing capital from another capitalist, thus indenturing yourself further through debt. You've just gotten yourself higher on the food chain, that's all. Credit is insidious in this regard – we can't seem to live with it or without it. The United States has a higher standard of living than most countries not because it's capitalist, but because most of its citizens are living a borrowed life on credit. Again, from Smith and Evans:

> All the notions of justice held by both the worker and the capitalist, all the mystifications of the capitalist mode of production, all capitalism's illusions about freedom, all the apologetic tricks of vulgar economics, have as their basis the appearance that wages are 'natural' and potentially 'fair.' **They are not, nor can they be.** It is not 'natural' for workers to be divorced from the means of production. This, we have seen, is the result of an agonising and bloody historical process – that of *expropriation*. Labour-power is sold to capital only because capital possesses a monopoly on the means of production. So-called 'free workers' --- who are free above all to alienate their labour for the privilege of exploitation – experience a travesty of freedom.[47]

Why is this happening? We touched on this at the beginning of the chapter. The primary obstacles to cooperation are political and psychological. The working population is neither creative nor well organized. Folks raised under capitalism become conditioned to take orders and be subservient. Emotionally, they are heavily invested in all kinds of authoritarian relations and seldom challenge the existing power structure.[48]

349

Will we ever be able to produce cooperatively, for shared use rather than for profit? The answer to that question depends on us. None of this is simple. What makes it murkier than it was fifty years ago is the fact that capitalism has changed, and what we have today bears little resemblance to its original form. Today the words 'capitalist' and 'worker' are not mutually exclusive, for one. Secondly, the power structures in many corporations are immense. There is no longer only one boss – there are many in the form of middle managers and what have you. Yet they do not necessarily own the business. Even with stock options, unions, and cooperative work forces, we still have to deal with the bottom line, which is always *profits* – not people. And as long as people are secondary to profits, exploitation exists.

The ideology of communism as presented by Marx advocates the abolition of private property to some extent. Even though he says, "Communism deprives no man of the power to appropriate the products of society; all that it does is to deprive him of the power to subjugate the labour of others by means of such appropriation."[49] Still, any attempt to redistribute property in this day and age is unrealistic. Ideology aside, Marx's greatest contribution to humanity was in his analysis of capitalism and pointing out its incompatibility with true freedom.

Money is not evil. It's energy, and all depends on how it's used. Many courageous pioneers are leading the way in economic reform, showing how worker-owned businesses can survive and thrive against all odds. Altruistic CEOs who want to make a positive contribution to the world in the way they treat their employees do exist. Still, it is like chipping away at an iceberg with an ice pick. Revolution may be the only option yet. But I cannot overemphasize that first means a revolution from *within*.

The Socialist Party of the United States is a benign organization whose ideals and principles are worthy and sound, yet the Party leaves much to be desired in terms of effectiveness – making an impact – applying those principles.[50] I've often

350

said that if they just got rid of the "S" word, then maybe people would embrace their platform because I've yet to find one person who disagrees with it in principle. But the Party can't seem to get a foot in the door edgewise as long as they call themselves 'socialists' because Americans are so brainwashed to fear and hate that word. They equate it with communism and anti-Americanism. The U.S. Socialist Party preaches a democratic socialism – a socialism that would enhance and empower democracy – not cripple it. The laws that brought us Social Security, the eight-hour workday, and minimum wage were all originally Socialist Party initiatives later adopted by Democrats and liberals who got them passed in Congress. Few people know that and fewer still are taught it. Still, it may be as Audre Lorde prophesizes: "The Master's tools will never dismantle the Master's house." I'm not ready to concede just yet though. Reform is better than nothing at all.

Personally, I do not believe that any "ism" – whether it be capitalism, socialism, communism, or whatever ism – is going to solve our problems. These systems are just methods by which we govern ourselves. Systems can be used for the benefit of humanity or abused, and capitalism is more often abused by the muddlers than it is not.

Capitalism is the economic arrangement preferred by muddlers because it's a model of muddling itself. But remember, capitalism is not the same thing as free enterprise. Free enterprise is unrestricted economic activity in a free and open market. This is why entrepreneurs are often called the backbone of the free enterprise system. A pure capitalist, on the other hand, lives for profit, which does not necessarily require free enterprise but can co-exist with it. A purely financial capitalist who profits off the manipulation of money alone (investors, bankers, stockbrokers) does best in a closed enterprise system because there is little or no competition. They love monopolies. This is why it's so scary when banks begin to merge. It's why we have anti-trust laws. The further away we get from monopolies, the more capitalism deteriorates. That has been the trend within the last century. Yet instead of empowering the people and entrepreneurs, the power is subtly shifting to new kinds of monopolies – corporate institutions specializing in information management which control most all other enterprises. This brings us to discover yet another major tool of the muddlers: censorship and the manufacturing of consent through a controlled media. First, let's define *freedom of expression*.

The Gift: Freedom of Expression

If you were born in America – you were born with a priceless gift. But even today in the land of liberty, some folks would like to take it away from you. So watch out, lest we lose this precious gift that's called Freedom of Expression.

Though remarkable as it was as a blueprint for self-government, the Constitution in 1787 was deeply flawed because it had no bill of rights. Those early Americans wanted strong guarantees that their new government would not trample on their newly found freedoms. So the Constitution was not ratified until 1791 when the first ten amendments that we know as the Bill of Rights became the law of the land.

The First Amendment is first because it's the most important:

> **CONGRESS SHALL MAKE NO LAW RESPECTING AN ESTABLISHMENT OF RELIGION, OR PROHIBITING THE FREE EXERCISE THEREOF; OR ABRIDGING THE FREEDOM OF SPEECH, OR OF THE PRESS; OR THE RIGHT OF THE PEOPLE PEACEABLY TO ASSEMBLE, AND TO PETITION THE GOVERNMENT FOR A REDRESS OF GRIEVANCES.**

This is the gift – the right that we call freedom of expression today. But our government's forefathers and representatives conveniently ignored the First Amendment for over a hundred years. Just seven years after adopting the Bill of

Rights, Congress passed the Alien and Sedition Act that made it a crime for anyone to publish malicious writings against the government. In Virginia before the Civil War, anyone who spoke against slavery was imprisoned for one year. In 1912, Margaret Sanger was arrested for giving a lecture on birth control. During World War I, Eugene Debs was sentenced to ten years in prison just for telling a rally of peaceful workers that they were fit for something better than cannon fodder. And as late as 1923, the year my mother was born, author Upton Sinclair was arrested for trying to read the text of the First Amendment at a union rally!

This is why the American Civil Liberties Union was founded in 1920. Free speech rights still need constant, vigilant protection because new questions keep coming up, such as what are we going to do with the Internet, and old questions keep coming back such as what to do about flag desecration, if anything. It's the job of the United States Supreme Court to answer these questions using the First Amendment as its guide.

In 1919, the Supreme Court unanimously upheld the conviction of a Socialist Party member for distributing anti-war leaflets. But a few months later, two dissenting opinions would form the cornerstone of our modern First Amendment law. Justices Oliver Wendell Holmes and Louis D. Brandeis argued that speech could only be punished if it presented a "clear and present danger" of imminent harm. Mere political viewpoints, they said, were protected by the First Amendment. Eventually, they convinced the other judges, and the right to free speech became a little more secure until the 1950s.

In the era of McCarthyism, many political activists were jailed for supporting communist views. It wasn't until 1969 that the Supreme Court established a new standard. In striking down the conviction of a Ku Klux Klan member, they said that speech could be suppressed only if it is intended and likely to produce imminent lawless action. All other speech, even speech that advocates violence, is protected. This is the standard that prevails today.

So what does protected speech include? Well, as we all know, it isn't limited to pure speech in the form of words. It also protects symbolic speech – nonverbal expression with the purpose to communicate ideas, like art. The flag in the toilet may be lousy art to some, but it is symbolic speech and therefore protected. This idea of symbolic speech came about in the 1969 Supreme Court decision, *Tinker v. Des Moines*. In this decision, the Court said that students had a right to wear black armbands in protest of the Viet Nam war.

The government can place limited restrictions on protected speech, such as requiring permits for demonstrations. But a permit cannot be denied on the basis of speech content because that would be viewpoint discrimination. The government can also intervene when certain protest goes too far such as in blocking building entrances or intimidating people. Hate speech is protected. If only popular ideas were protected, we wouldn't need a First Amendment. History teaches us that the first target of government repression is never the last. If we don't defend the free speech rights of the most unpopular and repugnant among us, even if their views are anti-First Amendment, then no one's liberty is secure. As one federal judge put it, tolerating hateful speech is really the best protection we have against fascism or totalitarianism.

So what speech is not protected? Yelling fire in a crowded theater, defamatory falsehoods that are expressed with malice, and material deemed legally obscene. However, the tests that the court uses to determine exactly what is obscene have not been very helpful. So this is an area of First Amendment law that is constantly challenged and subject to government abuse. It's clear that the battles will continue well into the 21st century. Therefore, according to the American Civil Liberties Union, protecting the gift of freedom of expression is essential to a free society for three reasons:

1. It's the foundation of self-fulfillment. The right to communicate freely with each other affirms the dignity and worth of every human being, allowing us to realize

our full human potential. So as a means to an end, freedom of expression deserves society's greatest protection.

2. Freedom of expression is vital to the attainment of knowledge and the search for truth. As John Stuart Mill wrote, enlightened judgment is possible only when all facts and ideas are considered and tested against opposing views. Therefore all points of view, even those we consider bad or harmful, should be represented in society's "marketplace of ideas."

3. Freedom of expression is necessary in a democracy because it gives us important leverage against government excess and corruption. If the American people are to be the masters of their fate and an elected government, they must be well informed and have access to all information, ideas, and points of view. Mass ignorance is the breeding ground for all tyranny and oppression.[51]

I urge you to enjoy, cherish and protect YOUR gift as well as that of your neighbors. Because the truth is, conspiracy or no, that in coming for one they come for all. We are so blessed with this gift. The best way to show our gratitude is to keep it sacred and secure for everyone.

Noam Chomsky on the Media

Noam Chomsky is one of the ten most quoted writers of our day. The *Chicago Tribune* once ranked him 8th among all the great intellectual minds of the Western hemisphere. The *New York Times* once said that Chomsky is "arguably the most important intellectual alive." His ideas are completely original and supported by facts that cannot be disputed – however unsettling they may be.

The fact that he's not a major public icon is proof that one of his main theses is true. The major media don't want you to know about him. Why? Because if too many people listened to Chomsky talking about how huge corporations are running the world and especially the major media, people might begin to question the authenticity of our so-called 'freedom.'

You might be wondering, if his ideas are so threatening, then why hasn't he been put out of commission somehow? Well, for one, that would bring more attention to his ideas and then we might really begin to change things; and second, he is also a leading expert in linguistics, holding a prestigious teaching position at MIT.

Chomsky's thoughts on the media and politics are what get most people fired up. One of his most revealing theories is about the media's role in manipulating us – or in manufacturing consent. Did you see the movie, *Wag the Dog*? What happened in that film Chomsky would say happens everyday in differing degrees.

Some fundamental truths underlying Chomsky's reasoning are:

1. Our government lies to us;
2. Corporations and the government unite to create a ruling elite;
3. The two major political parties are identical with regard to most issues that affect us because they're really just two factions of "the business party";
4. The news media do not give a full, balanced picture of political events; and
5. Even though the United States is called a democracy, most of us are locked out of any meaningful participation in the decision-making processes.[52]

In order for democracy to be authentically 'democratic,' the media have to do two things: First, it must report the news fairly, completely, without bias; and second, the media must function as a public watchdog against abuses of power. Chomsky feels that the media fail miserably in both regards.

He believes that the mass media is just a public relations industry for the rich and powerful, and that its sole function is to sell to the public rather than inform them.

Chomsky wrote a book called *Necessary Illusions – Thought Control in Democratic Societies*. We usually associate thought control with totalitarian countries. Who ever heard of such a thing happening in a democracy where everyone is supposed to be free and equal? Well Chomsky reminds us that even though journalists constantly use buzzwords such as democracy, capitalism, and equality, we hardly hear any genuine discussion of what these words really mean and how they apply to our lives. Chomsky took it on himself to ask these questions.

First, he found that there were two opposing viewpoints regarding the role of media in democracy. Former U.S. Justice William Powell articulated the view that most of us like to hold. He said that the press performs a crucial function in effecting the First Amendment by enabling the public to assert meaningful control over the political process. The opposing view, however, goes all the way back to the time of our forefathers. James Mill was the father of John Stuart Mill, one of the main guys who influenced the authors of our Constitution. Mill said that the media's role was to "train the minds of the people to virtuous attachment to their government." I must repeat that: *train the minds of the people to virtuous attachment to their government.* This goes right along with something that John Jay, another founding father said: "Those who own the country should run it."

Politics then becomes an interaction among groups of investors who compete for control of the state. We are made to believe that these groups of investors have our best interests at heart by something called *the manufacturing of consent,* and this happens through our major media. How? Because our major media are owned and controlled by these groups of investors or ruling elite, otherwise known as Corporate America. This is not a conspiracy theory. You talk to any public relations expert and they will admit this is true.

In the United States, the government and the corporations cannot maintain control with brute force as they can in third world dictatorships. They have to use a more subtle technique: Propaganda. Chomsky says the two targets for this propaganda are: (1) the political class which is the 20% of the population which is educated and expected to play some role in decision making – managers, attorneys, and so on, so they must be deeply indoctrinated; and (2) the other 80% which is expected to take orders and go along without thinking, and who usually pay the bills, which probably translates to most of us.

Again, it is important to remember that these leaders who believe it is necessary to fool the public may not even be aware of their deception because they themselves are trained to believe that they are doing it in our best interests. Oliver North is a classic example of this.

After Watergate, in 1975, the Trilateral Commission published a paper called "The Crisis of Democracy." They wrote that public participation in decision-making was a threat to the elite governing class. They viewed the media as a notable new source of power that had contributed to an excess of democracy and a resulting reduction of governmental authority. They also said that if journalists don't impose certain new standards of professionalism, then "the alternative could well be regulation by the government."

The news industry is also a "guided market system" – not only guided by government but also largely guided by *profit*. Information that is guided to suit any agenda, whether political or financial, is propaganda. Therefore, ownership determines content. How do the owners of the *New York Times* control content while managing to remain practically invisible?

Chomsky's Propaganda Model explains how. This model consists of five news filters that one at a time -- remove all "undesirable elements" from ever finding their way into your mind or your living room.

FILTER 1. MONEY. The great wealth of the owners, the fact that ownership of media is concentrated in a few huge corporate conglomerates, and the fact that media corporations, like other corporations, exist only to make a profit.

FILTER 2. ADVERTISING is their primary source of income.

FILTER 3. RELIANCE ON INFORMATION provided by government, business, and "experts" with ties to both.

FILTER 4. FLAK as a means of disciplining the media.

FILTER 5. "ANTI-(fill in the blank)" as a national religion and control mechanism. This used to be Anti-Communism but since the fall of the Soviet Union, it's more likely to be Anti-Terrorism.

Let's expound on these filters a bit.

Filter No. 1: It's practically impossible to start your own media company, much less compete with the biggies, without tremendous wealth. In 1982, fifty corporations owned all major media outlets (and this includes print media, radio, television books and movies). In 1993, this number had shrunk to twenty. I shudder to think of what it is today!

Filter No. 2: Advertising distorts the news because it makes the media more accountable to its advertisers than the community. An example: In 1985, TV station WNET ran a documentary called "Hungry for Profit" that criticized the activities of multinational corporations exploiting natural resources in the third world. The CEOs of Gulf and Western Corporations pulled their funding from the station on the grounds that the program was "virulently anti-business if not anti-American." That's why you rarely see this type of programming anywhere, even on public TV. Advertising sponsors will also object to programming that explores complex and disturbing issues that may "disrupt the buying mood." TV audiences are not thought of as citizens but consumers. Advertisers want entertainment – good time programming, so that the real issue becomes, "Am I having enough fun? Maybe I ought to buy one of those. . .Yeah!"

Filter No. 3: Reporters cannot be everywhere at once so they're usually stationed outside the usual places to be fed the usual lines by the usual suspects, I mean "experts" – White

House, Pentagon, Congress, corporate public relations departments. Even if it appears that they've tagged a so-called independent expert – on closer look, that expert usually has ties to the government or the corporation as a former employee or consultant. These sources are rarely checked for reliability. The information is deemed credible by virtue of where it came from.

Filter No. 4: Flak is a word used to describe the negative reactions media get from critics when they get out of line. For instance – an angry letter to the editor by a government official, a phone call from an offended CEO threatening to sue, or a big sponsor threatening to pull advertising. Flak also comes from independent organizations pretending to be media watchdogs. For instance, in the early 90s, the group Accuracy in Media thrived on mostly large donations from corporations including at least eight oil companies. They pressured the media to follow the corporate agenda and a right-wing foreign policy. The Center for Media and Public Affairs was created in the 1980s as a "nonprofit, nonpartisan" research institute – but two of its major movers and shakers were the ultra-conservative Patrick Buchanan and President Ronald Reagan.

These supposedly neutral watchdog groups often portray the media as left wing and liberal when it is already dangerously pro-business, pro-government, and pro-status quo. Shows such as Crossfire pit two people against each other with opposing viewpoints – supposedly one left and one right. But political insiders know that the one who is supposed to be liberal is really moderate or center and the conservative is just to the right of that. So any view left to center is rarely represented. Yet the public is duped into thinking they heard both sides.

Filter No. 5: Anti-Communism – and now anti-terrorism or anti-Ben Ladin or whoever. These devils by whatever name always seem to threaten the one thing that all Americans have in common – "American Interests" -- and everyone likes to rally around that flag. But there's just one problem: No one ever defines what those interests are. Are they your interests? Are they my interests? Chomsky would say that they're the

360

interests of the corporate conglomerates whose bottom line is the almighty dollar – not me, not you. Blood for oil. Remember that? It is happening again as I write these words on the eve of war with Iraq.

But don't take Chomsky's word for any of this. He wants you to check it out for yourself. How? Well it's really very simple. Find out who the owners of the media are – who are the sponsors. Does the programming reflect your values or their values? With a newspaper, simply measure the column space devoted to coverage of a certain subject and compare it with amounts devoted to other subjects. Ask yourself: Which story does the paper feel is most important? Try to pick the media that spend the most time or the space on subjects that you consider most important, if they do at all. Or better yet, talk to the reporters. Many a reporter will have at least one horror story to tell about being fired or almost being fired when they did not tow the company line.

So, to summarize Chomsky's position on the media, the media's function is NOT to inform the public, but to SELL to the public. What is it selling us? To paraphrase author David Cogswell, it's selling us this story about how we the people run our own country, that we are, in some meaningful sense, a democracy. It has sold us this dangerous delusion that our opinions are freely formed, not coerced, conned or manufactured in accordance with the designs of a handful of rich people. But perhaps the most dangerous story of all is the story of a fake history that leaves out the major players and leaves little semblance of reality. Chomsky asks us, "Why is it that the propaganda system is geared to suppressing any inquiry into the role of corporations in foreign policy?"[53] Before we answer that question, let's get a better look at exactly what corporations are, where they came from, and where they're going.

Corporations as Kingdoms

Corporations had their birth in Europe, as did the American legal system and many American traditions. In early English law, corporations were a way of legally establishing a state sanctioned project in order to serve some public function. Suppose the King wanted to build a major road from the west coast of England to the east. In order to do this he would need to procure labor, materials, and living quarters and provisions for the laboring men. Of course he would need capital to do this. So to get the money to finance his project, he would issue a royal charter intended to attract capital by defining privileges for prospective shareholders. The corporation was not only registered with the state, it was actually an agency of the state because the state retained control of it. One of these corporations gave birth to the United States colonies: the Massachusetts Bay Company, which King Charles I chartered in 1628 for colonizing the New World.

Back in those days, there were far more restrictions on corporations than today. For one, the corporation could only engage in activities related to its chartered purpose. Second, its charter was granted for a limited period of time and could be revoked if the corporation caused harm or exceeded its authority. Third, the owners and managers were held accountable for any criminal acts committed by the corporation. Fourth, the corporation was barred from participating in politics. Fifth, a corporation could not own stock in other corporations or own any other property outside the purpose of the charter. And sixth, the charter had to serve a public interest; profit for shareholders was a means to that end only and no other.

Even with all those restrictions, corporations exercised a great deal of power, and became greedy for more. When Charles II attempted to investigate the Massachusetts Bay Company in 1664, its shareholders vigorously protested. The King replied that giving the corporation authority over the subjects within its jurisdiction was not the same as making them its subjects or giving them supreme authority. In other words, they could not create a "sub-kingdom" of his kingdom. Thomas Hobbes, 17th century philosopher and tutor to Charles II, called the corporations "worms in body politic."

Naturally, the early American colonists felt that corporations were a real threat to their newly found ideals of unalienable rights to life, liberty and the pursuit of happiness. The Boston tea party not only protested against the English crown but also against the British East India Company for its monopoly on Eastern trade. When the colonists began to draft the U.S. Constitution in 1787, someone proposed giving the federal government power to charter corporations. According to Madison, the proposal was dropped because most of the delegates were repelled by the idea of corporations continuing to act as state monopolies dominating commerce.[54] Instead, they left it to the individual states to charter corporations in a very limited fashion. As a result, each state established its own bank with its own currency.

By the early 1800s, only about 334 corporations existed in the United States. This was still one too many for President Thomas Jefferson who later remarked, "I hope we shall crush in its birth the aristocracy of our moneyed corporations which dare already to challenge our government to a trial of strength and bid defiance to the laws of our country." Jefferson enacting a trade embargo of France and Britain only added fuel to the fire. American manufacturers sought to form corporations of their own in order to meet the demands of a growing domestic market. The corporate focus shifted from the public good to profits first. The Supreme Court was called upon to resolve this conflict, and set a pro-business precedent under Justice John Marshall in *Flecker v. Peck* (1810) deciding that contracts were sanctified and inviolable.

It was also under Marshall that the Supreme Court finally granted the federal government the power to charter corporations. The 1819 decision of *McCullough v. Maryland* broadened interpretation of the proper and necessary clause of

Article 1 of the Constitution. The issue at hand was whether or not the state of Maryland could tax the national bank that resided in that state. The Supreme Court said no, and that in order to establish a national currency, the federal government through Congress could incorporate a national bank not subject to state laws. The result of this decision established the concept of implied powers, which greatly extended the influence of the federal government.

Alexander Hamilton was behind this movement from the very beginning, as he organized the first central bank of the United States as Secretary of the Treasury during George Washington's term. Hamilton wanted the federal government to assume all state debt into one national debt. Then the federal government would continue to borrow money from Hamilton's central bank, which would be privately owned and operated. In order to pay for this deepening debt, Hamilton suggested the very tactic the revolutionaries fought against – taxation without representation. Sure enough, Hamilton pushed through a tax on distilled liquor, which resulted in the Whisky Rebellion of 1794. The whisky makers called for another revolution, so Hamilton got Washington to send out the militia to crush their rebellion.

While Madison and Jefferson agreed that a national currency should be issued, they opposed the establishment of a privately owned central bank which they viewed as dangerous and unconstitutional. Just as Jefferson warned, this institution created major financial upsets in 1893 and 1907 and had a negative influence on foreign affairs.[55] This bank, after several lapsed and renewed charters, became what is known today as the Federal Reserve Bank.

After the Marshall court rulings, legislators kept a tight rein on the corporate chartering process. For example, in 1832, President Andrew Jackson vetoed a motion to extend the charter of the Second Bank of the United States because it had become so corrupt. In fact, many banks were acting in opposition to the public interest giving rise to a wave of antitrust legislation. But everything changed after the Civil War.

The chaos and corruption of the Reconstruction period saw corporations making enormous profits from procurement contracts and then funneling those profits into buying political influence. Abraham Lincoln was so alarmed by this trend that in 1865 he prophesized, "I see in the near future a crisis approaching that unnerves me and causes me to tremble for the safety of my country. As a result of the war, corporations have been enthroned and an era of corruption in high places will follow, and the money power of the country will endeavor to prolong its reign by working upon the prejudices of the people until all wealth is aggregated in a few hands and the Republic is destroyed."

Then something really, really stupid happened. In the 1886 decision of *Santa Clara County v. Southern Pacific Railroad*, the Supreme Court inadvertently decided that a corporation was a "natural person" constitutionally speaking, subject to the protection of the Bill of Rights and the Fourteenth Amendment just like ordinary people. I say inadvertently because the issue of corporate personhood was not before the Court. The Justices made a comment to that effect that got transcribed into the headnotes of the case. Subsequent Court rulings used those comments to establish new precedents. This incident changed the course of history, and yet according to future Supreme Court Justice William O. Douglas, it clearly could not be supported by "history, logic or reason." As author Joel Bleifuss points out, corporations are fictional characters that ". . .feel no pain. They do not need clean air to breathe, potable water to drink or healthy food to eat. Their only goal is to grow bigger and more powerful."[56] Yet now the country was ordered to treat them as flesh and blood beings with the right of free speech, when women and minorities did not even have such rights! The Supreme Court had already ruled that women were not "persons" for the purposes of the Fourteenth Amendment in *Minor v. Happersett*. So now we see, the machine is born, and it is a scary ghost that continues to haunt us to this day.

The Fourteenth Amendment was originally enacted to protect the rights of Negroes after emancipation, establishing that "No state shall make or enforce any law which shall abridge the privileges or immunities of the citizens of the United States; nor shall any State deprive any person of life, liberty, or property, without due process of law; nor deny to any person within its jurisdiction the equal protection of the laws." The State of California wanted to impose certain taxes on the Railroad that the Railroad viewed as excessive. The Court used the provisions of this amendment to assert that basically the state could not tax the corporation any differently than it did individuals. Ironically, this decision opened the door to other decisions that essentially repealed laws originally enacted to protect people (especially Negroes) from corporate harm.

This new doctrine of corporate personhood created an interesting legal contradiction according to author David Korten:

> The corporation is owned by its shareholders and is therefore their property. If it is also a legal person, then it is a person owned by others and thus exists in a condition of slavery – a status explicitly forbidden by the Thirteenth Amendment to the Constitution. So is a corporation a person illegally held in servitude by its shareholders? Or is it a person who enjoys the rights of personhood that take precedence over the presumed ownership rights of its shareholders? So far as I have been able to determine, this contradiction has not been directly addressed by the courts.[57]

And neither has the constitutionality of a corporation's illegitimate personhood. For a more detailed explanation of what corporate personhood is and why it is bad for our society, see William Meyers' *The Santa Clara Blues: Corporate Personhood versus Democracy.*[58]

It took about fourteen years for corporate moguls and their lawyers to achieve this nonsensical feat. By the time they got to the Supreme Court, the Justices had already exposed their partiality to moneyed interests to the extent that they refused to

366

even hear arguments on the issue. Before the lawyers got the chance to say anything, Chief Justice Waite announced: "The court does not wish to hear argument on the question whether the provision in the Fourteenth Amendment to the Constitution, which forbids a State to deny to any person within its jurisdiction the equal protection of the laws, applies to these corporations. We are all of the opinion that it does." This comment is what got transcribed into the headnotes of the case and subsequently motivated all further rulings of this nature. This is what is so amazingly incredible about this historic event. It wasn't even a proper Supreme Court ruling. The issue itself was never given the due process it deserved!

After the *Santa Clara* decision, many lower court rulings that had given freed slaves equal protection in such matters as travel and interstate commerce were overturned on the basis that the protection imposed unreasonable burdens on a corporation's ability to do business. This led to one of the ugliest Supreme Court decisions ever: *Plessy v. Ferguson* (1896) that held that black persons should be forced into "separate but equal" accommodations, thus ringing in the era of Jim Crow that would last for over half a century. The injustice of the *Plessy* ruling was not overruled until *Brown v. Board of Education* in 1954.

Now that corporations had more freedom from state restrictions, they grew into huge trusts and conglomerates in violation of their charters. They amassed great wealth through exploiting the nation's natural resources, creating their own private fiefdoms – factory-centered company towns that by today's standards would rival most prisons. Workers who attempted to organize and resist the inhumane working conditions so prevalent in those towns were quickly silenced through blacklisting and even gunfire when needed. Fear of unemployment became a tool in the hands of the boss who learned to exploit it to his own advantage.

While workers in America need not fear gunfire as they once did, they continue to suffer the same kinds of manipulations resulting in a more subtle form of slavery. If you want to "get ahead" beyond merely "staying afloat" – you must find a second job or "agree" to work overtime. In fact, if you are an "exempt" professional, in all likelihood you are expected to work way past the minimum of forty hours a week without direct compensation or else your career is in jeopardy. This dangerous pattern of behavior leads to burnout, a serious job induced stress-related condition that often results in death. Workers and their careers continue to suffer from chronic bad health conditions brought about by job related stress. The job with the best health insurance benefits becomes the most attractive for this reason alone. It's absurd.

Companies and their cultures have so much control over our lives that they are the equivalent of private governments. This is especially true of the Fortune 500 companies which in some regards act as extensions of state government by virtue of their development and allocation of natural resources, government contracts and other socially significant functions they perform. According to author Timberg,

> The modern state undeniably delegates political power to large private corporations . . . Furthermore, the activities authorized for a large corporation involve such functions as price-fixing, the division of markets, the setting of wages, and the general development of local communities, functions which in a pre-Industrial Revolution era had been the primary responsibility of the State.[59]

William Kalle Lasn, author of *Culture Jam: The Uncooling of America*, writes, "In 1997, fifty-one of the world's hundred largest economies were corporations, not countries. The top five hundred corporations controlled forty-two percent of the world's wealth. Today corporations freely buy each other's stocks and shares. They lobby legislators and bankroll elections. They manage our broadcast airwaves, set our industrial, economic and cultural agendas, and grow as big and powerful as they damn well please."[60] And yet, if you are not a shareholder, you have little or no say in their decisions – those decisions that invariably affect you and yours. Even if you are a shareholder, there is no guarantee you will be valued and held harmless from the corporation's egregious acts. Witness the recent Enron scandal among countless others. Modern history has shown us that while our government maintains political sovereignty, corporations exercise economic sovereignty. This is why our democracy is not complete – there is no economic democracy and no democracy at all in the workplace.

No Freedom at Work

Most American citizens know that when they cross the border into Mexico or any foreign country, they leave the Constitution and the Bill of Rights behind them. But few know that they do the same thing each day when they go to work. Unless you work directly for the government, you have no freedom of expression in the workplace. You are not entitled to free speech – but the corporation is. If you are the victim of wrongdoing on the part of the corporation and try to bring the corporation to justice, you must buy your way through the legal system. Lawyers cost money, which often means not being able to afford to bring a case at all, or at a minimum – going into deep debt or even bankruptcy. Not only does the corporation have the legal and economic advantage here (for a few hundred thousand dollars in legal costs rarely affects the corporate bottom line), their legal costs are a tax-deductible expense! The ordinary, natural person is a second-class citizen in the eyes of the law compared to the illegitimate corporate "person" who has all the privileges.

After the *Santa Clara* decision, corporate free speech rights expanded to the point of diminishing free speech rights of American citizens as individuals and as a population. How did this happen?

In Massachusetts, once there was a state law that made it a crime for corporations to spend money to influence voters on issues that did not directly relate to the corporation's business. A graduated income tax was proposed and the First National

Bank wanted to publicly oppose it, so they challenged that law. The Supreme Court in *First National Bank v. Bellotti* decided in the bank's favor, stating that the First Amendment "goes beyond protection of the press and the self-expression of individuals to prohibit government from limiting the stock of information from which members of the public may draw."[61] However, there were four dissenting Justices who warned of the dangers of this opinion on several grounds. For one, they asserted that corporate speech deserved less protection because it was profit-motivated and did nothing to further the purpose of the First Amendment values of self-expression. Secondly, it could not reasonably further First Amendment values because there could be no unanimity among shareholders with conflicting political views. And third, because corporations are in a position to control vast amounts of economic power, there was a real danger of the corporations "using that wealth to acquire an unfair advantage in the political process."[62] Besides, as Justice Rehnquist noted, a corporation has the privilege of perpetual life and limited liability unlike an individual, substantially increasing the dangers of that risk. Legal scholar, Terry Ann Halbert notes,

> Indeed, the dissenting opinions in Bellotti correctly perceived that the critical element for effective free speech is access to an audience. Corporate speech acquires a superior effectiveness compared to individual speech because the former can afford a vastly more expensive "megaphone." The issue then becomes one of amplification of ideas rather than the right to express ideas. The first amendment was never designed, and should not be used, to protect the rights of a small minority of American citizens acting through the "person" of a corporation to amplify their particular beliefs in such an omnipotent manner.[63]

Private employers can get away with far more than governmental employers. For instance, a private employer can make you work on a project that benefits the political campaign of a candidate that you do not endorse. If you do not cooperate, you can be fired. Suppose you work for a corporation that has a contract with a company that is getting some bad press due to its poor environmental record. You happen to be a member of the Sierra Club that is opposing that company in the courts or in the legislature. If your employer finds out about your membership in the Sierra Club, they can accuse you of disloyalty and fire you on those grounds. Sound outrageous? It is -- and it's perfectly legal. In recent years, a whole new kind of discrimination has come to light in these matters – it's called "lifestyle discrimination." Although it's still a gray area in the law, it is a growing concern for many civil libertarians -- especially in light of continuing erosion of our civil liberties.

It is true that many states along with the federal government have laws that protect whistleblowers, but those laws are getting weaker as well. Employees are finding it increasingly difficult to prosecute such claims because of the legal costs involved and the permanent damage that is done to their health and reputation – especially when it comes to finding new employment. Corporations find ways to legally retaliate and harass the employee who is deemed a troublemaker for all time.

The only solution to these dilemmas is to make the corporation a "nonperson" or "constitutionalize" it – holding it constitutionally accountable in the same way we hold the government accountable. This speaks directly to the fact that corporations are private governments in themselves and therefore should be treated as such. The ideas and opinions of ordinary Americans who lack the resources to amplify their ideas competively have very little forum as it is – and none at all in the workplace. If we cannot be free to exchange ideas, beliefs, and opinions in the workplace without harassment – then on what public stage can we? The only airwaves that are open to us are the isolated venues of talk radio, which are also limited and colored to a large extent by the ideological views of the host. There is no guarantee your letter to the editor of a newspaper will be published without editing, if at all, either.

We can join a single issue group that speaks on our behalf such as a union or the ACLU, but what about those passionate concerns which have no active coalition for support? What about unpopular or controversial views? Yes, there's the Internet, and right now it might be the very last bastion of democracy in our world. So we should fight to preserve freedom there at all costs if nowhere else.[64]

Of course all this requires courage, and as Justice Brandeis once remarked, tolerance is one of the greatest acts of civic courage. Perhaps an even greater act of courage requires the discipline to exercise freedom responsibly. Free speech can be abused. The tenuous balance between politically correct speech and workplace harassment is a real problem. In short, censorship is a complicated subject. Not always are disputable incidents black or white, but usually somewhere in between. If we genuinely want freedom, we must be prepared to live with the possibility that it may be abused from time to time. In this respect, it may be helpful to remember the following words of attorney and legal scholar, Stanley Ingber:

> Freedom is not related to self-government simply as a mechanism for stymieing official abuse; freedom in its broadest sense is self-government, viewed as active engagement in a self-directive process in all aspects of life. Thus, constitutional consideration must focus on more than vindicating the rights of victims of government wrongs. Attention must also be given to the overall life situation of community members that dictates their self-perception, molds their character, and thereby determines their ability to create and function in a free and democratic society. The values that a community hopes its citizens exude, therefore, must inhere in the community's institutional arrangements.
>
> Consequently, if we exclude institutional settings from first-amendment coverage, the concept of a society founded on virtuous popular participation is likely to remain unfamiliar and foreign, perforce

making its attainment unrealistic. We then are left with a free speech liberty that serves only a symbolic role in our culture, merely allowing us to feel good about ourselves, our community, and our nation while we remain an essentially closed society. If daily life trains us unquestioningly to accept or to wield authority, we cannot expect an essentially symbolic free speech right – a right extraneous to the development of a courageous, self-possessed, and tolerant polity – to serve any function other than to legitimize an entrenched status quo.[65]

The most insidious form of censorship is self-censorship. Out of fear of losing their jobs, millions of people engage in this self-destructive behavior every day when they go to work. This is how the chief dominators – corporations -- have accomplished their prolonged stranglehold on our lives and our liberty. It is ironic that most of the time they don't have to censor us because we do it for them. This all goes back to what I initially talked about in the beginning of this chapter: the psychological dynamics of authoritarianism, repression and obedience. Repression breeds hatred – of self and others. We are not only alienated from the means of production, but we are alienated from our own sense of self and well-being by restrictions on our freedom of self-expression. Ingber reiterates:

The workplace is a significant learning environment, of crucial importance to the development of an individual's personal identity. It is the one location where employees convene daily and where they share common interests; therefore, it is also where they seek to persuade fellow workers in matters related to their status as employees. Consequently, it can readily serve as a locus of personal and collective realization, growth, and expression.[66]

Middle managers and supervisors often internalize the dominator/muddling values of their corporate bosses so that the oppression/repression mechanics trickle down the ladder to encompass the whole hierarchy of the corporate kingdom. Have you ever suffered at the hands of a frustrated "bottom feeder"? Maybe you didn't get your copy job back from the copy center on time because of a power struggle between the supervisor of the copy center and the minimum wage clerk operating one of the machines. Various scenarios such as that one are endless. And the frustration is not always left at the office. The clerk goes home to beat up on his wife who beats up on the kid who beats up on the dog. Where does it end? This hurts us all in the long run because what affects one person eventually affects the entire community. So we find that our freedom entails learning to use a double-edged sword. According to Ingber,

> Although the workplace may represent for many the situs of greatest potential for personal fulfillment, it also provides the greatest possibility of interpersonal domination. Long ago, deTocqueville cautioned against the rise of a new form of aristocracy that would convert owners and managers into petty despots and reduce workers to mechanically organized, dependent operatives, a condition incompatible with full democratic citizenship. . . Yet democracy ostensibly is based on faith in the ability of people to rule themselves intelligently and responsibly. If the workplace is structured to deny this faith and treat employees autocratically, it may diminish irreparably the employees' confidence in their overall ability to participate meaningfully in political activities and other community affairs.[67]

Prolonged harassment and workplace abuse in whatever form can result in the disorder known as chronic post-traumatic stress syndrome. Worker advocates claim that this syndrome is more of an injury than a disorder but can manifest in both paradigms. However it appears, the costs to society are enormous in loss of time, money, resources, and productivity.

Yet employers are rarely held accountable for this growing epidemic.

Occupational sociologists emphasize that work behavior involves social and interpersonal skills as well as physical and intellectual skills. An employee's work can have great personal meaning in their life – both economically and socially. It can have a deep affect on the employee's sense of well-being and self-esteem. The mind and body are one, and therefore all stress that is experienced on a psychological level has a physical pay off eventually. An assault on a person's well-being that happens at work can be extremely damaging to that person on all fronts and to everyone around them. This is how we are thoroughly consumed by the machine. The corporation as machine combined with our shameful complicity not only dehumanizes us, enslaves us and makes us second-class citizens, it eventually kills us. Ingber agrees:

> This mechanical, structured model views organizations as instruments designed to attain stated goals. It is the form of organization, lauded by Max Weber as "the most rational known means of exercising authority over human beings," that ascended rapidly in turn-of-the-century America. From this organizational perspective, the machine is the bureaucratic metaphor, and workers are viewed merely as parts of the machine. Predetermined organizational goals are perceived as unrelated to the needs of fungible workers, whose feelings are of little significance. For this system to operate, workers must obey their superiors and adjust to the structure of their workplace. The rhetoric of this organizational structure is so pervasive that the proposition that efficient decision making requires specialization, expertise, and a chain of command goes largely unchallenged.[68]

We don't have to take it anymore. We can get involved or remain in the jaws of the machine. If we choose freedom, we must believe in ourselves and our ability to organize and impact, and stop deferring to so-called "experts" and bosses because that undermines the whole premise of representative democracy.. Studies (and common sense) indicate that worker participation in decision/policy making and opportunities for on-the-job self-expression promote worker satisfaction, reduce alienation and job related stress, and facilitate intra-office cooperation instead of competition.[69] We can applaud the efforts of those brave CEOs, companies and unions who have made progress toward freedom within the limited confines of capitalism by building models based on these ideas, but that is not enough. We must go to our legislatures and demand that the same protections for public employees be granted to private employees. We must insist that the Bill of Rights and Constitution apply to our jobs as well as to any other sphere of communal activity. Ingber reminds us,

> If free speech is neglected in the day-to-day context of the workplace, we risk breeding caution and stifling initiative. We will not be worthy of respect as a people if we foster only the virtue of obedience. The communal value of the First Amendment is its fostering of a citizenry that values personal integrity, truth, and courage and the willingness to risk positions, criticism, and the misunderstandings that so often come when people do heroic things. The responsibility for promoting these constitutional virtues lies with all institutions, not merely with courts. Yet this responsibility generally is forsaken in the workplace precisely because courts cannot impose it upon private employers.[70]

We must get our own game together. We must choose to become inspirational examples, not demoralized victims. In the early days of union organizing in the nightmarish company towns, company bosses often hired preachers to promote a religious dogma that encouraged workers to focus on happiness in the hereafter rather than the present moment. The lyrics of a popular organizing song referred to this as the old "pie in the sky" trick. While our corporations no longer openly engage this strategy, they substitute high priests of materialism -- industrial psychologists, organizational consultants, team builders, and human resource managers specializing in stress-reduction workshops to employ similar diversionary tactics. Well don't be deceived. It may help to improve poor working conditions to relieve some temporary stress caused by those conditions in the first place, but until the conditions themselves are obliterated, the problem is not resolved, and you're just continuing to bank on that illusory pie in the sky. You'll never see it. Why? Because you've got to make your own pie out of real stuff in the here and now – not tomorrow. Or at least demand your fair share of the one that exists.

If you can partner up with a legislator in proposing a new law, great. But that process alone does not guarantee results because the government cannot be completely trusted either. In fact, corporations and the government are not the adversaries they once were – they are cozy bedfellows in this muddling frenzy. They are partners in crime. Don't be fooled by conservative propaganda – corporate welfare exists. To understand why and how this affects the muddling process, we turn to Chomsky again.

Chomsky on World Politics

Chomsky says that the free market system is only a theory; that it doesn't really exist. The government provides a safety net insuring that businesses will survive and thrive, even if the market does not support those businesses. This safety net is comprised of a complex system of tax laws, loopholes, and complicated regulatory mechanisms. The economy, according to Chomsky, is rigged. Government makes massive subsidies to business disguised as defense programs or tax structures that channel the money into specific areas. Chomsky says since World War II, a program to suburbanize America has greatly contributed to these subsidies. Specifically,

> The Federal Highways Acts of 1944, 1956, and 1968,
> funneled billions of taxpayer dollars into a national
> highway system that was the brainchild of Alfred
> Sloan, chairman of GM. It made the American
> economy dependent on gasoline-powered
> transportation and gave the oil industry a virtual
> energy monopoly. This dependency would lead
> eventually to events like the Gulf War, in which
> hundreds of thousands of Iraqis were killed to ensure
> U.S. control of Middle Eastern oil.[71]

This is about to happen again as I'm writing this. Will we ever learn?

One such muddling happened in the 1940s when General Motors, Standard Oil, and Firestone Rubber Company colluded to systematically buy up and dismantle electric transit systems in over forty-five cities and replace them with GM buses. GM partners were subsequently convicted of criminal conspiracy and fined a measly $5,000. The world has never been the same since.

Capital gains cuts, investment subsidies, increased tax exemptions for estates, reduced health and safety regulations, increased military expenditures and other "entitlement" programs combine to make a welfare system for the rich. Foreign policy is a cover for economic imperialism – a more subtle form of colonialism for the modern age. The U.S. spreads economic control, not democracy. It goes into a third world country setting up shop under the pretext of furthering democracy and human rights, when its real purpose is to maintain a client state ruled by terror which serves the interests of a business and military elite. This was especially the case when communism was a real threat to corporate interests.

George Kennan was a State Department planner who wrote "Policy Planning Study 23" in 1948, explaining the rationale and detailed workings behind establishing the system of military client states that has been operative since World War II. Chomsky is not making this up. It was a deliberate and focused project. These are Kennan's words:

378

> . . . we have about 50 percent of the world's wealth,
> but only about 6 percent of its population. . . In this
> situation we cannot fail to be the object of envy and
> resentment. Our real task in the coming period is to
> devise a pattern of relationships that will permit us to
> *maintain this disparity* . . . To do so we will have to
> dispense with sentimentality and daydreaming; and
> our attention will have to be concentrated everywhere
> on our immediate national objectives. . . We should
> cease to talk about vague and. . . unreal objectives
> such as human rights, the raising of living standards
> and democratization. (Emphasis added.)[72]

Kennan recommended a policy of noninterference when confronted with violent repression in these client states. He felt that a strong regime was a better defense against communism than a liberal one where the people had the opportunity to become more informed. So there is no conspiracy here. It is in our laws and historical documents for all to see.

An educated American citizenry would not tolerate its government applying brute force in order to dominate the world economy. So the government does it covertly through these puppet client states with the aid of the Central Intelligence Agency (CIA), National Security Agency (NSA), and whatever other subagencies exist to keep the plan going. This is the real New World Order and its agenda. It has nothing to do with such secret societies as the Illuminati, Bilderbergs, or what have you. It is just plain economics, and we all play a role.

Corporate interests backed by military power practically "own" the natural resources in these client state countries. Shamefully, the oil that is produced in Iraq does not further the living standards of its own people. Most people think that this was the fault of Iraq's brutal dictator, Saddam Hussein, and it appears that this is largely true. But who brought Saddam to power in the first place? Just two years before the Gulf War, George W.'s father and then Secretary of State James Baker made sure that Saddam got another $1 billion in loan

379

guarantees, even though the Treasury Department said that Iraq's credit was poor and even though Saddam was continuing to gas Kurds and torture dissidents in his own country. Yet the State Department insisted this loan was justified because Iraq was "very important to U.S. interests in the Middle East," was "influential in the peace process," and "a key to maintaining stability in the region, offering great trade opportunities for U.S. companies."[73]

Sometimes the people in these client states wish to wean themselves from their imperialist parents and initiate independence movements through land reforms or nationalization of industries. This happened in Central America in the mid-1980s. The result was an illegal war against the "Communist threat" that eventually gave us the Iran-Contra scandal. The killing that the U.S. backed contras engaged in was not ordinary. "A major element is brutal, sadistic torture – beating infants against rocks, hanging women by their feet with their breasts cut off and the skin of their faces peeled back so they will bleed to death, chopping people's heads off and putting them on stakes. The point is to crush independent nationalism and popular forces that might bring about meaningful democracy."[74] This kind of thing still goes on – indigenous peoples are still being massacred – yet we hear little, if nothing, about it. Chomsky again harps on the media for this because the same corporate elite responsible for backing the government-sponsored violence in these countries controls the media:

> These are not just academic exercises. We're not talking about the media on Mars or in the 18th Century. There are real human beings who are suffering and being tortured and starving because of policies we are involved in because we as citizens of a democratic society are . . .directly responsible for the actions of our government. What the media are doing is ensuring that we don't act on our responsibilities.[75]

Sometimes a client state dictator becomes a little too independent for the U.S. government/corporate elite, so plans are made to overthrow him and replace him with another. This is what happened with Noriega in Panama. Suddenly we heard about human rights violations that were never reported before, and the military moves in under the pretext of stopping a brutal dictator.

Now that communism is no longer the major threat, government/corporate interests push the menace of terrorism. Of course the definition of terrorism does not apply to us, only to "them." And "them" is whoever happens to be threatening corporate interests at the time. Islamic fundamentalism only becomes a problem when it gets "out of control" and turns into something like a nationalist independence movement. The most extreme Islamic fundamentalist country is the U.S. ally, Saudi Arabia – a family dictatorship serving as an obedient loyal U.S. client state.

I know it's difficult to come to terms with all this. None of us wants to believe that our government has a hand in all this torture, brutality, and genocide, but the evidence can be found if one is willing to read documents other than what the mainstream media provide. But we have to ask these questions and be open to the possibility of unpleasant truths if we're ever going to change things. As Chomsky indicates,

> To ask serious questions about the nature and behavior of one's own society is often difficult and unpleasant; difficult because the answers are generally concealed, and unpleasant because the answers are often not only ugly... but also painful. To understand the truth about these matters is to be led to action that may not be easy to undertake and that may even carry significant personal costs. In contrast, the easy way is to succumb to the demands of the powerful, to avoid searching questions, and to accept the doctrine that is hammered home incessantly by the propaganda system. This is, no doubt, the main reason for the easy victory of

dominant ideologies, for the general tendency to
remain silent or to keep fairly close to official
doctrine with regard to the behavior of one's own
state and its allies. . . while lining up to condemn the
real or alleged crimes of its enemies.[76]

The history we've been taught in school is largely false.
We are told only what the government/corporate elite wants us
to know about certain founding fathers. For instance, Thomas
Jefferson was against the developing capitalism in this country
and remarked that it was going to lead to a form of absolutism
worse than the one we fought against. According to Chomsky,
the pattern began long ago. Corporate tyranny sprang from the
same roots as fascism and Bolshevism:

> We think of corporations as immutable, but they were
> designed. It's a conscious design which did as Adam
> Smith said: the principal architects of policy
> consolidate state power and use it for their interests.
> It was certainly not popular will. There isn't any
> legislation about it. It's basically court decisions and
> lawyers' decisions, which created a form of private
> tyranny which is now more massive in many ways
> than even state tyranny was. . .

> Transnational corporations now have an enormous
> role in the world economy. These are just incredible
> private tyrannies. They make totalitarian states look
> mild by comparison.[77]

Yet there would be no tyrants if we did not bow down to
their tyranny. It all comes down to us as individuals with free
will. Our educational system is deeply entrenched in the
propaganda system. It doesn't matter whether it's public school
sponsored by the state or private schools sponsored by corporate
interests and religion. The controllers are two sides of the same
coin. Republicans and Democrats are two factions of the same
political party – the business party. They play the game of
adversaries, but remember that's just a diversionary tactic. It's

all for show. Any differences at all in viewpoint or political platform are really not that substantial. And this is why so little changes, election after election. We've got to rise above it all and see through their games. Chomsky has hope as long as we cultivate the courage to develop and maintain critical thinking skills, questioning everything -- refusing to take things at face value acquiescently. It would be nice to have the luxury of believing that what is revealed to us on the evening news by the pretty anchorwoman is sufficient and complete, but it is not. We are tired. It's difficult to be aware and think critically when one is tired. But remember, that too is a part of the machine's agenda. The machine does not want us to be at our peak during what little time we have to ourselves. So we have to make a special effort to keep our eyes open – to look for other ways – other avenues of obtaining critical information – information that can lead us to act toward freedom. Certainly this means sacrificing some of our leisure time in order to do this for the benefit of one and all. Are you willing?

Now let's turn our attention to how these muddlers control the arena of public information concerning UFOs, ETs, and the ramifications of full disclosure.

Towards Full Disclosure

> The pursuit of truth requires the ability to see beyond the appearance of things to the meaning and substance behind the forms. In no field of study and research is this more essential than that of UFOlogy, a field beset by mystery, partial information, misinformation and deliberate disinformation. And, alas, in no field is there so great a deficiency of this very quality.
>
> -- Steven M. Greer, M.D.

Imagine a world where the following takes place:

General health condition of the human body is ascertained in less than five minutes by running a hand-held diagnostic scanner over it. Treatment is prescribed for any abnormalities that are found without the need for further tests. Cancer is curable.

World hunger and famine are obsolete. All countries have technology in place that is not dependent on so-called fossil fuels and antiquated agricultural methods using pesticides. Fresh water is produced from salt water with no great effort or expense.

Zero Point energy is freely accessible to everyone. There are no roads, no railroad tracks, no shipping channels. All transportation takes place above ground in flying vehicles that rely on anti-gravitational technology for propulsion. Environmental pollution is a thing of the past.

What year do you think this is? Way off into the future? What year do you think it could be? Same answer? Way off into the future? Wrong: 1950. It could have been 1950. The technology needed to actualize such a world existed and was available on our planet as early as 1950. Needless to say, it was not made available to the general public or we wouldn't be in the horrible shape we're in today.

Who had it or has it, and why hasn't it been disclosed to the world for the benefit of one and all? A group of greedy individuals is hoarding it for the benefit of a few and possible harm to many, because this same advanced technology can be put to evil uses as well – military projects and psychological warfare to keep the general population under control. Whose control? The muddlers, of course.

This scenario may sound like conspiracy but it is no theory. Testimony from hundreds of witnesses to this effect has been fully documented and recorded by a man who will surely someday be perceived as one of the most courageous, tenacious, and visionary pioneers of the 20th century – Dr. Steven M. Greer.

Dr. Steven Greer is a specialist in emergency medicine and former chairman of the department of emergency medicine at Caldwell Memorial Hospital in North Carolina. He is a lifetime member of Alpha Omega Alpha, the nation's most prestigious medical honor society. Dr. Greer left a very successful career in medicine to fully devote himself to the study of extraterrestrial intelligence (ETI), by founding the Center for the Study of Extraterrestrial Intelligence (CSETI) in 1990, and then later the Disclosure Project (www.DisclosureProject.org) in June of 2000.

For over a decade, CSETI has trained and deployed teams of investigators out in the field to observe, record, and often interact with ETI. Having experienced a great deal of success in these endeavors, CSETI has grown into a worldwide organization that continues to investigate, analyze, educate and promote understanding of ETI with compelling results.

The Disclosure Project is a nonprofit research project working to fully disclose the facts about extraterrestrials, UFOs, and advanced energy and propulsion systems that remain classified. It is hoped that disclosure of this information will result in new technologies to end pollution and stave off ecological disaster, leading to long-term solutions to the energy crisis and to the beginning of an era of peaceful relations with extraterrestrial civilizations.

This is no X-Files. This is the truth. It has been the greatest kept secret in modern history, but not for long. Instead of trying to summarize Dr. Greer's efforts in my own words, I'm going to cut directly to the chase and reproduce bits of witness testimony verbatim.

The Cover-Up: UFOs and Advanced Technologies

Mercury and Gemini Astronaut, Colonel Gordon Cooper:

> A saucer flew right over [us], put down three landing gears, and landed out on the dry lakebed. [The cameramen] went out there with their cameras towards the UFO... I had a chance to hold [the film] up to the window. Good close-up shots. There was no doubt in my mind that it was made someplace other than this earth.[78]

FAA Division Chief of Accidents and Investigations, John Callahan:

> The UFO was bouncing around the 747. [It] was a huge ball with lights running around it... Well, I've been involved in a lot of cover-ups with the FAA. When we gave the presentation to the Reagan staff, they had all those people swear that this never happened. But they never had me swear it never happened. I can tell you what I've seen with my own eyes. I've got a videotape. I've got the voice tape. I've got the reports that were filed that will confirm what I've been telling you. [79]

Former Chief of Defense, British Royal Navy, Admiral Lord Hill-Norton:

> I have frequently been asked by a person of my background – a former Chief of the Defense Staff, a former Chairman of the NATO Military Committee – why I think there is a cover-up [of] the facts about UFOs. I believe governments fear that if they did disclose those facts, people would panic. I don't believe that at all. There is a serious possibility that we are being visited by people from outer space. It behooves us to find out who they are, where they come from, and what they want. [80]

Former Director of the CIA, Vice Admiral R.H. Hillenkoetter:

> It is time for the truth to be brought out in open Congressional hearings. Behind the scenes, high-ranking Air Force officers are soberly concerned about the UFOs. But through official secrecy and ridicule, many citizens are led to believe the unknown flying objects are nonsense. To hide the facts, the Air Force has silenced its personnel. [81]

US Navy Pilot, Lieutenant Frederick Fox:

> There is a [military] publication called JANAP 146E
> that has a section that says you will not reveal any
> information regarding the UFO phenomenon under
> penalty of $10,000 fine and ten years in jail. So the
> secret has been kept.[82]

Marine Corps, Corporal Jonathan Weygandt:

> [The UFO] was buried in the side of a cliff. When I
> first saw it, I was scared. I think the creatures calmed
> me... [Later] I was arrested [by an Air Force officer].
> He was saying, "Do you like the Constitution?" I'm
> like, "Yeah." He said, "We don't obey. We just do
> what we want. And if you tell anybody [about us or
> the UFO], you will just come up missing."[83]

Corporate Manager of Fairchild Industries, Spokesperson
for Wernher von Braun, Dr. Carol Rosin:

> Von Braun [rocket science pioneer] told me [in 1976]
> the reasons for space-based weaponry were all based
> on a lie. He said the strategy was that first the
> Russians, then the terrorists are going to be
> considered the enemy. The next enemy was
> asteroids. "The last card is the alien card, and all of it
> is a lie."... I was at a meeting in Fairchild Industries
> in the War Room... The conversation [was] about
> how they were going to antagonize these enemies,
> and there was going to be a Gulf War. Now this is
> 1977!"[84]

US Air Force, FAA, Captain Robert Salas:

> [The security guard called and] said, "Sir, there's a
> glowing red object hovering outside the front gate.
> I've got all the men out here with their weapons
> drawn." We lost between 16 to 18 ICBMs [nuclear-

tipped InterContinental Ballistic Missiles] at the same time UFOs were in the area... [A high-ranking Air Force Officer] said, "Stop the investigation; do no more on this and do not write a final report." I heard that many of the guards that reported this incident were sent off to Viet Nam.[85]

US Air Force Lieutenant, Professor Robert Jacobs:

So this thing [UFO] fires a beam of light at the warhead, hits it and then it moves to the other side and fires another beam of light. And the warhead tumbles out of space. What message would I interpret from that? [The UFOs were telling us] don't mess with nuclear warheads. Major Mannsman said, "You are never to speak of this again." After an article [about the incident years later], people would call and start screaming at me. One night somebody blew up my mailbox.[86]

Russian Space Communications Center, Major General Vasily Alexeyev:

They came up with a table with pictures of all the shapes of UFOs that had ever been recorded – about fifty... The study of UFOs may reveal some new forms of energy to us, or at least bring us closer to a solution.[87]

US Army, National Guard Reserve, Brigadier General Stephen Lovekin:

Colonel Holomon brought out a piece of metallic debris. He explained that this was the material that had come from a New Mexico crash in 1947 of an extraterrestrial craft... I got an opportunity to travel with President [Eisenhower]. He was very, very interested what made [the UFOs] go... But Eisenhower got sold out. He realized that the [study of these technologies] was not going to be in the best hands... I think secrecy has been enforced because [advanced UFO-based technologies] would destroy an economy designed by certain capitalists in this country to maintain their corporations from here to eternity.[88]

US Marine Corps, Captain Bill Uhouse:

The [flight] simulator they used was for the extraterrestrial craft they had – a 30 meter one that crashed in Arizona, back in 1953. I was inside the actual alien craft for a start-up. There are probably two or three dozen [flying saucers] that we built.[89]

US Air Force, Lockheed Skunkworks Engineer, Don Phillips:

We've got these things [developed from UFO technology] that are handheld scanners that scan the body and determine what the condition is. We can also treat from the same scanner. And we have ones that can cure cancer. Again, politics, and God bless them, the FDA, and other people whose financial interests could be damaged keep these out of view.[90]

US Air Force, Aerospace Illustrator, Mark McCandlish:

This [US made] antigravitiy propulsion system – this flying saucer – was one of three that were in this hangar at Norton Air Force Base. They called [it] the Alien Reproduction Vehicle [ARV], also nicknamed the Flux Liner.[91]

US Air Force, NRO Operative, Sergeant Dan Morris:

I became part of a group that would investigate, gather the information and in the beginning it was still under the Blue Book, Snowbird and different covert programs. I would go interview people who claimed they had seen something and try to convince them they hadn't seen something or that they were hallucinating. Well, if that didn't work, another team would come in and give all the threats. And threaten them and their family and so on and so forth. And they would be in charge of discrediting them, making them look foolish and so on and so forth. Now if that didn't work, then there was another team that put an end to that problem, one way or another... UFOs are both extraterrestrial and manmade... It's not that our government doesn't want us to know that there are other people on other planets. What the people in power don't want us to know is that this free energy [from energy generators developed with UFO technology] is available to everybody. So secrecy about the UFOs is because of the energy issue. When this knowledge is found out by the people, they will demand that our government release this technology, and it will change the world.[92]

US Air Force, Colonel Charles Brown:

I was getting 20 to 30% improvement in efficiency on an internal combustion engine. I sponsored the US Army race team on a racing car, [and] we won a race. [Then] the Federal Trade Commission performed an illegal act. I lost my vehicle, about $100,000 worth of equipment, and a test vehicle was stolen... So in three weeks, psychologically I was wiped out.[93]

US Army, Ph.D. in Nuclear Engineering, Colonel Thomas E. Bearden:

Probably 50 inventors have invented [virtually cost-free energy systems]. If we use these systems, we can clean up this biosphere. But, what we have is a situation where the entire structure of science, industry, and the patent office are against you. And

390

behind this, we have a few people who are quite wealthy. The more powerful the agency, the more they will resort not only to legal, but to extra-legal means to suppress their competition. Lethal force is used.[94]

Former NASA contractor employee, Donna Hare:

During the '70s... I did have secret clearance... I walked into a restricted area... And there they developed the film from the moon and satellite pictures, everything that's done by NASA. One of the gentlemen I had been friends with... pointed my attention to one area of this mosaic... They were aerial looking down... And then, with a smile on his face he said, look over there. And I looked. And in one of the photo panels I saw a round white dot. And at the time it was very crisp, very sharp lines on it. And I said to him what is that? Is that a dot on the emulsion? And then he's grinning and he says dots on the emulsion don't leave round shadows on the ground. And there was a round shadow at the correct angle with the sun shining on the trees. I looked at him and I was pretty startled because I had worked there several years and had never seen anything like this, never heard of anything like this. And I said, is this a UFO? And he's smiling at me and he says, I can't tell you that... What I knew he meant was, it was [a UFO] but he couldn't tell me. So I just said, what are you going to do with this information? And he said, well, we always have to airbrush them out before we sell them to the public. And I was just amazed that they had a protocol in place for getting rid of UFO pictures on these things.[95]

Disclosure Project, Founder and Director, Steven M. Greer, M.D.:

The situation is so dire that senior Joint Chiefs of Staff leaders in the Pentagon who I have briefed have no more access to such projects than any other civilian – unless they are on the 'inside.' The government is really quite outside the loop. We have insiders and scientists who can prove that we do in fact possess energy generation systems capable of completely and permanently replacing all forms of currently used energy generation and transportation systems. Every single person who is concerned about the environment and the human future should call for urgent hearings to allow these technologies to be disclosed, declassified and safely applied.[96]

The above testimony is from a small fraction of more than a hundred and growing witnesses who have bravely risked their reputations, careers, and sometimes even their lives – to come forward for the sake of public disclosure. Many of these witnesses are military officers who have taken a national security oath not to reveal these facts. Many potential witnesses have not come forward because they do not want to break the oath. However, Dr. Greer makes it clear that such an oath is not binding because it involves extra-constitutional activity. All the secrecy, black projects, and cover-up processes involved in the witnessed activities are not legal because they lack the constitutional oversight of the United States Congress, and therefore the oath does not apply.

Problems concerning accountability for all this are not simple. No single entity, whether it be a person, corporation, military subcontractor, or government agency, can be wholly indicted because these operations are classified top secret and are often unacknowledged and tightly compartmentalized. Therefore, the majority of the personnel and often times leaders of these organizations know nothing about them. This very specialized compartmentalization allows these operations to exist without those involved even knowing that their work is related to the UFO/ET subject. Those persons in high places who are familiar with the operations often find their hands tied, which can be very frustrating.

Let's take Barry Goldwater for example. Barry Goldwater, former Republican Senator from Arizona and ex-presidential candidate, is the founder of the modern conservative movement. He is well respected by Republicans and Democrats alike for his rugged individualism, integrity, and ability to see both sides of an issue. He was also a general in the Air Force Reserves and is well respected in the military. He once met with Dr. Greer in order to discuss these covert activities and relayed the following story. According to Dr. Greer, it is general knowledge that the blue room at Wright Patterson Air Force Base contains much evidence for these covert activities. Barry Goldwater went to the commander of Wright Patterson, four-star General Curtis Lemay, and asked for access into the blue room. General Lemay turned to him and said something to this effect, "Goddammit Barry, I can't even get into that area anymore. And if you ever ask me a question about this again, I will personally see that you are court-martialed."[97]

Barry Goldwater is not the only high public official who has tried to pierce the veil of secrecy. Dr. Greer was the first person to brief the Clinton Administration and Clinton's CIA director, Admiral James Woolsey on this subject. President Carter and many other high-ranking government officials have attempted to find out more information about what is going on but were completely cut off or silenced.

Much of this secret system and covert cartel was constructed during the administration of President Truman. When Eisenhower took office, it was all he could do to leave us with a warning:

> In the councils of Government, we must guard against the acquisition of unwarranted influence, whether sought or unsought, by the Military Industrial Complex. The potential for the disastrous rise of misplaced power exists, and will persist. We must never let the weight of this combination endanger our liberties or democractic processes. We should take nothing for granted. Only an alert and knowledgeable citizenry can compel the proper

meshing of the huge industrial and military machinery of defense with our peaceful methods and goals so that security and liberty may prosper together." (January, 1961.)

It was the main reason why President Kennedy was assassinated. He was getting very close to the truth and about to reveal it. Marilyn Monroe's death was timely too, in light of the fact that government documents reveal she was being wiretapped and watched closely by the CIA because she threatened to tell the public what Kennedy told her about "the visit by the President at a secret air base for the purpose of inspecting things from outer space."[98] Dr. Greer, through the Freedom of Information Act, has obtained many internal memorandums from the government and military sources that support this premise. Photocopies of these documents are reproduced in his book, *Disclosure,* along with transcriptions of hundreds of witness interviews and even diagrams of ARVs (Alien Reproduction Vehicles). Four hours of the videotaped testimony can be purchased directly from The Disclosure Project web site (http://www.DisclosureProject.org.)

These USAPS (Unacknowledged Special Access Projects) were designed to operate outside of the law and have violated U.S. and international law for decades. In 1952, President Truman created the National Security Agency (NSA) partly for this purpose by Executive Order. Many laws that are just mechanisms to create loopholes in existing law are created by Executive Order, and this is one way that Congressional oversight is avoided. The NSA, CFR and other organizations previously mentioned operate in consort with an international cartel in order to carry out these USAPS. Many U.S. corporations having a hand in these USAPS are successful manufacturers in the aerospace industry, such as McDonnell-Douglas (now under the auspices of Boeing), and Lockheed-Skunkworks. The Rand Corporation and TRW have also been frequent targets for these USAPS. Yet we cannot wholesale indict any one of them because such projects remain 'unacknowledged.' Personnel are only briefed to the extent needed in order to carry out their small end of the project. Little is revealed about the project, and what is exchanged is only on the basis of a need to know.

Another quasi-governmental, quasi-private entity known as PI-40 focuses on getting the work out to private contractors. They are also involved in active disinformation, public deception, so-called abductions and mutilations, reconnaissance and UFO tracking, space-based weapons systems, and specialized liaison groups with strong connections to the media. Because of the complexity of our funny money system, money-laundering and alternate means of funding for these USAPS are easy to structure:

> An Air Force source has told us that deep black projects can escape any direct oversight by having funds "hidden" in other projects. For example, $1 billion may be allocated for secret aerospace research and development, with certain projects cited as beneficiaries of this funding. In reality, however, $600 million may be used for those 'acknowledged' secret projects while the remaining $400 million is used for 'unacknowledged' projects.[99]

The muddlers continue to launder money through dummy projects while the real funds are diverted to USAPS that Congress, the President, and the American people know nothing about. Dr. Greer has spoken to other witnesses in government who acknowledge such operations:

> In 1994, Dick D'Amato who was senior counsel for the Senate Appropriations Committee under then Chairman Senator Byrd personally told me that somewhere between $40 billion and $80 billion was going into projects that they could not penetrate – even with a top-secret clearance and a Senate subpoena. He said he was sure money was going into UFO related projects but they could not penetrate them. I remember he said, "Dr. Greer, you are

dealing with the Varsity Team of all black projects –
good luck."[100]

Large defense contractors such as SAIC (Science
Applications International Corporation) in San Diego are often
merely fronts for these kinds of operations. Bell Labs, the
"innovation engine" behind Lucent Technologies has also been
intimately involved in this work. A few ET technologies that
have been "reverse-engineered" or copied in black projects have
been allowed to surface in the market, such as fiber-optics.
Still, many more technologies that could tremendously benefit
society are being shelved. Because of the laws protecting
confidential and proprietary interests of private industry, it is
virtually impossible to penetrate these fronts. The testing of
secret technology related to these USAPS usually takes place at
equally impenetrable military bases such as Edwards Air Force
Base and the infamous compound known as Area 51 in the
Nevada desert. Witnesses who are not silenced by fear, threats,
or "suicide" are often silenced with cash payments of over a
million dollars or more. This is especially true for witnesses in
the private industry sector. Dr. Greer has been offered
substantial sums of money in an effort to get him to stand down.
Fortunately, he cannot be bought.[101]

On May 9, 2001, Dr. Greer and many government, military
and private sector witnesses came before the National Press
Conference in order to get this information out to the public.
The conference was one of the largest ever attended by viewers
online. The videotapes of this conference are also available,
along with a set specially created for and hand delivered to
members of Congress, the executive branch, NASA officials
and senior military/Pentagon personnel prior to the press
conference. I encourage everyone to obtain copies of these and
Dr. Greer's books, and to distribute them as widely as possible.

As of this writing, the press conference in conjunction with
public response to the efforts of the Disclosure Project, has not
been enough to persuade Congress to open up congressional
hearings on this subject. Therefore, Dr. Greer and friends are

working on a second strategy. Rather than wait for this shape-shifting shadowy, para-governmental and transnational entity to disclose these earth-saving technologies on their own watch, a select group of inventors, researchers, scientists and like-minded individuals have undertaken the task of replicating and producing these technologies on their own.

The energy sector of our economy is worth over six trillion dollars a year. Obviously, the immediate extinction of the internal combustion engine, among other things, would shake it up big time. Realistically recognizing that new technologies could dangerously cripple current industry causing a short-term adverse economic effect, Dr. Greer and consultants are also working on ways to avert such crises. Gradual introduction and phasing in of clean energy technologies while phasing out the old is a given. Redeployment and diversification of industrial and natural resources is essential so that no one gets left out. We, the taxpayers, have already paid for the development of these technologies, although the funds were illegally manipulated. Therefore, we need not incur the economic burden of further research and development.

In the meantime, we must continue to put pressure on the powers that be to fully disclose the truth about UFOs and advanced technologies and to stop the lies. Our future depends on it, literally.

You may be asking, why haven't the muddlers gotten rid of Dr. Greer? His strategy is simple. He tells us that you cannot beat them at their own game. There is no such thing as a private conversation with today's technology. Therefore, counter-spy tactics are futile. We can't even begin to match them in skill. You cannot hide from them. There is no safe place left on the planet where they will not find you. Your only hope is to "stay in the light" he says, meaning to surround yourself with thousands of other people dedicated to the same cause. By doing so, a collective presence creates an electric shield the muddlers don't dare touch without being severely burned. This is also why efforts to discredit Dr. Greer have not been totally successful. With enough supporters, friends, and sympathetic insiders, those efforts could easily backfire. This is good advice for anyone thinking about going up against the machine. To do so alone is suicide. You must "seek refuge in the sangha," as Buddhists say.

Cosmic Deception and the Art of Muddling

Yes, 9-11 was a part of this. It is highly speculated that the minds of the pilots who crashed the jets into the World Trade Center and the Pentagon were being controlled by advanced psychotronic technology in the hands of the muddlers. This is the playing of the "terrorist card" Von Braun warned us about. As a result, we are experiencing the most violent assault on our civil liberties in U.S. history. But for the muddlers, that is not enough. In fact, it's only the beginning. As I write these words, the Bush administration is pushing for another multi-billion dollar package for "spaced-based" weapons of mass destruction, though it is clear that Iraq and other officially recognized terrorist groups have never had them, and never will. No, the real terrorists are those who live on our own soil – executing USAPs, disinformation, and plans for future evil deeds, such as a hoaxed extraterrestrial invasion. Such an invasion would ideally set us up for dramatic rescue by the military at the small price of imposing permanent martial law upon our nation, of course.

Hollywood has been employed for preparing us for this hoaxed invasion with movies like "Independence Day" and other Sci-Fi series. With over seventy per cent of the public accepting the reality of UFOs and over fifty per cent believing the government is involved in a cover-up, ridicule is no longer sufficient for keeping a lid on these stranger than fiction facts. Therefore, the only logical alternative is to make sure that when the time comes for the government to completely "fess up," the public has already been programmed to believe that any and all extraterrestrials are evil alien demons out to get us all.

The muddlers already possess the space ships. ARVs (Alien Reproduction Vehicles) manufactured by Lockheed,

Northrup and others are ready to go. Mind control and holographic projection technologies are fully operational for simulating abduction and other ET-related events. This hijacking of the legitimate disclosure process by the muddlers is a real possibility. Yet if this show should actually occur, Dr. Greer reminds us not to be deceived.

If such evil alien demons really existed and really wanted to get us, they could have gotten us a long time ago with their superior technology. And if visiting aliens really posed a threat to humanity by releasing a foreign fatal virus, then why was a 1982 law passed by Congress making contact with ETs illegal and quarantining those having had exposure with them, repealed?

Remember, most anything can be faked today. We are bombarded with special effects inside and outside of the movie theatre. The only way to find out the truth is to investigate these phenomena for yourself. In so doing, learning about the ways and means to detect fraud is your best defense strategy. Therefore let's examine various muddling techniques.

Beware of false polarities, especially presented in a Machiavellian context. The Libertarian Party and conservative talk show hosts such as Rush Limbaugh use this technique regularly. For instance, they will tell you that they're for "small government" if any government at all, and less government interference in private affairs, especially related to business. Then they will turn around and support anti-reproductive choice legislation. This makes no sense. A true conservative, as Barry Goldwater has pointed out, will be against government regulation of *any* private affairs, including reproductive rights. Therefore, another motive must be involved. Question it. Liberal activists, such as Ralph Nader, will rally for consumer rights. Yet this is nearly an oxymoron. Remember Chomsky – the muddlers *want* consumers but not activists. They want people indentured to the almighty bank, too busy making money trying to stay one step ahead of the bill collectors so they don't have time to pay attention to what's really going on, much less do anything about it. President Bush publicly announced he was against any legislation that would condone gay marriage because "it was against the Bible." He is pandering to a certain constituency here and nothing more. It is absurd to raise the issue because it is a *non-issue*. Our government is based on the separation of church and state. Therefore bringing the Bible into it is entirely irrelevant! These are subtle muddling techniques that are quite common, if not commonly recognized. Why? Because it requires the use of common sense, which actually atrophies with disuse. Therefore, keep that brain switch turned on! It's not that difficult.

Beware of disinformation. Mixing truth with lies makes the lies more believable. The Internet is a powerful tool for the people *and* the muddlers. The need for discernment and discrimination in evaluating what is read cannot be emphasized enough. Most of what is out there on this topic is pure disinformation. According to Dr. Greer,

> Disinformation is false information which is deliberately provided to groups or individuals for the purpose of obfuscating an issue, and/or effecting a specific psychological response (such as denial, disbelief, fear, ridicule, etc.). Covert attempts designed to minimize accurate knowledge of UFOs/ETs have used disinformation and psychological warfare techniques for over 40 years, and these techniques and related technologies have become increasingly sophisticated and effective, especially since the 1960s. The most effective disinformation is information which is related to a truth, at least in part, but which is then embellished and deliberately distorted by combining disinformation with the information. The presence of a minimal but adequate degree of truth enables the false information to be more readily accepted, or for the intended psychological response to occur.[102]

The two major of kinds of disinformation are active and passive. Passive disinformation is conveying false information via conventional means; for example, denying or falsifying data in UFO reports, ridiculing and discrediting individuals, and propagating fear. Active disinformation involves hoaxing UFO/ETI phenomena and using psychotronic devices for mind control and inducing hallucinations. Cattle mutilations are an example of active disinformation.

The book *MILABS: Military Mind Control and Alien Abduction* by Dr. Helmut Lammer and Marion Lammer, reveals much about the art of active disinformation. In 1994, the Clinton administration appointed a panel to investigate over four hundred government backed bio-medical experiments on humans between 1944 and 1975. Of all these studies, the experiments subjecting unknowing patients to radiation treatment received the most media attention. The mind-control projects previously known as CHATTER, BLUEBIRD and ARTICHOKE along with a host of others were subsumed under the umbrella project called MKULTRA that later became MKSEARCH.[103] MKULTRA research focused on the use of implants, hallucinogens, hypnosis, sensory deprivation, classical conditioning and supersensory power for nefarious purposes. Combining these techniques with staged drama simulating ET abduction or Satanic ritual abuse became a powerful way to control witnesses, especially children, and to create multiple personalities in victims who could then be used by the military and CIA as puppets. Once kidnapped, the victims are often fitted with a brain implant, which is really a tiny radio transmitter. Disturbing electronic frequencies and "voices" can then be transmitted directly into their minds from a distance. Hallucinations are often electronically generated as well as severe mood changes. Practicing physicians have treated victims and survivors of these dark experiments, found and surgically removed these implants, and even testified before Congressional committees on this subject.

Most alleged abductees have had more than one abduction experience. The reason for this is because once the covert military/intelligence operations target a person (and it's usually during that person's childhood) for use in these experiments, they find it convenient to continue to use that person throughout their life. The unfortunate victim becomes stigmatized with a life-long diagnosis of mental illness and therefore automatically deemed unreliable as a credible witness, no matter what they see. Therefore it makes sense why the majority of abductees report seeing military personnel somehow involved in their abduction scenario.

"Black helicopters" frequently harass abductees at their homes in an effort to keep them silenced, confused and frightened. These helicopters are often deployed from FEMA underground facilities, where sightings and abductions frequently occur.[104] The kidnappers usually attempt to induce amnesia in their victims with drugs or electric shocks, but sometimes they do not completely succeed. Therefore, it is not uncommon for abductees to remember seeing many strange things. One of the most commonly reported scenarios is seeing rows of fetuses floating in giant glass tubes and other strange phenomena transpiring in medical laboratories. The victims are most likely witnessing the results of covert genetic engineering and cloning experiments that have been underway for some time. That is also why so many abduction experiences involve invasive sexual probing. The MILAB scientists need a fresh supply of genetic material for their research.

These covert programs involving the forced kidnapping, torture and abuse of ordinary citizens like you and me are financed with our tax dollars. From Dr. Greer's research and testimony from inside witnesses who have worked on these projects, it is estimated that 99% of all abduction experiences are of this nature – completely hoaxed – and have nothing to do with genuine ETI contact.

It is easy to recognize how full disclosure benefits countless individuals and humanity as a whole in countless ways. For the sake of preserving the planet, our future, and all lives that share it, what could be more important?

What makes Dr. Greer tick? What motivates him to continue with what seems like such an impossible mission? What are the rewards? The same that can be said of all true

402

adepts. It is something that cannot be adequately described in words, yet he gives it a good shot:

> On a personal level, it's been catastrophic. I gave up a quarter of a million dollars per year as an emergency medical doctor to do this work. Financially and professionally, it's been disastrous. And in dealing with the media, it's been ruinous. This is a topic where you open yourself up to every kind of slander and defamation of character. I've also seen far too few people willing to take action.

> From a selfish point of view, one could never endure the challenges. What keeps me motivated, however, is that it is an unselfish endeavor.

> I have a deeply spiritual connection to God and I'm convinced that we're in a time whose hallmark is universal peace. And those of us who are working together to create this all over the world – whether or not they are connected to my group – understand when I say that this is a purpose that transcends one's selfish interests.

> To help establish a stable humanity on earth that can co-exist peacefully with civilizations from space is the greatest challenge of the time in which we live. And whatever God-given gifts each of us has should be brought forward to achieve that end. That's why I've given up my medical practice for now to do this work.

> Aside from that, when you asked about the rewards, I must say just how incredibly fascinating all these experiences have been. To be out on a remote desert landscape with our team and have the experience of contact with an advanced civilization hovering above us in a spacecraft! It has been astounding and wonderful.

The other rewards have been working with many wonderful people, the core of whom are completely pure hearted and deeply spiritual. For example, two of the closest friends of the Dalai Lama are on our advisory team.

On balance, one has to view this effort almost like the path of a bodhisattva, where you're willing to sacrifice your own personal interest because – let's face it – unless you're willing to publicly state that you were just molested by aliens, there is no money in this field. If I were to make such statements, I would have hundreds of millions of dollars being thrown at me by the intelligence community, which is why the alien abduction subculture is so financially well-put.

But if you're doing anything meaningful, there is absolutely no monetary return – nothing at all. And that's one of the sad realities that most people have no knowledge of. And it's one I don't normally speak about. But since you asked, that's the truth of it.[105]

Greer is not a pessimist, however. He views all the current turmoil of this dark age as the last "death gasps" of an era, and foresees with certainty the dawning of an age of lasting peace and enlightenment. How it happens and how soon it happens is up to us. As he says,

It's not just me. It's everyone who joins with us. When we all pull together, it will happen. It could have happened a hundred years ago. But the timing isn't relevant now; it's the conscious effort of humans that's relevant. Our intention and consciousness will have to be put into action to make it so – and if we make it so, it will be so. That's how we need to view it in order to make it happen. The potential for it is now. Universal peace is like a ripe fruit ready to fall into our hands.[106]

404

Seeing Outside the Window

The UFOlogy community shares serious literary deficiencies, spiritually and politically speaking. It behooves us all to do our part in dispelling the disinformation that's out there, especially in connection with occultism and spiritual practice.

So I ask you again to ponder the question Glinda posed to Dorothy upon her arrival in Munchkin Land, "Are you a good witch or a bad witch?" And why, when Dorothy was in the castle of the Wicked Witch, she could not voluntarily hand over the ruby red slippers? First, it is obvious that Glinda recognized that Dorothy had power. Secondly, she was really asking Dorothy what it was that she was going to do with that power. Dorothy, for the life of her, couldn't give it away, no matter how hard she tried. Distracted and then hypnotized by the appearance of her imprisonment, she had not yet recognized that it was a result of her own doing and that she had the power to undo it. Disintegrated and isolated, she felt helpless to help herself.

We cannot escape the fact that each of us has power and that each of us has responsibility for how we use that power. The lessons of the Wicked Witch are about our daily power struggles with ourselves and others based on the illusion of separateness. We don't just find ourselves visiting her castle once, but repeatedly. Some of us may feel that we live there.

Looking out the window, we see our avenue of escape. The Tin Man, the Scarecrow, and the Cowardly Lion come trudging up the mountain, led by Toto. Next we see how Dorothy's three companions are able to sneak into the castle – by ambushing some guards and donning their costumes for disguise. This is a secret strategy that needs no elaboration if meditated upon.

But before any of this happens, another important event occurs that we should not overlook. In the forest while the flying monkeys were abducting Dorothy, some of them attacked

Scarecrow and tore him apart, leaving him in separate pieces all over the place. Self-consciousness is shattered yet retains self-awareness. He cannot put himself back together on his own and must rely on the good will of the Tin Man and the Cowardly Lion. Only Love (the Tin Man) and Courage/Will/Faith (Cowardly Lion) can restore our sense of autonomy, impetus and confidence to act in these troubled times. Until our shattered minds are made whole again and integrated with every other aspect of our being, we cannot help anyone – not even ourselves.

Our society has too many shattered scarecrows, sitting on their couches watching T.V., allowing apathy to get the best of them. How many of us say, "What can I do? I'm just one person." Are you really?

We only recognize our unity with others and all life after our seeming separateness is challenged. Conscious integration cannot occur unless our separate sense of identity has been attacked and torn asunder in some way, some place. We can thank the muddlers for doing the ugly deed and bringing this most necessary task to our attention. Bless them, for they have the most difficult role of all.

"And if I be lifted up, I will lift all others unto myself," said Jesus. In making ourselves whole, the world is healed. This integration process involves every single aspect of our being. We turn our attention to a most important aspect that is not commonly recognized as such, in the next chapter.

---

[1] John D. Rankin, *The Mystic Keys of Hermes*, CSA Printing and Bindery, Inc., Second Printing, 1977, p. 45.

[2] *Id.*, p. 49-50.

[3] Lawrence S. Wrightman, Ph.D., *Social Psychology*, Second edition, Brooks/Cole Publishing Company, 1977, p. 584-587.

[4] Riane Eisler, *The Chalice and the Blade*, Harper Collins, 1988, p. 35.

[5] Gerda Lerner, *The Creation of Patriarchy*, Oxford University Press, 1986.

[6] Mary Daly, *Gyn/Ecology: The Metaethics of Radical Feminism*, Beacon Press, 1978.

[7] Maurice Brinton, *The Irrational in Politics*, Black Rose Books, 1974.

[8] Laurence Gardner, *Genesis of the Grail Kings*, Fair Wind Publishers, 2001, p. 6. Reprinted with permission.

[9] *Id.*, p.129-130.

[10] *Id.*, p.89.

[11] William Bramley, *The Gods of Eden*, Avon Books, 1989.

[12] *Id.*, p. 53.

[13] *Id.*, p. 85.

[14] *Id.*, p. 86.

[15] *Id.*, p. 166.

[16] Michael Howard, *The Occult Conspiracy: Secret Societies – Their Influence and Power in World History,* Destiny Books, 1989.

[17] *Id.*, p. 178.

[18] *Id.*, pp. 128-129.

[19] *Id.*, p. 39.

[20] Eliphas Levi, *Transcendental Magic,* Samuel Weiser, 1972, pp. 191-193.

[21] Howard, p. 75.

[22] *Id.,* p. 82.

[23] Paul Foster Case, *The Great Seal of the United States: Its History, Symbolism and Message for the New Age*, J. F. Rowny Press, 1935, pp. 9-10.

[24] Howard, p. 86.

[25] *Id.*, p. 61.

[26] *Id.*

[27] *Id.*, p. 68.

[28] Holly Sklar (editor) *Trilateralism – an overview (excerpted from the book Trilateralism)*, South End Press (1980), published at http://www.thirdworldtraveler.com/Trilaterialism/Trilateralism_overview.html.

[29] *Id.*

[30] *Id.*

[31] *Id.*

[32] *Id.*

[33] *Id.*

[34] *Id.*

[35] Edward S. Herman and Noam Chomsky, *Manufacturing Consent: The Political Economy of the Mass Media*, Pantheon Books, 1988.

[36] Roger Scruton, *A Dictionary of Political Thought,* Hill and Wang, 1982, p. 116.

[37] *Id.*, p. 32.

[38] *Id.*, p. 117.

[39] Bramley, p. 218.

[40] *Id.*, p. 219.

[41] *Id.* p. 220.

[42] Rius, *Marx for Beginners*, Random House, Inc., 1976, p. 14.

[43] Scruton, p. 80.

[44] David Smith and Phil Evans, *Marx's Kapital for Beginners*, Random House, Inc., 1982, p. 37.

[45] *Id.*, p.49.

[46] *Id.*, p. 167-168.

[47] *Id.*, p. 171.

[48] *Id.*, p. 62.

[49] Karl Marx, Friedrich Engles, *The Communist Manifesto*, Penguin Books (1888, 1967), p. 99.

[50] For a complete list and explanation of these principles, see http://sp-usa.org/about/principles.html.

[51] American Civil Liberties Union, http://www.aclu.org.

[52] David Cogswell, *Chomsky for Beginners*, Writers and Readers Publishing, 1996.

[53] *Id.*, p. 101.

[54] Farrand ed., *2 Madison's Records of the Federal Convention of 1787* (1937), p. 325.

[55] Bramley, p. 291.

[56] Joel Bleifuss, *Know Thine Enemy: A Brief History of Corporations*, from <u>In These Times</u> magazine, February, 1998.

[57] David C. Korten, p. 185, reprinted with permission of the publisher, from *The Post-Corporate World: Life After Capitalism,* copyright © 1999 by David C. Korten, Berrett-Koehler Publishers, Inc., San Francisco, CA. All rights reserved. http://www.bkconnection.com.

[58] William Meyers, *The Santa Clara Blues: Corporate Personhood versus Democracy,* http://www.iiipublishing.com/afd/santaclara.html.

[59] Timberg, quoted in Arthur S. Miller, "The Corporation as a Private Government in the World Community", 46 Virginia Law Review 8 (1960).

[60] William Kalle Lasn, *Culture Jam: The Uncooling of America*, Morrow/Eaglebrook, 1999.

[61] Terry Ann Halbert, "The First Amendment in the Workplace: An Analysis and Call for Reform," 17 Seton Hall Law Review 42 (1987).

[62] *Id.*

[63] *Id.*, p. 51.

[64] The Electronic Frontier Foundation is the place to go for this: http://www.eff.org

[65] Stanley Ingber, "Rediscovering the Communal Worth of Individual Rights: The First Amendment in Institutional Contexts," 69 Texas Law Review 1 (1990), p. 52.

[66] *Id.*, p. 53.

[67] *Id.*, p. 54.

[68] *Id.*, p. 60-61.

[69] *Id.*, p. 62.

[70] *Id.*, p. 65.

[71] Cogswell, p. 113.

[72] Quoted in Cogswell, p. 121.

[73] *Id.*, p. 115.

[74] *Id.*, p. 132.

[75] *Id.*, p. 126.

[76] *Id.*, p. 135.

[77] Noam Chomsky interviewed by David Barsamian, "Rollback: The Return of Predatory Capitalism," reprinted in Alternative Press Review, Vol. 2, Number 3, (1996).

[78] Steven M. Greer, MD, ed., transcribed in *Disclosure*, Crossing Point, Inc., 2002, pp. 226-227. Reprinted with permission. Also on Disclosure Video; see also Gordon Cooper and Bruce Henderson, *Leap of Faith: An Astronaut's Journey into the Unknown*, pp. 80-91, 194-200.

[79] Greer, pp. 80-85.

[80] *Id.*, pp. 305-307.

[81] *Id.*, p. 58. See also *The New York Times*, Sunday, February 28, 1960: "Air Force Order on 'Saucers' Sighted," p. L30.

[82] Greer, pp. 145-146.

[83] *Id.*, pp. 275-277.

[84] *Id.*, p. 255-259.

[85] *Id.*, pp. 168-171.

[86] *Id.*, pp. 184, 187.

[87] *Id.*, pp. 345-347.

[88] *Id.*, pp. 230-236.

[89] *Id.*, pp. 384-385.

[90] *Id.*, p. 381.

[91] *Id.*, p. 501.

[92] *Id.*, pp. 38, 364.

[93] *Id.*, p. 247-251.

[94] *Id.*, pp. 534-542. See also www.chenier.org.

[95] *Id.*, pp. 419-420.

[96] *Id.*, pp. 14, 15, 567. See also www.disclosureproject.org and www.seaspower.com.

[97] Personal dialogue with Dr. Greer in February, 2003.

[98] Steven M. Greer, M.D., *Extraterrestrial Contact*, Crossing Point, Inc., 1999, p. 398. Reprinted with permission.

[99] Greer, 1999, p. 429.

[100] Greer, 2001, p. 455.

[101] *Id.*, p. 296. Also from private dialogue with Dr. Greer in February, 2003.

[102] Greer, 1999.

[103] Lammer, p. 21.

[104] *Id.*, p. 39.

[105] From an interview with Greer by Paula Peterson entitled "To Take Our Place Among the Stars" in *Spirit of Ma'at*, Vol. 3, March 2003, www.spiritofmaat.com. Reprinted with permission.

[106] *Id.*

PART 5

Reclaiming the Broomstick

It is only with the heart that one can see rightly;
what is essential is invisible to the eye.

-- from *The Little Prince*
by Antoine de Saint Exupery

CHAPTER 8

AWAKENING THE DRAGON:
THE PHYSIOLOGY OF AWARENESS

Dorothy and company escape the clutches of the evil
kingdom when they leave the poppy field and when the wicked
witch is melted. Both times, however, they are led to Oz. At
Oz they find that they still have more challenges, maybe more
subtle ones, but they're still challenges. It is an interesting
paradox.

Reality is a Rubber Band – Transcendence is a Lie

All paradox is rooted in the law of impermanence. For
example, we are at the same time limited and not limited by our
physical bodies. On a relative scale, our bodies present
limitations regarding what can and cannot be done with them.
Yet can those limitations be transcended? Not really. Our
reality merely expands – our capacity to respond to truth. Once
the physical body develops beyond the previous limitation, the
limitation no longer exists. There is no "transcendence." To
transcend something means that it must still exist. In this case,
the limitations disappear – they no longer exist. Therefore, they
have not been transcended. They have *changed* – just like us –
just like our bodies. In their place, new limitations appear. This
is where the law of impermanence comes into play. Energy
never disappears – it just changes shape. This is the law of
One; The Emerald Tablet of Hermes; the Korean Chung-Bu-
Kyung or Heavenly Code; the Tibetan Prajna Paramita; the Tao.

Reality is elastic – capable of stretching beyond its so-
called original size. Therefore, size matters not, as Yoda says.
What matters is the intrinsic nature of the rubber band – what it
can do – what purpose does it serve. What it looks like doesn't
matter. This also involves the law of polarity. This is why it's
so easy to fall back down to hell after experiencing the heights
of heaven. Does it mean that heaven or our capacity to

experience heaven no longer exists? Not really. It just means our perspective has changed. This is why sacred outlook is so important. It's a way to keep the rubber band stretched, fulfilling its purpose. An unused rubber band is meaningless. Therefore, whenever we feel that something is meaningless, it just means that we're not recognizing and actualizing its potential. The rubber band is not bad. Mustn't throw it away. Just use it. Allow your reality to expand and look at what surrounds it. Contracting, shrinking, and expanding universes must be contracting and expanding in something, right? Mingling with space/energy opens awareness to infinite possibilities.

On a relative scale, we know that rubber bands come in all different sizes and strengths and can be broken if stretched too far. Similarly, it's important to recognize one's limitations. If you try to encompass more than what you're prepared for (and preparation is training, learning, practicing) -- there is a danger of breaking and destroying your sense of intrinsic meaning. If this happens, then the maker just gets another rubber band – and it's usually stronger. Perhaps it had to break for that reason, so that next time around, reality could stretch further. The rubber band breaks and is discarded. The intrinsic purpose of the rubber band becomes invisible, and what remains is apparent empty space. Yet lo and behold, a new, different, better rubber band emerges on the scene. Its intrinsic nature and purpose was never lost – it simply found new form. Empty space became filled with new rubber bandness. The energy of that space poured into the rubber band – giving it energy and purpose. Rubber bandness did not disappear with the rubber band. It just found a new home.

It's the law of evolution. Who is in control of the rubber bands? The creator -- the user of the rubber bands. Who is the creator/user? Can the creator/user and the rubber band become one? Then you're in the next universe. Another paradox – a new set of limitations has appeared to you. Just like *The Fool* in the Tarot – when one mountain summit is reached, there's always another one, a bit higher than the one before.   So congratulations! Life goes on…

Star Seed

Being is elastic – especially when it comes to our bodies. And as long as we're in our bodies, spiritual experience has a biological component.   Spirit and matter are fully integrated, whether we intellectually accept that fact or not.   As the Qabalistic phrase goes, "The Kingdom of Spirit is embodied in my flesh."

Consider the following tune:

> Away in a manger, no crib for a bed. The little Lord Jesus lay down his sweet head. The stars in the sky looked down where he lay. The little Lord Jesus asleep in the hay.

The story told in this lovely Christmas carol is symbolic of the process by which Christ consciousness is awakened within us.

Jesus was born in Bethlehem. The word 'Bethlehem' in Hebrew means 'house of bread.' Jesus was born in the house of bread.   Turns out, the house of bread is our abdomen, specifically the small intestine. Most people might think that the dawning of enlightenment is located in the head in a higher chakra. Well it's not. It's in the belly.

What's a manger like? Well, it's a crude, rustic place where farm animals are gathered around, slowly chewing their cud and producing a whole lot of shit. What exactly are they chewing? The very thing that baby Jesus is sleeping in -- hay. Meanwhile, the stars are looking down on him, so there's a cosmic connection going on too.

The light that liberates is born in animal flesh – the organs most intimately linked with digestion. The stars are watching as if they have a special investment in it. A star child has materialized in animal flesh on Earth. Christ-consciousness is born. The shit that's lying around is the byproduct of the very

414

substance that illuminates us. Therefore, in the old alchemical tales, this represents the stone that the builders refused because it is so commonplace. Shit is not the magical substance, but a substance found in it is.

Jesus was born of a virgin. The symbol for the astrological sign of Virgo is the virgin. The region of the physical body associated with Virgo is the belly. The virgin's milk in alchemical texts is referred to as "an oily water which will not wet the hand." That's because it never *sees* the hand. It is no mysterious substance. It is simply chyle. Flash to a medical encyclopedia for clear, helpful definitions:

> Chyle: a milky fluid consisting of lymph and emulsified fat that forms in the small intestine during digestion.
>
> Lymph: body fluid containing white cells: a fluid containing white cells, chiefly lymphocytes, that is drained from tissue spaces by the vessels in the lymphatic system. It can transport bacteria, viruses and cancer cells. Colorless in hue, lymph draining the intestines can turn opalescent from fatty globules absorbed from a meal.
>
> Lymphatic system: a network of vessels that transports fluid, fats, proteins and lymphocytes to the bloodstream as lymph, and removes microorganisms and other debris from tissues.

Chyle is white because the emulsified globules of animal fat are composed of three complex compounds: stearine, palmitin and olein. Each one of these compounds is a combination of the three elements of oxygen, hydrogen, and carbon. In esoteric terminology, oxygen is fire, hydrogen is water, and carbon is earth.

Chyle is absorbed into the lacteals, lymphatic vessels in the small intestine, where it is picked up by lymphocytes and transported through the thoracic duct into the bloodstream.

Chyle releases finer forces into the bloodstream that can then be directed to the brain for energizing particular centers in the frontal lobe responsible for providing the physiological basis for illumination. Mercury is the alchemical force related to the brain, and Mercury, astrologically speaking, is exalted in the sign of Virgo, corresponding to the abdominal region. So see, it starts in the belly – not in the head!

Why is this so important to know? Because you can't reach this state by just sitting on a cushion meditating all day, contrary to purveyors of particular brands of newage. We must exercise! And there are exercises specifically designed to facilitate this process. But first, let's examine those head centers involved.

Dragon Treasure: The Spirit Gland

If the body is a temple, church or cathedral, it must have within it a special place where the Holy of Holies is thought to reside transmitting the spiritual truths. In my Order, Builders of the Adytum, the word 'adytum' refers not only to this body or temple, but also to that specific holy place or altar within the temple where the Divine Presence shines forth in all its glory. The adytum is the purified and perfected pineal gland.

We're all born with a pineal gland. In the brains of an adept, however, it is a highly developed crystallized structure. When working in close conjunction with the pituitary gland, it is more capable of receiving and transmitting 'higher frequencies' than ordinary pineal glands. Yet keep in mind that it's not just a crystallized pineal gland that makes an adept an adept. The other energy centers in the body must be fully charged, refined, and functionally synergized, operating in perfect equilibrium so that the temple stands on a secure foundation. For instance, if the heart is not equally developed so that it is an eternally open channel for endless streams of compassion, the temple will become top heavy and crash. This is what happened to Darth Vader, the villain in the *Star Wars* movies. To put it simply, he was all in his "head" with very

416

little "heart." But because the pineal gland is so essential to multidimensional perception, it is critical that we gain a proper understanding of this gateway to "other-worldly" experience – particularly experiences involving contact with extraterrestrial intelligence.

Derived from the Latin 'pineus' and 'pinus' referring to the pine, the pineal gland is shaped like a little bitty pinecone, small enough to sit on the end of your finger. It is the most unique organ in the brain because it is the only one not paired. Every other part of the brain has two halves, such as right frontal lobe and left frontal lobe. The pineal gland stands alone, and scientists had no clue of its real function until recently. Descartes, however, was on to something when he called it "the seat of the soul." He felt that the pineal gland was where spirit met flesh.

The pineal gland is like an eye, and in some animals, that's how it works. This third eye has a cornea, retina, and lens and is particularly light sensitive. It also helps regulate skin coloration and body temperature. In humans, it is buried more deeply within the brain, and so it is not as sensitive to light as it is in other animals, yet it seems to be deeply impacted by the absence of light.

The pineal gland emerges in the growing fetus exactly when gender is defined -- about 49 days from the date of conception. Interestingly, the Tibetan *Book of the Dead* states it takes 49 days after death for a soul to reincarnate.[1] Is there a relationship? Also, at this early stage, the pineal gland is not really a part of the brain yet. It grows out of specialized tissues in the roof of the mouth. Then it eventually migrates to a strategic location in the brain where it can easily access cerebrospinal fluid and be close to the centers that control emotion and sensation. In fact, it sits right on top of these specialized brain tissues so that anything that's secreted by the pineal gland gets into them immediately.

The pineal gland produces the hormone melatonin associated with the functions of sleep and dreaming. Melatonin is also implicated in DNA repair mechanisms and antioxidant activity helping to prevent dementia. It is usually produced in the body at nighttime because light turns it off. The neurotransmitters regulating melatonin synthesis are noradrenaline and adrenaline secreted from nearby nerve endings. These neurotransmitters are different from the ones produced by the adrenal glands. Noradrenaline and adrenaline secreted by the adrenal glands regulate our responses to stress. Interestingly, the stress-related hormones never make it to the pineal gland because the gland is protected by something called the blood-brain barrier. This is why the pineal gland prefers not to make melatonin during the day; it's too busy getting rid of the stress cells.

This is the secret behind the effectiveness of dark room retreats. After spending over a week in complete darkness, just relaxing, sleeping and meditating, the pineal gland becomes highly activated. Because this can precipitate strange experiences, it is recommended to take these kinds of retreats under the supervision of a trusted teacher.

This is probably why darkness gets such a bad rap. It's associated with scary things that go bump in the night, when really it's just a time when supernormal events are more likely to occur – pleasant and not so pleasant. The true light of spirit is the light that is generated from within. Therefore, we find another truth revealed in seeming paradox: The light is found in the darkness, and the darkness is the light.

The interpretation of 'Om Mani Pedme Hung' as "the jewel is in the lotus" refers to the dragon's treasure (the perfected, crystallized pineal gland) that is fully integrated with the corresponding vortex, chakra or divine energy center. Yet the golden treasure will not be released without facing the dragon.

DMT: The Spirit Molecule

The following information comes from the revolutionary research of Rick Strassman, M.D., memorialized in his book entitled, *DMT – The Spirit Molecule.*[2] Strassman's pioneering research into the biology of near-death and mystical experiences revealed that an extraordinary little molecule known as DMT is the most active ingredient in these experiences, neurochemically speaking.

DMT, short for di-methyl-tryptamine, is a naturally occurring psychedelic drug in the human body. Dr. Strassman prefers the term 'psychedelic' as opposed to 'hallucinogen' because hallucinogen only emphasizes the perceptual effects of these drugs. Psychedelic means 'mind-manifesting' and so the emphasis is on revealing what's in the mind, uncovering thoughts and feelings -- not just restricting it to special effects. Psychedelic drugs come from two families: tryptamines and phenethylamines. Mescaline and Ecstasy are phenethylamines. Tryptamine is derived from the amino acid, tryptophan. Tryptamine based drugs include serotonin, LSD, ibogaine, psilocybin (found in some mushrooms), and DMT -- all similar in chemical structure. Exactly how these drugs make us feel or see things is still unknown. As Dr. Strassman indicates,

> It is important to remember that while we understand a great deal about the pharmacology of psychedelics, we know nearly nothing about how changes in brain chemistry *directly* relate to subjective, or inner, experience. This is as true for psychedelics as it is for Prozac. That is, we are far from comprehending how activating particular serotonin receptors translates into a new thought or emotion. We don't "feel" a serotonin receptor blockade; rather, we feel ecstasy. We don't "see" frontal lobe activation; instead, we observe angels or demons.[3]

Therefore, causality is a non-issue and should probably stay so. To reduce experience to mechanistic molecular interactions is far from fulfilling. Instead of trying to decide what came first, the chicken or the egg, it's more helpful and realistic to assume that they have always existed together in synergized being – a unified multidimensional dynamic living process – rather than a separative one-dimensional static duality. Integrative medicine recognizes that although our physical existence is immensely important, it's not the only aspect of our being.   Levels of reality are not disjointed; they are interpenetrating.   To assign causality to one dimension is shortsighted.

So where is DMT found other than in our bodies? It is found throughout the plant and animal kingdoms, meaning practically everywhere. It is thought to be most abundant in the plants of Latin America around the Amazon River. Indigenous peoples have long known about it and concocted medicinal drinks with it.

It's the endogenous DMT -- the DMT made within the body that concerns us. For a long time, scientists couldn't figure out why it was there. Psychiatrists speculated that it might be the culprit behind mental illness. Studies during the 1960s suggested a relationship to psychosis, but nothing conclusive. Progress in this research was hampered during the 1970s by growing anti-drug sentiment. Congress passed a law placing DMT in a highly restricted category. Two decades later Strassman finally got the approval and resources needed to conduct his research, and only after a marathon of jumping through legal and academic hoops.   After careful screening, volunteers were recruited to receive regulated dosages of DMT in a controlled experimental setting for studying the effects of DMT. The results were nothing less than astounding.

Strassman found that the brain favors DMT over all the other drugs. He says it's like a "brain food" because the brain routinely processes it very quickly as if it is needed for proper functioning.   The only time DMT results in extraordinary experiences is when its levels reach a particular threshold. And where is DMT produced? You guessed it – the pineal gland.

Strassman declares that DMT is the spirit molecule – not that it is more 'spiritual' than other molecules – rather it is more instrumental in precipitating spiritual experiences than other biological mechanisms. It is a tool -- a vehicle -- a trigger:

> A spirit molecule needs to elicit, with reasonable
> reliability, certain psychological states we consider

"spiritual." These are feelings of extraordinary joy, timelessness, and a certainty that what we are experiencing is "more real than real." Such a substance may lead us to an acceptance of the coexistence of opposites, such as life and death, good and evil; a knowledge that consciousness continues after death; a deep understanding of the basic unity of all phenomena; and a sense of wisdom or love pervading all existence.

A spirit molecule also leads us to spiritual realms. These worlds usually are invisible to us and our instruments and are not accessible using our normal state of consciousness. However, just as likely as the theory that these worlds exist "only in our minds" is that they are, in reality, "outside" of us and freestanding. If we simply change our brain's receiving abilities, we can apprehend and interact with them.[4]

This is precisely what Strassman found in his studies.

Extreme stress can cause a breakthrough of the pineal security system in the blood brain barrier. Strassman speculated that in some cases, the pineal gland might secrete DMT when the stress hormones reach this ultimate threshold. Irregular amounts of DMT completely immobilize the body and overwhelm the psyche with intense emotional and visual imagery. Patients diagnosed as psychotic might simply have a damaged pineal shield. Stress certainly exacerbates psychotic symptoms, thus shattering the shield.

Melatonin by itself is not enough to produce dreams while sleeping. Melatonin and DMT are suspected to somehow team up precipitating the dream state. Meditation can produce similar states, thus activating pineal DMT response. Strassman states,

> In a similar way, meditative techniques using sound, sight, or the mind may generate particular wave patterns whose fields induce resonance in the brain.

Millennia of human trial and error have determined that certain "sacred" words, visual images, and mental exercises exert uniquely desired effects. Such effects may occur because of the specific fields they generate within the brain. These fields cause multiple systems to vibrate and pulse at certain frequencies. We can feel our minds and bodies resonate with these spiritual exercises. Of course, the pineal gland also is buzzing at these same frequencies.[5]

Substantial amounts of DMT are released during transitional life experiences which are naturally stressful, such as birth, death, and near-death events. Perhaps the pineal gland is the major gateway enabling the soul to "enter" and "exit" this plane of existence. The volunteers in Dr. Strassman's study always experienced intense psychedelic imagery and overpowering emotions. However, they also reported a feeling that the mind had separated from the body. Phrases like, "I no longer had a body" or "My body dissolved – I was pure awareness" were typical. The sensation of moving away from or out of the body was reported in terms like "falling," "lifting up," or "flying."[6] The experience of space was not limited to three dimensions either. Volunteers reported not being able to distinguish "in front" from "behind," even though colors and imagery were brighter than what is experienced in a normal state. "Four-dimensional" or "beyond dimensionality" were words commonly used to describe this effect.

Even though most volunteers felt they were "out" of their bodies, they reported a profound awareness of what they described as DNA. Examples from four separate individuals:

"There were spirals of what looked like DNA, red and green."

"The visuals were dropping back into tubes, like protozoa, like the inside of a cell, seeing the DNA twirling and spiraling. They looked gelatinlike, like tubes, inside which were cellular activities…"

"There was a spiral DNA-type thing made out of incredibly bright cubes. I "felt" the boxes at the same time that my consciousness shifted."

"I felt the DMT release my soul's energy and push it through the DNA. It's what happened when I lost my body. There were spirals that reminded me of things I've seen at Chaco Canyon. Maybe that was DNA. Maybe the ancients knew that. The DNA is backed into the universe like space travel. One needs to travel without one's body. It's ridiculous to think about space travel in little ships."[7]

Often there was a clear association made between words and numbers:

"… There were all these colors and then there were all these numbers, Roman numerals. The numbers became words…"

"… They were 3-D circles and cones with shading. They moved around a lot. It was almost like looking at an alphabet, but it wasn't English. It was like a fantasy alphabet, a cross between runes and Russian or Arabic writing. It felt like there was some information in it, like it was data. It wasn't just random."

"Like seeing panels with a cut-out shape, rounded edges, hieroglyphics of some sort…"

"It was Mayan hieroglyphics… The hieroglyphics turned into a room, like I was a child."

"It's like threads of words or DNA or something. They're all around there, they're everywhere… When I looked around, it seemed like the meaning or

423

symbols were there. Some kind of core of reality where all meaning is stored."[8]

Another common experience was entering into some kind of holding space – that a room or place had been specially created for them, and then foreign life forms acting as guides would come meet them. When in these holding rooms, the participants often felt like they were little children in some sort of nursery. The life forms took on many different shapes. Words often used to describe them were "clowns," "elves," "reptiles," "mantises," "bees," "spiders," "cacti," "insects," and "stick figures." In at least one experiment, a subject noted "blue-skinned hands." Always they were referred to as beings of some kind in the context of aliens, entities or guides. The interesting thing about these contact experiences is that they only happen with DMT. Other psychedelic drugs produce no such contact effects.[9]

Many scenarios described parallel those reported by UFO abductees, yet not at all negative or unpleasant. One male, for example, found himself on an operating-room table being examined by four strange entities with very advanced technology. He insists that this was more real than dream-like:

> "DMT has shown me the reality that there is infinite variation on reality. There is the real possibility of adjacent dimensions. It may not be so simple as that there's alien planets with their own societies. This is too proximal. It's not like some kind of drug. It's more like an experience of a new technology than a drug.
>
> "You can choose to attend to this or not. It will continue to progress without you paying attention. You return not to where you left off, but to where things have gone since you left. It's not a hallucination, but an observation. When I'm there, I'm not intoxicated. I'm lucid and sober."[10]

Multiple volunteers had experiences like this. When communicating with these other beings, it was more like communicating through some type of body awareness rather than words or thoughts -- as if mutual energy was shared. According to Strassman,

> There are surprising and remarkable consistencies among volunteers' reports of contact with nonmaterial beings. Sound and vibration build until the scene almost explosively shifts to an "alien" realm. Volunteers find themselves on a bed or in a landing bay, research environment, or high-technology room. The highly intelligent beings of this "other" world are interested in the subject, seemingly ready for his or her arrival and wasting no time in "getting to work." There might be one particular being clearly in charge, directing the others. Volunteers frequently comment about the emotional quality of the relationships: loving, caring, or professionally detached.
>
> Their "business" appeared to be testing, examining, probing, and even modifying the volunteer's mind and body. Sometimes testing came first, and after results were satisfactory, further interactions took place. They also communicated with the volunteers, attempting to convey information by gestures, telepathy or visual imagery. The purpose of the contact was uncertain, but several subjects felt a benevolent attempt on the beings' part to improve us individually or as a race.[11]

It appears that DMT is enabling access to other dimensions where some extraterrestrials reside. More than several experiences support this. These volunteers were not allowed to interact with each other, and none were familiar with common descriptions of aliens in the UFO/ET literature, yet most all of them saw beings that matched these descriptions – particularly beings of an insect or reptilian nature, or who were humanoid with elongated heads, for instance. Ancient texts refer to such beings as well, and clay figurines of beings with elongated heads have been unearthed at several archeological sites in the Middle East.

Another interesting scenario reported with consistency was the beings interacting with what appeared to be sophisticated technology. Many of them were observed at what appeared to be computer terminals or console panels of spacecraft. The important element about the interactions, however, was that they seemed to be controlling the technology with their minds. Recall that CAT or TAC – consciousness assisted technology and technology assisted consciousness – is a common communication device among extraterrestrials as reported by Dr. Greer and other CSETI members. Rotating lights are frequently seen in extraterrestrial craft as part of this technology.

A male DMT study volunteer had one such contact experience involving beings he described as "guardians" or "gatekeepers," including one with an elongated head. He reported:

> "They were pouring communication into me but it was just so intense. I couldn't bear it. There were rays of psychedelic yellow light coming out of the face of the reassuring entity. She was trying to communicate with me. She seemed very concerned for me, and the effects I was experiencing due to her attempts at communicating."

> "There was something outlined in green, right in front of me and above me here. It was rotating and doing things. She was showing me, it seemed like, how to use this thing. It resembled a computer terminal. I believe she wanted me to try to communicate with her through that device. But I couldn't figure it out."[12]

One volunteer ended up on what he said was another planet. He was greeted by some friendly cloaked beings who stated they were pleased to see him again and excited that we had discovered this technology. They wanted to know more about his body and told him that humans exist on many levels. They became concerned that he needed to get back in order to have his blood monitored. Dr. Strassman and his staff were monitoring all vital signs during these experiments, so this seemed perfectly logical.

One volunteer reported that while in deep space, she encountered some beings who told her that there were many things they could share with us once we learned how to make more extended contact. When returning to her body, she said that although she always believed we were never alone in the universe, she had no idea we could contact these beings within our inner space. She thought it could only happen with flying saucers in outer space.[13]

The deep mystical and cosmic states of consciousness often triggered by DMT intrigued Dr. Strassman more than the contact experiences. The traditional features of a mystical experience fit precisely what many of the volunteers experienced. The sense of self, time and space are profoundly altered if not annihilated. In most cases personal identity is replaced with direct experience of the underlying unity and interdependence of all existence. This experience is not always pleasant for everyone. Some persons find it destabilizing and overpowering.

Many volunteers had some experience with recreational drugs, mainly LSD and hallucinogenic mushrooms. When contrasting those experiences with the ones with DMT, they all reported that with DMT, there was much more intensity and a complete feeling of helplessness. In other words, with LSD and mushrooms they felt they had some measure of control in building up to and filtering the experience. With DMT that control was lost, and yet it was precisely in losing this control that many of them found relief. For example, one volunteer related, "DMT shook some things loose, as it was so shattering.

I now find I have more control over my reality by letting go; it's a paradox. I've found that the DMT experience intensified verbal, visual, and musical abilities. Overall, DMT showed me another level or process I needed to see. Nothing I thought or felt made any difference in terms of controlling the sessions. I learned the beneficial aspects of losing control."[14]

All volunteers interviewed in follow up sessions reported life changes identical to those reported by people having undergone profound mystical or near-death experiences. Among these were a stronger sense of self, less fear of death, and a greater appreciation for life. Many of them cut down on drinking and other destructive behaviors. Some were inspired by their revelations, and many found comfort in the confirmation of other dimensions of reality previously unknown to them. Though these studies revealed no immediate psychotherapeutic benefits to the administration of DMT, the important discoveries certainly warranted future research.

For example, volunteers were unanimously emphatic about their experiences being completely real and unlike typical dream experiences. In listening to the descriptions of these experiences, Dr. Strassman repeatedly thought, "This sounds like nothing I've ever heard about in my therapy patients' dream life. It is much more bizarre, well-remembered, and internally consistent."[15]

It is obvious that DMT provides easy access to other levels of reality – to other planes of existence. Theoretical physicists speak of these planes as parallel universes or multiverses. Scientists base this theory on the phenomenon of interference or the interaction of invisible light particles with visible ones resulting in an unusual deflection or "bending" of the light. This is explained by studies into the nature of dark matter and dark energy.

Scientists estimate that at least 95 percent of the mass of the universe is comprised of dark matter and dark energy, meaning that it is invisible. Although it's invisible, we know it exists because of its gravitational effects. It appears to "hold" everything together so that without it, the universe would fall

428

apart. Scientists speculate certain undiscovered particles will lead to a better understanding of how dark matter and dark energy work. These particles are currently called *WIMPS* or weakly interacting massive particles. Scientists say that these WIMPS surround us, and that there could be at least a billion of them streaming through our bodies every second, traveling at over a million miles per hour. But because they only interact very weakly with light matter, most of them will pass through us unhindered. Dr. Strassman believes that DMT might alter something in the brain that makes it possible to perceive these WIMPS interacting with light matter as they pass through us.[16]

These multiverses can be accessed and explored by bending light or frequency in such a way that exposes the WIMPS. Then for just an instant, different dimensions can "open up" and "merge" with each other. Although spiritual sages and extraterrestrial beings have learned how to do this on their own with and without external technology, it is clear that something about our inner instrumentation needs to change before we can do the same.

The capacities of the human body far surpass any afforded to us by external drugs or material technology. Yet the inner technology of the mind is invariably chemical to some degree, as body and spirit are one. We already have the equipment. It just needs to be developed and refined so that we can "tune" into these other levels of reality with ease. We just need to find the appropriate switches and learn how to turn them on. DMT may be pointing at one.

Apparently, we cannot access these other levels of reality while in ordinary physiological states. Something about our physiology needs to change for us to be able to approach them with regularity. The discovery of the spirit molecule may provide just one more piece of the puzzle or map for tracking the relative biological processes.

The Dragon Body

There are many different kinds of dragons. Much can be learned about them from fairy tales and mythological lore. Yet like most legends, they are formed around a seed of truth. Dragons are universal. Dragons are symbolic. Dragons are real.

Behind all forms, essence is most important. That's why there can be so many different kinds of dragons, yet only one essence of dragon or "dragoness." My favorite form of dragon is the Western magical dragon associated with medieval legend. It has a chunky, scaly reptilian physique, a long tail, horse-like head, and huge wings. It has a forked tongue, flies and breathes fire. It is not mean or bad. It is simply dragon. The reptilian body signifies that it is a creature of earth. The wings say it is a creature of heaven. Therefore, earthly powers and celestial forces are united in the dragon.

The dragons associated with the reptilian race of extraterrestrials probably did not look like this. Nevertheless, something inspired the development of these various types of dragons. It could have been the extraterrestrial craft itself – an object made of scale-like metals with the wings of a bird, breathing smoke and fire upon take off and landing. Weapons from these craft could have literally scorched the earth as the stories tell us. Yet the most important dragon and the one that concerns us the most in our tumultuous lives, is the dragon within – particularly what we call "the dragon body."

The reptilian brain is at the core of the human brain. It is the oldest and most primitive part, largely relegated to bodily function and instinctual response. The pineal gland sits on top of this oldest of brains. The pearl of great price in the middle of the dragon's forehead -- the priceless treasure that the dragon guards deep inside its cave, is that crystallized pineal gland. Chinese Taoism taught that the spirit of "the Way" or the Tao was a dragon, guardian of the Flaming Pearl representing spiritual perfection. When the fire of the kundalini ignites the pineal gland, it glows with such brightness that the being is

430

truly illumined. Yet another interesting paradox presents itself. The physical head during this state is very cool. Most of the fire is felt in the belly.

The electromagnetic energy body surrounds and interpenetrates the physical body and provides its foundation. This is the dragon body. When the physical body is discarded, the dragon body becomes the main vehicle for the soul. In advanced states of awareness, this dragon body shines brightly with all the brilliant colors of a rainbow. Buddhists talk about "the rainbow body" that sometimes accompanies the death of an adept. Upon dying, the physical body is reabsorbed into its original light essence, producing waves of rainbow light, leaving nothing behind but the hair and nails of the corpse.[17]

The vital life force expressed through the dragon body and ultimately the physical, is called Qi or Ki (pronounced *kee*), an Eastern term. Sometimes it is called prana. It is the cosmic energy or "force" that gives everything life -- even inanimate, inorganic objects. It also acts like cosmic glue, holding things together. The aura is a part of this energy body or force field. With training, the aura can be seen, sometimes in full color. Qigong refers to breathing and exercise techniques that cultivate and increase Qi in the body, ultimately improving health and spiritual awareness.

The Qi is distributed through the body in meridians and nadis much like blood veins. Qi is highly concentrated in the blood, which is often considered the animating life force of the physical body. Many legends speak of the powers of the dragon's blood. In China, the blood of a dragon was considered dangerous. However in European lore, "heroes bathed in it to create invulnerability or drank it to become wise."[18]

Eastern Serpents of Wisdom created an entire science of esoteric energy anatomy. While Western alchemy embraces similar teachings, a practical system of methodology was not openly cultivated and handed down in the mystery schools as it was in the East. Therefore, this is perhaps the Eastern tradition's greatest contribution to the West. For that reason I will focus on Qigong empowerment techniques of Eastern

431

origin, though pointing out particular correspondences in Western alchemy as I proceed.

As the microcosm is a reflection of the macrocosm according to Hermetic law, the human dragon body as an etheric grid system is a reflection of the universal one or the dragon body of the cosmos. Both are intimately interconnected and intertwined, providing the basis for the effectiveness of various astrological systems. According to Pinkham,

> The human etheric grid is referred to in various traditions as the etheric body, the Pranamya Kosha (the sheath of Prana), and the human Dragon Body. As a manifestation of the Dragon this subtle body is well endowed with "serpent" symbolism. It has, for example, 14 or 2X7 major meridians, which represent the Dragon's 2 opposing principles and its 7 aspects. These 14 meridians are traditionally divided into 2 principal vessels, corresponding to the Dragon's male and female principles, and 12 major channels, which correspond to the 12 signs of the Dragon's Zodiacal body. Of the 12 major channels, 6 are yin and 6 are yang, thus reflecting the 6 feminine and 6 masculine signs of the Zodiac. The human Dragon Body also contains seven major vortexes or chakras corresponding to the seven principles of the Dragon.[19]

Tarot Key number 18, *The Moon*, is all about the physical body. From the moon drips 18 red-yellow *Yods* (the Hebrew letter corresponding to "I"). The red represents blood and the yellow represents air. When the oxygen in the air enters the bloodstream through the lungs, energy is born. Therefore the Yods in the next Tarot Key, number 19, *The Sun*, turn to orange. Life force or Qi is extracted from food, water and air through respiration and digestion. This life force sustains the dragon body. Becoming conscious of this process, paying attention to it, sensitizing oneself to it through visualization and exercise, increases one's receptivity to it, eventually resulting in the regeneration of the physical body and mind. At this point we become *as little children* as oft repeated in the Christian tale. Yet before the body can regenerate, it must heal. Any damage that has been done must be repaired. Realigning our personal grid system or dragon body with the cosmic flow most effectively does this. In this regard, the phrases "tuning into cosmic energy" -- getting "in harmony with the universe" or "going with the flow" can be taken literally.

I cannot overemphasize how important this is. In the last chapter, I talked about how the muddlers' greatest weapon – their "death star" – is nothing secret, covert, or mysterious. It is simply **stress**. Systematically overstressing the populace by reinforcing through legislation, public policy, and media propaganda the social infrastructure of an unjust, oppressive economy and workplace debilitates the psyche, destroys the body and weakens the spiritual resolve of the individual. The high priests of materialism tout the benefits of stress-management when stress elimination should be the goal. They attempt to normalize an abnormal lifestyle by putting all the responsibility on the shoulders of the individual when it should be a joint effort.

Studies show that sustained increased levels of cortisol, the stress hormone secreted by the adrenal glands and controlled by the pituitary gland (corresponding to one of the head chakras), can diminish the pituitary's ability to regulate its levels, thus weakening the immune system and metabolic functions. This is especially true for women because of the role that estrogen plays in prolonging the stress response. Individuals suffering from post-traumatic stress syndrome suffer from real brain damage. Prolonged hyper-arousal and neurophysiological activation due to trauma, chronic or acute, changes the brain producing a 'state' memory and makes the individual more vulnerable to other kinds of illnesses.[20] In children this is particularly tragic because normal brain development is arrested.

Some scientists feel that abnormal patterns of catecholamine activity associated with prolonged 'alarm reactions' induced by traumatic events during infancy and childhood can result in altered development of the central nervous system. This altered development includes a 'dysregulated' brainstem which then results in numerous symptoms including affective lability, increased anxiety and sleep abnormalities.[21] When the child grows older, the patterns get etched in the brain big time.

When a human is exposed to real or perceived danger, a series of complex, interactive neurophysiological reactions occur in the brain, the autonomic nervous system, the hypothalamic-pituitary adrenocortical axis and the immune system. Acute stress interferes with the release of epinephrine (adrenalin) and cortisol producing abnormal levels. Usually this activation is rapid and reversible. But when the stressful event is of sufficient duration, intensity or frequency, these changes are not reversible. Stress induced sensitization occurs – the neurochemical systems mediating the stress response change, becoming more sensitive to future stressful events. This alters gene expression of a variety of important structural and regulatory proteins, giving rise to all the symptoms usually associated with such a disorder. Yet as some scientists are learning, "disorder" is no longer the appropriate term. Blatantly, it's an *injury* that is inflicted. It is no mental illness, but rather a neurological breakdown due to psychic assault that can happen at any age. According to author David Kinchin,

> A stress breakdown is a natural and normal conclusion to a period of prolonged negative stress; the body is saying "I'm not designed to operate under these conditions of prolonged negative stress so I am going to do something dramatic to *ensure* that you reduce or eliminate the stress otherwise your body may suffer irreparable damage; you must take action now." . . . Often the cause of negative stress in an organisation can be traced to the behavior of one individual . . . Unfortunately, the person who suffers a *stress* breakdown is often treated as if they have had a *mental* breakdown; they are sent to a psychiatrist, prescribed drugs used to treat mental

illness, and may be encouraged – sometimes coerced – into becoming a patient in a psychiatric hospital. The sudden transition from professional working environment to a ward containing schizophrenics, drug addicts and other people with genuine long-term mental health problems *adds* to rather than alleviates the trauma. . . The person who is being bullied often thinks they are going mad. They are not; PTSD is an injury, *not* an illness. . . . A frequent diagnosis of stress breakdown is "brief reactive psychosis", especially if paranoia and suicidal thoughts predominate. . .The person who is being bullied will eventually say something like "*I think I'm being paranoid...*"; however they are correctly identifying *hypervigilance*, a key symptom of PTSD, but using the popular but misunderstood word *paranoia*. . . . The UK, and much of the Western world, adopts a *blame-the-victim* mentality as a way of avoiding having to deal with difficult issues. . . Sending employees on stress management courses may sound good on paper but coercing people to endure more stress without addressing the cause is going to result in further psychiatric injury.[22]

"Post Traumatic Stress Disorder (PTSD) is a natural emotional reaction to a deeply shocking and disturbing experience. It is a *normal* reaction to an *abnormal* situation."[23] Sometimes it results from one major life-threatening event. However, over the past decade, prolonged, chronic or complex PTSD has been recognized as a condition that can result from many types of shocking experiences including an accumulation of small, individual non-life threatening events.[24] This is typically what occurs to unfortunate victims of work-place abuse and harassment.

While we address these types of social injustices in our social spheres of influence, we also need to tend to those that have manifested in our bodies. We must heal the wounds -- the damage suffered as a result of this war. The preliminary action required is equipping the self with the appropriate armor and weaponry to fight back. Our best defense is the armor of a well-developed dragon body.

The only way to *well-being* is to awaken the dragon. We do this by healing, developing, nurturing, and strengthening our health on all levels of being, but particularly the physical. The physical body is the front line where immediate reinforcements are most needed. And now I'm going to say something pretty radical, but it's true. The reason why I know it's true is because I had to find out the hard way. The truth is that *no one should begin a program of spiritual study and practice without one that equally emphasizes health, physical fitness and qigong sensitivity training*. The health programs that are most effective and complimentary to spiritual practice are ones focusing on qigong empowerment because they deal directly with the developing dragon body, not indirectly. Programs that deal with it indirectly are those addressing only fitness and dietary concerns. While such programs are also necessary and beneficial, conscious integration and refinement of the energy body with the physical body provides so much more than diet and physical fitness alone.

Dahnhak and Healing Society

Qigong practice is body meditation. It is a restriction or focusing of consciousness on a certain aspect of being in order to expand or raise the frequency of that aspect. Qigong techniques vary widely. Any form of hatha yoga, tai chi, or martial art is a Qigong practice. Breath control is very important in all these practices. Tibetan energy yoga, for example, makes extensive use of different breathing techniques. Increasing capacity to store surplus prana helps to develop dormant abilities. One particular school, however, that has emerged in recent years, is having immediate and unprecedented effects on the life of its members. It is known as Dahnhak and was created by the Qigong Master, Dr. Ilchi Lee.

> *Dahnhak,* which I have taught to millions of people for the last twenty years, is not a set of techniques through which you can attain enlightenment. If it is enlightenment that you wish, then there is nothing that I can do for you, for *Dahnhak* is not a way to gain enlightenment but a way to actualize enlightenment. *Dahnhak* is a way to train yourself so that you can actualize the choices you have already made based upon your enlightenment.[25]

In other words, the prerequisite to succeeding in this program is to recognize inherent divinity – that you already have and are what you need to be; you only need to learn to actualize it. That is really the secret to any spiritual path. Dahnhak is one of the most effective ways to do this because it benefits every single aspect of being, particularly the body.

Over 5,000 years ago in an ancient Korean kingdom, *Shin-Sun-Do* (loosely translated as "Way of the Divine Person") was the founding principle and ruling ideology. Dahnhak's underlying principles have their roots in this ancient discipline. I suspect that its origins reach much further back, perhaps even to Lemurian times when burgeoning humanity needed assistance in becoming fully grounded in their new animal bodies. At any rate, this ancient discipline was revived and transformed into a modernized system of mind-body training by Dr. Ilchi Lee.

Dahnhak is essentially a Qigong empowerment technique that combines yoga, Tai Chi and meditation in Taoist fashion, recognizing the inherent unity of all things. The Shin-Sun-Do is codified in an ancient Korean sacred text known as the *Chun-Bu-Kyung* or the Heavenly Code. Each letter in the text has a meaning and number all its own, much like other sacred texts of the world. It is visually pleasing, and meditation on its symbolism can reveal much about the interrelationships between cosmic principle and energy and how they apply to current issues in your life, much like meditation on the Tarot can do. According to Dr. Lee:

The goal of *Dahnhak* is the recovery of the *Yuln'yo*, the natural rhythm of life that resides in humans and within all life, leading to a harmonious life. *Yuln'yo* is eternal life, light, sound, and vibration that exist wholly within and with itself. I describe this also as cosmic energy and cosmic mind. Even now, *Yuln'yo* is active within all life, beating and pulsing as the reality behind it. This is the energy that makes the Sun burn, Earth turn, and our hearts beat.[26]

Out of this practice emerges what Dr. Lee calls the *New Human* or "Earth Human." The goal of Healing Society is to heal the Earth through healing ourselves. A belief in some kind of God or religion is not necessary for this; only that such powers that we normally attribute to such Creator beings reside within us. One of the central tenets repeatedly emphasized in Dahnhak training is that "my body is not me but mine."

What makes the Dahnhak exercises different from other forms of Qigong empowerment is an emphasis on directly stimulating the organs of the body, especially the intestines. Primary focus on intestinal exercises strengthens them and rids them of toxins. This is essential for getting the body to a place where it can begin to reabsorb and better assimilate nutrients received from food substances. Naturally the processes involving chyle are facilitated. Certain internal energy channels are then opened, freeing energy blockages that previously prevented total healing. Extensive body tapping also promotes better circulation of the lymph system. In conjunction with exercises that enhance the mind/brain-body connection, astounding results are achieved. This is essential for the actualization of enlightenment.

Master healing graduates from the Dahnhak healing school are extraordinary in their abilities yet manifest a simple wisdom. While a Dahn Center is not an intellectual environment, a working partnership with the Korea Institute of Brain Science is providing rapid confirmation and systematic expansion of Dr. Lee's methodology. Any criticism of Dahnhak usually has its origins in a misunderstanding of its intention. Because it is Korean-based, cultural adaptation to Western society has not been easy. Most of the headmasters are Korean, not fluent in English; therefore unlike other traditions imported from the East, the translation of esoteric principles is still undergoing refinement. They also emphasize body awareness and listening with the heart over mental activity, and this can be a turn off to those more intellectually inclined. But there is a good reason for this. The area in the lower abdomen, the energy center known as the *Dahn-jon* corresponding to the Mars or naval chakra, is the anchor for all activity. It is the power center that keeps us grounded and fully present. Experiencing firsthand this very centralized awareness enables one to see past the cultural obstacles and sense directly the import of the teachings. A return to that open, natural, uninhibited and integrated awareness of body and mind that we experienced as children also facilitates the healing process. Westerners spend far too much time in their heads without adequate grounding, and this makes them less resistant to stress. The Dahnhak message is that you have to come back down to Earth before you can go back up.

The simplicity of Dr. Lee's approach makes these esoteric principles accessible to anyone, even little children. With the support of scientific research, Dr. Lee's Dahnhak technique of brain respiration is growing in popularity among elementary school educators. Persons from any race, creed, economic, or educational background can benefit from this training. The universal appeal of Dr. Lee's approach and the beautiful simplicity of his vision has assured him a place among the top 100 spiritual leaders of the world and garnered him an invitation to speak before the United Nations.

Newcomers may get the impression that Dahnhak is some simplistic New Age cult. But it is not. As I always say, ye shall know them by their fruits. They get results and they get them faster than traditional medicine and even other qigong methods. Many individuals have entered their doors on the verge of dying, and within six months they are completely healed, transformed, and often on the path to becoming healers

439

themselves. I am one of them so I should know. I can say in all honesty that Dahnhak may be largely responsible for saving my life. That's not to say that it's been all fun and easy because it has not. In the very beginning, "healing symptoms" are commonly experienced, yet they are often misinterpreted as an exacerbation of illness. When blocked energy is becoming freed, it often manifests in unusual symptoms of pain or discomfort. These symptoms only last a few weeks however, and then classes become more enjoyable. You might begin a session completely drained of energy, yet at the end you are completely revitalized. Everyone progresses at their own pace of course, and the atmosphere is one of support and gentle encouragement. It is also one of those few places where you can experience unconditional love and a true concern for your well-being. And there is no better environment for healing than that!

Dahnhak makes the direct realization and practice of the principles learned in any other mystery school more readily accessible because it is based on a body awareness of those principles. In the Qabalah, the sephirah known as Yesod marks the integration point of the etheric or dragon body with the physical. Therefore it is appropriately called the *Foundation*. If your foundation is not strong, the adytum cannot be built.

Cosmic energy is not just some warm fuzzy New Age idea -- it's a reality. Dahnhak teaches how to feel it, control it and use it, not just know about it. It is applied, engaged enlightenment and radically transformative. It is truly "the Way" of all ways.

My feeling that the roots of this energy practice go all the way back to Lemurian times is supported by the pervasiveness of the symbol of the Big Dipper in Korean culture and in particular, the iconography connected with Dahnhak. Previously mentioned, the Big Dipper is considered to be one of the head chakras of a great cosmic being. It could be that extraterrestrial ancestors from that constellation had much to do with the dissemination of these teachings in the Far East.

Like most spiritual leaders, Dr. Lee does not come right out and admit this. However, in one of his books, he tells a story about some "gods" that decided to do a grand experiment about fifty billion years ago.[27] They wanted to see if diverse life forms could learn to live together in harmony. So they created Earth, seeded it with the appropriate conditions and copied their own genetic material into life forms so that these life forms would retain their image. They allowed the life forms to evolve and further diversify into new species for millions of years without interfering with the process. The domineering dinosaurs, however, became a threat to the survival of the project. So the gods unleashed a virus that selectively destroyed them. This set the stage for phase two of the project: To unleash the power of creativity. They needed a creature that could get past the law of evolution and begin to work the law of revolution or divine creativity. The chosen creature was the human being. In Master Lee's words,

> A grand controversy ensued. One side argued that following the original intent of the experiment, they had to unlock the divine creative potential in humans to see if one created could develop into a creator and establish a peaceful and harmonious community among diverse life forms. The other side argued that such a power, once unleashed, would tempt the humans to lord it over other species and eventually to destroy themselves and the Earth because their intellectual capacities would not be able to deal with their divine creativity.

> Those that favored unlocking the divine creative potential wore white robes and the opposition wore black. The division represented a more fundamental division among the gods: one side wanted to expand the use of the divine creativity in all areas of the universe and, accordingly, went around planting seeds of divine information. The other side wanted to limit the use of divine creativity, and was

441

consequently busy scooping up the seeds of divine information that the white-robed ones had scattered.

However, knowing that they represented opposite but necessary sides that brought a balanced tension to the universe, each side respected the work of the other.[28]

So after considerable debate, the gods reached a compromise. The divine creative potential would be unlocked in humans on the condition that if humans failed, the gods would later switch robes, indicating a general change in the direction of the universe. They agreed to this because they recognized that even gods must take responsibility for their choices.

According to Dr. Lee, the gods used a virus that when embedded in human cells worked to unlock and activate genes for divine creativity. There is such an independent life form that resides in the human cell. But it's not a virus – it's a bacteria. It's called mitochondria -- the powerhouse of the human cell. George Lucas of *Stars Wars* fame admits to loosely basing his *midichlorians* on these elusive creatures. Midichlorians are the physical vehicles for the Force. These little beings live in symbiosis with our bodies. They do not share our DNA and are completely separate entities. Yet without them, our lives would be bereft of any and all energy. The other side of the coin, however, is that they could not live without us either. The lives of mitochondria are sustained by the raw materials we provide to them. In return, they manufacture adenosine tri-phosphate (ATP) which stores energy in a form that our bodies can burn for fuel.

According to Dr. Ilchi Lee, the divine creative power had two modes of expression: the creative mode and the enlightenment mode. These modes did not immediately synchronize as the gods had hoped. Instead, humans, drunk on the illusion of seemingly separate power not recognizing their inherent oneness with divinity ran the creative mode to the extreme, thus monopolizing the Earth's resources and threatening the survival of all other species. Seeing that their project again was in jeopardy, the gods decided to allow certain members of the white-robed faction to make an appearance on Earth in various guises in order to boost activation of the enlightenment mode embedded in the human psyche. At first they did this through mating with the humans, hoping that their offspring would become appropriate role models. Later they appeared as inspirational teachers to provide limited guidance to humanity, mostly by setting an example. In most cases, however, the humans merely twisted the teachings and idolized the teachers, giving birth to religion. Although a few humans were able to synchronize the modes, find the way and rediscover the balance, the majority began to stagnate.

The explosion of the atomic bomb, like a "great disturbance in the Force," jolted the gods out of complacency. They met again to discuss the future of their project. Basically, communication with humans has increased since that time, stopping short of direct interference. World War II indeed sparked an unprecedented wave of UFO sightings and extraterrestrial contact.

Dr. Ilchi Lee believes we have a limited window of time in which to change our ways before the Earth is completely destroyed, the choice ultimately being our own. Choosing to focus on healing is a result of perceiving the divinity within. Helping all of us to make that choice is his mission.

Meditation: Dragon Mind

In the early 1980s, scientists began taking a serious look at the physical and psychological benefits to meditation and found that there are many. Recently, scientists have taken their research one step further by studying the role meditation plays in sustaining positive states of awareness and diminishing the effect of destructive emotions. The Mind and Life Research Institute, a nonprofit organization based in Boulder, Colorado, partnered up with the Dalai Lama and other Tibetan Buddhist monks in order to determine exactly what is happening inside their brains during meditation that enables them to attain such high levels of equanimity. Preliminary results from the initial projects were so compelling that the best-selling author of *Emotional Intelligence*, Daniel Goleman, published a book about it entitled, *Destructive Emotions.*

Goleman asserts that the central purpose of spiritual practice is to recognize and transform destructive emotions.[29] Scientists found that indeed, dharma practice not only alleviates destructive emotions, but it does so in a way that alters the way the brain functions.

Parts of the brain can be stimulated in various ways – neurochemically, electrically, magnetically, and with plain physical force. Deep inside the brain in the limbic system, there's a little structure called the amygdala that becomes highly active whenever disturbing emotions are felt, particularly aggression. For instance, a tumor on this part of the brain might provide the stimulation for extremely aggressive behavior. This is exactly what happened to Charles Whitman, the sniper who killed himself after killing fourteen people from the campus tower at the University of Texas in August of 1966. An autopsy revealed that he had a malignant tumor on his amygdala.[30]

When in a state of agitation, there is much activity in the amygdala and the right prefrontal cortex of the brain. When positive states prevail however, such as optimism, hope, and feelings of loving-kindness, those areas of the brain are quiet and the left prefrontal cortex of the brain shows more activity. Most people's brains stay somewhere around the middle, although some show a tendency toward right or left tilted activity. Those who show more tilt to the left are less prone to experiencing destructive emotions, and those who show more tilt to the right are predisposed to bad moods.

Richard Davidson, Ph.D., one of the scientists leading the research at the Mind-Life Institute, taught beginning meditation mindfulness practices to a bunch of stressed out scientists at a biotech firm. After these scientists meditated on average of three hours per day after a period of about two months, Davidson found that not only had they begun to enjoy their work again and remain calmer, a noted shift in activity was observed between the right prefrontal cortex to the left. From this it was concluded that even beginning meditation practice could produce a significant shift in the brain. When they hooked up the Tibetan monks to the machines, these guys had the highest values for leftward tilt they'd ever seen.

All in all, the research is showing that the brain is elastic. Permanent changes in the brain can be effected with systematic, repeated experiences. This is what Goleman refers to as an altered *trait* of consciousness in contrast to the altered *state*. Anyone who meditates or does drugs can easily experience an altered state such as bliss, rapture, or pleasant visions. These states, however, are not the goal for the serious practitioner. In fact, Buddhist tradition warns that these epiphenomena can become serious distractions and seductive lures impeding progress. If not careful, an unhealthy attachment to them could become a crutch. The goal of genuine spiritual practice is not in the achievement of these states, but in stabilizing the underlying ability of insight that led to those experiences. This eventually establishes the "altered trait" – an enduring change that continues to benefit the practitioner and others in multidimensional ways. Meditation used merely to intensify and sharpen one's ability to focus is limited to worldly accomplishments. Meditation used to develop and strengthen insight and compassion reaps genuine spiritual rewards.

Paul Ekman, a professor of psychology at the University of California San Francisco Medical School, is one of the world's foremost experts on the physiology of emotions. For decades his landmark studies on facial expressions and how people interpret them has had a lasting impact upon many fields. For instance, Ekman found that so far there are at least eighteen different types of smiles, and that anatomically, a true smile can be distinguished from a fake one with practice. He also discovered "microexpressions" -- fleeting facial expressions lasting less than a twentieth of a second. People vary widely on their ability to correctly interpret microexpressions. Ekman found that individuals who like to think that they are good at it,

445

such as judges, psychotherapists and police officers, aren't really better than the average person. The occupational group that tested higher for this was secret service agents. But when he measured seasoned meditation practitioners, these folks had a 99 percent accuracy rating, the highest of all.[31] Scientists suspect that it may be a sharpened perceptual ability or enhanced empathy that gives meditators this advantage.

Probably more than once in this book I have quoted the words of Jesus, "If I be lifted up, I lift all others unto myself." The point I'm trying to make is that undertaking a spiritual practice is never intrinsically selfish as it might appear to some. Self-improvement in any form is going to rub off on others inevitably. For one, if others are happy, they are more likely to treat you well and want you to be happy too. But it's more than that, as Ekman and other scientists participating in the Mind-Life projects will vouch. Journalist Marshall Glickman writes,

> Before Ekman was invited to Mind and Life VIII in Dharamsala, he had little interest in Buddhism and was skeptical of reports about scientists who had been changed by their meetings with the Dalai Lama. As it turned out, Ekman's own first encounter with His Holiness was profound. . . Ekman relates that he had "what some people would call a mystical, transforming experience." A private meeting with His Holiness left Ekman "inexplicably suffused with physical warmth... a wonderful kind of warmth throughout my whole body and face. It was palpable. I felt a kind of goodness I'd never felt before."

> The effects of that meeting continued long after the conference. Ekman's connection with the Dalai Lama helped dissolve much of his long-held anger, which Ekman traces to a very difficult relationship with his father. "About once a week for the last fifty years, I've had an anger attack that I regretted," Ekman says. But after his encounter with His Holiness, "I didn't even have an angry impulse for the next four months, and no full episode of erupting

446

in anger for the whole of last year." Ekman left Dharamsala a changed man, professionally as well as emotionally: his research took a new direction after he agreed to administer the Cultivating Emotional Balance project, a key Mind and Life initiative.[32]

To a person with increased sensitivity, this is the mark of another – especially an adept. They simply radiate. These people are truly illumined. So what are they adept at? This is it.

Learning to generate and hold right thought and feeling can produce profound physiological changes. Destructive thoughts and emotions likewise damage the brain and body. While some scientists may continue to argue that changes in the body precede and actually cause corresponding behavior, studies such as the ones done at the Mind-Life Institute are clearly showing that the opposite is more likely. The tumor on Whitman's amygdala didn't "cause" him to become violent. It is more probable that a life-long pattern of negative and destructive emotions and thought-patterns precipitated the creation of the tumor, eventually triggering the violent behavior. This is in accordance with occult principle and is also applicable to other scenarios. While an individual can be born with genetically related diseases and neurochemical imbalances, these too were more than likely karmic carry-overs from past lifetimes. This is also why neurochemical imbalances are never really "healed" by medication. The medication simply holds the symptoms in check by altering the chemistry in the brain. Sometimes this results in a "retraining" of the brain leading to healing, sometimes not. A complete healing and recovery from mental and emotional disorder can only occur through long time cultivation and practice of the appropriate mental and emotional states, as the meditation research is showing.

Granted, in most cases, psychopharmacological treatment is warranted and often necessary in the beginning. Sometimes a severely depressed person is simply unable to move at all, let alone climb out of a deep black hole without assistance. Sometimes it is too late and the brain needs that neurochemical kick-start. Then over time, the brain and the personality learn the correct neurochemical sequencing of feeling and thinking so that a new pattern can begin to be established. If proper motivation has been cultivated along with a genuine desire to learn to generate positive thoughts and feelings on a regular basis, eventually a slow withdrawal from medication is possible. But it is not easy. Old habits are difficult to break – especially those that have been neurochemically etched in the brain. But it is possible:

> Neuroplasticity – the ability of the brain to generate new nerve cells and neural connections, thereby altering emotions, behavior, and perceptions – is the major story in neuroscience of the past decade, overturning basic assumptions about brain structure and functioning.[33]

As Goleman emphasizes, meditation shapes the brain. Therefore, the implications for introducing it to young children when their brains are still developing are enormous. If children can learn these skills early on, we are one step closer to healing the planet, for they are the future. Reducing destructive emotions is the goal of Life-Mind's cultivating emotional balance project. The researchers are looking to develop a program that combines mindfulness practice and elements of Western psychology that can be taught to people with no background in meditation. The Institute hopes to include non-Buddhist contemplative traditions in future research. This is good because Dr. Ilchi Lee already has such a program in place that is proving extraordinarily successful. Most people who join Dahn centers have no previous meditation training. Dr. Lee's Brain Respiration program practiced in many elementary schools is becoming increasingly popular because it is fun and effective.

Kundalini: Dragon Fire

Author Mark Amaru Pinkham writes,

> When the snake (the Kundalini) reunites with the
> eagle (the brain) in the upper branches of the "yogic
> tree of life" (the spine) a person becomes a "Serpent
> of Wisdom."[34]

Birds are sometimes symbols for the enlightened brain.
Important ones in Western spiritual tradition are the dove -- a
Christian symbol, and the swan -- sacred to the medieval
knights of the Holy Grail. The brain has two wings – a left and
right hemisphere, and conjoining them is connective tissue
called the corpus collasum and the third eye, known as the
pineal gland. The pineal gland is still highly operative in birds.
The eagle is one of the three symbols for the Zodiacal sign
Scorpio, the other two being the scorpion and the serpent or
lizard. All three creatures combined make up a kind of dragon
when you think about it. Scorpio is said to evolve or transform
through stages corresponding to these creatures.   Mars and
Pluto rule Scorpio. Mars is the planet corresponding to the
navel chakra or energy center known as the *Dahn-jon*
previously discussed. Pluto is the planet assigned to Tarot Key
20, *Judgment*, corresponding to the spiritual stage of
regeneration. One of those altered traits earned by the hard
working spiritual aspirant is the "Perpetual Intelligence" of the
awakened adept. This is the doorway to the Fifth Kingdom that
bestows the completely unobstructed, unwavering perception
and experience of Cosmic Consciousness.

The spinal cord is a tube. In many young children it is
open, enabling the kundalini to go up and down. This is what
gives them the "sight" to see humans and animals that most
adults deem imaginary. As we grow older, the tube closes so
that at puberty, when the Mars force becomes concentrated, the
kundalini cannot be propelled upwards prematurely damaging
the brain.   Therefore what appears to impede our progress

toward spiritual illumination really protects us. When an occultist seeks the metaphysical vision however, the Mars force is applied to destroy the cells that keep the lower end of the spinal tube sealed. When it's reopened, we become "as little children" again.

The Mars force related reproductive functions of the body are intimately associated with Scorpio. Therefore, the dragon fire or kundalini lies dormant, coiled in that region of the energy body near the base of the spine. Many branches of the Eastern mystery schools aim to awaken the kundalini directly through various kinds of meditations and physical exercises. The Western mystery schools, however, teach that direct concentration on this energy is unnecessary and often dangerous. The main reason for this goes back to one of the essential differences between the Eastern and Western methods. Traditionally, the Eastern schools were able to teach these techniques openly because their students were completely cloistered and under the constant supervision of a teacher. Therefore, if a problem was encountered, an expert could deal with it firsthand. Such controlled environments offered ideal circumstances for these kinds of practices with a minimum of stress and outside distraction.

In the West, however, it was a different story. People who were suspected of such practices were burned at the stake. Therefore much of the knowledge remained hidden and secretly coded. Nevertheless, many unsuspecting aspirants stumbled upon the keys and inadvertently unlocked the gates, sometimes prematurely and unprepared. Without the guidance and supervision of someone who had gone before, the consequences were disastrous more often than not. And although we hear stories about the crazy yogis of the East, at least they're still recognized as yogis. In the West they are called idiots, fools, dangerously deranged, severely deluded, profoundly retarded, and schizophrenic at best. Because of society's lack of understanding of this sacred phenomenon, these unfortunate seekers usually end up captured, confined and forgotten, lingering on until death in some institution somewhere. I'm talking about mainly European based Western culture here, not indigenous ones. The American Indian shamans had it better. Craziness due to prematurely awakened kundalini was seen as a sign of advanced spirituality, and therefore a person manifesting such symptoms was often chosen as a spiritual leader.

Environmental conditions are key for the proper awakening of the kundalini without damaging side effects, as the Eastern teachers were well aware. The only reason why things go wrong with this process in the West is the major obstacle previously mentioned – *stress*. If the dragon energy on its way up the spine encounters stress, imbalance or blockages, particularly in the endocrine system which is intimately integrated with the major chakras, then this will manifest in mental/emotional disorder, usually psychosis. Therefore, even past the age of persecution and complete secrecy, Western mystery schools continued to warn about the hazards of directly concentrating on these energy centers because of unavoidable social stress. Instead, certain safeguards were established. The Masters developed an intricate and powerful system of symbolic correspondences for this purpose that would ensure that the prerequisite of balance was met before the full awakening could occur. These correlations as I mentioned before, involve combinations of sound, color and imagery. So rather than focusing on the physical location of the Mars chakra, for instance, one would visualize Tarot Key Number 16, see the color red and chant the tone 'C'. And this is only done in the context of a larger more elaborate exercise that first centers on facilitating equilibrium in the functioning of all the chakras and the full grounding of the physical body. Following this much safer procedure ensures that the student will not progress at an uncomfortable pace. It is common sense and it works. It is also the best system for a school where one seldom has the luxury of one-on-one guidance and supervision from a fully present flesh and blood teacher.

In 1977, Itzhak Bentov wrote a fabulous little book called *Stalking the Wild Pendulum* – on the mechanics of consciousness. It is a primer for anyone wanting to learn more about the sonic foundations of the universe. Bentov puts forth a model for the *physio-kundalini syndrome.*[35] The syndrome is a progressive set of physiological symptoms that emerge as the kundalini rises up the spine. When the energy begins to seep into the brain it stimulates certain sections that correspond to various parts of the body, such as the knee, for instance. A person experiencing the phenomenon will imagine that something may be wrong with the knee when it's really the kundalini stimulating that particular part of the brain. Bentov explains that this stimulus moves along the cerebral cortex in acoustical standing waves in the cerebral ventricles triggered by heart sounds, which then cause vibrations in the walls of the ventricles. As the ventricles are filled with fluid, the vibrations are easily conducted to the gray matter between the two hemispheres. They will then polarize the cortex in a manner that simulates sensory stimulation from the toes on up to the head, in contrast to the usual right angle entrance of sensory signals. When the kundalini completes the full loop around the brain, blissful states are experienced due to the current's direct stimulation of the pleasure centers in the brain along the sensory cortex. Most of the bodily symptoms begin on the left side of the body while the right hemisphere is stimulated, correlating to meditative, feeling and spatial states.[36]

Bentov believes that periodic exposure to certain mechanical or acoustical vibration can trigger the symptoms as well. The main point he makes, however, is that in a normally healthy, relaxed individual, these symptoms go unnoticed. Only when areas of stress are encountered will the symptoms become disruptive. Therefore, trauma victims with any degree of spiritual sensitivity are especially susceptible to this phenomenon. Bentov states,

> All that was described above may happen to people *spontaneously*, that is, to people who do not meditate. However, it is usually associated then with much more trauma and results very frequently in the hospitalization of such people. The usual diagnosis will be schizophrenia. The reason for this is that they

have been catapulted suddenly into a situation in which they are functioning in more than one reality. They can see and hear things occurring in our neighboring realities, that is the astral or other higher realities, because their "frequency response" has been broadened.[37]

This is why a gradual systematic evolution of this process such as meditation affords is so important. Occult training by those who have gone before is equally helpful for sorting through the confusion that sometimes occurs when the seeker tries to share unusual experiences with those not open to such realities. This is why the esoteric traditions are quick to admonish silence in most cases. Exile, alienation, excommunication, stigmatization, and institutionalization are not viable options. Such recommendations by those who profess to care are inhumane, abusive, and shortsighted. Fortunately, the more that is learned about these states of consciousness in the lab, the less tendency is there for these kinds of misunderstandings to develop. Holistic, integrative medicine has made some progress addressing these sensitive issues.

An accelerated nervous system requires accelerated thinking. Bentov observed that the purpose of the physio-kundalini syndrome seems to be to "unite the cerebrospinal and the autonomic nervous systems, thus providing for a possible control of autonomic functions such as respiration, cardiac function, blood flow, etc., through the cerebrospinal system."[38] This is exactly what is seen when yogis and advanced meditators are studied under laboratory conditions. They are able to control heartbeat, breathing, superficial blood circulation, and many other body functions previously thought by Western scientists to be inaccessible to the mind. This is all a part of awakening and developing the dragon body.

Siegfried is one of the music dramas in Richard Wagner's masterpiece, *Der Ring des Niebelung*; the Ring Cycle. The sleeping hero, Siegfried, is awakened by the sweet song of a bird. He tries to answer the bird by calling back to it, but instead awakens a slumbering dragon. Siegfried admires the fierceness of the dragon before he slays it. Impressed by Siegfried's courage, the dragon on his last breath warns Siegfried of impending treachery. When Siegfried draws his sword from the dragon's body, a few drops of dragon blood fall upon his hand. Instinctively, he tastes it. As a result, he is suddenly in tune with all the mysteries of nature. He understands the unspoken language of the wind and all the forest animals -- especially the birds.

The dragon, in this instance, represents deep powers latent in the soul which must be integrated with the rest of our being. Esotericist Corinne Heline writes,

> This episode illustrates one of the more profound arcana of alchemistry. Blood is, in a special sense, the medium of the ego, the selfhood. As the blood stream is purified by sustaining the body on pure food and the mind with exalted thought, the ego is better able to use its body as an instrument of spiritual activity. Thus, an individual becomes more and more attuned to the Soul of Nature and acquires an intuitive knowledge of natural law and phenomena.
>
> This intuitive knowledge is no mere blind instinct or vague sensing. The voice of the bird symbolizes the awakened and spiritualized intuition of the heart which, in its essence, is the voice of Spirit itself, whose admonitions are never wrong. When the aspirant learns to follow this voice he unerringly walks on the Path of Wisdom.[39]

It is a powerful thing to have a dragon by your side. It takes courage, wisdom, and some measure of restraint. The sword is the sword of Truth, and it is always double-edged. Dragons, magic rings, magic helmets, magic carpets, and holy grails are not inherently good or evil. Like all symbols of power, it depends on how we wield them. Greed enslaves us to the object of power. Returning the object to its source, unconfined and unpossessed, brings the rewards of service to a greater good and freedom for all.

Like a maze of mirrors, there are dragons within dragons within dragons. Let us now become acquainted with the dragon body of the Earth herself.

Earth Energy: Dragon Breath

Adepts use their dragon power through their awakened dragon bodies to accomplish many things. In the tale of King Arthur, Merlin "awakens" the dragon so that he can help Uther shape-shift into the form of Gorlois in order to deceive Igraine, although not without painful consequence. The world suddenly becomes enveloped in a mysterious mist. This mist, Merlin says, is the dragon's breath. Merlin invoked his own dragon power while simultaneously calling upon the dragon energy of the earth. According to Gareth Knight, the dragon also represents an ancient form of earth energy long forgotten by humanity:

> Folk memories remain of this hidden knowledge, which accounts for the interest in ley lines and power centers associated with megalithic sites. Some of these are natural earth forces, comprising a whole range of gravitational, magnetic and more subtle force-fields. Others are man-made channels for these forces, in much the same way that physical water resources may be utilized not only as natural rivers and lakes but by dams, reservoirs and canals.[40]

These lines of energy are the meridians and nadis of the Earth's dragon or etheric body. Our extraterrestrial ancestors knew all about them and used them for navigational purposes, similar to railways.

It is thought that the Earth grid was fully energized in Atlantean times, the cross points giving rise to huge energy vortices that functioned like acupoints in the Earth. These smaller versions of the Aurora Borealis looked very much like the mouth of a dragon, with moving streams of energy wavering back and forth hundreds of feet high. Therefore ley lines also became known as dragon lines.

The "wars of the gods" diverted the grid energy, causing great damage to the Earth's ecosphere. Some authors say a decision was made to shut down or switch off the vortices so that they could no longer be used for destructive purposes. The disabling of the vortices is partially responsible for the legends about slaying dragons. These actions somehow detached the grid from the Earth, which had a corresponding effect in the dragon bodies of the developing humans.

It is said that this grid waves around the earth like a banner, and every two thousand years or so it gets a little closer. Some authors speculate that the last time it was nearest was when Christ appeared on Earth, and that the next time will be when the Anunnaki return. Regardless, the powers of the grid and our dragon bodies are not out of reach. In fact, I do not feel that the grid system was ever completely dismantled. I suspect that our genetic codes were scrambled, somehow making the grid less accessible.

Too many legends hint at a golden age before the cycle of life began, when all living creatures coexisted in harmony, not needing to feed on one another. The primeval ages of Earth before the fall in frequency were a time when the grid was stronger and played a more active role in holding the planet together. As the crust began to cool and harden, the creatures had to resort to recycling energy through blood shed. Yet the "Shining Ones" continued to subsist on light alone. The Egyptians called them the Henmemet. Folklore remembers them as the elves. The Shining Ones were no doubt a faction of our extraterrestrial ancestors who retained their ability to plug into the grid and use its cosmic energy for all their needs. Their dragon bodies were fully integrated with the dragon body of the Earth, enabling them to tap into what physicists call zero point energy. As we have learned, this ability lies dormant and locked within each of us even today. Part of the Great Work is rediscovering the keys – the treasure that is guarded by the dragon – and returning it to its source, to be freely shared by all. We do this on the microcosmic scale by learning to reawaken the dragon within. Dr. Greer and others working toward full disclosure in the field of free energy devices, are affecting the macrocosm through their generous efforts, until someday, the entire Earth and all of her inhabitants will be liberated from the bonds of ignorance and exploitation.

DNA: Dragon Blood

DNA – it's called the building blocks of life. Short for deoxyribonucleic acid, it's a chemical structure that forms chromosomes. Genes are parts of chromosomes that dictate the traits of the physical body.

When the human genome was finally decoded, scientists were humbled to discover that it was only slightly double the 13,601 genes of a fruit fly and the 19,008 genes of the roundworm. In an overall comparison, our genes only separate us from chimpanzees by one percent and thirty percent from the mouse. Most of our functional genes are identical to the genes of plants and animals. Although we still appear to be the most complex organism on the planet, it's not by much. By virtue of the Scarecrow's "superior brain" though, we know we've got something all the others 'ain't' got, but what is it?

There happens to be 223 little genes in our genome – (just 223!) – that do not have the required predecessors on the genomic evolutionary tree. In other words, these 223 enigmatic genes have no connection with any other genome on the planet. So how did we get them?

Scientists postulate that instead of the normal evolutionary vertical rise in genetic material, we were recent *recipients* of a "horizontal transfer." But from whom or what? Well, *we* know, don't we? But scientists can't bring themselves to admit it yet. Therefore, they are calling the mysterious donor "bacteria" for now. Yet these 223 genes have been shown to be responsible for important neurological enzymes exclusive to the mitochondrial portion of DNA, meaning its origins would have to go all the way back to the original "Eve" because mitochondria is only inherited from the mother. Modern science has traced this original "Eve" all the way back to a human female living in Africa around 300,000 years ago. This precisely matches the time period when the Anunnaki first created humans as reported in the early Sumerian records.

What is it that separates us from our primate ancestors? It's not the size of our brains but what our brains can do — which must come from those 223 little genes. Yes, it is the DNA of our Anunnaki ancestors.[41]

This explains why we have approximately 4000 genetically related diseases, and the rest of the planet's creatures have hardly any at all. We're a strange hybrid, to say the least. This also explains why humans have more difficulty than other primates giving birth and raising their offspring, anatomically and psychologically. The Anunnaki did not foresee all the problems that their genetic tinkering with homo erectus would produce.[42]

But here we are, and there's not much we can do but play the cards we were dealt. Predictably, we're following in the footsteps of the Anunnaki with the advent of cloning and genetic engineering in our brave new world. Let's hope and pray we don't make the same mistakes they did!

Having barely reached the frontier of genetic science, it will be a while before all the mystery is unraveled. What possible new discoveries will come to light in the not too distant future? We may find we have more than two strands of DNA. Scientists experimenting with 4-D physics such as Dr. Noel Huntley theorize two biological strands with an additional eleven electromagnetic strands.[43] Talk of twelve-stranded DNA has been coming through in channeling circles for some time. Barbara Marciniak's Pleiadians say that the tiny strands are infinitesimal light-encoded filaments that act like fiber optics. Each of the twelve strands corresponds to a chakra center. When these strands mature, we are supposed to have access to free energy and manifest supernormal abilities.[44] Mary-Margareht Rose of "The Messenger" says that ten of the twelve strands were disconnected when humans were in their infancy, with the two remaining strands limited to the functions of survival and reproduction.[45] Sumerian records hint at such an experiment conducted by the Anunnaki.

We know that some of our extraterrestrial ancestors evidenced these abilities, and we know that we inherited these same abilities as children of the Creator. Sages and ordinary men and women walking among us even now have been exercising many of these abilities for some time.

Lee Carroll channels a being called Kryon. In Book VI of the Kryon Series, Carroll writes that the existence of these additional strands of DNA is difficult to prove because they are "invisible" and "electromagnetic."[46] Difficult to prove, indeed! Most science professionals I've queried on this matter just laugh. Yet one wonders why it keeps popping up in the literature. Remember, based on the reality of dark matter and dark energy, scientists speculate we know very little about 95% of the universe. To say there's a lot more to learn about this is an understatement.

I asked Marcia Schafer (an extraterrestrial contactee, intuitive, and author with a background in the health profession) what she thought of this idea of twelve-stranded DNA. Schafer feels that the secret lies in the codons or the ladders rather than in the strands themselves. At any rate, it will be exciting to watch for future developments in this fascinating new field of research.

Regarding the relationship between sacred language and mathematics, it appears that DNA has its own language characteristics based on the Fibonacci number series.[47] GeNum Labs concludes that the supra-code of DNA is a universal bio-mathematical law that can be translated into resonant frequencies or "music." It is a natural harmony providing global cohesion and stability to all living organisms:

> We have discovered a mathematical law controlling the self-organization of T C A G nucleotides within DNA. The sequential sets of DNA nucleotides are

organized in long-range structures entitled "RESONANCES". A resonance is a particular proportion doing a partition of DNA according with "Fibonacci's Number series" (1 2 3 5 8 13 21 34 55 89 144 etc...) [These] are the same proportions [as] those controlling morphology of natural organisms as Nautilus, apple-pines, etc...[48]

Another author likens DNA to a living language of layered meanings reflective of the Holy Qabalah. YHVH is the Hebrew tetragrammation for Yod Heh Vau Heh, a holy name for God. Erik Davis writes,

> DNA is an information system, with a sender-message-receiver form. DNA's basic code consists of four different nucleotides which are multiplied along the linear strand of the double helix (while YHVH contains only three letters, it also includes four units). The arrangement of these four "letters" (AGCT) produces "words" (called codons) which combine into instructions for the cell. Through copying itself, DNA sends its instruction code through messenger RNA, which delivers the message to factories in the cell, which then copy the code into a sequence of amino acids. This linear string of amino acids then literally *folds* into three-dimensional proteins. These proteins are the building blocks for the life of the world.

> Some DNA messages code for specific proteins, while others concern structural commands and other information: how to edit and arrange the information, when to start and stop, etc. And 97% of the original DNA seems to be junk, random noise that means and produces nothing. Recently, in order to retrieve the meaningful "words" buried in the babble of "AGGCAGCTTGA..." some scientists began using linguistic techniques originally developed to decipher ancient languages, many of

which, like DNA, are written without spaces between words...

... a virus ... mystified scientists because its DNA was much too short to code for all the proteins that it was commanding the host cell to produce. Scientists then discovered that the viral DNA *superimposed* different instruction sequences on top of another, so that its sequence would have different meanings depending on where you started reading the letters.[49]

So DNA replicates the same teaching methods sages have been using for years to communicate esoteric truths. Occult principle is embodied in our very cells. As above, so below.

Some esoteric literature references a lost mother tongue or the "language of light" otherwise known as Hiburu.[50] A primal seed language, this ancient form of Hebrew is supposed to be a natural language, the forms of the letters emerging from phosphene flare patterns in the brain. These alphabetic shapes begin in a spinning vortex, translating into light, embodied neurologically into our biological being.

Author Paul White reports that many contemporary scientists see DNA as a "shimmering waveform configuration" resembling the Qabalistic Tree of Life. It's a live vibrating process – not a static structure, easily modified by light, radiation, magnetic fields or sonic pulses. He suggests this "language of light" might well be the legacy of Thoth/Enoch.[51]

DNA is the matrix of biological being – the juncture between force and form. The double helix emerges from a spiraling vortex spawning all the alphabets of sacred languages according to researchers in sacred geometry. There really is no such thing as "sacred" geometry any more than there is "sacred" anything. Once we make something "sacred" we separate it from the rest, exclusionary thinking sets in, and intellectual elitism rears its ugly head(s). A search on the Internet regarding DNA, Hebrew letters, and hands will show you some. Mathematical systems for decoding religious texts written in Hebrew or any other "sacred" alphabet are quite common. But

461

these systems are not the best way or only way to make sense of these texts. The oldest and most reliable method, as always, is meditation. And no one can "own" the ideas that emerge from that because they are expressions of spiritual principle.

The Hermetic Axiom – as above, so below – teaches that all geometry is divine. The basis of the logarithmic spiral is the Golden Section seen in nature and in Euclid's 5 by 8 rectangle demonstrating that the lesser part is to the greater part as is the greater part to the whole.

This also reveals the spiritual significance of the perfect 5th and octave in music. The lines of the pentagram, a five-pointed star figure representing the human being, are divided in exact extreme and mean proportion of the Golden Section. Five is also the number of mediation. We are children of the stars, or in Biblical terms, man is the mediator between God and nature. We have five physical senses and five fingers on each hand. We use our hands to "sense" reality, integrating inner perceptions with externals. Hands gestures are a primary form of communication. That they can be visualized as spiraling geometric shapes or letters of the alphabet is nothing new. This premise underlies sign language and the art of mudra – gestures of power.

Mudra is a Sanskrit word meaning "sign" or "seal." The root "mud" means to please or delight. "Dru" means to draw forth. Therefore, the performance of mudras gives pleasure to the object of reference which in turn rebounds on the practitioner. It is a visual alphabet that obtains results that go beyond ordinary speech, much like music. But instead of playing a musical instrument, the hands are playing with prana or Qi – cosmic energy.52

Almost all iconographic representations of spiritual leaders and saints show them exhibiting some kind of mudra or symbolic gesture. Mudras are common to both Eastern and Western traditions, and each one has a specific effect. Many forms of Qigong bodywork such as Tai Chi and Yoga incorporate the use of mudras into their practices. So you see, there are many turns, twists, and levels in the cosmic spiral of energy awareness of which DNA is only one.

The Truth about Vampires

The subject of vampires has more to do with our topic than suspected. This is the complicated story of the vampire.

Several years ago, my Toastmasters Club asked me to give a fact-finding report on the issue of whether vampires truly exist. I summarized my findings with various facts and anecdotal evidence, and at the end of my report, they had enough information to decide for themselves whether or not vampires really exist. I invite you to keep an open mind as you read this because it was our conclusion that they do.

It all depends on what you mean by "vampire." We're all familiar with the Dracula stereotype. Vampires are supposed to sleep in coffins during the day, and at night they come out to suck the blood of innocent victims. They are repelled by such things as garlic, crucifixes and sunlight. You know the story. Well that's about all it is – a story. A myth. But all myths have some basis in fact or they wouldn't exist. Every culture in the world recognizes the vampire.

Historically, Dracula was partially based on Vlad Tepes – a cruel Romanian ruler of the 15th century. He was also known as Vlad the Impaler because he threw his victims on sharp stakes. Rumor had it that he would also dip his bread in their blood. However, according to Dracula scholar, Elizabeth Miller, there is no evidence of this.[53]

About 100 years later, Elizabeth Bathory came along – the sadistic Slavic countess who tortured and killed over 600 victims – mostly young women who were her servants. She bathed in their blood because she thought it kept her skin looking young. Even in the 20th century we find serial killers who think that they are vampires. In the mid 1990s, 21-year-old Joshua Rudiger (who claimed to be a 2000-year-old vampire) pleaded not guilty to charges he murdered a homeless woman and slashed three other people in San Francisco. Fortunately,

463

these are isolated cases yet the ones we hear most about because of the sensationalism. But is this an accurate description of most modern day vampires? No!

Contrary to popular belief, most vampires are harmless, law-abiding citizens. They are as diverse a people as any other subculture. Generally, they look no different from the next person. Like others, they commonly don't agree with each other – not even on theories of vampirism. They might be straight, they might be gay. They might be Republican, they might be Democrat. They might teach elementary school, they might work in a bar. They might even go to church – I read about one who was a minister. Startling facts?

For more detail, I recommend the book, *Piercing the Darkness: Undercover with Vampires in America Today*, by Katherine Ramsland, a long time investigative journalist and best-selling author of the biographies of Anne Rice and Dean Koontz. If you are interested in reading her book, prepare yourself for some graphic scenes. Though it is well written and deeply insightful, some sections read like S&M pornography. Still, like it says on the flap, it is an extraordinary investigative memoir that "takes you directly into the world of the urban vampire: a transgressive arena of dark energy and heat that overlaps with S&M, bondage, and Goth cults. Here you will learn the distinctions between Bloodists, Classicals, Nighttimers, and Inheritors. You will visit the members-only clubs where "liquid electricity" (blood) is the favored currency of intimate exchange, and explore the "feeding circles" that avoid the risk of AIDS. You will hang out with lovers whose sex toy is a razor and meet others who shun normality as we would shun the secret practices they hold sacred."[54]

So what are these practices? What exactly do modern-day vampires have in common? Well, only that they call themselves vampires. However, we can generally say that there are five categories: (1) 'Dead' blood drinkers, (2) living blood drinkers, (3) intentional psychic vampires, (4) unintentional psychic vampires, and (5) roleplayers.

The first category, dead blood drinkers, is the traditional vampire whose existence is most difficult to prove. However, cases in Europe as late as 1917 have supported their existence. Corpses suspected of being vampires were dug up only to reveal that the decomposing process had been radically slowed. Some appeared to breathe. Driving a wooden stake through the heart sometimes ended the plague of vampirism in that area. There are several theories about how such vampires could exist. Demonic possession of the corpse is one theory among those who believe in demons. The most commonly held belief, however, is that the soul of the dead person has some unfinished business to tend to and is trying to keep their body alive for that purpose. These people typically died violent deaths or committed suicide.

The second category is the living blood drinkers. These are mortals who simply enjoy drinking blood for whatever reason. Some feel that their bodies physically require it; some just enjoy it and experience a sense of euphoria from it. Even among self-proclaimed vampires it is hotly debated on whether the body actually requires drinking blood to stay alive. We know that some genetic conditions and physical diseases produce a craving for blood and sensitivity to sunlight. But not all living blood drinkers have this condition, and not all people who have this condition are vampires and drink blood. For some, it could simply be a psychological addiction. But surveys show that a population of this type of vampire genuinely begins to feel bad if they don't feed at least once a week.

In recent years, the discovery of a "royal vampire" -- an exceptional living blood drinker -- has been intimately linked with our extraterrestrial origins and the grail bloodline. This vampire sheds much light on certain mysteries of the physiological processes of the dragon body and the real basis for many of our religious rituals, fairy tales and folklore.

How, exactly, do these blood-drinking vampires feed? Do they prey upon unwilling innocent victims? Fortunately, most of them do not. They feed consensually among themselves in monogamous relationships or have what's called a safe circle of donors.   Some web sites are devoted to promoting safe bloodletting techniques, much like safe sex, because obviously this is a very dangerous practice that could cause illness or even death.   These conscientious vampires go to great lengths to promote necessary precautions.   For instance, one rule is that you should never drink blood from a donor who has not been tested for AIDS or other diseases.   This testing can be done at no cost through any blood bank.   In drinking the blood, sucking from an open wound is discouraged because the bacteria in the mouth could infect the wound.   Most vampires allow their donors to make the incision and simply lick the blood from the body as it runs away from the wound.   Some vampires are trained phlebotomists who draw the blood safely and then drink it.   The "royal vampire" only drinks menstrual blood, and there are preferred techniques for that.

These practices occur between consensual adults. Sometimes they occur in public places like vampire clubs in New York and Los Angeles.   Sometimes they occur in ritual settings or at private social gatherings.   Sometimes they are practiced as part of sex, and here we find the overlapping of the vampire subculture with the S&M sex scene.   Though again, not all vampires are into S&M, and not all blood fetishists call themselves vampires.   That's important to remember.   Many couples engage in oral sex involving some exchange and possible ingestion of bodily fluids.   When people kiss they usually can't avoid exchanging saliva.   The blood is just one more bodily fluid.   Yet there is something about it being outside the body that grosses most people out.   You might swallow your partner's saliva while you're kissing, but if they spit it out in a glass would you drink it?   There's that psychological barrier that once overcome apparently causes some individuals to experience erotic pleasure.

Of course there are blood-drinking psychopaths out there, but they are rare because the number one rule for real vampires is: NEVER DRINK SOMEONE'S BLOOD WITHOUT THEIR PERMISSION because that is a crime and can get you into a lot of trouble!   As Katherine Ramsland discovered, investigating these people had its risks because some "crazies" are inevitably attracted to this scene.

The third category of vampire is the intentional psychic vampire. This vampire is considered the most dangerous because their identities are difficult to ascertain. Two surveys showed that about one out of five people are attacked by this kind of vampire at least once in their lives. These vampires are individuals who deliberately feed off the psychic energy of others. Some of the symptoms of an attack are to wake up in the middle of the night with a sense of dread, then feeling pressure on the chest and a paralysis lasting several minutes. The next morning, the victim usually feels drained of energy. Ways to protect yourself from these attacks are discussed in the book, *Vampires – The Occult Truth* by Konstantinos.[55]

The fourth category of vampire is the unintentional psychic vampire. Again, these are ordinary individuals who are *unaware* that they feed off the psychic energies of others. These people are often elderly or seriously ill. Low on energy, they unconsciously seek that energy elsewhere. Most of us have had the experience of being in a room with someone who made us feel uncomfortable or who has a tendency to drain us of energy and we don't know why. Well they might be a psychic vampire – intentional or unintentional, sucking on our psychic vortices or chakras.

The fifth category of vampire is the role-player. These people play elaborate games and fantasies, online and off. They usually take on an identity like a character from an Anne Rice novel, and just fantasize and role-play as vampires. They tend to live a gothic lifestyle but most of them don't drink blood. In fact, I found it amusing that during my online search, I came across many websites devoted to "real" vampires that boldly state "NO ROLE PLAYERS WELCOME." So as I said, not even all vampires get along!

Many young people are attracted to the vampire and gothic scene, and this raises concerns for many parents. From my research, it appears that most vampires are responsible individuals and many are parents themselves. Most websites openly discourage children from viewing them. I even found an educational site that took great pains to instruct young people – especially young females – on the dangers of communicating with people in online chat rooms who profess to be vampires and especially those who promise to turn them into one. No real vampire will ever offer to "turn a person" -- and most believe that it cannot be done – at least not the way movies portray it. More than one young girl has been misled by such a predator and consequently harmed. This website gives these young women a good dose of reality, albeit a scary one.

So if your child or teenager seems to be obsessed with this kind of stuff or dresses in black all the time, is there any reason to be alarmed? According to psychologist, Dr. Barbara Kirwin who was interviewed by Katherine Ramsland, the answer is no, most of the time. Each case must be considered on its individual merits. Dr. Kirwin says that most kids she sees are really very bright but are just not making it in the banal, materialistic culture of privilege. But they don't want to get involved with sex, drugs, and alcohol either. So their sense of vampirism gives them an alternate spiritual reality. The media dismiss them as deviant but Dr. Kirwin says that's too shallow. There's a difference between noncomformity and real antisocial pathological deviance. Great minds deviating from the norm is how progress occurs. But she does make this interesting comment: "Baby Boomer parents seem to have a psychic vampire style that consumes their children's youth. These kids are wearing the same fashions their parents wore 20 years ago, they listen to similar music, and there's just nothing that's theirs anymore."[56] So kids are just acting out what's happening to them, and simply exploring and developing their sense of individuality like typical teenagers. As one young vampire says, "The vampire is about the search for something genuine in an era when almost anything can be faked... Feeling is what's risky now. Being cut represents that." Ramsland found that the vampire often appears to be a means of self-reinvention for those who wish to distance themselves from a family or culture that no longer nurtures them in order to rediscover themselves purely as individuals: "They're beyond the reach of the banal, which seeks alternatively to suck the life out of them."[57]

Ramsland found no exact profile of the vampire or of those attracted to vampires:

> Some are paranoid, some trusting; some view themselves as outsiders, some don't; some are borderline mentally ill, some are healthy; some like to present themselves as dangerous, others as nurturing and harmless; some thrive on the image that they love or need blood; others find this disgusting. In other words, the vampire fills a need for characters larger than life who enable us to venture to the edge, to look into the abyss, to test ourselves.[58]

Still, I believe the most revealing statement about vampires was made by Anne Rice in the prologue to the video release of *Interview with the Vampire*. She says, "Remember, this movie is not about vampires. It's about us."

The vampire is a symbol of immortality. It is also a reminder that we cannot exist alone. We are all interdependent. We all feed on the life energies of each other and the universe – especially the plant and animal kingdoms. Anne Rice's fictional vampire Lestat said, "God kills indiscriminately and so shall we. For no creatures under God are as we are, none so like him as ourselves." In the last supper, Jesus passed around the cup and said, "Drink this – this is my blood." Esoteric mysteries surround the blood. Life and death are two sides of the same coin. This life energy is constantly recycled. Therefore, to me, the vampire as metaphor is far more powerful than the real thing. It doesn't have to be all negative. In fact, the vampire, like all beings, is evolving. We've exposed a code of ethics among real-life vampires like those mentioned above and among fictional vampires who only feed on bad guys. Children are treated to a vegetarian Count Duckula who teaches them to be tolerant of those who seem different. Who says we can't have vampire heroes like the fictional Vampirella who defend us against evil vampires from outer space in fiction OR real life? Because as we've seen, truth is often stranger than fiction. And no better is this illustrated than in the story of...

Royal Vampires and Dragon Courts

Our expert, Katherine Ramsland, devoted another book to the biology of the vampire, drawing upon her skills as a forensic psychologist.[59] Yet surprisingly, she omits perhaps one of the most important discoveries about this mysterious creature in recent years – and that is the phenomenon of the "royal vampire."

All across the Internet ugly rumors and deliberate disinformation abound about evil alien shape-shifting reptiles drinking the blood of ritually sacrificed innocent victims, like vampire gods from outer space. In contrast, there is a story about a benevolent willing donor by the name of Jesus Christ who symbolically offered his blood and body at the last supper, ritually memorialized to this day in the practice of Holy Communion. The truth, believe it or not, is somewhere in between these two legends and was lost in the mists of time until recently.

Before the fall, *the Shining Ones* did not need to ingest outer substance in order to maintain some form of embodiment on the planet. Some of them still don't. Yet some beings do, like humans. But unlike humans, they had something we didn't, and they were spoiled by that privilege. Supernormal powers and incredibly long life spans were those privileges, and over-attachment to them was their downfall. Something happened to a faction of our extraterrestrial ancestors that made them need to depend on a divine elixir to prolong their lives and continue to manifest those supernormal powers in an *unnatural* way. This is my take on a story offered by authors 'in the veins' of Sir Laurence Gardner and Prince Nicholas de Vere.

As previously discussed, something happens to the blood of an enlightened person. Author Hugh Colmer says, "Our blood

470

is as good as the state of our consciousness so as we purify our thoughts so we purify our blood."[60]   Blood is precious for in the blood lies our power and will to live. It is the animating life force of our physical existence. Yet blood can also be a carrier for death as the AIDS virus has taught us. Throughout history, humanity has had a love/hate relationship with blood. It has been worshipped and feared for many reasons. Colmer relates,

> The codes of consciousness stored in our blood course through our veins and connect us to our ancestors. Our blood stores all of the information of our cosmic experiences which manifest in our bodies through our blood. Our blood is rich with the geometric codes of life inherent in all things that reorganize themselves and evolve spiritually. Our thoughts are recorded by our blood according to our feelings and radiated through our morphogenetic fields for all to learn from.[61]

In battle it was often customary to drink the blood of the fallen foe in order to assimilate their courage. Native Americans ate the heart and drank the blood of the slaughtered buffalo in order to take on its strength.

The blood of a virgin is supposed to be particularly special. In legend, sacrificing a virgin to the dragon often saved the village. Women in Italy had an old custom of saving a few drops of their menstrual blood in a small vial. If a woman could get the man of her choice to ingest this blood somehow, it was believed that he would be bound to her forever.[62]

A taboo against a woman's menstrual blood exists in many cultures. This blood was feared because of its power, literally and symbolically. Therefore the patriarchal leaders taught it was unclean and that women were to be shunned during their periods. This negative conditioning continues to some degree in many cultures. Young women are no longer taught to honor and revere this sacred power that belongs to them alone. Instead of first menstruation being a sacred rite of passage filled with awe and wonder, it is a painful time of doubt, humiliation, and even a fear of dying – a part of "Eve's curse." Actually, the menstrual period is a time of heightened sensitivity – sexually, emotionally, and psychically. In ancient times, wise women knew this and used this time for solitude, solace and reflection. It was a sacred time when a woman was more in touch with herself.[63] Today, many people and men especially look at it as a time to avoid women because of PMS and all the bitchiness that comes from that. Well I'm inclined to believe, as does Clarissa Pinkola Estés, that a woman's frustration during PMS arises from the fact that she is not taking enough time out to rest, revivify and renew herself as she should. Instead, she is thwarted by her own social conditioning and that of those around her. Instead of heeding her intuition and self-nurturing instincts and going off alone somewhere, she continues to let the demands of work, friends, and family bleed her dry. In this context, society is the vampire.

Flowers are the sexual organs of plants. In esoteric tradition, the yoni or female organ is often represented by a lotus, lily, or rose. Sometimes the chakras or energy vortices are also referred to as lotus blossoms. Many Mesopotamian goddesses have names based on the Sumerian word for lily, such as Lilith. According to Colmer, Lilith was the world's first free-thinking virgin who refused to submit to Adam's attempt at sexual domination.[64] To control women is to control their sexuality because this was the key to dynastic lineage and privilege. This was nothing new to the Anunnaki.

It was also the key to the Anunnaki's continued survival as the dominant force on the planet and their so-called "immortality." Because some of them had lost the ability to accomplish the inner alchemy, they resorted to an outer alchemy, a cheap imitation of the real thing. But hey – it worked, at least for a while.

In Laurence Gardner's book *Genesis of the Grail Kings*, notably distinguished for its exemplary scholarship, he discusses this methodology at length. You want to know why the virgin's blood was so special? Because they drank it -- literally. Yes, you read that right. This was the beginning of a bloodline of royal vampires that eventually culminated in the legend of Count Dracula.

The ancient ones venerated the menstrual blood of their goddesses and called it "star fire." The fire of the *kundalini* is what feeds the star in the head – the pineal gland. In order for the pineal and pituitary glands to do their jobs properly and release the natural DMT within the body, the bloodstream and nervous system must be saturated with enormous amounts of certain hormones and chemical substances, such as oxytocin, prolactin, serotonin, adenosyne triphosphate, dopamine, telomerase (currently under investigation for its anti-aging properties), retinal, and melatonin especially. Menstrual blood is rich in all these substances. The Anunnaki, generally speaking, had more concentrated amounts of these substances in their blood. Therefore, the royal Anunnaki females willingly shared their menstrual blood in order to replenish what was being lost, and this was done in a sacred ritual. As a result of partaking of the sacred star fire, the Anunnaki effectively *regenerated* their physical bodies and therefore kept the kundalini loop working. Remember the Gnostic symbol of the Ouroboros – the serpent biting its own tale? That's the loop I'm talking about. The dragon body becomes a complete body of light endlessly circulating the cosmic energy between the etheric counterpart of the physical body and the zero point energy that's all around us. Remember, we're always plugged into this energy. We just don't have the switch completely turned on. That's what this alchemy is all about – turning the switch on and leaving it on so that a continuous circuit is permanently established. But first we have to do some rewiring.

These hormonal secretions conduct (like water) magnetic resonances and higher frequencies processed through the pineal/pituitary "radio-receiver." For the whole system to work properly for the benefit of one and all, a strong anchoring of these frequencies must occur in the heart center and be synchronized with all the other chakras. Unfortunately, many of the Anunnaki neglected this important step in the process.

473

The regenerative process involves the kundalini climbing up the thirty-three vertebrae of the spinal column, which incidentally, correspond to the thirty-three degrees of Freemasonry. The virgin's blood was especially coveted for this process because the hormones are strongest right after puberty.

The sacred star fire, the red elixir, had to be drunk out of something, and this is the origin of the Holy Grail. A cup, chalice or bowl by its very shape is symbolic of the womb. Yet the Holy Grail contained the blood of Christ. Obviously, Jesus Christ didn't have periods. No, this blood came from his wounds as he bled on the cross. Yet less than a day before this event, he was passing a cup around to his disciples saying, "This is my blood. Drink this in remembrance of me." So what's that all about? What's really going on here?

The New Testament of the Bible is supposed to be an addition to the Old. Therefore, contradictory edicts and customs abound. After the flood, the Lord gave Noah a strange command. Genesis 9:3-6 in the Old Testament reads as follows:

> Every moving thing that liveth shall be meat for you; even as the green herb have I given you all things. But flesh with the life thereof, *which is the blood thereof,* shall ye not eat. . . Whoso sheddeth man's blood, by man shall his blood be shed: for in the image of God made he man. (Emphasis added.)

The Lord ordered Noah and his descendants not to ingest blood. This implies it was a practice for some. Remember Noah is part of that royal priestly bloodline and was Enki's protégé. If it weren't for Enki, humanity would have been completely destroyed. Because we know the Biblical account is an edited version of the original Sumerian records, any reference to "the Lord" in the Old Testament could be either Enlil or Enki. We have to ask ourselves then, which one was "the Lord" in this particular instance? Gardner says it was Enlil, the wrathful Jehovah who hated people. Therefore, for him to prohibit humans from drinking blood certainly could not have been for their benefit. Surely, the motive must have been to impede the spiritual development of humanity in order to keep them as slaves. This would make sense if it were Enlil who said this. But look at the verse again: "for in the image of God made he man." Enlil didn't make man. Enki and Ninhursag did. Who is talking to who here? The pronouns "you" and "he" are not clear. The words "Lord" and "God" could mean two different things as well.

I suspect another mistranslation here. Common sense tells us that if Enlil didn't like Noah and wanted him dead, then what would he be doing going out of his way to tell him to go replenish the earth and multiply, and dictate to him what he can have and do and what not. He could care less. It had to be Enki, who, as before the flood, was continuing to provide guidance to Noah and his family. The wise and beneficent Lord making such a command must have had a good, well-intended reason for it. And this was it: Continuing to ingest star fire in the form of menstrual blood is "black" or bad magic, which in the long run will do you more harm than good. There was and still is a better way.

That this was Enki's command makes more sense in light of occult principle, and it appears to be supported by Sitchin's research into the records. A chapter from *The Lost Book of Enki* tells the story about Enlil plotting against Adapa who had been summoned to Nibiru by Anu. Remember Adapa was the human offspring fathered by Enki. Prior to Adapa's departure, Enki warned him:

> Adapa, to Nibiru, the planet whence we had come, you will be going, Before Anu our king you will come, to his majesty you will be presented... A bread on Earth not found they to you will give; the bread is death, do not eat! In a chalice an elixir to drink they to you will give; the elixir is death, do not drink![65]

Aside from drinking the blood, bloodletting of any kind, whether it's an animal or a human, whether in the context of a sacrificial ritual or a heinous crime, releases a vital invisible etheric energy that can be scooped up and redirected by the bloodletter. Primitive shamans and hoodoo practitioners know this well. Some sociopaths have been known to thrive on the rush they get at the moment of killing when the life energy is released from their victim. It's a high they can't describe. Dean Corll, the infamous mass murderer of teenage boys in Houston during the early 1970s, combined homosexual torture with bloodletting in order to increase his magnetic powers. Using sex and/or bloodletting in magic gets immediate, powerful results, but usually with negative karmic consequences.

A sacred sexuality practice exists in the Western and Eastern traditions. But the purpose is not for accumulating power or material benefit. If done with a consensual partner heterosexually and with love, the act becomes a higher communion with the Beloved and a vehicle for recognizing oneness with the Higher Self. Seeing your sexual partner as a deity helps to awaken the divinity within.

Mixing sexual juices and imbibing them in ritual is one of the more ancient, primitive and secret magical practices prevalent in occult traditions all over the world. As late as the 19th century, Western occultists such as Aleister Crowley were writing about it. Some writers speculate that the concept behind his "Scarlet Woman" was derived from the ancient Egyptian practices surrounding the star fire mysteries. Sometimes these practices are combined with those geared toward perpetuating the bloodline or furthering an esoteric lineage. For instance, in Tibet, in order to enhance the power of the lineage, a lama would arrange for one of his disciples to marry a woman with fairy or dakini characteristics (read: ET). The sole object of the union would be to produce a child destined to carry on the spiritual lineage of the lama. The couple would cloister in extended retreat and participate in many elaborate preparatory rituals that would strengthen the bond between each other and with the lama. Finally, in the midst of a *kyilkhor* or magic circle, just like the Great Rite or Great Marriage of the Old Religion, they would have sexual intercourse and conceive the magical child.

The famous Tibetan Buddhist sage Marpa is reported to have participated in such a rite for his married disciple Ngog Chosdor. Lama Alexandra David-Neel describes the details:

> When their retreat had come to an end, the initiations having been duly conferred on both husband and wife, the *kyilkhor* erected and all the ceremonies concluded, Marpa shut himself up with his own wife Dagmedma and the young couple in his private oratory. There the Lama took his place on his ritual throne along with his fairy-wife, whilst Ngog Chosdor and his wife remained folded in each other's arms at his feet. Marpa received his sperm in a goblet made of a human skull, and after mixing with it various ingredients supposed to possess magical properties, the potion was drunk by the disciple and his wife.[66]

According to David-Neel, this practice is reserved for an exclusive group of initiates and rarely taught. Again, as with Western alchemy, the Eastern equivalent has symbolic and literal aspects. Mating happens on all levels, and you don't have to have physical sex to conceive a magical child!

Prince Nicholas de Vere who proudly informs us these rites are still practiced by 21st century royalty, claims that these royal vampires only take blood from voluntary females. In ritual, the menstruating sacred donor or goddess-princess is sexually stimulated until she "ejaculates." The juices combine, creating star fire and are either collected in a cup or sucked out with a straw. Drinking the star fire prolongs the life of the donor and the donee.[67]

In order to prolong and perpetuate the royal bloodline, babies are made of course. Sometimes this is done in ritual too, like the 'Great Marriage' that Arthur completed with his half-sister, Morgaine. Viviane de Lac, Lady of the Lake, and Merlin, the Druid wizard, arranged this magical union. Lancelot was the son of Viviane and he was known as Lancelot de Lac (of the Lake) and Lancelot of the Dragon Blood. Gardner traces the word 'lake' back to the old Grail dynasty House del Acqs, meaning 'of the waters' having its origins in the queenly Lady of the Lake tradition:

> The Rosi-crusis (or Dew-cup) – the emblem of the Holy Grail – was itself identified with the Messianic blood held within the sacred chalice of the maternal womb. It can, accordingly, be seen that the styles de Lac and del Acqs are entirely synonymous, as are the historical traditions of the Dragon and the Grail. These conjoined traditions are especially significant in the story of the 'blood and water' which flowed from Jesus's side at the Crucifixion – being emblematic of the fact that he was truly a kingly dhynast of the Shining Ones.[68]

This brings us back to Jesus. Why was he symbolically sharing his blood, and why was this ritual memorialized in the act of Holy Communion by the church, especially since the earlier edict outlawed such a practice? Gardner thinks it's a throwback to the ritual of ingesting star fire. We know that Jesus descended through the same royal bloodline that began with Noah. We know he participated in Gnostic rituals with the Essenes. We know that he and Mary Magdalene were mates and that the bloodline was perpetuated through their descendants. We know that in the West, their spiritual tradition eventually branched off into many forms, including the Knights Templar and the Rosicrucians -- the people of the "rosy cross."

Gardner connects the Rosy Cross with the Holy Grail as follows:

> The Rosi-crucis (whose supporters were called Rosicrucians) is often misidentified as if it referred to a Rosy (or Red) cross – but in fact the term has a

rather different origin. It stems from the old Greek 'rosi', meaning 'dew', and from 'crucis' meaning 'fire-cup' (as in the word 'crucible'). Hence, the Rosi-crucis was the dew-cup of fire – or fiery cup of the waters.[69]

The waters, of course, are the byproducts of a woman's menstrual cycle known as star fire. Gardner contends that this practice of ingesting star fire continued among certain descendents in the lineage of the royal bloodline, including Jesus. He says it's the origin of what the muddlers popularized as "the black mass" which was co-opted, sanitized, and disguised by the Roman Catholic church as the "white mass" ritual of Holy Communion. Women were feared and hated because they were the holders of the royal lineage and the powerful star fire. Mary Magdalene and other women were priestesses in this bloodline providing star fire, ministry and babies. The Church couldn't have that. Therefore, any reference to "power in the blood" had to be about a man's blood, in particular, the blood of Jesus, their version of "God" -- who was to forevermore replace the goddess in worship of the divine.

That's an interesting argument. I agree that the Church mounted a massive campaign to erase women from history and religion. What I don't agree with is that Jesus drank star fire. Why? Because he didn't *need* to. He had his own. He practiced real alchemy -- not a counterfeit substitute.

Gardner says all the legends about witches, elves, fairies, sprites, pixies, and other supernatural beings were about real people – descendants of the Anunnaki – the royal bloodline. In addition, all the fairy tales and folklore about seeking the captured or missing bride or princess is all about this phenomenon. In the medieval period, the royal bloodline was persecuted and had to go into hiding because of the Church's campaign to destroy them. Many of the old families were killed off and their females burned at the stake as witches. Therefore, carriers of the bloodline, the royal princesses, were in short supply. So princely heroes go on epic adventures looking to rescue their Sleeping Beauties, Cinderellas, and Snow Whites in order to perpetuate the bloodline before they are left to rot away in a dungeon somewhere or fed a poisoned apple. Lohengrins, Parsifals, and other noble knights go off in search of the Holy Grail so they can get their star fire fix before they rot away or die from a poisoned apple too. Well, all I can say is that fortunately, there is more than one way to interpret a story.

Gardner provides convincing evidence that most elves and fairies were probably our extraterrestrial ancestors, and I've always agreed with that. But they were no more a part of a royal bloodline than you or me or your pet hamster because there is no such thing as a *royal* bloodline period. The technology of genetic engineering was lost and replaced with medieval breeding experiments that were nothing more than sophisticated magical rituals. **All blood is equally precious and capable of transformation.** The true and invisible Rosicrucian Order is truly invisible as Paul Foster Case says because its strength and purpose do not rely on physical structure for subsistence – neither is it limited by any. No one is barred from such an order based on class, creed, color, I.Q., bloodline, or for any other reason. The door is open to all who knock.

I believe that Jesus, the Serpent of Wisdom that he was, along with genuine Gnostics, Rosicrucians, Knights Templars and other followers of the Western Mysteries in the tradition of Enki, created ritual that would reinforce the sacred principles through their symbolic meaning, and that is why he chose to emblematically share his blood with his disciples in a powerful acknowledgment that his blood was *their* blood – his power was *their* power – his claim to divinity was *their* claim to divinity. "And you will do even greater things than I...."

"Do this in remembrance of me" means make yourself an embodiment of the Holy Grail – the Sacred Adytum – a receptacle for the Holy Spirit or cosmic energy to shine forth for the benefit of one and all. It is the temple not made with hands, but with the inner conviction, devotion and understanding of a true spiritual aspirant, whose compassion and wisdom together complete the transmutation of the personality into the gold of fully illumined awareness. As one of my teachers is fond of saying, Jesus was the great example – not the great exception.

Of course any good wizard can go bad. Throughout the centuries there were many who strayed from the straight and narrow of their traditions, taking what they perceived as a short cut to illumination with drugs, experimenting with star fire, and other harmful methods. This is where Dracula comes into the picture.

Gardner says that Dracula was feared for his extensive knowledge of occultism and alchemy more than for his streak of cruelty because he was a descendant of the royal bloodline that formed into the sacred 'Order of the Dragon.' I don't doubt this. However, I suspect he was one of the good wizards gone bad. Perhaps he was the model for Saruman, the white wizard turned evil in Tolkien's *Lord of the Rings.*

I don't want to minimize Gardner's invaluable contribution to this research. He is a meticulous scholar and extraordinary author in his own right. His historical discoveries about the true origin of the legends of Ring lore, for instance, are profound.[70] His findings also appear to fill in some missing links about the migration of the Atlanteans into Europe before reaching Mesopotamia and the route they took to the British Isles.

Remember a possible Kurgan civilization and invasion predated Sumer. In September of 2000, the Associated Press reported on the archeological finding of a settlement at the bottom of the Black Sea at least 7,000 years old. This is around the same time archeologists date the foundation of Catal Huyuk in Anatolia. Not long after these settlements were founded Ubaid culture sprang up in Mesopotamia where artifacts reveal a kind of being with an elongated head and disproportionately large, slanted eyes. An interesting archeological discovery was made in the Transylvanian region of Romania, a country that borders the Black Sea. Clay tablets found underneath an ancient village revealed inscriptions in symbols that were to turn up in Mesopotamia much later. According to Gardner, this was the region of the Scythian Wood Lords, the Transylvanian fairy race from whence the ancient king tribe of Tuadhe d'Anu emerged. The Tuadhe d'Anu or 'tribe of Anu' (remembering Anu as the father of Enlil and Enki), were the same as the Tuatha de Danaan of Irish legend. The Tuatha de Danaan were immigrants from Atlantis. This suggests that the Anunnaki settled in the European regions before migrating to Egypt and Mesopotamia.

According to Gardner, these Scythian Wood Lords were the elves depicted in Tolkien's *Lord of the Rings.* They were masters of a transcendent intellect known as the Sidhe, not unlike the Sanskrit word present in many Tibetan Buddhist chants, 'siddhi,' referring to psychic ability. Gardner writes,

> The concept of calling the princely race of the Grail the Shining Ones, while also defining them as Elves, dates well back into ancient Bible times and can be traced into Mesopotamia (modern Iraq) and Canaan (Palestine). The ancient word 'El', which was used to identify a god or lofty-one (as in El Elyon and El Shaddai) actually meant Shining in old Mesopotamian Sumer. To the north in Babylonia, the derivative 'Ellu' meant Shining One, as did 'Ilu' in Akkad. Subsequently, the word spread across Europe to become 'Ellyl' in Wales, 'Aillil' in Ireland, and 'Elf' in Saxony and England.
>
> The plural of El was Elohim, the very word used in old Bible texts to denote the gods, but strategically mistranslated to conform to the Judeo-Christian 'One God' image. Interestingly, in Gaelic Cornwall, South West England, the word 'el' was the equivalent of the Anglo-Saxon 'engel' and the old French 'angele' which, in English, became 'angel'.[71]

Tolkien was an Oxford professor of English and Anglo-Saxon with a love of history and mythology. When asked about the approximate setting for Middle Earth, he estimated 4000 B.C.E. That times perfectly with the establishment of our Anunnaki settlements. Instinctively knowing that folktale and mythology were veils for truth, he fictionalized his own historical analysis of those times.

Gardner states that the Ring was one of the primary ruling devices of the Anunnaki overlords. Over time, instead of wearing or holding them, the rulers began to place them on their heads, and this is the origin of the crown. In legend, the Saxon god Wotan distributed nine rings to rule nine worlds, retaining the ninth ring to control all the others. Therefore, Wotan is equated with the Sumerian Lord Anu:

> The contested ownership of the One Ring, as related in The Lord of the Rings, is little different to the enduring quest for the Holy Grail; they are both quests for the maintenance of sovereignty. But, in both fact and fiction, the Ring and the Grail are seen to be misappropriated by those who perceive them as weapons of power.[72]

Gardner suggests that the ousting of the so-called royal bloodline was a misappropriation of the Ring. Prince Nicholas de Vere has no doubt. Claiming to be a descendent of this bloodline and admittedly a royal vampire, his website is filled with elitist diatribe, whining, and sour grapes about the horrible injustice done to him and his sovereign family by the "client peasant race" of humanity. He believes that humans at one time hired the Sovereign Dragons to be their rulers because after all, it's just not in our blood. Divine right is inherited – not made, and therefore these royal vampires are rightful shepherds of the human flock, exclaims De Vere. The website says that he and Gardner at one time were buddies in the closed fraternity known as "The Dragon Court." But then they had a falling out and Gardner was asked to leave. De Vere claims that he's the one who introduced Gardner to his family's archive of ancient historical documents elaborating on the purpose of star fire and the vampire ritual used to extract it; therefore he should get credit for it.[73]

But let's take a closer look at Tolkien's take on this whole thing again. The Ring was intrinsically evil and no good in anyone's hands. The initial act of forging the Ring was the real misappropriation. The esoteric truth behind this parable is also reflected in Wagner's music drama epic, the Ring Cycle mentioned previously. It's not that power or even misuse of power corrupts. It goes deeper than that. It's more like these words out of the handbook given to the reluctant Messiah in Richard Bach's tale:

The original sin is to limit the Is. Don't.[74]

It all hinges around what the Ring is made of – gold. Gold is metallic light with a frequency above all other metals. Gold is crystallized sunrays. It is symbolic of the ultimate cosmic energy and life giving force of the Sun. It is the real and symbolic source of all inner and outer illumination. Like the river of the Rhinegold where it was found, it must remain free-flowing and uncorrupted for peace and harmony to prevail. Heline states:

It is said that the golden veins running through the earth are magnetic channels for cosmic forces of a particularly beneficial nature; that if gold had not been misused to enslave the race, it would have attracted to the earth fertility, plenty and every material and spiritual blessing. Paradise would not have been lost.[75]

The gold in the veins of our planet is equivalent to the blood of the Dragon body of Mother Earth. What did the Anunnaki originally come to Earth for? Gold. Raping the Earth and then forging its precious lifeblood into a ring is symbolic of limiting and constricting the free-flowing cosmic energy of the world. And this is exactly what these vampires accomplished in more ways than one. Contesting ownership of the ring is not a quest for divine sovereignty -- it's a fight for power and control.

For a long time, gold translated to money. The characters in the Ring Cycle who steal the gold ring and attempt to hoard it and use it for evil purpose are giants and dwarves whom Heline equates with Atlantean races, most likely our extraterrestrial ancestors. To continue with her esoteric analysis of Wagner's Ring cycle:

> The evil lies not in gold (money) itself, but in its abuse. Its deflection from free-flowing channels of commerce (the Rhine) wherein it is available for the exchange needs of the multitudes, and its appropriation by giants of finance (Fafner and Fasolt) who thereby acquire power over the lives of those who lack it, violate cosmic law and bring ruin upon the social order in which such an economy is operative.[76]

This is why the Old World Order of Wotan or Anu has to be overthrown. The Funny Money system is fundamentally evil. That Richard Wagner was well aware that this was the primary message of the story is evidenced by the following statement from his biography:

> The task must be to cultivate mankind and to bring about the greatest well-being of all... when as many active human beings as the earth can support would unite in well-organized societies to enrich and bless one another by the interchange of their various, multifold activities. God will enlighten us so that we may find the right law by which this principle may be introduced into actual life. The demonic idea of money, with all its hideous attendant evils of public and secret usury, swindling with the currency, interest, and the speculation of bankers, will vanish like a bad nightmare.[77]

Socialists analyze the Ring legend likewise. The point is that when you have a divisive split in society between the "haves" and "have-nots" trouble ensues. The fact that the Anunnaki could not see this from the very beginning of their mining and genetic engineering exploits is evidence that their blood did NOT give them any special ability to be good rulers. They were crappy at it -- I mean, what a sham! Not that humans are any better -- yet, for look at our role models. But we're coming along. At least most of us have outgrown the false belief in the biological basis of elitism and "Divine Right" rule, which might mean that sociologically, we're further along than the Anunnaki were when they first arrived on the planet.

There is another reason why the capture and confinement of gold is unnatural and harmful. According to Heline:

> Gold is also a transmitter of astral or psychic forces. If we think in terms of the collective soul of the world we perceive how it is possible for gold, due to constant association with envy, hatred, jealousy, greed and war, to become a focusing point for evil so that even to possess it tends to awaken corresponding qualities in the individual soul. It is even thought by many esotericists that the veins of gold in the earth serve as mediums for explosive gases which ultimate in earthquakes, volcanoes, tidal waves and other destructive phenomena, whereby nature effects retribution upon the human race for its vandalism.[78]

The Anunnaki's use of gold extended further than the salvation of their sovereignty on Earth and their atmosphere on Nibiru. They used it for the salvation of their psychic abilities in conjunction with star fire.

Monatomic Gold: Dragon Wings

Not only did the Anunnaki feed on star fire, they also manufactured a "star stone" that was equally important to maintaining their longevity. Gardner relates:

> On one of the rock tables near to the Mount Serabit cave entrance is a representation of Tuthmosis IV in the presence of Hathor. Before him are two offering stands topped with lotus flowers and behind him is a man bearing a loaf of white bread. Another stela

details the mason Ankhib offering two conical bread-cakes to the king and there are similar portrayals elsewhere in the temple complex. Perhaps one of the most significant is a depiction of Hathor and Amenhotep III. The goddess, complete with horns and solar disc, holds a necklace in one hand, while offering the emblem of life and dominion to the pharaoh with the other. Behind her is the treasurer Sobekhotep, who holds in readiness a conical shem of 'white bread'. Treasurer Sobekhotep is very importantly described elsewhere in the temple as the Overseer of the secrets of the House of Gold, who brought the noble Precious Stone to his majesty'.[79]

Some scholars such as Gardner and Sitchin believe that the Biblical references to 'manna' and the Egyptian references to a special white powder are one in the same. The Mesopotamian word for it was shem-an-na or "highward fire-stone." Turns out that there is a way of transforming gold into an edible white power. This is the special 'bread' or 'stone' that was fed to the kings. What it did was make them high as a kite. It was also used in aviation for its anti-gravitic properties.

Only recently has modern science discovered that this is possible based on advances in quantum mechanics. White powdered "fire-stone" is a superconductive material that can be manufactured from metallic gold and platinum-group metals. These metals on the Periodic Table are known as the transition elements and include rhodium, palladium, ruthenium, gold, platinum, iridium, osmium and silver. They can all be transmuted into a monatomic state that manifests in a white powder. Per Gardner,

> The monatomic state occurs when the time-forward and time-reverse electrons correlate around the nucleus of a substance so that its individual atoms cannot bind together as a solid. Instead, it becomes a powder of single atoms. In this condition the atoms lose their chemical reactivity, changing the

configuration of their nuclei to an elongated shape which is called "asymmetrical high spin."[80]

Stories exist, mainly derived from ancient texts and alchemical treatises, alleging that a magical white powder or "philosopher's stone" could be made by transmuting base metals into a purified gold. In the Bible, Moses burns the golden calf, turns it into a white powder and feeds it to the Israelites. Before the quantum age, scientists did not understand how this was possible because ordinarily gold just melts when it's heated. Now they can make this white powder with the metals through a complicated process involving heating, cooling, distilling, electrical arcing and other factors. The white powder possesses the properties of a superconductor with many functions. Superconductivity results when high-spin atoms exchange energy with no net loss. Applying an electromagnetic field to these high-spin atoms triggers the energy flow.

The white powder, when ingested, stimulates the endocrine and nervous system in such a way that turns the body into one great big superconductor. This can prematurely open the head chakras, much like the administration of high dosages of DMT, allowing for the manifestation of heightened perception and extraordinary psychic ability.

Medical science in recent years has been experimenting with the possible healing properties of this white powder. They know for instance, that monatomic ruthenium will correct damaged DNA in cancer cells thus eliminating the cancer. A treatment procedure is not yet available because the nanotechnology has not been perfected as of this writing. Surgeons are not trained to work on individual atoms! Still, this minor obstacle has not deterred people from experimenting with the white powder. David Hudson, creator of a processing technique for the powder, witnessed a stage four cancer patient take it orally for 45 days, by which time the cancer entirely disappeared. The powder has the same effect on AIDS.[81]

Tests with samples of high-spin atoms show that when repeatedly subjected to a heating and cooling process with inert gasses, the substance fluctuates between 400% of its starting weight to less than zero. Finally, after removing the sample from the pan, the pan begins to levitate; yet weighing more than it did with the substance in it. Since gravity is the interaction of subatomic particles with zero point energy, the scientists suggested that somehow the white powder was bending space-time in ways previously proposed by quantum researchers. In other words, the white powder was still there but invisible because it was resonating in a different dimension. Subsequent tests confirmed this was the case.

The concept that space is not exactly empty but can be bent and distorted is neither new to science fiction or quantum scientists. The aerospace industry is applying these principles to the development of anti-gravitic propulsion systems. Have you ever wondered how the Stars Wars characters (or real extraterrestrials for that matter) could travel across the galaxies faster than the speed of light or in 'warp drive' and not suffer from Einstein's time dilation effect? It's because these spaceships can "...rest in warp bubbles between space-time distortions – so on that basis (whatever the distance theoretically traversed) the passage of time would be the same inside the bubble as that which passed outside."[82]

This also explains the secret to the technology that enabled our ancestors to build such monolithic monuments as Stonehenge and the pyramids. It might be in honor of that feat that the ancient ones shaped the sacred manna into cones resembling the pyramids. The pyramids were not tombs. They were spaceports. Evidence suggests the Anunnaki also used this technology to create 'stargates' through which people could pass. According to Gardner, the King's Chamber was designed with superconducting properties able to transport pharaohs into another dimension through the Meissner Field, the body's polar magnetic aura. Certain passages from the Egyptian *Book of the Dead* support this.[83]

David Hudson has a patent on this stuff, which he calls Orbitally Rearranged Monatomic Elements after ORME, the golden tree of life. Instead of gold, he uses rhodium and iridium because they appear naturally in the human body and in a host of other natural substances. He says that according to the ancient Egyptians, we must feed our light bodies as well as our physical bodies. He believes the white powder is the ultimate food for the light body.

500 milligrams per day was fed to a guy who after six days began to hear a very high frequency sound that wouldn't go away. But it wasn't unpleasant. He said he loved it, that it was like nectar to his brain. The sound just kept getting louder and louder. After sixty days he began to experience vivid dreams, visions and revelations. Finally, light beings appeared and began to teach him through telepathy:

> He said, "Dave, the sound seems to originate about 8 inches above my head, it comes into my brain, it's like a hat band around my head, and it just roars here in my head. I can feel the vibration all through my body." Well, he only sleeps about an hour and a half to two hours now, he doesn't need 7-8 hours like most of us... something strange happened. He said it began down the pelvis... came up over his stomach, up over his chest, up over his head, and he said, "My whole body was involved in this energy... I felt hot... like if someone came up and touched me they would burn their hand. Then all of a sudden, out of the top of my head, goes this column of energy.""[84]

This sounds just like the kundalini. Since this happened, the guy sees through playing cards, predicts the future, and feels at one with everything. Hudson says an Egyptian ritual from a book called *Secrets of the Golden Flower* by Richard Wilhelm estimates the length of this process to be about ten months, after which time the person becomes a light being capable of levitation and bi-location. Whether this particular guy has completed this "Egyptian Rite of Passage" he does not say.

The Book of Isaiah prophesies that a latter day David, a descendant from the royal bloodline, would come along and plant the Golden Tree of Life. Nostradamus predicted that by

1999 the occult gold would be known to science. A cousin of Hudson's joined the Mormon Church and did her genealogy. She found out that Hudson's great-great-great grandmother was a daughter in the de Guise family -- a family prominently placed in the "royal bloodline" or Holy Grail lineage. Surprised? Therefore Hudson believes he is this David.[85]

He admits that his substance is not the answer to everything, but that it unlocks the door to the answer. In other words, once everyone experiences total oneness with everything and everyone and has perfect telepathic contact with one another, there will be no more greed, no more lies, no more exploitation, and no more wars. We will no longer need to kill plants and animals for food because we will be fed on the resonance fields of the universe. We can travel anywhere just by thinking about it, experience immortality, and live happily ever after, just like the Holy Grail fairy tale says.

I'd genuinely like to believe this but history tells us differently. The Anunnaki took this stuff. Did it stop them from killing each other and having wars? No. Similarly, throughout the ages, sages with similar powers and abilities have appeared, and not all of them have been so kind and compassionate. Some of them, in fact, have committed great acts of evil and harm towards others, and in turn, to themselves.

It is true that when many people have a mystical experience where they feel this overwhelming oneness with everything, it changes their lives and they become better persons. That is certainly a primary objective. Yet this does not always happen because other factors and variables are at play. The 'Dark Side' is very seductive, and to use another cliché, the road to hell is paved with good intentions.

A wise old rabbi warned Hudson of this possibility. Hudson introduces his lecture with this story, but seems to have forgotten it by the end:

> When I became interested in this alchemy... I began
> to do all sorts of reading, and one of the things I came
> across immediately was the Melchizedek priesthood

and the white powder of gold associated with the Melchizedek priesthood. So I went to Rabbi Plotkin at Temple Beth Israel in Phoenix, and I asked the Rabbi, who is one of the most knowledgeable rabbis in Arizona, I said, "Rabbi, have you ever heard of the white powder of gold?" And he said, "Oh yes, Mr. Hudson. But to our knowledge no one's known how to make it since the destruction of the first temple." He said, "The white powder of gold is the magic. It can be used for white magic *or black magic.*" (Emphasis added.)[86]

While we should certainly and understandably get very excited about a possible cure for cancer, we must also heed the words of the Rabbi. If the other connections are not properly made, particularly with the heart, supernormal abilities can be very damaging and destructive. The only way to ensure that the prerequisites to lasting spiritual illumination are met thus solidifying and perpetuating the correct *Foundation*, is to accomplish the inner alchemy with one's own elements. All we need is already in the body. The body is already endowed with a miraculous healing and transformative power. We just need to learn how to access it, trigger it and turn it on, redirect it, stabilize it and facilitate the process as said before. This is exactly what the Mystery Schools teach.

Some evidence suggests that the more we rely on outer substances and chemicals to acquire desired states of consciousness, the less we are able to generate them on our own. It's as if the drug or agent tears down or wears away the neurochemical pathways and tissues necessary to achieve those states. In all likelihood, this is what happened to the Anunnaki who took these substances.

In 1918, Mary Anne Atwood published a little treatise called *A Suggestive Inquiry of the Hermetic Mystery.*[87] In it she documents the harmful consequences of abusing these substances in an effort to complete the Great Work. Many prominent individuals have died from it. And more than one magician has been destroyed by greed, addiction, and spiritual sloth.

Laurence Gardner conducted an Institute in Tempe, Arizona on November 24, 2003, reporting on the latest research regarding the effects of white powder. He told us that we could go the long 25-year route of a Tibetan monk in order to attain these superior states or "take this stuff." For one, it's not that simple. Secondly, such a statement reflects a misunderstanding of Tibetan Buddhism. The "state" is not the goal as the monk well knows. What separates the humble monk from the rest is not the seeking of the state but the cultivated trait. The cultivated trait is heart-felt compassion that serves as a sure and sound anchor for any "state" that should arise. No powder can give you that.

Delusion by the illusion of separateness cannot be erased by a drug. It cannot be overcome by intellectually recognizing the oneness of all things. The process must begin with a self-generated feeling – genuine compassion – unconditional love. Attitude and motive are all important. Emotions have a physics and geometry all their own. Taking white powder interferes with the waveforms generated by the heart in the development and expression of genuine compassion. So while the user is initially drunk on the illusory sensation of universal love and cosmic bliss, it is a transitory "state" – not the cultivated *trait*.

Heart-Brain Synchronization: The Key to Harmony

The heart as the source of energy field coherence in the human body is a scientifically proven fact. Groundbreaking biomedical research conducted by the Institute of HeartMath and confirmed by independent peer review reveals that the heart is not just a circulatory pump, but also a powerful brain in itself capable of profoundly influencing health, perception, emotions, behaviors, and performance. An important goal of the HeartMath Institute is to clarify the physiological components of emotions. While other researchers have focused on the effects of destructive emotions, the HeartMath Institute

493

emphasizes the role of positive emotions in their work, such as appreciation, love, care, and compassion. They have found that when these emotions are prevalent, clear changes occur in the activity patterns of the brain, heart, autonomic nervous system, immune system, and hormonal system. These changes result in improved health and cognitive abilities, increased longevity, and an enhanced ability to understand others.[88] What is even more significant, however, from an occult perspective, is that a person's heart has been found to influence another person's brain signals at a distance. Before we talk about that, let's look at how the heart and brain work together.

Up until recently, researchers have focused on how the brain influences the heart and other organs. Now they know that dialogue is a two-way street and that the heart can actually initiate 'conversation' so to speak. In fact, the brain and the heart keep a line of communication open between each other at all times. The heart talks to the brain via four channels: (1) neurological communication (nervous system); (2) biomechanical communication (pulse waves), (3) biochemical communication (hormones); and (4) energetic communication (electromagnetic fields). Emotions have their own cardiac rhythmic activity that directly influences the brain's ability to function. A particularly beneficial physiological mode of functioning is called *physiological coherence* characterized by increased efficiency, order, and harmony in all body systems. When the physical body is in this state, emotional stability and cognitive performance are at their peak.

Being coherent or in a state of coherence is not just a metaphor for having it all together; it can be measured. In mathematics and physics, coherence is usually described in reference to a single sine wave's ability to retain strength, order, and stability. Physiological systems in the body generate their own waveforms which can be measured with appropriate equipment like the electro-encephalogram (EEG) and the electrocardiogram (ECG), for instance. Physiological coherence then describes stability and order in the system's waveform reflecting the rhythmic activity of that system over a specific amount of time. A coherent heart rate variability waveform promotes increased coherence between the rhythmic patterns produced by other systems, resulting in a synchronization and entrainment between heart rhythms, respiratory rhythms and blood pressure oscillations.[89]

Heart rate variability (HRV) is a measure of the naturally occurring beat-to-beat changes in heart rate, and has its own waveform. Traditionally, this waveform has served as an indicator of neurocardiac fitness and autonomic nervous system function. The autonomic nervous system (ANS) controls the body's regulatory functions – those automatic functions we usually don't have to worry about, such as breathing. The ANS has two branches: the sympathetic branch that mediates functions that accompany arousal or excitement, and the parasympathetic branch that mediates functions that occur in a relaxed state.

There is a difference between "coherence" and "entrainment." Entrainment occurs when two or more waveforms begin to oscillate at the same frequency. They become phase or frequency locked. This is often called cross-coherence. Physiological coherence embraces entrainment, resonance and synchronization. These physiological phenomena manifest when interactions among the various systems are most ordered and harmonious. Heart rhythms show increased parasympathetic activity and synchronization with the brain, accompanied by entrainment between diverse physiological systems. In this state, the body is a veritable "harmony hut" and natural regenerative processes are facilitated.

> There is increased cardiac output in conjunction with increased efficiency in fluid exchange, filtration, and absorption between the capillaries and tissues; increased ability of the cardiovascular system to adapt to circulatory requirements; and increased temporal synchronization of cells throughout the body. This results in increased system-wide energy efficiency and metabolic energy savings.[90]

The increased absorption ability is crucial for the Great Work. The production, synthesis and absorption of the important elements from chyle is a preliminary procedure for the physiological process of enlightenment, remember. Better energy efficiency means more mitochondria; therefore more fuel for the fire!

While it is possible for a natural physiological coherence to spontaneously occur for brief moments, it is rarely observed in an extended state. The research indicates, however, that an individual can sustain this state for prolonged periods by self-generating positive emotions.

> Using a positive emotion to drive the coherent mode allows it to emerge naturally, and results in changes in the patterns of afferent information flowing from the heart to the respiratory and other brain centers. This, in turn, makes it easier to sustain the positive emotional state and coherent mode for longer periods, even during challenging situations.[91]

When this happens, it's called psychophysiological coherence. In this state, increased synchronization and harmony occur among all systems, and the person becomes more efficient and effective at whatever they are doing. The researchers have observed numerous benefits to psychophysiological coherence including reduced stress, anxiety and depression; decreased burnout and fatigue; enhanced immunity and hormonal balance; improved cognitive performance and enhanced learning; increased organizational effectiveness; and overall improvement in health.

Stress is characterized by high levels of desynchronization between systems and a lack of psychophysiological coherence. When this state is sustained, especially in the ANS, the nervous system and all the organs become overburdened and unable to transfer information efficiently. This is how stress kills, literally. The antidote to this, researchers have found, is positive emotions generated by the heart. A coherent heart pulls

496

other physiological oscillators into synchronization with its rhythms, resulting in multi-system entrainment. The heart is better at this task than the brain because the heart's electromagnetic field is the most powerful rhythmic field produced by the human body. It not only permeates every cell in the body, but also extends out in all directions into the space around it. Sensitive technology can measure this field several feet away from the body. Therefore, researchers conclude that the heart's field is an important, if not the most important, carrier of information that we possess.

This is nothing new to Ageless Wisdom or to the countless mystics who have left behind paintings of various saints and religious figures. Though these figures are usually adorned by a halo around the head representing illumination, the more vibrant light is emanating from the heart.

Harmony, peace, and "good vibes" are not metaphors; they are physiological realities. They can be measured in waveforms of frequency in Hertz. More specifically, when the heart is functioning in the internal coherence mode, the amplitude spectrum measured by an ECG exhibits a harmonic series.[92] On the ECG graph, frustration, an incoherent waveform, manifests as harsh, inconsistent and irregular spikes. The emotion of appreciation on the other hand, a coherent waveform, makes smooth, orderly, and graceful spikes.

These highly ordered and coherent HRV patterns are also associated with enhanced cardiovascular function. Mean power spectral density analysis of the waveforms in one study revealed that the increased activity in the parasympathetic system resulting from the positive emotional state of gratitude helps to protect the heart, possibly preventing heart disease. Due to these findings, techniques using this wave comparison technology are being developed into biomedical applications for patients with heart problems and hypertension.[93]

Intentionally altering emotional states by focusing on the heart modifies neurological input from the heart to the brain. Not only does this result in the numerous benefits listed above, but it also feels good. If done for a particularly long time, it can get you high! You don't have to sit on a cushion chanting "om mani pedme hung" for hours at a time either (though that works too.) You can simply invent your own exercise and do it anywhere. I have a favorite one I like to practice while riding in a vehicle. I look at each passing vehicle and project, "Bless you and love you infinitely!" Of course the phrase needs to be accompanied with the feeling, but after long-term repetition the feeling usually arises if it wasn't there already.

At my Dahn Center, when we're doing a particularly difficult exercise, headmaster says, "Smile. Change your energy. Enjoy your pain!" It's funny, but it works. Not only does the humor help relieve some of the tension, but for a brief moment the body gets a little boost of energy that helps to keep it going. The research shows that as people learn to sustain heart-focused positive feeling states, the brain can be brought into entrainment with the heart. This is why it's so important to surround yourself with supportive people who help elicit these positive emotions. This, I think, is the purpose of a true sangha, church, or spiritual organization of any kind.

I used to get really turned off to what I called "harmony hut" environments. I realized that it wasn't "being in harmony" that distressed me. It was that in most cases, the feelings in those environments were contrived, and I was just picking it up. Most people were faking it for the sake of appearance, self-righteousness or some other egocentric reason. There is a place for acting kindly when you don't really feel it. Not only is it good manners, it also helps to get you in the habit of thinking about your energy so you can begin to redirect it. However, when it's overly done, when the words or acts of kindness are compensatory or used deceptively in order to disguise true motive and feeling, then real harm is done. Even when used in a non-malicious manner, for instance, when trying to hide or suppress deep feelings of anger, loss, or pain, it is harmful. Why? Because feelings that need to be expressed are turned back inward, thus producing real damage to the well-being of the one experiencing the feelings. This is basic psychology. But now we know that the physiological component is equally significant. Negative emotions are the roots of all disease or "dis-ease."

Lama Surya Das's most recent book, *Letting Go of the Person You Used to Be: Lessons on Change, Loss, and Spiritual Transformation* addresses these issues and could not be more timely. One of the messages in this book is about the importance of dealing with these negative emotions head-on. The message is particularly important for spiritual aspirants. Why? Because it matters not how many times you recite the purification chant of Vajrasattva or how many bows you do or how many meditation hours you log in your weekly planner – if you do not deal directly with the negative feelings weighing you down, you will not heal. If you do not heal, you cannot spiritually progress, period. It's that simple.

Of course, the teachings in his tradition, like those in the Western, are being reinforced and supported by current research. Sounding like something right out of the HeartMath studies, Surya quotes Tarthang Tulku:

> When positive or joyous feelings and attitudes pass through each organ and circulate throughout our whole system, our physical and chemical energies are transformed and balanced.[94]

Not only do we heal, but we also help heal others by healing ourselves. This is partly how healers heal. So when we talk about picking up vibes from other people, it's literal. One of the key findings of a HeartMath study was that when people are in proximity to one another or touch one another, one's heartbeat signal is registered in the other person's brainwaves.[95]

Positive feeling vibrations mingled with healing energies are transmitted through the aura and hands of the healer. Western science has ignored this concept until these recent studies. The healer, experiencing a caring, positive attitude toward the patient, automatically produces a coherent HRV. Since the heart's electromagnetic field is the strongest and most powerful in the body, it only makes sense that this would facilitate the energy exchange between both persons through the field. Indeed, analyzed waveforms in a study testing this idea showed a clear transference of electrical energy between two people. While person A's ECG signal and person B's respondent EEG signals are strongest when in physical contact with each other, the signals are still detectable when they are in proximity without contact.

Coherent electromagnetic fields, through a form of resonance, are often detected and amplified by biological tissue. The fact that our brains can register the cardiac waveforms of another human being partly explains how our emotions impact others at a basic physiological level. Key findings of another study reveal that these registered vibrations can produce synchronization between one person's brainwaves and another person's heartbeats. However, the synchronization was more dependent on the degree of coherence in the *receiving subject's* heart rhythms. Therefore, individuals in a physiologically coherent state are more sensitive to the subtle electromagnetic information encoded in the heart signals of those around them. This supports data gathered from the use of a HeartMath technique called *Intuitive Listening.* This technique focuses on openness, empathy, and neutrality in developing listening and communication skills. Heartfelt connections between people are established by increased heart rhythm coherence generated by the parties synchronized with each other's brainwaves.

These findings have a dark side too in connection with the topic of psychic vampirism previously discussed. If you are in a living or working environment where negative people and hostility surround you, get out. 'Wet blankets' and 'party poopers' are real. If we choose to associate with negative or depressed people all the time, we will become that way too. It's a physiological fact. Only very strong witches can hold their own around such people. One of the best weapons of defense is music. The Institute of HeartMath is also involved with research that shows that facilitative music enhances mood and boosts immunity.

Therefore, enlightenment must be a function of the heart as much as it is a function of the head. If a person's heartwaves are incoherent with negative emotions, greed, lust for power, or self-aggrandizement, the attainment of enhanced perceptual and psychic ability will backfire. No matter how well intended thoughts may be, thinking is in the brain. And if the brain is not synchronized with a coherent compassionate heart, only chaos will ensue. The person becomes out of balance and vulnerable, succumbing to "the dark side of the Force."

Going to the opposite extreme is not the answer either. Neurotheology, an attempt to relegate all spiritual experience to physiology, makes for interesting study, but is too narrow a perspective in light of the complexity of numerous variables. We don't want to fall into the same trap as the Anunnaki and become irresponsible, arrogant gods of creation. Eugenics is the dark side to genetic engineering and will continue to rear its ugly head as long as the cloning debate continues. Bioethics must become central to continuing advances in biotechnology.

In the meantime, we, as individuals, have our own ethics to consider, and must claim responsibility for our own actions. A person who resorts to the use of white powder in this work is a person not in sync. If their systems were fully synchronized, the necessary waveform for the induction of the sought-after states would have already done its magic. We're never going to be able to just pop a pill made up of the spirit molecule or drink a modern rendition of 'star fire' to properly spiritually unfold because that diminishes the body's natural ability to do so on its own. We cannot become dependent on physical substances above and beyond that needed to sustain baseline.

If these emotional energies affect every organ in our body down to the cellular level, they surely affect the structure and maintenance of DNA. Many researchers believe that an overuse of the white powder may damage DNA in the long run. Continued use of the white powder overstresses the endocrine system (because the correct wiring or foundation for it was never established) which then begins to break down. The white powder then loses its effectiveness because the user becomes habituated to it. This is the nature of the addiction process.

It's the divine, sweet music of the heart that awakens the kundalini. The heart's own sound waves based on the expression of genuine wonder and compassion generate the magical harmonic frequencies necessary to charm the snake up the spine transforming the pineal/pituitary axis into fully blossomed golden flowers.

Bottom line, this self-steering process, engaging will and innate creative power is what leads us to the promise of enlightenment and immortality. A passive "let the drug do it for me" attitude just doesn't cut it. Some writers suggest that the Anunnaki who came in search of gold for this purpose might have done so out of necessity – that their previous planetary environments were so polluted and their ecosystems so damaged, that their bodies might have lost the power to regenerate on their own. I seriously doubt that. Otherwise, where would we have gotten the gene to do so? No, I think what really happened was that a few of them decided to take a short cut and so suffered the consequences.

A careful examination of the golden calf episode in the Bible in Chapter 32 of Exodus, raises questions we would do well to consider. Clearly "the Lord" was not happy about the Israelites making a golden calf. But then why did Moses turn it into white powder and feed it to them anyway? It would not matter if the Lord in this case were either Enlil or Enki because they would both have their own reasons for admonishing the Israelites not to partake of the white powder. Enlil wouldn't want them to have it because it put them on equal footing with the Anunnaki. Enki wouldn't want them to have it because it's bad for them. But Moses made it and fed it to them anyway. In the end, "the Lord plagued the people, because they made the calf." It was because they made the *calf* -- not the white powder. The issue was not whether or not they should partake of the white powder but who should control access to it. This was muddling and political maneuvering to disempower the people so they would depend on another for enlightenment – a guru – a god, whatever. "God" forbid they find out they could do this on their own! Therefore the traditional interpretation of the story -- condemning idolatry -- is accurate as well. "Thou shalt have no other gods before me." How can we be expected to actualize our innate divinity when we're always praying to someone else's?

Another analogy might go like this: Suppose you want your child to become one of the greatest artists of all time. So you purchase most of the supplies necessary for this – all except for blank sheets of paper or canvases. Instead, you buy her coloring books that already have the pictures drawn with the lines imprinted on the page. The child ends up coloring between the lines and nothing more. She never develops into a great, original artist. She never cultivates creativity and actualizes her true potential. If she's exceptionally bright, she might receive a spark of inspiration and discover a way to procure her own blank papers and canvases. But it's doubtful. Cultural conditioning is partly to blame. Pop culture does not value or teach the mechanics of independent thinking and creative bliss to our children. Therefore they turn to video games, cults, sex, alcohol, drugs, and other addictive agents. We don't need the stimulus of external fire when we learn to tap into our own inner, eternal and unfed flame.

The only way to develop our own creative resources and divine power is to use them – not somebody else's. It's not that drugs and medicine or even reliance on them are bad. It's the mental and emotional attitude that results from an *over-attachment* or *addiction* to them that does the harm. Because remember, anecdotal evidence and the studies on brain elasticity indicate that sometimes a drug can help train the brain to make new neurochemical pathways if the right attitude is present. If the mental/emotional/energy healing does not occur however, the new neurochemical pathways will turn into ruts and damage the brain. And if the healing is not anchored in the heart, it is not anchored at all. It's a precarious balancing act. But it's our choice.

To be on the safe side, I choose to stick to the old traditional alchemical ways of generating my own internal 'star fire' and 'gold stone' with my own music. That way I know my foundation is real and secure.

Interestingly, some channeled information from extraterrestrial sources warns about the use of the white powder gold. The chief danger seems to be the possibility of physical contamination with heavy metals. Toxins accumulate in the belly where this process begins. However, according to Gardner, after the metal assumes the form of a powder, it is no longer toxic.[96] Either way, transmutation of the personality into the fully awakened being is done not with gold powder, but with a heart of gold.

Reclaiming the Witch's Broomstick

It's an unsuspecting Hobbit that returns the ring of gold to Mount Doom. And it's Dorothy Gale from Kansas, the small and meek, who liquidates the wicked witch. What do they have in common? Humble origins, innocent integrity, unrelenting vision, single-minded purpose, and loyal friends representing being true to oneself.

When the Wizard says, "Bring me the broomstick of the Wicked Witch of the West," Dorothy and crew are clearly overwhelmed and uncertain whether this is even possible. Yet they set out on their journey anyway. That is what a spiritual aspirant does. Against seemingly insurmountable odds, we "go for the gold" as it were.

It is possible and it can be done, but it takes persistence, a lot of imagination and engaged creativity. It also involves facing fear and overcoming it. Reclaiming the broomstick from the Wicked Witch is a metaphor for reclaiming rightful ownership and control over one's own kundalini and dragon body – one's own source of power. So long as we believe it's not in our power to do so, the power remains in the hands of the muddlers represented by the Wicked Witch. As long as we continue to give our outer gold away to the priests, gurus, doctors, and New Age marketers of magical powders and potions, our inner gold diminishes in brightness.

The Good Witch tells Dorothy, "The sooner you get out of Oz altogether, the safer you'll sleep." Dorothy replies, "I'd give anything to get out of Oz altogether." The key word: *altogether.* Being altogether means being complete -- recognizing our inherent wholeness as we are. Dorothy's companions were not missing their coveted items. They just *thought* they were. Scarecrow had a brain all along. Tin Man had a heart all along. And the Cowardly Lion had courage from the very beginning. They just had to *realize* it. Same with Dorothy. Only after Dorothy returns to Oz with the broomstick of the Wicked Witch does she realize (with a little prompting from Glinda) that she always had the power to get back home. Where was it? In her ruby red slippers.

The folk tale of *The Red Shoes* has many different versions and meanings. In one version, an orphaned girl exchanges her hand-made red shoes for shiny store-bought ones. Yet there is a hidden price. The new shoes are cursed and compel her to dance uncontrollably until she dances herself to death.

Figuratively, shoes protect and defend our grounding ability and our feet – what we stand on. The feet are also symbols for freedom and mobility. Without shoes, it's hard to go anywhere. Red, being the color of blood, denotes sacrifice. Willing sacrifice for something strongly desired is one thing; red bloodshed in that case is the blood of life. But when the sacrifice is unwilling or becomes too much and too long, blood that is shed is the loss of life. According to Estés, this is what occurs in the fairy tale. The child is forced to give up her handmade shoes, and chooses counterfeit ones as a substitute. The counterfeit shoes are beautiful and magical all right; they keep her dancing seemingly forever. But that's just the problem. She dances herself to death.

According to Estés, the loss of the handmade red shoes represents the loss of a "self-designed life" made with the passionate vitality of our own values, dreams, hopes and wishes. It represents all the poor choices that led us down a road we did not intend to take. Perhaps we chose the stability and security of a dead-end job over an adventurous and risky but more fulfilling career in the arts. Perhaps we married the wrong person for the right reasons or the right person for the wrong reasons. Perhaps we simply decided to put our own health and happiness on the back burner while we tended to someone else's. It could be any number of things. Sometimes we think it's too late to turn around, but it's not.

The store-bought red shoes made by someone else are never a fully satisfying substitute for the *homemade* ones. But we treat them as if they are. Out of desperation we cling to them and become slaves to them. Unwise choices and addictions occur when the instinct is injured. These addictions can take many forms – negative thinking, abusive relationships, abusive situations, alcohol and drugs – whatever. Like the counterfeit red shoes, they just don't come off that easily. Why does this happen? How do our instincts become injured? While Estés is talking about mainly women here, the same can be said for men:

> Sometimes it is difficult for us to realize when we are losing our instincts, for it is often an insidious process that does not occur all in one day, but rather over a long period of time. Too, the loss or deadening of instinct is often entirely supported by the surrounding culture, and sometimes even by other women who endure the loss of instinct as a way of achieving belonging in a culture that keeps no nourishing habitat for the natural woman.[97]

Natural woman – let alone natural anything. Acting naturally does not come easy for anyone anymore. There's too much risk involved. People are too busy conforming, being nice, saying things they don't really mean – going along with the crowd because they don't want to appear different. This all goes back to taking the easy way out. It's not being true to oneself. Estés reminds us,

To follow such a lifeless value system causes loss of soul-linkage in the extreme. Regardless of collective affiliations or influences, our challenge in behalf of the wild soul and our creative spirit is to *not* merge with any collective, but to distinguish ourselves from those who surround us, building bridges back to them as we choose. We decide which bridges will become strong and well traveled, and which will remain sketchy and empty. And the collectives we favor with relationship will be those that offer the most support for our soul and creative life.[98]

Spiritual aspirants have to be especially mindful of this or they will not survive. The blood of our bodies and our souls is just too precious to waste. It is our strength, our energy, our life.

The ruby red slippers are representative of Dorothy's blood too, and in particular, her menstrual blood. Again, Estés reminds us:

It is said that in the matriarchal cultures of ancient India, Egypt, parts of Asia, and Turkey – which are believed to have influenced our concept of the feminine soul for thousands of miles in all directions – the bequeathing of henna and other red pigments to young girls, so that they could stain their feet with it, was a central feature in threshold rites. One of the most important threshold rites regarded first menstruation. This rite celebrated the crossing from childhood into the profound ability to bring forth life from one's belly, to carry the attendant sexual power and all peripheral womanly powers. The ceremony was concerned with red blood in all its stages: the uterine blood of menstruation, delivery of a child, miscarriage, all running downward toward the feet. As you can see, the original red shoes had many meanings.[99]

Dorothy doesn't give her red slippers to anyone else. At one point, yes, she agrees to let the wicked witch have them in exchange for preserving the life of Toto. But she finds that it's impossible. As long as she's *alive*, the shoes will not come off her feet. That's important for it means that as long as the blood is being supported by the inner fire and vital energy, we still own it. It's only when the vital energy is gone that the life is drained from us, and this is usually due to injured instinct. Toto represents instinct and he's not injured although the witch is making threats.

Dorothy doesn't give away her blood. She doesn't let the vampires suck it dry. She refuses to be a factory for the progeny of a sham sovereignty. Her own sovereignty is all that matters. She uses her ruby red slippers as the grounding vehicle and foundation for her own ability to thrive and navigate the journey. And she requires no one's permission and no one's assistance. The Tin Man, Cowardly Lion, and Scarecrow (and Toto too!) are all aspects of her being. They provide everything she needs to complete the journey and go back home.

Taking the white powder is a crude and dangerous substitute for the real thing. It is not the natural way. It's like exchanging the handmade shoes for the counterfeit ones. Addiction to it is certain death. Believing in the lie of a special, exclusive, sacred bloodline that bestows special powers and privileges us mere mortals can never have is equally absurd and destructive. We know it's a lie because their continued attempts at genetic manipulation through incestuous intermarriage did not work. It just further corrupted a gene pool that was already damaged by the destructive effects of ancestral over use of white powder and star fire. Granted, maybe every once in a while, a recessive gene popped up that contained the super-charged mitochondrial superconducting magical "mysterical" element, but so what? Psychics are a dime a dozen. And it's no guarantee that you're going to have your shit together better than anyone else.

While I will defend the civil rights of vampires as much as anyone's, the need to be a vampire or identify with one is redundant. As was said earlier, we are all vampires in a sense because we all feed on cosmic energy and the energy of everyone and everything. But to think that one must depend on the source of that energy as always coming from or being "another" – external to oneself – and to the point of addiction – is coming from a perspective of lack, not abundance. We already have everything we need. We need not become vampires to actualize it. The Goddess within is sufficient. Her riches are exhaustless. In the words of an ancient Qabalistic text,

> *From the exhaustless riches of its limitless substance,*
> *I draw all things needful, both spiritual and material.*

There are no chosen people. The desire to become special is something we all have to get over. Why? Because we're all, each and every one of us, already special! In the words of Dr. Ilchi Lee:

> This relative "specialness" is not just a matter of freedom of individual expression. It carries the unmistakable scent of competition that spirals ever upwards. All expressions of life are already special by definition. The specialness of life is absolute and not subject to a relative comparison... What is the basic compelling force being the drive to become special? It is the craving for attention that comes from the need for recognition. Turned inside out, it is the twisted expression of an ego with an inferiority complex.[100]

Dr. Lee reminds us, character comes before enlightenment. "God" is not to be worshipped but to be used. And "my body is not me, but mine." Don't give it away. Retain your sovereignty. Recognize your own true worth as a co-creator in the divine plan. This is what will get you home and keep you there.

Just *three* clicks of the heels, and you're there. Three is a magical number that appears frequently in fairy tales. In the true and authentic alchemy, coordination of three special substances are involved in this operation: sulpher (rajas), salt (tamas), and mercury (sattva). Sulphur represents the subtle fiery energy that fills the seemingly empty spaces between subatomic particles or "soul." It is invisible and subject to mental manipulation. Salt represents subconsciousness and "the body." Mercury represents superconsiousness or "spirit" -- containing everything – the source. Mercury is exalted in Virgo. Remember Virgo is the sign that governs the abdominal region. Virgo is also the sign of the virgin – the mystical bride of the dragon. Christ was born of the virgin within – whose blood, soul, and body were purified by the inner fire of the unfed flame. His dragon wings were earned, not given, and fueled by an aspiration that led to one of the most complete embodiments of Love and Wisdom the world has ever known. Because of this, the world has never been the same. He is not the chosen one. He is not the only one. Yet his essence – his blood – his life – is in our own.

Awakening the dragon is building the adytum is completing the Great Work is living the Dharma is experiencing the Great Natural Perfection is the embodiment of Spirit in our flesh. Every single aspect of our being is involved. It is establishing the kingdom of heaven on Earth as was predicted. It is here and now. And it's all within. Enjoy!

---

[1] Rick Strassman, M.D., *DMT: The Spirit Molecule*, Park Street Press, 2001.

[2] *Id.*, p. 81.

[3] *Id.*, p. 39.

[4] *Id.*, p. 54.

[5] *Id.*, p. 74.

[6] *Id.*, p. 146.

[7] *Id.*, pp. 177-178.

[8] *Id.*, pp. 178-179, 181.

[9] *Id.*, p. 182.

[10] *Id.*, p. 195.

[11] *Id.*, p. 199.

[12] *Id.*, p. 209.

[13] *Id.*, pp. 214-215.

[14] *Id.*, pp. 270-271.

[15] *Id.*, p. 314.

[16] *Id.*, pp. 318-319.

[17] Sogyal Rinpoche, *The Tibetan Book of Living and Dying,* Harper Books, 1992, p. 168.

[18] D.J. Conway, *Dancing with Dragons*, Llewellyn Publications, 1997, p. 19.

[19] Mark Amaru Pinkham, *The Return of the Serpents of Wisdom*, Adventures Unlimited Press, 1997, p. 338. Reprinted with permission.

[20] Bruce D. Perry, M.D., Ph.D. et al., "Persisting Psychophysiological Effects of Traumatic Stress: The Memory of 'States'," *Violence Update,* 1:98), 1-11, 1991.

[21] Perry, B., M.D., Ph.D., "Neurological Sequelae of Childhood Trauma: Post-traumatic Stress Disorders in Children. The Child Trauma Academy: *Catecholamine Function in Post-Traumatic Stress Disorder: Emerging Concept, 1997..*

[22] David Kinchin, "Complex PTSD and Trauma Caused by Bullying, Harassment and Abuse," *Post Traumatic Stress Disorder: The Invisible Injury*, UK: Success Unlimited, reprinted at www.bullyonline.org.

[23] *Id.*

[24] *Id.*

[25] Dr. Ilchi Lee, *The Twelve Enlightenments for Healing Society*, Hampton Roads Publishing, 2002, p. 103. Reprinted with permission.

[26] *Id.*, p. 104.

[27] *Id.*, pp. 80-83.

[28] *Id.*

[29] "Taming Destructive Emotions," an interview with Daniel Goleman, *Tricycle: The Buddhist Review,* Spring, 2003, p. 75.

[30] Neil R. Carson, *The Physiology of Behavior,* Allyn and Bacon, 1977, p. 455.

[31] Goleman in *Tricycle*, p. 78.

[32] Marshall Glickman, "The Lama in the Lab," *Tricycle: The Buddhist Review,* Spring, 2003, p. 73. Reprinted with permission.

[33] *Id.*, p. 72.

[34] Pinkham, p. 352.

[35] Itzhak Bentov, *Stalking the Wild Pendulum,* Bantam Books, 1977, pp. 212-233.

[36] *Id.*, p. 220.

[37] *Id.*, p. 222.

[38] *Id.,* pp. 225-226.

[39] Corinne Heline, *Esoteric Music Based on the Musical Seership of Richard Wagner,* New Age Press, 1980, pp. 249-250. Reprinted with permission.

[40] Gareth Knight, *The Secret Tradition in Arthurian Legend*, Samuel Weiser, Inc., 1996, p. 35. Reprinted by permission from Red Wheel/Weiser.

[41] Zecharia Sitchin, "The Case of Adam's Alien Genes," published at http://www.sitchin.com/adam.htm; see also Neil Freer, "An Expanded Context for Genetic Exploration and Explanation" published at http://www.neilfreer.com/index11.htm.

[42] Flindt, Max H. and Binder, Otto O., *Mankind: Child of the Stars*, Ozark Publishing, 1999, pp. 135-163.

[43] Noel Huntley, http://www.users.globalnet.co.uk/~noelh.

[44] Barbara Marciniak, http://home-2.worldonline.nl/~gibbon/dna.htm.

[45] Mary-Margareht Rose, http://www.themessenger.cc.

[46] *Id.*

[47] Jean-Claude Perez, "The DNA Supra-Code: Discovery, Proves and Evidence of the Hidden Language of DNA," September, 2000, geNum lab, http://www.genum.com/dna_supracode/dan_supracode.htm.

[48] *Id.*

[49] Erik Davis, "Tongues of Fire, Whirlwinds of Noise: Images of Spiritual Information," *Gnosis*, No. 23, Spring, 1992. Reprinted with permission.

[50] Paul White, "The Secrets of Thoth," http://www. newage.com/au/library/thoth.html.

[51] *Id.*

[52] Sabrina Mesko, *Gestures of Power*, Sounds True Video, 1997. This is an excellent instructional video!

[53] From private e-mail correspondence with Ms. Miller.

[54] Katherine Ramsland, *Piercing the Darkness: Undercover with Vampires in America Today*, HarperPrism, 1998.

[55] Konstantinos, *Vampires: The Occult Truth*, Llewellyn Publications, 1996.

[56] Ramsland, p. 240.

[57] *Id.*, p. 239.

[58] *Id.*

[59] Katherine Ramsland, *The Science of Vampires*, Berkley Boulevard Books, 2002.

[60] Hugh Colmer, "Celestial Fire: Virgin Blood," http://www.crosscircle.com/celestial_%20Fire.htm. Reprinted with permission.

[61] *Id.*

[62] *Id.*

[63] Clarissa Pinkola Estés, *Women Who Run With the Wolves*, Ballantine Books, 1992, p. 293.

[64] Colmer, see Internet citation above.

[65] Zecharia Sitchin, *The Lost Book of Enki*, Bear & Company, 2002, p. 174.

[66] Alexandra David-Neel, *Initiations and Initiates in Tibet*, Dover Publications, 1931 (1993), pp. 37-38.

[67] Nicholas De Vere, "From Transylvania to Tunbridge Wells", http://www.dragoncourt.org.

[68] Gardner, "Realm of the Ring Lords" lecture, http://www.geocities.com/CapitolHill/Parliament/3460/lords1.html; see also *Realm of the Ring Lords*, Fair Winds Press, 2002. Reprinted with permission.

[69] *Id.*

[70] *Id.*; also see book of the same title.

[71] *Id.*

[72] *Id.*

[73] See DeVere at http://www.geocities.com/newworldorder_themovie/DragonsRant.

[74] Richard Bach, *Illusions: The Adventures of a Reluctant Messiah*, Dell Publishing, 1977, p. 128.

[75] Heline, p. 243.

[76] *Id.*, p. 244.

[77] *Id.*, p. 206.

[78] *Id.*, p. 243.

[79] Laurence Gardner, *Genesis of the Grail* Kings, Fair Winds Press, 2001, pp. 253-254. Reprinted with permission.

[80] Laurence Gardner, "The Powder of Projection: 21st-Century Science Casts New Light on an Ancient Mystery," *Atlantis Rising*, No. 40, July/August, 2003, p. 39. Reprinted with permission.

[81] David Hudson, "Superconductivity and Modern Alchemy: Has the Philosopher's Stone Been Found?" published at http://www.karenlyster.com/hudson.html.

[82] Gardner, 2003, p. 67.

[83] Gardner, 2001, p. 257.

[84] Hudson, see previous Internet citation.

[85] *Id.*

[86] *Id.*

[87] Mary Anne Atwood, *A Suggestive Inquiry of the Hermetic Mystery*, William Tait, 1918.

[88] http://www.heartmath.org/research/research-overview.html.

[89] *Id.*

[90] *Id.*

[91] *Id.*

[92] *Id.*

[93] *Id.*

[94] Lama Surya Das quoting Tarthang Tulku in *Letting Go of the Person You Used to Be: Lessons on Change, Loss, and Spiritual Transformation,* Broadway Books, 2003, p. 113.

[95] http://www.heartmath.org, previously cited.

[96] from a lecture given by Sir Laurence Gardner in Tempe, Arizona, November 24, 2003.

[97] Estés, pp. 249-250.

[98] *Id.*, p. 227.

[99] *Id.*, p. 235.

[100] Lee, p. 47.

PART 6

Closing Encounters

If you learn music, you'll learn history. If you learn music, you'll learn mathematics. If you learn music, you'll learn most all there is to learn.

-- Edgar Cayce

CHAPTER 9

MUSIC IS KEY: THE MAGIC OF SOUND, COLOR, AND IMAGERY

A universally accepted definition of music is not necessary or even possible. To an avant-garde musician, a couple of kids banging garbage can lids in the alley is music; to others, merely noise. Animals make a peculiar music all their own. And what about silence? Well sure enough, the American composer John Cage composed a piece called 4'33" – four minutes and thirty-three seconds of silence. In performing this composition, the musician walks out on stage, sits down in front of any instrument that might be at hand, and continues to sit for four minutes and thirty-three seconds. He makes no noise and does not play an instrument. Is that music?

Music is art and art is experience, and experience is whatever we want it to be. But always there are sounds, so always there is music. Music is first and foremost vibration. I'm limiting my discussion to music as "organized sound" or sound which has been created and arranged in such a way to be presented to others in a form usually recognizable as music. Words sometimes stand in the way of true understanding. That's why I always suggest that the best way to learn about music is simply to listen to it.

The Elements of Music

What most of us recognize as music is usually comprised of one or any combination of three elements: rhythm, melody, and harmony. Rhythm is musical time. Tones are either short or long, and these lengths are constructed into note values indicated by the notation of meter. Rhythm is also pulse – the beat. It can be regular, irregular or both. Rhythm can be strong or weak, accented or not, or both. Either way, it keeps on moving. Melody is musical line – a succession of single tones perceived by the mind as a unity, like words making up a sentence. All the tones, like the words, relate to one another in such a way as to convey meaning. They make a recognizable pattern that can be repeated. They can go up or down or stay the same, but they're always moving forward. Melody is always going somewhere. Harmony is musical space. Harmony is created by the relationship of tones to each other as they are played together or in close proximity to one another. The blending of tonal values creates harmony. Harmony is to music what depth perspective is to visual art. Playing or singing two or more melodic lines together creates harmony. Harmony is also background or foreground – especially if the rhythmic changes emphasize shifts in harmony, such as playing chords on guitar. I like to think of harmony as encapsulating – surrounding everything, like space.

Other factors influence these three dimensions of music. There's tempo for example, which is musical speed. Tempo is how fast or slow the music is played. Dynamics refers to musical volume – how loud or soft the music is. Tempo and dynamics enable music to be especially expressive. Another aspect of musical sound is timbre which is like musical color. Timbre is the unique quality of sound produced by individual instruments. Timbre enables us to distinguish between the sounds of a flute and a violin, for instance. Timbre is often determined by the physical structure of the instrument and how it's played.

Form is musical structure and design. A basic musical form is three-part or "A-B-A." Any song which has three parts consisting of a first and last verse and a chorus in the middle fits this form. Obviously form ranges from the very simple to the highly complex. Often complexity in form is the standard by which great genius in artistic expression is judged.

Then there is musical style. Style is the way something comes across – the individual's unique manner of presentation. Style can be broad or narrow, old or new. It can even be timeless. Style is the essence of a work of art. Style reflects the original identity of a century, decade, a small group of people like a rock band, or a singular individual. It's how we distinguish between genres of music and musicians. Style is the way you do it. And no matter what anyone says, you can never be without style. You have your own style somewhere in there, even if you can't pin it down. Being yourself is being your own style. Being in style is simply "being." Think about that one.

All these various elements provide the essential building blocks for music from an acoustic perspective.

The Psychology of Music

The psychology of music as it's taught in most universities is the study of the observable effects of music on behavior. The word "observable" is key because conventional academia seldom allow for the subjective effects of music to be recorded. The reason is because they do not believe that the subjective aspects are measurable unless they're accounted for in terms of heart rate, blood pressure, or galvanic skin response. These music psychologists also tend to tear apart the elements of music until music is reduced to practically nothing and is lost underneath the analysis of it. In discussing the language aspects of music, they talk about "designative meaning" – "embodied meaning" – and "alleged" mode and key effects. Well, music is not on trial here so we can do away with the word "alleged" right now. Beethoven felt that different musical keys had their own individual effects, same as many other musicians and nonmusicians. If different keys are felt to have different effects, then they do – at least according to individual perception and experience. The effects may not be identical for all, but an effect is an effect all the same.

Other facets of the conventional psychology of music include observations on musical taste sometimes leading to the absurdity of "measuring" musical taste. I don't believe musical taste can be measured any more than culinary taste can. Can you measure how bad or good spinach tastes to me? Of course not because I'm the only one who possesses my taste buds. I can tell you how I think it tastes, or I can spit it out with a look of disgust on my face and you can infer something from that behavior, but you cannot pin it down to an accurate measurement of some kind. So it's not really taste that's being measured, but only what one *reports* about taste. These scientists also like to pretend they can measure musical ability. Don't let them fool you though. We all have our own individual and diverse yardsticks to go by.

Music psychology is often applied to industry and therapy. For instance, most of us have experienced the retail outlet that plays some kind of programmed music in the background because some research suggested that certain types of music put people in a buying mood. I don't know about you, but this technique doesn't work with me. I can remember many occasions where I deliberately left the store before I bought anything simply because I did *not* like the music being played. But then that may just be me. I'm hypersensitive to music and so not one of those people who can easily ignore it or who doesn't even hear it half the time.

The psychology of music spawned the scientific discipline of music therapy. Music therapy as defined by the National Association for Music Therapy as using music as a *tool* in therapy. A registered music therapist receives certification through a national board after obtaining a college degree from an approved school and after serving an internship in an approved clinical setting. Though many researchers have traced the development of music therapy in its purest sense to ancient times, today the field has a narrow focus and is highly regulated. In defense of the discipline however, music therapists have had astounding success in the treatment of autistic children. Still, tasks are limited to activities having specific objectives with a measurable outcome. For instance, a music therapist might help a moderately to severely retarded child learn to put toothpaste on a toothbrush to the tune of "Twinkle, Twinkle Little Star." They often lead groups of geriatric patients in a round of wheelchair eurhythmics, which is simply moving to music. These tasks do not require much creativity, but demand patience and skill writing out behavioral objectives and strategies. Like Dr. Michel says, these music therapists are first and foremost behavioral scientists.[1] Music to them may or may not be an art, but it is certainly a tool in a mechanistic approach to well-being. Thank goodness it is only one approach.

Music as a Universal Language – Literally

Music can mean a lot of different things to a lot of different people. And no matter what music means to anyone, experiencing it evokes feelings in response to it. In that sense, the *experience* of music is truly universal.

The idea that music is a universal language has been disputed. The small minority of dissidents are primarily scientists and linguists so caught up in their own areas of specialization, their limited scope prevents them from seeing beyond cultural differences to similarities in context. For instance: Nearly all human societies use music as a form of communication or self-expression. Just because a student from Malaysia might not understand the meaning of a Beatles song doesn't mean that they don't recognize the fact that the music is a vehicle for communication. In that context alone, music is a universal language. All language, whether it be comprised of words, tones, squeaks, grunts or chirps – is SOUND – and SOUND is VIBRATION; and VIBRATION is the foundation for all existence.

Assuming that music is a universal language, we can borrow from linguistics to enhance our understanding of it. Mastering music theory is much like mastering the mechanics of a foreign language. But being well versed in the mechanics of any language alone will not help us understand why it has specific effects on particular people. Particular combinations of words or musical tones can have a profound effect on the human psyche – and most linguists and musicologists are at a loss to explain why. Researchers in the psychology of music have attempted to get at the bottom of this but haven't had much success. Why? Because similar to many UFOlogists, these scientists choose to study phenomena from a limited, restricted, materialist point of view. We're dealing with multidimensions that encompass not just the physical and psychological realms, but the spiritual realm as well. Two personal stories out of the 1980s illustrate this.

On a cool spring evening in 1982, Dr. John Miller's advanced meditation class at North Texas State University had a pleasant surprise in store for them. Four men and seven women were to participate in an experiment involving an unusual experience with music. The guest speaker for the evening had chosen four musical compositions for them to listen to during meditation. These were her instructions:

> There are specific colors, symbolism, and imagery connected with these musical compositions. Your purpose in meditation is to discover these colors, symbols, and images as you are listening to the music. After each piece, you will remain silent and write down a total description of the colors, symbols, and images you received. After the conclusion of the experiment, I will collect your papers for analyzing later. So this is kind of like an ESP experiment, except that the *music* is serving as a transmitter instead of a person.

The lights were dimmed, Dr. Miller led them into the meditative state, and the music began. In the darkness one could see the faint outlines of human figures against the shadowy backdrop of a flickering candle flame. A haunting flute melody led them into its own inner world.

After all was said and done, data examined, and results determined, the students' experience with that little flute melody provided the most convincing evidence of all -- experiential evidence that music communicates to us far more than we suspect.

This particular composition was completely unknown. The only persons in the world who had ever heard this music before were the composer and the flutist. More importantly, this music was structurally organized and highly integrated with the specific colors, symbolism, and numerology of an ancient archetypal image. Everyone saw the two predominant colors of the image. Everyone also experienced the corresponding imagery and symbolism to some degree.

What does this mean and what is it good for? First, another example.

On November 14, 1985, the San Antonio City Council voted seven to three to censor rock concerts for children under age thirteen not accompanied by a parent or a guardian. The city became the first in the nation to enact an ordinance restricting certain language about violence and explicit sex in artistic performances. Promoters and directors of events in city-owned facilities were held responsible for advertising certain performers as "unsuitable" for children, and violations were punishable by a maximum fine of $200.00. Supporters of the ordinance didn't think it was strict enough. Opponents were outraged and called it an embarrassment to the city, locally and nationally.

It didn't stop rock'n'roll in San Antonio. One only needed to listen to Joe Anthony's "Godfather of Rock" show Saturday nights on KISS, 99.5 FM, and hear the hoards of young rockers call in and request their favorite tunes – particularly songs by hard rock heavy metal bands such as AC/DC, Judas Priest, and others of the "Filthy Fifteen." Joe ends the conversation not with "goodbye" but with "rock 'n' roll!" The kids respond, "rock 'n' roll!" It's a ritual. And to some, these rituals take on strong religious overtones:

> The narration or ritual repetition of sacred texts and ceremonies, and the worship of such a figure (any hero-god image) with dances, hymns, prayers, and sacrifices, grip the audience with numinous emotions (as if with magic spells) and exalts the individual to an identification with the hero.[2]

Now if that doesn't sound like a rock concert, what does?

522

During this dark decade fundamentalist Christians felt particularly threatened by this music, and sought to influence government to censor this form of freedom of expression. But it was more than one religion's fear of being replaced by a pseudo-religion; it was symbolic of a coming change in social consciousness. What tried to occur in the late sixties was trying to occur once more with added strength and determination. The political power behind the music of the sixties and early seventies didn't fully lead to liberation because the people are the politics. Muddlers know this well and fully use it to their advantage. "Yippies" become "yuppies" addicted to consumerism and indentured to the world of work and spiraling personal debt. The popular music begins to reflect this, the new movement is stopped in its tracks and the power wanes. Still the flame smolders in the occasional song of protest, and has the potential to blaze forth again, as foretold in Rage Against the Machine's "Wake Up" auspiciously played at the end of the movie, *The Matrix*.

Music has the power to change minds, hearts and souls. Therefore, it has the power to change the world. It also has the power to change the very molecular composition of our physical bodies, especially in healing. It has the power to move stones, as has been demonstrated by contemporary Tibetan monks and ancient cultures. Further and most importantly, it has the power to communicate where words cannot – it can cross cultural, ethnic and religious boundaries – it can even cross worldly boundaries as a particularly effective means by which to communicate with ETs – peoples of different worlds -- as has already been demonstrated by CSETI and others working within a CE-5 context.

Again, why is this true? Because as was said earlier, music is first and foremost vibration – and so is everything else. And yet it's more than that – as everything is as well. It's certainly more than just a form of entertainment. Some research and anecdotal experience suggests that the properties of music may be just as important to our psychic bodies as food is to our physical bodies. If this is true, then that would mean that our personal "diet" of music can be too much or too little, nutritious or unhealthy. Yet music, like food, is neither good nor bad in itself; it all depends on what we do with it.

Music Parapsychology and the Esoteric Psychology of Music

This was my special area of research in graduate school which I naively thought was going to lead to the advent of a new discipline called music parapsychology. But unlike most pioneers who go on to accomplish great things, I allowed personal problems and responsibilities to distract me from the goal, and alas, my mission was postponed. Finally, others have taken up where I left off, and that is good. Still, I have yet to see anyone come close to the conclusions I reached in graduate school. Therefore, let me tell you how I got there, because we all must begin somewhere.

I began as a small child of four hiding underneath my parents' bed in a ridiculous ballet suit. Why was I hiding? Because I didn't want to go to ballet class. Why did I not want to go to ballet class? Because the teacher was insisting that we learn to "gallop." I knew how to skip, but for some reason, I couldn't bring myself to "gallop." So I wouldn't come out from underneath the bed until my mother promised I wouldn't have to go. It worked! (My first successful political protest.)

So my mother, the wise soul that she was, took another look at what my talents might be and noticed that I spent a lot of time just fiddling around on the piano though I could barely reach the keyboard. She asked if I would rather take piano lessons. I agreed, as this seemed more interesting and certainly more sensible than "galloping."

According to my mother's observations, I was deeply affected by music for my age. Even before I could barely walk, whenever she put music on the stereo – especially classical music -- I would crawl up into the huge reclining chair in the den and sit still for hours just listening. It was as if the music held me in some sort of trance.

President John F. Kennedy was assassinated when I was in second grade. The fact that he bore my namesake only added to my sadness. When I got home from school, I went straight to the piano and began improvising my own variations on the theme of "America."

Some people are so moved by the sounds of certain strains of music that they cry. I am one of those. According to researcher/musician/recording artist Steven Halpern, this is good because it means the music is reaching the soul. "Crying is a holistically human sound experience. Crying is a sign that you are in touch with your soul. It is also a sign to others that you are present at the level of soul."[3]

I've had countless mystical experiences while listening to music, and not just with classical music. One of my most exhilarating moments was at the 1975 Rolling Stones concert at the Cottonbowl Stadium in Dallas, Texas, and I wasn't on drugs. The music was my drug!

Everyone at one time or another is drawn to a song with which they feel a special affinity, and whenever they hear that song the same feelings are evoked. This phenomenon is not exclusive to love and love-lost songs. Sometimes some of us read messages in lyrics that somehow seem to have a personalized meaning for us, regardless of what the lyricist intended. Special events in our lives are often tagged by songs that were popular during that time. These are some of the lighter ways in which the power of music affects us, and may result from the power of association more than the direct power of music. Most of us have no problem accepting this power.

What is not universally accepted, however, is that the music of a particular time not only reflects, but also projects, enhances, and changes predominant states of mass consciousness, and that this is part of a divine plan for the evolution of humanity. A metaphysical book by the late British composer, Cyril Scott, entitled, *Music: Its Secret Influence Throughout the Ages,* explores this idea at length.[4] Scott summarizes the specific influence of the music of particular classical composers, yet he reveals an unwarranted bias towards other forms of music, particularly jazz and popular music. This is unfortunate because not only is it elitist -- it completely ignores the occult truth that nothing is good or bad in itself. All depends on how it's used.

My love for music was so deep that I wanted to devote my entire life to it. This love propelled me through years of music lessons, music collecting, and composing music, eventually going to college and getting a degree in music. But it wasn't enough for me to simply bask in that love and enjoy it; I wanted to know *why* it made me feel that way. I wanted to know *how* it was so deeply transformative. What was it about music that literally made me want to dedicate my whole life to it?

During my undergraduate years, I began to research the esoteric or little known occult or spiritual aspects and effects of music on my own. I joined a witch's coven to become familiar with the use of music in a ritual and healing setting. At the same time, I attended Unity Church of Christianity for a different perspective on sacred music. I read all the books I could get my hands on about this subject, and there were few. I attended numerous rock concerts in an effort to experience that approach to the transformative power of music. I had countless questions about how music changes our consciousness, and I soon discovered that most musicians, musicologists, including witches and Christians – didn't have a clue.

So I turned to the study of music therapy. I spent two semesters of graduate work in this area at Texas Women's University in Denton, Texas in the early eighties. At that time, music therapy was a marginal discipline, struggling to retain its academic credibility by adhering to a rigid and mechanistic scientific approach to research and application that severely limited any creativity on the part of the students. Behaviorism was "in" and therefore the field was intensely regulated and excluded any recognition of a therapeutic power inherent in the music itself. Music was reduced to slave status, nothing more. Disillusioned with this approach, I left T.W.U. and went next door to North Texas State University, known today as University of North Texas, an institution long recognized for its distinguished music school. At first, I focused on composition because I'd been writing songs since I was big enough to reach the keyboard. But due to the intensive course work in psychology I was exposed to during my brief encounter with music therapy, I opted for the interdisciplinary program essentially resulting in a dual degree in music and psychology. When thesis time came, no professor would even consider my proposed topic which was something like, "The Mysticism of Sound: Occult, Mystical, and Spiritual Effects of Music." I was forced, fortunately, for my own good, to make the project an experimental study entitled, "Sound, Color, and Imagery Correlations Manifesting in the Nature of Psi." Three professors had to sign off on this special research project – one from each of the main disciplines involved: music, psychology and philosophy. The surprising results of this little study combined with other course work in parapsychology and personal study in psychotronics opened my eyes to the secret power of music more than anything previously encountered.

I composed a piece for solo flute entitled "The Fool" that was based on the sound/color correlations of the Tarot key by that name. Since the predominant color of the key and what it represents is yellow, and since yellow correlates to the tone E, I composed the piece centric on E. Keep in mind that this was music not previously heard by anyone except me and the flutist who recorded it for me. Without telling some meditation students anything about the music, I asked them to listen to it while meditating with the goal of the meditation being to receive the colors, symbols, and imagery associated with the music. Afterwards, I asked them to write down the imagery and symbolism received. All of them recorded imagery and symbolism related to *The Fool*. Of course, there were variations on some of the symbols, however, the correlation was clear. All the subjects saw yellow as the predominant color. Because the data was nonparametric, statistical significance could not be determined. This was a pilot study so I didn't have a baseline. It became clear to me that too many variables were at play anyway. For instance, was the music somehow

527

transmitting this imagery to them, or was it just my own telepathic suggestions? Maybe it was just the extraordinary abilities of the students or a combination of all these things. Who knows? At any rate, this was the most important outcome of the study, and the one that haunts me to this day.

The following section is comprised of excerpts from the study, the results of which are incorporated into a discussion of the role of music in relation to extraterrestrial intelligence and renewing the cosmic connection. The study was conducted during the spring of 1982 at N.T.S.U. While the review of the pertinent literature may be dated, the general conclusions are not.

The Experiment

Sound, Color, and Imagery Correlations Manifesting in the Nature of Psi

Introduction

An esoteric psychology of music outside most academic circles explores the unconventional, metaphysical, or occult aspects of sound and music. Numerous books in the esoteric literature explore (1) what the various religious, mystical and occult traditions teach about the power of sound, color and imagery, (2) the use of sound, color and imagery in healing, ritual, and meditation, and (3) a metaphysical interpretation of the creative process: mystical, spiritual, or paranormal experiences composers often have which sometimes include the projection of archetypal images and symbolism into their music, consciously and unconsciously. To my knowledge, the research in this area remains historical, anecdotal, and philosophical. This study may be the first attempt to experimentally test some of these esoteric ideas related to music. Therefore, I propose the advent of a new discipline called "music parapsychology" - - the study of the unconventional or paranormal aspects and effects of sound and music from a scientific perspective.

528

The first part of the study tested the ability of subjects to properly assess the musical tones corresponding to two colors taken from a sound-color scale widely used by occult aspirants in a particular branch of the Third Order of the Western Mystery Tradition. (See Table 1.) Therefore, Tarot and astrological correspondences are also noted in the table. The second part of the study tested the ability of subjects to receive and assess colors, images, and archetypal symbolism associated with specific music while listening to the music during meditation.

In the first test, musical tones correlated with colors were the targets, whereas in the second test the colors were the targets, associated with the predominant harmonic structure of the music. So it is assumed that these sound-color correlations manifest in the context of pitch and key. For Instance, "F" as yellow-green may refer to a particular pitch in a musical composition or to the center of tonality or key of a piece, such as F Major, F Minor, or F Lydian mode. This is how a particular piece of music could correspond to a general color while containing various pitches, because it is the key or major harmony predominating from the particular combinations of those pitches that produces the color. This variable is noted in the description of the particular music used.

Table 1

SOUND-COLOR SCALE[5]

MUSICAL TONE	COLOR	TAROT KEY	ASTROLOGICAL CORRESPONDENCE
C	Red	4, 16, 20	Aries, Mars, Pluto
C Sharp (D Flat)	Red-Orange	5	Taurus
D	Orange	6, 19	Gemini, Sun
D Sharp (E Flat)	Yellow-Orange	7	Cancer

E	Yellow	0, 1, 8	Uranus, Mercury, Leo
F	Yellow-Green	9	Virgo
F Sharp (G Flat)	Green	3, 11	Venus, Libra
G	Blue-Green	13	Scorpio
G Sharp (A Flat)	Blue	2, 12, 14	Moon, Neptune, Sagittarius
A	Blue-Violet	15, 21	Capricorn, Saturn
A Sharp (B Flat)	Violet	10, 17	Jupiter, Aquarius
B	Red-Violet	18	Pisces

Review of Literature

The notion that the communicative aspects and effects of music only exist if they can be quantified solely in the cognitive and physiological realms is a major obstacle in music research. The unconscious and precognitive realms are totally ignored.[6] Perhaps the most significant and frequent way music communicates thoughts, feelings, ideas, or images, is the same way most psi phenomena occur – through a psychic medium or in a telepathic nature like ESP.

At the 28th International Conference of the Parapsychology Foundation, Dr. Paul Byers presented a paper entitled "Nonverbal Communication and ESP." Since music also operates as nonverbal communication, the correlation is obvious. Byers feels that information can be *shared* rather than transmitted, and that the communication is more a matter of dynamic relationships rather than cause-effect events. In support of his idea, he cites several research studies indicating that communication is analogous to message transfer -- particularly studies indicating that eye contact between people can affect arousal level, even though no finite or concrete bits of information are transferred. Byers draws a holistic conclusion suggesting that reality is much different from what we normally perceive it to be, and that the external world is only a vibrational *representation* of reality; in essence, reality is only constructed within the mind.

Dr. Martin Ruderfer, New York engineer and physicist, represented an entirely different perspective in his paper entitled "Neutrino Theory of Psi Phenomenon." His insights might reveal how the subtler or disguised vibrations of music are communicated. Ruderfer feels that telepathy might result when a remote brain detects electrical activity in the brain broadcast by the neutrino sea. He states that neutrinos have several properties which make them possible carriers of such information: (1) They represent a form of unobserved energy, and the interaction of such energy can account for psi, (2) They can interact with matter, (3) They can energetically couple with living cells, (4) The properties of neutrino scattering (such as immunity to physical barriers) match the properties required for the extrasensory transfer of information, (5) Such neutrino scattering has been observed by scientists, and (6) This scattering is intrinsically detectable by living tissue.[7] Ruderfer also pointed out that psi often seems to be guided by some kind of intelligence inferring that the mind is not wholly contained within the brain. He proposes an X factor coming into play as an information source during psi interactions having access to past and future events affecting our lives.

Dr. Luther D. Rudolph suggests that elementary particles might not directly interact with the brain, but instead create a field effect to which the brain might be sensitive.[8] It has long been held by occultists that the subtler effects of music occur through the interactions of the vibratory rates of the colors in the aura or energy-field surrounding and interpenetrating the body.[9] This field has partially been photographed with Kirlian photography. An energy process at subatomic levels where vibration is seen to consolidate into mass long before any physical evidence of a tumor or disease emerges has also been observed by clairvoyants and via Kirlian motion pictures. This suggests that physiological processes and potential disorders

531

arise out of an imbalance or disorganization on mental and emotional levels first, thus outwardly reflecting our internal states of awareness.[10]

Dr. William Tiller of Stanford University has done experiments using ultrasonic waves in affecting the colloidal structure of individual cells.[11] This colloidal structure has also been found to be extremely sensitive to the impact of thought and feeling patterns as well. Occultism teaches that thoughts and feelings have their own vibratory frequencies roughly corresponding to those within the spectrum of color.

Psychotronics, sometimes linked with radionics and psychoenergetics, is basically the study of the interaction of the psyche with electronic waves, and the generation and interaction of those waves by such psychic media as brain cells or electronic instruments.[12] The sensor can be a life-system or an electromechanical device. Implicit in the operation of psychotronics principles is that everything in our environment vibrates, and vibration of whatever kind can either be measured or perceived by sentient systems, and that the very basis of life is vibration itself. Vibratory motion that is harmonious within and throughout various systems is beneficial to those systems. Accordingly, inharmonious motion can have an adverse effect on those systems.

At the 1980 United States Psychotronics Association Conference, Joan Orion discussed a study by Dr. Valerie Hunt, a specialist in kinesiology at UCLA. Dr. Hunt's study involved a model of mind-body changes at the subatomic level relating changes in coherence and structural integration to the holographic model. This model particularly applied to myofosseal tissue, which can be likened to "guide-wires" serving to align and support body mass and the gravitation of the electromagnetic field, with the assumption that improved efficiency of this system must involve energy-field coherence. Reactions were observed on the oscilloscope, sonar equipment, and voice print equipment using FM frequencies. In recording the various voice prints (frequencies of sounds taken off the human body in this case), electrodes were placed in the approximate area of the chakras. Immediate correlations were found between what was happening in the physical tissue and in the color around the body and the way in which the tissue changed.

For instance, an audience was exposed to the voice print of "red" taken from bodies in intense pain. This particular print had a siren-type form in it that made the audience feel very uncomfortable. Electronic adjustments eliminated the siren sound, and the audience began to adapt more easily to the red in their own auras. Yellow was the color perceived to be the most musical wandering tone, always prevalent within the mental processes of intellectualization and memorization, taking on very broad waves resembling an uneven sine wave with an occasional slow rounded peak. Yellow is the color attributed to much of Bach's music by Cyril Scott, who states that the "mission" of this music – along with most contrapuntal music – was to enhance and develop the intellectual capacities of the human being.[13]

Expressed in proportional numbers only, Dr. Hunt's team found the color red to correspond to a range of 0 to 6,000 Hertz. Pain was recorded in frequencies in the range of 100 to 300 Hertz, meaning that the body has to "down gear" tremendously from its potential to go into pain, regardless of I.Q. They found that colors such as blue, white, and violet corresponding to higher frequencies up to 250,000 (the highest taken off the human body) were found to disrupt lower frequencies, thus eliminating pain. Sonograms and waveform frequency analysis were used in these experiments along with a unique living instrument – a clairvoyant. The clairvoyant's observations immediately coincided with and were confirmed by data recorded by the mechanical instrumentation.

Dr. Hunt's team was also able to make direct correlations between creative imaging and sensory awareness techniques in the induction of higher frequency states in the energy field.[14] The fact that Dr. Hunt's frequencies do not exactly correlate with those from the spectrum of visible light does not negate the findings. No data has ever indicated that the eye and brain processing centers only interpret colors in the high Kilohertz frequencies.

Music is first and foremost vibration and so is life. Ancient mystery schools of Ageless Wisdom have long taught that the nucleus of every human cell is formed around a seed atom of perfection, and healing involves the release of that perfection so that it can become manifest in the mind and body through musical vibration.[15]   Many treatises describe the various philosophical approaches to the mysticism of sound and music, from the use of sound, mantra and chanting in ritual and meditation, to the specific effects of various composers' music in the transformation of states of consciousness.   The Sufis strongly believe that music leads to liberation of the soul and to union with God.[16]   Cyril Scott's book, written from a theosophical slant, discusses this aspect of music in detail. Scott says that music shapes our souls through predominant colors emitted by the vibrations of the music blending with the colors in our auras.   Whatever quality the color represents will increase that quality in the human soul through the principle of sympathetic resonance.[17]   In light of recent psychotronics research, this proposition is not as outlandish as it may initially seem, especially when considering the following statement by Dr. William Tiller:

> A basic idea in radionics is that each individual organism or material radiates and absorbs energy via a unique wave field which exhibits certain geometrical frequency and radiation-type characteristics. This is an extended force field that exists around all forms of matter whether they be animate or inanimate. A useful analogy here is the physical atom that is continually radiating electromagnetic energy in the forms of waves because of its oscillating electric dipole moment and its thermal vibrations. Regions of space associated with a given phase angle of the wave constitute a three dimensional network of points in resonance with the particular gland of the entity. The capability

of scanning the waveform of the gland exists for the detection of any abnormalities. Likewise, if energy having the normal or healthy waveform of the gland is "pumped" into any of these specific network points, the gland will be driven in the normal or healthy mode. This produces a tendency for its structure to reorganize itself in closer alignment with the normal structure; healing of the gland occurs. Cells born in the presence of this polarizing field tend to grow in a healthier configuration which weakens the original field of the abnormal or diseased structure.[18]

Author Corrine Heline believes that music and sound have a particular place in releasing or reawakening an inherent divinity or pattern of perfection within us all.[19] Scott writes that certain music was inspired and created specifically for this task – for raising our own "vibratory rate" so to speak, in order to perceive spiritual or universal truth more readily than before, whether the composer was conscious of the process or not.[20]

Bonewits, in a talk entitled "A Psychic Exploration of Music" given at the 1974 Gnostic Aquarian Festival, discussed many important factors involving the unconscious receptive and projective qualities of the communicative aspects of music. She suggested that anyone undertaking a serious study of composers speaking on the creative process will find a peculiar phrase almost appearing with the consistency of a stereotype. It's a phrase in which the composer describes composition as a kind of "fishing process" – usually saying something to the effect that "something *fell into me*" or "something came *through* me." Ageless Wisdom teaches that a collective fabric of sound surrounds us at all times, similar to C.G. Jung's collective unconscious, from which musical patterns or motifs can be drawn in the same manner as symbols and archetypal images. This collective fabric is like the subconscious mind of God. What we consider our own individual subconsciousness is just a bay or small inlet merging into this great ocean of infinite awareness. This principle accounts for many cases of simultaneous scientific discovery and also illustrates the mechanics of telepathy. It also reveals how music communicates its deeper messages. Everything is interconnected. On the physical plane, this "cosmic consciousness" is demonstrated by the innumerable patterns of subatomic radiations constantly emitted and traveling at infinite speeds, uniting all life into an eternal now – an omnipresence or Absolute Intelligence – "the Force" – "God" – or whatever term is preferred.[21]

This principle is supported by research into the application of the holographic model of the brain. The search for memory and subconsciousness in the brain continues, but the claims of Ageless Wisdom are slowly surfacing in the scientific world through this holographic concept. When a person "loses" his memory, for instance, from a concussion or stroke, occultism teaches that the memory is still there. It is *not* lost but only appears to be because the brain has become incapable of registering the *vibration* of that memory, much like a damaged instrument. A broken key on a piano can be struck repeatedly, and even though the sound may not register in audible frequencies, the pitch in potentiality is still there. This principle suggests that the brain itself is not the source of thought, but only an instrument for its translation or registration. The brain receives thought-waves much in the same way a radio receives radio waves.

At the International Congress on Psychotronics Research in 1979, R. D. Snyder explained:

> The hologram can store the whole in each part, each part can generate the whole; in addition, space and time are elastic within this model, much like the reported experiences of altered states of consciousness.[22]

Dr. Douglas Dean says that the holographic model is a "monstrous attack on our everyday view of the world."[23] He explains that the world of appearances is not the first reality, but the second; that the primary reality is an enfolded order or implicate reality, the secondary is the unfolded or explicate reality. The world of appearances then is nothing more than a holographic projection based on a "frequency domain" void of time and space, which can explain precognition and clairvoyance. Telepathy is the united waveform of the consciousness of two people. Dr. Dean further states that if the noosphere (collective-consciousness enveloping the earth) is the large hologram of which each brain is a part, two minds joined in the same hologram could communicate. Dr. I. Wiesenberger of Prague, discussing the importance of the subconscious components of the human inner information fields, states, "...its deepest layer is probably identical with the ultimate reality which underlies the whole Cosmos."[24]

The second part of this study is based on the supposition of a collective fabric of sound, color and vibration of which most people remain unaware. The act of inspired composition is then likened to a "raid on the infinite."[25] This "raid" is a passive and receptive state inasmuch as it is an active and projective state of consciously organizing the ideas and writing down the notes. To use an analogy made by Bonewits: A tribal chief of ancient days probably listened to the sounds of nature, the sounds of a spear thrown into the air, and the sounds of wild beasts. He then translated these sounds into a pattern that was taught to the tribe and which served to put them into the state of consciousness known as "the hunt." Each time this happened, the process became more deeply embedded in the racial consciousness of humankind, and this is why future composers would sometimes unknowingly but very vividly draw upon similar musical motifs originally belonging to their ancient ancestors. Musical scholars have found many of Bach's and Purcell's tunes to be highly reminiscent of pagan dance tunes.[26] Bonewits proposes that this unconscious process has been with artists for a very long time – the subconscious memory of the original purpose of sound and music as a shamanistic art for the transformation of consciousness.

This is equally true of composers in the Western musical tradition, whether they are partly aware, totally aware, or totally unaware of the process. A review of the biographical literature produces much anecdotal evidence in support of this. Composers often describe these kinds of experiences. Gustav Mahler, for instance, upon completing his First Symphony, claimed he did not even recognize it when he conducted it.[27] Edward Elgar claimed that all he had to do was stretch out his hand and take whatever music he needed from the air around him.[28] In a letter to a friend, Richard Wagner writes:

> There must be some indescribable inner sense which is altogether clear and active only when the outer senses are as in a dream. When I strictly neither hear nor see distinctly, this sense is at its keenest, and it functions as creative calm. I can call it by no other name, merely I know that this calm of mine works from within to without; with it I am at the spirit's center.[29]

Wagner's "center" easily corresponds to the Absolute Self or "grand archetype" of all creation. Archetypal projection is seen perhaps most vividly in the esoteric analysis of the meaning of the mythological symbolism in Wagner's epic *Ring Cycle*, discussed at length by Corinne Heline in her book on that topic.[30] How this works musically is explained as follows: The definition of archetype is "the original pattern or model from which all other things of the same kind are made; prototype."[31] Musical themes act in an archetypal manner – they serve as prototypes or seed-ideas from which the whole music of a composition emerges and grows. The archetypal musical themes seem to become activated by the archetypes in the composer's own psyche, which are in turn stimulated by a higher source – the "Self" or universal center within us all as one, according to metaphysical doctrine. This is exactly how Wagner's *Leitmotifs* work.

In German, leitmotiv means "leading motive." This term was coined by H. Von Zogen, a friend of Wagner's, to refer to the fundamental method of composition Wagner used in his later operas or "music dramas" as he preferred to call them. Specifically, the leitmotiv is the musical representation of the acting characters, typical situations, and recurrent ideas in musical motives or themes. The leitmotivs are not generally used as fixed melodies but are very flexibly woven together with frequent and sometimes elaborate modifications according to the particular dramatic event in which they are heard at a given moment. For instance, the presence of Brunnhilde, a leading character in one of Wagner's music dramas, is not always a prerequisite for her motive to be heard. It can and does occur whenever someone is thinking of her in conjunction with all the other motives relevant to that particular moment in the opera. Another example: A transfiguration of a theme often represents a transformation of the idea, character, or situation it symbolizes. Many composers after Wagner have used this musical technique, such as the contemporary popular composer, John Williams, in his screen scores for the *Star Wars* movies.

The archetypal patterns of music materialized in the sand formations of Chladni's geometric figures on a glass plate when played with a violin bow. They may be materially discerned in the music of many composers upon careful scrutiny. Erno Lendvai demonstrated that much of Bela Bartok's music is based on the Fibinacci Series and the Golden Section. The Fibinacci Series and the Golden Section are universal mathematical laws primarily reflected in the symmetrical formation of a pine cone, snowflake, and other natural forms. The series goes 3, 5, 8, 13 and so on, the numbers being derived from adding the sum of the equation to the second digit to get the next one. For example, $1 + 2 = 3$, $2 + 3 = 5$, $3 + 5 = 8$, and so on. Bartok never once specifically referred to these laws in his writing as a basis for his compositions, yet he once stated, "We should follow nature."[32]   Therefore it is not certain whether this was a conscious process for Bartok or not.

Subconsciousness responds more readily to images than to the spoken word because imagery is its native language. The symbols   work   on   the   subconscious   directly,   and subconsciousness understands their meanings whether the conscious mind does or not. Early humans first communicated through the use of pictures before the evolving concrete mentality learned the language of words and alphabets, so this original universal language of images and symbols is innate. It is true that one can take, make, associate or program a symbol into practically anything, such as is the case with classical conditioning, but that does not lessen the force or impact of the universal archetypal symbols which consistently occur.

Jung showed that that mandala or "magic circle" – the symbol of complete unity and wholeness -- is prevalent in all cultures. When photographing a vibrating steel disc, sound waves produce a visually striking mandala form.[33] Jung considered the most significant archetype of all to be the "Self" pictorially represented by the mandala, because it gives unity and stability to the entire structure of the personality, its instrument of expression.

Donington in *Wagner's 'Ring' and Its Symbols*, states that

> What a symbol can do when it impinges upon us is to bring to a sharp and effectual focus an experience or realization previously latent in potentiality. The result is a concentration of energy which may alter the balance of inner forces so substantially as to amount to a change in the personality; a change to which both symbol and personality contribute. It is one of the most important facts about symbolism that the personality is capable of growing by means of the symbols it assimilates.[34]

To Donington, however, the term "unconscious" seems inappropriate in describing how symbols work. He feels they incorporate both realms – conscious and unconscious – in their functions:

> We are conscious of the symbols. We may not be, in the rational sense, conscious of their meaning, though

540

their meaning is working on us through our intuition.[35]

Donington concludes:

> Like other experiences which have roots in the unconscious, a work of art contains more meanings than an onion has skins. We can get to the centre of an onion, but we cannot get to the centre of a work of art. There is always another meaning underneath.[36]

Description of the Music

For the second part of this study, four musical pieces were selected that must be analyzed in order to explain how the colors, images, and symbolism used as criteria are derived. The colors, symbols and images attributed to each piece are broken down into three weighted levels of significance. Primary hits are direct hits and equal three points. Secondary hits are indirectly related colors and symbolism and are worth two points. Distantly related or modified forms are hits worth one point. This takes into account the theory that each individual will differ with varying degrees of receptivity to these colors, images, and symbols. Just as a lampshade can color light according to its temperament, so can a person's individual subconsciousness color a pure image or symbol according to the individual's psychic disposition. For instance, a very sensitive subject may receive the Holy Grail symbol in its purest and unaltered form. Someone less "attuned" may register only the slightest semblance of a grail form, such as a bowl or a coffee cup. Misses are defined as colors, images and symbols seen by subjects not listed under any level of significance, and counted an average of two points against every hit.

A. Symphony No. 6 (The Pastoral) in F Major, Op. 68 by Ludwig Van Beethoven, Movement 1: Allegro ma non troppo. (Awakening of Cheerful and Serene Impressions on Arriving in the Country.)

541

This piece was selected for its color potential. Unlike most Beethoven symphonies and radically different from the previous one (the Fifth), this symphony and particularly its first movement are very stable in virtually all elements, especially harmony. Most of the modulations are treated traditionally, and the harmony and motivic structure are repetitive, almost "drone" sounding at times. It is believed that this was intentional on Beethoven's part because he was trying to depict the simple-mindedness of peasants enjoying the countryside. This symphony was one of the first truly programmatic symphonies to be written, each movement receiving a specific descriptive title for its mood. Figuratively speaking, harmony has always been associated with color in music, but occultism teaches it is also literal. In the particular sound-color scale tested in this study, "F" is yellow-green – the color so often seen in nature's blooms in early springtime. The first movement emphasizes harmony more than the specific development of particular themes. In fact, any development in the development section is minimal. What predominates is two striking harmonic shifts. The exposition typically begins in the tonic key of F major (yellow-green) and predictably modulates to the dominant of C major (red) in measures 78-79. Briefly returning to the tonic, it enters the development section going immediately into a prolonged B-flat Major (violet) in measure 151 until it suddenly shifts to a prolonged D Major (orange) in measure 163. This abrupt and accentuated harmonic shift occurs once more except this time the change is from G Major (blue-green) in measure 200 to E Major (yellow) in measure 219. Since harmony or "color" is the predominant factor at play in this movement, it is safe to assume that color should be the predominant visual target received, particularly the colors involved: yellow-green, violet, orange, blue-green, and yellow, with some red interspersed here and there. Symbols and other imagery involved might incorporate scenes of a pastoral countryside, as is indicated by the subtitle of the movement.

Imagery related to the lifestyle of peasants is also a strong possibility.

B.   Lohengrin, Prelude to Act I, by Richard Wagner

This piece is chosen for its imagery which Wagner vividly described:

> Out of the clear blue aether of the sky, there seems to condense a wonderful yet at first hardly perceptible vision, and out of this there gradually emerges, ever more and more, an angel host bearing in its midst the sacred Grail. As it approaches earth it pours out exquisite odours like streams of gold, ravishing the senses of the beholder. The glory of the vision grows and grows until it seems as if the rapture must be shattered and dispersed by the very vehemence of its own expansion. The vision draws nearer and the climax is reached when at last the Grail is revealed in all its glorious reality, radiating fiery beams and shaking the soul with emotion. The beholder sinks on his knees in adoring self-annihilation. The Grail pours out its light like a benediction and consecrates him to its services; then the flames gradually die away and the angel host soars up again to the ethereal heights in tender joy, having made pure once more the heart of men by the sacred blessing of the Grail.[37]

The libretto of the opera is based on the medieval legend of Lohengrin, a Knight of the Holy Grail. Therefore secondary symbolism could consist of knight imagery – a sword, a shield, and the swan-drawn boat he appears in. Colors would be of bright intensity shimmering in high octaves of white, gold, silver, and pastels. The key of the piece is B-Flat, and so violet is a strong possibility according to the sound-color scale being tested.

C.   Quatour pour la Fin de Temps (Quartet for the End of Time) by Olivier Messiaen. Section II: "Vocalise, pour l'ange qui annonce la fin du temps" (Vocalize, for the angel who announces the end of time.)

Olivier Messiaen (born in Avignon, France, December 10, 1908), is a very important 20th century composer, thought to be totally independent in style yet greatly contributing to the development of modern music since before World War II by his works and his teaching. Particularly known for his complex formulated musical structures, he devised his own musical language that incorporated the use of different modes of limited transposition along with the use of nonretrogradable rhythms. He was especially known for his ametrical music, the use of Hindu rhythms, and what he called "bird song." His teacher, Paul Dukas, often told him, "Listen to the birds – they are great masters!"[38] All these various techniques summed up what Messiaen considers the most important aspect of his music appropriately labeled "the charm of impossibilities." By this he meant that music should give us listening pleasure, but at the same time, be able to express some noble sentiments; the most noble of all – spiritual sentiments he felt were exalted by the theology and truths of his Roman Catholic faith. He explains:

> This charm, at once voluptuous and contemplative resides particularly in certain mathematical impossibilities of the modal and rhythmic domains.[39]

More notably, Messiaen openly admits to being a pronounced chromosthesiac and perhaps even clairvoyant, as illustrated from the following statement from his important theoretical treatise, *The Technique of My Musical Language:*

> All these investigations ought not to make us forget the natural harmony, the true unique, voluptuous pretty by essence, willed by melody, issued from it, pre-existent in it, having always been enclosed in it, awaiting manifestation. My secret desire of enchanted gorgeousness in harmony has pushed me toward those swords of fire, those sudden stars, those

flows of blue-orange lavas, those planets of
turquoise, those violet shades, those garnets of long-
haired arborescence, those wheelings of sounds and
colors in a jumble of rainbows which I have spoken
with love in the preface of my *Quartet for the End of
Time*; such a gushing out of chords should
necessarily be filtered; it is the sacred instinct of a
natural and true harmony which alone, can so charge
itself.[40]

Messiaen's *Quartet for the End of Time* contains one of the
most profound examples of archetypal projection in music.
Jung and others point to universal archetypes. Ageless Wisdom
further develops them into 22 specific images or "keys"
collectively called the Tarot. The imagery of the Tarot is
deeply embedded within the *Quatour pour la Fin du Temps*,
unbeknownst to most people and probably even Messiaen.

This programmatic quartet was composed while Messiaen
was held captive in a Nazi concentration camp during World
War II. It was written for the only instruments and musicians
that were accessible to him: piano, clarinet, violin, and cello.
Drawing upon his deep inner strength and religious faith,
Messiaen centered the music on a major theme depicting "the
Angel who announces the end of time." A natural mystic, he
describes this angel in brilliant detail and color in the preface to
his quartet. Quoting from the Biblical *Revelation of St. John*, he
writes:

And I saw a mighty Angel come down from heaven,
clothed with a cloud; and a rainbow was upon his
head, and his face was as it were the sun, and his feet
a pillar of fire. He set his right foot upon the sea and
his left foot upon the earth, and standing steadfast on
the sea and on the earth, he lifted up his hand to
heaven and swore by Him that liveth forever and
ever, that there shall be no more time; but in the day
of the trumpet of the Seventh Angel, the mystery of
God shall be finished.[41]

The *Quartet* is divided into eight major sections, each with a subtitle; two which specifically refer to the "angel who announces the end of time." These sections are also where Messiaen attributes his blue-orange chords described at length in his preface. In Tarot, Key 14 called *Temperance* is the identical image of the angel that Messiaen describes. In metaphysics, this angel is known as Michael, Archangel of the South. He is also the Archangel of Fire and of the sun, so he wears a solar disc on his forehead.

In occultism, the four archangels represent four basic aspects of the Higher Self. Michael in Key 14 represents that aspect which "tempers," putting us through the necessary trials for the purification of personality in order to unfold a deeper spiritual awareness. This key also has other implications, but that is a major attribution, obviously relevant to Messiaen's experience in the Nazi concentration camp. It is no wonder he called upon this force for the strength and inspiration he greatly needed, for the Hebrew letter assigned to this key is Samekh (◘), which means "crutch" or "prop." It is also an interesting synchronicity that Messiaen was born under the sun sign of Sagittarius – the key's astrological correlation. Therefore, it was natural for him to feel a strong affinity for the sustaining force represented by this key.

The relationships do not stop there. There is a rainbow above the angel's head. In the sound-color scale in use here, each of the rainbow's colors corresponds to the six tones in Messiaen's first mode of limited transposition also known as the whole tone scale: Red = C, orange = D, yellow = E, green = F-Sharp, blue = G-Sharp, and violet = A-Sharp. Also, each Tarot key has a general color and keynote assigned to it with all its other attributions. According to this particular system, the general color assigned to Key 14, *Temperance*, depicting the angel, is BLUE, and its keynote is G-Sharp or A-Flat. Taking the next most relative Tarot key to this one, we have Key 19 in Tarot, *The Sun*, remembering Michael as the Archangel of the sun. The color attributed to this key is ORANGE, and its keynote is D. Combining G-Sharp or A-Flat (BLUE) and D

(ORANGE) together produces an augmented 4th or tritone; an interval considered sacred by Messiaen and the Russian composer Alexander Scriabin. Look again, and we also have Messiaen's BLUE-ORANGE chords! However, in examining the musical score, D and G-Sharp or A-Flat are only slightly emphasized, even though they are played together as a tritone in several piano chords in the part particularly designated as "blue-orange" and for the "angel who announces the end of time."

Could this really be coincidence? There's also another key closely linked symbolically to this quartet, and that is Key 6, *The Lovers*, to which is assigned the color orange and the keynote D, also like *The Sun*. The angel in this key is Raphael, Archangel of the East and of Mercury. He represents the superconscious aspect of the Self, and being "clothed in a cloud" (remembering the quotation from St. John) indicates that this aspect is partially hidden from us at our present stage of evolution. The man and woman appear to be Adam and Eve, but really represent the two forms of specialization through which the Life Force expresses. The man is also a symbol for self-consciousness, and the woman is a symbol for subconsciousness.[42]

The Hebrew letter assigned to this key is Zain (ז), meaning "sword". The symbolism of the sword has many implications, but the most obvious one is cleavage. Another title for this key is "The Disposing Intelligence" governing the faculty of discrimination and the analytical ability of the mind which tears things apart only to put them back together again for better understanding. The astrological attribution to this key is Gemini, The Twins, ruled by Mercury, sphere of the mind. The twins of Gemini are graphically depicted by *The Lovers* revealing the Hermetic doctrine that all opposites are different aspects of the ONE THING although they may appear complementary.[43]

Messiaen mentions "swords of fire" in his preface to the Quartet, and fire represents the solar force of purification and regeneration symbolized by the sun in all keys relevant to this Quartet. The sun is the natural symbol of enlightenment.

Messiaen quotes from St. John concerning the angel's head "as it were the sun." The Hebrew letter assigned to Key 19, *The Sun*, is Resh (ר), meaning "head" or "face." The sun in this key has a face that is smiling down upon two children, just as Raphael is smiling down on the two lovers in Key 6. Here the male and female children still represent self-consciousness and subconsciousness, except now they have joined hands as one under the full influence of the sun (superconsciousness). They have both consciously begun to recognize their oneness, and so are reborn, representing a regenerated humanity.[44] They know they are literally children, offspring, or "extensions" of the sun. "And a little child shall lead them..." All savior archetypes such as Jesus Christ, Horus, and Apollo among others, have been symbolized by the sun. The Angel or Higher Self also represents the Christ within, and some occultists allege that the sun is the physical body of the Christ, encompassing all of us in his infinite love and light which sustains all life.

A fifth sunflower in this key which has yet to bloom symbolizes the fifth stage of our evolution where we will become as Jesus Christ himself. This is what he meant when he said, "And you will do even greater things than I," according to esoteric Christianity. The other four sunflowers correspond to the mineral, plant, animal, and human kingdoms of development. The new "superhuman" species is still beyond the majority of humanity's present level of attainment, and this is represented by the mountain in the background of Key 6.[45]

Key 20, *Judgment*, is another image related to this music. In this key, the fifth stage is finally realized, again symbolizing "in the day of the trumpet of the Seventh Angel, the mystery of God shall be consummated." This key represents the attainment of a multidimensional or cosmic consciousness where there is no time! Neither is there space as we know it. It represents the full reawakening of superconsciousness or the Christ child in a more direct sense. This angel is Gabriel, Archangel of the West, Water, and of the Moon. The Hebrew letter here is Shin, (ש), meaning "tooth" or "fire," relating to assimilation and purification. The color assigned to this key is red, and the tone is C. Whether or not this somehow ties into the Quartet has yet to be seen by me. But Mahler's Symphony No. 2 in C Minor is called "The Resurrection Symphony," obviously related to the symbolism in this key. Gabriel's trumpet is aimed at a child rising from a coffin. It might seem that the symbols in this key are giving a clue as to the true purpose of sound or music in accordance with Ageless Wisdom: To awaken or "resurrect" the divinity within us all as one.

Whether or not Messiaen consciously knew what he was doing here does not matter. The fact remains that he did it. Being a devout Roman Catholic and perhaps an orthodox one as well, he might be horrified at the thought of his Quartet having so much occult imagery imbedded in it. Bach as a devout Lutheran might have reacted similarly if anyone had told him he was composing pagan dance tunes. Whether or not Messiaen's chords are literally "blue-orange" must be tested by future research. He saw them as blue-orange at least, and it would be interesting to see if a clairvoyant also saw them as blue-orange when played. Therefore, the colors, imagery, and symbolism to be tested for in this composition are specifically spelled out by Messiaen and the Tarot.

D.   The Fool, for solo flute, by Judy Kennedy.

The colors, imagery, and symbolism in this music are also intimately linked to a specific Tarot key. But this time the projection was completely deliberate on the composer's part. The composition is very short, but highly integrated and strictly organized according to the gematria (Qabalistic numerology), colors, and symbolism of Key 0 in the Tarot, called *The Fool*. (See Appendix 3.)

In this key, the predominant colors corresponding to their tones are: yellow = E, yellow-green = F, green = F-Sharp or G-Flat, violet = A-Sharp or B-Flat, and red = C. The general keynote assigned to this key is E and the color is yellow. Therefore, the piece is centric on E, and the other tones function as secondary tonal centers for quartal harmonies structured in

6/4 position, but leaving out the third and substituting a major second. So a C chord would be built: G, C, *D*, G, and not G, C, E, G. Each chord, naturally broken for the flute, is built this way and is based on one of the five major colors as its tonal center. The chord may not always start on the fifth, but all the notes must be played to make up the chord. All intervals are possible between these five tones except for the minor third and its inversion, the major sixth. These intervals determine the relationships between the chords. They serve as tonal polarities in each of the nine sections of the piece. For example, in the first section, a minor second is used, meaning that the E chord must go up a minor second to establish its tonal polarity to F. So a chord built B, E, F-Sharp, B is immediately followed by a chord built C, F, G, C, and it cannot go anywhere else except alternate between those two poles in that particular section; those two quartal harmonies centered on E and F.

Aleph (א) meaning "ox" is the Hebrew letter assigned to this key. In gematria, the value of the word "Aleph" is 111 which reduces to 3: $1+1+1 = 3$. Important esoteric ideas associated with the number 3 are expansion, augmentation, and multiplication. These ideas are reflected in the music along with the basic meaning of *The Fool* representing the Life Force which in its most abstract expression is free, unbound, high-spirited, and fiery in nature. It is the superconscious "egg" (0) from which the world is "hatched." 111 divided by $3 = 37$. 37 is the number of a divine name representing the Self or center of all creation. There are exactly 37 notes in each of the nine sections of the piece. Key 9 has a very special relationship to Key 0 in Tarot, and that is one reason for nine sections. There are three major sections subdivided into three subsections, each making up nine in all because 9 times $37 = 333$. $3+3+3 = 9$, and 333 divided by $3 = 111$, the number of Aleph. All three major sections have their own tempo and meter.

37 is divided by 1 through 9, giving the motivic basis for each individual section. For example: In section 1, 37 divided by $9 = 4$ with 1 left over. This calls for a 9 note motive which could be played either inverted, in retrograde, or any way, just

as long as the 9 note motive is played four times with one remaining note. The remaining note could be any note out of the two quartal harmonies serving as the main polarity for that particular section.

E centricity occurs because each section's 37th note must be E regardless of whether it is in the tonal polarity or not. E is yellow, so yellow preponderance is predicted. E or yellow is assigned to The Fool, whose colors, imagery, and symbolism would be expected to result from this music, because it was specifically composed for it.

Results

The first part of the study on sound-color correlations involved testing the ability of 61 subjects to hear the note "C" when viewing the color red and to hear the note "F-sharp" when viewing the color green. The second part of the study tested 11 subjects who were students of a meditation class for the reception of colors, imagery, and archetypal symbolism associated with specific music during meditation. Of course, the subjects were initially screened to ensure unfamiliarity with the music.

For the first test, results were not statistically significant. Post-analysis of the data suggested that this was probably due to methodological error. The experimental setting was not ideal, and unexpected variables had not been totally eliminated. Similar problems prevailed with the second test, so only a descriptive analysis of the data was possible. A separate analysis was made for images and colors in each piece of music. Likewise, in analyzing written data, images which could be self-contained were separated from the others and counted as a unit (hit or miss) in accordance with a predetermined listed inventory of possible hits. For example, in analyzing the statement, "...butterflies in a field of yellow flowers...", four distinct units are implied: (1) butterflies, (2) field, (3) flowers, and (4) yellow. The proportion of the percentage of hits with confidence intervals for each piece was calculated by color and by imagery. Ratios of hits in points were calculated in relation to misses in points.

The data indicated that subjects expressed greater accuracy in determining colors than symbols or imagery. One possible explanation for this is that color perception generally has a far more limited range than image perception. There are an infinite number of images to draw from, but only about twelve to eighteen colors. Eighteen was the range chosen for the test because only eighteen different colors appeared in the subjects' total perceptions. Most of these were within the primary and secondary range of colors. Very few blends were perceived such as yellow-orange or blue-green, and only one uncommon color was perceived – "bluish-gray." Blue-orange, not really a natural color blend, was counted as two colors, both blue and orange, in order to make up blue-orange. This is a primary hit for the Messiaen. Two out of the eleven subjects saw blue-orange and five saw blue. Since that is such an uncommon color combination, I think that just two subjects seeing it is significant.

A review of the raw data suggests the occurrence of many significant events, but when the misses (colors and imagery stated not listed as significant) are counted as two points against every possible hit at one, two, or three points, the proportions appear nonsignificant. My statistician told me that if the probability problem were ever corrected, particularly regarding finding a proper measurement tool for ranges and establishing the criteria for chance occurrence, the data might look much different.

When reading the written descriptions, even though there might not be many hits in terms of specific symbols in a particular Tarot key, there were accuracies expressed in other ideas related to the symbolism or general meaning of the key. For example: The following is word-for-word raw data from one subject (female, age 50, accounting clerk) describing her experience of *The Fool* by Judy Kennedy:

The colors of green and yellow were dominant, bursting forth from a central point – sparking – an image of struggle – growth and finally being free. Like grass.

Black space with planets and stars – I felt as though I could step from one to the other. Looked down to see what I think was earth surrounded by smoke and glowing as though on fire.

A small flame – orange and pink and bordered in violet. It got larger and larger. I walked up to it with no fear and it engulfed me – I started walking forward to apparent nothingness – unafraid – and felt I was anticipating the end of the song and?

This subject has three primary hits, four secondary hits, and one indirectly related or modified form hit. The Fool is often said to represent attainment after long hard struggle, for he climbed the mountain, reached the summit and is free in his contemplation of even greater goals – higher mountain peaks beyond him. The Fool is the Life Force in all its potential for growth and courage, inevitably leading one to jump off the cliff into apparent nothingness; however, nothing is something or it wouldn't have a name... This is a popular meditation in associating oneself with The Fool.

What seems so significant is the frequency with which these hits appeared. For instance, with the Kennedy piece, all eleven subjects got direct hits on color. They all saw yellow and white as predominant. Six subjects saw intense sunny light. Two subjects saw fire or a flame. Two subjects saw mountains. Six subjects saw height symbolism. One subject saw a "large bird" (an eagle?). Four subjects saw birds. Three subjects saw flowers. Two subjects saw planets or stars. Four subjects saw sun symbolism. One subject saw small animals. Three subjects saw butterflies (flying insects). Two subjects saw space symbolism. One subject saw loops. Four subjects saw dancing. Someone might think that the music, if it sounded like dance music, would evoke dance imagery, but that is not the case with this piece. The rhythms and meter are irregular, so there is no steady pulse. The composition is interpreted very freely and does not sound like a dance tune at all. Not listed as significant yet seen by more than one subject: Four saw a lush forest landscape; three saw droplets of color or water; five saw "in and out" or "appearing and disappearing" imagery; five reported a flowing feeling; four saw water; two saw Pan or a satyr; the next most predominant colors were blue and orange. Now why did this happen? A parapsychologist might infer that there was more going on than what the music was responsible for alone. To what degree were the subjects unconsciously influencing each other's perceptions telepathically?

Messiaen significant hits: Two subjects saw blue-orange and five saw blue. Red was the next most predominant color, seen by four. Two subjects saw violet. One subject saw a mountain. One subject saw water and land coming together, like a shore. One subject saw a human figure. One subject saw children. Two subjects saw a path. One subject saw a real "sudden star." One subject saw a spherical object. Two subjects saw "monumental" or "great blocks of stone" imagery. This piece had the least amount of significant hits, contrary to my expectations. However, something else happened which might be very significant. Nearly everyone described a mood that Messiaen might have felt when he was composing this music. He was confined to a Nazi concentration camp in the most deplorable of conditions. We might assume that music inspired by an angel would convey beautiful, uplifting, and inspirational feelings – and it does for me – but this might be because I've learned to associate that imagery with it. Obviously, ten of the eleven subjects felt quite differently. Here are their descriptions:

1. In a desert searching for truth… enlightenment, etc. – finally got to the mountain but silly demons there, as if the search had led nowhere!

2. A man appears lost – unfamiliar with anything... ends with feeling of awe.
3. Intimidating, frightening environment on the astral level... ends with abrupt solitude and quiet.
4. Heavy darkness... trying to pierce this... finally come to rest.
5. Disjointed emotions... things slipping away... unpleasant eerie thoughts and feelings.
6. A journey through darkness... dark colors, mental, everything at odd angles.
7. A large machine – silver or metallic... could not tell purpose but at times felt it was searching for me...
8. In a dark cave frightened... escaped, became depressed and began crying. The feeling of sadness was gradually replaced by feelings of a quiet acceptance and at the end it seemed as though a resolution of sorts had occurred...
9. Mental... disorganization at beginning and end... geometric figures crashing into each other... felt very heavy – trodding through a long endless dark tunnel... very effortful – tiresome... suits a very depressed mood.
10. Calm, melancholy serenity, basically astral, kind of desolate.

Was it the unconventionality of the music perhaps – the unfamiliar dissonance that evoked this kind of imagery, possibly paired with subjective reactions? I must admit, the first time I ever heard this music as an undergraduate, I got strange feelings too. It was so unlike anything I'd ever heard. But the more I listened to it, the more I liked it. Now I love it. To me, it's one of the most beautiful, mystical and inspirational compositions I've ever heard. But this was not the reaction of most of the subjects. Only one subject expressed a real liking for this music. Afterwards she asked me where she could find a recording of it. Perhaps she was the only one who had nothing negative to say about it.

Wagner: Most significant hits were with color. However, eight out of eleven subjects commented positively about what they felt was the highly spiritual nature of the piece. This was the favorite music played that evening. It is not surprising because it is believed that Wagner specifically composed it for this effect.[46] One subject had a particular "Lohengrin"-like experience. She wrote:

> Waiting in a mist of color for a symbol of an expression of love, goodness, perfection in the form of a human being. The person touched others as he processionally walked through the solemn crowd awaiting "his arrival"...

One person even saw a white swan and a wooden boat with a sail!

Beethoven: There were more significant hits with the Beethoven than with any other piece. Ten out of the eleven subjects received strong countryside or festivity imagery. Three saw horseback riding. Seven emphasize green, three yellow, and two red. There were no misses regarding color, and "cheerful impressions" prevail. Candidly, this was probably due more to the objective characteristics of the music than any subjective psi phenomena. The music matches the imagery well, reflecting Beethoven's genius for depicting the mood in the sound of the music. After all, he intended it to sound that way. If I ever do another experiment like this, I probably won't use the Beethoven for that reason. It may have been just too familiar sounding. But my composition was totally unfamiliar, and there were several hits with it. So who is to say what's really at play?

Conclusion

The first test needs to be repeated so the methodological errors can be corrected. The second test needs to be repeated too, maybe with the individuals tested separately and in an environment more conducive to relaxation. Nothing had ever been done like this before to my knowledge, so I had nothing to serve as a control condition, a baseline, or to compare or establish significance against. A music professor told me how he once played some programmatic music to a class who didn't get any of the imagery right. That was probably because they were not in the proper state of awareness to receive anything in the first place. So a control group of listeners in a beta state would serve no useful purpose because I was not testing whether or not the reception occurs during the meditative state, but rather what specific symbols, colors and imagery occurred period. The "during meditation" part was taken for granted and considered to be a critical variable. As one of my teachers says, you can't expect to catch any fish by jumping around and making noise! It's the same principle when fishing for colors, symbols, imagery, and anything else that comes out of the sea of subconsciousness. A meditative or quiet still state of mind is imperative.

Therefore due to the lack of adequate controls and probability criteria, this study is not conclusive of anything, although it certainly suggests there might be something to the theory if the right tests are applied – frequency tests especially. Counting how many times a specific image or symbol occurs consistently might indicate some level of significance, even if it isn't listed as a significant hit. This phenomenon occurred strongly with my piece. Overall, the experiment proved very fruitful as a learning experience, and inevitably points toward more positive results with future research.

> For now we see through a glass darkly; but then face
> to face; now I know in part; but then shall I know
> even as also I am known.

>   -- Paul, Corinthians 13:12

*   *   *

So that was my little study. The results, however unclear, warrant further research. Looking back now, I am amazed my professors allowed me to do it at all. Initially, because it was at the Master's degree level, they really didn't care what I did just as long as I stuck to the empirical approach. But after the results were reviewed, they expressed great consternation and subjected me to such ridicule that it almost cost me my degree. I had to threaten litigation alleging civil rights discrimination before the administration allowed me to complete the program and receive my degree. It was a nightmare. In any event, that was enough exposure to the academic ivory tower to turn me off from pursuing further studies there indefinitely. Mature hindsight now enables me to see the unfortunate side to that because this is an area where great strides in research could be made, given the proper funding and direction.

The academic forum was probably not the proper one for this kind of research at that time. Not only was I trying to do an originally designed experimental study (which would not typically be done until the doctoral level), I was also trying to test ideas and theories which did not completely fit into the tidy box of current scientific understanding, practically guaranteeing their exclusion from serious academic consideration. I know this now and recognize my mistake. Still, I'm glad I did it, because I confirmed to myself the rightness and worthiness of this kind of iconoclastic pioneering into unchartered territory.

No one to my knowledge had ever done this before. I found experimental studies in parapsychology where music had been the specific target in psi research, but no studies where music served as the transmitting agent itself.[47] No one can deny the outstanding results obtained with my own composition, *The Fool*, in spite of the methodological problems. Still the reason for that success is unknown. Was it the music transmitting the imagery, or was it just my own telepathic suggestions? Perhaps it was both. Maybe it was the extraordinary abilities of the students or a combination of all these variables. We may never know. What's important is that it worked. I could only conclude that music is one of the best, if not the best -- medium for the direct communication of nonverbal thoughts, ideas, and imagery, and that these extraordinary powers are not being used to their fullest advantage.

How the Magic Works

Scientific research since the time of my study sheds additional light on this subject.   Today I am proud to say that there are many excellent researchers making progress in this area resulting in a new discipline altogether.   As I predicted over 25 years ago, it is truly interdisciplinary in nature.   This new discipline has many names, depending on the focus of the researcher, such as bioacoustics, psychoacoustics, and neuroacoustics.   Today it is not uncommon to find academics at various symposiums presenting papers on "the biophysics of music," "sonic alchemy," the neurophysiology of music," and "sound healing."   Pioneers in energy research – radionics, psychotronics, and radiaesthesia – have also made great contributions to this field.   So-called "medical intuitives" are jumping on the bandwagon, incorporating sound and music into their holistic therapies based on much of this research.

Cymatic therapy is a 'sound medicine' that was developed by the British osteopath Peter Guy Manners.   He based his therapy on the theory that each part of the body has its own unique vibratory rate.   Therefore, sound is directly applied to the body for healing in order to correct disrupted frequencies. Neuromuscular problems in particular, such as arthritis and osteoporosis benefit from this type of treatment.[48]

There's nothing mystical about this when you consider that the human nervous system, by its very nature, is acoustical. When a nerve cell fires an impulse to be transmitted through the nervous system in order to communicate information to another part of the body, it does so through *changes in frequency*, with energy intensity directly related to the rate of firing of nerve impulses.   The changing electrical energy is an audio-frequency waveform, thus creating an audio-frequency magnetic biofield. Scientists such as Dr. Valerie Hunt of UCLA, Dr. William Tiller of Stanford University, and others have been testing and measuring these fields for some time.

Scientists say that music triggers three neurophysiological processes in the brain:

> First, because music is nonverbal, it can move through the auditory cortex directly to the center of the limbic system, the midbrain network that governs most of our emotional experience as well as basic metabolic responses like body temperature, blood pressure, and heart rate. Second, music may be able to activate the flow of stored memory across the corpus callosum, a collection of fibers connecting the left and right sides of the brain, helping the two to work in harmony. And third, music may be able to excite calling agents called peptides, or stimulate endorphins, natural opiates secreted by the hypothalamus that produce a feeling akin to being in love.[49]

That helps to explain my early mystical experiences with music. It also supports other research unequivocally showing that children who study music in their early years are generally better at other subjects. They're usually happier as well. When both hemispheres of the brain are acting in harmony -- processing and integrating information in concert, the natural result is a child less prone to emotional and mental imbalance. I've always believed that I have a musical body as well as a physical, emotional, mental, and spiritual body. When it's not nurtured, I get moody!

Rhythm entrainment is also another important aspect of the power of sound, music and vibration. Have you ever gone for a hike with a group of people, and noticed that after a while, you're all marching in step to the same beat? Women who work closely together in an office setting sometimes find that they begin their periods around the same time of the month. Suppose you're sitting outside at sunset listening to the crickets sounding off randomly. An hour later, they're all chirping in unison. This biological process is called entrainment. It's a way that nature saves energy by having periodic events close

560

enough in frequency occur in step or in phase with each other. You can set up a row of ticking clocks and get this same effect after a while. Sound vibration and light dominate this process – music and color. Therefore, think of all the possibilities inherent in the use of this principle.

Ageless Wisdom has always taught that each and every thing in the universe – organic, inorganic, sentient or nonsentient – has its very own unique vibratory signature always broadcasting. Even the smallest subatomic particles when in motion are not really particles at all but waveforms. Wherever you have a waveform, you have frequency. Wherever there is frequency, there is vibration. Wherever there is vibration, on some level you have sound. And that's where it all begins according to practically every spiritual tradition on the planet. The Bible says, "In the beginning was the Word." Hopi spider woman *sang* everything into creation, and so on.

Much nonuniformity exists in the variety of sound-color scales marketed by New Agers. From my experience, I find the sound-color scale I tested to be the most accurate and effective. The harmonics of color are approximately forty octaves higher than audible sound. Therefore, if we could add that many octaves to the right half of the keyboard, the notes played at the higher end would be in color rather than in sound.[50] The correlations or harmonics between musical tones and reflected light or color work like this: A single musical note is a specific vibratory rate. Continuously doubling those pulsations causes the vibration to ascend through several octaves – from the octave of electricity to the octaves expressed as heat and light. The medium in this realm is subtler than the medium of air where the sound waves are first created. The precise correlation between the sound and the color is difficult to test because these mediums are so different. This is probably one reason for the discrepancy between the various sound-color scales, yet Ageless Wisdom teaches that exact correlations exist.

When vibration changes, form changes. Early pioneers in energy medicine immediately recognized the value of determining the waveform of a healthy organ and then "beaming" that energy into unhealthy organs in order to realign them into a healthy pattern of vibration. Dr. Valerie Hunt can diagnose disease by measuring incoherency in a biofield long before it manifests in a materially observable form. Similarly, many clairvoyants can see these incoherent biofields, and usually report them as irregularities in the color and intensity of the aura prior to diagnosis. Kirlian photography is often used to capture this phenomenon on film.[51]

Even today's most sophisticated medical instrumentation like CT scans, sonograms and MRIs operate on this principle. The pictures generated by this equipment are made possible by processing the energy pulses and frequency patterns in the body. Additionally, the principle of sympathetic resonance applies to biological life forms as well as to inanimate objects.

Finally, many musicians and composers are incorporating these exciting new discoveries into their own music and artistic performances. Steven Halpern, Tom Kenyon, Joshua Leeds, and Silvia Nakkach are just a few. These composers are consciously creating music with the intention to induce altered states, heal, and transform consciousness. Still, I believe composers and musicians who may not even be aware of the process make the greatest impact. Their creative geniuses act as inspired mediums – channeling archetypal forces and transformative vibrations from that limitless source that transcends the personal, thus influencing the group mind of a society as well as the individual. As a result, humanity is able to more easily adapt to changing paradigms essential for the continued survival and transformation of the species. According to Heline,

> All great musical composers have been connected, consciously or unconsciously, with this source of music – a fact which enabled them to become masters of their art. Their compositions contain specific messages brought through from high realms for the definite purpose of bettering world conditions and bestowing upon mankind greater illumination.[52]

562

The above still pertains to contemporary composers and musicians as well, and is not limited to those in the so-called classical genre of music. For instance, the timeless music of many groups from the era of "classic rock" (Pink Floyd, The Rolling Stones, Led Zeppelin, and The Moody Blues just to name a few) is probably more responsible for some of the deepest spiritual transformations in the group consciousness of humanity than all the priests and rabbis of the world combined. The same thing can be said of many movie directors, producers and other artists. I know that sounds radical, and I know of no evidence to support it, *today*. Nevertheless, I feel it is true.

The Dark Side of the Force

Of course, music, like sound, like any expression of energy, is truly a dual-edged sword. It's neither good nor bad in itself. All depends on how it's used. Shamans of indigenous cultures have always known this, as related by author Dane Rudhyar:

> Magic is a purposeful act of will focused by a particular form and directed toward a particular entity or being; and for the primitive, magic-oriented consciousness, all modes of existence, all beings, are alive. They are specialized forms taken by the One Life for the performance of a particular function. The magic-working shaman is able to resonate to the essential character or quality of this function, and by so doing uncover its Name. Every specialized form taken by the One Life has its Name – or, from the point of view of a much later development of the human mind, its archetype.[53]

For ages, aspirants of the Western and Eastern mystery traditions have been taught the secret uses of sound and color, especially for healing and the cultivation of spiritual awareness. These techniques are also used for tuning and balancing the chakras. Because the potential for misuse of these energies is great, students are usually only taught these techniques after

563

many years of other kinds of preliminary practices. For example, the Western mystery tradition that uses the sound-color scale that I tested does not give out instructions on how to use these correlations until after at least six to seven years of other course work.

The reasons are simple. The main work at hand is not the development of supersensory powers but the transmutation of personality so that the aspirant can become a better attuned instrument for the reception and transmission of those energies -- which will in turn serve others in the transmutation of their personalities. Our first responsibility is to tend our own gardens. Compassion and wisdom merge and strengthen through the awakening of our innate divine perfection until our personalities are fully transmuted, delusions destroyed, and motivations purified. Modern Buddhism calls this awakening the Buddha within – becoming more aware of our natural enlightened state. Jesus put it this way, "If I be lifted up, I will lift all others unto myself." To be able to heal others, the healer must be healed first. It's just common sense. Of course this process is not always linear and sequential. Most of us are doing the and/and dance rather than the either/or, and that's okay. The important thing to remember is that the focus is spiritual awakening, and through and from that, all else emerges.

Being awakened or enlightened is still no assurance that a person will not misuse or misapply these occult principles at some time in their practice. It just makes it less likely because the student is more likely to have suffered first-hand consequences of similar errors from other misapplications of occult energy in the early stages of their spiritual practice. Therefore, experience is important.

We must also never forget that these particular energies combined – sound and color – and especially with the added reinforcement of imagery – are among the most potent and powerful tools in the universe. Ancient civilizations used this power to build the megalithic monuments around the world, such as Stonehenge and the Egyptian pyramids. They also used it as a weapon in warfare.

Does that sound strange? Well remember the old adage that truth is stranger than fiction. The United States military, long before the cold war, had in its possession weapons of this kind based on the principles of psychotronics. What is far more horrifying is that these weapons have been used against its own citizens in massive mind control experiments and the staged simulation of UFO/ET abductions.

Let us examine the occult principles of sound and color to see how this works. Remember the definition of occult is that which is ordinarily hidden from view. However, current advances in scientific research are lifting the veil on these ancient techniques and validating their effectiveness in new technologies every day.

Sound waves can be constructive or destructive, as is the case with most energy forms. The Swiss doctor Hans Jenny, a pioneer in cymatics, was one of the first scientists in the last century to document the formative powers of sound. He conducted a series of experiments to determine the effects of sound vibration on various materials such as plastics, liquids, powders and other substances. Before and after photographs clearly reveal coherent organic geometric shapes forming out of the unshaped inorganic matter as a result of exposure to different sound frequencies. These blobs of material began to form into shapes resembling living creatures like starfish, human cells, and other microscopic life, in the same manner that Chladni got the sand to form into geometric patterns on a glass plate by sliding a violin bow across its edge. This is a simple, basic illustration of the constructive power of sound.

Regarding the destructive power of sound, the principle of sympathetic resonance brings to mind the all too familiar image of the opera singer breaking a glass with her high "C". Well, according to the mystic/seer Edgar Cayce and Corinne Heline, this is exactly what occurred on the lost continent of Atlantis; not shattering glasses, but shattering people -- actual physical bodies – with the magnified power of sound.[54] If every object and creature has its own unique vibratory rate, whether it be a specific keynote, a song, or any kind of sonic frequency pattern, once that personal key signature is determined, the means to mess with that lock so to speak is also available. Sanskrit and Tibetan texts also reinforce this concept when discussing the power of mantras. Author Peter Hamel reiterates,

> According to the laws of vibration and acoustic proportion, a body can be disintegrated by means of its 'own note' or basic resonance-frequency, provided that this frequency is known in the case of the body in question: Each organism exhibits its own vibratory rate, and so does every inanimate object from the grain of sand to the mountain and even to each planet and sun. When this rate of vibration is known, the organism or form can, by occult use of it, be disintegrated – or, for that matter, cognised and brought into awareness.[55]

The second migration from Atlantis was responsible for bringing this power to the area associated with the Far East, and so knowledge of its uses were preserved in their mystery schools. Heline comments as follows:

> Speech was developed by the Atlanteans, a sort of *singing speech.* Their intoned words projected power into any object named, and by that power the object could be reshaped in accordance with an individual's will. The chants and mantras of all ancient religions had their origin in this *singing speech...* in the Atlanteans' practically unlimited power lay the seed of ultimate decadence and destruction... The *singing speech* of consecrated Temple-Initiates was made over to evil and destructive ends. Literally, "blasts" of tone, attuned to the keynote of a person or an object, were used to ruthlessly destroy human life and property.[56]

This is precisely how modern psychotronic mind control devices work.[57] Once someone's brain wave patterns in the form of a personalized sound print are deduced and vulnerably exposed, other amplified waveforms can be aimed at that person with the sole purpose of disrupting or jamming those frequencies, just like radio signals. This then opens the doorway to memory tampering, induced hallucinations, and a whole house of horrors – without the perpetrators even having to be physically present. Like radio these destructive waveforms can be broadcast from a distance. And as was mentioned earlier, the quintessential "lone nut" mad scientist is not to be worried about. The real threat is an entire panel of them sanitized with the "Good Housekeeping" seal of the United States government and its black op allies.

Do we have any countermeasures for this? Well, yes we do. And believe it or not, the best countermeasure is simple prayer, meditation, and spiritual affirmation coupled with a strong faith and belief in a higher power. How so you ask? Just follow the same principle. Prayer, chanting, mantra, or any focused activity like meditation is just another way of controlling your own brain waves and modifying your personal sound print. This too is being scientifically tested and proven.

Jonathan Goldman and other researchers in energy work, psychoacoustics, and sacred geometry, are finding that engaging in spiritual practices like prayer and sacred chanting helps to build a light vehicle or *merkabah* on the subtle planes above the body. This light vehicle can be used in many different ways – for healing, as a shield or protective cloaking device, or even as a means for transporting messages to other beings. Not only can clairvoyants and other sensitives see or feel this energy form, but biofield energy measurement devices have also been able to record the formation of these shapes. Sometimes they're simple three dimensional geometric patterns like pyramids or tetrahedrons. On other occasions, for example with advanced practitioners like Tibetan monks, elaborate forms can arise according to whatever detailed visualization they're projecting. The sound vibrations create, consolidate, anchor, and energize the visualized forms which can then take on a life of their own. Old school occultists called these things "thought forms." It's also the origin of the witch's familiar, genies, and other servants of the practiced magician. In science fiction terms the equivalent would be an android, robot, or clone of some kind. Corinne Heline says, "When rightly performed, music in certain keys is a strong factor in the materialization of disembodied spirits."[58]

A member of Builders of the Adytum, for example, spends hours honing their ability to visualize symbols related to the Qabalah and Tarot. Rituals are prescribed dealing with the direct manipulation of this imagery in conjunction with sound and color in order to produce specific effects in consciousness. An Eastern aspirant following the tantric Vajrayana path of Tibetan Buddhism will do the same with images of Buddhas, deities, and wrathful dharma protectors. These practices more often than not are accompanied by their corresponding chants or mantras with color also playing an important role.

But again, such formal elaboration is not necessary to effectively protect yourself. Many victims of psychic attack have successfully defended themselves with a simple prayer or repeated affirmation. This is how Dr. Greer fended off a psychotronic attempt on his life by the shadow government.[59] Much depends on the strength, personal nerve and self-confidence of the victim. Still, as was mentioned before, the best defense for any kind of psychic attack or psychotronic manipulation is the transmutation of your own personality. *The only way anyone can harm another person is if that other person already has within themselves the harmful element the attacker is seeking to reinforce.* The harmful elements are usually just negative thoughts and emotions. Fear, lack of faith and succumbing to the power of negative suggestion can weaken personal resolve. This is why there is no more powerful protection than the genuine heart-felt vibration of love and compassion.

This is reinforced by research into the effect of sound vibration on the colloidal system by Dr. Tiller and other scientists. Colloid comes from a Greek word meaning "glue." The colloidal system is likened to etheric connective tissue linking the mind to the body. Like an invisible matrix of energy, it holds everything together. Remember, every thought, feeling, and image creates a vibrating vortex in this energy field. Certain conditions cause the colloids to condense or crystallize into forms commonly recognized as "dis-ease." As one researcher noted,

> It is so important that the surface of the colloidal field be positively charged. And it is very simple: *maintain enthusiasm.* When you pour love and interest into whatever you are doing, you are automatically insulating this field against inharmonious conditions. Internal harmony is an insulator against external inharmony.[60]

So we see that the sages of ancient wisdom and mystical prophets of love were right all along. We don't need to wait for science to catch up, although it's nice that it is doing so for the benefit of those skeptics out there!

This same principle is what strengthens and characterizes certain musical performances as extraordinary. Sound is a carrier wave for consciousness. A performer who is "in the zone" and loving what they're doing is literally absorbed in and by the music. So not only does the music convey the original thoughts and feelings of the composer, but also those of the performer if they are not already one and the same.

A final note about the darker uses of sound, color and imagery. There was a time in the evolution of humanity where people were more susceptible to manipulation by these forces, and that was during the time of Atlantis as was said. This magic had its beginning in those days when the behavior of a person was controlled more by tribal, hive or group mentality than individual will. Mass hypnosis was the rule, not the exception. This ancient form of 'glamour' magic is still practiced today at rock concerts, evangelical revivals, motivational workshops, in movies and in television commercials. As Gareth Knight observes,

> The modern exploiters of these old Atlantean magical techniques are to be found, not in occult fraternities, but in the creative departments of advertising agencies. Indeed, time spent studying television commercials in an analytical fashion is perhaps one of the best introductions to the use of rhythm, vowel sounds, background music or sound effects, and associated visual images.[61]

This is just another example of unsuspecting persons being witches and not knowing it!

Dancing with Stones

Tibetan Buddhist music sounds very strange to most Western ears. For one, the instruments are radically unique. Secondly, Tibetans developed a system called overtone chanting which is a technique found in many indigenous shamanistic traditions around the world. Basically, the chanter learns to create multiple overtones or vocal harmonies by singing two or more tones simultaneously. While chanting one tone, the additional tones are reached by resonating certain cavities in the human body which in turn produce the overtones. Such chanting creates a powerful reverberation within the practitioner's body and in the surrounding environment. The force is so powerful, that when it's combined with the sounds of other instruments in just the right way, it can literally levitate and move stones.

You are not likely to see this demonstrated unless you become an advanced practitioner yourself. It's simply not taught as it used to be. And it's not something that one can simply pick up as a new skill. It is best understood in the context of the more esoteric teachings of Tibetan Buddhism because this type of music does not come from the personal human dimension at all. It has its roots in shamanistic and animistic aspects of the old Bon religion of the Himalayas, which were eventually integrated into the tantric form of Mahayana Buddhism.[62] However, this phenomenon has been observed and recorded by Western eyes on more than one occasion during the first half of the 20th century.

In the 1950s, the Swedish writer and engineer, Henry Kjellson, recorded the observations of two different men who witnessed this phenomenon while visiting Tibet.[63] Dr. Jarl, a Swedish doctor, watched monks using sound to levitate and move great blocks of stone while he was visiting a friend at a remote monastery in southwestern Tibet during the 1920s or 30s. A detailed accounting with drawings and diagrams of exactly what took place were given to Dr. Kjellson and published in his book. Andrew Collins duplicates these diagrams and a detailed description of the event in his book, *Gods of Eden*.

The monks were constructing a huge wall of stone blocks against some high cliffs near the monastery. 240 monks participated in this process along with an enormous Tibetan orchestra with a wide variety of strange instruments. Nothing was random about this operation at all. Distances were precisely marked and measured, and each monk and instrument was strategically placed relative to the stone block that was about to be levitated and moved. After about four minutes of playing their instruments, the stone block began to wobble until it finally lifted into the air. The monks lifted their instruments accordingly as if to guide the stone block, and kept playing until the stone block reached its destination. As soon as the monks were satisfied with the block's location, they stopped the music and the block fell into place. The whole process was repeated with each stone block to be moved.

The second story recorded by Kjellson was relayed to him by Mr. Linauer, an Austrian filmmaker. Linauer visited a remote monastery in northern Tibet during the 1930s. The monks showed him two strange instruments that when played together would emit an inaudible resonance wave that produced a temporary weightlessness in stone blocks. The monks told

Linauer that this was an ancient secret sonic technology that had been in use for centuries. The monks also admitted that they had other devices that could disintegrate and dissolve physical matter in addition to moving it. The monks must have trusted Linauer because they also confided that foreigners were usually never allowed to see these kinds of operations for fear that the technology would be stolen and perhaps misused.

Today many lamas and exiled Tibetans relish stories about the times when such amazing feats were commonplace. Sadly, in large part due to the Chinese invasion of Tibet during the 1950s, we may never be able to determine the extent to which such a technology existed and was used by the Tibetans prior to that time.

Collins points to the Tibetan meditation practice of dzogchen as evidence that such feats transpired, according to what Shardza Tashi Gyaltsen writes in the classic, *Heart Drops of Dharmakaya: Dzogchen Practice of the Bon Tradition*:

> The channels become completely purified and through them divinities and beings appear. At this time all the normal thoughts which are mixed with ignorance are completely purified and liberated. Awareness and wisdoms directly appear. At that time you can focus on rocks and move them if you want to. Your mind can make imprints in rock; there is no attachment with the material body.[64]

The author is actually referring to a particular dzogchen practice called *Togel*, which means "leaping over." According to Lama Surya Das, a more accurate way of describing it is "being through." In fact, whenever Surya is guiding his students in meditation, he often says, "See through and be through everything." Normally, students take such instructions figuratively, as most people might tend to read the foregoing statement by Gyaltsen. However, no rule excludes such experiences from transpiring materially, because as we've learned, there is little difference. Nothing is as solid as it seems, and we are not what we appear to be. Neither are the rocks.

Reality is essentially liquid in essence and can be shaped accordingly.

The Tibetans, however, are not the only culture professing to have had such a sonic technology at one time or another. Christians are familiar with the story about the fall of the Tower of Babel by the sounds of trumpets. First Creation stories of the Incas in South America reveal a time when their ancestors were able to transport stones through the air carried on the sounds of horns.[65] Mayan legend speaks of an ancient race of dwarfs who could "whistle" heavy rocks into place.[66] Pausanias, a 2nd century Greek geographer wrote that Amphion erected the walls of Thebes with his harp.[67] Interestingly, Amphion was a son of Jupiter, and we know that many of these olden gods were extraterrestrials subsequently mythologized.

Modern research shows that the ancient Egyptians may have used similar technology in constructing the pyramids. It is confirmed that they used an ultrasonic drilling technology whereby an inaudible high-pitched sound causes a diamond-tipped drill-bit to vibrate at incredibly fast rates.[68] This technology enabled them to cut through heavy stone with extreme precision. Similar technology in use today was only invented within the last century.

Clearly this advanced technology was just a small sampling of what our extraterrestrial ancestors brought to Earth. Like any technology used for the betterment of humanity, it always had the potential to be abused, and so it was. Most of these technologies were lost to humanity after the flood except where hidden away and preciously guarded within the small enclaves of those faithful disciples to the early Serpents of Wisdom. Therefore an echo or vestige of this wondrous power was preserved in the mystery schools of Ageless Wisdom to be handed down to us today in these rudimentary techniques involving sound, color, and imagery.

Music of the Spheres and Modern Day Stargates

Anyone who's ever seen the unforgettable film classic "Close Encounters of the Third Kind" will recall the beautiful little melody that evolves into the major thematic motif for the entire screen score. At first, it appears to permeate the Earth's atmosphere emerging out of the collective unconscious of humanity – from the Indians chanting the melody and pointing up to the sky when asked where it came from – to the little boy playing the tune on his toy xylophone. Finally, the French scientist is able to map it out mathematically, correlate it with specific colors, and then use it in contact with the ETs as a way of communicating with them. Incidentally, this movie was loosely based on an event that took place in 1954 at what is now Edwards Air Force Base.[69] Whether or not sounds and colors were used in the contact context, however, is unknown to me.

Linda Tucker of P.U.R.E. Research, has documented many events tracing sound to UFO encounters.[70] Sometimes the sounds appear to come directly from the craft – sometimes the sounds are heard before or after the craft appears. Many times, a craft will appear silently and make no sound at all. And sometimes not all persons present will hear the identical sounds if any. Another frequent phenomenon is the sound of "beeping tones" heard in locations where there have been sightings of UFOs, particularly in crop circles. During the 1960s and 70s, many of these cases were investigated by the Air Force and Department of Civil Defense. Tucker contacted Dr. Ronald Stearman, an aerospace professor who was interested in analyzing these sounds. Using some of the most advanced acoustical analysis software, Dr. Stearman sampled several recordings with a digital signal analyzer and converted the data into a graph depicting the sound in the frequency domain. The signals were further filtered using variable speed analysis and strip chart time domain studies to determine other characteristics of the sound. The preliminary results of this study showed that the sounds are remarkably similar:

The peaks associated with the beep frequencies all
match up at about 1050 HZ. with the median beep-
frequency interval occurring at approximately 1.7 HZ
... The beeps are roughly spaced at 0.6 to 0.7
seconds apart. The common spectral peak
frequencies of the first four recordings varied only by
7 percent. This variation was expected due to the
various types of recorders and generations of source
tapes available for use... [71]

What this means exactly has not yet been determined.
What we do know, however, is that anomalous electromagnetic
effects often appear in conjunction with these sounds.
Electrical failures and erratic equipment behavior are often
noted in the vicinity of these events, and many times these
sounds are heard broadcast over regular radio waves. Unusual
animal and insect behavior has been observed in response to
these sounds.[72] In fact, animals often sense the presence of
UFOs long before humans, indicating the possible occurrence of
frequency emissions outside the spectrum of our normal hearing
range.

Crop circle researcher Colin Andrews recorded sound
sequences heard inside of a crop circle believed to have come
from the UFO craft that made the crop circle in question.
Professional musician and CSETI member, Charlie Balogh,
determined that these sounds were simple sine waves, and then
produced a "distilled version" of them with the pure tones of a
synthesizer. The prominent tones in this sound sequence are
"E" and "G". CSETI teams often broadcast the distilled version
while trying to initiate contact with ETI. According to CSETI
members, fruitful results have been obtained from this activity.
Balogh says,

I believe it is the tones themselves that are important
and that it isn't necessary to use a copy of the original
tape to achieve the goal desired during the CSETI
contact protocols. I like to think of the tones as a sort
of cosmic birdcall, somewhat like an airport beacon

or a sonic lighthouse signaling the fieldwork team's location. Only time will tell if I'm correct.[73]

The specific tones of E and G have Qabalistic significance. Yet I have not determined if that means anything in this instance.

Many CSETI members have had unusual experiences while simply playing the tape recording of the beeping tones. Balogh relates, "...after playing the tones for about 15 or 20 minutes, I've heard the same tones played back to me when I've been by myself and with the group. Some folks have even heard them after they've gone back to their hotel rooms during a training. They sometimes come from one direction and also from all directions. Not very loud, but definitely audible."[74] As another CSETI member explains, it's as if the ETs are saying, "Hi there! Glad you got our message!"

CSETI teams have also been successful establishing contact when playing a recording of a musical composition by Michaele de Cygne believed to be a musical translation of mathematical fractals from Mayan calendar calculations. In listening to this music, the musical interval of the tritone is predominant in the harmonic structure. The Russian composer, Alexander Scriabin and the French composer, Olivier Messiaen, both considered the tritone to be sacred. This makes sense to me because esoterically, according to theory behind the sound-color scale I tested, the colors corresponding to the two notes in a tritone are always opposites that when combined become gray, symbolizing the inherent unity of all things. Could it be that this creates a kind of universal cosmic 'signature' that transcends cultural or planetary differences, making it easier for beings who have mastered nondual reality (like ETs) to recognize, 'lock on' and respond to?

The sacred Mayan calendar, called the Tzolk'in, can be broken down into thirteen specific harmonic sequences, which de Cygne translated into music. The Mayans believed the origin of these cycles to come from a divine source, which de Cygne calls "the Great Harmonic Matrix/Mother." It is probably more accurate to say that the calendar system was given to the Mayans or their ancestors by a representative of the Divine, who we know from Zecharia Sitchin's work to be a version of Quetzalcoatl --the "feathered serpent god" – one of the ruling Anunnaki.[75] At any rate, de Cygne explains the calendar as follows:

> The cycles/harmonics of Energies embodied by the Tzolk'in are believed to originate from the Divine Consciousness of the Great Mother/Spirit/Father, emanating (or being transmitted) throughout the galaxy via the electromagnetic waves surging from our galactic core. The Qualities of the Energies expressed by the Tzolk'in's harmonic interactions or permutations are constant, on all planes, in all dimensions. These permutations, which I'll refer to herein as "Harmonic Patterns" are believed to compose the vibratory Framework of all existence throughout the universe. Being universally constant, these Harmonic Patterns are evident (and encoded) in the formation (measure) and cycles (movement) of galactic, stellar and planetary systems as well as in the "fibers" of our spirits and souls (our etheric bodies), in the neuronal networks of our body's central nervous system and in the molecular structure and harmonic spirals of DNA. Thus, the Tzolk'in expresses an universal, harmonic lattice which engenders the composition of the forms and transformations of all that exists, in all dimensions, including the Harmonic Patterns (of Spirit and Nature) which spawn all aspects of Consciousness and Being as well as DNA. (While this may seem fantastic, sci-fi or "new age hoop-dedoo" to many, this ancient understanding is being validated by empirical science on a daily basis.) Observing the embodiment of these Patterns in the planetary, solar, galactic systems, the Maya recognized the correlations between macrocosmic cycles and those of the subtler realms of existence, including the psyche and spirit. (As sacred archetypes, these

Patterns are represented in the gamut of the world's religions and spiritual traditions.) Eventually, the Tzolk'in revealed Itself to them as Vinculum, a scientific and esoteric Model that functions as a Tie bonding all religions, all sciences and all religions with all sciences and (most profoundly) as an Harmonic Matrix embodying and expressing an universal, binary Code by Which all aspects of the human being and the Cosmos are inherently unified, brought into universal alignment and synchronized to effect the expression of Divine Being throughout the human being via the individual's spiritual/mental, psychic/astral and physical/material bodies.[76]

Debbie Foch, CSETI Coordinator, says that they believe the de Cygne music "... is a Fibonacci sequence, and the sound expands our consciousness as well as helping more of the phase shifted/dematerialized objects/beings to "bleed through" or be projected into our visible reality."[77] This explanation rides well with what was related about the ability of some spiritual practitioners to use sound in an effort to materialize their visualizations. CSETI teams often amplify the tones or music with a transceiver when trying to establish contact. They feel that using as many bands of the communication spectrum as is possible increases the probability for contact, and I am told that their success rate using this technique is nearly 100 percent.[78]

As of this writing, CSETI has not done much with the color end of the spectrum in their contact efforts except for using lasers in conjunction with amplifying tones as a means of marking their location for the ETs' benefit. But the color of the laser is random and not specifically chosen for any particular purpose. At any rate, it does appear that sounds and colors are an integral aspect of the language of contact between ETs and humans thus far, as would be expected.

If everything has its own unique vibratory rate or frequency pattern or "song" as I prefer to think, from the smallest subatomic particle to the largest galaxy and beyond – then the ancient idea of the 'music of the spheres' is not a simple metaphor after all. Pythagorus, the Greek philosopher who was a contemporary of Buddha (500 B.C.E.) said, "The octave formed a circle and gave our noble earth its form."[79] Two dimensionally, this is represented by the infinity sign which looks like a figure 8 on its side, untwisting itself and forming a complete circle. Meditation on that symbolism reveals much.

Pythagorus is accredited as being the first western thinker to associate music with numbers. He also created the diatonic scale of seven notes, which gave rise to his doctrine of the music of the spheres. Heline states:

> According to his calculations the distance from the Moon to the Earth corresponded to one tone; the distance from the Moon to Mercury equaled a semitone; from Mercury to Venus one and one-half tones; Sun to Mars one tone; Mars to Jupiter, a semitone; Jupiter to Saturn, a semitone; and Saturn to the fixed stars, or zodiac, one and one-half tones.[80]

All musical scales consist of patterns of five, seven, or twelve tones. These numbers are fundamental to all structures in the universe, like the Golden Mean and the Fibonacci Series. Musical intervals (the distance between any two notes) are the result of the ratios between their frequencies. The astronomer Johannes Kepler (1571-1630) found that these intervals correspond to the ratios of each planet's angular velocities seen from the sun. A renaissance era treatise relates a vision of Hermes Trismegistus describing the descent of the soul through the Solar System. As the soul passes each celestial body, it takes on the psychological qualities of those bodies in varying degrees, and these expressions of energy can be seen in the natal horoscope of an individual. In her book, *Music, Mysticism and Magic*, Jocelyn Godwin writes, "Each incarnate being therefore sounds, as it were, a different chord of the planetary or psychological harmonies, and it is this that causes *musica humana* (the music of the human being) to resemble *musica mundana* (the music of the worlds or spheres)."[81]

NASA released some recordings of planetary music. The United States space probe Voyager discovered that the magnetosphere of Saturn emits peculiar waves. When these waves are transposed into audible sound by speeding them up, they sound like a slow, dreamy tune when played on a synthesizer.[82]

The astrological natal or birth chart is a diagram of the earth and sky at the exact moment a person is born. As no two individuals are alike, no two astrological charts are the same. Specific placements of the planets and the aspects between them in minutes and degrees are reflected in the natal chart of an individual, which is a complete 360 degree circle. Complex mathematical calculations determine the placement of the planets and their relationships to each other in zodiac signs and houses of the chart. Therefore, many musicians intuitively perceive that a person's chart could be said to represent the keynote or "song" of that individual. The astrological aspects can be translated into musical intervals. Composer/pianist Gerald Jay Markoe has attempted to translate astrological charts of various individuals into music. Whether or not this technique can be tested for accuracy and eventually evolve into an exact science remains to be seen. It certainly suggests a way in which such frequency patterns could be ascertained. Maybe this is how the Atlanteans found the original sound or keynote for a human being.

Peter Michael Hamel, in his book, *Through Music to the Self*, writes:

> The construction of a 'musical' cosmology, and the harmonic correspondences between the laws of music and of atomic physics, are thus not just mere esoteric speculation. Contemporary research has ventured into the field of 'occult' phenomena and revealed a scientific basis for many of our intuitive and mystic intimations.[83]

For instance, one mystic scientist, Wilfried Kruger, discovered that the musical proportions governing musical

580

intervals are the proportions found in the shells of the atomic nucleus. He also states that the structure of the major scale otherwise known as the Gregorian Ionic mode, can be demonstrated in the nucleus of an oxygen atom:

'The eighth atom of the periodic table, the oxygen atom (O), *the* basis of our breathing, reacts under radiation (heating, burning) with almost all elements. Its nucleus contains eight protons. Our scale has eight notes. The two notes at each end of the octave coincide almost exactly, and through their oscillation-ratio create the strongest resonance.' The 'magic numbers' (2, 8, 20, 28, 50, 82, and 126) for whose discovery Maria Goeppert-Mayer and Hans D. Jensen received the Nobel Prize for Physics in 1963, give to the atomic nucleus (e.g., in the case of oxygen, whose atomic number is 8) a special stability. An atom comprises a nucleus and a shell. The nucleus consists of protons and neutrons. The shell consists of inner and outer shells that surround the nucleus concentrically. The inner and outer shells are full of electrons. Wilfried Kruger now compared the spacings of the inner atom with those of the scale, consequently found the structures of both minor scales in the atomic nucleus and finally arrived at the following deduction in respect of the harmonic scale: 'With the harmonic minor scale we face a synthesis between the vertically-orientated forces of the inner atom and the horizontally-orientated forces binding the molecule together... In the case of the carbon atom (atomic number: 6) the scale can contain only six notes. The "carbon-scale is a hexachord... Likewise one of the deepest secrets of the Pythagorean secret teachings, the sacred *Tetraktys*, is traced in Kruger's work to the prime elements of organic life, the nucleic acids. This *Tetraktys* comprised the four intervals of the octave, fifth, fourth and second, according to whose governing laws, under the terms of the Pythagorean teachings, the life of the world and creation itself unfolds.[84]

Because these universal principles of vibration and resonance are embedded in everything, places as well as people have their own frequency patterns. Might this be the basis for a theory of 'stargates' – portals through which UFOs and ETs have always been able to pass through more easily? We know that special areas of the Earth show variations in resonance, and that our brain waves can become entrained to those varying frequencies often resulting in mystical states. The electromagnetic grid and energy ley lines play into this concept as well when considering why certain places have long been considered sacred or special throughout history. Indigenous peoples speak often of sacred mountains, magical wells, and other places of power. This may also explain why UFO sightings are more common in some areas than others. In fact, studies measuring and documenting the magnetic effects and other anomalies at such places have shown that something to that effect is occurring.[85] Steven Halpern explains:

> It has been shown that the entire body as a total system vibrates at a fundamental rate of approximately 7.8 to 8 cycles per second (inaudible) when it is allowed to come into its most natural, relaxed state of being. The frequency of brain waves produced in this deeply relaxed (alpha) state, as in meditation, is also in the 8 cycles per second range.
> This is no accident. Physicists have shown that the earth itself vibrates at this same fundamental frequency of 8 cycles per second. This is known as the Schumann resonance, and is a function of the speed of electro-magnetic radiations divided by the circumference of the earth. The nervous system of all life forms are attuned to this fundamental frequency. Thus there is a resonance between the human instrument in a natural relaxed state and the electrically charged layers of the earth's atmosphere.
> This suggests that the phrase *"being in harmony with oneself and the universe"* might be more than a beautiful, poetic image.[86]

Could it be that each and every individual has within themselves their own individual stargate based on their own unique frequency pattern? And by tuning into such an original pattern (the "Self" in mystical terms), the personality can be realigned into a more perfect reflection and thus expression of that divinity within? Archetypal symbols and mandalas open up interdimensional doorways in the psyche, and all archetypes, from the simple to the complex, are essentially crystallized sound waves.

Itzhak Bentov, another scientist/mystic, even describes the difference between the absolute and relative realities in vibratory terms:

> What was the nature of our reality before the vibratory motion started? Clearly, the nonvibratory state is the basis of the latter, which appeared when the vibratory motion arose and became our physical manifest reality. The nonvibratory base we may call the *absolute protospace.*
>
> At the risk of complicating things a little bit, we can also define the absolute as being an *infinitely* fine relative, that is, where the size of the waves is so minute and their frequency is so high that they are invisible. When this happens, we have a surface that appears calm and smooth but contains a tremendous energy and is *full of creative potential.* This is the actual definition of the absolute (to the extent that it can be defined); it is a high-energy creative potential plus intelligence. The "intelligence" adds a *self-organizing capability* to any entity in creation. Therefore, the ripples of the "relative" arise in a surface that appears to be smooth but is actually vibrant with potential creative energy. The smaller the amplitude of the waves, the higher the energy contained by the surface. As the waves become so small that the crests and valleys, which are the points of rest, come so close to each other as to overlap,

then a state of rest is reached, in which motion is just potential motion and the energy of the system becomes infinitely large.

The absolute is thus a state in which *contrasting concepts become reconciled* and fused. *Movement and rest fuse into one.*

Ours, then is a vibratory reality – from subnuclear to atomic, to molecular, to macrolevels. *Everything is oscillating between two states of rest.* Everything is producing "sound."[87]

Spoken like a true Qabalist!

To provide a comprehensive treatment of sound, color, music, and the creative process as they relate to universal principle is beyond the scope of this book. Authors have written entire books on this subject, and more could still be written. Suffice it to say however, that within the study of music itself -- all the mysteries of the universe are revealed in one form or another.

Music, Political Power and Freedom

Because music as a force in and of itself is so powerful, when coupled with political protest and resistance, it can and often does becomes explosive. This combustibility seems to have peaked in the 1960s and again in the 1980s. That this phenomenon occurred when our civil liberties were under renewed and vigorous attack is no coincidence.

Initially I planned to develop this theme to demonstrate its relationship to my topic in terms of how our government tries to control us, and how it is so important to fight censorship on all fronts for this reason. It's just one more way the muddlers try to hide the truth. Instead, I will pray that such truth is self-evident and leave you to consider this:

I believe that one can tell a lot about another person just by perusing their music library. If a person's library contains only one kind of music, watch out. It's like eating only one kind of food. Something will be lacking in their mental and emotional health. Doesn't matter what kind of music it is either. The more genres of music -- the more diverse the collection, the "sounder" the person. Having said that, little room is left for discrimination of any kind of music.

Unfortunately, the media which is controlled by the controlling corporations, do not wish you to be so open-minded, tolerant, and appreciative of such diversity and visionary art. Therefore, only selected types of music get aggressively marketed, and it's a very narrow sampling. It's up to you to seek out the rest. I encourage you to do so, not just for your own sake but for everyone's benefit.

Dissonance, angry music, even silly music has its place. Not one kind of music is "better" for your health than another, no matter what some New Agers might try to sell you. Studies suggest that listening to a type of music that you don't like while eating, for example, causes more stress, therefore more indigestion – than music that is labeled calm and relaxing. We are all different. And if you listen, you will know what you need.

If you hear music that offends you, just don't buy it. Censorship is never the way. We must never look to government, the music industry, or any other organization to do our job or the job of parents -- to make our decisions for us about our health, our musical tastes or about anything because that's the first step towards fascism. Musicians and artists who put their art and their lives on the line for what they believe in – give them voice – even if you don't like what they say. They still have as much right to say it as anyone. Stand up for them as you would for yourself. You will not be standing alone.

Journalist Stuart Goldman, interviewing Jello Biafra of the defunct punk rock bank, *The Dead Kennedys*, wrote:

> The trend towards censorship today – which goes hand in hand with the rampant narcissism and empty-headed patriotism so in vogue in America – is

stronger than ever. In fact, the climate in America today is frighteningly reminiscent of that which existed in pre-Hitler Germany. In view of this, we are more than ever in need of true outlaws – which doesn't mean a self-serving simpleton like Willie Nelson or some stupid rock and roll moron yelling "fuck the establishment." No, real rebels are those who aren't afraid to go against majority opinion, no matter what the cost personally or in terms of their careers. If the American system is to remain viable, it depends on people who are willing to be disruptive, and more – willing to fight for the right to be disruptive. This stance, and not empty ballyhooing of *this* cause or *that* issue, is the real essence of freedom.[88]

Though Goldman wrote that in 1986, it is nonetheless true today. And though the music of Willie Nelson and hard rockers singing "fuck you!" can be great music and has its place, we still need more than just that and as much variety as possible because music is the very breath and blood of our lives. The moment we allow that gift to be taken from us, we've lost it all and the muddlers have already won.

So sing your song. No one else can do it for you. And in so singing – the music will never die. True freedom comes from that and that alone. It wasn't a great big battleship that blew up the Death Star. It wasn't an army of hobbits, elves and dwarves who threw the ring back into Mount Doom. It wasn't the Kansas militia that recovered the broomstick of the Wicked Witch. It was one person – a unique individual – the hero with a thousand faces. The ocean could not exist without all those countless individual drops of water. That's the beautiful paradox about it. You make a difference by you just being yourself as Mr. Rogers says. It's got to start somewhere. It might as well start with you. Play on!

---

[1] Donald E. Michel, *Music Therapy: An Introduction to Therapy and Special Education Through Music*, Charles C. Thomas, 1976.

[2] Carl G. Jung, *Man and His Symbols*, Aldus Books Limited, 1964, p. 79.

[3] Steven Halpern with Louis Savary, *Sound Health: The Music and Sounds that Make Us Whole*, Harper & Row, 1985, p.160.

[4] Cyril Scott, *Music: Its Secret Influence Throughout the Ages*, 3rd ed., Samuel Weiser, 1973.

[5] Paul Foster Case, *Highlights of Tarot*, 7th ed., Builders of the Adytum, 1970, pp. 46-47.

[6] Madsen and Madsen's *Experimental Research in Music* (1978), often used as a textbook in music therapy classes, is a perfect example of this kind of bias.

[7] Scott D. Rogo, "Communication and Parapsychology: A Report on the 28th International Conference of the Parapsychology Foundation," *Parapsychology Review*, X/6, Nov.-Dec. 1979, pp. 1-7.

[8] *Id.*, p. 6.

[9] Corrine Heline, *Music: The Keynote of Human Evolution*, New Age Press, 1965; Corrine Heline, *Esoteric Music Based on the Musical Seership of Richard Wagner,* 3rd ed., New Age Press, 1970; Corrine Heline, *Healing and Regeneration Through Music*, 15th ed., New Age Press, 1974; Scott, 1973.

[10] Mikol Davis and Earle Lane, *Rainbows of Life: The Promise of Kirlian Photography*, Harper & Row, 1978.

[11] Laurel E. Keyes, *Toning: The Creative Power of the Voice*, DeVorss & Co., 1973.

[12] William Bise, "Natural and Artificial Pulsed Electronic Waves and Life Function," *United States Psychotronics Association Newsletter*, III/1, Spring, 1981, pp. 5-7.

[13] Scott, p. 58.

[14] Joan Orion, "Training in Energy Awareness," a cassette tape recording of a lecture given at the United States Psychotronics Conference in Dayton, Ohio, 1980.

[15] Keyes, 1973.

[16] Sufi Inayat Khan, "The Mysticism of Sound," "Music," "The Power of the Word," "Cosmic Language," *The Sufi Message of Hazrat Inayat Khan,* Vol. II, 4th ed., Servire Wassenaar, 1976.

[17] Originally, this theory was to be tested too with the use of several clairvoyants isolated in soundproof booths observing what was occurring in the atmosphere around human subjects listening to music and in their auras. Unfortunately, after speaking with several clairvoyants, it was decided that there were far too many variables involved to do this experiment, given the limited resources available and lack of adequate controls.

[18] Keyes, pp. 67-68.

[19] Heline, 1965.

[20] Scott, 1973.

[21] Itzhak Bentov, *Stalking the Wild Pendulum,* 4th ed., Bantam, 1979.

[22] Benson Herbert, "Fourth International Congress on Psychotronic Research," *Parapsychology Review*, II/1, Jan.-Feb. 1980, pp. 11-17.

[23] *Id.*, p. 16.

[24] *Id.*.

[25] George Rochberg, "A Raid on the Infinite," *Psi Factors in Creativity* – Proceedings of an International Conference held in France, June, 1969, ed. Allan Angoff & Betty Shapin, Parapsychology Foundation, Inc., 1970.

[26] R. Bonewits, "A Psychic Exploration of Music," The Gnosticon Tapes, Gnostic Aquarian Festival, 1974.

[27] *Id.*

[28] Robert Donington, *Wagner's 'Ring' and Its Symbols – The Music and the Myth,* Faber & Faber, 1963.

[29] Heline, 1970, p. 129.

[30] *Id.*

[31] A Webster dictionary dated 1966 that I used in 1982.

[32] Erno Lendvai, *Bela Bartok: An Analysis of His Music*, 1971: rev. reprint: Kahn & Averhill, 1979.

[33] M. L. von Franz, "Science and the Unconscious," *Man and His Symbols*, ed. by Carl G. Jung, Doubleday, 1964.

[34] Donington, p. 20.

[35] *Id.*, p. 23.

[36] *Id.*, p. 20.

[37] Heline, 1970, pp. 108-109.

[38] Olivier Messiaen, *Technique de Mon Language Musical*, Alphonse Leduc, 1944, p. 34.

[39] *Id.*, p. 13.

[40] *Id.*, p. 52.

[41] Olivier Messiaen, "Preface," *Quatour pour la fin du temps,* Durand & Cie, 1942, p. 1.

[42] Case, pp. 29-30.

[43] *Id.*

[44] *Id.*, p. 43.

[45] *Id.*, pp. 42-43.

[46] Heline, 1970.

[47] See H.H. J. Keil, "A GESP Test with Favorite Music Targets," *The Journal of Parapsychology*, Vol. 20 (1985), pp. 35-44; Kathleen Altom and William G. Braud, "Clairvoyant and Telepathic Impressions of Musical Targets," in J.D. Morris et al. (Eds,) *Research in Parapsychology* (1975), pp. 171-174.

[48] Pamela Bloom, "Soul Music," *New Age Journal,* March/April, 1987, p. 59.

[49] *Id.*, p. 59, quoting from M. Critchley and R.A. Henson (eds.), *Music and the Brain: Studies in the Neurology of Music.*

[50] Halpern, pp. 182-183.

[51] Davis & Lane, 1978; Stanley Krippner and Daniel Rubin (eds.), *The Kirlian Aura: Photographing the Galaxies of Life*, Doubleday, 1974.

[52] Heline, 1965, p. 135

[53] Dane Rudhyar, *The Magic of Tone and the Art of Music*, Shambhala, 1982, p. 16.

[54] Heline, 1965, p. 35.

[55] Peter Michael Hamel, *Through Music to the Self,* Element Books, 1978, p. 109, referencing Evans-Wentz: Appendix to the *Tibetan Book of the Dead*, London, 1927.

[56] Heline, 1965, pp. 34-35.

[57] Dr. Helmut Lammer and Marion Lammer, *Milabs: Military Mind Control and Alien Abduction*, IllumiNet Press, 1999; Thomas E. Bearden, *Excalibur Briefing: Explaining Paranormal Phenomena*, Walnut Hill, 1980.

[58] Heline, 1965, pp. 47-48.

[59] Related to myself and others by Dr. Greer in February of 2003.

[60] Ralph M. DeBit, *Colloidal Structure*, Rowny Press, 1957, quoted by Laurel Elizabeth Keyes in *Toning: The Creative Power of the Voice*, DeVorss & Company, 1973, p.41.

[61] Gareth Knight, *The Secret Tradition in Arthurian Legend,* Samuel Weiser, Inc., 1996, p. 120.

[62] Hamel, p. 71.

[63] Andrew Collins, *Gods of Eden*, Bear & Co., 1998, p. 65.

[64] Shardza Tashi Gyaltsen, *Heart Drops of Dharmakaya: Dzogchen Practice of the Bon Tradition*, Snow Lion Publications, 2002, p. 102. Reprinted with permission.

[65] Collins, p. 60.

[66] *Id.*, p. 61.

[67] *Id.*, p. 62.

[68] *Id.*, p. 55.

[69] Milton William Cooper, *Behold a Pale Horse*, Light Technology Publishing, 1991, p. 204. Be advised that while this book has some fascinating information in it, there is also much muddling.

[70] Linda Tucker, "Tracing Sound to UFO Encounters," *MUFON UFO Journal*, Oct. 1994, No. 318.

[71] *Id.*

[72] *Id.*

[73] From the CSETI Working Group Training Kit, 1995.

[74] From a personal e-mail exchange with Charlie Balogh dated May 3, 2003. Used by permission.

[75] Zecharia Sitchin, *The Lost Realms*, Avon Books, 1990.

[76] Michaele de Cygne, as published on her personal website: http://cirrus.spaceports.com/~solomoon/musicresume.html.

[77] From personal e-mail exchange with Debbie Foch, dated May 2, 2003. Used by permission.

[78] *Id.*

[79] Heline, 1965, p. 57.

[80] Corinne Heline, *Healing and Regeneration Through Music*, New Age Press, Inc., 1974, p. 6.

[81] Joscelyn Godwin, *Music, Mysticism and Magic: A Sourcebook*, Arkana, 1976, p. 14.

[82] Thomas Vaczy Hightower, "The Musical Octave," previously published online at http://home3.inet.tele.dk/hitower/octave2.html.

[83] Hamel, p. 106.

[84] Hamel, p. 107.

[85] Paul Devereux, John Steele and David Kubrin, *Earthmind: Communicating with the Living World of Gaia,* Destiny Books, 1992.

[86] Halpern, pp. 38-39.

[87] Itzhak Bentov, *Stalking the Wild Pendulum*, Bantam Books, 1977, pp. 110-111.

[88] Stuart Goldman, from an interview with Jello Biafra published in *The Reader – Los Angeles's Free Weekly*, Friday, June 20, 1986, Vol. 8, No. 35.

PART 7

Going Home

Remember, we say that a flower is blooming whether it is in half, three-quarters, or full bloom.

-- Clarissa Pinkola Estés

CHAPTER 10

DOROTHY WAKES UP: MEANWHILE, BACK AT THE RANCH...

My goodness! What a journey we've had. Was it a dream?

Simple Summary

In Part One, we learned all about the esoteric mystery schools behind the world's spiritual traditions. We explored what it means to be a spiritual aspirant on the Path and the true purpose of that Path. In Part Two, we learned what occultism really is and how and why it's such an integral part of the Path. We looked at the principles, techniques, the teaching methods, and established a cosmological context for their applications. In Part Three, we discovered the landscape and the environment where these applications are made, which revealed their extraterrestrial origins. We learned all about our extraterrestrial ancestors, their impact on history and how the mystery schools evolved up to the present day. In Part Four, we began to wake up and open our eyes. What we see at first is not at all pleasant. We encountered the inner and outer obstacles on the Path, how these obstacles came about, who put them there and why. In Part Five, we begin to arm ourselves for the rest of the journey. We learned all about the physiology of awareness so that we can take back the power that rightly belongs to us. We begin to heal so the world can heal. In Part Six, we discover perhaps the greatest key to all of this -- one which will strengthen our ability to communicate with all beings and therefore enable us to better understand ourselves, others, and the nature of the universe. And here we are now in Part Seven – Going Home.

There's No Place Like Home

We all know "There's no place like home." But what does that mean exactly? Jesse Stewart writes:

> Describing with words what Dorothy possibly means by, "There's no place like home" is almost impossible. This statement points to something that can hardly be articulated. Because both book and film act only as mediums of the message, they each have their limitations as to how much of Dorothy's paradigm shift and new understanding they can convey. What is needed is for each of us to become active in our imaginations, to fill in for ourselves what may be the message of the story.[1]

However your home was when you were growing up, however it is now, however you would like it to be -- home is vital to all of us. The word "homeless" brings up unimaginable fears for most people. Yet there are people precisely in that condition. There are also many folks who have a home but feel as if they do not belong. Or how about certain orphans, who despite having the most loving adoptive parents, still feel alienated because they don't know where they came from?

Home is not necessarily a family, nor is it a house. Home is whatever you want it to be. So if we take the word figuratively, it could even mean more than previously imagined, as in *The Wizard of Oz*.

In an earlier chapter, I wrote about home representing the source of our true being – the Higher Self – God – or something along those lines. To me, home represents the ultimate – the place where we are completely secure, completely loved, and completely nurtured. It's a refuge -- a place where we can set anchor and rest. It's a place that belongs to us alone, where we can be just as wild and as free as the heart allows. It's where the heart is. It's inside of each of us.

We may share it with others -- we may not. One thing is for certain. Home is where we live. Do we take it with us or do we leave it behind when we go to work each day? That's up to us. As Stewart says, what we do with this concept is up to each of us as individuals. Still, it is a universal concept with universal meaning and application to a large degree.

Beyond the Wall: Rogers Waters and "Home"

There is a musician who I consider one of my most important mentors. His inimitable artistry delivers a spiritual alchemy beyond compare. He is a recognized artistic genius. He's a spiritual warrior. He's a bleeding heart. He is a mesmerizing magician. He's a fearless prophet. He's a brutal visionary. He's a reflection of us all. He is Roger Waters.[2]

Roger Waters was the bass player, lead vocalist, and master mind for the original rock group *Pink Floyd*. When the band split up, his magic didn't stop. It continued to manifest in his solo work. He continues to gift us with extraordinary music which is as thought provoking as it is enjoyable. I've always wanted to write a tribute to him but nothing I could say seemed like enough. His contributions speak for themselves. Yet I feel like I owe him as much gratitude as I do my spiritual mentors. Words alone are inadequate for describing his impact on the world of music, the world itself, and me. I am not alone in feeling this way.

I bring him up in this final chapter because *home* is an underlying theme that runs all through his music. *The Wall*, which was made into a movie and considered by some to be his greatest masterpiece, is a modern music drama. It is a psychological study in the psychosocial dynamics of authoritarianism and domination within the self and between the individual psyche and society at large. In the beginning of Chapter 7, I spoke at length about this. Waters exposes, explores and develops these dynamics in the story of *The Wall*. On a deeper level, the lyrics in the music reflecting the events in the life of the main character, Pink, reveal deeper archetypal conflicts within all of us which play out as our projections in the arena of dominator society.

Waters admits that Pink is partly biographical and partly autobiographical. The events that happen in the life of Pink partly reflect events in his own life and events in the life of Syd

594

Barrett, a beloved band member who was lost to madness.[3] Waters' father was killed in World War II – so was Pink's.

On the surface, it appears that Waters' treatment of women in *The Wall* is a bit biased. He admits he was partly influenced by some painful relationship experiences when he wrote the music. Yet true to the Hermetic Axiom, he was in the spiritual process of coming to terms with his own anima – the female archetypal aspect of his being in Jungian terminology. The shadow side of the anima only presents when there is some kind of repression going on. A rejection of that energy, which is just as essential to a man's psyche as the animus (male archetype) is to a woman's, will result in it coming out in a destructive form in order to get one's attention. Therefore, the microcosm of Pink was having a hard time with women.

This is nothing specific to Pink. We all go through this at one time or another in our psychosocial development. A period of painful relationships is a sign that the psyche is ready to re-integrate – that the ground is fertile for planting the seeds for the eventual meeting and union with the mature masculine or mature feminine because the psyche itself is maturing. Growth is a process of tearing down and rebuilding. Even biologically our bodies are constantly shedding dead cells in order to replace them with new ones.

But Pink doesn't let go of the dead cells so he can heal. He holds onto them, buries them deep inside, and they become smelly rotten targets for the worms. Instead of facing his difficulties and working through them, he chooses to withdraw, further alienating himself from the divine feminine. This leads to a psychotic break with reality. He was ripe for this because from the beginning of his life he never had the opportunity to establish a toehold for the development of an adequate sense of autonomy with healthy boundaries due to the absence of his father. There was no balance. He never knew his father, meaning he never learned how to actualize himself in the world – never learned how to solve problems for himself – never learned how to stand up for himself. A strong single mother can teach these skills to her son, but Pink's mother did not. She hid inside her sense of loss, becoming unavailable for the child. Whatever attention she showered on him was compensatory – smothering – overprotective – a recipe for codependency. He never learned to rely on himself because he didn't have the proper role models.

> *Mama's gonna make all of your nightmares come true*
> *Mama's gonna put all of her fears into you,*
> *Mama's gonna keep you right here under her wing.*
> *She won't let you fly but she might let you sing,*
> *Mama's gonna keep baby cosy and warm.*
> *Ooh babe, ooh babe, ooh babe,*
> *of course Mama's gonna help build the wall.*[4]

The construction of the wall -- the tower of self-isolation, begins.

A sign that something is wrong with Pink's developing masculine archetype is seen when it manifests as the cruel authoritarian schoolmaster who attacks his sense of self-worth. Pink the schoolboy is punished and publicly ridiculed for self-expression through his poetry, which is also an assault on the feminine or creative aspect of his being. He turns to cigarettes and voyeurism to ease the pain. He grows up to be a rock star, does drugs, and gets married. By then the addiction has claimed him. He neglects his wife for his drugs and music, so she turns to someone else for comfort. This illicit affair devastates him. It's the straw that breaks the camel's back, representing a complete betrayal by his anima, and this is just too much.

At this point in the movie, we are treated to some brilliant original animation by artist Gerald Scarfe. The symbolism of this scene is all about the tension between the male and female energies. It shows how unhealthy relationships, the violation of fragile boundaries, and exploited sexuality as a form of domination set the stage for the scourge of war and global domination. The macrocosm reflects the microcosm. All are interrelated. Death, loss, suffering, sacrifice – it's an intense, visually graphic animation where shapeshifting symbols tell the story better than words ever could.

Pink becomes unresponsive and hypnotized by television. When a female groupie tries to break the spell, he erupts into a rage, letting loose emotional steam that had been building up for some time. We are taken on a tour through Pink's mind in order to see what's really going on. The images are deeply surreal and symbolic.

Here we have trauma messing with the kundalini, as described in Chapter 8. Pink has a genuine 'peak' experience. Through the psychotic revelation, he catches a glimpse of an alternate reality and possibly a way out of his pain. Initially it manifests as a manic state of hyper-arousal when everything seems all too real and all too clear, but it does not last.

> *I don't need no arms around me,*
> *And I don't need no drugs to calm me*
> *I have seen the writing on the wall.*
> *Don't think I need anything at all.*
> *Oh no, don't think I'll need anything at all.*
> *All in all it was all just bricks in the wall,*
> *All in all you were all just bricks in the wall.*[5]

He sings, "Goodbye, Cruel World." Instead of giving in to suicide, he retreats into the inmost recesses of his mind. The song, "Hey You" represents one last rhetorical call for help. The word 'home' first appears. "Open your heart, I'm coming home." But the wall was too high by then and the worms ate into his brain. On an abstract level, the merging of the microcosm and macrocosm is seen in the song "Is There Anybody Out There?" with Pink trapped behind the wall. This song is followed by "Nobody Home." He's trying to call into Higher Self Central but no one answers because he's shut it out. We hear "Vera," lamenting the loss of the sacred feminine. The song "Bring the Boys Back Home" is a call to society. We sacrifice our boys to dominator ideology early on in their lives so that they march off to war in service to the machine unquestioningly. They never knew home really – they never knew *principle-centered beingness* characterized by equilibrium between the masculine and feminine archetypes – a spiritual equanimity. If they did – if all of us did with any degree of consistency, there would be no war and no patriarchy – no dominator society.

Pink becomes "Comfortably Numb." This is my favorite song on the album. In it we hear the phrase, "Is there anybody *in* there?" We've gone from "out there" to "in there." The two worlds meet and become inseparable; the boundaries between self and other are indistinguishable. Pink is lost.

The psychotic break is complete. His manager and crew must break down the door and medicate him in order to get him to a state of minimal functioning so that the "show can go on." But the worms, having eaten into his brain, have him thoroughly possessed. Having nowhere to run, he internalizes the values of his oppressors and becomes like them -- a cruel, unfeeling fascist.

> *There must be some mistake,*
> *I didn't mean to let them take away my soul.*
> *Am I too old? Is it too late?*
> *Ooh Ma, Ooh Pa!*
> *Where has the feeling gone?*
> *Ooh Ma, Ooh pa!*
> *Will I remember the songs?*
> *Ooh ah! The show must go on.*[6]

The pendulum swings again. After a brutal campaign of violence against those "who don't look right" – excess has run its course, defenses are loosened, the mask is torn off, and we hear

> *Stop! I wanna go home,*
> *Take off this uniform and leave the show*
> *And I'm waiting in this cell because I have to know*
> *Have I been guilty all this time?*[7]

Pink, reduced to a helpless, faceless, lifeless-looking rag doll of not even an adult – the animation looks more like a child – is put on trial. He has fully sacrificed himself to the demons now. All his accusers – the schoolmaster, his mother and his wife – all reflections of his shadow self that consume him, confront him. Finally he is forced to face the music.

> *Good morning, worm your honour*
> *The crown will plainly show the prisoner who now*
> *stands before you*
> *Was caught redhanded showing feelings*
> *Feelings of an almost human nature.*
> *This will not do.*[8]

The Judge is a giant worm – oppressor supreme of the psyche. He is not gentle and shows no mercy. Pink is held accountable for everything that's happened to him. He is found guilty and sentenced to tear down the wall and be exposed before his peers.

Here we learn a great lesson. Though it appears that the Judge is meting out an excessively cruel and unusual punishment, he's actually doing Pink a favor. So it is with the muddlers in our lives. They challenge us, push our buttons, and make us see what needs to be changed within us – because they are our reflections on some level or another. When others victimize us, it means that in some way we have compromised ourselves. Otherwise, we never would've found ourselves in that position. So what is it? Are we not tending to the home front?

On Waters' solo album, *Radio K.A.O.S.*, he's got a song entitled *Home*. The first verse lists a bunch of cities that could be home for some people – ending with the line, "Everybody got somewhere they call home." Then there's a verse that goes:

> *When they overrun the defences*
> *A minor invasion put down to expenses*
> *Will you go down to the airport lounge*
> *Will you accept your second class status*

599

A nation of waitresses and waiters
Will you mix their martinis
Will you stand still for it
Or will you take to the hills[9]

The third verse lists things that could mean home, like a tract of arable land, a cabin, a bend in the river, and so on, then ending with the line, "Everybody got something they call home." Fourth verse:

When the cowboys and Arabs draw down
On each other at noon
In the cool dusty air of the city boardroom
Will you stand by a passive spectator
Of the market dictators
Will you discreetly withdraw
With your ear pressed to the boardroom door
Will you hear when the lion within you roars
Will you take to the hills[10]

Fifth verse places various types of people after the words 'could be' -- like a cyclist, a saint, a Vietnam Vet, a cop, a thief, a cripple, a dentist, on and on and on, until it gets to could be...

... the soldier in the white cravat
Who turns the key in spite of the fact
That this is the end of the cat and the mouse
Who dwelt in the house
Where the laughter rang and the tears were spilt
The house that Jack built ...
Bang, bang, shoot, shoot
White gloved thumb, Lord thy will be done
He was always a good boy his mother said
He'll do his duty when he's grown, yeah
Everybody got someone they call home.[11]

This is the same message as "Bring the Boys Back Home" but with more depth and urgency. The house is not a home. And I don't believe the word "call" in this instance is a noun in

as much as it's a verb. It's time to start calling people home –
to come home – away from the madness of the current social
system controlled by "The Powers that Be," which is the title of
another song on the album. That song is all about the muddlers.
And …

> *If you see them come*
> *You better run – run*
> *You better run on home.*[12]

Radio K.A.O.S. is a story about another hero's journey.
Instead of a hobbit or a young girl from Kansas, the hero is a
kid named Billy – a disabled computer hacker who saves the
world from nuclear destruction.

> *Now the satellite's confused*
> *'Cause on Saturday night*
> *The airwaves were full of compassion and light*
> *And his silicon heart warmed*
> *To the sight of a billion candles burning...*

> *I'm not saying the battle is won*
> *But on Saturday night all those kids in the sun*
> *Wrested technology's sword from the hand of the*
> *War Lords*
> *Oh, oh, oh, the tide is turning.*[13]

And so it is. There is hope. A regenerated humanity
become as little children can stop the madness threatening to
destroy the world. But the opposite of war is not the peace of
complacency. No, Waters warns us against this trend in his
next work, *Amused to Death*.

A book could be written analyzing the symbolism in this
work. Waters wrote it around the time of the first Gulf War.
News coverage of the war was very much like watching a video
game. One of my favorite songs on this one is "The Bravery of
Being out of Range" -- a musical social commentary that speaks
for itself. There is a reference to home in a tune called "Three

Wishes." It's about a guy who is granted three wishes by a genie. He uses them all up on frivolous requests. Then he remembers that there's someone he's "just learned to miss" and he asks the genie to "bring her home." Genie says sorry, you've used up your last wish. Still, "he wants her to come home." I believe this is about the divine feminine again. From *Radio K.A.O.S.*, in the tune called "The Powers that Be," Waters calls upon the "Sisters of Mercy" to join with their brothers and "put a stop to the soap opera state." In the final tune of *Amused to Death*, it's as if he's putting out another call to "western woman." He's invoking the balance and reminding us that we all have a role to play in this. We can't complete the work so long as we are fighting each other. From *The Wall*, "United we stand – divided we fall."

The tune *Perfect Sense (I)* is especially poignant because in it, alien anthropologists arrive on Earth to discover that our species has become extinct. Only after eliminating every other reason for our demise, they concluded that we amused ourselves to death. The symbolism in these songs is more obtuse than in his other works. I still haven't finished my analysis. One thing is for sure. Waters, on some level, is keenly aware of our true history and extraterrestrial origins:

> *The monkey sat on a pile of stones*
> *And stared at the broken bone in his hand*
> *And the strains of a Viennese quartet*
> *Rang out across the land*
> *The monkey looked up at the stars*
> *And he thought to himself*
> *Memory is a stranger*
> *History is for fools*
> *And he cleaned his hands*
> *In a pool of holy writing*
> *Turned his back on the garden*
> *And set out for the nearest town*
> *Hold on hold on soldier*
> *When you add it all up*
> *The years and the marrowbone*

There's an ounce of gold
And an ounce of pride in each ledger
And the Germans killed the Jews
And the Jews killed the Arabs
And the Arabs killed the hostages
And that is the news
And is it any wonder
That the monkey's confused
He said Mama Mama
The President's a fool
Why do I have to keep reading
These technical manuals
And the joint chiefs of staff
And the brokers on Wall Street said
Don't make us laugh
You're a smart kid
Time is linear
Memory is a stranger
History's for fools
Man is a tool in the hands
Of the great God Almighty
And they gave him command
Of a nuclear submarine
And sent him back in search of
The Garden of Eden.[14]

According to biographer Karl Dallas, Waters once complained that fans sometimes read too much into music lyrics. Still, whether or not Waters intended certain meanings to be derived from the music is not the issue. As I explained in the previous chapter, sometimes composers unconsciously and synchronistically project symbolism into their music.

Speaking of synchronicity, there is a theory that Pink Floyd's *Dark Side of the Moon* is synchronized to *The Wizard of Oz*. If you begin playing the album at the end of the third lion roar right before the movie begins, the scenes in the movie clearly correspond to certain words in the lyrics of the songs. For instance, the song "Brain Damage" begins just as Scarecrow launches into "If I Only Had a Brain." When the

Good Witch Glinda confronts the Wicked Witch, the lyrics "And who knows which is which" are sung. When Dorothy leaves Professor Marvel to return to Aunt Em, the album is playing "Home, home again." And so on. All the band members deny this was deliberate except for Waters who has no comment. So who knows?

To me, the fact that this juxtaposition of the music on the movie is even possible and that Waters wrote a work about alien anthropologists is enough synchronicity for me to include him in my book! I look forward to his next contribution.

The Lion's Roar

Roger Waters singing, "Will you hear when the lion within you roars?" -- is a call to your true self – that part of you that refuses slavery and bondage to ignorance. It's the part of you that speaks to your own sovereignty and no one else's -- that fully acknowledges that you are king of your own forest. It's not the cowardly lion that hides in the forest but the courageous lion which ventures beyond the forest, and in so doing changes the world because he himself has changed. It's the part of you that cherishes freedom, justice and equality and is willing to fight for it. What is it that set us free? The Truth. Well, the truth is just another word for the Dharma and the Great Work. It's interesting that in Buddhism the Dharma is called "the lion's roar."

Way back in the mid-1980s, President Ronald Reagan's preposterous positions greatly angered me. Yet every time I watched him on television, something about him pulled at my heart strings. He was really a very likeable fellow. I told myself, "Oh that's because he's Aquarius!" Finally I realized, no – he's just another human being -- an *Earth* human, no less. It's the same way with President George W. Bush. Though I get frustrated with his policies and listen to what many perceive to be a remarkable lack of intelligence in his words, when I look at him closely and listen with my heart, I just see a little boy with responsibilities far greater than he should be asked to bear.

Yet he manages to keep a smile, and my compassion begins to flow.

There's a scene in the movie *The Pianist* that really brings this *home*. The movie is based on a true story. Adrien Brody plays Wladyslaw Szpilman, a popular Jewish-Polish pianist during the 1940s. Szpilman, having escaped capture during World War II, hid out for most of the war. As the Germans were leaving Warsaw, a German officer, Captain Wilm Hosenfeld, found Szpilman foraging for food in a war-torn villa. Rather than kill him on the spot, Captain Hosenfeld asked him to play a piece on the piano. The Captain told him to remain hidden, left, and later returned with food. He said it wouldn't be long before the Allies entered the city and Szpilman would be saved. In a later scene, some Jewish men walk past a temporary enclosure with imprisoned German soldiers. They taunt them. Hosenfeld, now on the other side of the fence runs up to the Jewish men and asks if they know Szpilman, the great pianist. One of them replies that he does. Hosenfeld relays that he helped Szpilman and asks them to let Szpilman know his whereabouts. Unfortunately, Szpilman was unable to secure Hosenfeld's release, and the Captain later died in a Russian concentration camp. The memory of Hosenfeld and his good deed, however, lives on in the movie and is memorialized in Szpilman's biography along with extracts from Hosenfeld's diary commenting on the insanity of war.

Christmas Eve, 1914, out of the front line trenches of 'no man's land' during World War I, British and German soldiers called a brief truce in order to celebrate Christmas with one another. They joined arms, sang Christmas carols, and shared food and drink. One British soldier wrote in his diary, "It doesn't seem right to be killing each other at Christmas time." Perhaps if these men had realized that every day could be Christmas when the Christ consciousness within each and every one of us is born and is not just something that only Jesus had – then peace might have lasted. The fact that this event even occurred is a testament to its possibility. Sharing the Christmas

Spirit is sharing the Holy Spirit within us all, at all times, in all ways.

These stories are only two examples illustrating the truth that we are all the same deep down. Muddlers are people too. We are no different. We are all Buddhas – perhaps unawakened, but Buddhas nonetheless. A Buddha is a Buddha whether she's sleeping or awake. So we look through the roles others play – behind the masks – beyond the acts of evil – and see what really drives them. It's the same thing that drives us – a longing for peace and happiness. We're just going about it in different ways. Some ways are more skillful than others. As I mentioned before, the muddlers have the most difficult roles of all. They suffer the greatest karmic burden. Most of the time, they shoulder greater responsibilities as well.

Esoterically, it is said that if Hitler's heart could have been turned, he very well may have arisen to the level of Christ. Why? Because of the law of polarity remember. The pendulum swings as low as it swings high. A person capable of greatest evil is also capable of greatest good. While I believe that the traditional story about Mary Magdalene being a whore and then achieving salvation through turning to Christ is not entirely factual, the symbolism of the tale teaches a great truth. She became his number one disciple. Yet she was the one who had erred the most according to the traditional teaching.

This same principle can be applied to the weak, the sick and the downtrodden. Whenever you see anyone wallowing in the mud of life, you are seeing the beginning of a glorious lotus bloom. Alcoholics, after joining Alcoholics Anonymous and becoming sober, sometimes become exceptionally spiritually aware. People who have undergone great suffering -- whether by their own hands or another's -- know what it's like to be down in the gutter. They often become our greatest guides -- our greatest teachers because they've been there. And every single one of them will tell you that they had help in finding their way out, that they could not have done it alone. When asked what that help was, they point to a higher power within themselves. By the grace of that power, whether it picked them

606

up directly or came through other people – the deed was done. They were "saved."

In the Eastern tradition of Mahayana Buddhism, we find this principle expressed in the tantric teachings of Vimalakirti. The eminent Buddhist scholar Robert Thurman explains,

> Vimalakirti's reconciliation of dichotomies is so thoroughgoing that he shocks the disciples by his advocacy of the most horrible things as being part of the bodhisattva's path. The bodhisattva may commit the five deadly sins, may follow the false heterodox teachings, may entertain the sixty-two false views, may consort with all the passions, and so on. Even the Maras, or devils, that plague the various universes are said to be bodhisattvas dwelling in inconceivable liberation – playing the devil, as it were, in order to develop living beings.[15]

How do you begin to actualize this principle in your daily life? Well, there are many occult practices that will enable you to do this. There is one, in particular, that is not as "occult" as it once was. It is a popular meditation practiced by Buddhists based on what's called "The Four Immeasurables" -- "The Four Divine Abodes" -- "The Four Brahma Viharas" or "The Four Noblest Qualities of Mind." They are:

1. Loving-kindness -- friendly happiness;
2. Compassion and empathy;
3. Sympathetic joy; and
4. Equanimity – peace of mind.

Lama Surya Das calls these *The Four Heartitudes* or attitudes of the heart.[16] These traits are cultivated by realizing that we are the same as everyone else in three ways:

1. We all have difficulties and suffer;
2. We all want to be free of difficulty and suffering; and
3. Deep down inside, we all have innate goodness.

607

In realizing these truths, we recognize that what we know about other people is really just a very small sliver of their total being; that they are each and every one a billion more things than what we normally associate with them -- such as friend, stranger, or enemy. This theory can be tested any place where there's social interaction. For instance, suppose you are at the mall on Saturday afternoon. You walk into a store and suddenly you see your long lost high school buddy, Bob. You are overjoyed and think, "Oh there's my friend, Bob. How nice!" So you both stand there and chat for a while, exchange phone numbers, then each of you are off on your own separate ways again. Bob walks down the mall and suddenly sees a coworker whom he detests and considers his sworn enemy. This coworker is always trying to sabotage Bob, which often results in abusive verbal sparring. He's the last person Bob wants to see, especially today on his day off. So Bob ducks into another store and hides behind a clothes rack until the despised coworker walks past. While Bob is hiding behind the clothes rack, a mother and her small child walk past him as if he's not even there, not at all noticing him or his odd behavior. As far as they are concerned, he's just part of the mall scenery, as are all the other strangers around them. In less than thirty minutes, Bob has been a friend, an enemy, and a stranger. And that's not the least of him. He's so much more than that – more than any of us will probably ever know.

This truth applies to all of us. The way to get past the slivers of anyone and beyond these artificial labels we stick on each other is to practice an affirmation meditation and prayer known as the Four Immeasurable Aspirations. Each aspiration corresponds to one of the Four Heartitudes. Each lineage has its own translation, but the words are loosely constructed as follows:

May all beings enjoy happiness and the root of happiness (corresponding to loving-kindness);

May all beings be free from suffering and the root of suffering (corresponding to compassion and empathy);
May all beings remain undivided from the sacred joy which is free from suffering (corresponding to sympathetic joy);
May all beings come to dwell in the great equanimity beyond attachment and aversion to anything and everyone (corresponding to equanimity and peace of mind.)

The meditation goes like this: First, get relaxed and comfortable. Then visualize someone who you really admire, love, or care about, and repeat the four aspirations with them in mind: "May [name] enjoy happiness and the root of happiness. May she be free from suffering and the root of suffering. May she remain undivided from the sacred joy which is free from suffering. May she come to dwell in the great equanimity beyond attachment and aversion to anything and everyone." Really feel it in your heart as you are repeating these aspirations. You can do this silently or out loud. This initial person corresponds to the category of friend. Then pick someone who you don't know -- a stranger. Maybe it's the clerk at the grocery store or someone you see walking their dog on the way to work each day. It doesn't matter who it is as long as it's someone who falls under the artificial label of stranger. Then say the four aspirations directed toward them: "May he [or she] ..." and so on. Then the third person you pick must come under the enemy category. They don't have to be a bonafide enemy. They can be a muddler or just someone you don't like. Then say the four aspirations with them in mind. If it's too difficult to do this with a particular person, start with someone it's easier to feel that way toward – maybe an actor you don't care for so that it seems less personal at first. But that's the general idea. The more you do this, the easier it gets. With practice it becomes second nature, and it's truly liberating.

As Earth Humans I feel we should extend this practice off planet as well – direct it to any and all extraterrestrial acquaintances we might be fortunate enough to make. And let's not forget the least of us on this planet – all the living creatures sharing this beautiful Earth with us. As Albert Schweitzer said, "Until he extends his circle of compassion to all living things, man will not himself find peace."

When we change our hearts, the hearts around us change, and that changes the world. Transformation is inevitable. The innate goodness that we share with everyone enables us to do this. It is an expression of the Will to Good which eternally creates and sustains the universe. It is the only real will there is, contrary to popular opinion. Our seemingly little wills are but reflections of the one. When we try to control it and lord over it, it cannot do its job properly. Letting go of the delusion that we are separate from one another allows that One Will to emerge unobstructed -- with clarity and perfection. It is instinctual – it is intuitive. It is the mark of the Wild Woman, as Clarissa Pinkola Estés would say – that part of us which is not tame but is free. It is being true to the Spirit in the Soul in the Body through Heart-Mind synchronization.

It brings to mind a program I saw on public television about horses and their trainers. All the best trainers in the world agree that it's not about the rider. No matter how great the rider thinks he or she is, it's not about them. It's all about the horse. And when that's realized, the rider and the horse become as one. In no greater instance can you see this than with a champion cutting horse.

Competitive cutting horses are horses that have been trained to separate one cow from the herd and block it from returning to the herd. The training to get a horse to do this is actually a kind of 'untraining' -- particularly of the rider. Rather than jerk the reins around in an attempt to control the horse forcing the desired movements, the reins are loosened and the horse is allowed to mirror the movements of the cow. They do this instinctively. In fact, it is a penalty for the rider if they raise their hands any time at all during the process.

It is exactly as Yoda says: We must unlearn what we have learned. This is why dzogchen is so effective. As Lama Surya

Das so often says, "Nothing to do – rest in the view." Effortless being is what leads to skillful living.

There was so much I wanted to say in this concluding chapter. But now as I'm writing this, it all seems irrelevant. Yet while we're on the subject of horses, I want to say one more thing. We are already familiar with "the horse of a different color." There is another scene early on in the *Wizard of Oz* with horses. As the tornado is approaching the farm, the farmhands are told to let the horses loose. If the twister were to strike the barn with the horses all tied up or confined to their stalls, they would be killed. So they are set free. It was agreed that the horses were better off free – that they would know what it was they needed to do to take care of themselves. They were trusted.

When I was a young girl, I spent five weeks each summer at a popular camp in east Texas. One of my favorite activities was horseback riding. I often got to ride this stubborn Palomino mare named Sue. On the trail, sometimes Sue would suddenly stop and stand stiff as stone as she leisurely bent her head down to get some grass. It was almost impossible to get her going again. I usually had to give her a sharp little tap on the hiney with a switch. She'd begin to walk again however begrudgingly -- just dragging her hooves, like she was so tired. But on the way back, about 500 yards from the stable, Sue magically transformed. Suddenly, she'd prick up her ears and break into a frisky little trot. It was all I could do to restrain her from cantering. At first I thought this was just Sue. But then I noticed the same thing would happen when I rode the other horses. I asked the riding master about this. She said, "Oh, they know they're going home. That's why they do that."

Once we know we're going home, we somehow find the energy we need to get us there – or perhaps it finds us. Like the horses, it becomes easy and natural. Is it because we've gotten back into the stream and we're going with the flow? Perhaps.

What about other animals? We've all heard miracle stories about cats and dogs taken hundreds of miles from their homes. Yet somehow they manage to find their way back. It's as if they have some kind of supersensory homing device that we cannot even begin to fathom. Do we have one of our own?

I believe so. Once we make the decision to take that first step on the Path that leads back home, it's as if we are swept up in a kind of irresistible momentum. No matter how many obstacles we encounter on the way, we still keep going. When we fall, something always pulls us back up. Somehow we manage to overcome the obstacles. We've opened up to who we really are and where we're really going. Letting go and letting God – however you understand that energy – is the only way to be because it is what you are made of – it is your true Self.

There are many yellow brick roads. No matter which one you follow, if you keep going, you'll eventually get home. It is evolution. We want to go home. It's where we belong. So yes, "There's no place like home." Could it be because it's not really a place at all, but a state of being?

> *And if I ever go looking for my heart's desire again, I won't go looking any further than my own backyard, because if it's not there, I never lost it to begin with.*

We are beyond the rainbow now. The cosmic connection is renewed. The lion is roaring. Dorothy is awakening. Meanwhile, back at the ranch. . . Well, we know what to do.

---

[1] Jesse Stewart, *Secrets of the Yellow Brick Road: A Map for the Modern Spiritual Journey*, SunShine Press Publications, 1997, p. 147. Reprinted with permission.

[2] A heart-felt thanks to Roger Waters and his publishers for permission to reprint partial lyrics from his songs.

[3] Karl Dallas, *Pink Floyd: Bricks in the Wall*, Shapolsky Publishers, 1987, p. 80.

[4] MOTHER from *The Wall* (All Lyrics by George Roger Waters) © 1979 Roger Waters Music Overseas Ltd./Warner Chappell Artemis Music Ltd. All Rights Reserved. Used by Permission. Warner Bros. Publications Inc., Miami, FL 33014.

[5] ANOTHER BRICK IN THE WALL (PART 3) from *The Wall* (All Lyrics by George Roger Waters) © 1979 Roger Waters Music Overseas Ltd./Warner Chappell Artemis Music Ltd. All Rights Reserved. Used by Permission. Warner Bros. Publications Inc., Miami, FL 33014.

[6] SHOW MUST GO ON from *The Wall* (All Lyrics by George Roger Waters) © 1979 Roger Waters Music Overseas Ltd./Warner Chappell Artemis Music Ltd. All Rights Reserved. Used by Permission. Warner Bros. Publications Inc., Miami, FL 33014.

[7] STOP from *The Wall* (All Lyrics by George Roger Waters) © 1979 Roger Waters Music Overseas Ltd./Warner Chappell Artemis Music Ltd. All Rights Reserved. Used by Permission. Warner Bros. Publications Inc., Miami, FL 33014.

[8] TRIAL from *The Wall* (All Lyrics by George Roger Waters) © 1979 Roger Waters Music Overseas Ltd./Warner Chappell Artemis Music Ltd. All Rights Reserved. Used by Permission. Warner Bros. Publications Inc., Miami, FL 33014.

[9] HOME (Waters) © 1987 Pink Floyd Music Publishers, Inc. Used by permission.

[10] *Id.*

[11] *Id.*

[12] THE POWERS THAT BE (Waters) © 1987 Pink Floyd Music Publishers, Inc. Used by permission.

[13] THE TIDE IS TURNING (AFTER LIVE AID) (Waters) © 1987 Pink Floyd Music Publishers, Inc. Used by permission.

[14] PERFECT SENSE Part 1 (Waters) © 1988 Pink Floyd Music Publishers, Inc. Used by permission.

[15] Robert A.F. Thurman, *The Holy Teaching of Vimalakirti*, Pennsylvania State University Press, 1988, p. 7.

[16] Lama Surya Das, *Awakening the Buddha Within*, Broadway Books, 1997, p. 293.

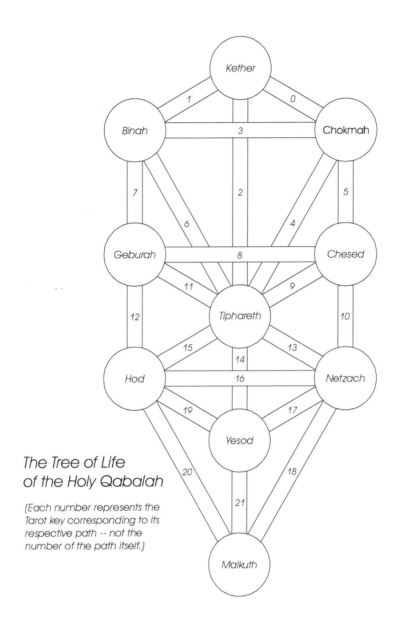

*The Tree of Life
of the Holy Qabalah*

(Each number represents the
Tarot key corresponding to its
respective path -- not the
number of the path itself.)

APPENDIX 2

A COSMIC CHRONOLOGY

The information that is italicized is highly speculative and based on a summary of Jelaila Starr's work. The non-italicized information comes from the work of Zecharia Sitchin, other scientists, anthropologists, archeologists, and various sources.

BILLIONS OF YEARS AGO TO 18 MILLION YEARS B.C.E.

Formation of worlds. Sirius B implodes creating Sirius A and C. Planet Tiamat and planet/battlestar Nibiru created near Pleiades. Reptiles rapidly evolve on Aln. Felines seed Avyon in the Lyran Constellation for the new Human race. Humans move to Avalon after evolving from aquatic primate to bipedal form. Reptiles arrive on Avalon causing civil wars. Humans migrate to Sirius B from Avyon, Avalon and the Vegan Star System. Sirian Humans split into etheric and physical groups. Physical Humans establish new colony on Aln, becoming Orion Humans. Reptiles conquer and enslave Orion Humans. Orion rebels form "the Black League" in opposition to the Reptiles. Orion rebels and Etheric Sirians migrate to Tiamat. Some Etheric Sirians begin to incarnate in animals bodies on Tiamat. The remaining Etheric Sirians become "Christos Sirians" forming a spiritual hierarchy to provide custodial protection and guidance to Sirians in animal bodies. Reptiles arrive on Tiamat. Pleiadians from Avyon arrive on Tiamat for genetically upgrading primate bodies to human bodies. A rare period of peace prevails between Reptiles and Humans until Reptiles destroy Avyon. Avyon Pleiadians move to Nibiru and oversee evolution of Humans on Tiamat developing agriculture. Orion Reptiles arrive on Tiamat instigating conflict between Humans and Reptiles. Black League Orions ally with Tiamat Humans. Conflict lasts for at least 10,000 years. Reptiles destroy Human colonies. Mass exodus of Humans from Tiamat. Nibiru blows up Aln and Tiamat creating Earth and the asteroid belt. Surviving friendly Reptiles provided sanctuary on Nibiru; surviving hostile Reptiles found underground colonies on new planet Earth. Galactic Federation forms to oversee Human exodus and control Nibiru. Great galactic wars begin, lasting for millions of years. Earth reseeded by Felines with help of Christos Sirians. Etheric Sirians evolving in animal bodies become known as "Earth Sirians." Etheric Sirians evolving as dolphins and whales known as "Aquatic Sirians" maintain biosphere of planet. Lyran Human colony of Hybornea established on Earth after millions of years.

18 MILLION YEARS TO 480,000 B.C.E.

Lemurian civilization flourishes. Human kingdom on Earth raised to mental level of self-consciousness. Earliest hominids begin to individualize. Reptiles based on nearby Maldek attack Hybornea and Human colonies on Venus and Mars. Nibiru destroys Maldek ending Galactic Wars, yet becomes severely damaged as a result. A few Nibiruans return to Earth to aid in the developing civilizations of Atlantis and Mu, offshoots of Lemuria. Felines modify "white" race DNA to produce racial differences between colonists in Atlantis (origin of "red" races) and Mu (origin of "yellow" races.)

480,000 B.C.E. TO 300,000 B.C.E.

Nibiruans form treaty with Reptilians by marriage of Pleiadian Anu with Reptilian Dragon Queen Dramin, whose offspring is Enki. A large group of Nibiruans (the Anunnaki) headed by Enki land on Earth in search of gold to reconstruct force field of Nibiru. Human primates at stage of Homo Erectus. Anunnaki colonize Mesopotamian region. Enki's half-brother and half-sister, Enlil and Ninhursag (*1/2 Feline*) arrive. Enki oversees mining operations in Africa. Enlil and Ninhursag cultivate "Garden of Eden" compound. *A long period of peace prevails.*

300,000 B.C.E. TO 148,000 B.C.E.

Mining conditions worsen in Africa, and Anunnaki miners revolt. Miners take Enlil hostage yet Enki secures his release. Enlil accuses Enki of inciting riots. Matter is brought before Nibiruan high council. Decision made to create worker race to mine gold with *Christos Sirians supervising transition of souls from Earth Sirians to new worker race.* Anunnaki DNA combined with that of Homo Erectus to produce Homo Sapiens by Enki and Ninhursag. Homo Sapiens genetically upgraded with ability to procreate, resulting in Homo Sapiens Sapiens. **Modern science traces our genetic ancestry back to one particular African female during this time, as all mitochondria is inherited from the mother.** Selected humans taught to read, write, and telepath.

148,000 B.C.E. – 100,000 B.C.E.

Massive migration of Earth and Etheric Sirian souls into new worker race – Earth Humanity. Human civilization regresses while other ETs (e.g. Andromedans, etc.) continue to colonize planet. Ice Age begins. Earliest archeological evidence of humans intentionally burying dead.

100,000 B.C.E. – 75,000 B.C.E.

Warming trend begins. Earth humans at CroMagnon stage. Anunnaki mate with Earth Humanity producing very tall offspring.

75,000 B.C.E. – 25,000 B.C.E.

Cooling trend begins. So-called "lost civilizations" flourishing. Migrations from these civilizations begin to regions later known as the Americas and Europe. Earliest archeological evidence of human settlement in the Americas. Neandertals roaming European region and eastern Asia. Earliest evidence of cave art and mining for red ochre. Galactic Federation provides *"Christos upgrade"* to Earth Humanity's DNA by combining the *Reptilian*/Human genes from Enki with the *Feline, Carian* and Human genes from Ninhursag, producing the original "Adam and Eve" humans. Humans of Anunnaki parentage given custodial responsibilities. Enki establishes "The Brotherhood of the Snake" – origin of the Mystery Schools -- for the education of their new Human children. Enlil forces conspire to slow down Humanity's rapid spiritual evolution by expelling them from "Garden of Eden" compound and restricting entry into Mystery Schools.

25,000 B.C.E. – 11,000 B.C.E.

Earliest archeological evidence of agriculture. Leaders of the Mystery Schools split into pure and corrupted factions. Political disputes and territorial conflicts abound, pushing Humanity into further degeneration and sole preoccupation with survival. *Marduk, offspring of Enki and Reptilian princess, rises to power in Atlantis.* Marduk, through advanced technology, *crashes a comet into Lemuria, destroying the continent. Nibiru thwarts Marduk's applying same strategy to civilizations of Rama and Yu by redirecting comet to collide into Atlantis destroying that continent.* Galactic Federation withholds information from Humanity regarding impending deluge due to Marduk's warring and the orbital shift caused by Nibiru's passing. Enki in opposition to the Federation salvages selected Humans ("Noah" and his family) and animal and plant species for reseeding Earth after the great deluge.

11,000 B.C.E. – 3,700 B.C.E.

Mesopotamian region resettled by Enlil, Enki, and Human descendants. Enki's descendants rise to power in Egypt. Ubaid culture flourishing. Kurgan waves begin. Enlil's descendants dispatched to South America for gold. *Pleiadian descendants* of Enlil representing younger generation (including "Inanna" and "Seth") begin to struggle with older generation for power. War rages between Enlil and Enki factions over pyramids and other space facilities. Ninhursag ends war and claims control of space facilities. Enki's son, Thoth, rules Egypt peacefully for about 5,000 years. Neolithic Age underway.

3,700 B.C.E. – 2,000 B.C.E.

Nibiru establishes monarchy style of government on Earth through bloodline of "Priest-Kings" half Nibiruan/*Pleiadian* and half Earth-Human. Marduk instigates Babylonian debacle. *Human settlements dispursed, "language" deliberately confused, and last genetic change implemented by disconnecting 10 of the 12 strands of DNA and infusing astral bodies with implants containing dormant codes.* Marduk conquers Egypt. Thoth flees to South America where he becomes known as "Quetzalcoatl – the White Plumed Serpent." Inanna establishes rule over Indus Valley. Rise of the Akkadian Empire. *Marduk wages war with Inanna from a military base on Mars.* Space facilities destroyed with nuclear technology ("Sodom and Gomorrah"), and pyramid records are hidden from Marduk. Earth Human royal line continues through Abraham, Moses and their descendants. Marduk's forces steadily gain control resulting in patriarchy, slavery, and oppressive religion. Minoan Crete, one of the last Goddess-centered matriarchal strongholds, crumbles. Anunnaki phase off planet. Mystery Schools go underground.

Important Note: Dates, purposes, and frequency of the genetic manipulations of Earth hominids vary among Zecharia Sitchin, Jelaila Starr, R.A. Boulay, and Laurence Gardner. Sitchin contends that the first genetic experiment resulted in the births of "Adam" and "Eve." Starr contends that there were three genetic manipulations: the first occurring around 350,000 B.C.E., granting humanity the ability to procreate; the second "Christos" upgrade occurring around 40,000 B.C.E. resulting in the creation of "Adam" and "Eve;" and a third genetic tampering occurring around 3,000 B.C.E. disconnecting certain strands of DNA resulting in a suppression of our psychic abilities. Boulay contends that the first genetic creation resulted in a hybrid slave species that was largely Reptilian and could not procreate, and that the second genetic tampering resulted in the creation of "Adam" – Homo Sapiens with dominant mammalian traits, a significantly shorter lifespan and the ability to procreate. Gardner contends that the first upgrade or second genetic manipulation resulting in "Adapa" was around 10,000 B.C.E., and that this was the original Adam and first postdiluvian king, resulting in the "royal bloodline." However traditional archeology points to the origin of Homo Sapiens Sapiens otherwise known as CroMagon man being around 130,000 B.C.E. Therefore, it is important not to take to any of this information as absolute fact. Even in modern, conventional science, dates for the origins of events and archeological artifacts are constantly changing, due to advances in technology and new archeological findings.

618

APPENDIX 3

Modern spiritual practice includes coloring one's own Tarot keys for strong, solid consciousness imprinting. Color *The Fool* as follows:

white: sun, rose, eye on purse, dog, Fool's undergarment, mountain snow
yellow: sky, shoes, Fool's hair, circles/wheels on Fool's robe
gold: tip of stick under purse, star on Fool's robe, belt
silver: moon on Fool's robe
red: feather, purse, inner robe lining, wheel spokes, flame in circle
yellow-green: Fool's legs (stockings)
green: cap, rose leaves, foliage background on robe
light violet: tall mountains
dark violet: foothills
brown: eagle on purse, cliff

BIBLIOGRAPHY AND RECOMMENDED SOURCES

Alder, Vera Stanley. *The Finding of the Third Eye,* Samuel Weiser, Inc., 1938, 1973.

Allione, Tsultrim. *Women of Wisdom*, Snow Lion Publications, 2000.

Altom, Kathleen and Braude, William G. "Clairvoyant and Telepathic Impressions of Musical Targets," in J.D. Morris et al. (eds.) *Research in Parapsychology*, 1975.

American Buddhist Center, http://www.americanbuddha.org.

American Civil Liberties Union. http://www.aclu.org.

Atwood, Mary Ann. *A Suggestive Inquiry of the Hermetic Mystery,* William Tait, 1918.

Bach, Richard. *Illusions: the Adventures of a Reluctant Messiah*, Dell Publishing, 1977.

Bailey, Alice A. *A Treatise on White Magic*, Lucis Publishing Co., 1951.

Bailey, Alice A. *Esoteric Astrology*, Lucis Publishing Co., 1951.

Bailey, Alice A. *Esoteric Psychology, Vol. I*, Lucis Publishing Co., 1936.

Bearden, Thomas E. *Excalibur Briefing: Explaining Paranormal Phenomena*, Walnut Hill, 1980.

Beer, Robert. *The Encyclopedia of Tibetan Symbols and Motifs,* Serindia Publications, 1999.

Bentov, Itzhak. *Stalking the Wild Pendulum,* Bantam Books, 1977.

Bernard, Roy. http://www.kormet.org/pipermail/levnet/2000~July/014959.html.

Berzin, Alexander. *Relating to a Spiritual Teacher*, Snow Lion Publications, 1977.

Beutlich, Robert. "Quarks, Occult Chemistry and the String Model," a paper presented at the 1980 United States Psychotronics Association Conference.

Bise, William. "Natural and Artificial Pulsed Electronic Waves and Life Function," *United States Psychotronics Association Newsletter,* III/1, Spring, 1981.

Bleifuss, Joel. "Know Thine Enemy: A Brief History of Corporations," *In These Times*, February, 1998.

Bloom, Pamela. "Soul Music," *New Age Journal,* March/April, 1987.

Bonewits, R. "A Psychic Exploration of Music," *The Gnosticon Tapes*, Gnostic Aquarian Festival, 1974.

Boulay, R.A. *Flying Serpents and Dragons,* The Book Tree, 1999.

Bradley, Marion Zimmer. *The Mists of Avalon*, Ballantine Books, 1982.

Bramley, William. *The Gods of Eden*, Avon Books, 1990.

Bridges, Vincent. "The UFO Enigma (Part 3)," published at http://www.magicjourney.com/artandarchives/SS3.html.

Brinton, Maurice. *The Irrational in Politics,* Black Rose Books, 1974.

Builders of the Adytum, Ltd., (BOTA). 5101 N. Figueroa Street, Los Angeles, CA 90042-0278, http://www.bota.org/main.html.

Butler, W.E. "Concerning Contacts, Control, and Communication," published at http://www.houseofthehorizion.org/public/documents.php?id=172

Campbell, Joseph, with Moyers, Bill. *The Power of Myth*, Anchor Books Doubleday, 1988.

Campbell, Joseph. *The Hero With A Thousand Faces*, MJF Books, 1949.

Capra, Fritjof. *The Tao of Physics*, Bantam Books, 1975.

Case, Paul Foster. *Highlights of Tarot*, Builders of the Adytum, Ltd., 1970.

Case, Paul Foster. *The Book of Tokens: Tarot Meditations*, Builders of the Adytum, 1960.

Case, Paul Foster. *The Great Seal of the United States: Its History, Symbolism and Message for the New Age*, Builders of the Adytum, Ltd., 1935, 1976.

Case, Paul Foster. *The True and Invisible Rosicrucian Order,* Samuel Weiser, Inc., 1985. Red Wheel/Weiser.

Chogyam, Ngakpa. *Wearing the Body of Visions*, Aro Books, 1995.

Childress, David Hatcher. *Vimana Aircraft of Ancient India & Atlantis,* Adventures Unlimited Press, 2001.

Chomsky, Noam interviewed by David Barsamian. "Rollback: The Return of Predatory Capitalism," reprinted in Alternative Press Review, Vol. 2, Number 3, 1996.

Chomsky, Noam and Edward S. Harman. *Manufacturing Consent: The Political Economy of the Mass Media,* Pantheon Books, 1988.

Christensen, Kevin. "A Model of Mormon Spiritual Experience," (February, 2002), published at http://www2.ida.net/graphics/shirtail/spiritua.htm.

Cogswell, David. *Chomsky for Beginners,* Writers and Readers Publishing, 1996.

Collins, Andrew. *Gods of Eden*, Bear & Co., 1998.

Colmer, Hugh. "Celestial Fire: Virgin Blood," http://www.crosscircle.com/celestial_%20Fire.htm.

Conway, D.J. *Dancing with Dragons,* Llewellyn Publications, 1997.

Cooper, Milton William. *Behold a Pale Horse,* Light Technology Publishing, 1991.

Covey, Stephen R. *The Divine Center,* Publishers Press, 1982.

Covey, Stephen R. *The 7 Habits of Highly Effective People*, Simon & Schuster, 1989.

Crowley, Aleister. *Magick in Theory and Practice,* Castle Books.

CSETI Working Group Training Kit, 1995. http://www.cseti.org.

Cygne, Michaele de. Published at http://cirrus.spaceports.com/~solomoon/musicresume, html.

Dallas, Karl. *Pink Floyd: Bricks in the Wall*, Shapolsky Publishers, 1987.

Daly, Mary. *Gyn/Ecology: The Metaethics of Radical Feminism*, Beacon Press, 1978.

Das, Lama Surya. *Awakening the Buddha Within,* Broadway Books, 1997.

Das, Lama Surya. *Awakening to the Sacred,* Broadway Books, 1999.

Das, Lama Surya. *Awakening the Buddhist Heart,* Broadway Books, 2000.

Das, Lama Surya. *Dancing With Life: Dzogchen View, Meditation and Action,* Dzogchen Publications, 1996.

Das, Lama Surya. *Letting Go of the Person You Used to Be,* Broadway Books, 2003.

Das, Lama Surya. *Tibetan Dream Yoga,* Sounds True Audio Cassettes, 2000.

David-Neel, Alexandra. *Initiations and Initiates in Tibet,* Dover Publications, 1931,1993.

David-Neel, Alexandra. *Magic and Mystery in Tibet,* Dover Publications, 1931, 1971.

Davis, Erik. "Tongues of Fire, Whirlwinds of Noise: Images of Spiritual Information," *Gnosis,* No. 23, Spring, 1992.

Davis, Mikol and Lane, Earl. *Rainbows of Life: The Promise of Kirlian Photography,* Harper & Row, 1978.

De Saint Exupéry, Antoine. *The Little Prince,* Harvest/HJB Books, 1971.

DeVere, Nicholas. "From Transylvania to Tunbridge Wells," http://www.dragoncourt.org, and http://www.geocities.com/newworldorder_themovie/DragonsRant.

Devereux, Paul, Steele, John and Kubrin, David. *Earthmind: Communicating with the Living World of Gaia,* Destiny Books, 1992.

Donington, Robert. *Wagner's 'Ring' and Its Symbols – The Music and the Myth,* Faber & Faber, 1963.

Dossey, Larry, M.D. *Healing Words: The Power of Prayer and the Practice of Medicine,* Harper San Francisco, 1993.

Dossey, Larry, M.D. *Prayer is Good Medicine: How to Reap the Healing Benefits of Prayer,* Harper San Francisco, 1996.

Edmunds, Albert J. "A Buddhist Genesis" translated from Digha Nikaya 27, published at http://essenes.crosswinds.net/budgenesis.html.

Eisler, Riane. *The Chalice and the Blade,* Harper Collins, 1988.

The Electronic Frontier Foundation. http://www.eff.org.

Estés, Clarissa Pinkola. *Women Who Run With the Wolves: Myths and Stories of the Wild Woman Archetype,* Ballantine Books, 1992.

Farrand, ed. *2 Madison's Records of the Federal Convention of 1787,* 1937.

Flindt, H. Max, and Binder, Otto O. *Mankind: Child of the Stars,* Ozark Mountain Publishing, 1999.

Fortune, Dion. *Sane Occultism,* Samuel Weiser, Inc., 1967. Red Wheel/Weiser.

Fortune, Dion. *The Cosmic Doctrine,* Helios Book Service, Ltd., 1966.

Fortune, Dion. *The Esoteric Orders and Their Work,* 1928, reprinted by Llewellyn Publications, 1971. Red Wheel/Weiser.

Franz, M.L. von. "Science and the Unconscious," *Man and His Symbols,* ed. By Carl G. Jung, Doubleday, 1964.

622

Freer, Neil. "An Expanded Context for Genetic Exploration and Explanation," published at http://www.neilfreer.com/index11.htm.

Freer, Neil. "The Alien Question: An Expanded Perspective," a white paper published at http://www.neilfree.com/index20.htm.

Freer, Neil. *God Games: What Do You Do Forever?*, The Book Tree, 1999.

Gardner, Laurence. "Realm of the Ring Lords," http://www.sunnyjohn.com/gardner/realmoftheringlords2.htm.

Gardner, Laurence. "The Powder of Projection: 21st-Century Science Casts a New Light on an Ancient Mystery," *Atlantis Rising,* Number. 40, July/August, 2003.

Gardner, Laurence. *Bloodline of the Holy Grail: The Hidden Lineage of Jesus Revealed,* Barnes & Noble Books, 1997.

Gardner, Laurence. *Genesis of the Grail Kings*, Fair Winds Press, 2001.

Glickman, Marshall. "The Lama in the Lab," *Tricycle: The Buddhist Review,* Spring, 2003.

Godwin, Joscelyn. *Music, Mysticism and Magic: A Sourcebook,* Arkana, 1976.

Goldman, Stuart. "Interview with Jello Biafra," *Reader – Los Angeles's Free Weekly*, Vol. 8, No. 35, June 20, 1986.

Goleman, Daniel. "Taming Destructive Emotions," *Tricycle Magazine,* Spring, 2003.

Green, Joey. *The Zen of Oz: Ten Spiritual Lessons from Over the Rainbow*, Renaissance Books, 1998.

Greene, Brian. *The Elegant Universe: Superstrings, Hidden Dimensions, and the Quest for the Ultimate Theory,* Vintage, 2000.

Greenfield, Allen H. *Secret Cipher of the Ufonauts,* IllumiNet Press, 1994.

Greer, Mary K. *Women of the Golden Dawn: Rebels and Priestesses,* Park Street Press, 1995.

Greer, Steven M. *Disclosure: Military and Government Witnesses Reveal the Greatest Secrets in Modern History*, Crossing Point, Inc., 2001 See also http://www.DisclosureProject.org, and http://www.cseti.org.

Greer, Steven M., M.D., *Extraterrestrial Contact: The Evidence and Implications,* Crossing Point, Inc., 1999.

Gyaltsen, Shardza Tashi. *Heart Drops of Dharmakaya: Dzogchen Practice of the Bon Tradition*, Snow Lion Publications, 2002.

H.H. the Dalai Lama. Tsong-ka-pa and Jeffrey Hopkins, *Tantra in Tibet*, Snow Lion Publications, 1977.

Halbert, Terry Ann. "The First Amendment in the Workplace: An Analysis and Call for Reform," 17 Seton Hall Law Review 42 (1987).

Hall, Edward T. *The Silent Language,* Anchor Books, 1973.

Halpern, Steven with Savary, Louis. *Sound Health: The Music and Sounds that Make Us Whole,* Harper & Row, 1985.

Hamel, Peter Michael. *Through Music to the Self,* Element Books, 1978.

Hanh, Thich Nhat. *Living Buddha, Living Christ,* Riverhead Books, 1997.

HeartMath Institute. http://www.heartmatch.org.

Heline, Corinne. *Esoteric Music Based on the Musical Seership of Richard Wagner*, New Age Press, 1980.

Heline, Corrine. *Healing and Regeneration Through Music,* New Age Press, 1974.

Heline, Corrine. *Music: The Keynote of Human Evolution*, New Age Press, 1965.

Herbert, Benson. "Fourth International Congress on Psychotronic Research," *Parapsychology Review*, II/1, Jan.-Feb. 1980.

Hightower, Thomas Vaczy. "The Musical Octave," previously published at http:home3.inet.tele.dk/hitower/octave2.html.

Hixon, Lex. *Mother of the Buddhas: Meditation on the Prajnaparamita Sutra,* Quest Books, 1993.

Holy Bible, King James Version.

Howard, Michael. *The Occult Conspiracy*, Destiny Books, 1989.

Hudson, David. "Superconductivity and Modern Alchemy: Has the Philosopher's Stone Been Found?" at http://www.karenlyster.com/hudson.html.

Hulse, David Allen. *The Eastern Mysteries,* Llewellyn Publications, 2000.

Hulse, David Allen. *The Western Mysteries,* Llewellyn Publications, 2000.

Huntley, Noel. Published at http://www.users.globalnet.co.uk/~neolh.

Ingber, Stanley. "Rediscovering the Communal Worth of Individual Rights: The First Amendment in Institutional Contexts," 69 *Texas Law Review* 1 (1990).

International Kalachakra Network. http://www.kalachakranet.org/resources.shambhala.html.

Jacobi, Jolande and Hull, R.F.C. (eds.) *C.G. Jung Psychological Reflections: A New Anthology of His Writing,* Princeton University Press, 1953.

Jenkins, Palden. "The Great Taboo – It's the Neighbours! ETs and Humanity," http://www.palden.co.uk.

Jones, Kathy. "Spinning the Wheel of Ana," 1990, 2000 published at http://wwwlisleofavalon.uk/local/h-pages/kathyj/ap-ana.html.

Jung, Carl G. et al., *Man and His Symbols*, Aldus Books Ltd., 1964.

Keil, H.H.J. "A GESP Test with Favorite Music Targets," *The Journal of Parapsychology,* Vol. 20, 1985.

Kellerman, Dana F., ed. *New Webster's Dictionary,* Delair Publishing, 1981.

Kennedy, Judy. "Sound, Color, and Imagery Correlations Manifesting in the Nature of Psi," experimental study and paper, North Texas State University, 1982.

Keyes, Laurel E. *Toning: The Creative Power of the Voice,* DeVorss & Co., 1973.

Khan, Sufi Inayat. *The Sufi Message of Hazrat Inayat Khan*, Vol. II, 4rth ed., Servire Wassenaar, 1976.

Khenpo, Nyoshul. *Natural Great Perfection*, Snow Lion Publications, 1995, translated by Lama Surya Das.

Kinchin, David. "Complex PTSD and Trauma Caused by Bullying, Harassment and Abuse," *Post Traumatic Stress Disorder: The Invisible Injury,* UK: Success Unlimited, reprinted at http://www.bullyonline.org., 2002.

Knight, Gareth. *A Practical Guide to Qabalistic Symbolism, Vol. 1,* Helios Book Service, 1965.

Knight, Gareth. *A Practical Guide to Qabalistic Symbolism, Vol. II,* Helios Book Service, 1965.

Knight, Gareth. *The Secret Tradition in Arthurian Legend*, Samuel Weiser, Inc., 1996. Red Wheel/Weiser.

Konstantinos. *Vampires: The Occult Truth*, Llewellyn Publications, 1996.

Korten, David C. *The Post-Corporate World: Life After Capitalism,* Berrett-Koehler Publishers, 1999.

Krippner, Stanley and Rubin, Daniel (Eds.). *The Kirlian Aura: Photographing the Galaxies of Life*, Doubleday, 1974.

Laing, R.D. *The Politics of Experience,* Ballantine Books, 1967.

Lammer, Helmut and Lammer, Marion. *MILABS: Military Mind Control and Alien Abduction*, IllumiNet Press, 1999.

Lasn, William Kalle. *Culture Jam: The Uncooling of America*, Morrow/Eaglebrook, 1999.

Lee, Ilchi, Dr. *The Twelve Enlightenments for Healing Society,* Hampton Roads Publishing, 2002.

Lendvai, Erno. *Bela Bartok: An Analysis of His Music*, 1971: rev. reprint: Kahn & Averhill, 1979.

Lerner, Gerda. *The Creation of Patriarchy (Women & History, Vol. 1),* Oxford University Press, 1987.

Levi, Eliphas. *Transcendental Magic,* Samuel Weiser, Inc., 1972.

Lewis, C.S. *The Chronicles of Narnia,* Collier Books, 1980.

Madsen, Clifford K. and Madsen, Charles H. *Experimental Research in Music,* Contemporary Publishing Company, 1978.

Marciniak, Barbara. Published at http://www.home-2.worldonlin.nl/~gibbon/dna.htm.

Markale, Jean. *The Druids: Celtic Priests of Nature*, Inner Traditions International, 1999.

Marx, Karl and Engles, Friedrich. *The Communist Manifesto*, Penguin Books, 1888, 1967.

Matthews, Clayton. *Secret Psychic Organizations*, Sherbourne Press, 1969.

Mesko, Sabrina. *Gestures of Power*, Sounds True Video, 1997.

Messiaen, Olivier. "Preface," *Quatour pour la fin du temps,* Durand & Cie, 1942.

Messiaen, Olivier. *Technique de Mon Language Musical,* Alphonse Leduc, 1944.

Meyers, William. "The Santa Clara Blues: Corporate Personhood versus Democracy," published at http://www.iiipublishing.com/afd/santaclara.html.

Michel, Donald E. *Music Therapy: An Introduction to Therapy and Special Education Through Music,* Charles C. Thomas, 1976.

Miller, Arthur S. "The Corporation as Private Government in the World Community," 46 *Virginia Law Review* 8 (1960).

Monahan, Scott. "History on the Rocks," a Rocky Mountain PBS documentary, transcript at http://www.archaeoastronomy.com/doctans.html.

Nasrai, Yesai. Order of the Nazorean Essenes can be found at http:/www.essenes.net.

The New York Times. Sunday, February 28, 1960.

Noel, Daniel, Ed. *Seeing Castaneda: Reactions to "Don Juan" Writings of Carlos Castaneda,* Perigee Books, 1976.

Norbu, Chogyal Namkhai. *The Practice for the Naga*, Shang-Shung Edizioni (Italy), 1995.

Nyland, Edo. *Linguistic Archeology,* Trafford Publishing, 2001, also published at http://www.islandnet.com/~edonon/linguist.htm.

Nyland, Edo. *Odysseus and the Sea Peoples,* Trafford Publishing, 2001.

Orion, Joan. "Training in Energy Awareness," paper given at the United States Psychotronics Association Conference in Dayton, Ohio, 1980.

Owens, Lance. "Joseph Smith: America's Hermetic Prophet," *Gnosis: A Journal of the Western Inner Traditions*, Spring, 1995.

Pagels, Elaine. *The Gnostic Gospels*, Vintage Books, 1981.

Perez, Jean-Claude. "The DNA Supra-Code: Discovery, Proves and Evidence of the Hidden Language of DNA," GeNum Lab, 2000, published at http://www.genum.com/dna_supracode/dan_supracode.htm.

Perry, Bruce D., M.D., Ph.D. et al. "Persisting Psychophysiological Effects of Traumatic Stress: The Memory of 'States'," *Violence Update,* 1:98, 1991.

Perry, Bruce, M.D., Ph.D. "Neurological Sequelae of Childhood Trauma: Post-traumatic Stress Disorders in Children," *Catecholamine Function in Post-Traumatic Stress Disorder: Emerging Concepts,* The Child Trauma Academy, 1997.

Peterson, Paula. "To Take Our Place Among the Stars," (interviewing Dr. Steven M. Greer), *Spirit of Ma'at,* Vol. 3, March, 2003, published at http://www.spiritofmaat.com.

Pickett, Joseph P. et al., ed. *The American Heritage Dictionary,* 4th Ed., 2000.

Pinkham, Mark Amaru. *The Return of the Serpents of Wisdom,* Adventures Unlimited Press, 1997.

Plotkin, Edward. *The Four Yogas of Enlightenment: Guide to Don Juan's Nagualism and Esoteric Buddhism,* http://www.FourYogas.com, 2000.

Plutarch, translated by Babbitt. *Plutarch's Moralia, Vol. V.*, Harvard University Press, 1962.

Ramsland, Katherine. *Piercing the Darkness: Undercover with Vampires in America Today,* HarperPrism, 1998.

Ramsland, Katherine. *The Science of Vampires*, Berkley Boulevard Books, 2002.

Rankin, John D. *The Mystic Keys of Hermes*, CSA Press, 1977.

Ray, Reginald A. *Secrets of the Vajra World*, Shambhala, 2002.

Regardie, Israel. *The Golden Dawn*, 6th ed., Llewellyn Books, 1993.

Richmond, M. Temple. *Sirius*, Source Publications, 1997.

Rinpoche, Bokar. *Chenrezig Lord of Love: Principles and Methods of Deity Meditation*, ClearPoint Press, 2001.

Rinpoche, Sogyal. *The Tibetan Book of Living and Dying*, Rigpa Fellowship, 1992.

Rinpoche, Tenzin Wangyal. *The Tibetan Yogas of Dream and Sleep,* Snow Lion Publications, 1998.

Rius. *Marx for Beginners*, Random House, Inc., 1976.

Roberts, Mark. http:home.earthlink.net/~pleiadesx.

Rochberg, George. "A Raid on the Infinite," *Psi Factors in Creativity*, Proceedings of an International Conference held in France, 1969, (Allan Angoff & Betty Shapin, editors), Parapsychology Foundation, 1970.

Rogo, Scott. D. "Communication and Parapsychology: A Report on the 28th International Conference of the Parapsychology Foundation," *Parapsychology Review,* X/6, Nov.-Dec. 1979.

Rose, Mary-Margareht. Previously published at http://www.themessenger.cc/Nov99/Earth%20MAPA.htm.

Rosen, Steven M. "Toward Legitimizing Parapsychology: More Data and Less "Blind Faith," *Parapsychology Review,* Nov.-Dec., 1979.

Royal, Dr. "A.T.P. The Currency of Life" published at http://www.royal-health.com/atp.htm, 2003.

Royal, Lyssa. "Transmission dated August 29, 1995," Royal Priest Research published at http://www.lyssaroyal.com.

Rudhyar, Dane. *The Magic of Tone and the Art of Music,* Shambhala, 1982.

Schafer, Marcia. *Confessions of an Intergalactic Anthropologist*, Cosmic Destiny Press, 1999.

Schlain, Leonard. *The Alphabet Versus the Goddess: The Conflict Between Word and Image*, Viking, 1998.

Schlemmer, Phyllis V. *The Only Planet of Choice*, Gateway Books, 1994.

Scientific American. August 25, 2003.

Scott, Cyril. *Music: Its Secret Influence Throughout the Ages,* 3rd Edition, Samuel Weiser, Inc., 1973.

Scruton, Roger. *A Dictionary of Political Thought*, Hill and Wang, 1982.

Sheridan, Sally. "Tibet, Shambhala and UFO's," published at http://www.sacred-texts.com/ufo/tibetufo.htm.

Sitchin, Zecharia. "The Case of Adam's Alien Genes," published at
http://www.sitchin.com.

Sitchin, Zecharia. "The Case of the Evil Wind," published at
http://www.sitchin.com.

Sitchin, Zecharia. "The Case of the Intelligent Designer," published at
http://www.sitchin.com.

Sitchin, Zecharia. "The Case of the Layered Asteroid," published at
http://www.sitchin.com.

Sitchin, Zecharia. "The Case of the Lurking Planet," published at
http://www.sitchin.com.

Sitchin, Zecharia. "The Case of the Missing Elephant," published at
http://www.sitchin.com.

Sitchin, Zecharia. "The Olmec Enigma: Astronaut Corroborates Sitchin,"
published at http://www.sitchin.com.

Sitchin, Zecharia. *The 12th Planet: Book I of the Earth Chronicles,* Avon
Books, 1976.

Sitchin, Zecharia. *The Cosmic Code: Book VI of the Earth Chronicles,*
Avon Books, 1998.

Sitchin, Zecharia. *The Lost Book of Enki*, Bear & Co., 2002.

Sitchin, Zecharia. *The Lost Realms: Book IV of the Earth Chronicles*, Avon
Books, 1990.

Sitchin, Zecharia. *The Wars of Gods and Men: Book III of the Earth
Chronicles,* Bear & Co., Inc., 1985.

Sklar, Holly, ed. *Trilateralism,* South End Press, 1980.

Smith, David and Evans, Phil. *Marx's Kapital for Beginners*, Random
House, Inc., 1982.

Smith, Joseph. *The Pearl of Great Price.*

Smoley, Richard and Kinney, Jay. *Hidden Wisdom: A Guide to the Western
Inner Traditions*, Arkana, 1999.

The Socialist Party of the United States. http://sp-
usa.org/about/principles.html.

Squire, Charles. *Celtic Myth and Legend, Poetry and Romance,* Crown
Publishers, 1979.

Starr, Jelaila. *We Are the Nibiruans,* Granite Publishing, 1999.

Stewart, Jesse. *Secrets of the Yellow Brick Road,* Sunshine Press, 1997.

Strassman, Rick, M.D. *DMT: The Spirit Molecule*, Park Street Press, 2001.

Temple, Robert. *The Sirius Mystery*, Destiny Books, 1998.

Three Initiates. *The Kybalion: A Study of Hermetic Philosophy of Ancient
Egypt and Greece*, Yogi Publication Society, 1912, 1940.

Thurman, Robert A.F. *The Holy Teaching of Vimalakirti,* (a Mahayana
scripture translated by Thurman), The Pennsylvania State University
Press, 1988.

Tolkien, J.R.R. *The Lord of the Rings*, Ballantine Books, 1981.

Tomas. *Creative Victory: Reflections on the Process of Power from the
Collected Works of Carlos Castaneda*, Samuel Weiser, Inc., 1995.

628

Tucker, Linda. "Tracing Sound to UFO Encounters," *MUFON UFO Journal*, Oct. 1994.

Tyson, Donald. "The Enochian Apocalypse," *Gnosis Magazine*, Summer, 1996.

Vessantara. *Meeting the Buddhas: A Guide to Buddhas, Bodhisattvas, and Tantric Deities,* Windhorse Publications, 1993.

Von Daniken, Erich. *The Return of the Gods*, Vega, 1995.

Walker, Barbara G. *The Woman's Encyclopedia of Myths and Secrets*, Harper San Francisco, 1983.

Wapnick, Kenneth. "Mysticism and Schizophrenia," *The Journal of Transpersonal Psychology,* Fall, 1969, Vol. 1, No. 2.

Waters, Frank. *Book of the Hopi*, Penguin Books, 1963.

Waters, Roger. Various lyrics from songs published by Roger Waters Music Overseas Ltd./Warner Chappell Artemis Music Ltd., Los Angeles, CA., and Pink Floyd Music Publishers, Inc., London, England.

White, Paul. "The Secrets of Thoth," published at http://www.newage.com/au/library/thoth.html.

Whorf, Benjamin Lee. *Language, Thought, and Reality,* from Selected Writings of Benjamin Lee Whorf, published jointly by the Technology Press and John Wiley & Sons of New York, reprinted in Edward T. Hall, *The Silent Language,* Anchor Books, 1973.

Wilber, Ken. *The Marriage of Sense and Soul: Integrating Science with Religion*, Random House, 1998.

Winston, Shirley Rabb. *Music as the Bridge – Based on the Edgar Cayce Readings*, A.R.E. Press, 1972.

Wrightman, Lawrence. S., Ph.D. *Social Psychology,* Second Edition, Brooks/Cole Publishing Company, 1977.

Zukav, Gary. *The Dancing Wu Li Masters: An Overview of the New Physics*, Bantam Books, 1979.

INDEX

633

634

635

639

Kennedy, i, vii, 394, 525, 549, 552, 553,
  624, 667
Kether, 31, 32
Ki, xiii, 216, 431, 432
kinesiology, 532
king, 36, 121, 137, 142, 180, 184, 194,
  212, 250, 258, 261, 263, 264, 287,
  307, 310, 348, 476, 478, 482, 487,
  604, 618
King Arthur, 171, 192, 194, 290, 455,
  512, 589, 625
kingdom, 42, 191, 218, 249, 250, 252,
  255, 259, 260, 261, 318, 362, 373,
  412, 420, 437, 469, 510, 548, 616
Kirlian, 531, 562, 587, 589, 622, 625
Knights Templar, 20, 245, 315, 318, 323,
  479, 480
koan, 235
Kolob, 240
Korea, 336, 412, 437, 438, 440
Ku Klux Klan, 353
kundalini, 44, 86, 179, 181, 261, 264, 430,
  449, 450, 451, 452, 453, 473, 474,
  490, 502, 505, 597
Kurgans, 258, 304, 306, 311, 481, 617
Kybalion, 50, 52, 70, 71, 78, 124, 628
Lady of the Lake, 478
lake, 38, 69, 262, 455, 478
Lakota, 198
lama, 39, 43, 50, 93, 100, 103, 104, 105,
  108, 248, 249, 253, 268, 270, 276,
  279, 286, 410, 418, 477, 572, 598,
  623, 626
Lama Surya Das, vii, 12, 19, 21, 36, 39,
  40, 42, 43, 49, 50, 51, 52, 73, 84, 86,
  89, 90, 92, 94, 102, 106, 125, 154,
  159, 164, 249, 266, 499, 514, 572,
  607, 611, 613, 622
Lancelot, 478
language, xiii, 9, 16, 20, 26, 54, 61, 68,
  119, 127, 133, 167, 177, 181, 202,
  203, 204, 205, 206, 209, 210, 211,
  212, 213, 214, 215, 216, 218, 219,
  220, 221, 222, 224, 226, 240, 268,
  272, 282, 304, 454, 459, 460, 461,
  518, 520, 522, 539, 544, 578, 618
Lapdron, Machig, iv, 267, 268, 269
lasers, 153, 578
Latin, xi, xii, 29, 205, 220, 326, 417, 420
LDS Church, 232
Led Zeppelin, 563
legend, xiii, 16, 136, 150, 171, 188, 189,
  190, 192, 193, 194, 200, 203, 212,
  213, 214, 228, 249, 250, 254, 259,
  262, 274, 310, 318, 320, 430, 431,

456, 470, 471, 473, 479, 481, 482,
  483, 486, 543, 573
Lehi, 238
Leitmotif, 538
Lemuria, 15, 170, 171, 180, 189, 196,
  255, 273, 437, 440, 616, 617
Lenin, 343
Levi, Eliphas, 87, 125, 320, 407, 625
levitation, 152, 167, 489, 491, 570, 571
ley lines, 455, 456, 582
liberty, 119, 321, 323, 329, 352, 354, 362,
  365, 371, 372, 373, 393, 398, 584
libido, 60, 170
library, 26, 195, 214, 219, 276, 584
life force, 59, 170, 182, 185, 193, 262,
  277, 431, 432, 471
lifestyle, 3, 19, 109, 231, 300, 305, 371,
  433, 467, 543
lightening, 96, 233
lighthouse, 576
Limitless Light, 226
lineage, 104, 105, 116, 180, 186, 264,
  268, 274, 279, 281, 287, 472, 476,
  479, 491, 608
lion, 98, 115, 142, 284, 311, 319, 600,
  603, 604, 612
lizard, 146, 449
Lockheed, 389, 394, 398
Lohengrin, 543, 556
longevity, 487, 494
Lord, 125, 137, 175, 182, 190, 209, 210,
  217, 240, 260, 320, 386, 414, 474,
  475, 481, 482, 483, 502, 600, 627, 628
Lord of the Rings, 190, 481, 482, 483, 628
Lot, 158
lotus, 75, 85, 259, 280, 418, 472, 487, 606
love, vii, x, 2, 10, 12, 36, 67, 71, 72, 95,
  103, 105, 109, 121, 124, 141, 142,
  173, 176, 217, 220, 227, 243, 270,
  298, 313, 321, 322, 337, 351, 421,
  425, 440, 444, 464, 469, 471, 476,
  483, 490, 493, 494, 498, 525, 526,
  545, 548, 555, 556, 560, 568, 569,
  593, 608, 609
LSD, 419, 427
lucid dreaming, 92
Lucifer, 319, 320, 322, 323
Lugh, 191, 192
Luke, 71, 72, 296
lunar, 206, 318
Lutheran, 342, 549
lymph, 415, 438
Lyran, 141, 615
M Theory, 7
Machiavelli, Niccolo, 313
Machiavellian, 241, 246, 314, 399

642

646

649

Spirit, v, xii, 6, 9, 12, 31, 56, 58, 63, 64,
66, 70, 74, 75, 77, 80, 81, 82, 83, 86,
96, 106, 147, 160, 169, 179, 182, 183,
188, 193, 219, 220, 222, 235, 236,
237, 243, 258, 279, 285, 303, 324,
410, 414, 416, 417, 418, 420, 421,
429, 430, 454, 481, 501, 507, 510,
538, 568, 577, 606, 610, 623, 626, 628
St. John, 203, 545, 547, 548
Stalin, Joseph, 215, 343
Standard Oil, 378
star, 14, 75, 76, 83, 88, 93, 139, 149, 150,
161, 162, 173, 174, 175, 176, 178,
196, 198, 199, 200, 203, 212, 219,
228, 233, 240, 268, 275, 283, 307,
315, 319, 320, 322, 325, 393, 414,
433, 473, 474, 475, 476, 478, 479,
480, 481, 484, 486, 487, 489, 501,
504, 508, 544, 553, 554, 579, 596, 602
star fire, 473, 474, 475, 476, 478, 479,
480, 481, 484, 486, 487, 501, 504, 508
Star Wars, 71, 73, 296, 416, 539
stargate, 141, 208, 223, 490, 582, 583
starseed, 146, 268
stereotypy, 300, 301, 463, 535
stigmatization, 453
stone, 85, 192, 205, 234, 308, 415, 487,
488, 504, 523, 554, 570, 571, 573,
602, 611, 619
Stone of Fal, 191
Stonehenge, 15, 190, 489, 565
stress, 105, 347, 367, 374, 375, 376, 418,
421, 422, 433, 434, 439, 450, 451,
452, 496, 497, 585
Stuarts, 286, 287
style, 14, 45, 64, 65, 67, 79, 89, 102, 103,
107, 109, 189, 255, 300, 333, 468,
478, 517, 544, 618
Subaru, 202
subliminal, 176, 202, 254
submission, 300, 301, 334
suicide, 396, 398, 435, 465, 597
Sulphur, 86, 510
Sumer, 134, 217, 247, 283, 311, 481, 482
Sumerian, 48, 133, 134, 135, 140, 149,
170, 185, 203, 212, 247, 248, 263,
273, 283, 311, 458, 459, 472, 475, 483
Sun, 14, 16, 17, 86, 149, 160, 162, 175,
176, 187, 188, 207, 216, 322, 432,
437, 438, 484, 529, 546, 547, 548, 579
superconductor, 487, 488
supernatural, 152, 165, 186, 193, 220,
225, 267, 479
supernormal, 8, 26, 152, 270, 418, 458,
471, 492

supersensory, ix, 8, 26, 100, 101, 102,
109, 152, 165, 186, 193, 220, 221,
225, 267, 270, 310, 401, 418, 458,
471, 479, 492, 564, 612
superstition, 8, 93, 300
Supreme Court, 353, 354, 363, 365, 366,
367, 369
swan, 449, 543, 556
swastika, 318
Swiss, 225, 565
sword, 96, 374, 454, 543, 544, 547, 563,
601
symbiosis, 442
symbolism, x, xiii, 11, 14, 20, 26, 32, 44,
48, 54, 55, 58, 59, 60, 61, 62, 63, 65,
66, 76, 87, 89, 96, 97, 99, 100, 119,
120, 143, 150, 170, 172, 179, 180,
181, 182, 184, 189, 192, 193, 195,
201, 203, 207, 211, 221, 225, 235,
237, 238, 245, 254, 256, 258, 264,
266, 268, 282, 286, 304, 305, 317,
318, 319, 322, 323, 324, 325, 326,
327, 353, 372, 414, 415, 424, 430,
432, 437, 440, 449, 451, 454, 462,
469, 473, 474, 477, 480, 482, 484,
485, 505, 521, 522, 523, 527, 528,
529, 535, 538, 539, 540, 541, 543,
547, 549, 551, 552, 553, 556, 557,
568, 579, 583, 596, 597, 601, 602,
603, 606
symphony, 542
synagogue, 123
synchronicity, 97, 546, 603, 604
Tables of Testimony, 186
tablet, 133, 308, 482
taboo, 166, 471
tai chi, 436
Taliesin, 192
talisman, 235
Tamas, 86
Tantra, 15, 43, 45, 49, 50, 93, 94, 96, 97,
98, 106, 116, 250, 257, 264, 265, 272,
276, 279, 568, 571, 607
tantrikas, 82
Taoism, 10, 21, 217, 218, 264, 279, 412,
430, 437, 621
Tara, vii, 93, 195, 254
Tarot, 20, 26, 32, 51, 61, 62, 63, 83, 89,
97, 98, 165, 177, 178, 182, 205, 282,
284, 322, 325, 413, 432, 437, 449,
451, 527, 529, 545, 546, 549, 550,
552, 568, 587, 621, 667
Tattva, 87, 88
Taurus, 174, 200, 529
teacher, vii, x, 12, 40, 43, 47, 50, 65, 68,
69, 89, 90, 92, 100, 101, 102, 103,

650

651

tumor, 444, 447, 531
tyranny, 35, 184, 287, 328, 355, 382
Tzolkin calendar, 220
Ubaid, 482, 617
UFOlogy, 128, 154, 216, 224, 249, 268, 383, 405
ultrasonic, 532, 573
Unacknowledged Special Access Projects (USAPS), 145, 146, 394, 395, 396
underground, 19, 38, 40, 48, 137, 145, 146, 180, 225, 249, 252, 326, 402, 615, 618
Unidentified Flying Object (UFO), iv, v, viii, x, xi, xii, xiv, 82, 128, 129, 132, 139, 140, 145, 152, 153, 154, 156, 159, 165, 169, 171, 173, 178, 199, 205, 216, 219, 224, 225, 239, 247, 258, 260, 262, 267, 268, 275, 291, 292, 316, 383, 385, 386, 387, 388, 389, 390, 391, 392, 395, 397, 398, 400, 424, 425, 443, 565, 574, 575, 582, 589, 620, 627, 629
Unitarian Church, 4
United States of America, viii, 11, 16, 17, 20, 21, 22, 27, 39, 40, 43, 51, 98, 103, 142, 146, 156, 162, 166, 179, 181, 196, 197, 198, 206, 207, 209, 223, 229, 231, 234, 236, 243, 249, 260, 271, 272, 273, 291, 303, 314, 317, 323, 324, 325, 326, 330, 331, 333, 335, 336, 343, 346, 349, 350, 352, 353, 354, 355, 356, 357, 359, 360, 361, 362, 363, 364, 365, 367, 368, 369, 370, 375, 377, 378, 379, 380, 381, 392, 394, 395, 398, 407, 408, 420, 451, 464, 512, 516, 525, 532, 565, 567, 573, 580, 585, 587, 617, 618, 620, 621, 625, 626, 627, 628
Unity, Church of Christianity, 4, 34, 67, 282, 526, 667
Universal Product Code, 205
Unmanifest, 226
Uranus, 530
Ursa Major, 250
use-value, 344, 345
uterus, 182
vajra, 93, 96
Vajrayana, iv, 17, 93, 94, 96, 265, 272, 568
Valiant Thor, 146
Valle, Jacque, 225
value, viii, 3, 4, 19, 35, 39, 41, 62, 124, 161, 204, 217, 218, 231, 232, 283, 301, 306, 336, 337, 339, 340, 341, 344, 345, 346, 347, 348, 361, 370,

372, 373, 376, 383, 445, 503, 506, 507, 516, 550, 561, 598
Vampirella, 470
vampires, 100, 193, 230, 262, 463, 464, 465, 466, 467, 468, 469, 470, 472, 473, 477, 483, 485, 500, 508, 509
Vayu, 86, 88
VCV formula, 209
Vedanta, 275
Vedic, 195, 254, 257
vegetarian, 109, 324, 470
vehicles, 18, 57, 139, 140, 168, 169, 179, 202, 210, 235, 253, 384, 390, 420, 431, 442, 476, 498, 508, 520, 567
Venus, 146, 319, 530, 579, 616
vibration, 61, 64, 81, 83, 87, 88, 91, 121, 161, 169, 171, 177, 258, 269, 270, 282, 422, 425, 438, 452, 490, 500, 516, 523, 531, 532, 534, 535, 536, 537, 559, 560, 561, 562, 565, 566, 567, 568, 573, 577, 578, 582, 583, 584
Victoria, Queen, 214
videotapes, 396
Viet Nam, 302, 354, 388
View, 37, 51, 622
Vimaanika Shastra, 256
Vimalakirti, 56, 78, 607, 613, 628
virgin, 47, 415, 471, 472, 473, 474, 510
Virgin Mary, 217
Virgo, 415, 416, 510, 530
virus, 315, 399, 415, 441, 442, 461, 471
Vishnu, 149
visualization, 26, 65, 69, 74, 75, 76, 90, 94, 98, 269, 285, 432, 451, 567, 568, 578, 609
Viviane de Lac, 478
Von Braun, Wernher, 387
vortex, 64, 418, 455, 456, 461, 462, 467, 472, 569
Voyager, 580
Waco, 336
Wag the Dog, 356
wages, 109, 338, 348, 349, 351, 368, 373
Wagner, Richard, 64, 453, 484, 485, 512, 538, 540, 543, 555, 587, 588, 622, 624
Wales, 286, 482
walk-in, 140, 147, 268
Wall, the, 594, 595, 602, 612, 613
wand, 96, 97, 100, 117, 182, 191, 256
war, 41, 142, 144, 146, 156, 158, 166, 188, 192, 196, 223, 240, 252, 254, 255, 302, 305, 312, 313, 314, 315, 325, 341, 353, 354, 360, 364, 380, 384, 400, 435, 456, 486, 491, 565, 596, 597, 601, 605, 615, 617, 618
warp, 489

About the Author

Judy Kennedy is a creative artist with an unwavering commitment to civil liberties – especially freedom of expression, continual cultivation of spiritual awareness, and a passion for principle-centered living. A natural intuitive, her writing reveals a heightened ability to see connections between things, people and events not ordinarily discerned. Some of her credentials:

- Student and teacher of music, meditation, astrology and the Western Mystery Traditions since 1972 (including affiliations with Wicca, Unity – Church of Esoteric Christianity, and Builders of the Adytum – Temple of Tarot and Holy Qabalah)
- Personal work and study under a Dzogchen Master and Lama in the Eastern Mystery Tradition of Tibetan Buddhism
- **Bachelor of Arts** degree in Music with a minor in Journalism and Political Science
- **Master of Arts** degree in Interdisciplinary Studies (Music, Psychology, and Philosophy)
- Graduate studies in Music Therapy, Parapsychology, and Psychophysiology
- Continuing certified education in Law with over 15 years experience as a legal researcher, litigation paralegal, with personal trial experience
- Successful completion of the CSETI (Center for the Study of Extraterrestrial Intelligence) Ambassadors to the Universe Advanced Research Training
- Published writer/speaker (ATM Toastmasters)

She currently shares a home in the rural wilderness of southern Arizona with her mate, her "kids" (a wide assortment of domesticated animals), and the beautiful, bountiful wildlife of the Sonoran Desert.